Equity in
Commercial Law

Head Office: 100 Harris Street PYRMONT NSW 2009
Tel: (02) 8587 7000 Fax: (02) 8587 7100
For all sales inquiries please ring 1800 650 522
(for calls within Australia only)

INTERNATIONAL AGENTS & DISTRIBUTORS

NORTH, CENTRAL & SOUTH AMERICA,
CARIBBEAN
Carswell Co
Ontario, Canada

HONG KONG
Sweet & Maxwell Asia
Hysan Avenue, Causeway Bay
Hong Kong

MALAYSIA
Sweet & Maxwell Asia
Petaling Jaya, Selangor

NEW ZEALAND, PACIFIC ISLANDS
Brooker's Ltd
Wellington

SINGAPORE
Sweet & Maxwell Asia
Battery Road

EUROPE, MIDDLE EAST AND AFRICA
ISM Europe, Middle East & Africa
Sweet & Maxwell Ltd
Andover, Hampshire

AUSTRALIA, PAPUA NEW GUINEA
Thomson Legal & Regulatory Ltd
Pyrmont, Sydney

JAPAN, KOREA, TAIWAN
ISM Asia Operations
Thomson Legal & Regulatory
Pyrmont, Sydney

Equity in Commercial Law

edited by

Simone Degeling

James Edelman

Lawbook Co. 2005

Published in Sydney by

Lawbook Co.
    100 Harris Street, Pyrmont, NSW

National Library of Australia
    Cataloguing-in-Publication entry

Equity in commercial law.

    Includes index.
    ISBN 0 455 22208 8.

    1. Equity. I. Degeling, Simone. II. Edelman, James.

    346.004

Editor: Lara Weeks
Product Developer: Catherine Fitzgerald

Typeset in 10.25/12 pt Minion by Midland Typesetters, Maryborough, Victoria

Printed by Ligare Pty Ltd, Riverwood, NSW

In memory of Peter Birks.

צֶדֶק צֶדֶק תִּרְדֹּף

Foreword

More than 130 years ago, the British Parliament enacted the *Judicature Act 1873*, ending the segregation of common law and equity in different courts. However, as Sir Anthony Mason notes in the opening chapter of this book, it is clear that the Act, and its progeny in the Commonwealth countries, merely had a procedural effect and did not bring about fusion of the substantive rules of common law and equity. Therefore, despite the passage of time, the fusion of law and equity remains a live issue today, subject to debate by academics, practitioners and judges alike. This book demonstrates just how lively the debate can be.

Academics are fascinated by the interplay between the common law and equity in the context of modern commercial law. Since the enactment of the Judicature Acts, many variants of the law-equity merger have grown up, furnishing excellent material for legal historians and encouraging comparative studies. In addition, a particularly spirited debate (dubbed by some as the "fusion wars") has developed around many of the core concerns and needs of modern commercial law, such as certainty in business dealings, flexibility to accommodate diverse and changing marketplaces, and fairness and justice for all parties. The debate turns on whether the needs of commerce are better served through fusion or through maintaining discrete boundaries between equity and the common law. Several of the authors in this book also touch on a related topic: the blurring in law of the distinction between obligations and property. The role of equity in commercial law remains a vital contemporary academic concern and this book will no doubt enliven the debates that have been underway since the late nineteenth century.

Although there is a high level of academic interest in these debates, the debates are far from purely academic. The relationship between the common law and equity and the question of fusion engage the interest of practising lawyers and the bench as well. One need only look as far as the pleadings filed by commercial litigants to get a sense of the interrelationship of the common law and equity in practice. Litigants who might once have framed their claims in either common law *or* equity, now seek both common law *and* equitable remedies. One such example is the rise in popularity of breach of fiduciary duty as an alternative cause of action on facts that would once have prompted an action framed solely in negligence. The authors provocatively explore whether legal and equitable remedies serve the same primary functions, or whether equitable remedies serve a distinct function and provide a valuable corrective tool against the blunt force of the common law. As is evident in the chapters of this book, there are diverse views about the expansion or contraction of equity in relation to the common law, the overlapping spheres of these two domains, the relationship of common law and equity to statutory law, and the propriety and necessity of analogy between these areas of law.

This book will contribute much to the discourse on equity in commercial law, delineating the essential points of contention in the fusion debate. It sets out the strengths and weaknesses of blending and borrowing between the common law and equity. This will be particularly useful to trial judges who often do not have the luxury of stepping back and viewing the development of the law as a whole when faced with the need to make a decision in a particular case.

Lawyers looking for the most appropriate remedies for their clients will also be interested in the pros and cons of the fusion debate. As a point of strategy, they will wish to assess whether their clients are better served through diversity in the law (that is, the argument that preserving distinct equitable doctrines makes the law more resilient and equipped to deal with factually diverse situations), or through the consistency and rationality that is said to result from the fusion of equity and the common law (for example, the treating of like cases alike), and to develop their arguments accordingly.

Although this book grew out of a conference held in Australia, the fruits of that conference will be relevant throughout the common law world. The authors have done a particularly fine job of placing the fusion debate in context for specific areas of commercial law and in providing case examples from England, Canada, Australia, and New Zealand. The chapters dealing with property, choice of law, trusts and fiduciaries, unjust enrichment, gain-based and punitive remedies, and specific performance, show how equitable doctrine has been formed – and is being reformed – often in conjunction with the common law. These chapters explore whether equity should, as the maxim says, follow the common law, for example, in imposing strict liability for unjust enrichment or retaining a fault requirement in equity. They highlight where equity differs from the common law (for example, equity's rules for choice of law are less well-defined than the common law's). They also provide differing views about how courts treat fiduciary duties – at times as analogous to common law duties; at other times as distinct equitable obligations.

This is a fascinating and comprehensive collection that indicates where courts might take equity in the future. Courts may find guidance here to assist them in developing equity in a manner that builds on its strengths, and situates it within a effective and efficient system of law (including statutes and common law). For, while equity often takes a back seat to the common law (its more forceful and dominant sibling), equity is an effective backseat driver. Equity provides essential direction to the courts as they struggle to navigate their way through modern commercial legal quandaries.

I commend the authors and editors on this achievement which will, without doubt, assist in further developments in the law of equity in Australia, England, Canada and New Zealand. *Equity in Commercial Law*, dedicated to the late Peter Birks, is a great tribute to a scholar whose work on the doctrine of unjust enrichment and the law of restitution contributed mightily to clarifying the roles of law and equity in the modern legal framework.

Beverley McLachlin
Ottawa, Ontario
Canada
August 2005

Contributors

Professor Andrew Burrows QC is Norton Rose Professor of Commercial Law at the University of Oxford and Fellow of St. Hugh's College Oxford.

Professor Michael Bryan is Professor of Law at the University of Melbourne.

Professor Robert Chambers is Professor of Law at the University of Alberta until June 2006 and then Professor of Law at King's College, London University.

Dr Simone Degeling is Senior Lecturer in Law at the University of New South Wales.

Dr James Edelman is Fellow and Tutor in Law at Keble College, CUF Lecturer in Law at the University of Oxford and Adjunct Professor of Law at the University of Western Australia.

Dr Joshua Getzler is Fellow and Tutor in Law at St Hugh's College Oxford and CUF Lecturer in Law at the University of Oxford.

Professor Ross Grantham is Professor of Commercial Law at the University of Queensland.

The Hon Justice William Gummow AC is a Justice of the High Court of Australia.

The Hon Justice David Hayton is now a Justice of the Caribbean Court of Justice, having been Professor of Law, King's College, London University.

Professor Steve Hedley is Professor of Law at University College Cork.

The Hon Justice JD Heydon AC is a Justice of the High Court of Australia.

The Hon Sir Anthony Mason AC KBE is a former Chief Justice of the High Court of Australia.

The Hon Justice Keith Mason AC is President of the New South Wales Court of Appeal.

Professor Mitchell McInnes is Professor of Law at the University of Alberta.

The Right Honourable Beverley McLachlin, PC is Chief Justice of Canada.

The Right Hon Lord Millett is a Lord of Appeal in Ordinary and Justice of the Court of Final Appeal of Hong Kong.

Professor Charles Rickett is Sir Gerard Brennan Professor of Law at the University of Queensland.

Professor Lionel Smith is James McGill Professor of Law, Faculty of Law and Institute of Comparative Law, McGill University. During 2004-05 he was a Visiting Researcher at the Swiss Institute of Comparative Law, Lausanne, Switzerland.

Mr Robert Stevens is Fellow and Tutor in Law at Lady Margaret Hall and CUF Lecturer in Law at the University of Oxford.

Mr William Swadling is Fellow and Tutor in Law at Brasenose College and CUF Lecturer in Law at the University of Oxford.

Professor Sarah Worthington is Professor of Law and Deputy Director for Research and External Relations at the London School of Economics, and Barrister, 3/4 South Square, London.

Associate Professor Yeo Tiong Min is Associate Professor of Law at the National University of Singapore.

The Hon Justice Peter Young AO is Chief Judge in Equity in New South Wales.

Acknowledgments

Lawbook Co, part of Thomson Legal and Regulatory Limited, is grateful to the publishers, authors, and government departments, who have allowed us to reproduce extracts of their work in this book. The extracts attributed herein have been reprinted with permission of:

Attorney General's Department, Western Australia: www.wa.gov.au
Western Australia Reports (WAR).

Cambridge University Press, Cambridge UK: www.cup.cam.ac.uk
GD Libecap, 'A transactions-cost approach to the analysis of property rights' in E Brousseau and JM Galchant (eds), *The Economics of Contracts* (2002).
SM Waddams, *Dimensions of Private Law: Categories and Concepts in Anglo-American Legal Reasoning* (2003).
J Brunyate (ed), *Equity A Course of Lectures by F W Maitland* (revised 1947).

Canada Law Book, Inc: www.canadalawbook.ca
Dominion Law Reports (DLR).

Carswell, a division of Thomson Canada Limited: www.carswell.com
PD Finn, 'The Fiduciary Principle' in TG Youdan (ed), *Equity, Fiduciaries and Trusts* (1989).
British Columbia Law Reports (BCLR).

CCH Australia: www.cch.com.au
Australian Company Law Cases (ACLC).

Council of Law Reporting for New South Wales:
New South Wales Law Reports (NSWLR). © Council of Law Reporting for New South Wales.

Duckworth: www.ducknet.co.uk
Justinian's Institutes, translated by P Birks and G McLeod (1987).

Fontana Books (a division of HarperCollins, London): www.harpercollins.co.uk
J Hackney, *Understanding Equity and Trusts* (1987).

Hart Publishing, Oxford UK: www.hartpub.co.uk
P Birks, 'Receipt' in P Birks and A Pretto (eds), *Breach of Trust* (2002).
J Edelman, *Gain-Based Damages: Contract, Tort, Equity and Intellectual Property* (2002).

Harvard Law Review: www.harvardlawreview.org
OW Holmes, "The Path of the Law" (1897) 10 *Harvard Law Review* 457.

HMSO (Her Majesty's Stationery Office) UK: www.hmso.gov.uk
Judicature Commission UK, *First Report* (1869).

English Law Commission, Report No 247, *Aggravated, Exemplary and Restitutionary Damages* (1997).

The Incorporated Council of Law Reporting for England & Wales: www.iclr.co.uk
Appeal Cases Reports (AC).
Chancery Division Reports (Ch D).
Queen's Bench Division Reports (QB D).
Weekly Law Reports (WLR).

Israel Law Review (by the Faculty of Law, Hebrew University of Jerusalem): http:// law.mscc.huji.ac.il/law1/ilr
P Birks, "The Content of Fiduciary Obligation" (2000) 34 *Israel Law Review* 3.

Juta & Co Ltd: www.juta.co.za
Pretoria City Council v Levinson 1949 (3) SA 305.

The Lawbook Co. (a division of Thomson Legal & Regulatory Limited): www.thomson.com.au
PD Finn, *Fiduciary Obligations* (1977).
Commonwealth Law Reports (CLR).

Law Quarterly Review (by Sweet and Maxwell, London): www.sweetandmaxwell.co.uk
PJ Millett, "Restitution and Constructive Trusts" (1998) 114 *Law Quarterly Review* 399.

LexisNexis Butterworths, Sydney: www.lexisnexis.com.au
R Meagher, JD Heydon, M Leeming, *Meagher Gummow and Lehane's Equity: Doctrines and Remedies* (2002) 4th edition.
Australian Law Reports (ALR).
Butterworths Property Reports (BPR).

Modern Law Review (by Blackwell Publishing, UK): www.blackwellpublishing.com
RR Pennington, "The Genesis of the Floating Charge" (1960) 23 *Modern Law Review* 630.

Michigan Law Review (by the University of Michigan Law School and the Michigan Law Review Association): www.law.umich.edu
W Hohfeld, "The Relations Between Equity and Law," (1913) 11 *Michigan Law Review* 537.

New Zealand Council of Law Reporting:
New Zealand Law Reports (NZLR).

New Zealand Law Review (by the University of Auckland): http://nzlawreview.auckland.ac.nz/NZLR
P Birks, "Property and Unjust Enrichment: Categorical Truths" (1997) *New Zealand Law Review* 623.

Oxford Journal of Legal Studies (by Oxford University Press, Oxford): www.oup.com
A Burrows, "We do this at Common Law but that in Equity" (2002) 22 *Oxford Journal of Legal Studies* 1.

Oxford University Press (also Clarendon Press,Oxford): www.oup.com
G Elias, *Explaining Constructive Trusts* (1990).
AM Honoré, 'Ownership' in AG Guest (ed), *Oxford Essays in Jurisprudence* (1961).
P Birks, 'The Concept of a Civil Wrong' in D Owen (ed), *Philosophical Foundations of Tort Law* (1997).
P Birks, *An Introduction to the Law of Restitution* (1985).
J Penner, *The Idea of Property in Law* (1997).
S Milsom, *Historical Foundations of the Common Law* (1981), 2nd edition.

Recueil Des Cours (by Brill Academic Publishers): www.brill.nl
BA Wortley, "The General Principles of Private International Law from the English Standpoint" (1947) 71 *Recueil Des Cours* 1.

Restitution Law Review (by the School of Law, University of Bristol, UK): www.law.bris.ac.uk
P Birks, "Trusts Raised to Reverse Unjust Enrichment" [1996] *Restitution Law Review* 3.

Selden Society, London: www.selden-society.qmul.ac.uk
C St Germain, *Doctor and Student* (1974).

Sweet and Maxwell, London: www.sweetandmaxwell.co.uk
P Fitzgerald, *Salmond on Jurisprudence* (1966) 12th edition.
R Goode, *Principles of Corporate Insolvency* (1997) 2nd edition.
Appeal Cases (App Cas).
English Reports (ER).

Supreme Court of Canada: www.scc-csc.gc.ca
Supreme Court Reports (SCR).

University of Western Australian Law Review (by the University of Western Australia): www.lawreview.law.uwa.edu.au
P Birks, "The Law of Restitution at the End of an Epoch" (1999) 28 *Western Australian Law Review* 13. ©P Birks (1999).

William S Hein & Co Inc., Buffalo New York: www.wshein.com
G Spence, *The Equitable Jurisdiction of the Court of Chancery* (1981).

The Yale Law Journal (The Yale Law Journal Company and William S Hein Company): www.yalelawjournal.org
LL Fuller and WR Perdue, "The Reliance Interest in Contract Damages" (1936) 46 *Yale Law Journal* 52.

Every effort has been made to contact copyright holders and/or their agents. While every care has been taken to establish and acknowledge copyright, Lawbook Co. tenders its apology for any accidental infringement. The publisher would be pleased to come to a suitable agreement with the rightful owners in each case.

Contents

Gain-based and punitive remedies

Specific performance and contract

CONCLUSION

Table of Cases

Table of Statutes

Introduction

JAMES EDELMAN AND
SIMONE DEGELING

This book of essays arose from a conference on the law of equity which was held in Sydney in December 2004.[1] The month before the conference we wrote in the *Australian Bar Review* introducing the debate we expected at the conference:[2] is it legitimate to develop the laws of equity by reference to, or by analogy with, the common law and vice versa? We saw cases like *Hedley Byrne v Heller*[3] — in which the common law of negligent misstatement was developed by reference to equitable principles in *Nocton v Lord Ashburton*[4] — as lying at the heart of this debate. As the conference proceeded, a core consensus seemed to emerge as a response to this question. As one delegate, Jeremy Kirk, observed in an early question, no-one was arguing that all equitable doctrine should automatically be merged with the common law, nor was anyone arguing that development of the rules of equity could not consider parallel developments at common law. The process of analogical development is described by Sir Anthony Mason and Professor Burrows as fusion by analogy.[5] However, the extent to which analogies can be drawn between common law and equity remains a matter of great controversy. The nature of the relationship between common law and equity, and the extent to which analogy is possible, is the central issue explored in the chapters in Part I of this book. It is implicit in the chapters in Part II in which specific issues involving the relationship between common law and equity are considered.

In the first chapter of Part I, Sir Anthony Mason argues that principles of equity are more discretionary and conscience-based than those of common law but that convergence between the two systems is necessary where material inconsistencies exist. Sir Anthony makes the point that convergence, in appropriate cases, responds to the need for an orderly, coherent and principled development of the law and its rules, principles and remedies. In the second chapter Professor Smith accepts that a different set of moral norms underlie equitable principles but rejects discretion or conscience as material differences between equity and common law. Smith argues

---

1   *Fusion: The interaction of common law and equity*, conference hosted by the University of New South Wales and sponsored by Blake Dawson Waldron, Freehills, Mallesons Stephen Jaques and the *Australian Financial Review*. Over 300 lawyers attended.

2   J Edelman and S Degeling, "Fusion: The interaction of common law and equity" (2004) 25 *Australian Bar Review* 195.

3   [1964] AC 465.

4   [1914] AC 932.

5   See chapter 1 (Sir Anthony Mason); chapter 15 (Professor Andrew Burrows). See also chapter 10 where Dr Getzler refers to opposition to any analogical development as a fundamentalism that is historically false.

that the different norms are exemplified by equity's unique conversion of personal rights into property rights (a moral norm he describes as respect for other people's obligations) and the justiciability of motive in equity; two unique characteristics that he says lie at the core of equity's central institution — the trust. Therefore, although for different reasons, Sir Anthony Mason and Smith in the first two chapters both accept that equity and the common law have a history of integration and mutual learning but implicitly suggest hesitancy before drawing analogies between doctrines deriving from court systems with different moral underpinnings. The third chapter, by Justice Keith Mason, is less hesitant. Mason denies any unique characteristic of equitable doctrine apart from historical development. He argues that equitable doctrines should now take their proper place as part of a unified system of judge-made law, alongside and integrated with common law and statutory developments. Indeed, he remarks that "to my knowledge, no law school teaches 'common law' as a subject."

The different approaches to drawing analogies in the first three chapters emphasise that, even if fusion by analogy is accepted, it is only the beginning of the story. To what *extent* can analogies be drawn between common law and equity? Is it legitimate to speak of a taxonomy of legal events and to draw analogies at broad levels of generalisation? Each of the chapters in Part I, like most modern writing in private law, are part of a debate which has been shaped by the work of the late Professor Birks, whose passing deprived the conference of a paper he was to present entitled "The Curse of Duality". Like Justice Mason, Birks rejected the assertion that there was any difference between the morality underlying common law and equitable doctrine. Indeed, his work consistently demanded answers from his detractors:[6] most particularly, if the "overriding aim of all equitable principle is the prevention of unconscionable behaviour"[7] how is such behaviour to be identified? Can strict liability in equity really be based on "unconscionability"?[8] How are equitable principles to be developed by reference to this undefined notion of "conscience" when, as Justice Hayne has said extra-judicially, a term such as "unconscionable or unconscientious is a statement of a conclusion"?[9] And why is the common law not equally motivated to remedy unconscionable conduct?

One of Birks' grandest achievements was to propose a taxonomy of private law which separated legal events from legal responses and integrated equity and the common law into events of consent, wrongs, unjust enrichment and other events. Of course, as Birks acknowledged, he was not the first to propose a taxonomy of private law that assimilated the rules of equity. His work developed the classificatory schemes of two of the greatest jurists in history. The second century Roman jurist Gaius and the eighteenth century jurist and judge Sir William Blackstone both wrote that private law was comprised of contract, delict, quasi-contract and quasi-delict. In chapter 4 (the final chapter of Part I), the relevance of Gaius' work

---

6   P Birks, "Equity, conscience, and unjust enrichment" (1999) 23 *Melbourne University Law Review* 1.

7   *ACCC v Berbatis* (2000) 169 ALR 324 at 341.

8   Compare the rejection of the label "unconscionability" in different contexts by the Privy Council and the Supreme Court of Canada: *Royal Brunei Airlines v Tan* [1995] 2 AC 378 at 392; *Ryan v Moore* [2005] SCC 38 at [74].

9   K Hayne, "Letting Justice be Done without the Heavens Falling" (2002) 27 *Monash University Law Review* 12 at 16. See also *Garcia v National Australia Bank* (1998) 194 CLR 395 at 409[34]. See also P Birks, *Unjust Enrichment* (2nd edition, Oxford University Press, 2005) at 5-8.

to the development of the legal order in the twentieth and twenty-first centuries is dismissed by Professor Hedley who argues that it is concerned with a Roman system which, unlike modern law, conceived of an autonomous private law independent of government. Other commentators disagree with this.[10] But it is not the only objection. Another objection raised by Hedley is to dismiss Birks' work as a panglossian ordered and formal law that envisages far too little discretion for the judge and which constrains legal innovation by reference to abstract, intangible concepts. There is more than a trace here of Holmesian realism that law is merely the result desired by a majority of the judges that hear a particular case: "the prophecies of what the courts will do in fact, and nothing more pretentious, are what I mean by the law."[11] However, Hedley does not argue against *any* form of classification or taxonomy. Instead he argues that there is no single dominant taxonomy nor need there be one; a healthy legal pluralism "…arguably *demands* the co-existence of many and conflicting taxonomical concepts."

Hedley's closing paragraphs, which conclude Part I of the book, reflect the view of courts in most common law countries today which is an antipathy to categorical development and broad taxonomic ideas. With the exception of the recent addition of unjust enrichment, the common law of Australia, Canada and England (the countries considered in this book) seems to have settled upon a partial classification of private law into categories of contract, tort and trusts.[12] The many other areas of private law are miscellaneous events that are not part of any particular category of obligation. On the other hand, in the history of private common law our existing taxonomy is very young indeed. Professor Pollock wrote that "scientific" treatment of principles of English law only really began in "that classical period of our jurisprudence [between 1852 and 1875]".[13] Although the origin of the modern trust arose from the ashes of the executed use in the sixteenth and seventeenth centuries,[14] the modern law of contract did not completely emerge from its foundations of assumpsit until the mid-nineteenth century. In 1806, a translation of Pothier's *Traité des obligations* was published in England,[15] exposing English lawyers to the will theory of contract and there followed some of the key cases of the modern law in the mid-nineteenth century such as *Hadley v Baxendale* and *Smith v Hughes*.[16] Further, the law of tort, in the form we understand it today, did not even emerge until the

---

10 M Loughlin, *The Idea of Public Law* (Oxford University Press, Oxford, 2003); E Weinrib *The Idea of Private Law* (Harvard University Press, Harvard, 1995).

11 OW Holmes, 'The Path of the Law' (1897) in S Novick (ed) *The Collected Works of Justice Holmes* (University of Chicago Press, Chicago, 1994) Vol 3 at 393.

12 "…the three great sources of obligation in private law, contract, tort and trust": *Roxborough v Rothmans of Pall Mall Australia Ltd* (2001) 208 CLR 516 at [64] (Gummow J).

13 F Pollock, *The Law of Torts: A Treatise on the Principles of Obligation Arising from Civil Wrongs in the Common Law* (Stevens and Sons, London, 1887) at vii.

14 For the evolution of the trust after the *Statute of Uses 1535* 27 Henry VIII c10 see JH Baker, *An Introduction to English Legal History* (4th ed, Butterworths, London, 2002) at 248-258, 280-297.

15 W Evans, *A Treatise on the law of Obligations or Contracts by M Pothier* (A Strahan, London, 1806).

16 *Hadley v Baxendale* (1854) 9 Ex 241; 156 ER 145; *Smith v Hughes* (1871) LR 6 QB 597. See AWB Simpson, 'Innovation in Nineteenth Century Contract Law', in *Legal Theory and Legal History. Essays on the Common Law* (Hambledon Press, London, 1987) at 171-202, and DJ Ibbetson, *A Historical Introduction to the Law of Obligations* (Oxford University Press, Oxford, 999) at chapters 12 and 13.

mid-twentieth century after *Donoghue v Stevenson*[17] began the process of generalising a duty of care. Most recently of all, was the development of unjust enrichment which did not fully emerge from the miscellany of other private law legal events until 1954 in Canada,[18] 1987 in Australia[19] and 1991 in England.[20] In chapter 14, which was recently cited with judicial approval by Justice Mason,[21] Professor Grantham powerfully argues against any assimilation of this category of unjust enrichment back into general notions of equity.[22]

The second part of the book moves from these broad issues of taxonomy and the relationship of equity with common law to the operation of particular principles of equity in commercial law. It examines six major issues: the operation of principles of property law across common law and equity; the choice of law rules that should be applied in equity; the nature and operation of duties of fiduciaries and other trustees (particularly duties of care and skill owed by fiduciaries); the operation of restitutionary principles (particularly receipt based liability) in equity; money remedies of disgorgement, restitution and punishment in equity; and the relationship between equity and contract (particularly the nature of the rights of an purchaser under an executory contract that is specifically performable).

In chapters 5 and 6, Professor Worthington and Professor Rickett consider the operation of principles of property law across common law and equity. In *Yanner v Eaton* the High Court of Australia implicitly rejected Professor Hohfeld's concept of property or paucital rights as a multitude of rights in personam,[23] preferring a Benthamite 'thinghood' conception of property rights (as rights to an object or thing).[24] Against this, Worthington argues that modern equity has eliminated a coherent distinction between personal rights and property rights, particularly one based on thinghood. She illustrates her argument by reference to notions of assignability and excludability and argues that whether a person is said to have property rights to something depends on the reason the question is being asked. Rickett argues the opposite. Traversing through the history of property law, he argues that property is a distinct concept and he defends a thinghood conception of property rights. Rickett then considers the operation of one area of property law, the law of tracing and claiming (in particular, rules of tracing and claims to substitute assets).

In chapters 7 and 8, Professor Yeo and Mr Stevens both argue that there is no distinct and single set of rules for choice of law principles in equity. The effect of

---

17 [1932] AC 562.

18 *Deglman v Guaranty Trust Co of Canada* [1954] SCR 725.

19 *Pavey & Matthews Pty Ltd v Paul* (1987) 162 CLR 221; *David Securities Pty Limited v Commonwealth Bank of Australia* (1992) 175 CLR 353.

20 *Lipkin Gorman v Karpnale Ltd* [1991] 2 AC 548.

21 *Fostif Pty Ltd v Campbells Cash & Carry Pty Ltd* [2005] NSWCA 83 at [232]-[239].

22 Cf *Roxborough v Rothmans of Pall Mall Australia Ltd* (2001) 208 CLR 516 at [70]-[75] (Gummow J).

23 W Hohfeld, "Fundamental Legal Conceptions as Applied to Judicial Reasoning" (1917) 26 *Yale Law Journal* 710. See also W Hohfeld, *Fundamental Legal Conceptions* (Yale University Press, New Haven, 1923).

24 (1999) 201 CLR 351 at 365-366 (Gleeson CJ, Gaudron, Kirby and Hayne JJ). See J Bentham, *An Introduction to the Principles of Morals and Legislation* (Athlone Press, London, 1970, JH Burns and HLA Hart, eds) at 211.

their argument is that the prevailing approach in Australia (for example in *Parama-sivam* v *Flynn*)[25] — that there is a different choice of law methodology within equitable jurisprudence–needs to be reconsidered. Yeo shows that an argument for a single choice of law rule for equity cannot be defended on the basis of a jurisdic-tional analysis of equity or by invoking the peculiar nature of equity within the domestic law. He rejects the argument from *Paramasivam* v *Flynn* that such an approach to choice of law provides convenience and certainty and avoids the difficulty of having to ascertain the relevant foreign law. He reasons that this argument threatens to undermine the rationale of choice of law and is, in any event, counterbalanced by other considerations such as the possibility of modification by foreign law. Both Yeo and Stevens also argue that it is not possible to have separate categories of choice of law uniquely within equity. They both use the example of fiduciary duties and show that such separate categories would ignore the diverse sources of fiduciary duties. As Stevens expresses it, these duties are imposed by contract (agreement) as well as by operation or law (in which case the category of tort would be appropriate). As Yeo expresses it, fiduciary duties can be analysed as sourced in contract, tort, trusts, or the law of corporations.

Chapters 9, 10 and 11 consider aspects of the law relating to trustees and other fiduciaries. Particularly difficult issues in this area are the nature of duties of care and skill owed by fiduciaries and duties owed by custodial fiduciaries. In chapter 9, Justice Heydon undertakes a comprehensive examination of whether the duties of care and skill owed by company directors are fiduciary duties. He argues that the *Wheeler* doctrine[26] (that the duties of care and skill owed by company directors are not fiduciary duties) is based on a misunderstanding of authority and is insupportable in principle. This conclusion may affect the rules of causation and remoteness of damages and the availability of limitation periods and proprietary remedies and other associated actions (such as dishonest participation in a breach of fiduciary duty). Heydon describes the argument that different types of fiduciary duty should be treated differently in the application of these rules as the "idea that the equitable obligations of a fiduciary are to undergo a process of filleting". In relation to trustees he observes that there is a close relationship between the different duties as well as a basal principle underlying all the duties which is to keep trustees to their duty to protect their beneficiaries. It may follow from this reasoning that the same approach would also apply to the different fiduciary duties of directors (duties which evolved in equity by extension from the duties of trustees). In chapter 10, Dr Getzler also examines this issue. He also considers suggestions that different rules should apply to different types of fiduciary duty: custodial vs non-custodial fiduciary duties; duties of loyalty vs duties of skill and care; and between subjectively dishonest breaches vs less serious breaches. Getzler explains that the characterization of duty helps frame the relevant rules (such as causation, remoteness etc) that apply but he argues that all of these counterpoints are false: they rely on difficult distinctions between custodial trusts and fiduciary law; they ignore equitable policies of objectifying fraud and requiring prudence as a dimension of good faith; and they do not take into account the contexts shaping common law apportionment and mitigation doctrines within contract and tort, which differ from fiduciary contexts. With similarly wide-ranging

---

25 (1998) 160 ALR 203.
26 *Permanent Building Society (in liq) v Wheeler* (1994) 11 WAR 187.

and historical analysis, Getzler reaches the same conclusions as Heydon. On the other hand, their conclusions contrast with the approach of Justice Hayton. In chapter 11, Hayton focuses closely upon the precise nature of the unique duties of trustees and argues that it is not surprising that different duties should be treated differently. "There is a world of difference" between, on the one hand, the trustee's core obligations of fidelity to the terms of the trust and altruistic loyalty to the beneficiaries, and on the other, the trustee's duty of care and skill (where the trustee-beneficiary relationship is only an incidental factor in a negligence inquiry). Hayton's close focus on the nature of the trustee's duty (or, the Hohfeldian co-relative right of the beneficiaries) seeks to highlight a difference between a duty of performance in the former instance (particularly the obligation to maintain the trust assets) for which the remedy of substitutive compensation provides a substitute for the value of the trust assets (maintenance of which is the trustee's required performance) and a breach of a duty of care for which the remedy of compensation is reparative for financial loss suffered. An instructive parallel might be drawn with common law compensation for breach of contract and the emerging recognition of substitutive compensation for the duty of contractual performance (even in cases in which there has been no financial loss).[27]

Chapters 12, 13 and 14 all consider the operation of the law of unjust enrichment across equity and common law. We have mentioned Professor Grantham's chapter above and his thesis that unjust enrichment should not be subsumed into a notion of "unconscionability". Another extremely important current issue is the vexed doctrine of "knowing receipt" of assets obtained by a third party in breach of trust. Sir Anthony Mason, in the first chapter of the book, introduces this issue by observing that the law in this area is replete with arcane distinctions and quoting from Lord Millett who said, nine years ago that "the unsatisfactory and confused state into which the law in this area has fallen is little short of a disgrace."[28] In chapter 12, Lord Millett returns to this theme and is joined by Professor Bryan in chapter 13 in advocating recognition of a strict liability action in unjust enrichment against the recipient of trust assets (subject to defences such as change of position). Millett and Bryan, however, differ in their approach to the scope of unjust enrichment claims and in particular, whether claims to vindicate property rights are part of the law of unjust enrichment (Bryan) or based on a separate legal event based on the nature of a property right (Millett). As the law develops, it might be that both possibilities are recognised. Concurrent liability means that one action need not exclude another.[29]

The strict liability unjust enrichment claim against a recipient of trust assets that is advocated in chapters 12 and 13 (in England and Australia respectively) was first advanced by Professor Birks.[30] Birks' argument was that equity should follow the common law, which imposes strict liability upon the recipient of

---

27   This was described as the "broad ground" which was favoured by two Law Lords and assumed to be correct by a third in *Alfred McAlpine Construction Ltd v Panatown Ltd* [2001] 1 AC 518.

28   P Millett, "Equity — The Road Ahead" (1995-1996) 6 *King's College Law Journal* 1 at 10.

29   *Henderson v Merrett Syndicates Ltd* [1995] 2 AC 145.

30   P Birks, *An Introduction to the Law of Restitution* (rev edn, Clarendon Press, Oxford, 1989) at 477-478. His final writing on this topic forcefully maintained this position: P Birks, "Knowing Receipt: Re Montagu's Settlement Trusts Revisited" (2001) 2 *Global Jurist* 1; P Birks, 'Receipt' in P Birks and A Pretto (eds), *Breach of Trust* (Hart Publishing, Oxford, 2002) at chapter 7.

another's asset.[31] An irony of this debate is that in the mid-19th century the position was the opposite. The common law insisted upon fault whereas equity imposed strict liability. A controversial *obiter dictum* in advice to the House of Lords by 12 common law judges in *Marsh v Keating*[32] had suggested a requirement of knowledge or fault at common law. In contrast, in *Harrison v Pryce*, Lord Hardwicke ordered an account against a recipient of trust assets and said that the case "may be compared to that of a man's goods coming into the hands of different persons one after the other; in which case an action [strict liability] of trover may be brought against any of the persons who have ever had possession of the goods."[33] Although this decision is reported by both Barnadiston[34] and Atkins[35] and only Barnadiston reports this remark of Lord Hardwicke, Barnadiston's report has been observed to be more accurate than the very abbreviated Atkins report which even incorrectly records the order in the rolls.[36] Although Australian and Canadian law still insist upon fault[37] it is extremely likely that the House of Lords will adopt a strict liability approach at the next opportunity.[38]

Chapters 15 and 16 consider the operation of money remedies across common law and equity. In chapter 15, Professor Burrows, after discussing the background of the fusion debate and setting out the range of common law and equitable remedies, critiques the refusal by the majority of the New South Wales Court of Appeal in *Harris v Digital Pulse Pty Ltd*[39] to recognize the availability of punitive damages for a breach of fiduciary duty. Although he disagrees with the conclusion, Burrows observes, and applauds, the approach taken by all members of the court in *Harris* that development of equity by analogy with the common law was, in theory at least, possible. In chapter 16 Professor McInnes focuses upon disgorgement relief and shows that whilst disgorgement of profits is well recognized as a remedy which follows an accounting for profits it also has a respectable history at common law. This is not often recognised. McInnes also distinguishes disgorgement awards from restitutionary and compensatory awards, all of which are available at common law as well as in equity.

---

31 *Holiday v Sigil* (1826) 2 C & P 176; 172 ER 81.
32 (1834) 2 Cl and Fin 250 at 289-290; 6 ER 1149 at 1164. See criticism of this obiter dictum in *James v Oxley* (1939) 61 CLR 433 at 456.
33 (1740) Barnadiston 324 at 324; 27 ER 664 at 664.
34 *Harrison v Pryce* (1740) Barnadiston 324; 27 ER 664.
35 *Harrison v Harrison* (1740) 2 Atkins 121; 26 ER 476.
36 An observation by Sir Edward Sugden (later Lord St Leonards) in argument in *Marsh v Keating* (1834) 2 Cl and Fin 250 at 267; 6 ER 1149 at 1155.
37 *Consul Developments Pty Ltd v DPC Estates Pty Ltd* (1975) 132 CLR 373. In Canada see *Gold v Rosenberg* [1997] 3 SCR 767.
38 Judicial remarks of the Law Lords: *Criterion Properties Plc v Stratford UK Properties LLC* [2004] UKHL 28; [2004] 1 WLR 1846 at [4] (Lord Nicholls; Lord Walker agreeing); *Twinsectra Ltd v Yardley* [2002] UKHL 12; [2002] 2 AC 164 (Lord Millett). Extrajudicially in addition to Lord Millett's chapter in this book: Lord Hoffmann 'The Redundancy of Knowing Assistance' in P Birks (ed), *The Frontiers of Liability* (Vol 1, Oxford University Press Oxford, 1994) 27 at 29; Lord Nicholls, 'Knowing Receipt: The Need for a New Landmark', chapter 17 in W Cornish, R Nolan, J O' Sullivan and G Virgo (eds), *Restitution Past, Present and Future* (Hart Publishing, Oxford, 1998); Lord Walker, "Dishonesty and Unconscionable Conduct in Commercial Life: Some Reflections on Accessory Liability and Knowing Receipt" (2005) 27 *Sydney Law Review* 187.
39 (2003) 56 NSWLR 298.

Chapters 17, 18 and 19 consider specific performance. One topical issue, upon which the High Court of Australia and House of Lords may differ, is the correctness of the decision in *Lysaght v Edwards,* that the vendor of land under an executory contract of sale holds the land on constructive trust for the purchaser. Mr Swadling argues that this trust cannot be justified. Applying an analysis which seeks to identify the event to which the vendor-purchaser trust responds, he concludes that the trust rests on a fiction and has no rational basis. Swadling argues that the combination of this irrationality, and the undeserved insolvency priority afforded by such a trust, indicate a need for legislation to abolish the vendor-purchaser constructive trust. Professor Chambers takes a different view. Discussing the Supreme Court of Canada's decision in *Semelhago v Paramadevan*[40] and the High Court of Australia's decision in *Tanwar Enterprises v Cauchi*[41] Chambers supports the rule that specifically enforceable contracts of sale produce constructive trusts. Chambers defends this rule not merely on the basis of precedent, but also because it is integral to the law of property. In particular, he argues that the power to obtain title to an asset is specifically enforceable against other members of society (subject to defences that protect interests acquired for value in good faith). This section concludes with a thorough chapter by Justice Young, the NSW Chief Judge in Equity, who considers the broad role of equity in contract generally and surveys the impact of developments over the last 400 years.

In Australia, the body of learning relating to the doctrines and remedies of equity is very closely associated with three original authors of the unrivalled Australian text on the subject.[42] Although Justice Meagher is now retired from the New South Wales Court of Appeal and Justice Lehane has passed away, the judgments of Justice Gummow in the High Court of Australia and his extra-judicial writing continue as a driving force of Australian equity. A parallel in Canada is the writing of Chief Justice McLachlin. In almost every chapter in this book the reader will find references to the judgments and writing of these two judicial scholars. We are honoured that the scholarship in this book is introduced by McLachlin and concluded by Gummow.

This book and the conference which generated it could not have happened without the support and assistance of many people. Foremostly, to all the authors of the chapters that follow for their painstaking research, engaging conference presentations, and effort and assistance with redrafts and revisions. Although it is not possible to thank the many other individuals and institutions that supported the conference and this book, we wish to acknowledge the financial support, time and effort from the Australian Financial Review, Blake Dawson Waldron, Freehills, Mallesons Stephen Jaques and the University of New South Wales (the sponsors of the conference), Catherine Fitzgerald and Lara Weeks (from Thomson Lawbook Co.), Jane Kelly and Christopher Lemercier (from the University of New South Wales) and three truly exceptional students of ours: Andrew Lodder, Benjamin Spagnolo and Kristin Van Zwieten, who provided enormous assistance with organization of the conference and the proofreading of the chapters in this book.

---

40   *Semelhago v Paramadevan* [1996] 2 SCR 415
41   *Tanwar Enterprises v Cauchi* [2003] HCA 57; (2003) 77 ALJR 1853.
42   Justices Meagher, Gummow and Lehane. See R Meagher, J D Heydon, M Leeming (eds), *Meagher, Gummow and Lehane's Equity Doctrines and Remedies* (4th ed, LexisNexis Butterworths, Sydney, 2002).

PART I

THE FUSION DEBATE

1

Fusion

ANTHONY MASON

I begin by congratulating Simone Degeling and James Edelman on their success in organising the conference from which the chapters in this book derive. They have managed to bring together fragmented bands of warring academic and judicial tribespeople to discuss the Fusion Wars.

The Fusion Wars have been notable for the penchant of some participants to draw upon the language of metaphor, denigration and personal point-scoring. In equity, as in law, the language of metaphor and simile serves to confuse and confound rather than to clarify, as Lord Diplock's reference to the confluence of the Rhone and Saone so convincingly demonstrated. At a conference years ago one speaker was moved to say that, on the occasions when he visited the confluence of those two rivers, all he could see was an impenetrable fog. The impenetrability of that fog has obscured Lord Diplock's reputation in the eyes of Australian equity lawyers.

As for personal pointscoring, it is the weapon of political disputation and often serves to conceal the intellectual void that lurks behind. True it is that academic disputants, mainly historians and scientists, occasionally resort to the same weapons. There is no reason why judges and lawyers, whether practising or academic, should follow such unscholarly examples. To that extent, I agree with what the late Professor Birks said in his recent review in the *Law Quarterly Review* (LQR) of the 4th edition of Meagher, Gummow and Lehane.[1] But, with all respect to the reviewer, his reference to the notorious Butcher Heydrich in an earlier article did nothing to advance the case for restitution which he constructed against those equity lawyers who favoured an approach based on unconscionability. Indeed, his LQR review and his "Letter to America"[2] exhibited traces of the very flaws he identified in others, though his defenders will say that he used a rapier, not a meat cleaver.

So my first message, admittedly an unpopular one which will fall, I suspect, on some deaf ears, is that lawyers should return to the customs and convention of civilised discourse in devoting themselves to the tradition of high scholarship.

Once we move beyond the rhetoric, the metaphors and the personal pointscoring, some of the broad issues are easily resolved. On the narrow issue

---

1   (2004) 120 *Law Quarterly Review* 344.
2   P Birks, "A Letter to America: The New Restatement of Restitution" [2003] 3(2) *Global Jurist Frontiers* (Article 2) 1.

of fusion there is no support for Sir George Jessel's early view that the Judicature Acts had a substantive operation resulting in the instant merger of legal and equitable estates. To-day the accepted view is that the Judicature Acts had a procedural operation and that the Acts did not bring about automatic fusion of the rules of common law and equity.[3]

On the other hand, it is also clear that the Acts did not require the courts to treat the rules of common law and equity as if they must forever remain unchanged in frozen isolation. The courts were free, within the limits attaching to the judicial process, to develop those rules, as indeed the courts have proceeded to do in England for over a century since the Judicature system was introduced and in this jurisdiction (New South Wales) since 1970 when, as Sir Kenneth Jacobs once said, we belatedly made the "Great Leap Forward" to 1875.

Likewise, the Judicature Acts contained no prohibition against judicial development of equity rules by reference to common law principle and doctrine and vice versa. In other words, fusion by analogy, to use a term employed by Professor Burrows and others, was permissible.[4] Nonetheless my strong impression was that, here in New South Wales, the last surviving bastion of unreconstructed equity jurisprudence, there has been resistance to the notion that the principles of equity could, even in limited respects, be developed (or should I say "polluted") by reference to the common law.

I doubt that now anyone seriously maintains such an absolute proposition. Antipodean antiquarianism does not stretch quite that far – at least I don't think it does. Perhaps I should apologise to New Zealand lawyers for using the adjective "Antipodean". To imply that they are antiquarians is not quite cricket – to make such a suggestion is the equitable equivalent of bowling another underarm delivery. If our trans-Tasman colleagues have any shortcomings – and I am not suggesting they have – legal and equitable antiquarianism is not among them. Lord Cooke, who could not remotely be described as an antiquarian, would unhesitatingly repudiate such a suggestion.

Maitland predicted that the day would come when lawyers would cease to inquire whether a given rule would be a rule of equity or a rule of common law. The relative absence in contemporary United States jurisprudence of fusion controversy seems to vindicate Maitland's prediction, even if other explanations, including legislation, contribute to this phenomenon.

The difference in our situation – and I speak here with particular reference to Australia – is that we are pre-occupied with the past and with the dominant notion that history has lessons for us. No doubt it has, but not to the extent of dictating answers to present legal problems. Knowledge of history, in the law, as in other disciplines, is of fundamental importance in explaining how we have arrived where we are. It does not, however, provide us with infallible signposts to our destination. In combination with other relevant considerations, history may well carry us to our destination, but not on its own. Maitland, as

---

3   Discussed by K Mason, 'Fusion: Fallacy, Future or Finished?', chapter 3 in this book and Professor Smith, 'Fusion and Tradition', chapter 2 in this book.

4   A Burrows, 'Remedial Coherence and Punitive Damages in Equity', chapter 15 in this book. See also J Edelman, "A 'Fusion Fallacy' Fallacy?" (2003) 119 *Law Quarterly Review* 375 at 377.

Dr Getzler reminds us, saw a deep understanding of the history of the law as an indispensable foundation of our ability to transcend it.[5]

The pre-Judicature attitudes of mind and the language of Chancery judges and lawyers have been used to support a history-bound approach. To say that equity had no jurisdiction to award common law relief of a particular kind had and has a resonance of authority and finality about it. But what does such a statement mean? Simply that, because relief of that kind was awarded at common law and had not been awarded in equity, equity would not award it for breach of an equitable obligation. To say that equity had no jurisdiction to award exemplary damages means no more than that an award of exemplary damages was a common law remedy with no provenance in equity. The "no jurisdiction" formula, not infrequently invoked by Chancery judges and lawyers, did not reflect a judgment on the policy considerations which are now urged in favour of awarding exemplary damages for breach of equitable obligations in exceptional cases such as flagrant breaches of trust. How can the "no jurisdiction" formula afford a convincing answer to policy arguments not previously considered? Indeed, the effect of the Judicature Acts was to relegate that approach to the detritus of history.

If there be a real place for exemplary damages in a rational system of law, one would have thought that a flagrant breach of trust is an obvious candidate for such an award unless it be thought that other sanctions against an errant trustee are such that exemplary damages would serve no useful purpose.

A fundamental question, however, is whether there is a place for exemplary damages in our law. In this respect, I do not disagree with the result reached in *Harris v Digital Pulse Pty Ltd*,[6] though I would not speak in jurisdictional terms. I have never been an enthusiastic advocate for exemplary damages. It is a blunt instrument with the potential to do a lot of random damage. The American experience has been less than encouraging. It has generated wide-ranging detrimental economic consequences which have come about largely because American jury verdicts are respected, a problem that would not confront us to the same extent. Even so, exemplary damages do not lend themselves to thorough-going review, just as defamation damages were not readily reviewed under the old dispensation.

A narrower question is: do we need exemplary damages in equity? The question raises many other questions, one of which is whether exemplary damages would have a significant deterrent effect on breaches of trust and fiduciary duty. Intuitively, I suspect that the detriments would outweigh any gains. Exemplary damages might serve a useful purpose in defamation in alerting media proprietors and keeping them to their responsibilities – but that is another and very different story which is relevant to the broader question.

I am not a little surprised at the newly discovered enthusiasm for exemplary damages. There seems to be more support for it than there was a decade or so ago.

---

5   J Getzler, 'Am I my Beneficiary's Keeper? Fusion and Loss Based Fiduciary Remedies', chapter 10 in this book.

6   (2003) 56 NSWLR 298. The case is also discussed by A Burrows, 'Remedial Coherence and Punitive Damages in Equity', chapter 15 in this book.

Whether equity should adopt a particular common law rule or remedy in relation to breach of an equitable obligation, be it causation, contributory negligence, mitigation, measure of damages, remoteness of damage, must depend upon a variety of factors. In the case of some equitable rules or remedies, it may be that the differences between the relevant rules of common law and equity in relation to their origins, history, scope, reach and, more importantly, the duties which they create or the purposes which they serve, are so pronounced that assimilation or importation cannot be justified. Each rule may create a different duty or serve a different purpose and there may be a present need for each rule to serve its purpose.

Such differences, however, should not necessarily preclude an assimilation of common law and equity rules which lack a shared inheritance. Rules can transcend both their origins and their history and they can serve more than one purpose. This is simply to say that rules are not immutable; they are not inflexibly anchored in the past. They are capable of evolutionary adjustment in response to changes in circumstances and conditions and the need for orderly, coherent and principled development of the law and its rules, principles and remedies.

It follows that any fusion by analogy of particular rules or remedies must depend upon a thorough analysis of the relevant rules and remedies, taking account of factors already mentioned. Differences in origins and history are unlikely to be decisive except to the extent that they throw light on the scope of a duty or the purpose which a rule or remedy serves.

Even then, as I have said, it should not be assumed that the existence of a difference in scope of duty or in purpose which emerges on an analysis of rules and remedies will dictate an answer to the question which arises. The orderly, coherent and principled development of the law may point in another direction. The High Court of Australia recently identified the coherence of the law as an important factor in judicial elucidation of legal principle, as indeed it is.

It can scarcely be suggested that the complexity of the existing law governing unjust enrichment, knowing assistance and knowing receipt exhibits the hallmark of coherence. The law in this area is replete with arcane distinctions. Nine years ago, Lord Millett said:[7]

> "The unsatisfactory and confused state into which the law in this area has fallen is little short of a disgrace."

The intervening years have not brought greater certainty. We are still beset by fine distinctions and arguments about the different gradations of knowledge. Nine years ago, the Privy Council thought that commercial people would have no difficulty in recognising what is "dishonest" or "commercially unacceptable" conduct in the context of accessory liability for breach of trust.[8] The assumption underlying that statement is that the judges knew what "dishonest" meant. Now we know that judges are not agreed as to what "dishonest" means in that context.[9] Perhaps we should leave the definition of "dishonest" in the

---

7   P Millett, "Equity – The Road Ahead" (1995-1996) 6 *King's College Law Journal* 1 at 10.
8   *Royal Brunei Airlines v Tan* [1995] 2 AC 378 at 389.
9   *Twinsectra v Yardley* [2002] 2 AC 164.

context of commercial conduct to the judgment of commercial people. So much for the superior claims of "dishonest" conduct over "unconscionable" conduct in the search for certainty. There is an obvious case for charting a clearer approach to these and other problems.[10]

In such an exercise, a critical question is whether the different approaches and remedies which have evolved at common law and in equity in response to issues which, at least superficially, appear to share a good deal in common, should be maintained. There is no place for inconsistent treatment of like cases.

In *Bristol & West Building Society v Mothew*,[11] Lord Millett sought to identify some common ground where common law rules would apply to the liability of a fiduciary for breach of the duty of skill and care. He said:[12]

"Equitable compensation for breach of the duty of skill and care resembles common law damages in that it is awarded by way of compensation to the plaintiff for his loss. There is no reason in principle why the common law rules of causation, remoteness of damage and measure of damage should not be applied by analogy in such a case. It should not be confused with equitable compensation for breach of fiduciary duty, which may be awarded in lieu of rescission or specific restitution."

This approach, which was followed by the New Zealand Court of Appeal in *Bank of New Zealand v NZ Guardians Trust Co Ltd*[13] may be compared with that advocated by Lord Browne-Wilkinson in *Henderson v Merrett Syndicates.*[14] There his Lordship said that:[13]

"The duty of care imposed on bailees, carriers, trustees, directors, agents and others is the same duty; it arises from the circumstances in which the defendants were acting, not from their status or description."

On the other hand, the Australian High Court (to use a quaint expression favoured by overseas commentators – it seems to pitch the High Court of Australia at the same level as the English High Court or the New Zealand High Court) has expressed reservations about this in *Youyang Pty Limited v Minter Ellison*.[16] You will recall the passage.[17] It has its genesis in a judgment of McLachlin CJ in *Canson Enterprises Pty Ltd v Boughton & Co*.[18] After referring to the unique foundation and goals of equity, including the trust, the High Court asked the question whether there could be any assimilation, even in this limited way, between equitable compensation and common law compensatory damages.

The raising of the question seems to suggest that the unique nature of equity makes fusion by analogy inappropriate, at least in relation to equitable

---

10 See M Bryan, 'The Liability of the Recipient: Restitution at Common Law or Wrongdoing in Equity', chapter 13 in this book.

11 [1998] Ch 1. See now *Hilton v Barker Booth and Eastwood (a firm)* [2005] 1 All ER 651 which approves (at 660) *Mothew's* Case.

12 *Bristol & West Building Society v Mothew*, above n 11 at 17.

13 [1999] 1 NZLR 664 at 681.

14 [1995] 2 AC 145.

15 *Henderson v Merrett Syndicates*, above n 14 at 205.

16 (2003) 212 CLR 484.

17 *Youyang Pty Limited v Minter Ellison*, above n 16 at 500[39].

18 (1995) 85 DLR (4th) 129.

duties. The reference to trust duties may indicate that the thrust of the comment is directed to protecting trust territory from common law invaders. But the reference to the uniqueness of equity may indicate that a much larger expanse of territory is to be preserved from alien incursion.

It may be that Lord Browne-Wilkinson's view that all the duties of care to which he refers, particularly those applicable to trustees, arise from the circumstances, not from status, is open to question. Even if he be mistaken, the question is whether the duties of care differ or should differ significantly in scope and content. This question remains to be resolved authoritatively. In the case of the trustee, there are arguments for imposing a higher duty of care than that imposed by the common law. One is that the trustee, most notably the express or primary trustee with management and other duties to perform, should be kept up to his duties. On the other side, the virtue of having a single duty of care imposed, the standard being calibrated to the circumstances of the case, has its own attractions in terms of simplicity and may well be appropriate, particularly in the case of those who are not professional trustees.

At a level below that of the trustee, in the case of the fiduciary, the arguments for imposing a higher duty of care or standard of care than that imposed by the common law are certainly weaker. Here we are dealing with an indefinable miscellany of particular relationships, including bailees and ad hoc relationships. Why should every bailee who happens to be a fiduciary owe a higher duty of care than those who are not. And what about directors who are now subject to an array of statutory duties?

If, in *Mothew* and *Breen v Williams*,[19] the courts, apart from the obligation of full and frank disclosure, had not confined fiduciaries to proscriptive duties – the no conflict rule and the no unauthorised benefit rule – and had imposed positive fiduciary duties, there may have been a stronger case for differentiating the fiduciary's duty of care from that of the common law duty of care. That path was not followed.

Indeed, in *Breen v Williams*, Gummow J cautioned against translating into general fiduciary law particular principles developed in the administration of trusts. His Honour pointed out that the obligations of a trustee in a number of respects arise from a characteristic of the trust relationship not from the fiduciary relationship. He went on to say that trustee obligations do not "supply any proper foundations for the imposition on fiduciaries in general of a quasi-tortious duty to act solely in the best interests of their principal".[20]

Absent a relevant fiduciary duty, it is not easy to see why a non-trustee fiduciary should owe a higher duty than the common law duty of care. The argument that the miscellaneous band of non-trustee fiduciaries are not free and independent actors, unlike the common law defendant, but are bound to act in the interests of their principal, is not particularly compelling given the limited fiduciary duties acknowledged in *Mothew* and *Breen v Williams*. The argument comes from McLachlin CJ's judgment in *Canson Enterprises* and it is a reflection of the more expansive Canadian notion of the scope of the fiduciary relationship and the duties of a fiduciary.

---

19   (1996) 186 CLR 71.
20   *Breen v Williams*, above n 19 at 137.

Much rests on a comparison of the relevant duties. If their scope is relevantly the same or similar, there is certainly a case for fusion by analogy. And, in making the comparison we should avoid the temptation, to which lawyers sometimes succumb, of making a distinction for its own sake or, in the case of equity lawyers, for pointing out some difference simply for the purpose of preserving equity jurisprudence as an independent body of rules.

Generalised references to notions such as the "unique foundations and goals of equity" offer an insecure foundation for reasoning to a specific conclusion, in the absence of other compelling reasons. So also with the concept of vulnerability. It has emerged as a possible touchstone to the existence of a common law duty of care. If there is anything in this suggestion, it might tend to indicate that there is a basis for an analogy between the fiduciary's liability for negligence and the common law duty.

If we are looking for distinguishing features between the common law and equity, the former is a rule-based system, whereas equity has always relied upon the existence of discretions to alleviate the consequences of principles and doctrines. This difference – again a generalised difference – is not an answer to every prospect of fusion by analogy.

It would be a mistake to assume that it is only a matter of determining whether equity should follow common rules or offer common law remedies or vice versa. There are past examples of outstanding judges who have fashioned new principles applicable at common law or equity by drawing upon the companion body of law. Lord Mansfield had no hesitation in shaping the principles governing the action for money had and received by reference to the principles of equity and natural law.

In his intriguing work *The Mansfield Manuscripts and the Growth of English Law in the Eighteenth Century*,[21] James Oldham refers to Lord Mansfield's "inclination to accomplish individual justice whenever he could do so without harm to overriding principles[22] – an inclination which was scathingly criticised in Junius's letters".[23] This inclination mirrored his extensive private law practice in Chancery work when he was at the Bar.

More recently, Sir Owen Dixon in his judgments on estoppel succeeded in formulating new principles applicable at common law by reference to notions of equity and justice.[24] All the discussion about legalism and the enigmatic quality of his approach to the law tends to obscure the fact that he was an extremely creative judge. The enigmatic quality of his approach to the law reflected the underlying tensions in the role of the judge.

It so happens that the two judges whose creativity I invoke drew upon equity to enliven the common law. Reverse engineering is more difficult to identify. Perhaps the most interesting recent example of fusion by analogy is the

---

21 (University of North Carolina Press, Chapel Hill, 1992) at 100.

22 J Oldham, *The Mansfield Manuscripts and the Growth of English Law in the Eighteenth Century*, above n 21 referring to *Alderson v Temple* (1768) 4 Burr 2235; 98 ER 165.

23 J Oldham, *The Mansfield Manuscripts and the Growth of English Law in the Eighteenth Century*, above n 21 referring to Letter 41, in Junius *Letters*, 2:42.

24 *Thompson v Palmer* (1933) 49 CLR 507; *Grundt v Great Boulder Pty Gold Mines Ltd* (1937) 59 CLR 641.

award of gain-based damages at common law, endorsed by the House of Lords in *Attorney-General v Blake*,[25] and by the Supreme Court of Canada,[26] but so far not followed in Australia. Again, it was an illustration of what equity can do for the common law.[27]

The magnitude of the debate about fusion, while it has been instructive and enlightening, is somewhat removed from the judicial method which ordinarily informs the way in which judges go about deciding cases. There is no way in which a judge or a court can achieve comprehensive fusion by analogy overnight. There are instances to be found where judges legitimately adopt a "top down" approach and develop an overarching principle, just as Sir Owen Dixon did in the estoppel cases to which I referred. This is what Lord Millett and Lord Browne-Wilkinson endeavoured to do in *Mothew* and *Henderson* respectively. But the occasions where the attempt is justified do not often arise and, as the attempts of courts of final appeal to find the key to the common law duty of care demonstrate, even then the attempt does not always succeed. Fusion by analogy is necessarily a painstaking process which can only proceed on a case by case basis.

Is there then a case for law reform? The answer must be "yes". But is there a political will to engage in such an exercise? The answer is "probably not". In any event, my experience of many equity lawyers – notably the Australian strain – is that they would resist legislative intervention even more stoutly than the threat of common law importation.

---

25   [2001] 1 AC 268.
26   *Bank of Canada v Clarica Trust Co* [2002] 2 SCR 601.
27   See M McInnes, 'Account of Profits for Common Law Wrongs', chapter 16 in this book.

2

Fusion and Tradition

LIONEL SMITH[1]

THE IDEA OF A LEGAL TRADITION

A legal tradition is a way of understanding and solving legal problems.[2] The same legal problem may be approached in different ways by different legal traditions, even if ultimately they arrive at the same solution. They may use different terminology, and they may employ different legal abstractions as tools in the reasoning process. The result is that discourse that is intelligible within one tradition may not be intelligible within another.

Rationality is a tradition, although not especially a legal one.[3] There is also a rationality in tradition. This means more than that a tradition must be internally consistent. It also means there is good reason to feel bound by a tradition. An institutional commitment to a way of solving legal problems provides a rational reason to continue to solve them in that way, even though other equally rational ways are available. In other words, there is a certain irrationality in inconsistency.[4] This is why cases that are materially alike must be resolved similarly. It is also why judges, even more so than other people, may be reluctant to change course overtly; this represents an institutional inconsistency, not merely a personal one. In *Anderton v Ryan*,[5] the accused bought a video recorder believing it was stolen; but it was never proven that it was stolen. Charged with an attempt to handle stolen goods, she was acquitted by the House of Lords. A little later, in *R v Shivpuri*,[6] the accused thought he was carrying prohibited drugs but, presumably because the people for whom he was carrying had been duped, his suitcase was full of some "harmless vegetable matter." Nonetheless, his conviction on a charge of attempt was affirmed by the

---

1   I am grateful to the Social Sciences and Humanities Research Council of Canada for financial assistance and to the Swiss Institute of Comparative Law for its hospitality during 2004-2005.
2   HP Glenn, *Legal Traditions of the World* (2nd ed, Oxford University Press, Oxford, 2004).
3   HP Glenn, *Legal Traditions of the World*, above n 2 at 1-2.
4   See B Chapman, "Legal Analysis of Economics: Solving the Problem of Rational Commitment" (2004) 79 *Chicago-Kent Law Review* 471.
5   [1985] 1 AC 560.
6   [1987] 1 AC 1.

House. Lord Bridge was in the majority in both cases. The second speech must have been difficult to deliver. It is not just the difficulty of admitting a past mistake. Everyone makes mistakes. It is the implication for the system, and for the future. What kind of legal system makes a considered decision at the highest level and then reverses itself 371 days later? And what implications does this have for the new holding — is it any more secure than the previous one?

There is therefore a rational reason why a legal tradition is always understood as normative, in the sense that it is in some degree binding for the future. This is crystallised not only in the doctrine of precedent, but in the use of legal fictions, which amount to a kind of collective self-delusion that change is not happening when everyone knows that it is.[7] In certain kinds of discourse, an argument based purely on history is not a very good argument for the justi- fication of some present state of affairs. If I ask my son why I can't find my watch, and he answers that he has flushed it down the toilet, he has given a historical account that explains but fails to justify the current absence of the watch. With this kind of relationship between history and justification in mind, some legal analysts argue that legal history is of no value in justifying current law. But it is not only through the doctrine of precedent that prior decisions are relevant in a justificatory way. Academics cite cases too, although they are not bound by them; and they do not cite them only by way of saying that they agree with the reasoning (which they may well not). Rather, it is more often by way of saying that the issue has been resolved and the path chosen.[8] Together a body of decisions generates a way of knowing or an epistemology, which creates a rational reason to continue to act in a way that is consistent with that episte- mology and legitimate within that legal tradition. The binding force of tradition is by no means absolute, but that does not mean that it is nugatory.[9]

---

7   LL Fuller, *Legal Fictions* (Stanford University Press, Stanford, 1967); L Smith, "Constructive Trusts and Constructive Trustees" (1999) 58 *Cambridge Law Journal* 294 at 295.

8   P Birks, "Adjudication and interpretation in the common law: a century of change" (1994) 14 *Legal Studies* 156 at 164: "everyone would admit ... that law books cannot be safely relied upon as a simple alternative to cases, to do the same work which is normally done by cases."

9   OW Holmes famously said, "it is revolting to have no better reason for a rule of law than that so it was laid down in the time of Henry IV. It is still more revolting if the grounds upon which it was laid down have vanished long since, and the rule simply persists from blind imitation of the past": "The Path of the Law" (1897), 10 *Harvard Law Review* 457 at 469 (reprinted in OW Holmes, *Collected Legal Papers* (Harcourt, Brace & Co, New York, 1920) at 167 and in SM Novick (ed), *Collected Works of Justice Holmes* (University of Chicago Press, Chicago, 1995) Vol 3 at 391 and in (1998) 78 *Boston University Law Review* 699). That article as a whole, and his other writings, show that Holmes was very much alive to the normative force of history in legal tradition; there is a reason he was such an accomplished legal historian. Just before the sentences quoted above, he said, "history must be a part of the study, because without it we cannot know the precise scope of rules which it is our business to know. It is a part of the rational study, because it is the first step toward an enlightened scepticism, that is, toward a deliberate reconsideration of the worth of those rules." And elsewhere he said, "the past gives us our vocabulary and fixes the limits of our imagination; we cannot get away from it. There is, too, a peculiar logical pleasure in making manifest the continuity between what we are doing and what has been done before. But the present has a right to govern itself so far as it can; and it ought always to be remembered that historic continuity with the past is not a duty, it is only a necessity": OW Holmes, 'Learning and Science' in OW Holmes, *Collected Legal Papers*, at 139; also in SM Novick (ed), *Collected Works of Justice Holmes*, at 492.

Although the principles of Equity[10] do not constitute a complete system of law, it seems clear enough that Equity constitutes a legal tradition distinct from the common law. The two traditions have distinct (albeit frequently overlapping) histories. Before the Judicature Act reforms, the common law and Equity had different courts, judges and practitioners.[11] They had different methods of proof and different principles of civil procedure. They had different processes for the enforcement of their orders. They also had different vocabularies and different ways of addressing what they understood to be different sorts of questions.[12]

POLITICS OF FUSION

Kinds of fusion

The word "fusion" can function like a verbal hand grenade in many contexts. It is not at all clear that the participants in these discussions are all discussing the same thing. Some who are decried as "fusionists" by those opposed to them would not use that word to describe their position. In this section I will try to work out what are the substantial objectives of at least some participants to the debate.

I assume everyone agrees that what the Judicature Acts wrought was, at least, *procedural fusion*: one court, one judge, one set of lawyers to resolve a dispute. If this is the only kind of fusion that has occurred, then no case will be decided substantively differently than it would have been under the pre-Judicature Acts regime.

What more than that is desired by some, and is resisted by others? One possibility could be called *terminological fusion*. We could stop saying, "we do this at common law and that in equity," the title of the important contribution by Professor Burrows.[13] This may not be as trivial as it seems, because for many, it is the constant duality, which can be seen as a mere accident of history, that

---

10   I will use "Equity" for the system of courts and doctrine, and "equity" for the idea captured by the Latin *aequitas* or the French *équité*; Quebec Research Centre of Private and Comparative Law, *Private Law Dictionary* (2nd ed, Yvon Blais, Montreal, 1991), sv "equity." See also J Hackney, 'More Than a Trace of the Old Philosophy' in P Birks (ed), *The Classification of Obligations* (Clarendon Press, Oxford, 1997) at 123 n 2; S Worthington, *Equity* (Oxford University Press, Oxford, 2003) at 9 n 1.

11   In some places, such as New South Wales and England and Wales, there may continue to be a separate Equity or Chancery division of a unified court, which implies a continuing specialisation of the judiciary, and a continuing specialisation in the legal profession.

12   Although in some cases this distinctness may have been exaggerated for political purposes: S Gardner, "Equity, Estate Contracts and the Judicature Acts: *Walsh v Lonsdale* Revisited" (1987) 7 *Oxford Journal of Legal Studies* 60 at 92-94.

13   A Burrows, "We Do This At Common Law But That in Equity" (2002) 22 *Oxford Journal of Legal Studies* 1. The article, however, advocates substantive as well as terminological fusion. Burrows's arguments are further developed in A Burrows, *Fusing Common Law and Equity: Remedies, Restitution and Reform* (Hochelaga Lectures 2001, Sweet & Maxwell Asia, Hong Kong, 2002).

some find unacceptable.[14] A narrow terminological fusion could get rid of dual terminology without actually changing the substantive results of cases. In this sense, it would be outside the definition of the "fusion fallacy".[15]

To take one example, we could move from saying "at common law, a plaintiff is *entitled* to damages for breach of contract; but in equity, he *may* be able to obtain a decree of specific performance" to saying "a plaintiff is *entitled* to damages for breach of contract; but he *may* be able to obtain an order for specific performance". The same exercise could be conducted even in the domain of Equity's exclusive jurisdiction. We could describe a trust relationship without saying "equitable" or "legal". "A trust is a manner of holding property in which the holder, called a trustee, accountably administers property for the achievement of an abstract purpose or for the exclusive benefit of other persons, called beneficiaries (of which he may be one); the trust property is not available to personal creditors of the trustee." It is general enough to capture bare trusts, including constructive and resulting trusts.[16] It does not say that the trustee's obligations are Equitable in origin.[17] But a definition does not need an etymology, although we often find etymology interesting, and sometimes it is the very object of our study. You can define "palinode," the word that Lord MacKay of Clashfern applied to the speech of Lord Bridge in *R v Shivpuri*, without revealing its pedigree from Greek through Latin to modern Romance languages.[18]

Thirdly, of course, there is a more substantive sense of "fusion" which is what most people have in mind when they address the issue. *Substantive fusion* entails that the results of cases will be substantively different than they would have been under the pre-Judicature Acts regime. A topical example is the availability of punitive or exemplary damages for a breach of fiduciary obligation, vigorously aired in *Harris v Digital Pulse Pty Ltd*.[19]

Before addressing this in more detail, it is worth pausing to notice that terminological fusion, non-substantive in itself, is liable to lead to substantive

---

14   For example, P Birks, 'Definition and Division: A Meditation on *Institutes* 3.13' in P Birks (ed), *The Classification of Obligations* (Clarendon Press, Oxford, 1997) at 15-17 (although Birks also advocated substantive fusion).

15   R Meagher, JD Heydon, M Leeming, *Meagher Gummow and Lehane's Equity: Doctrines and Remedies* (4th ed, Butterworths, Sydney, 2002) at 54: the "fusion fallacy" is defined as a belief in substantive fusion.

16   This is why the definition omits any reference to duties of loyalty.

17   By contrast, see the definition in D Hayton, *Underhill and Hayton: Law of Trusts and Trustees* (16 ed, Butterworths, London, 2003) at 3.

18   "Palinode" is a poetical word for "retraction." Note, however, that Burrows observes ((2002) 22 *Oxford Journal of Legal Studies* 1 at 5) that even terminological fusion might be very difficult in some contexts. Can we reformulate, without "legal" and "Equitable", the rule that a bona fide purchaser for value of a legal interest, without notice of a pre-existing Equitable interest, is not bound by that Equitable interest? Ames argued that the true doctrine is indifferent to whether the bona fide purchaser acquired a legal or an equitable interest: 'Purchase for Value Without Notice' in JB Ames, *Lectures on Legal History, and Miscellaneous Legal Essays* (Harvard University Press, Cambridge, Massachusetts, 1913) at 253. This would make the reformulation more feasible.

19   (2003) 56 NSWLR 298, discussed by A Burrows, 'Remedial Coherence and Punitive Damages in Equity' in this book, at 391–402.

fusion. The debate in *Harris* arises partly because of a careful refusal to talk about "damages" for breach of fiduciary obligation, and instead to discuss "equitable compensation." If instead we say that damages just means a money order, usually compensatory, and so we might as well say "damages for breach of fiduciary obligation," then we may not even notice that there could be an issue to be addressed when someone asks for punitive damages for the breach of such an obligation. This seems to have happened in Canada.[20] A legal tradition is like a language — it partly *is* a language — and if a language is not used, or is used only in formal ways and not as a tool for the communication of ideas, it will die.[21]

Pro-fusion arguments

Why is there a call for substantive fusion? The argument is primarily based on rationality, and in particular on consistency. If two cases are materially alike, they should be resolved in the same way, whether the plaintiff's rights are legal or equitable. It is not easy to argue against the goal of treating like cases alike. This goal is part of the rule of law, but only, I think, because it is rational to treat like cases alike, and if the law is not rational it loses its normative force.

There is a sub-theme relating to discretion.[22] If Equitable remedies are discretionary, in a meaningful way, then there is not only a possibility that like cases will be treated differently, but an apparent acceptance of that outcome. The elimination of any such strong discretion in Equity can be seen as promoting consistency even within the sphere of Equity. More broadly, if no such discretion exists at common law, then its elimination also serves the goal of consistency between Equity and the common law. Discretion also creates uncertainty, which is a different vice from inconsistency.[23]

---

20   In *M (K) v M (H)* (1992) 96 DLR (4th) 289 at 337f, the Supreme Court of Canada affirmed a trial jury's award which included punitive damages, holding that such damages could be awarded for a breach of fiduciary duty. There was very little discussion, and this particular point does not seem to have been contested, the case being mainly about limitation periods (see (1992) 96 DLR (4th) 289 at 336g, 340c). When the Court recently restated the law of punitive damages, their availability for breaches of fiduciary duty was confirmed, again with little discussion but for a reference to *M (K) v M (H)*: see *Whiten v Pilot Insurance Co* (2002) 209 DLR (4th) 257 at [67]. Neither case mentioned the fact that McLachlin and L'Heureux-Dubé JJ, in the minority in *Norberg v Wynrib* (1992) 92 DLR (4th) 449 at 505-507, would have allowed such damages. There was more discussion there, but no suggestion that there was any particular difficulty in awarding punitive damages for the breach of an Equitable duty.

21   Compare the discussion of the decline of the Raeto-Romansch language in J Steinberg, *Why Switzerland?* (2nd ed, Cambridge University Press, Cambridge, 1996) at 147-50. It is a national language of Switzerland, appearing for example on bank notes, but (at 149) "Dictionaries and grammars cannot prevent emigration from the Alpine fastness." From 1941 to 1990 the percentage of Swiss for whom Raeto-Romansch is the principal language fell from 1.1% to 0.6%.

22   See for example P Birks, "Rights, Wrongs and Remedies" (2000) 20 *Oxford Journal of Legal Studies* 1 at 16-17, 22-24.

23   That is, even if like cases were all treated alike, still if people could not know their legal position in advance of a ruling, there would be a rule of law objection based on unknowable law: L Fuller, *The Morality of Law* (Yale University Press, New Haven, 1964), at 49-51 (defect of secret law), 63-65 (defect of vagueness).

I will not address in detail the argument about judicial discretion, but I am not convinced that there is a serious problem here. To choose a few comments of Lord Eldon and use them to argue that Equity has long ago abandoned judicial discretion is a misreading of history[24] and of the modern law.[25] Particularly in some contexts, the law needs discretion, and it is found in every legal system, whether or not it has a tradition of Equity.[26] It may be impossible to get rid of it.[27] One might reasonably wish to delimit discretion, perhaps especially insofar as its exercise affects non-parties to the litigation in question; but discretion, as such, does not seem necessarily to be inconsistent with the rule of law.[28]

Another sub-theme relates to the idea of "unconscionability". This concept may be attacked on the same ground as an overt claim to judicial discretion: that it too is liable to create unacceptable uncertainty.[29] This attack, however, loses its force if "unconscionability" is not a test but a conclusion. A liability conclusion, like "negligence", "breach of contract", or "unjust enrichment", is

---

24 See the careful analysis by D Klinck, "Lord Eldon on 'Equity'" (1999) 20.3 *Journal of Legal History* 51.

25 *Chan v Cresdon Pty Ltd* (1989) 168 CLR 242 at [25]; *Semelhago v Paramadevan,* (1996) 136 DLR (4th) 1 at [20]-[22]; *Co-operative Insurance Society Ltd v Argyll Stores (Holdings) Ltd* [1998] AC 1; *Mediterranean Shipping Co SA v Atlantic Container Line AB* (unreported, 3 December 1998 (Eng CA)); *Schmidt v Rosewood Trust Ltd* [2003] 2 AC 709.

26 CK Allen, *Law in the Making* (7th ed, Clarendon Press, Oxford, 1964) at 383-399, concluding (at 425), "an element of discretionary justice is and has always been essential to the efficient interpretation and application of law."

27 See J Getzler, 'Patterns of Fusion' in P Birks (ed), *The Classification of Obligations* (Clarendon Press, Oxford, 1997) at 192 ("principle of conservation of aggregate discretion"); K Barker and L Smith, 'Unjust Enrichment' in D Hayton (ed), *Law's Future(s)* (Hart Publishing, Oxford, 2000) at 430 ("Law of Conservation of Judicial Discretion").

28 Karl Llewellyn posited a "Law of Lawful Discretion": KN Llewellyn, *The Common Law Tradition: Deciding Appeals* (Little, Brown & Co, Boston, 1960) at 217-219; see also KN Llewellyn, *The Bramble Bush* (Oceana, New York, 1951) at 156. Endicott's resolution of the problem which vagueness in law presents to the ideal of the rule of law is very similar: T Endicott, *Vagueness in Law* (Oxford University Press, Oxford, 2000) at 197-203. It is impossible to make the law absolutely certain in advance, but the existence of discretion is acceptable if the discretion itself is administered according to the rule of law. Asked to describe this limitation on their powers, judges may speak in terms of an unwillingness to "cheat": see D Robertson, *Judicial Discretion in the House of Lords* (Oxford University Press, Oxford, 1997) at 17, 74.

29 Professor Birks also raised the concern that it was liable to turn the law of unjust enrichment into a subset of the law of wrongs: P Birks, *Unjust Enrichment* (2nd ed, Oxford University Press, Oxford, 2005) at 6. He was certainly correct that it is a distinctive and defining feature of obligations arising from unjust enrichment, and of other obligations to make restitution, that they do not depend on wrongdoing: L Smith, "Restitution: The Heart of Corrective Justice" (2001) 79 *Texas Law Review* 2115. But for the reasons explained in the text, I am not sure that the idea of "unconscionability" necessarily tends in that direction, although I agree that stating the liability conclusion as "unconscionability" to the *exclusion* of the liability conclusion "unjust enrichment" would be a mistake. The two liability conclusions are at different levels of generality. For this reason, I would suggest that Gummow J erred in his concurring judgment in *Roxborough v Rothmans of Pall Mall Australia Ltd* (2001) 208 CLR 516 at 543-544, in supposing that if some examples of "money had and received" are not explicable as based on unjust enrichment, it follows that money had and received is never explicable as based on unjust enrichment, and therefore that "good conscience" is a

always in some sense circular, since it states that the defendant is liable in some way but does not explain why. The conclusion is expressed in normative language, but the reason that the circularity objection is usually invalid is that the liability conclusion is not usually applied directly to the facts of the case; more detailed rules typically mediate between the facts and the generally-worded liability conclusion.[30] A generally-worded liability conclusion can, occasionally, be applied directly to the facts where the case is a novel one which does not fall within any established and regulated category.[31]

If this is correct, then it is true to say that "unconscionability" does not explain the liability.[32] But it is not clear that it purports to explain anything, except a historical link. If the basis of all Equitable intervention was, originally, the prevention of unconscionable conduct (conduct which, while legal, would imperil the defendant's immortal soul), then unconscientiousness serves only to state the conclusion, using the traditional language of Equity, that Equity will intervene.[33] This means that the term is a very wide one; it covers all Equitable intervention, whether based on dishonesty, breach of contract, or the simple innocent receipt by a donee of trust property.[34] It is at a higher level of generality than those explanations. The unconscionability that justifies a decree of specific performance co-exists with a wrongful breach of contract, while the unconscionability that requires an innocent donee of trust property to give it up only co-exists with a pre-existing and undestroyed trust interest. Unconscionability in this sense does not entail any especially high degree of judicial discretion.

Moreover, in this relatively neutral sense, unconscionability does not raise any particular concerns about like cases being treated alike. Common law

---

better explanation. The fact is that money had and received covers many kinds of claim (see J Edelman, "Money Had and Received: Modern Pleading of an Old Count" (2000) 8 *Restitution Law Review* 547); not all examples can be explained as unjust enrichment, but many (perhaps most) can. If all examples of money had and received are nonetheless to be understood as based on "good conscience", this only shows how wide that liability conclusion is.

30   For example, in *Soulos v Korkontzilas* (1997) 146 DLR (4th) 214 the majority of the Supreme Court of Canada stated that constructive trusts are based on "good conscience" but went on to specify a legal test to govern whether a gain acquired in breach of fiduciary obligation is held on such a trust. The Privy Council also rejected unconscionability as a legal test in *Royal Brunei Airlines Sdn Bhd v Tan* [1995] 2 AC 378 at 392. The High Court of Australia sounded the same note in *Tanwar Enterprises Pty. Ltd v Cauchi* (2003) 201 ALR 359 at 365-366, and the same view is propounded in R Meagher, JD Heydon, M Leeming, *Meagher Gummow and Lehane's Equity: Doctrines and Remedies* (4th ed, Butterworths, Sydney, 2002) at xii, xvi.

31   Gummow J's concurring judgment in *Roxborough v Rothmans of Pall Mall Australia Ltd.* (2001) 208 CLR 516 seems to take the view that "against conscience" is not generally to be applied directly to the facts, although (at 553) it may occasionally be necessary so to apply it.

32   P Birks, *Unjust Enrichment* (2nd ed, Oxford University Press, Oxford, 2005) at 5-6. Unjust enrichment, on its own, is also too vague to be applied generally to the facts, except in rare cases (at 274). But it is narrower than unconscientiousness, since it is confined to cases of defective wealth transfers, or, somewhat more widely, reversible defendants' gains; it does not reach cases of loss without gain.

33   See generally D Klinck, "The Unexamined 'Conscience' of Contemporary Canadian Equity" (2001) 46 *McGill Law Journal* 571, who shows that the idea of conscience has been variable over the centuries and remains ill-defined, but persists partly for reasons of tradition.

34   In some periods the phrase "equitable fraud" played a similar role.

judges have sometimes used the language of unconscientiousness.[35] The best-known example is Lord Mansfield, who also described the action for money had and received as "equitable."[36] Lord Mansfield, however, was an early and passionate advocate of the substantive fusion of law and equity.[37] His example, for whatever it may be worth today, lends no support to those who resist substantive fusion, but nor does it lend support to those who would banish references to unconscionability.

Anti-fusion arguments

How can we understand the position of those who stand against substantive fusion? Can anyone be opposed to rationality in law and legal discourse? I doubt it, but it is not so simple as that. One reaction may be that the two cases that are being compared are not really alike at all, and so rationality does not compel identical outcomes.[38] This is similar to Lord Goff's warning, adopted by Lord Cooke, not to fall prey to the temptation of elegance.[39]

More interesting, perhaps, are the attitudes of those who are *generally* opposed to substantive fusion, rather than those who may object that the project is misconceived in relation to particular doctrines.[40] Why should anyone take this position? One might argue that the Judicature Acts give no

---

35   LA Knafla, "Conscience in the English Common Law Tradition" (1976) 26 *University of Toronto Law Journal* 1 points out that changes in common law procedure between the late fifteenth and early seventeenth centuries allowed the common law to become much more flexible than it had been, and in some situations the judges took account of conscience; for example, a defendant in debt might be denied wager of law (examples at 9-10). Conscience also appears in the judgments of Parke and Rolfe BB in the seminal common law case *Kelly v Solari* (1841) 9 M & W 54 at 58-59; 152 ER 24 at 26. For other examples, see B Kremer, "Restitution and Unconscientiousness: Another View" (2003) 119 *Law Quarterly Review* 188.

36   Most famously in *Moses v Macferlan* (1760) 2 Burr 1005; 97 ER 676; see also *Sadler v Evans* (1766) 4 Burr 1984; 98 ER 34. For discussion, see ET Bishop, "Money Had and Received, An Equitable Action at Law" (1933) 7 *Southern California Law Review* 41, the concurring judgment of Gummow J in *Roxborough v Rothmans of Pall Mall Australia Ltd* (2001) 208 CLR 516, and the comment by B Kremer, "Restitution and Unconscientiousness: Another View", above n 35. See also *Bradford Corp v Ferrand* [1902] 2 Ch 655 at 662, and J Getzler, *A History of Water Rights at Common Law* (Oxford University Press, Oxford, 2004) at 217-220.

37   In this, he was largely isolated in his own day, although Blackstone agreed: W Holdsworth, *A History of English Law* (Methuen & Co, London, 1938) Vol XII at 584-599. I am grateful to Michele Graziadei for the reference to Holdsworth's discussion.

38   For example, I have argued that the case of a transfer by a trustee, of property held in trust for the plaintiff, to the defendant is not materially identical to the case in which the plaintiff makes a transfer directly to the defendant: "Unjust Enrichment, Property and the Structure of Trusts" (2000) 116 *Law Quarterly* Review 412, refined in L Smith, "Restitution: The Heart of Corrective Justice" (2001) 79 *Texas Law Review* 2115 especially 2157-2174.

39   R Goff, "The Search for Principle" in 69 *Proceedings of the British Academy* 169, reprinted in W Swadling and G Jones (eds), *The Search for Principle* (Oxford University Press, London, 1999) at 318; Lord Cooke of Thorndon, *Turning Points of the Common Law* (Sweet & Maxwell, London, 1997) at 48.

40   Most famously, R Meagher, JD Heydon, M Leeming, *Meagher Gummow and Lehane's Equity: Doctrines and Remedies* (4th ed, Butterworths, Sydney, 2002) at 52-54 and passim.

warrant for substantive fusion.[41] But such authority need not be found in the Judicature Acts. Both Equity and the common law are legal traditions, but if the binding force of legal tradition were absolute, neither system could ever change except by legislation. The fact is that both the common law and Equity are flexible and able to adapt to changing social circumstances. That flexibility owes nothing to the Judicature Acts. It would be absurd if the one change that neither could make was a change in the direction of the other's solution.

If hostility to substantive fusion is not based on a general resistance to change in legal norms, it may be better understood as an argument for the preservation of the distinctness of the Equitable tradition. In other words, it is not so much a concern that the particular Equitable solutions of legal issues are better or are better justified than any other, but rather that the legal tradition of Equity must be preserved. A similar reaction is commonly found where one legal tradition is under pressure from a foreign one. In the relatively small civil law jurisdictions of Quebec, Scotland, and Louisiana, there is always a resistance to what may be seen as incursions of the common law. One might say, "why resist a development of the law if it can be seen as an improvement, merely because it happens to be the common law solution?" To the beleaguered civil lawyer, however, that question must be answered with an eye on the wider world, not just on the immediate issue. If such arguments succeeded routinely, the identity of the civil law tradition in that jurisdiction could be rapidly diluted and destroyed.

The case of Equity and the common law, however, requires a closer look. The binding force of a legal tradition is expressed in the idea, "we have always done it this way; we have chosen a path, institutionally, and while we know there are other paths, we choose consistency". The consistency is with the past, as in any tradition. Where we are considering the interaction of Equity and the common law, however, we are looking at two traditions that govern the same polity. Equity cannot be seen in the same way as a civil law jurisdiction under threat from the common law, because the same people who are governed by Equity are also and at the same time governed by the common law. The call for consistency with the past runs up against the call for consistency of approach in the present.

How might an opponent of substantive fusion support the case that within a single political unit, and despite at least procedural fusion, we must not have substantive fusion, and, perhaps, we must also resist terminological fusion? How can that case be made, especially in the face of the arguments that rest on consistency and therefore rationality? Or in other words, what values are supported by the preservation of the Equitable heritage, which are so important that they can justify inconsistency, at least in terminology, and perhaps also in methods of reasoning, and perhaps even in outcomes (for example, whether or not exemplary damages are available)?

---

41   This is the main line taken in R Meagher, JD Heydon, M Leeming, *Meagher Gummow and Lehane's Equity: Doctrines and Remedies,* above n 40. Similarly, at 83, in reference to Burrows' argument (see n 13), they question whether judges have the authority to make the changes he advocates.

Sometimes we say that some traditions are worth preserving for their own sake. Consider a language. Tremendous efforts are made to preserve languages that are in danger of disappearing. An outsider might say, "let the language die. For one or two generations, the people who speak it will be unhappy to witness its demise. But after that, everyone will be better off because we will stop wasting resources on a futile effort to preserve it". History shows that this is an impoverished view of language. We might say that language is worth preserving for its own sake, but I think it is more accurate to say that language is a crucial part of identity, and identity is a crucial part of human dignity. A person may learn a language even as an adult as a sign of identity, to himself and others, regardless of whether he actually needs to speak it. We can also think of the Hebrew language. A thousand years ago it had almost ceased to exist except for ceremonial purposes. It was consciously revived in the late nineteenth century and is now the official language of the State of Israel.

There are other traditions which do not so clearly form a part of one's identity, and which will therefore yield more easily to cost-benefit or other utilitarian analysis. As a law professor at McGill, once a year I put on a funny costume at a graduation ceremony; as a tutor at Oxford, I wore fancy dress more frequently. These are traditions that will continue, but they could well yield if someone were being harmed by them, or even if they came to seem too strange.[42] Similarly, the English traditions for courtroom dress and etiquette have changed to various degrees in other places that inherited them.[43]

One reading of the stance against fusion is that it sees Equity as more like a language than like these other, more superficial traditions. If Equity, with its particular vocabulary and syntax of legal reasoning, is part of one's identity, then one can hardly be expected to give it up on the basis of an argument that things would be easier to understand if there was only one legal language in play. The European Union now has 20 official languages and the costs of translation are mind-boggling, but that does not mean it would make more sense to do everything in English or German.[44] To take another example, there are two sets of rules of the game of major league baseball, one for the American League and one for National League. These must be reconciled every time there is inter-league play, and every October for the ambitiously-titled World Series, which is played between the champion team of each league. The rule (or meta-rule) is that the rules of the home team apply.[45] This may seem awkward, but it

---

42   The Oxford tradition that a lecturer always wears a gown to lecture is just about gone, without any decision to that effect having been made to my knowledge.

43   In Canada, the practice of calling federally appointed judges "My Lord" is dying out, presumably because it is liable to make both the judge and the lawyer feel embarrassed or just silly. In England and Australia, barristers still wear wigs and gowns; in Canada, gowns only; in the United States, only the judge is gowned.

44   According to figures of the EU's Directorate-General for Translation (which translates written documents; oral translation is provided by the Directorate-General for Interpretation), total EU translation costs are roughly €1 157 700 000 per year: see http://europa.eu.int/comm/dgs/translation/navigation/faq/faq_facts_en.htm (visited 30 June 2005), where it is stated that the cost is about €2.55 per EU citizen per year; following the latest expansion, the EU population is roughly 454 million.

45   The basic rule in baseball is that every member of the team plays in the field and also bats in order. If a substitute is inserted for another player, that other player is out of the game. For

is far more feasible than would be getting agreement in favour of uniformity for one rule or the other.[46]

This interpretation of the anti-fusionist position is supported by this observation, that what is perceived as an attack on one's identity is liable to generate a rather more pointed and robust response than would be expected in ordinary legal discourse.[47] If some anti-fusionists are concerned to preserve the distinctiveness and identity of a community, then arguments based on transparency and rationality are unlikely to make much headway.[48]

We must also consider the possibility that the anti-fusionist is not so much an Equity conservative, but rather an Equity conservationist. Patrick Glenn argues for "sustainable diversity in law": "each major, complex legal tradition provides something to the world which the others do not, and probably cannot".[49] Just as genetic diversity allows a population to respond more flexibly to environmental change, diversity of legal traditions provides a resource for adaptability to unforeseen and complex problems.

SUSTAINABLE DIVERSITY

What does Equity provide that is different from what the common law provides? The most important differences may not be where we might expect to find them. Our concern is not with what has historically been different; for

---

about thirty years, the American League has had the "designated hitter" rule. Under this rule, a designated hitter bats in place of the pitcher, but does not play when the team is in the field. See also J Getzler, 'Patterns of Fusion' in P Birks (ed), *The Classification of Obligations* (Clarendon Press, Oxford, 1997) at 157 (red and blue numbers in two different mathematics); S Worthington, *Equity* (Oxford University Press, Oxford, 2003) at 4-5 (red and green teams playing by different rules).

46   The DH rule is a matter of lively debate. Those against it claim "traditionalist" credentials and argue that it takes some strategy out of the game; those in favour (taking a more "rationalist" line) argue that it leads to a better quality of game (pitchers are generally not the greatest hitters, and the rule also allows the extension of the career (as a DH) of a player who can still hit well but is not a strong contributor in the field). There is even a fusion thread: see www.halfbakery.com/idea/Improved_20DH_20rule (visited 24 June 2005): "I would propose that teams be allowed to select a designated hitter BUT require that pulling either the pitcher or DH out of the game would require pulling both and replacing them with either one or two new players." Under the existing rule, one can replace the DH without replacing the pitcher for whom he is hitting, and vice versa.

47   R Meagher, JD Heydon, M Leeming, *Meagher Gummow and Lehane's Equity: Doctrines and Remedies* (4th ed, Butterworths, Sydney, 2002) for example, at xi, xv, 54, 839.

48   The idea of Equity as an identity is surely reinforced in those jurisdictions that retain a "Chancery bar" and a Chancery or Equity division, despite Judicature Act reforms (see n 11). See the comments in this regard by Lord Justice Evershed, "Equity After Fusion: Federal or Confederate" (1948) 1 *Journal Of the Society of Public Teachers at Law* (ns) at 180-181. (Note also that this speech, delivered the same day that the Court of Appeal handed down its decision in *Re Diplock* [1948] Ch 465, affirmed on other points, [1951] AC 251, confirms (at 179) the reading (L Smith, *The Law of Tracing* (Clarendon Press, Oxford, 1997) at 126-129) that *Re Diplock* did *not* impose a requirement that there be a fiduciary relationship before a plaintiff could trace in Equity.) In England there is also a Chancery Bar Association, in addition to other Bar Associations for particular practice areas.

49   HP Glenn, *Legal Traditions of the World* (2nd ed, Oxford University Press, Oxford, 2004) at 357.

example, modes of proof or of enforcing judgments were different, but these procedural matters are now fused in a single body of civil procedure. Instead the question is what might be thought to remain distinct. We will notice that some strands of fusionist argument attempt to simplify legal discourse through reductionism, arguing that it is unproductive to have two sets of terminology or concepts in play. In at least some cases, this reductionist approach can inadvertently obscure what might be thought to be the distinctive contributions of Equity.

Differences of approach

A more flexible approach?

Aristotle's insight was that any attempt to lay down a set of rules in advance would always run up against situations that had not been envisaged by the rule-maker, and it was the role of equity to leaven the rule-based system with some flexibility.[50] Every developed legal system of the world, however, has equity in this sense.[51] And the common law, even in the narrow sense that excludes Equity, is a developed legal system. It is no doubt true that the presence of Equity allowed the common law to under-develop its own brand of equity, and to stand on the side of certainty and predictability, knowing all the while that in many cases, relief was available elsewhere.[52] But it is simply not the case that Equity is flexible while the common law is rigid.[53] There are perfectly good examples of the common law showing flexibility.[54] Conversely, there are

---

50   "And this is the nature of the equitable, a correction of law where it is defective owing to its universality." Aristotle, *Nicomachean Ethics* (trans WD Ross, Clarendon Press, Oxford, 1925) Book V at c 10.

51   J Story, *Commentaries on Equity Jurisprudence* (13 ed, Little, Brown & Co, Boston, 1886) at §§6-9; RA Newman, *Equity and Law: A Comparative Study* (Oceana, New York, 1961).

52   B Rudden, 'Equity as Alibi' in S Goldstein (ed), *Equity and Contemporary Legal Developments* (Sacher Institute, Jerusalem, 1992) at 30.

53   J Story, *Commentaries on Equity Jurisprudence*, above n 51 at §34: "Now such a notion is founded in the grossest mistake of our systems of jurisprudence." See also D Klinck, "'Nous sumus a arguer la consciens icy et nemy la ley': Equity in the Supreme Court of Canada' in JEC Brierley et al (eds), *Mélanges Presented by McGill Colleagues to Paul-André Crépeau* (Yvon Blais, Montreal, 1997) at 568-573; J Getzler, 'Patterns of Fusion' in P Birks (ed), *The Classification of Obligations* (Clarendon Press, Oxford, 1997) at 178-179; W Gummow, *Change and Continuity: Statute, Equity and Federalism* (Oxford University Press, Oxford, 1999) at 40-41, warning against a "triumphalist view of the historical mission of [E]quity". At 41 Gummow sets out a passage from LA Knafla ("Conscience in the English Common Law Tradition" (1976) 26 *University of Toronto Law Journal* 1) at 1, describing the contrast between a humanistic Chancery and a formalistic and unjust common law. As Gummow notes by describing the contrast as "triumphalist," this passage is not Knafla's view, but rather his parody of the view that may be taken by those unfamiliar with the details of the common law's history, which Knafla's article explores.

54   One might instance the development of negligence for pure economic loss, the duty to rescue that can arise in certain situations, and the duty of medical practitioners to warn of the risks of a proposed procedure. The common law has shown tremendous flexibility in the development during the last century of the law of unjust enrichment and administrative law. For other examples of equity in the common law, see n 36 above.

examples of inflexibility in Equity.[55] So here I think a reductionist line, which says that there is not much difference between common law and Equity as regards flexibility, is largely accurate.

A conscience-based approach?

It might also be claimed that Equity operates according to a different approach by arguing that Equity is a conscience-based jurisdiction. On this view, "unconscionability" is the touchstone of liability. I have already expressed the opinion that ultimately, "unconscionability" only states a liability conclusion.[56] In this sense, I would agree with reductionist approaches that say there is not much difference between the common law and Equity here.[57] At the same time, there is no way to understand the fact of Equity without this reference to unconscionability. The whole story of Equity as a separate juristic order would be impossible if it were not the case that in some sense, the basis of liability and justiciability is different from what it is in the common law. The idea of unconscionability is therefore embedded in tradition. It is not surprising that it should die hard.

A more discretionary approach?

Something quite similar can be said about any claim that Equity is peculiarly discretionary. On the one hand, all legal traditions find a place for discretion, albeit constrained so as to be deployed judicially.[58] Hence a reductionist can note that there is nothing special about Equity in this regard,[59] and that any discretion can be understood and rationalised in other terms, for example, as a series of available defences.[60] On the other hand, the discretionary nature of Equity is constantly reaffirmed.[61] Like the idea of conscience, the notion of discretion has deep historical roots in the Equitable tradition.

---

55 The system described by Charles Dickens in *Bleak House* was hardly a model of flexible justice, nor was it a passing phase: JH Baker, *An Introduction to English Legal History* (4th ed, Butterworths, London, 2002) at 111: "It is the height of irony that the court which originated to provide an escape from the defects of common-law procedure should in its later history have developed procedural defects worse by far than those of the law. For two centuries before Dickens wrote *Bleak House*, the word 'Chancery' had become synonymous with expense, delay and despair. That the court survived at all owed something to the vested interests of its officials but still more to the curious fact that expense and delay do not extinguish hope." One could also argue that despite the efforts of Lord Denning and others, English Equity ultimately failed to provide adequately for the equitable division of property on the breakdown of marriage or other close relationships of sharing. When it took over the administration of the estates of deceased persons from ecclesiastical courts, Equity also failed to solve the problem of inadequate testamentary provision for dependants, leading eventually to legislative intervention. Some would also instance the majority decision in *Harris v Digital Pulse Pty Ltd* (2003) 56 NSWLR 298 as inflexible.
56 See text at and following n 29.
57 See S Worthington, *Equity* (Oxford University Press, Oxford, 2003) at 298-303.
58 See text at and following n 24.
59 See S Worthington, *Equity*, above n 57 at 303-307.
60 A Burrows, "We Do This At Common Law But That in Equity" (2002) 22 *Oxford Journal of Legal Studies* 1 at 14-15.
61 See the cases at n 25.

Differences of underlying moral norms

I take it as a working assumption that judge-made legal norms (in a broad sense that includes those enforceable in Equity) should be justifiable on the basis of some underlying norm of morality or right conduct. These underlying norms do not need to be spelled out in every judgment. But there has to be some reason why the norm was developed and continues to be enforced.[62] I would argue that there are at least two examples of norms that are enforced routinely by Equity, but only sporadically by the common law, and that it is here that the true distinctiveness of Equity may lie. In other words, leaving aside the mass of detailed doctrine in both traditions, these are examples of situations in which Equity enforces a norm or value which the common law generally does not.

Respect for other people's obligations

This section can be introduced with a simple normative problem. Imagine that John owns a boat. He lends it to Mary, promising her that she can keep it for one month. After one week, Eleanor offers to buy the boat from John. John accepts her offer and Eleanor becomes the owner of the boat. Is she required to allow Mary to retain possession during the rest of the one-month period? Reasonable people could differ.[63] Many people would say that it depends upon whether Eleanor was aware of the arrangements between John and Mary, and some might think it was relevant whether Mary had paid for her one month of use, or whether it was in the nature of a gift.

In the Romanist tradition, the most fundamental distinction in private law is the one between obligations and property rights. A right of ownership binds everyone. Obligations bind only the parties to the obligation: the debtor is bound to the creditor. The common law, in the narrow sense that excludes Equity, basically follows this line. Both modern civil law and the common law in the narrow sense admit the possibility that someone can commit a wrongful act by interfering with the fulfilment of another person's obligation. But short of that fault-based wrong, obligations do not have effects except on the debtor and the creditor. Equity takes a different view. Some obligations systematically have third-party effects, without recourse to the law of wrongs. These are obligations that relate to the benefit of particular property, or an interest therein.

This approach is seen in a crucial technique of legal reasoning that underlies much of the original jurisdiction of Equity. At the risk of leaving out much doctrinal detail, it can be stated in this way. If a person is under an obligation, and the obligation relates to the benefit of particular property or an interest

---

62   I agree with OW Holmes: "The law is the witness and external deposit of our moral life. Its history is the history of the moral development of the race": "The Path of the Law" (1897) 10 *Harvard Law Review* 457 at 459; see n 9 for reprint citations.

63   This is effectively the nature of the issue that split the House of Lords in *Twinsectra Ltd v Yardley* [2002] 2 AC 164. As to whether Mr. Leach had acted "dishonestly", as Lord Hoffmann said at [23], Leach "thought that whether Mr. Yardley's use of the money would be contrary to the assurance he had given Mr. Sims or put Mr. Sims in breach of his undertaking was a matter between those two gentlemen." That is, Mr. Leach did not need to concern himself with dealings between other people, even though he was aware of them.

therein, then another person who comes into possession or control of that particular property — even though he does so without any personal culpability — is not allowed to get in the way of the fulfilment of the obligation.[64] The defendant can free himself of this constraint only by affirmative proof that he gave value in good faith without notice of the obligation, and that the interest he acquired was a common law interest and not an Equitable one only.[65] This is an example of the point made above, that "unconscionable" does not mean "culpable" but only liable: the heir or the good faith donee is caught by this principle, and his "conscience is affected", even though he may have no knowledge or notice and so not be guilty of any kind of wrongdoing. The representative of creditors is also caught, although he represents persons who are in good faith and who, for the most part, gave value.

This principle is not totally alien to the common law. First, as we have noted, the common law recognises that one person should not deliberately interfere in another person's performance of his obligations. But in this tort context, it looks for a level of cognition on the part of the defendant that allows us to understand the defendant as having committed a genuinely wrongful act. In that setting, of course, it is irrelevant whether the obligation relates to specific property or not. More interestingly, in one crucial context, the common law did exactly what Equity does routinely: it said that if the obligation does relate to specific property, then a recipient of that property must allow the obligation to be performed, even though the recipient does not owe the obligation, and without any finding that the recipient acted wrongfully. That context is the lease of land.[66] The lessee's rights were enforceable against a transferee from the lessor, and later against all the world, first in damages only, but later by specific recovery.[67]

In Equity, however, this principle is ubiquitous, and routinely turns an obligation relating to a particular asset into a kind of property right, held by the beneficiary or creditor of the obligation, in the particular asset. Effectively, people are bound by other people's obligations — not bound to perform them, but bound not to interfere with them. It explains the enforcement of uses against heirs and other transferees from the feoffee to uses, the equivalent of the modern trustee. It explains why express trust interests are enforceable against gratuitous transferees from the trustee, and therefore why those interests subsist in the trustee's bankruptcy. It explains the proprietary features of estate contracts. It explains why a promise to give a legal mortgage makes an Equitable mortgage. It explains why a promise to give an equitable charge on after-acquired property takes effect in Equity as soon as the property is

---

64 L Smith, 'Transfers' in P Birks and A Pretto (eds), *Breach of Trust* (Hart Publishing, Oxford, 2002) at 111.

65 Although it has been argued that even one who acquires only an Equitable interest should be able to take free of the prior interest: JB Ames, 'Purchase for Value Without Notice' in JB Ames, *Lectures on Legal History, and Miscellaneous Legal Essays* (Harvard University Press, Cambridge, Massachusetts, 1913).

66 JH Baker, *An Introduction to English Legal History* (4th ed, Butterworths, London, 2002) at 298-301.

67 Interestingly, Baker's view (above n 66) is that the common law judges were here following Chancery.

obtained, without the need for any new legal act, a principle that is the foundation of modern corporate finance in the countries of the common law tradition.[68]

Those are all cases in which the obligation relating to particular property arises from a promise. The principle, however, is even wider, and can operate where the obligation arises by operation of law. It may arise through a wrongful act, or through an unjust enrichment. A mistaken payment creates an obligation to return the payment, which is seen as an obligation relating to specific property, and so it makes a trust.[69] An insured who has been indemnified by his insurer and then recovers from a wrongdoer has been overindemnified, and must transfer the recovery to his insurer; this also makes a trust, or at least a lien.[70] As for wrongdoing, a person who acquires a bribe or secret benefit in breach of his duty of loyalty has an obligation to pay it to his principal, and this obligation, relating to specific property, makes a trust.[71] The principle can even be engaged by an obligation arising out of a judgment, which did not on its face impose a trust. If a judgment obliges a debtor to transfer specific property, this obligation becomes a trust even if the judgment did not say so.[72]

The principle underlies all of the law of equitable proprietary claims based upon tracing. The obligations here arise out of the accountability of a trustee, and this makes them less easy to identify more precisely by their source. To say that someone is accountable in respect of property means, on its face, only that they must provide information as to what happened to that property. But an obligation will exist in relation to what is revealed by the accounting; and if the obligation relates to specific property, it will be turned into a trust or a lien.[73] So if a trustee properly invests trust property, the investment is instantly held in trust on the basis of the trustee's voluntarily assumed obligation to so hold it; he need not declare a trust. If he improperly disposes of trust property, he will again have an obligation to hold those proceeds on trust; again, the obligation becomes a trust, as soon as the substitution is made, even though the

---

68   See R Nolan, "Property in a Fund" (2004) 120 *Law Quarterly* Review 108, explaining how property rights in a shifting fund (whether under an express trust or a floating charge) are merely rights in the constituent elements of the fund from time to time.

69   *Chase Manhattan Bank NA v Israel-British Bank (London) Ltd* [1981] Ch 105. See L Smith, "Unravelling Proprietary Restitution" (2004) 40 *Canadian Business Law Journal* 317.

70   *Mutual Life Assurance Co v Tucker* (1993) 119 NSR (2d) 417; 314 APR 417; *Lord Napier and Ettrick v Hunter* [1993] AC 713. Similarly, a mortgagee who has sold the mortgaged property and holds a surplus has an obligation to transfer it to the next mortgagee, or the mortgagor, and this obligation (relating to specific property) makes a trust. In England and Wales this is codified in *Law of Property Act 1925*, s 105.

71   *Attorney-General of Hong Kong v Reid* [1994] 1 AC 324; *Soulos v Korkontzilas* (1997) 146 DLR (4th) 214.

72   *Re Morris* 260 F 3d 654 (6th Cir 2001); *Mountney v Treharne* [2003] Ch 135.

73   The remedy called an "accounting of profits" is understood not to create a trust; this makes sense in the current discussion if the obligation revealed by the accounting is only to pay a sum of money, not to transfer specific assets. The obligation of an agent to his principal in respect of a bribe was understood in the same way in *Lister v Stubbs* (1890) 45 Ch D 1 and so no trust was found. How the line is drawn is a difficult question: S Gardner, "Two Maxims of Equity" (1995) 54 *Cambridge Law Journal* 60.

accounting process that will identify the proceeds only occurs later. The *accounting* process is a factual inquiry governed by legal principles, and those principles allow a beneficiary certain choices, including the choice to approve or not of unauthorised transactions. This is why tracing claimants have such a wide range of possibilities when the value being traced has been mixed. But the proprietary claim over the ultimate proceeds is built on the *obligation* of the trustee in respect of those specific proceeds, identified by that accounting process. This is why tracing looks for transactional links, and not causal links. If claims to traceable proceeds were only available against express trustees, the obligation that makes the trust or lien could be said to be based on consent: the trustee agrees to hold the trust property on trust, and that includes the proceeds of disposition.[74] Alternatively, it could be said to be based on wrongdoing, in the form of breach of trust. But even an innocent recipient of trust property will find that he holds traceable proceeds on trust.[75]

Justiciability of motive

Again, we can introduce this section with a simple normative illustration. Normatively, motive can be important. The difference between a "white lie" and a malevolent lie is not in the lying. In both cases, there is a lie: a deliberately false statement that is intended to deceive the hearer. The difference is in the motive. The teller of a white lie intends to deceive his hearer, but he does so out of a good motive: rightly or wrongly, he thinks it is better for the hearer to hear a falsehood than to hear the truth.

Legal liabilities, however, do not usually turn on the motives of the defendant. Instead there is an obligation to do or not to do, and the obligation may be a strict one, or an obligation to make reasonable efforts to bring about a result, or to take reasonable care not to bring about a result. The civil law tradition has an important qualification to this, in that there is usually a general obligation of good faith. The obligation requires, at least in part, an examination of motives. For example, why did the defendant break off pre-contractual negotiations? If his circumstances had changed, fair enough. But if it turns out that he was never seriously intending to contract but only wanted to string the plaintiff along, the result may well be different.[76] Pre-contractual negotiations are not binding and generally parties are at liberty to break them off. But there can be an examination into motive to determine whether this liberty has been abused ("abuse of rights") or used in bad faith.

---

74 This will be explicit in most formally created trusts, and is probably implicit in informally created ones. A power to alienate trust property in such a way as to leave nothing but a personal claim is possible (*Space Investments Ltd v Canadian Imperial Bank of Commerce Trust Co (Bahamas) Ltd* [1986] 1 WLR 1072; *Twinsectra Ltd v Yardley* [2002] 2 AC 164) but the presumption is the other way.

75 As illustrated by the "in rem" holding in *Re Diplock* [1948] Ch 465, affirmed on other points, [1951] AC 251.

76 R Zimmermann and S Whittaker (eds), *Good Faith in European Contract Law* (Oxford University Press, Oxford, 2000) especially at 236-257.

The common law traditionally refuses to make this kind of inquiry,[77] and those cases where it does so may be viewed as islands.[78] Equity, however, inquires into good faith as a matter of course, it being an ingredient of the defence of good faith purchase for value without notice.[79] But Equity has refined its willingness to inquire into motives to a higher pitch than any other legal tradition, in the form of the fiduciary duty of loyalty. That duty, at its core, requires that a person act with a particular motive: in general, he must make decisions based on what he perceives to be the best interests of the person to whom the duty was owed.[80] The strict rules about conflicts of interest and duty (and conflicts of duty and duty) often get most of the attention, but these are merely trip wires set up to keep people out of situations where they will be subjected to contradictory motivational pressures.[81] The obligation of loyalty could still exist perfectly well if the strict rules about conflicts were abolished; that would really only change the burden of proof.[82]

Equity's highly developed rules about duties of loyalty are one of the signal achievements of the English legal tradition. They are being imitated in some civil law jurisdictions.[83]

Reductionism

These two features of Equity arguably form the core of the law of trusts, which itself is the core of the original jurisdiction of Equity. The first feature, that obligations can affect people other than the debtor of the obligation, created the "proprietary" part of trusts. The second feature, the justiciability of motive, created the most distinctive feature of the "obligational" part of trusts.

We have noticed that one theme of fusionist discourse is reductionism. One could reduce the trust to its constituent components; it is a combination of property and obligation. Every legal system has these ideas, and indeed it is clear

---

77 *Mayor, Aldermen and Burgesses of the Borough of Bradford v Pickles* [1895] AC 587.
78 For example, in the law governing the acquisition of goods or bills of exchange from a non-owner; these parts of the common law find their source in the transnational law merchant, which was itself informed by the civil law.
79 And perhaps also part of an inquiry into "clean hands."
80 In some cases the duty cannot be expressed in this way; for example, in a charitable trust, or where a dispositive discretionary power is held in a fiduciary capacity, so that the exercise of the power will diminish the interests of trust beneficiaries. In these cases, the trustee must act in a way that he perceives will fulfil the purpose for which his powers were granted. See for example *Vatcher v Paull* [1915] AC 372 at 378; *Klug v Klug* [1918] 2 Ch 67; *McPhail v Doulton* [1971] AC 424 at 449, 457; *Re Hay's Settlement Trusts* [1982] 1 WLR 202 at 209; *Turner v Turner* [1984] Ch 100; *Re Beatty* [1990] 1 WLR 1503 at 1506; *Hayim v Citibank NA* [1987] AC 730 at 746; *Fox v Fox Estate* (1996) 28 OR (3d) 496, leave to appeal dismissed, [1996] SCCA No 241. But this is still a motivational inquiry.
81 L Smith, 'The Motive, Not the Deed', in J Getzler (ed), *Rationalizing Property, Equity and Trusts: Essays in Honour of Edward Burn* (LexisNexis, London, 2003) at 53.
82 See J Langbein, "Questioning the Trust Law Duty of Loyalty: Sole Interest or Best Interest?" (2005) 114 *Yale Law Journal* 929.
83 For Quebec, see *Civil Code of Québec*, especially Arts 322-326, 1309-1314, 2146-2147; for Swiss proposals, see L Thévenoz, *Trusts en Suisse — Trusts in Switzerland* (Schulthess, Zurich, 2001) especially at 319-320.

that there can be a recognisable trust without Equity.[84] On the reductionist approach, a trust is merely the combination of Equitable property and Equitable obligations, just as a sale of goods involves obligational and property aspects.

The reductionist approach, however, is a kind of translation, and as with all translations, it seems that something is lost in the process. To say that the beneficiary of a trust is the "Equitable owner" is a metaphor. His rights clearly have proprietary features, but just because we call them "Equitable ownership" does not permit us to assume that they are just like legal ownership, and from there, to say that to the extent that they are not so treated, something is wrong or irrational. Rationality requires like cases to be treated alike, but the fact is that legal ownership is significantly *unlike* a beneficial interest under a trust. In this case, reductionism may be a mistake.[85] There is no point trying to do now what the Statute of Uses failed to do in the sixteenth century. "Equitable ownership" arises from a different decision about what obligation *means*. It simply means something different — it has different effects — in the Equitable jurisdiction than in the common law, or in the civil law for that matter. Equity makes property rights out of obligations relating to specific property. It is no accident that while a property right, in the common law and in the civil law, can be understood as a relationship between the right-holder and a res, there is no such thing as "Equitable ownership" without another person — the trustee — who owes the obligations that generate the property rights.

In relation to fiduciary obligations, the reductionist school would simply treat them as part of contract law,[86] or perhaps part of tort law.[87] If this only means that the obligation must either be imposed by law or assumed by consent, then there is probably no harm in it. The difficulty is that it is likely to go further than that. Contract law and tort law are not familiar with the justiciability of motive and so cannot comprehend the fiduciary obligation. This might be addressed by other reductionist arguments: the fiduciary obligation is just a particular standard of disinterestedness that modifies some other obligation to improve another's position.[88] The problems with this are that it reduces the fiduciary obligation to a standard of care, and that it only explains the strict rules against conflicts of interest, not the underlying duty of loyalty that those rules exist to enforce. There is more to being loyal than avoiding conflicts.

Conclusions

Fusionists make a number of excellent arguments. Like cases should be treated alike. It is difficult to be sure we are doing this when we have two legal

---

84   See the *Civil Code of Québec*, Arts 1260-1298; G Gretton, "Trusts Without Equity" (2000) 49 *International and Comparative Law Quarterly* 599; T Honoré, 'Trusts: The Inessentials' in J Getzler (ed), *Rationalizing Property, Equity and Trusts: Essays in Honour of Edward Burn* (LexisNexis, London, 2003) at 7.

85   See n 38.

86   FH Easterbrook and DR Fischel, "Contract and Fiduciary Duty" (1993) 36 *Journal of Law & Economics* 425.

87   A Burrows, "We Do This At Common Law But That in Equity" (2002) 22 *Oxford Journal of Legal Studies* 1 at 9.

88   P Birks, "The Content of Fiduciary Obligation" (2000) 34 *Israel Law Review* 3.

traditions in play, with different terminology and perhaps enforcing different norms. It would be clearer if we had only one system of analysis and terminology, and it would help us in the pursuit of rational justice. Furthermore, such a system is certainly possible, just as it would have been possible to create a system with one legal tradition that produced the same results in actual cases as our dualistic system does.

But there are some other points that fusionists do not always notice. Tradition and history are normative, in every legal system. Duality is not necessarily a curse.[89] Not every difference is an injustice, and diversity can be a good thing.[90] Nor is discretion necessarily injustice. Complexity is not always worse than simplicity, if the complexity adds analytical power or permits the enforcement of additional normative standards.

Anti-fusionists may rely on arguments of that kind. But they should also take notice of some points. There is little point in making arguments that start from an undefended premise that Equity must remain "pure". This type of discourse, which sometimes takes on a quasi-religious tone, will not persuade anyone who needs to be persuaded; that is, anyone who does not already believe in the undefended premise.[91] More significantly, it is historically unfounded. There is a history of integration and mutual learning between the common law and Equity that goes back centuries.[92] There has also been fusion, as when the common law absorbed the law merchant, or when the Chancery took over the administration of the estates of deceased persons from ecclesiastical courts, or when English courts generally looked to Roman law for inspiration regarding water rights.[93]

History and tradition are normative, but they are not the only norms, and legal history teaches us that the normativity of tradition will eventually give way in the face of irrationality. And no legal tradition, Equity included, has reached such a state of perfection that it must be placed in a glass case and

---

89   D Klinck, "Review of S Worthington, *Equity*" (2004) 40 *Canadian Business Law Journal* 297 at 310-313.

90   For a similar argument against the harmonisation of contract law among the countries of the European Union, see E Descheemaeker, "Faut-il codifier le droit privé européen des contrats?" (2002) 47 *McGill Law Journal* 791.

91   R Meagher, JD Heydon, M Leeming, *Meagher Gummow and Lehane's Equity: Doctrines and Remedies* (4th ed, Butterworths, Sydney, 2002) at xi ("need for vigilant exposure and rooting out of error"; some jurisdictions must be counted as "lost"), 54 "(state of mind of the culprit cannot lessen the evil of the offence"), 57 ("the price for continued purity in doctrine will be an assiduity in exposing and rooting out false doctrine"). There is even a militant missionary tone; at xi, Lords Denning and Diplock are described as "cultural vandals" whose "attacks" have been "repelled" so that areas of the law have been subject to "reconquest"; the jurisdictions which are "lost" are so "for the present".

92   We have noticed that the common law learned from Equity regarding the protection of leases (see n 67). The common law also recognised trusts and the interests of those interested in the estates of deceased persons: see L Smith, "Tracing in *Taylor v Plumer*: Equity in the Court of King's Bench" [1995] *Lloyd's Maritime and Commercial Law Quarterly* 240. In the other direction, Chancellors often took the advice of the common law judges, as in *Bale v Marchall* (1457) 10 SS 143; see JH Baker, *An Introduction to English Legal History* (4th ed, Butterworths, London, 2002) at 108.

93   J Getzler, *A History of Water Rights at Common Law* (Oxford University Press, Oxford, 2004).

preserved from further change, on the ground that any change must necessarily be for the worse.

Arguments against fusion cannot therefore rely solely on the weight of tradition. Tradition puts a brake on change, but never stops it. Still less can they rest on any claim to "purity". Equity, like the common law and any other legal tradition, should rightly be constantly subjected to intellectual scrutiny, to test whether it makes sense. No friend of Equity should be afraid to engage with such scrutiny. I have suggested two possible avenues of engagement. One is particular, and one is more general.

The particular avenue is to question whether a suggested development makes sense even on its own terms. If the argument for change is built on the premise that like cases must be treated alike, then the argument does not apply unless the cases in question are really materially alike. The more general avenue rests on the idea that diversity may be better than uniformity. I have argued that Equity systematically enforces certain values that are not systematically enforced in the common law tradition. A reductionist approach to fusion could lead, perhaps inadvertently, to the loss of those values from the legal system.

3

Fusion: Fallacy, Future or Finished?

KEITH MASON*

The fusing of law and equity has been going on for centuries. It has generally been encouraged by all branches of government since the time that Chancery began behaving like a court of law. It reflects the law's striving for coherence and consistency.

James I intervened in 1615 to end the scandal of Chancellor Ellesmere's common injunctions being answered by Chief Justice Coke's writs of prohibition issued to the Court of Chancery. In the *Earl of Oxford's Case*[1] the King upheld Lord Ellesmere's jurisdiction to grant an injunction against executing a judgment in ejectment in the common law Courts. Chancery's jurisdiction to issue a common injunction was secured. The power would be abused from time to time, but the circuit-breaker was in place. Over the centuries, judges at common law and in equity moulded principles whereby the two "systems"[2] acted in aid of each other where appropriate, recognised and applied each other's rules when necessary to do so, and borrowed ideas from time to time. Movements towards a common Bar, especially strong in the colonies, encouraged the trend. In the nineteenth century Parliaments in England and elsewhere lent their hand, combining courts, sharing remedies across the board and promoting common procedures. Common procedures and fact-based pleadings encouraged plaintiffs to be less disciplined in confining themselves to traditional causes of action. But they also made courts contemplate both blended doctrines and the possible injustice of allowing plaintiffs to avoid the principled limitations of one cause of action/remedy by resort to another that differed only in name or history. Historical, and at times accidental differences between law and equity in dealing with the same facts, were no longer self-evidently justifiable.

The seeds of fusion have always lain in the judicial method. Significant developments since the Judicature Acts, especially in the late twentieth century,

---

*   I gratefully acknowledge the research assistance of Tim Breakspear and Michael Rehberg.
1   See 1 Ch Rep 1; 21 ER 485, which sets out the Chancellor's submissions.
2   There was also ecclesiastical and maritime law, each with their own later fusion stories to tell; see S Waddams, *Dimensions of Private Law* (Cambridge University Press, Cambridge, 2003) at 13-14.

have accelerated the fusion whose formal structure has been in place in most jurisdictions for well over a century. New South Wales was a very late arrival, but much groundwork was done there before 1972.

In these circumstances, questions about the institutional bifurcation of law and equity are becoming increasingly irrelevant, if not distracting. Legislation also covers many areas of former differentiation. Investigation of pedigree is being eclipsed by the greater need to have regard to the function served by a particular right or remedy and to the overlap of the parallel or discordant strands suggested by historical enquiries about "legal" and "equitable" rules.

DEFINING MODERN EQUITY IN AUSTRALIAN LAW

Assuming its meaningful existence in modern Australian law, one is still driven to concede that Equity:

- is regarded by the High Court as an unidentified portion of the constitutionally unified "common law" component of the "single system of jurisprudence" administered by the "integrated" or "unified" judicial system of Australia;[3]

- is administered throughout Australia in all courts of general jurisdiction with practically no distinguishing rules of procedure; and

- is as regulated by precedent as other branches of the law.[4]

What then is equity in modern Australian law? How is it defined by those who value its distinctiveness? What would an inquisitive layman (let us call him Socrates) be informed by an equity scholar?

Socrates would first be told about a body of largely non-statutory rules tracing historical roots to the decrees of the late medieval Chancellors who intervened in cases when the common law was defective or out of reach of disadvantaged suitors. Unless Socrates is a legal historian, this would be like describing Australian common law by reference to the Year Books or Australian statute law by reference to the Parliament of Edward I.

Pressed for a precise definition, the equity scholar would speak of that part of the law of England enforced exclusively in the Court of Chancery before its abolition in 1875. Memory jogged, the scholar would testily qualify the answer by additional reference to the equity jurisdiction of the English Court of Exchequer until 1842 and of the Palatine Courts of Chancery until 1971.

A glimmer of courteous recognition appears on Socrates' face. If he had technical understanding about the topic, dialogue would follow about the maxim of the Court of Chancery that *"Equity follows the Law"*. This would reveal that Chancery generally recognised and applied common law rules as well as its own "equity" rules. But Chancellors chose not to do so in particular cases; either (as with trusts) because the common law in a general field was

---

3   *Lange v Australian Broadcasting Corporation* (1997) 189 CLR 520 at 564; *Re Wakim; Ex parte McNally* (1999) 198 CLR 511 at 574[110]; *Lipohar v The Queen* (1999) 200 CLR 485 at 505[44]; *John Pfeiffer Pty Ltd v Rogerson* (2000) 203 CLR 503 at 534[66].

4   *Harris v Digital Pulse Pty Ltd* (2003) 56 NSWLR 298 at 419 (Heydon JA).

trumped by an in personam (equitable) right enforceable if necessary by a common injunction, or because there was a body of particular rules covering the same field in which law and equity were known before 1875 to be in conflict when addressing identical situations.[5] Our patient scholar would also acknowledge that equitable principles, doctrines and procedures were occasionally introduced into trials of actions at common law, for example by Lord Mansfield.[6]

The conversation might continue along the following lines:

Socrates: But what does this mean for Australia in 2004? Are you telling me that this body of Chancery Court law was received here in 1875 and that it applies to this day?

Should I look for an 1875 English textbook on the subject that I can place next to my copy of the third edition of *Bullen and Leake on Pleading*?

Scholar (drawing breath slowly through teeth):

Actually, Chancery law was almost certainly received into Australian law upon white settlement in 1788 because of a common law rule discussed in *Blackstone's Commentaries*. An 1828 Imperial statute confirmed the reception into eastern Australia of the general corpus of English Equity (along with common law, statute law and ecclesiastical law – but not matrimonial causes law).

But don't worry about the dates too much. In the latter part of the nineteenth century the Privy Council enforced legal uniformity throughout the Empire, and until late into the twentieth century Australian courts generally applied the rulings of all English courts slavishly. So, if an English court decided an equity case in say 1920, Australian law would fall in line, even in New South Wales which did not completely fuse the administration of law and equity until 1972.

In any event, your idea of getting an 1875 English textbook is pointless, unless you are a collector of historical works. You see, equity changed significantly in England after 1875. There have been major statutory developments and quite a few movements in the caselaw as well. There are doctrines like injunctions in public law, Mareva orders, Anton Pillar orders and promissory estoppel that would have shocked nineteenth century Chancellors. Some of these so-called "equitable" doctrines and remedies really stem from statute law or general law concepts like abuse of process developed across the board in recent years to prevent unconscionable use of legal rights. But, one may still speak of modern Equity, in reference to particular areas of English law derived from the pre-1875 Chancery law. Whether or not the progeny is legitimate, it represents a corpus of principle on a variety of topics that is binding in England today. You will read about it in the latest edition of *Snell*.

---

5   The body of rules said to be in "conflict or variance" was addressed in s 25 of the *Judicature Act 1873* (UK).

6   See *Roxburgh v Rothmans of Pall Mall Australia Ltd* (2001) 208 CLR 516 at 548[84] (Gummow J).

Oh, I forgot about trusts. It is a branch of property law that is part of equity, but not usually included in equity textbooks.

Socrates: Will *Snell* explain what unites and explains equity?

Scholar: No, because there is no common theme or principle. Besides, equity scholars don't often talk about theory, even when considering whether a modern precedent is in line with nineteenth century caselaw. There are some maxims of equity, but they have fairly limited application. Equity applies "common law" rules of precedent and of legal reasoning by analogy. Some remedies (now usually statutory, but originally exclusively equitable) are discretionary, unlike most original "common law" remedies. Of course, some "common law" remedies were and are discretionary also, and most equity doctrines are quite rigid (especially in property matters). All branches of the modern law grapple with notions of promise-keeping, good faith, privacy, abuse of process, unconscionability and estoppel, etc etc that were once largely (but never solely) equitable in origin.

Socrates: So *Snell's Equity* is where I can find modern Australian Equity?

Scholar: Certainly not. You see, the High Court of Australia has in recent decades declined to follow some of the English Equity cases. If you buy *Meagher, Gummow and Lehane*,[7] an excellent text, you will find many suggestions for additional departures from English equity, along with the occasional restrained criticism of the High Court itself. You would enjoy their treatment of Mareva orders which contains twelve pages proclaiming equity's lack of "jurisdiction" to award them, pouring scorn on any suggested statutory basis for this remedy, and concluding with a tiny, begrudging acknowledgement that the High Court has four times approved the remedy.

At this stage, Socrates mutters in his vernacular that *"It's all English to me"* and changes the topic. What he has learnt so far makes him wonder whether it matters to define or identify equity in the twenty-first century.

This chapter seeks to explore whether Socrates' original question does matter. The topic of fusion of law and equity generates interest and heat in certain circles, which of course is enough to justify the conference from which the chapters in this book derive. The relevance of the supposed law/equity divide has become a focus for those who endeavour to propound a rational, coherent and efficient scheme of Civil Obligations.

It is remedial and doctrinal fusion (or confusion) that generates most disputation, with claims ranging from those who believe fusion has already happened to those who believe that it is doctrinally impossible for "jurisdictional" reasons.

I want to start by unpacking the varieties of fusion, if only to identify matters of common ground and the true nature of underlying controversies.

---

7   R Meagher, JD Heydon, M Leeming, *Meagher, Gummow and Lehane's Equity: Doctrines and Remedies* (4th ed, Butterworths, Sydney, 2002) (hereafter referrred to as *Meagher, Gummow and Lehane*).

VARIETIES AND STAGES OF FUSION

When we speak about the fusion of law and equity we need to distinguish between four types of fusion: fusion of administration, procedure, remedies and doctrines. We must examine caselaw and legal theory as much as statutory developments. And we need to be on guard against distraction by sometimes fictional passwords like trustee, trust property and fiduciary.[8] Care is also needed in the use of different words to describe similar legal concepts and the use of the same word to serve different purposes.[9]

As fast as we distinguish the varieties of fusion, we must acknowledge that developments in one field have impacted on others. We inhabit a legal system that regards jurisdictional questions as primary, thinks of doctrines in terms of causes of action, views rights through remedies, and approaches remedies through procedure.

It is often stated that fusion of law and equity in England occurred in 1875, but this is quite misleading. Fusion of whatever nature represents an ongoing and interactive process, not an event that occurred in its definitive form at a particular moment of time. The processes and levels of integration (or non-integration) may differ from one law area to another. In any event, Judicature Acts are only constitutional in nature if you choose to treat them that way; and all Constitutions would surprise their founders more than a century after promulgation.

To my knowledge, debates about fusion have arisen in every legal system deriving from English law. Different attitudes about the relationship between law and equity are however, more than a product of when English law was received and when and how "law" and "equity" were statutorily fused. Academic cultures have also played their part.[10]

I shall hereafter use "general law" when referring to the inheritance of judge-made common law, equity, ecclesiastical and maritime law derived from English law. "Common law" in its stricter sense refers to the systems of law practised at trial level in England before 1875 in the Queens Bench, Exchequer and Common Pleas Courts. I suppose that is an accurate definition, although it is something of a mystery why no one treats "common law" in the same way as equity (usually spelt with a capital "E") in the present universe of discourse.

---

8   Equity's counterparts of "agent" (cf *Pinkstone v The Queen* (2004) 78 ALJR 797 at 808-809[60]). "Trust property" is often used fictionally to explain a company's right to trace and follow misdirected funds. Millett LJ described the use of "trust" as a precursor to a personal remedy as "nothing more than a formula for equitable relief" (*Paragon Finance plc v DB Thakerar & Co* [1999] 1 All ER 400 at 409). Labels touching the status of company directors ("trustee" or "agent") led to unseemly and expensive conflicts between Chancery and the Common Law Courts in the mid nineteenth century: see below.

9   Cf the variety of words used to describe an award of compensation (damages, compensation, indemnity, *Lord Cairns' Act* damages) and the use of "injunction" to describe orders that were never part of classical equity or which were or now are statutory (cf *Cardile v LED Builders Pty Ltd* (1999) 198 CLR 380 at 394[28], 412[80]).

10 The role of Sydney University Law School cannot be ignored. It has produced generations of well-informed defenders of equity. When I was an undergraduate, Sydney Law School prided itself on historically-based, black letter law. My teachers in equity were proud to be practition-ers in the world's last pre-Judicature system.

Can it be that common law scholars (if they exist in the same sense that we talk of equity scholars) have simply moved on? To my knowledge, no law school teaches "common law" as a subject.

In referring to a modern Judicature System, we envisage trial courts of general jurisdiction (subject to monetary limits in some cases) whose judges hear and determine disputes, whether arising under statute law or general law in all of its manifestations. These courts may have specialist lists, but litigants can advance claims and defences however arising. Proceedings will be moved sideways to appropriate judges or courts if commenced in an inappropriate forum or list. The choice of initiating process, pleading system, method of adducing evidence, interlocutory procedures, method of trial and right of appeal are generally unaffected by concerns as to whether asserted rights or defences are statutory, legal, equitable, ecclesiastical or maritime in derivation. There may be pockets of resistance in matters of practice (for example, the order of addresses), or culture (for example, the style or volume of counsel), but these are diminishing. Trial of "common law" matters by jury is now very exceptional.

Modern pleadings concentrate first on facts giving rise to substantive causes of action based, for example, on contract, tort, trust, statutory obligation etc. They then claim a variety of remedies in the alternative. Very few causes of action or remedies will be exclusively equitable in historical derivation and even these are now statutory in most cases.

Some court statutes, like the *Supreme Court Act 1970* (NSW), contain provisions re-enacting nineteenth century steps towards procedural fusion, but in a form that usually confers the power to award any variety of injunctions, declarations etc. This is not to imply that the reader does not need to know the circumstances in which the particular remedies are available. He or she is, however, more likely to go to the applicable specialist text on substantive law (torts, defamation, contract, trusts) or to practice books or books on remedies generally, rather than to equity texts to find the remedial and procedural rules referable to a field of law.[11]

Other statutes, like the *Trade Practices Act 1974* (Cth) offer a smorgasbord of remedies in terms that indicate the need for real caution lest judges wrongly assume that traditional "equitable" principles apply to the minority of available remedies that would have been available only in Chancery before 1875.[12] It can be misleading to approach statutes like the *Trade Practices Act* with preconceptions about the continuing role of equity doctrine, even when what formerly were purely equitable remedies like rescission and injunction are mentioned.

---

11   *Meagher, Gummow and Lehane* has many sections in which equity doctrines and remedies are helpfully explained in a context that includes the common law or statutory material referable to the single field of legal discourse (for example, assignments, misrepresentation, mistake, estoppel, duress, declarations, injunctions, set off, confidential information, passing off). At times, one might be excused for thinking that statute law had minimal impact (eg duties of company directors).

12   See *Akron Securities Ltd v Iliffe* (1997) 41 NSWLR 353; *Visy Paper Pty Ltd v Australian Competition and Consumer Commission* (2003) 216 CLR 1 at 10. This type of error could perhaps be described as a fusion denial fallacy. As to "fusion fallacies" see below.

In the twenty-first century it is hard to think of a non-Judicature system. Priestley JA once quipped that "even in New South Wales all common law judges are chancellors now".[13] Advocacy is becoming increasingly specialised, but the lines of division have nothing to do with any doctrinal common law/equity division. There may be different levels of complexity between different types of case, but this is presently irrelevant. I estimate that less than 10 per cent of the work done in the Equity Division of the Supreme Court of New South Wales involves equity in the sense explained to Socrates. Some is probate, much is contract, most is statutory (for example, *Family Provision Act, Corporations Act*, revenue law).

Occasionally we are reminded of the problems inherent in a pre-judicature system. This is when Parliament creates specialist courts with exclusive jurisdiction. Then it really can matter that the plaintiff has filed in the wrong court or that part of the matter in dispute lies outside that court's jurisdiction.

All four types of fusion of law and equity identified above were addressed in the *Judicature Act 1873* (UK), although it was not itself the original model for fusion.[14]

The *Judicature Act 1873* created a single Supreme Court of Judicature divided into the Court of Appeal and the High Court of Justice (with five Divisions, merged into three in 1881). Section 24 addressed the relationship between legal and equitable procedures, with the general object of securing a complete and final determination of all matters in controversy between the parties and avoiding multiplicity of proceedings. The section gave all branches of the Court power to administer equitable remedies, enabled equitable defences to be invoked, required all branches of the Court to recognise equitable titles, prohibited the issue of common injunctions within the Court and gave general power of determination of legal titles.

The predominant feature of the common law system of pleading had been the requirement that the plaintiff choose a cause of action in which to bring the claim. The parties thereafter exchanged pleadings that were designed to produce either an issue of law by way of demurrer or an issue of fact for decision by the jury. There were many technicalities and fictions, although some were abolished by pleading reforms in the mid-nineteenth century.

In Chancery, the plaintiff pleaded by Bill in equity, a complex, prolix and repetitive document. Once again mid-nineteenth century reforms removed a number of technical excrescences, requiring the Bill to state the material facts, matters and circumstances relied on.

The Rules of Court made under the Judicature Acts[15] prescribed the modern system of pleading which sought to combine the best features of the two former systems, the brevity and the simplified forms of the common law with the

---

13 *Renard Constructions (ME) Pty Ltd v Minister for Public Works* (1992) 26 NSWLR 234 at 269.

14 See *Meagher, Gummow and Lehane* at [2-010] discussing fusion that came to New York State in 1848.

15 The first Rules were a Schedule to the Act, accompanied by a Note – "Where no other provision is made by the Act or these Rules the present procedure and practice remain in force". The ambiguity of this direction had to be addressed as early as 1879 (see n 22 below).

equity principle of stating facts and not the legal conclusion which the pleader put upon the facts. This system enabled parties to allege in one process facts giving rise to causes of action, defences or replies recognised at law, in equity or by statute. The origin of a right did not need to be stated unless silence might take the opponent by surprise.

The *Judicature Act 1873* was mainly procedural in motivation. Lord Selborne LC said as much during the debate on the Bill. So too did Sir George Jessel MR in *Salt v Cooper* in 1880 when he said that the Act "simply transferred the old jurisdictions of the Courts of Law and Equity to the new tribunal, and then gave directions to the new tribunal as to the mode in which it should administer the combined jurisdictions".[16] Section 25 addressed areas of substantive clash, but initially it was thought that most bases had been covered and that the catch-all provision (subs 11) would have little work to do.

Contrary to what one sometimes reads, the reformers perceived that a system of fused administration might provide the means of ironing out inconsistencies and discordances in the practical administration of the law. Thus, the Judicature Commission responsible for the *Judicature Act* reported in 1869 that:[17]

> "The litigation arising out of Joint Stock Companies has constituted a very large proportion of the business which has engaged the attention of Court of Law and Equity for some years. Directors of Joint Stock Companies fill the double character of agents and trustees for the companies and shareholders; and the effect of their acts and representations has frequently been brought into question in both jurisdictions, and sometimes with opposite results. The expense thus needlessly incurred has been so great, and the perplexity thereby occasioned in the conduct of business so considerable, as to convince most persons, who have followed the development of this branch of the law, of the necessity that exists for a tribunal invested with full power of dealing with all the complicated rights and obligations springing out of such transactions, and of administering complete and appropriate relief, no matter whether the rights and obligations involved are what are called legal or equitable."

The merging of administration, procedure and remedies (with rule-making power that would enable further developments in that direction over the years to come) was the cornerstone of a system of fused administration of law and equity. But it was not the first or last legislative step on the topic in England. Earlier in the nineteenth century, statute provided the Common Law Courts with a limited power to grant injunctions;[18] and Chancery the power to decide legal titles,[19] together with a power to award damages[20] that with hindsight appears to have been unnecessary.[21]

As the years progressed after 1875, statute law and court rules further integrated common law and equity procedure. As early as 1879 the English

---

16   (1880) 16 Ch D 544 at 549. Lord Jessel expressed a different view in *Walsh v Lonsdale* (1882) 21 Ch D 9 at 14 when, in the context of estates in land, he said "there is only one Court, and equity rules prevail in it".
17   First Report, at 7.
18   *Common Law Procedure Act 1854.*
19   15 & 16 Vict c 86, s 62, a later version being 25 and 26 Vict c 42, s 1 (*Sir John Rolt's Act*).
20   *Chancery Amendment Act 1858* (known as *Lord Cairns' Act*).
21   See below.

Court of Appeal held that, in cases where no rule of practice was laid down by the Rules made under the *Judicature Act*, and there was a variance in the old practice of the Chancery and Common Law Courts, that practice was to prevail which was considered most convenient.[22] Procedural coalescence continued in the twentieth century with the gradual abolition of jury trial, greater use of the summons as an initiating process, increasing resort to evidence by affidavit or statement and other developments.

Other legal systems proceeded towards administrative, procedural, remedial and substantive fusion in different ways and at different times.[23]

Thus, administration within a single Supreme Court came to New South Wales from the founding of the colony, whereas full procedural and substantive fusion only arrived in 1972. But long before then, several of England's pre-1873, 1873 and post-1873 reforms were introduced piecemeal.

The English legislation of 1854 that had conferred on the common law Courts limited powers to grant injunctions and to recognise equitable defences was adopted in New South Wales by the *Common Law Procedure Act 1857*. But the latter provision was held to be only available in circumstances entitling the claiming of an absolute, perpetual unconditional injunction, otherwise it was still necessary to seek a common injunction in separate proceedings in the equity side of the Supreme Court. An attempt to plug this gap on condition that the proceedings were transferred into the jurisdiction of the Court in Equity was enacted in 1957.[24] Continuing difficulties with this provision were a fillip for the complete fusion enacted in New South Wales by the *Supreme Court Act 1970*.[25]

WHY LEGISLATION WAS NECESSARY IN NEW SOUTH WALES

New South Wales never had separate superior courts. The administration of law and equity was the business of the Supreme Court from the outset, with statutory backing from the time of the Second Charter of Justice in 1814. Yet this was insufficient to bring about the other varieties of fusion, however much the idea may have appealed to the first two Chief Justices of New South Wales.

In 1765, William Blackstone in his *Commentaries on the Laws of England*, formulated the general law rule of reception of English law into "settled" colonies, which all Australian colonies were later presumed to be. He proclaimed that "all the English laws then in being ... [were] immediately there

---

22 *Newbiggin-By-The-Sea Gas Co v Armstrong* (1879) 13 Ch D 310.

23 As to Canada, see PM Perrell, "A Legal History of the Fusion of Law and Equity in the Supreme Court of Ontario" (1988) *Advocates Quarterly* 472. As to the United States, see CT McCormick, "The Fusion of Law and Equity in United States Courts" (1928) 6 *NCL Rev* 283; DB Dobbs, *Law of Remedies* (2nd ed, West, St Paul, Minneapolis, 1993) at 148ff.

24 *Supreme Court Procedure Act 1957*, replacing s 98 of the *Common Law Procedure Act 1899*.

25 See *Meagher, Gummow and Lehane* at [1-260]. As to other Australian States, see [1-160]-[1-195].

in force". This principle was qualified by the statement that the colonists carried with them "only so much of the English law as is applicable to their own situation and the condition of an infant colony". The uncertain operation of Blackstone's rule had led to difficulties in New South Wales by the 1820s, but no one doubted that the general law of England (including Chancery law) was part of the colonists' inheritance.[26] Ellis Bent who was Judge-Advocate during Governor Macquarie's time granted equitable relief where appropriate, although he had no specific statutory authority to do so.[27] The Civil Supreme Court created under the second Charter of Justice in 1814 was declared, among other things, to be a Court of Equity having equitable jurisdiction.

Section 24 of the *Australian Courts Act 1828* (Imp), which applied in Australia by paramount force, was applicable to New South Wales as well as Tasmania, Victoria, Queensland and the Australian Capital Territory as they later emerged out of New South Wales. It provided that all laws and statutes in force in England on 25 July 1828 were to be applied "so far as the same can be applied". The Supreme Court of New South Wales founded in 1823 (which continues to this day) was a creature of statute and the royal prerogative. Its statutory parent was the *New South Wales Act 1823*.[28] The 1823 Act declared it lawful for the King to establish a court of judicature styled "the Supreme Court of New South Wales". The Act defined the principal jurisdictions of the Court, largely by reference to English models. Jurisdiction at common law was assimilated to the civil and criminal authority of the Judges of Kings Bench, Common Pleas and Exchequer in England. As a court of equity, the Supreme Court was to have the equitable jurisdiction exercised by the Lord High Chancellor within England. In 1828, this last grant of jurisdiction was supplemented by adding "and all such acts matters and things can or may be done by the said Lord High Chancellor within the realm of England in the exercise of the common law jurisdiction to him belonging".[29] This neatly makes my point that procedural and remedial fusion in England started long before the *Judicature Act 1873* (UK).

For New South Wales, the systems of common law and equity were never, as in England, to be administered by separate courts, but always by one and the same Supreme Court. But procedures and doctrines remained distinctive. A single judge wearing his equity wig could issue a common injunction directed at the prosecution or enforcement of common law proceedings or judgments pending before one of his brethren or in the Supreme Court generally.

A line was however firmly drawn when in 1882 Manning J purported to grant an injunction restraining certain proceedings pending an appeal to the Privy Council from a Full Court decision in a matter involving no grounds of

---

26   The Hon Justice B H McPherson CBE has very recently published a lecture entitled "How Equity reached the colonies" demonstrating that American colonists and scholars were not nearly as accepting that Chancery law was part of their legal system.

27   JM Bennett, *A History of the Supreme Court of New South Wales* (Lawbook Company, Sydney, 1974) at 94, 279.

28   4 George IV c 96, a temporary enactment rendered permanent by 9 George IV c 83, the *Australian Courts Act 1828*.

29   *Australian Courts Act 1828*, s 11.

equity. A Full Court was convened and Martin CJ gave his judicial brother a ticking off in the following terms:[30]

> "This was a very singular state of things ...
>
> The superior authority assumed by the Primary Judge to control the action of the Court cannot be submitted to for one moment, because, if it were allowed in this instance, we do not know where it would stop. We should find it applied in cases which altogether depend upon the common law principles, and which ought to be disposed of in a common law Court. His Honour is no more than a member of the Court. When sitting in equity in a suit disclosing equitable grounds, he would have the power exercised by him in this instance. But, where no such case was before him, he had no such power, still less had he a right to express an opinion condemnatory of the course taken by the Court in any case. I regret that His Honour has not only arrogated this position to himself, but that he should have gone out of his way to endeavour in an elaborate manner to throw discredit upon the judgment of the Court in a case triable only at common law."

All judges of the Supreme Court of New South Wales were vested with common law and equity jurisdiction. However, readiness and capacity to hear equity cases were largely dependent upon the individual judge's experience at the Bar, his learning and enthusiasm. For some judges, equity work went into the "too hard basket". The twice amoved John Walpole Willis fought to do these cases, going so far as to propose a separate Equity Court under his control as *"Chief Baron in Chancery"*. His colleagues and the Governor demurred.[31]

The nineteenth century judges in New South Wales were well aware that law and equity were different systems, each with their different procedures. Certainly by the 1840s any thought of adopting a single procedure was abandoned. English court dress, precedents and practice came to be followed with as much rigour as colonial conditions allowed. The Privy Council also curbed centrifugal tendencies, as elsewhere throughout the Empire. English reforming statutes were followed and adopted for use within the single Supreme Court. In 1850, the Full Court of the Supreme Court of New South Wales in *Bank of Australasia v Murray*[32] declined to grant any relief to a plaintiff who had proceeded by bill in equity instead of at common law. There the matter rested until the Queenslander Sir Samuel Griffith became the first Chief Justice of the High Court of Australia in 1903 (see below).[33]

The substantive and procedural rules pertaining to matters on the common law and equity "sides" of the Supreme Court of New South Wales operated in separate and seldom intersecting spheres, albeit administered by a single Supreme Court. The size of the Court never rose above seven in the nineteenth century. The shortage of judges skilled in equity and mid-century delays in

---

30　*Brown v Patterson* (1883) 4 NSWLR Eq 1A at 10, 11-12. It seems that the law reporter got the last laugh, by reporting the decision in the equity side of the NSWLR. On one definition, Manning J committed a "fusion fallacy" (see below).

31　JM Bennett, *A History of the Supreme Court of New South Wales*, above n 27 at 95.

32　(1850) 1 Legge 612.

33　According to McPherson, (above n 26), Queensland was the first place outside England to adopt the *Judicature Act* (in 1876).

handling equity matters actually encouraged moves to differentiate the Equity side of the Court. A Primary (later Chief) Judge in Equity was designated. There was even a proposal to create a separate building for Equity. The fusion reforms of the English *Judicature Act 1873* were resisted, although the judiciary and profession were divided on the issue.

Differing analyses of the nineteenth century milestones are offered by Dr JM Bennett in his many writings on the topic[34] and in an excellent Macquarie University Legal Research Thesis (regrettably still unpublished) by Justine Eloise Rogers, *Legal Argument and the Separateness of Equity in New South Wales 1824-1900.*[35] Rogers has, in my view, convincingly challenged Bennett's thesis that the failure to achieve substantive fusion from the springboard of a single Supreme Court represented a lack of will or possible misreading of the Charter of Justice on the part of the nineteenth century judges.

Echoes of the nineteenth, twentieth and twenty-first century debates about fusion and its consequences surfaced as early as the first volume of the *Commonwealth Law Reports.*

In *McLaughlin v Fosbery*[36] the High Court refused to overturn an order of the New South Wales Chief Judge in Equity staying all proceedings on an action for damages for assault and false imprisonment. The underlying dispute related to the confinement of the appellant, a lunatic, on the basis of an order by his committee. The High Court held that the Supreme Court ought to have stayed proceedings in the exercise of its inherent jurisdiction to stay vexatious actions, that is, reliant on the exercise of common law jurisdiction. It was therefore an error that the stay of the common law action had been granted by the Chief Judge in Equity in reliance on (Equity) lunacy jurisdiction. Since, however, the Full Court of the Supreme Court had power on appeal to disregard formal defects and irregularities in the proceedings, the High Court decided by majority to do the same. Accordingly the appeal was dismissed.

Griffith CJ (speaking for himself and Barton J) explained that the Supreme Court of New South Wales was:[37]

> "one Court, having under its original constitution all the powers which the Courts of Chancery and the Common Law and Ecclesiastical Courts had in England. Every Judge of the Court has the powers and authority of a Judge of the Court, and his powers are not in fact or in law impaired if he erroneously attributes the source of any particular power to the wrong Statute ....
>
> All powers of the Supreme Court of New South Wales are derived from Statute, and, in one sense, there are as many jurisdictions as there are Statutes conferring jurisdiction. But in another, and the truer sense, the jurisdiction of the Court, qua Court, is single, and an order of the Court made within its

---

34 See especially his *History of the Supreme Court of New South Wales* (Lawbook Company, Sydney, 1974). A fuller statement of his research on the present matter is his unpublished 1963 thesis, "The Separation of Jurisdictions in the Supreme Court of New South Wales 1824-1900" (a copy of which resides in that New South Wales Law Reform Commission Library).

35 Macquarie University, Law 514 Legal Research Project, Second Semester 2002. Copy made available by Mr G C Lindsay SC.

36 (1904) 1 CLR 546. See also *Maiden v Maiden* (1908) 7 CLR 727 where Isaacs J (a Victorian) agreed with Griffith CJ's views. Higgins J dissented on the point.

37 *McLaughlin v Fosbery*, above n 36 at 568, 569.

jurisdiction, in the sense that it is made by virtue of the authority vested in the Court by law, cannot be impeached merely because the formal documents describe it as made under a Statute different from that which actually confers the authority. If, as was formerly the case in England, but was never the case in New South Wales, the general judicial power of the State were distributed among several different Courts, an order of one Court not within its province could not be supported by showing that it could have been made by another Court. But this argument is not applicable to a single Court in which all the judicial power of the State is vested."

O'Connor J dissented strongly, stating:[38]

"It is said there is only the one Supreme Court invested with both common law and Equity powers, and that it is always open to the Court to apply any of its powers to facts that come before it. It is true that there is only one Supreme Court invested with all these powers, but ever since the establishment of the Court under the Charter of Justice its powers in Equity and its powers at common law have been exercised by separate divisions of the Court – separate not only in name and form, but administering in many respects different systems of jurisprudence. In many Statutes of this State the distinction is recognised. Take as an example, s 252 of the *Companies Act*, under which the rights of an applicant may vary considerably according as his application is made in the common law or in the Equity jurisdiction of the Court. It may or may not be convenient or necessary to have this separation of jurisdictions. That is not a matter for us to consider. The separation of jurisdictions exits, not as a mere matter of form or of headings, but as a substantial separation of different systems of jurisprudence, and so long as it does exist the Supreme Court could not, and would not, apply in the exercise of the one jurisdiction the principles of the other."

Griffith CJ's references to the universal judicial power to prevent abuse of process is interesting. This now frequently encountered judicial power is universally available to all courts to thwart a broad and undefined band of procedural and substantive chicanery.[39] Many fields in which it now operates would once have been the sole province of Chancery. This is one of many examples of developments in the general law that represent a form of substantive fusion where a composite principle claiming no particular derivation now covers the field.

By 1910 Griffith CJ abandoned any thought he may have had of using the single Supreme Court of New South Wales as a springboard for procedural fusion. In *Turner v The New South Wales Mont de Piete Deposit and Investment Co Ltd*,[40] the High Court held unanimously that the traditional separation of

---

38 *McLaughlin v Fosbery*, above n 36 at 574-575. O'Connor J had practised at the New South Wales Bar.

39 See *Smiles v Commissioner of Taxation (Cth)* (1992) 37 FCR 538; *Director of Public Prosecutions v Shirvanian* (1998) 44 NSWLR 129. According to Sir Victor Windeyer, the necessity for the common injunction to prevent dishonestly obtained judgments at law diminished when common law courts themselves took adequate steps to prevent the fraudulent abuse of their own processes (*Lectures on Legal History* (2nd ed revised, Lawbook Company, Sydney, 1957) at 260-261). Cf *CSR Ltd v Cigna Insurance Australia Ltd* (1997) 189 CLR 345 at 390-392.

40 (1910) 10 CLR 539.

law and equity within the Supreme Court of New South Wales had to be respected. Without additional statutory modification it was not possible to permit an equitable replication setting up an equitable title in a common law action in which the plaintiff commenced by pleading his legal title. Griffith CJ grumbled about "supposed ancient technicalities of the law, which are said to linger in New South Wales, after they have been abolished in, I believe, all the rest of His Majesty's dominions".[41] Similar comments were advanced by O'Connor J[42] and Isaacs J,[43] without quite so much grumble from O'Connor, the former New South Wales practitioner and Acting Judge of the Supreme Court of New South Wales.

Statutory reforms were introduced to the Supreme Court of New South Wales in stages, culminating in the fusion of administration of law and equity and adoption of a common pleading system with the *Supreme Court Act 1970*. Section 57 of that Act commands the Court to "administer concurrently all rules of law, including rules of equity". There were other borrowings from the English provisions.[44]

The early stirrings in the High Court nevertheless suggest that a bolder resort to existing judicial power might have broken the waters of separation for New South Wales, which had by 1900 become a legal Jurassic Park. They certainly affirm my proposition (developed below) that any distinction between law and equity is non-jurisdictional. The orthodoxy that redescended in 1910[45] indicated the need for additional statutory procedural fusion, but it did not condemn Law and Equity to permanently separate spheres of existence. The High Court of Australia would return to the integration of the general law in Australia after the last procedural barriers had been knocked down with the passing of the *Supreme Court Act 1970* in New South Wales. When it did, it brought in some (probably unnecessary) constitutional guns.[46]

SUBSTANTIVE FUSION ACHIEVED BY THE JUDICATURE ACT

Section 25 of the *Judicature Act 1873* (UK) also directly fused substantive law and equity. On the orthodox view, it did so, only to a limited degree. It is, however, possible to see s 25(11) as the statutory capping of a process that had started in 1615. Parliament confirmed equity's precedence as a matter of last resort (if Judges of a single Court could not sort out remedial and doctrinal differences between Law and Equity by their own devices).

The side-note to s 25 was "rules of law upon certain points". Subsections (1) to (10) dealt with particular conflicts between law and equity in respect of the same subject matter. The "conflicts or variances" thereby resolved related to assignments of choses in action, stipulations as to time in contract, the custody

---

41   *Turner v The New South Wales Mont de Piete Deposit and Investment Co Ltd*, above n 40 at 543.
42   *Turner v The New South Wales Mont de Piete Deposit and Investment Co Ltd*, above n 40 at 549.
43   *Turner v The New South Wales Mont de Piete Deposit and Investment Co Ltd*, above n 40 at 554.
44   See Part IV (ss 58-64).
45   See Sir Frederick Jordan, *Chapters on Equity in New South Wales* (6th ed, 1947) reprinted in Sir Frederick Jordan, *Select Legal Papers* (Legal Books, Sydney, 1983) at chapter 1.
46   See cases cited in n 3 above.

of infants, equitable waste, merger of estates, administration of insolvent estates and actions for trespass by mortgagors in possession. Resolution was generally in favour of Chancery's rule, but a statutory amalgam of law and equity was devised as regards assignments. The miscellany of topics is itself testimony to the extent to which the two systems were treading on each other's toes when administered separately.

Section 25(11) was the catch-all, providing:

> Generally in all matters not herein-before particularly mentioned, in which there is any conflict or variance between the rules of equity and the rules of the common law with reference to the same matter, the rules of equity shall prevail.

By the time that New South Wales took its great leap forward to the nineteenth century by enacting the *Supreme Court Act 1970*[47] most of the matters covered by s 25(1)-(10) of the *Judicature Act 1873* (UK) had already been addressed by the New South Wales Parliament. It was only thought necessary to enact a modern variant of subs (11).[48]

The framers of the English statute thought that s 25(11) would have little work to do. It turned out that they underestimated the situations in which later courts would discover direct "conflict or variance" between law and equity "with reference to the same matter". Later caselaw disclosed several topics where equity and law were seen to produce different outcomes on the same issue, areas where the pre-1875 Chancery rule prevailed in accordance with the subsection.[49]

Section 25 was never intended to do away with the distinction between law and equity. Maitland in his *Equity Lectures*[50] was, however, at pains to stress the general absence of conflict between law and equity, thereby explaining the minimal scope of s 25(11). He expounded equity as a gloss on the common law, albeit a collection of appendices between which there was no very close connexion. Using a Biblical metaphor, he stated that:

> "Equity had come not to destroy the law, but to fulfil it. Every jot and every tittle of the law was to be obeyed, but when all this has been done something might yet be needed, something that equity would require".

He illustrated his point by reference to the law of trusts.

There was a flaw in Maitland's gloss metaphor, with its message of continuing confluence between law and equity, like Ashburner's reference to "two streams of jurisdiction [which], though they run in the same channel, run side by side and do not mingle their waters".[51] Congruence, stemming from

---

47   It commenced on 1 July 1972.

48   Section 64, later re-enacted so as to apply to all courts in the *Law Reform (Law and Equity) Act 1972* (see *Pelechowski v Registrar, Court of Appeal* (1999) 198 CLR 435 at [33] and [37]). The New South Wales Law Reform Report on *Law and Equity* (LRC 13, 1971) at 9-10, documents the earlier adoption in New South Wales of subs (1) to (10) of s 25 of the *Judicature Act 1873* (UK). For example, subs (3)-(7) were addressed in the *Conveyancing Act 1919* (NSW).

49   See *Meagher, Gummow and Lehane* at [2-055]-[2-060].

50   J Brunyate (ed), *Equity A Course of Lectures by F W Maitland* (revised, Cambridge University Press, Cambridge, 1947).

51   D Browne, *Ashburner's Principles of Equity* (2nd ed, Butterworths, London, 1933) at 18.

Equity's supremacy before and after 1875, was a more accurate picture than confluence. Hohfeld answered Maitland in a famous article on "The Relations between Equity and Law" when he pointed out that: [52]

> "As against the proposition that there is no appreciable conflict between law and equity, the thesis of the present writer is this: while a large part of the rules of equity harmonise with the various rules of law, another large part of the rules of equity – more especially those relating to the so-called exclusive and auxiliary jurisdictions of equity – conflict with legal rules and, as a matter of substance, annul or negative the latter pro tanto. As just indicated, there is, it is believed, a very marked and constantly recurring conflict between equitable and legal rules relating to various jural relations; and whenever such conflict occurs, the equitable rule is, in the last analysis, paramount and determinative. Or, putting the matter in another way, the so-called legal rule in every such case has, to that extent, only an apparent validity and operation as a matter of genuine law. Though it may represent an important stage of thought in the solution of a given problem, and may also connote very important possibilities as to certain other, closely associated (and valid) jural relations, yet as regards the very relation in which it suffers direct competition with a rule of equity, such a conflicting rule of law is, pro tanto, of no greater force than an unconstitutional statute."

On this basis, Hohfeld wrote, s 25(11) had been added only out of an abundance of caution. Its fundamental idea was "anything but a novelty". [53]

Arguments that the *Judicature Act* directly changed substantive rules (outside the working out of s 25) have been rebuffed on the few occasions that they surfaced. One of the earliest examples is *Britain v Rossiter*[54] where the English Court of Appeal rejected a submission that the *Judicature Act* permitted damages to be awarded with respect to an unwritten contract where the conduct of the parties did not attract the doctrine of part performance that triggered resort to *Lord Cairns' Act* as a source of the power to award damages. The substantive doctrine of part performance as a key to *equitable* remedies was in truth too firmly fixed to justify further expansion of an already bold doctrine without clear legislative endorsement.

But it was or should have been equally clear that the *Judicature Act* did not forbid the continuing development of law and equity, including development in the direction of integration of principles, if the single Court otherwise considered this an appropriate application of earlier precedents. *Walsh v Lonsdale* was decided in 1883. Unloved for its boldness by *Meagher Gummow and Lehane's Equity*, and others, it nevertheless became undoubted authority for the proposition that a specifically enforceable agreement for lease would, in a *Judicature Act* court, be regarded as between the original parties as the equivalent of a lease at law.[55]

There is a more specific corollary to the proposition that s 25(11) and its counterparts have limited direct effect. Outside cases falling within its scope,

---

52   W Hohfeld, "The Relations Between Equity and Law" (1913) 11 *Michigan Law Review* 537 at 543-544.
53   W Hohfeld, "The Relations between Equity and Law", above n 52 at 545.
54   (1883) 11 QBD 123.
55   *Chan v Cresdon Pty Ltd* (1989) 168 CLR 242 at 252.

courts are free to develop the law in a principled manner by preferring legal rather than equitable analogies or precedents. This was the stance affirmed by the English Court of Appeal as early as 1879 in procedural matters.[56] A much more recent example is *AMEV-UDC Finance Ltd v Austin*[57] where, in the area of penalties, modern equity chose to follow the common law and, with the advent of the Judicature System, allow a discordant stream of equitable doctrine to "wither ... on the vine"[58] in the interests of coherence in the law generally. As I pointed out in *Harris*,[59] many of the instances when this borrowing has occurred (before and after 1875) are parked in equity texts under the rubrics of the maxim "equity follows the law" or equity's "concurrent jurisdiction".

I shall later suggest areas where similar developments might be expected.

Section 25(11) did not purport to stop or even affect the development of legal and equitable doctrine. Nothing in the *Judicature* reforms precluded the continuing trend towards a more integrated, internally-consistent and principled system of general law, a task assisted by progressive steps (before and after the *Judicature Act*) taken towards a single system of court administration, procedure and remedies.

Despite his attitude to s 25(11), Maitland in his lectures nevertheless forecast that: [60]

> "The bond which kept [these doctrines] under the head of Equity was the jurisdictional and procedural bond. All these matters were within the cognizance of courts of equity, and they were not within the cognizance of the courts of the common law. That bond is now broken by the judicature acts. Instead of it we find but a mere historical bond – 'these rules used to be dealt with by the Court of Chancery' – and the strength of that bond is being diminished year by year. The day will come when lawyers will cease to inquire whether a given rule be a rule of equity or a rule of the common law: suffice that it is a well-established rule administered by the High Court of Justice."

Maitland's prediction is yet to be fulfilled, although matters have hastened in the last couple of decades for reasons discussed below. For the moment, I draw attention to his observation that the procedural coalescence of the separate courts would be as much a trigger for fusion as s 25(11).

FUSION FALLACIES

It is not possible to discuss fusion without reference to the notion of "fusion fallacy" that is important to some equity scholars. The concept must be taken seriously, whether it represents an orthodox category, a fallacy in its own right, or those scholars' version of "ghosts of the past [that] stand in the path of justice clanking their medieval chains [for which] the proper course for the

---

56   *Newbiggin-By-The-Sea Gas Co v Armstrong* (1879) 13 Ch D 310.
57   (1986) 162 CLR 170.
58   *AMEV-UDC Finance Ltd v Austin*, above n 57 at 191, per Mason and Wilson JJ .
59   *Harris v Digital Pulse Pty Ltd* (2003) 56 NSWLR 298 at 326[143].
60   J Brunyate (ed), *Equity A Course of Lectures by F W Maitland* (revised, Cambridge University Press, Cambridge, 1947) at 20.

judge is to pass through them undeterred".[61] To those who believe in them, fusion fallacies are real and dangerous. The successive editions of Meagher, Gummow and Lehane present them as a rogues gallery invented by offending jurists who deserve to be pilloried to deter others.

The current edition of *Meagher Gummow and Lehane* commences its discussion of the topic[62] by pointing (correctly) to the minimalist and largely procedural intent of those responsible for drafting the English *Judicature Act*.

Meagher Gummow and Lehane then identify as "fusion fallacies" instances of change or development in relation to legal or equitable doctrines not deriving from s 25 or its counterparts, yet "stated or implied" to be a consequence of the Judicature system and thus dictated by statute. If one puts proper emphasis on the word "dictated"[63] there is little difficulty with this category of fallacy. I acknowledged it in *Harris v Digital Pulse Pty Ltd*.[64] But it is something of a non-existent bogeyman. In fact, the only authorities cited by *Meagher Gummow and Lehane* that contain reasoning invoking the *Judicature Act* to justify a change in doctrine are Sir George Jessel's short-lived decision in *Redgrave v Hurd*[65] where he relied upon the *Judicature Act* to justify damages for innocent misrepresentation; and the obiter dictum by Eve J in *Re Pryce*[66] that the Act precluded an action for damages for breach of a voluntary covenant.

On my reading, all of the other examples provided by the learned authors involve applying common law concepts to once exclusively equitable situations (occasionally doing the reverse) in contexts where the direct role of the *Judicature Act* is neither stated nor genuinely implied. Often this occurs with a relationship that has been within the cognisance of both law and equity for centuries but over which Equity claims some hegemony.[67] The cases held up as fusion fallacies may or may not have been correctly decided, but they should not be slated undeservedly for this type of fallacious reasoning. Furthermore, the cases are usually of such standing that they ought to be accepted as a point of departure to which the further development of legal principle must accommodate itself.

To illustrate my point, *Hedley Byrne & Co Ltd v Heller & Partners Ltd*[68] is criticised[69] for borrowing from *Nocton v Lord Ashburton*[70] the idea that

---

61   *United Australia Ltd v Barclays Bank Ltd* [1941] AC 1 at 29 per Lord Atkin.

62   *Meagher, Gummow and Lehane* at [2-100].

63   *Meagher, Gummow and Lehane* at [2-105]. See also A Dean, "What Did the Judicature Act Really Do?" (1935) 1 *Res Judicatae* 13.

64   Above n 59 at 326[139].

65   (1881) 20 Ch D 1 at 12. *Meagher, Gummow and Lehane* point out at [2-140] that "orthodoxy" was restored in *Smith v Chadwick* (1884) 9 App Cas 187. This fusion would occur later, by statute.

66   [1917] 1 Ch 234 at 241, referred to by *Meagher, Gummow and Lehane* at [2-170].

67   For example, company directors, who were regarded as both "agents" and "trustees" in the nineteenth century and solicitors, whose relationship with clients may in some respects be seen as contractual, fiduciary and (latterly) giving rise to a common law duty of care. Apart from trustees proper, the label "fiduciary" with reference to a relationship is often a warning that loose thinking and a claim of Equitable hegemony is about to follow.

68   [1964] AC 465.

69   *Meagher, Gummow and Lehane* at [2-135].

70   [1914] AC 932.

compensation may be awarded against a fiduciary who causes loss due to equitable fraud and applying that concept to explain an award of damages for misleading advice. If this is a fusion fallacy, the undoubted status of *Hedley Byrne* suggests that it may be time to move on, or at least to see this example as an indication that the fusion fallacy idea itself may be flawed. But the point I wish to emphasise is that to invoke the analogy of *Nocton* is not to state or imply (false) reliance on the *Judicature Act*. *Nocton* itself is treated as pure orthodoxy by *Meagher Gummow and Lehane* and others. It occupies a significant place in the history of fusion, but that is a separate story addressed below. It is, I suggest, irrelevant, unhelpful and misleading to criticise the *Hedley Byrne* doctrine by asking what provision of the judicature legislation permitted the recovery of common law damages for negligence merely because a breach of fiduciary duty had been established.[71]

Meagher Gummow and Lehane's critical analysis of *Cuckmere Brick Co Ltd v Mutual Finance Co Ltd* (mortgagee's duty when exercising power of sale),[72] the caselaw as to directors' duty of care,[73] exemplary damages for breach of all categories of fiduciary duty,[74] damages in equity[75] and the doctrine of *Walsh v Lonsdale*[76] do not support their thesis that these cases illustrate a fusion fallacy based upon wrongful application of the *Judicature Act*. This last proposition needs slight qualification as regards a small portion of the reasoning in *Walsh v Lonsdale*, but once again one is left to ponder about the nature of the supposed categorical error in such a well established doctrine.[77] *Cuckmere Brick* has never been accepted as good law in this country. This is not because of fear of the fusion fallacy, but because its formulation of the duty of "care" does not accommodate the true nature of the mortgagee's power of sale in the mortgagee's own interest.

Meagher Gummow and Lehane reveal their slide into a different type of fusion fallacy, where they state that (emphasis added):[78]

"The fusion fallacy involves the administration of a remedy, for example common law damages for breach of fiduciary duty, not previously available either at law or in equity, or in the modification of principles in one branch of the jurisdiction by *concepts which are imported from the other and thus are foreign*, for example by holding that the existence of a duty of care in tort may be tested by asking whether the parties concerned are in fiduciary relations."

The learned authors give the cases cited in my previous paragraph as examples of this phenomenon. They do not, in terms, brand the Mareva order as a fusion fallacy, but the jurisdictional language used by them to criticise the concept[79] and the categorical nature of their criticism of this now universally

---

71 Cf JD Heydon, "The Negligent Fiduciary" (1995) 111 *Law Quarterly Review* 1 at 3.
72 [1971] Ch 949. See *Meagher, Gummow and Lehane* at [2-150].
73 *Meagher, Gummow and Lehane* at [5-295]ff.
74 *Meagher, Gummow and Lehane* at [2-310].
75 *Meagher, Gummow and Lehane* at [2-155]. See further below.
76 (1882) 21 Ch D 9. See *Meagher, Gummow and Lehane* at [2-180].
77 See *Meagher, Gummow and Lehane* at [2-180]-[2-225].
78 *Meagher, Gummow and Lehane* at [2-105].
79 See *Meagher, Gummow and Lehane* at [21-435].

accepted right and remedy indicates to me that they would include it in their list. Perhaps they refrained out of concern that such labelling would raise eyebrows about the "fusion fallacy" concept itself, given that Mareva orders have been endorsed four times by the High Court of Australia in recent years.[80]

The fusion fallacy concept is often discussed in the language of Ashburner's metaphor referring to "two streams of jurisdiction".[81] But this language has its own built-in circularity of reasoning, because talk of want of jurisdiction (or even lack of power) signals a limitation that the body charged with the administration of the relevant principle is never free to cross. Herein lies a major problem for this "fusion fallacy" concept, because the law/equity divide ceased to be jurisdictional in this sense in New South Wales at least as early as 1814 and in England in 1875 when the Supreme Court of Judicature was created there.

Let us however permit the fusion fallacy believer to recast want of "jurisdiction" as a reference to the historical truth that there were some rights and remedies incapable of being obtained (even within a pre-Judicature single Supreme Court of New South Wales) unless claimed in a common law action or an equity suit respectively. If you filed the wrong process the Court would refuse to vindicate the extraneous right (or defence) and the litigant would be forced to commence fresh proceedings on the correct "side" of the Supreme Court (in New South Wales) or in the correct Court (in pre-Judicature Act England). This is really the sense in which Ashburner, Pettit and *Meagher Gummow and Lehane* speak of want of "jurisdiction" or power in the present area of discourse. But, if the *Judicature Act* did anything, it made this problem redundant by arming a single Court with a plenitude of statutory jurisdiction, with access to every conceivable remedy and jurisdiction to hear and determine all manner of disputes.

Meagher Gummow and Lehane's version of fusion fallacies goes well beyond substantive errors of law falsely attributed to (or said to be "dictated" by) the *Judicature Act* or its counterparts elsewhere. They are trying to make something special out of battles lost long ago that are no more than contestable decisions that ignored, overruled or blended earlier precedents. It is simply unhelpful to enter a debate about legal principles in twenty-first century Australia with such outdated tools whose root of title in England is now over 125 years old. Too many conveyances, consolidations, subdivisions, statutory dealings and other events have intervened to make it helpful or even relevant to think of how the doctrine or remedy might have stood in England in 1875 as regards the separate legal system that putatively administered it exclusively before then.

To harp about this particular class of "fallacy" is really a smokescreen for pursuing a goal to maintain the historical distinction between law and equity for its own sake. It is, in fact, harmful to legal development if it causes a judge to refrain from considering borrowing or blending ideas that may have been exclusively the province of one system in the distant past.

---

80 *Jackson v Sterling Industries Ltd* (1987) 162 CLR 612; *Patrick Stevedores Operations No 2 Pty Ltd v Maritime Union of Australia* (1998) 195 CLR 1; *Cardile v LED Builders Pty Ltd* (1999) 198 CLR 380; *Pelechowski v Registrar, Court of Appeal* (1999) 198 CLR 435.

81 See, for example, *Meagher, Gummow and Lehane* at [2-100]; P Pettit, *Equity and the Law of Trusts* (9th ed, Butterworths LexisNexis, London, 2001) at 9.

Post-Judicature Act Developments Encouraging More Complete Harmonisation

The fusion of administration, pleading and procedure presented opportunities to bold advocates to press new claims in a single proceeding and armed judges with tools to break down historical barriers and mindsets. But it would be wrong to conclude that the present-day relationship between law and equity is no more than the working out of the *Judicature Act* reforms. Several additional factors came into play in the second half of thetwentieth century.

First, there was the long-term impact of legal realist thinking and the more functional approach that often went with it. Influential judges like Lord Atkin and Lord Wright challenged black-letter ways of viewing precedent. Others like Lord Diplock sought to craft a more ordered legal universe. Others like Sir Anthony Mason encouraged examination of non-English precedents. Others, like Lord Denning and Lord Cooke, "pushed the envelope" in their quest for rationality and indivualised justice. Others like Deane J quietly slipped natural law concepts into legal discourse. Academic lawyers were openly cited for the first time, some of them becoming judges in the ultimate courts of appeal. Some of those academics, like Professor Birks, forced judges to respond to a vigorous modern debate about the structure of the law of civil obligations.

These judges and academics have all drawn their share of criticism, especially from those wedded to preserving equity intact. But their influence in debate about the framework of the law has been significant, to some degree because their more conservative brethren have tended not to enter such structural debates, proclaiming equity's pragmatism as a virtue as well as an explanation.

I do not, however, imply that any judge or commentator stands in a particular "camp" or even that bright line camps exists. (My recently retired colleague, Mr Justice Meagher, may be the exception for his uncompromising certainty on these issues. He would not, I think, like to be thought of as having a tenderly nuanced view on the topics addressed in this chapter.)

In recent years, Gummow J has made extremely important contributions about the continuing role of equitable principles and the distinctiveness of Australian equity, which (as he points out) is much more comfortable than its English counterpart with discretionary remedialism.[82] These matters may readily be accepted. Birks' sharply defined roadmaps of the universe of civil obligations with their emphasis on rights and not remedies have little prospect of acceptance in this country. This, however, has little bearing on the "fusion debate", which is no more concerned with dumbing down the sharp edges of the law of trusts, tracing, injunctions, unconscionability etc than with restricting the nuanced and principled development of the law of patents, negligence or real property. My point is that a proper understanding of the law concerning any of these topics is actually hindered by viewing them as if a "common law"

---

82 See WMC Gummow, *Change and Continuity: Statute, Equity and Federalism* (Oxford University Press, Oxford, 1999), his *Australian Law Journal* article referred to at n 147 below and his judgments generally.

or "equity" label revealed anything in common or even useful about the principles highlighted for discussion. Gummow J has generally pressed for coherence and rationality, emphasising the importance of substance over form and calling for proper acknowledgement of the role of statute law in shaping the general law and its structures. In his words, "the spirit of the times is unfavourable to the preservation of existing legal fictions and hostile to the creation of new ones."[83]

These developments in legal thinking at the appellate level mean that traditional equity cannot presume that an ancient pedigree is enough to command recognition, or even attention, in a post-Judicature Act world.

Secondly, and of particular significance in Australia, is the recent assertion by the High Court of the unity of the Australian legal system, especially the unity of the "common law of Australia".[84] This concept appears at times in a constitutional garb, but its main reinforcement stems from the Court's legitimate assertion of primacy and independence as the ultimate arbiter of legal disputes in this country. A badge of that unity is the frequently cited notion of coherence, a fundamental legal norm that assumes and works towards integration of legal principles.[85] Integration requires the general law not to be at odds with constitutional and statutory provisions and principles, and not to be at odds with policies found within itself. Coherence sets the law the aim of "devis[ing] principles which provide a way of solving disputes between private persons (including of course corporations); **rivalry** between principles, as opposed to a study of their interaction and interrelation, is unlikely to be productive".[86]

A third development has been the march of statute law (especially federal statute law) into the heartland of the general law, equity included. In some key areas, this has made many of the traditional law/equity distinctions simply irrelevant. For practical purposes, the *Trade Practices Act 1974* (Cth) and the cognate State and Territory Fair Trading Acts have created several equitable redundancies, with their overarching norm of proscribed misleading or deceptive conduct and their smorgasbord of remedies, old and new. The *Corporations Act 2001* (Cth) has rendered most of the duties of company directors and officers statutory, again with a comprehensive array of civil and criminal remedies. There is a limited preservation of the general law, but its impact is likely to be minimal.[87] In *Rich v Australian Securities Investments Commission*[88] the High Court was at pains to scotch the notion that there is any meaningful distinction between "punitive" and "protective" functions with respect to a statutory power to impose a range of civil sanctions on delinquent company

---

83   *Scott v Davis* (2000) 204 CLR 333 at 376[128]. I do not think that his reference to "legal fictions" was intended to exclude equitable ones.

84   See cases cited in n 3.

85   See generally *Sullivan v Moody* (2001) 207 CLR 562 and *Tame v New South Wales* (2002) 211 CLR 317. See also K Mason, "The Unity of the Law" (1998) 4 *Torts Law Journal* 1.

86   Gummow J in *Hill v Van Erp* (1997) 188 CLR 159 at 231, quoting F Reynolds, "Contract and Tort: The View from the Contract Side of the Fence" (1993) 5 *Canterbury Law Review* 280 at 281.

87   Sections 179, 191 and 192.

88   (2004) 209 ALR 271.

officers. The distinction was described as "elusive" at best and suffering the same difficulties as attempts to classify all proceedings as either civil or criminal.[89] This suggests to me that it is unhelpful to think of the vast corpus of "equity" as definable by reference to such concepts, at least in the area of company officers.[90]

A lawyer who failed to avail her or his client of the mechanisms and added protections of statutory assignment of a cause of action (compared to an assignment recognised only "in equity") would be a prime candidate for a professional negligence claim. The nearly ubiquitous Torrens system attracts the same comment, as well as the observation that its detailed regulation of priorities in interests in land overreach much traditional equity learning. Detailed rules as to caveats have pushed interlocutory injunctions to the margins in that field.

I am not suggesting that "equitable" rights and remedies are excluded altogether from this statutory world. As part of an integrated general law they will continue to play a role, but along with the tort of deceit, contractual claims and statutory claims that do not have supporters claiming that special recognition is vital to an understanding of their elements or the structure of law itself. Statutes may also exercise gravitational influence upon general law doctrines, and equity has not been immune from this process.

Fourthly, most modern textbooks present their topics systematically, discussing rights in broadly-recognised categories and proceeding to address all appropriate remedies. The practitioner exploring a contract issue will go to authorities such as Treitel and Carter for a complete exposition of contractual rights and remedies (statutory, common law and equitable; personal, proprietary or restitutionary). Likewise with specialist areas like trade practices, real property, corporations law, industrial law, defamation, agency and intellectual property. Procedure texts and services will be consulted for practical and tactical concerns. This is not to imply that the treatment of equitable rights and remedies in Equity texts is deficient, but the searcher is necessarily taken away from the particular context of interest. Of course the equity texts may offer analogies as they present doctrines and remedies across different topics of law as perceived by the modern practitioner. But in a sense this reinforces my thesis about the mutual interaction of all sources of law and the undesirability of hiding it away under increasingly irrelevant historical categories. Some equity texts (most notably *Meagher Gummow and Lehane*) are seeking to meet readers' demand by including discussion about common law and statutory remedies that have superseded, or that run in parallel with, "equitable" remedies. Again, this illustrates my thesis.

Fifthly, there has been the direct challenge from the restitution theorists, most notably Goff, Jones and Birks. They have sought to explain a sizeable portion of traditional Equity under the concept of unjust enrichment and to use this as an analogical bridge to related common law doctrines and remedies. Every edition of Goff and Jones, *The Law of Restitution*[91] commences:

---

89   *Rich v Australian Securities Investments Commission*, above n 88 at 280-281.
90   Cf *Harris v Digital Pulse Pty Ltd* (2003) 56 NSWLR 298.
91   First edition in 1966 to the sixth edition in 2002.

"The law of restitution is the law relating to all claims, quasi-contractual or otherwise, which are founded upon the principle of unjust enrichment. Restitutionary claims are to be found in equity as well as at law."

Unjust enrichment theory may come in several varieties, but all offer a theoretical template for seeing workable analogies between "common law" and "equitable" doctrines addressing a wide range of frequently encountered legal relationships. Aspects of the template may be contestable, but the law-equity crossovers are already acknowledged by the equity textwriters, who (usually) deal with the topics by acknowledging the related, parallel or subsumed "common law" principles covering approximately the same field.

I have written recently about these developments in Australian law, drawing particular attention to restitution theory's offer to explain and integrate areas where traditional equity's contribution is incomplete, generally unprincipled and at times discordant (vis-à-vis a near parallel common law right).[92] Areas that have recently developed or are in the process of developing in this direction include the recovery of money paid under mistake, unauthorised use or detention of land and goods, improper pressure, recovery of misdirected or stolen funds and non-contractual claims for contribution.[93]

A related development, but worth separate mention, is the recent but now orthodox insight that tracing and following are universally applicable processes concerned with identifying property as it changes various forms and passes through various hands. General law rules are involved, most notably the principle that money is currency, with protection afforded to persons who give value without notice of defect in title. Tracing and following operate independently of the (legal and equitable) causes of action to which the processes are appurtenant. The scholarship of Professor Smith and the judicial scholarship of Lord Millett have been particularly influential in this area.[94] We now see that there is nothing peculiarly legal or equitable about tracing and following, but that these processes may be the prelude to the application of "legal" and "equitable" remedies and rights, both personal and proprietary, designed to vindicate the title of the owner who has lost possession of something of value, often through a species of "legal" or "equitable" (but most likely statutory) wrongdoing.[95]

This area of discourse leads inevitably into discussion of notions of property, a topic addressed by the House of Lords in *Foskett v McKeown*. It was in this area that the Birks took such a categorical stance in recent years, with his

---

92   K Mason, "Where has Australian restitution law got to and where is it going?" (2003) 77 *Australian Law Journal* 358.

93   See generally A Burrows, "We Do this at Common Law But That in Equity" (2002) 22 *Oxford Journal of Legal Studies* 1. Particularly as to misdirected funds, see *Koorootang Nominees Pty Ltd v Australian and New Zealand Banking Group Ltd* [1998] 3 VR 16 at 100-105 (Hansen J). As to overlapping legal and equitable doctrines and remedies touching the unauthorized use of land and goods, see K Mason and JW Carter, *Restitution Law in Australia* (Butterworths, Sydney, 1995) at chapter 16.

94   See L Smith, *The Law of Tracing* (Clarendon Press, Oxford, 1997); *Boscawen v Bajwa* [1996] 1 WLR 328 at 334 (Millett LJ), *Foskett v McKeown* [2001] 1 AC 102.

95   Most wrongful receipt claims stem from breaches of statutory duties of company directors with regard to company funds.

passionate distrust of the discretionary remedialism that is the law in this country.[96] Much is still to be resolved about the remedial constructive trust as both a personal and a proprietary remedy, but if there is one area where equity has placed its discretionary, pragmatic yet principled mark in Australian law, it is this one.[97] It can also be stated with confidence that Australian law no longer subscribes to the view, stated in *Re Diplock*[98] and awaiting its coup de grâce in England, that a fiduciary relationship must first be identified before an "equitable" remedy based on tracing or following can be granted. These are all significant developments, but none are inconsistent with viewing legal doctrine as a unified whole, understood meaningfully without reference to pre-1873 notions.

Finally, there occurred in the latter part of the twentieth century a belated but inevitable realisation that the complete administrative and procedural fusion effected by the Judicature Acts has changed life forever. Lord Diplock bemoaned the fact that "the innate conservatism of English lawyers may have made them slow to recognise" the effect of fusing the two legal systems. Other jurisdictions, like Canada and New Zealand, were not as slow; and their generally pro-fusionist jurists have (like Lord Diplock) received strong rebuke from certain New South Wales quarters. Worldwide experience does however confirm that the greater the time lapse from a *Judicature Act* reform, the less important are the traditional law/equity distinctions. This is particularly so in the United States, despite a constitutional embargo there on complete integration, stemming from a preserved right to trial by jury in "suits at common law". Whether the distance of time breeds sloppy ahistoricity or puts things in their proper perspective will probably depend on whether the question is asked of a committed fusionist, a fusion-sceptic or a committed anti-fusionist.

DAMAGES IN EQUITY: A CASE STUDY

The question of exemplary damages for breach of an exclusively fiduciary duty has been addressed recently in New Zealand,[99] Canada[100] and Australia[101] and has proved a catalyst for discussion about the fusion of law and equity. Fusion-related questions arise if only because most "fiduciary relationships" bear "common law" and "equitable" faces on opposite sides of the same coin and because of the availability of parallel rights and remedies "at common law", "in equity" or under statute.

---

96 See, for example, P Birks, "Rights, Wrongs, and Remedies" (2000) 20 *Oxford Journal of Legal Studies* 1.

97 See *Bathurst City Council v PWC Properties Pty Ltd* (1998) 195 CLR 566 at 585; *Giumelli v Giumelli* (1999) 196 CLR 101 at 113, 127; *Parsons v McBain* (2001) 109 FCR 120; *Kais v Turvey* (1994) 11 WAR 357; *Ikeuchi v Liu* (2001) 160 FLR 94; *Hancock Family Memorial Foundation Ltd v Porteous* (2000) 22 WAR 198; *Robins v Incentive Dynamics Pty Ltd (in liq)* (2003) 45 ACSR 244; (2003) 175 FLR 286.

98 [1948] Ch 465 at 520-521, 532, 540.

99 *Aquaculture Corporation v New Zealand Green Mussel Co Ltd* [1990] 3 NZLR 299.

100 *M(K) v M(H)* [1992] 3 SCR 6; *Whiten v Pilot Insurance Co* (2002) 209 DLR (4th) 257 at 287[67].

101 *Harris v Digital Pulse Pty Ltd* (2003) 56 NSWLR 298.

But the wider topic of damages in equity has been a fascinating touchstone for developments over a century and a half that illustrate several points in the current debate.

A trustee whose breach causes loss falls under an "equitable" obligation to make good the loss to the trust property, a duty to put the trust estate in the same position as if the breach of trust had not been committed.[102] The obligation was described by James and Baggallay LJJ as an "equitable debt or liability in the nature of debt"[103] and by Street J as an "obligation to make restitution".[104] The former expression was used to emphasise the distinction between an obligation of Equity's creation and a (common law) specialty debt that would only arise if the trustee was bound by a covenant in the trust instrument that gave such effect to a breach thereof.[105] But equity's curious choice of the word "debt" showed that it was borrowing an idea from the common law, with its emphasis on the immediacy of the obligation and the absence of any requirement to prove any more than unauthorised conduct. Street J brought out this point in *Re Dawson*, when he stated that "considerations of causation, foreseeability and reasonableness do not readily enter into the matter"[106] and when he observed[107] that:

> "The principles embodied in this approach do not appear to involve any inquiry as to whether the loss was caused by or flowed from the breach. Rather the inquiry in each instance would appear to be whether the loss would have happened if there had been no breach."

The "debt" analogy was Chancery's way of saying that relief would follow as of course if loss were proved. It required statutory intervention before the strictness of the old Chancery law was lifted by enactment permitting the court to relieve a trustee who had acted honestly, reasonably and in circumstances fairly justifying excusal. This was an area where remedial equity was every bit as stringent as the common law.

In its original form, *Lord Cairns' Act* conferred power on the Court of Chancery to award damages in addition to or in substitution for an injunction "in all cases in which the Court of Chancery has jurisdiction to entertain an application for an injunction". This statutory power enabled the Court to give damages even where they were unavailable in a court of common law, because, for instance the injury was merely threatened or apprehended or where the right was purely equitable. The Act was widely adopted.[108]

---

102 See generally RP Meagher and WMC Gummow, *Jacob's Law of Trusts* (6th ed, Butterworths, Sydney, 1997) at [2203].

103 *Ex parte Adamson; Re Collie* (1878) 8 Ch D 807 at 819. See also *Wickstead v Browne* (1992) 30 NSWLR 1 at 14-15.

104 *Re Dawson* [1966] NSWR 211 at 216.

105 *Wynch v Grant* (1854) 2 Drew 312; 61 ER 739. The equitable derivation of the remedy also had consequences for the ready availability of compound interest or an account of profits against particular defaulting trustees or fiduciaries.

106 *Re Dawson*, above n 104 at 215. Note that he did not exclude such factors altogether.

107 *Re Dawson*, above n 104 at 215.

108 In New South Wales it was adopted by the *Equity Act 1880* and the provision deriving from it is now found in s 68 of the *Supreme Court Act 1970*.

In 1883 the statute was repealed in England.[109] The omission may have been inadvertent and the provision was re-enacted there in 1981. In 1924 the point was taken, in *Leeds Industrial Co-Operative Society Ltd v Slack*,[110] when damages were sought in lieu of an injunction *quia timet*. The House of Lords brushed aside the submission that power to award such damages had gone with the repeal of *Lord Cairns' Act* in 1883. The reasoning of some of the Law Lords is an extremely forced reading of certain savings clauses and it has been widely criticised.[111] Lords Sumner and Carson proceeded directly to the same conclusion on the basis that the *Judicature Act* rendered *Lord Cairns' Act* unnecessary.[112] Some may see this as a gross fusion fallacy, but it again illustrates my point about such "fallacies" being discoverable in all the right places.

Pettit's *Equity and the Law of Trusts*[113] and *Meagher Gummow and Lehane* [114] cite Goff J's statement in *Grant v Dawkins*[115] in which he doubted Chancery's power to award damages before the passing of *Lord Cairns' Act* in 1858. *Meagher Gummow and Lehane* also states[116] that "equity had no power to award damages as they were known at law". Sir Frederick Jordan in his highly influential *Chapters in Equity in New South Wales*[117] stated that: "until *Lord Cairns' Act* [Chancery] had no power to award damages".

These learned authors treat damages and "equitable compensation" as falling within categorically distinct spheres, a proposition that I question below. But more significantly, the researches of Peter McDermott have exploded the issue directly. His article on the "Jurisdiction of the Court of Chancery to Award Damages"[118] discloses statutory and non-statutory awards of damages well prior to *Lord Cairns' Act*. He demonstrates that by the early nineteenth century Chancery would award or assess damages (at law) in appropriate instances, where it had the machinery to do so and if it considered that its equitable jurisdiction had been genuinely invoked in the first place.[119]

There was a hardening of attitude under the Chancellorship of Lord Eldon in this as in several other aspects of Equity,[120] justifying Atiyah's observation

---

109 *Statute Law Revision and Civil Procedure Act 1883*, s 3.

110 [1924] AC 851.

111 See PM McDermott, *Equitable Damages* (Butterworths, Sydney, 1994) at 42-43, citing Jolowicz, Heuston, Bennion and Atiyah.

112 *Leeds Industrial Corporative Society Ltd v Slack*, above n 110 at 872-873 per Lord Sumner, at 873 per Lord Carson. This had been the view of Lord Esher in *Chapman, Morsons & Co v Guardians of Auckland Union* (1889) 23 QBD 294 at 299. See also *Board v Board* [1919] AC 956 at 962.

113 PH Pettit, *Equity and the Law of Trusts* (9th ed, LexisNexis UK, London, 2001) at 552.

114 *Meagher, Gummow and Lehane* at [23-030].

115 [1973] 3 All ER 897 at 899, 900.

116 *Meagher, Gummow and Lehane* at [1-225].

117 Sir Frederick Jordan, *Chapters in Equity in New South Wales* (6th ed, 1947) reprinted in Sir Frederick Jordan, *Select Legal Papers* (Legal Books, Sydney, 1983) at 13.

118 PM McDermott, "Jurisdiction of the Court of Chancery to Award Damages" (1992) 108 *Law Quarterly Review* 652. *Meagher, Gummow and Lehane* acknowledge the existence of this article at [23-025], but in effect as a footnote that leads to no revision of the thesis in the text.

119 See the cases cited by PM McDermott, "Jurisdiction of the Court of Chancery to Award Damages", above n 118 at 661-664.

120 See *Todd v Gee* (1810) 17 Ves 273; 34 ER 106.

that: "the Court of Chancery itself went into a period of decline from which it never wholly recovered. Partly, if not directly, this decline was due to the purely fortuitous nature of Lord Eldon's disposition".[121] Chancery's unwillingness to award damages during the early nineteenth century was seen by some writers at the time to have been jurisdictional, in the sense of establishing an absence of power.[122]

But Turner LJ reasserted Chancery's power in 1855 in *Phelps v Prothero*[123] and there were American decisions to similar effect.[124] McDermott[125] cites several other decisions, including those of Shadwell VC, Sir James Knight Bruce VC, Lord Langdale and Owen CJ in Eq as to Chancery's inherent power (in a proper case) to award damages rather than compel a creditor to have recourse to law, or as ancillary to equitable relief.

In *Raineri v Miles*,[126] Lord Edmund-Davies saw *Phelps* as authority for the proposition that, upon a vendor's default, a purchaser who proceeded in a court of equity "could recover damages whether or not he had also sought specific performance". His Lordship added:[127]

"The fact is that for some years before the Judicature Acts of 1873 and 1875 the common law and Chancery courts had been mutually making increasingly friendly overtures, and these had modified the attitudes of each."

This observation is echoed in the judgments of the Supreme Court of Canada in *Canson Enterprises Ltd v Boughton & Co*.[128] Like *Harris*, this was a case about remedies flowing from breach of "fiduciary" duty. There were significant differences in opinion, but the whole Court recognised that discriminate borrowing between common law and equitable concepts was appropriate.[129] In McLachlin J's words "we may take wisdom when we find it, and accept such insights offered by the law of tort… as may prove useful."

In *Raineri*,[130] Lord Edmund-Davies gave examples of the "assimilative process" that was accelerated by the *Common Law Procedure Act 1854* and *Lord Cairns' Act 1858*. In *King v Poggioli*[131] Starke J had spoken to similar effect.

The provision in the *Lord Cairns' Act* enabling the Court of Chancery to award damages for breaches of obligations not sounding in damages at law was all the more curious in light of Chancery's longstanding power to require defaulting trustees to do just that. Yet the first clear indication that equity embraced an inherent power to award compensation with respect to breaches

---

121   PS Atiyah, *The Rise and Fall of Freedom of Contract* (Oxford University Press, Oxford, 1979) at 392-393.
122   PM McDermott, *Equitable Damages* (Butterworths, Sydney, 1994) cites Fonblanque, Hovenden, Maddock and an 1832 edition of Bacon's Abridgment.
123   (1855) 7 De GM & G 722 at 734; 44 ER 280 at 285.
124   See PM McDermott, *Equitable Damages*, above n 122 at 668-669.
125   PM McDermott, *Equitable Damages*, above n 122 at 670-672.
126   [1981] AC 1050 at 1081.
127   *Raineri v Miles*, above n 126 at 1082.
128   [1991] 3 SCR 534.
129   *Canson Enterprises Ltd v Boughton & Co*, above n 128. See esp McLachlin J at 545-546, La Forest J at 587-588.
130   *Raineri v Miles*, above n 126 at 1081.
131   (1923) 32 CLR 222 at 246. See also *Minter v Geraghty* (1981) 38 ALR 68 at 80.

of fiduciary duty occurred in England with the seminal decision in *Nocton v Lord Ashburton*.[132] There is earlier authority in the Supreme Court of Victoria to like effect,[133] although the 1927 decision of Dixon AJ pointing this out in *McKenzie v McDonald*[134] is usually regarded as the root of title for equitable damages/compensation in this country. Nowadays equitable damages is so much a part of the landscape that it has its own textbook.[135]

The principles relating to this remedy are not applied uniformly to all equitable obligations or all categories of breach, and they do not necessarily replicate the rules as to assessing damages at common law. For some categories of fiduciary relationships and in some situations at least the rules as to remoteness and the time of assessment of compensation are much stricter than for breach of contract. But this observation contributes little to the fusion debate. Different rules on these matters may apply as between intentional torts and the tort of negligence[136] and contractual damages are also nuanced and contextual.[137] Common law analogies may offer assistance in many situations (for example in understanding the normative approaches involved in most causation enquiries in the law). The massive academic and judicial debate about different categories of fiduciaries, much of it focussing on *Target Holdings Ltd v Redferns*[138] and *Henderson v Merrett Syndicates Ltd*,[139] suggests that the idea of holding a single "equity" line on the approach to assessing compensation for equitable wrongs is both doomed and distracting.[140]

One lesson to be derived from the late emergence of non-statutory equitable damages or compensation is pointed out by *Meagher Gummow and Lehane*.[141] There was really no need for *Lord Cairns' Act* to have conferred on Chancery the power to award "damages" for breaches of purely equitable obligations. In other words, the general law (then on its Chancery side) contained within itself the capacity to develop by providing this additional remedy.

Another lesson is that the use of "damages" as an equitable remedy for infringements of equitable rights has legislative endorsement, with the consequence that judicial language to similar effect[142] should not be decried as a fusion fallacy.[143]

---

132 [1914] AC 932.

133 See *Robinson v Abbott* (1893) 20 VLR 346.

134 [1927] VLR 134.

135 PM McDermott, *Equitable Damages* (Butterworths, Sydney, 1994).

136 See *Palmer Bruyn & Parker Pty Ltd v Parsons* (2001) 208 CLR 388.

137 *Commonwealth v Amann Aviation Pty Ltd* (1991) 174 CLR 64.

138 [1996] 1 AC 421.

139 [1995] 2 AC 145.

140 See CEF Rickett, "Equitable Compensation: Towards a Blueprint?" (2003) 25 *Sydney Law Review* 31. See also J Getzler, 'Am I my beneficiary's keeper? Fusion and loss-based fiduciary remedies' in this book at chapter 10.

141 *Meagher, Gummow and Lehane* at [23-010].

142 For example in *Seager v Copydex* (No 2) [1969] 2 All ER 718; *Talbot v General Television Corp Pty Ltd* [1980] VR 224; *Aquaculture Corp v New Zealand Mussel Co Ltd* [1990] 3 NZLR 299; *Attorney-General v Observer Ltd* [1990] 1 AC 109 at 286 and *Wentworth v Woollahra Municipal Council* (1982) 149 CLR 672 at 676.

143 See *Meagher, Gummow and Lehane* at [2-155]. See also my remarks in *Harris v Digital Pulse Pty Ltd* (2003) 56 NSWLR 298 at 322[118]-[129].

Labels can operate as signposts, but they can also be misleading either because they may conflate separate concepts or (when different labels are seized upon as automatic indicators of distinctive legal concepts) because they may impede parallels or analogies being drawn (that is, principled fusion). The brickbats are shared equally between the common law and equity when one considers the proven capacity of words such as trustee, agent, trust property, fiduciary, damages, compensation and injunction to generate their own misleading fictions and confusion. Confusion as to whether company directors should be seen as "agents", thereby attracting entry to common law courts or as "trustees", thereby attracting entry to Chancery, offers an early example of the unhelpful dangers of labels and how perceiving differences that do not really exist and justifying them by a law/equity divide can be positively harmful.[144]

This brings me to the issue of exemplary damages. My views are set out in *Harris v Digital Pulse Pty Ltd*, but they did not prevail in the New South Wales Court of Appeal. It is appropriate for me to leave it to others to analyse the reasoning in the three judgments. I content myself with the observation that it is satisfying that the disagreement within the Court did not turn on arid historical disputation about Chancery's traditional jurisdiction. Issue was properly joined as to the scope and function of remedies protective of fiduciary relationships, the gravitational pull of contractual and/or tortious principles for assessing damages generally and in relation to the very relationships involved, and the characterisation of such relationships by reference to their function and the analogy of contract.[145]

WHAT IS THE FUSION DEBATE ALL ABOUT?

It will be apparent from what I have written that I share Lord Goff's view in *Lord Napier v Hunter* that:[146]

"… our task nowadays is to see the two strands of authority, at law and in equity, moulded into a coherent whole".

But it does not follow that historical differences between different concepts and principles are to be glossed over for the mere sake of simplicity or uniformity. If a doctrine can *genuinely* be described as equitable this may at least warn against insouciant or unprincipled fusing of doctrines.

Equity in Australia is vibrant and in no way past the age of child-bearing. Justice Gummow's recent article "Equity: too successful?"[147] outlines a body of jurisprudence that is vibrantly self-assured and that appears much more comfortable with discretion and pragmatism than English equity. But it does not

---

144 See text referable to n 17 above.
145 Spigelman CJ did not find it necessary to join Heydon JA in ruling that the Supreme Court of New South Wales lacked power to award exemplary damages for any equitable wrongs. The Chief Justice limited his remarks to breach of fiduciary duties arising in the context of a contractual relationship. See A Burrows, 'Remedial Coherence and Punitive Damages in Equity' in this book at chapter 15.
146 [1993] AC 713 at 743.
147 WMC Gummow, "Equity: too Successful" (2003) 77 *Australian Law Journal* 30.

follow that when judges administer "equity" in Australia they are using different methods or applying different underlying values than when dealing with concepts deriving from the common law or litigation relating to statute law.

Anthony Duggan warns against viewing appellate judges as having split personalities, applying different values and principles when deciding cases in equity, at common law and under statute. His thesis is that, despite the emphasis on altruism in the "new equity rhetoric", actual case outcomes really reflect efficiency concerns. Equity's promotion of "other regarding" behaviour is achieved by appealing to actors' self-interest, not their better nature.[148] It is indeed possible to detect a trend towards a stricter view of unconscionability and even greater equity deference to contractually negotiated (that is, "common law") outcomes since then.[149]

The process of greater integration has and will continue to gather pace to the extent that all branches of the general law use common concepts and common terminology (or at least realise that different language does not necessarily import different principles).[150]

Our adversary system allows plaintiffs to put their best foot forward and to plead claims in the alternative. Properly advised, plaintiffs will still choose to press an equitable/common law/statutory right or remedy if it is in their interests and to seek to blend the best of all worlds if that helps too.

But courts are not always obliged to go along with such a trisected view of the law. Parallel universes are not to be fostered for their own sakes. Defendants have rights too. And it is sometimes necessary or appropriate for the values inherent in one legal concept to mean that it takes primacy, or even occupies a field to the exclusion of others. In recent years, these sorts of issues have been addressed as regards the relationship of contract and tort,[151] contract and restitution,[152] negligence and defamation[153] and in other areas. Where remedies are seen as discretionary, principles have been developed to identify when they should issue.

These various enquiries are assisted by reference to the policies found in the precedents for triggering legal recognition of the right or remedy. But they are hindered by glib and unhelpful labelling based upon categories such as "common law", "equity", "statutory". In *Harris*, Heydon JA and I expressed differing views about equity's "punitive" function. I remain to be convinced that any overriding and helpful pattern can be detected at such a level of historical abstraction.[154]

---

148 AJ Duggan, "Is Equity Efficient?" (1997) 113 *Law Quarterly Review* 601 at 602. See also L Smith, "Fusion and Tradition" in this book at chapter 2.

149 *Bridgewater v Leahy* (1998) 194 CLR 457; *Tanwar Enterprises Pty Ltd v Cauchi* (2003) 217 CLR 315.

150 This probably explains why the Equity traditionalists fight so hard to retain traditional or distinctive labels.

151 *Hawkins v Clayton* (1988) 164 CLR 539.

152 *Dimskal Shipping Co SA v International Transport Workers Federation (the Evia Luck)* [1992] 2 AC 152 at 165; *Roxburgh v Rothmans of Pall Mall Australia Ltd* (2001) 208 CLR 516 at [58], [75], [95], [166], [197].

153 *Tame v New South Wales* (2002) 211 CLR 317 at 335[28], 342[58], 361[123].

154 Cf *Rich v Australian Securities Investments Commission* (2004) 209 ALR 271.

However, the accumulated judicial wisdom of the ages remains a starting (and usually finishing) point for decision-making, even at the appellate level. The tectonic plates under particular precedents shift slowly, even though pressure builds up in places.

It is helpful to distinguish between rights and remedies in this area of discourse.

As regards rights, law and equity may offer different legacies that plaintiffs may choose at will. If the discordance is so direct a "conflict or variance" as to engage s 25(11) of the *Judicature Act* or its counterpart, statute decrees that equity trumps law. But this provision is seldom engaged nowadays.

Nevertheless, the general law has developed techniques for choosing and/or fusing traditional legal and equitable principles. Sometimes the legal and equitable rights overlap to such a degree that the appellate guardians of the general law are ashamed to recognise the existence of nearly parallel, but ultimately divergent universes. In those cases the better right is allowed to cover the field, bringing with it the associated doctrines that may distinguish it in detail from its legal or equitable cousin. Often the doctrine that prevails is that which developed more flexibly, that is, usually that which was once fostered exclusively in Chancery. This phenomenon is discernible as regards the atrophying of the common law actions for account, contribution and recoupment. As regards the latter two "restitutionary" causes of action, courts have recognised that equitable principles now provide all the answers.[155] *Meagher Gummow and Lehane*[156] accept this as a situation where equitable principles cover the field. A similar development has been recognised in the law of privilege, where the privilege against exposure to penalties has long been recognised by the general law and is no longer simply a rule of equity relating to discovery.[157]

These developments are not the outworking of s 25(11) of the *Judicature Act* and they illustrate the general law's capacity (by techniques deserving to be labeled "fusion fallacies" by those who believe in them) for a rule from one "system" to "somehow annihilate" the situation prevailing in the other.[158] It is likely that estoppel by representation may also be developing in this manner.[159]

"Common law" doctrines may supplant or modify rules of equity. Short-circuiting of the traditional law/equity divide may also occur in the interests of justice. *AMEV–UDC Finance Ltd v Austin* (discussed above) is an example of the equitable doctrine yielding place to the better common law rule in the hands of a post-Judicature Act court. A fascinating development is also occurring in the heartland of the paradigmatic exclusively equitable institution, the trust, and it is occurring with due acknowledgment of the influence of the *Judicature Act*. A body of caselaw now recognises that a beneficiary can

---

155   *Cunningham-Reid v Public Trustee* [1944] KB 602; *Armstrong v Commissioner for Stamp Duties* (1967) 69 SR (NSW) 38 at 48; *Burke v LFOT Pty Ltd* (2002) 209 CLR 282 at 299[38]).
156   *Meagher, Gummow and Lehane* at [10-010].
157   *Daniels Corporation International Pty Ltd v Australian Competition and Consumer Commission* (2002) 213 CLR 543 at 554[13].
158   Cf JD Heydon, "The Negligent Fiduciary" (1995) 111 *Law Quarterly Review* 1 at 3.
159   See *Commonwealth v Verwayen* (1990) 170 CLR 394 at 412 (Mason CJ), 431-40 (Deane J).

in "exceptional circumstances" claim on behalf of the trust damages for breach of a "common law" obligation where the trustee disappears or neglects to act.[160] One assumes that Maitland would have been shocked by this sensible elision that cannot be explained away by assuming a fictional appointment of replacement plaintiff trustees.

Lord Browne-Wilkinson's speech in *Henderson* and the decision of the Western Australian Full Court in *Permanent Building Society (in liq) v Wheeler*[161] concerning the duty of care of company directors are other examples of this beneficent phenomenon, although I realise that these are fighting words and that an opposite position will be advanced in other chapters in this book. Unlike for trustees, Chancery never asserted a monopoly over directors. Indeed, in its reflective moments, equity has acknowledged the dangers of loose thinking prompted by invocation of the "fiduciary" label.[162] There is in my view no reason, beyond history, why (over a century after the English *Judicature Act*) equity should assert as of right that the law about a director's duty of care should continue to be worked out according to "its" rules, without at least offering justification for separate treatment. A fortiori, where this may produce a lengthy list of discordances affecting not just the immediate parties but also third parties.[163] As with the overlap between contractual and tortious claims upon professional people, these differences call to be justified, not merely identified, unless the law is to abandon concern for coherence and to risk ever-widening circles of liability by always giving plaintiffs the logical consequences of their demands, without questioning the justice of defendants' positions.

Sometimes it is the very differences between two sets of rights that lead appellate courts to choose which system has primacy. This phenomenon has already been mentioned. To take an example away from the present area, the notions of allocation of risk and the doctrine of efficient breach have seen contractual solutions squeeze out tortious alternatives in appropriate cases. The fusing of common law and equitable rights may partake of this process also. There is, of course, no reason why blending may not borrow the best of both worlds (if you are not troubled by an accusation of committing a fusion fallacy).

Turning to remedies, the processes of fusion are conceptually much simpler. Since the early nineteenth century Parliaments have been giving equitable powers to common law courts and common law powers to equity courts.[164] The *Judicature Act* was the culmination of this statutory process. But the courts have been acting in aid of each other and borrowing from each other for much longer. The process gathered pace in the nineteenth century and received a

---

160 *Parker-Tweedale v Dunbar Bank Plc (No 1)* [1991] Ch 12 at 19-20; *Lidden v Composite Buyers Ltd* (1996) 67 FCR 560 (Finn J); *Lamru Pty Ltd v Kation Pty Ltd* (1998) 44 NSWLR 432.

161 (1994) 11 WAR 187 discussed by JD Heydon "Are Duties of Company Directors to Exercise Care and Skill Fiduciary", chapter 9 in this book.

162 *Re Coomber* [1911] 1 Ch 723 at 728-9 per Fletcher Moulton LJ.

163 See JD Heydon, "The Negligent Fiduciary", above n 158 suggesting different outcomes in relation to measure of damages, limitation, contribution, contributory negligence, conditionality of remedy, unclean hands, exemplary damages and causation.

164 See WS Holdsworth, *A History of English Law* (Sweet & Maxwell, London), Vol xv at 122-127.

significant fillip with the *Judicature Act* reforms to procedure.[165] Unless false fear of committing a fusion fallacy stands in the way, there is simply no jurisdictional or power-related impediment to complete adaptation of remedies. Chancery in its auxiliary and concurrent jurisdictions was always pleased to assist common law whenever appropriate. Within a single court there is no continuing impediment to the "cross over" of remedies, whether it be "damages" in aid of equitable rights or the full gamut of equitable remedies in aid of common law rights. I am not saying this should happen invariably, but (at least with discretionary remedies) there is no problem with adapting them to new situations if justified by the analogical application of precedent or the proper application of general principles. Courts faced with choices in this area will have to examine the values and functions underlying the remedies: but they should be doing this anyway.[166]

Nothing herein stops the principled and coherent development of a general law of remedies. Some remedies will issue as of course, others will have special requirements and/or be discretionary. Appropriate principles in that regard can continue to be developed without the need to hearken back to false stereotypes of a long receding pre-Judicature Act system.

CONCLUSION

The general law, of whatever derivation, is largely found in precedent, operates within ever-diminishing interstices between statute law, and is developed according to common principles of judicial method supervised in each law area by an ultimate appellate Court.

It is no longer true to describe common law as a single system, or to brand it as rigid, rule-driven, incapable of change and disproportionate. These were its badges at the time when the Court of Chancery flowered "to soften and mollify the Extremity of the Law", to use Lord Ellesmere's phrase in his successful claim for equity's supremacy before James I.[167] The early nineteenth century Court of Chancery depicted in *Bleak House* itself needed statutory reform and a judicial wake-up call every bit as much as the Common Law Courts of that era.

Much water has flown under the bridge since the enactments culminating in the Judicature Acts throughout the "common law" world. Equitable doctrines and remedies have become available in all courts of general jurisdiction, if judges (following the tradition of the Chancellors) think them appropriate for application or adoption in accordance with the judicial method, or are required to take them into account by modern statutes. A misapplication of precedent, principle or legal policy will be corrected on appeal. Disagreements will ultimately be resolved in the highest courts.

---

165 Priestley JA pointed out that the *"crossover of remedies"* is more advanced in the United States than in England or Australia (LJ Priestley, "A Guide to a Comparison of Australian and United States Contract Law" (1989) 12 *University of New South Wales Law Journal* 4 at 29).

166 See D Laycock, "The Triumph of Equity" (1993) 56 *Law and Contemporary Problems* 54 at 81.

167 *Earl of Oxford's Case* (1615) 1 Ch Rep 1 at 7; 21 ER 485 at 486.

Equity may take some of the credit for this state of affairs, because for centuries her Chancellors prevailed through use of the common injunction, before the nineteenth century her doctrines tended to be more nuanced than those of the common law, and because her ultimate supremacy in things deemed equitable was affirmed by Parliament. In one sense, success has come with a loss of distinctive identity, because of the theoretical postulate of an undivided and coherent legal system.

But equity cannot take all of the credit for the modern legal system. Common law doctrines and remedies have in the last century moved apace, especially in the areas of procedure, remedies, contract, property, restitution and commercial law where equity and common law claim continuing and interacting roles. Statutory reforms have been very significant. The general law has developed the ubiquitous idea of abuse of process to check and frustrate unconscientious resort to legal rights and remedies.

In short, the myth of equity as saviour is now so outdated that its continued promulgation is as harmful to the understanding of the structure and development of the civil law as it is fictitious. "Equitable" doctrines should now take their proper place as part of a unified system of judge-made law, alongside and integrated with "common law" and statutory developments in those and other areas of legal discourse.

Fusionists come in all shapes and sizes, generally united by concerns for coherence, rationality, efficiency and respect for general principles that serve as guides in legal education and appellate decision-making. Anti-fusionists may also share these goals, but they are generally united in their greater respect for a static legal framework and their love of history.

One aim in this chapter has been to demonstrate the historicity of the ongoing quest for realising the values served by "fusion" in its many guises. Let me conclude by invoking historical support for Maitland's vision of a more complete fusion.

Blackstone in his 1768 *Commentaries*[168] observed that:

"there cannot be a greater solecism, than that in two sovereign independent courts, established in the same country, exercising concurrent jurisdiction, and over the same subject matter, there should exist in a single instance two different rules of property clashing with or contradicting each other".

Australia's greatest judicial legal historian, Sir Victor Windeyer wrote in *Felton v Mulligan*:[169]

"Mine may be an ingenuous view, but to me it seems that the law that a court must apply and administer, in the exercise of whatever jurisdiction pertains to it, may be derived from different concerns, but that it is still, so far as any particular case is concerned, a single though composite body of law."

Debate about the fusion of law and Equity goes back for centuries. And for centuries it has been bedevilled by confusion stemming from the use of a single metaphor to do work on many different fronts. The metaphor may change but

---

168 Vol 3 at chapter 27.
169 (1971) 124 CLR 367 at 392.

the idea of capturing the impact over time of a single event remains. There have been the metaphors of fusion, confluence, integration, interaction and inter-mingling. Justice Tipping has offered the metaphor of a rope in which discrete strands work separately yet together to do the task required of the whole rope. He offers "intertwining".[170]

For some, the debate is seen in terms of exegesis of a statutory event occurring at a single point of time in the legal history of a particular law area. For England, the date was 1875. If the fusion debate starts and finishes from this premise, the debaters will discover much in common. But they will be viewing a sliver of ancient history, like an MRI image of a thin slice of a living body at a moment of time long past. The academic and judicial guardians of the modern law can do much better than this.

---

170 Tipping J, "Causation at Law and in Equity: Do We Have Fusion?" (2000) 7 *Cambridge Law Review* 443.

4

Rival Taxonomies Within Obligations: Is There a Problem?

STEVE HEDLEY

Some aspects of the debate over the continued existence of equity are predictable enough. On the one side, you have those who refer to equity's history, its oddly moralistic concepts, and its refusal (despite centuries of development) to fit itself into neat categories. Surely, these people say, such a vague conception does not deserve to live any longer – let us put it out of its misery.[1] On the other side, you have those who see common values and themes in equitable doctrines, as well as a continuing need to correct the common law. Has the common law really become so perfect, they protest, that it has outgrown the need for equitable adjustment? When did this remarkable transformation occur?[2] Examples of both can be found in this book.

If that issue is fairly stated, this writer would align himself with the second school of thought. For as long as we have common law, it will have imperfections, and so we will need equity to correct it. If some say that equity is dying, then the fact must be admitted – but so is the common law. The great legal innovations today are statutory, not common law; when new law is needed, it is made by the legislature, whereas common law is only ever made slowly and interstitially. In the eye of history, the common law is slowly being whittled away, and presumably at some point in the future there will be none of it left. But while it is here, equity is needed too. My view would therefore be that equity will last as long as the common law will; how long *that* is, is anyone's guess, though we can see easily enough which way things are heading.

None of this, however, is the topic of this chapter, except tangentially; and none of this is what has motivated the loudest and most powerful attacks on equity in recent years. The flak has come from a quite different direction.

---

1   See for example, J Mummery, 'Commercial notions and equitable potions' in S Worthington (ed), *Commercial Law and Commercial Practice* (Hart Publishing, Oxford, 2003) at 29.

2   See for example, J Martin, "Fusion, Fallacy and Confusion: A Comparative Study" [1994] *Conveyancer and Property Lawyer* 13; WMC Gummow, "Equity: Too Successful?" (2003) 77 *Australian Law Journal* 30.

THE TAXONOMICAL ATTACK ON EQUITY

The bulk of the attack on equity has actually been on quite different grounds. A taxonomy in private law has been produced, and loudly asserted as fundamental to the area. It has been said that private law must be divided into a law of property and a law of obligations, and that the law of obligations in its turn must be divided into liabilities arising from four categories of causative events – consent, wrongs, unjust enrichment, and other events.[3]

Why does this have anything to do with equity? Equity has co-existed in the past with any number of other notions, and so it is not, at first sight, at all obvious what the problem is. But those promoting this taxonomy say that it is an all-or-nothing deal. If it is used to classify legal obligations, then those who do so may not use any other classifying concepts – they cannot talk about whether the liabilities are legal or equitable, or indeed put them into any sort of conceptual boxes that are not allowed for by the taxonomy. Is use of the taxonomy avoidable? Apparently not, according to its proponents; they suggest that a refusal to use it is a denial of the need for any sort of conceptual order within private law, little better than an argument that judges should have complete discretion to decide cases as they wish. Choose, they say: either use the taxonomy, or embrace chaos – there is no third possibility. And the notion of "equity" is only open to those who have chosen chaos.[4]

So the attacks on equity are part of a wider pattern of forays into private law, by which the taxonomists strike at whatever cannot be fitted into their scheme. A separate and distinct "equity" is one of the things they have been loudest about – the need to distinguish law from equity cuts right across their scheme of taxonomy. It is not that equity has done anything wrong – the mere fact that it exists is reason enough to condemn it. Other parts of the same attack have been the insistence on a coherent law of unjust enrichment, which must be quite distinct from the law of consent/promise and the law of wrongs, as well as not distinguishing between law and equity. This puts them at odds both with those, like Professor Grantham, who think unjust enrichment exists but has a quite different basis,[5] and those, like myself, who don't think it has any coherence at all.[6] While they trumpet it less openly, this taxonomical school of thought also takes controversial stances in relation to consent and to wrongs, wanting to base the law of contract and the law of torts on narrow and traditional versions of responsibility – contract is based on consent/promise and nothing else, tort is based on wrongdoing and nothing else. This, they say,

---

3   See for example, P Birks, "The Law of Restitution at the End of an Epoch" (1999) 28 *Western Australian Law Review* 13.

4   See especially P Birks, "Equity in the Modern Law – An Exercise in Taxonomy" (1996) 26 *Western Australian Law Review* 1.

5   R Grantham, 'The Equitable Basis Of The Law Of Restitution', at chapter 14 in this book. See also G Virgo, 'Restitution Through the Looking Glass' in J Getzler, *Rationalizing Property, Equity and Trusts* (LexisNexis UK, London, 2003) at 82; E Sherwin, "Restitution and Equity: An Analysis of the Principle of Unjust Enrichment" (2001) 79 *Texas Law Review* 2083.

6   S Hedley, *Restitution: Its division and ordering* (Sweet and Maxwell, London, 2001).

is orthodoxy, though it looks to me like an extremely conservative view of the law.[7]

I have attempted over a number of years, in various articles, to get some account of the credentials of this taxonomy. What is supposed to be so wonderful about it, I have asked; so wonderful, indeed, that any legal idea that conflicts with it must be jettisoned immediately. After all, there are any number of legal taxonomies or ways of dividing up the law. You frequently find seemingly incompatible taxonomies going around together, often in the same book or the same judgment or even inside the same skull, without any demonstrable harm being done to anyone. Why, then, are we supposed to drop everything in favour of this new taxonomy of obligations? Yet I have to say that, so far at least, the results of my enquiries has been mostly negative. The only public answers from the pro-taxonomists have been rather general ones: such as, that you either believe in legal principles and in treating like cases alike, in which case you will go for the taxonomy, or you believe in unprincipled chaos, in which case you won't.[8] That's a little too vague to amount to an argument, I think. There are many possible different principles to choose from, many different criteria to decide whether like cases are really being treated alike. And no one side of the argument can claim a monopoly on coherence or principled thought.

So many of the claims of the pro-taxonomists – their attacks on equity included – rest on the simple proposition that their taxonomy is superb and must not be tinkered with. Yet they have never explained why this should be so. It is not hard to write texts within obligations without using the taxonomy – I have done it myself, so have a number of others – and it is certainly not obvious that these texts lack coherence. The taxonomists have not argued, and could not argue, that the principal equity texts are incoherent or meaningless; on the contrary, these books are usually models of order – just not the sort of order that the taxonomists approve of. So, to all appearances, the taxonomical attack on equity is weak. It is simply not true that equity texts are incoherent or fail to treat like cases alike. And if they offend against some principle of order in legal thought, we have not yet been given any clear account of what that principle is.

So if the taxonomists want to maintain their claim of the incoherence of equity, they have work to do. To help this process along a bit, I thought I would look a little closer at the taxonomy they are using – not so much its detailed application to obligations, but the broader legal system it portrays.

THE GAIAN TAXONOMY

The taxonomy is reproduced as an appendix to this chapter (Appendix 1) showing the way obligations is supposedly structured, while Appendix 2 shows the bigger legal system into which obligations fit. Ultimately most of this can be traced back to Gaius, writing in the second century AD, though some prefer to credit Justinian, and there are some elements here which neither might have

---

7   S Hedley, *Restitution: Its division and ordering,* above n 6 at 63-66.
8   A Burrows, *The Law of Restitution* (2nd ed, Butterworths, London, 2002) at 13-15.

recognised or approved – and the whole elaboration of the civil law to fit into these categories took many centuries. As you can see, the idea that there is a distinct "law of obligations" is only a very small part of the scheme, and it assumes that we have already made a number of earlier distinctions at a higher level of generality: dividing public law from private; dividing private law into the law of persons, the law of things, and the law of actions; and finally dividing the law of things into property and obligations.[9]

What do lawyers make of this? People whose primary legal background is civil law, or who for some other reason studied Roman law at an early age, probably find that this reminds them of law school. It may or may not remind them of anything they encountered later. Common lawyers generally are likely to find it a little bit strange, but not grossly so. We do make some of the distinctions here, particularly that between public and private law, and between obligations and property. The truth is the civil law concepts have always been around in the books for common lawyers to use if this seemed like a good idea, and so over the centuries an awful lot of civil law has been absorbed into common law. What has looked good has been appropriated to common law uses, and the result is that common law and civil law do not look so strange to one another as might be supposed.

The civil law distinctions therefore have their uses – no objection can be made to the use of the civilian classification where its utility has been demonstrated. A possible use is for the structuring of books such as the gargantuan *English Private Law*, which try to take a very broad view of an entire legal system – every such book needs a structure, and this modified Roman law one is as good as any.[10] It would be quite another matter, though, for common lawyers to adopt this whole classification lock stock and barrel, and expel from the common law anything that does not fit into it. The real battle is not whether this civil law structure can be used by those who wish to – this does not appear to be in dispute – but whether it should have some sort of exclusivity, sweeping away all other ways of viewing the law – including ways that distinguish law from equity. That is what the taxonomists claim, and that is what I am opposing.

But the literature lacks much detailed consideration of the point. The few that have looked at it tend to resort to generalities. The taxonomists have simply claimed that it's a choice between their conceptual scheme and chaos; the anti-taxonomists, such as myself, have simply replied that this is nonsense.

---

9   On the Gaian scheme from a common law point of view see especially G Samuel, "Classification of obligations and the impact of constructivist epistemologies" (1997) 17 *Legal Studies* 448.

10 P Birks (ed), *English Private Law* (Oxford University Press, Oxford, 2000); see also the companion publication, D Feldman (ed), *English Public Law* (Oxford University Press, Oxford, 2004). On the scheme itself see especially 'Introduction' at xxxv-l. For debate sparked by the book see G Samuel, "*English Private Law*: Old and New Thinking in the Taxonomy Debate" (2004) 24 *Oxford Journal of Legal Studies* 335; P Matthews, "Book review – *English Private Law*" (2002) 6 *Jersey Law Review* (1) 115; E Descheemaeker, "Mapping the Common Law: On a Recent English Attempt and its Links with Scottish Jurisprudence" [2003] *Juridical Review* (4) 295; N Kasirer, "*English Private Law*, Outside In" (2003) 3 *Oxford University Commonwealth Law Journal* (Winter) 249.

What I hope to do here is to put it all in sharper focus. I want to ask first, how satisfactory is this Gaian taxonomy today; secondly, to ask why it is said that we need a single taxonomy anyway; and thirdly, to consider the trade-off between the need for structure and the need for development of the law. I hope at least to open the area up for debate rather more, to show what is at stake in asking whether we should accept the taxonomists' structure for the law or not.

Satisfactoriness of the Gaian Taxonomy

When we ask, as the taxonomists so rarely do, what there is to be said for or against their taxonomy, we see at once a wide array of issues. This is particularly so when we look inwards, at the content of obligations, as I have argued elsewhere.[11] But equally there is scope for argument when we look outside, and ask why it is "obligations" that must form a unit in the first place. Why, precisely, is it vital to adhere to Gaius' scheme – so very vital, indeed, that notions of equity or indeed anything that does not fit it must be discarded?

In fact, the Gaian model begs questions at every turn. No doubt it embodied good ideas at one time; in the form we now have it, it looks like a splendid model for the legal system in the 18th or possibly even early 19th century – and of course it was in the early-to-middle 19th century that it was increasingly embodied in national codes in continental Europe. But as a model for today, it looks odd, even whimsical.

The biggest question starts at the top – how much sense it makes today to draw a sharp line between the public and the private. It made great sense in Gaius' day, of course, and again there were reasons why it made good sense to the French and others in their code-making days.[12] But in the 20th and 21st centuries, with the role of government so massively grown, it is hard to see that there is any part of the law that is not influenced by official public policy, whether expressed through statute or through other mechanisms. We cannot really distinguish any more, I suggest, between a "public" law where the government says what should happen, and a "private" law where the courts just say what is fair between citizens. The government intervenes at every point. The common law has not been a self-sufficient entity for many years – the bits of the common law that are left are there because Parliament has decided that they should be there, and the other bits have been abolished by statute. And quite right too – it is for Parliament to decide on the general legal framework, including deciding which areas should be left to be regulated by the common law. We no longer live in a world where the government regulates only a small number of "public law" issues, leaving all the "private

---

11   For the internal structure of obligations, see appendix 1 below. For discussion see S Hedley, 'The taxonomic approach to restitution' in A Hudson (ed), *New Perspectives on Property Law: Obligations and Restitution* (Cavendish Publishing, London, 2004) at 151. For a more socio-logical slant see H Collins, 'Legal Classifications as the Production of Knowledge Systems' in P Birks (ed), *The Classification of Obligations* (Oxford University Press, Oxford, 1997) at 57.

12   For discussion see J Allison, *A Continental Distinction in the Common Law* (Oxford University Press, Oxford, 1996).

law" issues to the common law. Unlike the position in Gaius' day, the government regulates all.[13]

So to those who support the Gaian scheme, the role of the government is the great unmentionable here, the vast elephant in the room which they pretend they can't see. And a certain amount of legal scholarship can be done on that pretend basis. You can do useful work in contract while pretending that contracts are actually written by the parties to them – as opposed to the reality that they are written by corporate bodies, who will come under hostile supervision from the state if they appear to be imposing the wrong sorts of terms. Or again, you can do some useful work in tort by just treating it as a moral exercise in determining fault, without noting how carefully the definition of fault has been tweaked to fit in with current notions of public policy. Best of all, you can pretend that it's just a stroke of luck when defendants in tort actions happen to be insured, as if this was just a lucky chance, and not the result of a very deliberate government policy that this should happen. It's so easy just to pretend, and so long as you are simply looking at the detail it doesn't do too much harm. But to do serious work on the structure of the law, to ask intelligent questions about where "obligations" is and where it is going, you have to deal with the realities. And one of the realities is that common law liabilities are shaped by government policies, made to do the job that the government wants them to do, and modified or abolished if they seem to be doing more harm than good. There is nothing autonomous about private law any more.

The persons/things/actions distinction, so vital to the Gaian scheme, also seems dubious today, if indeed it is comprehensible. Again, there was a time when it made sense. What sort of a "person" you were was probably the most important thing determining your rights – were you slave or free? Roman or foreign? Woman or man? Married or single? By making a nod towards the social status people had (the "persons" bit), and another nod to the other legal rights they had (the "things" bit), the Gaian classification was firmly rooted in social reality. Whether or not someone was a slave was a crucial part of understanding the rights they had, and Gaius would have been remiss if he had not included it in his scheme. But there is very little of that left. Most of the old law of persons, of status, has been swept away, and quite right too. There are no different sorts of people with different sets of rights. There are only people, and they have equal rights. There are a few bits left where we still feel we have to distinguish. The law still, though grudgingly, concedes that children cannot have quite the same status as adults; and we have not quite abolished the law on marriage either, though with every year it becomes less status-like and more contract-like. The truth is that this persons/things/actions division, so vital to Gaius, is really of very little use today. Certainly it is hard to see how it is so important that it must influence the very way we classify private law.[14]

---

13   MW Hesselink, "The Structure of the New European Private Law" (2002) 6 *Electronic Journal of Comparative Law* (4) (www.ejcl.org/64/art64-2.html).

14   On viewing the distinction through modern eyes see G Samuel, "*English Private Law*: Old and New Thinking in the Taxonomy Debate", above n 10.

As to the property/obligations divide, what is its continued relevance? This isn't an easy distinction any more. It is one of the most hotly contested distinctions in private law theory today, as several contributions to this book testify. I suppose the last time at which this distinction would have made sense in common law terms would have been in the late feudal period. The law of property would then have been one thing, the law of personal rights a different thing. Of course, by "property" they meant real property, land – which is why remedies protecting chattels are regarded as merely personal even today. But then this neat distinction, between real rights and personal rights, ran into the industrial revolution, and the great explosion of new forms of wealth that it generated. Today, there is really no agreement as to what is property and what is a mere personal right. Is money "property", or does it depend on the form in which it is held? Is your right to your job a "property" right? When are contract rights also "property" rights? Is "intellectual property" really "property"? Can information be "property"? Is a milk quota "property"? Is an Internet domain name "property"? All these and more questions are routinely debated throughout the legal world. From the simple distinction proposed by Gaius, we now have an enormous complex of issues – not because we are any more prone to argue than the Romans were, but because we are incomparably richer, and the forms of our wealth incomparably more various. The distinction between property and obligation, so simple and so obvious to Gaius, is now anything but.

I would guess that a certain type of taxonomist is going to say at this point: this is all very well, but it is history. Who cares where this taxonomy comes from – if it's good, then surely it doesn't matter what its origins are. There are three points in reply to this.

First, most of those who favour this sort of taxonomy have been driven by the historical model, the wish to be part of what they saw as the great Gaian tradition. Certainly the great jurist Professor Birks was in this mould. He quite openly admitted that he was modelling himself on Roman sources, trying, as he saw it, to bring the shapeless common law into the ordered civil law fold.[15] Indeed, he famously argued – rather misguidedly in my view – that the Roman classification was a great intellectual invention, on a par with Darwin's theory of evolution.[16] Of course, Birks knew discretion was often the better part of valour, and that just as there were times to emphasise this point, there were also times to de-emphasise it, or even not mention it at all. He would never have lectured a room-full of proud English common lawyers as to how they should abandon centuries' worth of common law thought, on the ground that rational thought wasn't an English trait. So most of what Birks wrote simply asserted

---

15   See especially P Birks, 'Definition and Division: A Meditation on *Institutes* 3.13' in P Birks (ed), *The Classification of Obligations* (Oxford University Press, Oxford, 1997) at 1. For some of the debate sparked by that book see D Campbell, "Classification and the Crisis of the Common Law" (1999) 26 *Journal of Law and Society* 369; S Smith, "Taking Law Seriously" (2000) 50 *University of Toronto Law* 241.

16   P Birks, 'Definition and Division: A Meditation on *Institutes* 3.13', above n 15 at 2. Cf G Samuel, "Can Gaius Really be Compared to Darwin?" (2000) 49 *International & Comparative Law Quarterly* 297.

this taxonomy baldly, not with an argument to support it, but just daring people to tell him he was wrong. As to his real reason, it was to make the common law more Roman, and when he thought the audience would be receptive to this viewpoint, he made no secret of it.

Secondly, there has been a tendency in the pro-taxonomy camp to say that we should have nothing to do with equity because it is a historical creation, and that we should attend to the needs of the present not the past. Professor Burrows especially urges us not to be "slaves to history",[17] and other writers have referred to the history of the equitable jurisdiction as some sort of an argument against it. But, with respect, this makes no sense at all. All legal argument is historical up to a point. I am not sure what it would mean for a lawyer not to be a slave to history. Adopting the taxonomy doesn't free us from history, it simply means that we take our running orders from Gaius rather than from assorted Lord Chancellors. Legal schemes and taxonomies are all human creations, by different rational people at different times and places. Announcing that one scheme is "rational" whereas the alternatives are "historical" just won't do.

Thirdly, it is also true, of course, that we should search for rational reasons for the scheme we want to follow. If we have to be slaves of dead jurists, let us at least make an intelligent choice of master. All the schemes on offer are historical, and each has its own sort of rationality. Asserting a rigid taxonomy seems to be just a way of imposing a particular theory of the law, without going through the tedious business of explaining why it's a good theory to have. But no good case has been made, in my view, that one is any more rational than the others. And certainly a mere repetition by one school that their method is rational, but that the other is merely historical, carries us no further.

WHETHER WE CAN ONLY HAVE ONE TAXONOMY

Most of the trouble here is caused by an assumption that there can only be one taxonomy – that somehow rational legal argument is impossible unless everyone agrees on the same scheme for liabilities. If that's really so, of course, then very few legal arguments are rational, and we are in a very deep hole indeed.

This argument has always struck me as a wild exaggeration. Of course, lawyers need to agree on some things if legal argument is not to be completely chaotic. By and large we do, and while obviously the disagreements are fun and make a lot of noise, they are the exception. Even seemingly fundamental disagreements about how to structure the law can only happen because we already fundamentally agree on what sort of things the law contains, we are just not sure what pattern to put them in. A certain amount of pluralism is a healthy sign in any institution; it is far from clear that the imposition of a greater degree of order is useful.

What is the argument against this? Why is the imposition of a single taxonomy supposed to be a good idea? For Birks, it was all obvious. For him it was axiomatic that common law systems were inherently disordered and

---

17   A Burrows, 'Remedial Coherence and Punitive Damages in Equity', chapter 15 in this book at 382.

irrational – this was so obvious to him that he never thought it necessary to document it or argue for it. For him, it was enough just to state that anyone who relied on considerations of conscience must be unprincipled,[18] or that when he looked at equity he felt like he was looking at a woolly mammoth in a museum.[19] He left the justification of these rather bizarre propositions to his followers.

Some such have felt under rather more of an obligation to justify themselves, and I'll look at them briefly.

First, Burrows has been saying that those who do not accept the preferred taxonomy are guilty of a fundamental legal error. They are not treating like cases alike, but are drawing irrational distinctions between equity cases and legal cases. If equity cases really are different, he says, then those differences must be stated in terms compatible with the taxonomy; if the differences are not real, then we shouldn't perpetuate history by pretending that there is a difference.[20] This seems to me to misunderstand what equity is all about. Equity is there to correct the common law, to do justice where the common law does not. If the common law says two cases are identical, then it may be equity's job to step in and say that they are different, for some reason deriving from conscience or whatever. And of course its language and concepts jar with those of the common law – that is the whole point. If equity's interventions seem to lack a single theme, that may be because the common law's errors lack a single theme – there are lots of things wrong with it, perhaps not all related to one another. Surely we can accept that some bits of the law are fine and others need equitable modification; surely that is not "incoherence". And if it is hard to understand the pattern of equitable modification from a common law perspective, that may simply mean that the common law perspective is wrong.

I say all of this without prejudice to the particular disputes we had during the conference from which the chapters of this book derive. It's the big picture that matters, not the examples. It doesn't matter, except as a sample issue, whether you think equity should have followed the common law in the *Digital Pulse* case,[21] or what you make of the issue of trustees' contributory negligence.[22] And no doubt there are some areas of equity that can usefully be integrated with common law. But the big question is whether the common law has outgrown the need for equitable intervention completely. Has the common law become so perfect that it never needs to be corrected; or, perhaps, is equity's method of intervention so flawed somehow that it can't do the job any more? Someone who claims that should indeed be arguing for the abolition of equity as a category. But Burrows doesn't claim that. On the contrary, he thinks that

---

18   P Birks, "Equity, Conscience and Unjust Enrichment" (1999) 23 *Melbourne University Law Review* 1.

19   P Birks, "Book review of *Meagher, Gummow and Lehane* (4th ed, 2002)" (2004) 120 *Law Quarterly Review* 344.

20   See especially A Burrows, "We Do This at Common Law But That in Equity" (2002) 22 *Oxford Journal of Legal Studies* 1.

21   See A Burrows, 'Remedial Coherence and Punitive Damages in Equity', at chapter 15 in this book.

22   See J Getzler, 'Am I My Beneficiary's Keeper? Fusion and Loss-Based Fiduciary Remedies', at chapter 10 in this book.

many equitable interventions are still useful and indeed vital, and he's made that absolutely plain.[23] That being so, it seems to me that he should be supporting equity, not giving encouragement to those who would abolish it. He concedes the need for special equitable intervention sometimes; he just objects to some particular examples of it. Well, no-one said that equity was perfect; and the case for equity does not have to pretend that everything done in its name has always been good. Burrows should be saying, it seems to me, that equity should be made better than it is, not that it should be swept away.

The other recent writer to justify the need for a taxonomy is Professor McKendrick – he wasn't writing specifically about equity, but rather about the need for a unified taxonomy. McKendrick argues for the taxonomy on six grounds: that like cases should be treated alike; that otherwise, anomalies and inconsistencies in the law will remain unexposed; that taxonomy keeps the law "on the right track"; that it makes the law more accessible; that it is more "economic", presumably in the sense of intellectual economy rather than financial economy; and that it promotes legal elegance[24].

Summarising this, I suppose there are really two main claims, one empirical and one ideological. The empirical is that a precise and detailed taxonomy makes the law easier to apply, more user-friendly if you like. The ideological claim is that a law which is more satisfying to a logician should be more satisfying to everyone else – that logical clarity is good in itself.

The empirical claim – that applying a uniform taxonomy would make it easier for people to understand that law – is very interesting if true. Anything that makes law easier to understand should be welcomed. But empirical claims need empirical validation. It is far from obvious that greater logic in the law saves anyone any time or resources. A logically precise scheme is not always an easy one to apply. The most pure logical disciplines – such as philosophy and mathematics – certainly do not have the reputation of being the easiest. Is there any evidence that legal research is a more speedy or fair process in nations with more logical legal systems? Is it easier or cheaper to resolve law cases in continental Europe – which by and large accepts the taxonomy – than it is in common law countries? Are users of legal services any better served there than here? I know of no evidence to that effect, and the pro-taxonomists don't seem to be on the verge of producing any.

As to the ideological claim, that a more logical and structured legal system is a better one in itself, I need only refer you to the pride and joy of the taxonomical school, namely the theory of unjust enrichment. This has been in a constant state of flux throughout the whole of its life. Bold theoretical claims are made, and praised by all as fundamental contributions to the area. Then their author withdraws them, and we argue for years about whether he was right to do so, and whether the new theory he's put in its place is any better. Meanwhile, different theorists go off in different directions, and consensus

---

23   For example, A Burrows, "We Do This At Common Law But That In Equity", above n 20 at 5 (his "first category").

24   E McKendrick, 'Taxonomy: does it matter?' in D Johnston and R Zimmermann (eds), *Unjustified Enrichment – Key Issues in Comparative Perspective* (Cambridge University Press, Cambridge, 2002) at 627, 632-638.

become unattainable. Now you can look at all that in different ways. I've found the academic debate very invigorating and productive, and if the conclusions I've drawn from it haven't been the same as everyone else's, that is no surprise – consensus on such issues is often hard to get. But if someone is now claiming that this has all made the law simpler or easy to apply, then they should not be surprised if general hilarity ensues. One thing is clear about unjust enrichment law: it is *not* easy to apply or understand. So if the argument for the taxonomy is supposed to be that it makes things simpler, then I think it refutes itself.

My difficulty in this regard has always been the high level of exaggeration in the pro-taxonomy argument. Common law legal systems are not in chaos, in any practical sense, and claiming that they are serves no purpose. There is no obvious difficulty in finding out the law, so long as you have enough time, brain-power and up-to-date law books – and if the process is any better or easier in civil law countries, this has not come to the attention of comparative lawyers. All we have is the same false claim from the pro-taxonomists, repeating like a broken record: that anyone who doesn't adopt their way of thinking is irrational. Such a claim requires a weighty justification if it is to be taken seriously; so far we have received none at all.

How Hard Should Any Taxonomy Be Pushed?

The final issue is about the price that must be paid for any rigid taxonomy – a loss of legal flexibility, of the ability to respond to new situations as they emerge. It is obvious enough that the more rigid the taxonomical scheme imposed on the law is, the less scope the law has to respond to new situations, or to recognise old problems in new forms, let alone to deal with entirely new problems. A certain amount of theoretical incoherence is a necessary price for allowing both common law and equity to develop; allowing both to develop is necessary if they are not to become irrelevant to the needs of today.[25] Obviously there will be legitimate concerns over the degree of flexibility equity that should be allowed – the debate about "discretionary remedialism" comes to mind[26] – but only those who see no point at all in equity's distinct heritage will want to confine it to the same tools as the common has. The whole point of equity is that it is different from common law.

No doubt a case could be made, and no doubt some of the other contributors to this book would be happy to make it, that equity is no longer the right tool for adapting the law to the needs of the present and the near future, that other and better ways can be found. Where the common law needs to be adapted or fine-tuned, this need can sometimes be met by statute rather than

---

25   For particular problem areas see for example, B Horrigan, "The Expansion of Fairness-Based Business Regulation – Unconscionability, Good Faith and the Law's Informed Conscience" (2004) 32 *Australian Business Law Review* 159; A Hudson, "If We Did Not Have Equity, We Would Have To Make It" (2002) 7 *Queen Mary Law Journal* 14.

26   For contributions to that debate – including surveys of the literature – see especially S Evans, "Defending Discretionary Remedialism" (2001) 23 *Sydney Law Review* 463; D Jensen, "The Rights and Wrongs of Discretionary Remedialism" [2003] *Singapore Journal of Legal Studies* 178.

by equity. I feel the force of this, but I am not yet convinced that the statutory method is so very superior, so completely attuned to the country's needs that we can risk abandoning equity, which has proved so useful up to now. Equity has been far from static: it has adapted to new situations before, and may well do so again.[27] But be that as it may, no-one should doubt the need for flexibility in the law, for ensuring that its development is not driven solely by questions of logical consistency but also by the needs of those it affects. We do not know what tomorrow's problems will be. We should therefore be slow to conclude that any particular tool should be ruled out in advance as useless, or as inappropriate for modern needs.

CONCLUSION

To conclude, therefore, no good case has been made for sweeping away the distinction between law and equity. Those who say that it is irrational have themselves shown no great regard for rationality in their argument. Those who say that it is a merely historical distinction have equally relied on history for their argument. And those who say that maintaining the distinction unnecessarily complicates the law have probably done more than anyone else in introducing unnecessary complications in recent years. There is no demonstrated need for a rigid taxonomical scheme; indeed, a healthy pluralism arguably demands the co-existence of many and conflicting taxonomical concepts.

It is said that, if we look to the long term, equity is a dying tradition. Perhaps. But in the long term we are all dead: equity is indeed dying, and so is the common law which it both supports and corrects. But for as long as there is a common law, there will be a need of doctrines to correct and fine-tune its application; and it seems to me that the equity tradition is still a valuable part of that, despite the taxonomical impurities it has. Long live the incoherent common law, and incoherent equity to correct it as necessary.

---

27 On changes in the nature of equitable doctrines over time see J Getzler, 'Patterns of Fusion' in P Birks (ed), *The Classification of Obligations* (Oxford University Press, Oxford, 1997) at 157.

Appendix 1

THE "GRID" WHICH, IN THE MODERNISED GAIAN STRUCTURE, IS SAID TO ORGANISE OBLIGATIONS.

Rights by goal (down), and by causative events (across)	Consent	Wrongs	Unjust enrichment	Other events
Restitution	1	6	11	16
Compensation	2	7	12	17
Punishment	3	8	13	18
Perfection	4	9	14	19
Other goals	5	10	15	20

The precise detail of the grid, and the explanation of whether each of the boxes has content, has changed somewhat over the years. This version is from: 'The Law of Restitution at the End of an Epoch' (1999) 28 Western Australian Law Review *13 at 17.*

On the grid, see especially:

P Birks, "The Law of Restitution at the End of an Epoch" (1999) 28 *Western Australian Law Review* 13.

S Hedley, 'The taxonomic approach to restitution' in A Hudson (ed), *New Perspectives on Property Law: Obligations and Restitution* (Cavendish Publishing, London, 2004) at 151.

J Dietrich, 'The "other" category in the classification of obligations' in A Robertson (ed), *The Law of Obligations: Connections and Boundaries* (UCL Press, London, 2004) at 111.

Appendix 2

THE MODERNISED GAIAN STRUCTURE OF THE LAW

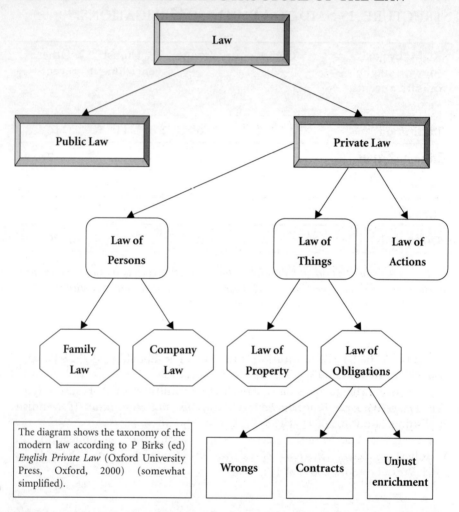

The diagram shows the taxonomy of the modern law according to P Birks (ed) *English Private Law* (Oxford University Press, Oxford, 2000) (somewhat simplified).

Much scholarly energy has gone into justifying the lowest level of distinctions here, with higher ones rather unwisely being taken for granted. Most "defences" of "taxonomy" have actually been defences of this precise model, rather than of the need for a taxonomy (of this sort) per se. See especially E McKendrick, 'Taxonomy: does it matter?' in D Johnston and R Zimmermann (eds), *Unjustified Enrichment – Key Issues in Comparative Perspective* (Cambridge University Press, Cambridge, 2002) at 627; E Descheemaeker, "Mapping the Common Law: On a Recent English Attempt and its Links with Scottish Jurisprudence" [2003] *Juridical Review* (4) 295. There has been little serious consideration of alternatives, or of whether multiple taxonomies may simultaneously be entertained; though see P Matthews, "Book review of *English Private Law*" (2002) 6 *Jersey Law Review* (1) 115.

PART II

EQUITABLE DOCTRINE AND REMEDIES IN COMMERCIAL LAW

5

The Disappearing Divide Between Property and Obligation: The Impact of Aligning Legal Analysis and Commercial Expectation

SARAH WORTHINGTON

"There is nothing which so generally strikes the imagination, and engages the affections of mankind, as the right of property."[1]

The thesis of this chapter is simple and startling. It is that equity, acceding to persistent commercial pressure, has effectively eliminated the divide between property and obligation, or between property rights and personal rights. Equity has achieved this in partnership with the common law and statute, but equity initiated the process and played a dramatic and innovative developmental role.

This idea, that there has been a collapse of boundaries, is no mean assertion, especially given the widely perceived importance of property, and the general assumption that there is a sharp doctrinal and functional divide between property and obligation. Most lawyers are familiar with Professor Sir Roy Goode's 1987 article on ownership and obligation. He notes that all legal systems sharply distinguish "property rights from mere personal rights to the delivery or transfer of an asset. I *own* property; I am *owed* performance of a transfer obligation."[2] Important consequences follow from the distinction, or so we always assume.

Lawyers are not the only ones to observe the division. Economists, too, are passionate advocates:[3]

---

1   Sir William Blackstone, *Commentaries on the Laws of England* (T Payne, London, 1791), Vol II at 2.

2   RM Goode, "Ownership and Obligation in Commercial Transactions" (1987) 103 *Law Quarterly Review* 433 at 433 (emphasis in original).

3   GD Libecap, 'A transactions-cost approach to the analysis of property rights' in E Brousseau and J-M Galchant (eds), *The Economics of Contracts* (Cambridge University Press, Cambridge, 2002) at 140.

"Property rights … are among the most critical social institutions, providing the basis for resource-use decisions and for the assignment of wealth and political power. As such, the property regime profoundly influences both economic performance and income distribution in all economies. Property rights define the accepted array of resource uses, determine who has decision-making authority, and describe who will receive the associated rewards and costs of those decisions. Accordingly, the prevailing system of property rights establishes incentives and time-horizons for investment in physical and human capital, production, and exchange. Cross-country differences in property rights result in important differences in economic development and growth. … The property-rights structure is also critical for the environment and natural resource use … [and] for establishing and protecting individual social and political rights within a society."

All this warms the hearts of property lawyers. But doubts soon surface. Fifteen pages later, this same economist notes that "It is useful to view property rights as contractual outcomes negotiated by parties".[4] And Goode, still focusing on the divide between "owe" and "own", observes a mere five pages into his analysis that "most *obligations* owed by B to A to transfer an asset to A are *proprietary* in nature rather than merely personal".[5] He puts this down to equitable developments.

The difficulties are equally clear to many undergraduates. The typical common law classification scheme suggests that property is divided into real and personal property; personal property is, in turn, divided into choses in possession and choses in action (tangible and intangible property respectively).[6] And then comes the rub. Not all choses in action are property: put more starkly, not all obligations are property. Those "choses" that are not property, or "property rights", are merely personal rights, or personal obligations. The boundary is never defined. Indeed, it is often described as subject to revision according to social and political norms.

Lack of a definitive boundary does nothing to diminish academic vigour in asserting the importance of the divide. This is not a matter of pure semantics or irrelevant jurisprudence. The distinction is critical for the very practical reason that property rights appear better protected than personal rights. Criminal law, tort law and public/constitutional law may all afford property rights additional protection, but the starkest illustrations of the benefits of property rights are seen as insolvency protection, and as the opportunity to recover windfall gains (or unauthorised profits) when property rights have been misused. These special protective rights are not unqualified, but the general perception is that they operate to protect property rights, not personal rights.

---

4   GD Libecap, 'A transactions-cost approach to the analysis of property rights', above n 3 at 155.

5   RM Goode, "Ownership and Obligation in Commercial Transactions", above n 2 at 438 (emphasis added).

6   It is possible to make the scheme more specific by dividing personal property first into chattels real (leases) and chattels personal (other), and then dividing the latter into choses in possession and choses in action. Choses in action can then be further subdivided into documentary intangibles and pure intangibles, but neither of these complications affects the point being made.

It contradicts this perception to suggest that the supposed divide between property and obligation (and especially between proprietary and non-proprietary intangibles) is no longer sustainable. In supporting this claim, this chapter proceeds in two parts. The first part considers the historical development of a dramatically expanded notion of property. It shows how obligations, or personal rights, have been increasingly treated as property. The second and longer part demonstrates how each of the traditional tests commonly regarded as useful in distinguishing between property and obligation is disintegrating. Attributes once thought to be specific to "property" are increasingly being accorded to all manner of rights. In sum, these two parts suggest that not only is the class of property rights expanding, but that rights that continue to be labelled as "personal" are receiving "proprietary" protection. In short, the doctrinal and functional divide between property and obligation is disappearing.

EXPANDING THE NOTION OF PROPERTY: TURNING OBLIGATION INTO PROPERTY

The goal in this section is simply to show that, over time, certain types of once purely personal obligations have come to be treated as property. The transition has been largely the result of equity's incursions, although common law and statutory developments have supported and reinforced the change. The assertion is not controversial, and the detail needs only to be summarised here.[7] Of course, the assertion depends on the definition of property. This issue is revisited in the next section, where some of the most commonly accepted divisions between property and obligation are examined. For the moment, it is enough to adopt the widely accepted notion that property is "usable wealth". From amongst a long list of rights of enjoyment typically associated with ownership or other proprietary interests,[8] the choice is made that the truly essential features of property rights are that right-holders can *transfer* their rights, and can *exclude* third parties from interfering with their rights. These twin attributes of "transferability" and "excludability" characterise property rights.[9] Put another way, those with property rights can control allocation and access.

The early common law approach was to accord proprietary status to real property (land) and to tangible personal property (goods), but not to intangible property. Intangible property was not assignable; it was not usable wealth. This boundary between property and obligation accords with the (now

---

7   Further detail appears in S Worthington, *Equity* (Oxford University Press, Oxford, 2003) at chapter 3 (although there the argument is simply that equity has dramatically expanded the notion of property, not that there is no longer a division between proprietary and personal rights). Also see the more general discussion in S Worthington, *Personal Property Law: Text and Materials* (Hart Publications, Oxford, 2000) at chapters 1 and 8.

8   For these, see AM Honoré, 'Ownership' in AG Guest (ed), *Oxford Essays in Jurisprudence* (Oxford University Press, Oxford, 1961) at 107.

9   K Gray, "Property in Thin Air" (1991) 50 *Cambridge Law Journal* 252.

crude) view of property as a "thing". Tangible "things" were accorded proprietary advantages and proprietary protection; intangible "things" were
characterised as personal rights against specific parties, and were not regarded
as proprietary.

Equity completely overturned this state of affairs. It dramatically expanded
the category of 'property', or proprietary rights, by acting on two fronts. The
story is well known.[10] First, it permitted the assignment of "personal obligations" that were unassignable at common law. Debts, shares and other
contractual claims thus became usable wealth. The possibility was further
extended to include rights to future benefits: claims to future dividends,
interest payments, royalties and such like could all be sold immediately, in
advance of entitlement to the underlying payment, for value.[11] In this way,
future benefits could be capitalised immediately and put to their most efficient
use by those agreeing to the exchange.

Sceptics might suggest that this expansion is too limited to contribute to the
agenda suggested here. It permits the assignment of the *benefits* of personal
contracts; the burdens remain with the original obligor. To take the simplest of
examples, a creditor can assign the benefit of the debt owed to her, but the
debtor cannot assign his obligation to pay his creditor, unless, of course, his
creditor consents to substitute performance from the transferee.[12] However,
this rather limited form of assignment of benefits, not burdens, accords with
the predominant commercial pressure to convert these contractual rights into
"usable wealth". It is the benefits, not the burdens, that the parties are keen to
assign, so as to capitalise their value. Indeed, precisely analogous rules apply to
transfers of tangible property, where it is exceedingly difficult (although not
impossible) to ensure that positive burdens run with the property.[13] Buyer One
may agree with his Seller that the fire breaks will be cleared annually on his
newly acquired farm, or that an artistic object will be displayed only in certain
ways. If the farm or the artwork is transferred to a new buyer, Seller can rarely
insist that Buyer Two comply with the same restrictions, unless the two have
contracted directly with each other to that effect. In some circumstances, this
inability to ensure that positive burdens run with tangible and intangible assets
can reduce the economic value of the assets in question. The next section makes
it clear that all three branches of the law — equity, common law and statute —
have made advances to improve matters on this front, while balancing the need
to protect Buyer Two from unexpected burdens. But the difficulties across the

---

10   See S Worthington, *Equity*, above n 7 at chapter 3, for the detail, but all these new rights are
     uncontroversially regarded as assignable, and also as attracting some powers to exclude third
     parties. This is addressed in more detail later in this chapter.
11   Taking care, of course, not to contract to transfer the *money* to be received in the future, but
     rather to transfer the existing *right* to the future income stream: *Norman v Federal Commis-
     sioner of Taxation* (1963) 109 CLR 9.
12   The three-way agreement between debtor, creditor and transferee is typically achieved by
     novation of the original debtor/creditor contract.
13   B Rudden, 'Economic Theory v Property Law: The *Numerus Clausus* Problem' in J Eekelaar
     and J Bell (eds), *Oxford Essays in Jurisprudence* (3rd series, Oxford University Press, Oxford,
     1987) at 239.

board only serve to reinforce the similarities in treating tangible and intangible assets as "property".

As well as expanding the class of rights that were assignable, equity's second strategy was simply to create completely new forms of property. It did this by permitting novel divisions of certain "bundles of rights" (property rights) that the common law had previously regarded as indivisible, and then, over time, re-classifying these novel bundles as "property" rather than "obligation".

To understand this second strategy, it is necessary to go back a step. Dividing property between different parties is commercially attractive. At common law, such divisions are possible. Tangible things (land and goods) can be co-owned, with several owners sharing the sum total of the relevant property rights. In the simplest case, a division of rights between co-owners can give them interests that are qualitatively the same, even if quantitatively different. Co-ownership of a horse, for example, might divide ownership rights ½ : ¼ : ¼. More sophisticated strategies allow different parties to have different *types* of interests in the same asset, not merely different shares of the interest. With tangible personal property, the common law allowed the parties to split ownership and possession between different parties. With land, the common law went even further, and allowed different parties to have sequential ownership interests along a time-line, via the doctrine of estates. In this way, the practical and commercial benefits of divided property ownership were recognised and accommodated by the common law. Although these common law options for divided ownership appear limited (especially for tangible personal property), their innovative potential should not be underestimated. For example, the simple division of ownership and possession of goods permits different forms of leases (with all manner of associated covenants), hire-purchase agreements, pledges, contractual liens, retention of title sales, bailments, and more.

Equity dramatically expanded upon these rather meagre common law possibilities for divided interests. It did this through the creation of trusts and charges. These two structures are often assumed to be equity's greatest legacy to the law. Their enormous commercial significance goes without saying. These devices began as contractual arrangements ("personal obligations"), and slowly evolved until they were unequivocally recognised as delivering new (divided) property interests in the underlying tangible or intangible assets.[14] The terms "trust" and "charge" disguise the enormous flexibility permitted within these categories. Taking each in turn, "trusts" permit the division of interests according to the common law model (that is, shared and sequential ownership) regardless of the nature of the underlying asset. But this is just the start. Trusts enable endless innovation and division, limited only by the imagination of interested commercial parties. Assets can be sub-divided at will, and different types of rights can be parcelled out to different parties.[15] Using the trust, for

---

14   Again, see S Worthington, *Equity* (Oxford University Press, Oxford, 2003) at chapter 3. "Asset" is used very loosely as shorthand for bundles of rights, whether proprietary or personal.

15   H Hansmann and U Mattei, "The Functions of Trust Law: A Comparative Legal and Economic Approach" (1998) 73 *New York University Law Review* 434; S Worthington, 'The Commercial Utility of the Trust Vehicle' in D Hayton (ed), *Extending the Boundaries of Trusts and Similar Ring-Fenced Funds* (Kluwer, The Hague, 2002) at 135.

example, rights associated with company shares can be divided to give certain parties the voting rights, others the dividend rights, and still others the rights to bonus issues. Even this does not exhaust the divided rights that are possible because of the trust. Consider the many formal and informal arrangements that are now considered to deliver trust structures of divided ownership. The best known include *Quistclose* trusts,[16] building retention trusts,[17] and constructive trusts arising in response to contracts of sale[18] or, occasionally, family agreements.[19]

"Equitable charges" are a more recent legal innovation. They evolved in a similar fashion to trusts, however, and now provide enormous flexibility in enabling contracting parties to structure security arrangements that accommo-date their individual needs and circumstances. The rapid evolution and growing commercial significance of equitable charges can be seen clearly in the evolving debates surrounding the granting of security over after-acquired assets,[20] the recognition of floating charges[21] and automatic crystallisation clauses,[22] and, most recently, the possibility that a lending bank could take a charge (a "charge back") over the debtor's account with the same bank.[23] The ability of well-advised creditors to protect themselves against their debtor's insolvency using such devices quickly led to parliament providing statutory protection for certain classes of unsecured third parties, especially against floating charge holders.[24] This, in turn, led to a fresh round of debates (still on-going) about the accurate characterisation of parties' arrangements as creating these vulnerable floating charges rather than some other form of proprietary protection such as a fixed charge,[25] or a contractual lien in the context of con-struction contracts,[26] or legal ownership or a trust in the context of retention of title agreements.[27] For our purposes, the outcomes of these debates are not important in themselves. What is important is that they serve to reinforce,

---

16   W Swadling (ed), *The Quistclose Trust: Critical Essays* (Hart Publishing, Oxford, 2004).

17   See *Mac-Jordan Construction Ltd v Brookmount Erostin Ltd (in rec)* [1992] BCLC 350.

18   Other than sales of goods, where the *Sale of Goods Act 1979* (UK) and its Commonwealth equivalents provide an even more aggressive default rule, so that *legal* property is rebuttably presumed to pass to the buyer at the time of the contract of sale, notwithstanding that delivery and payment of the price occur at some later stage.

19   The relevant cases are listed in S Worthington, *Proprietary Interests in Commercial Transac-tions* (Oxford University Press, Oxford, 1996) at chapters 3 and 8; S Worthington, *Personal Property Law: Text and Materials* (Hart Publications, Oxford, 2000) at chapters 3.9 and 4.10-4.14.

20   *Holroyd v Marshall* (1862) 10 HLC 191; 11 ER 999.

21   *Re Yorkshire Woolcombers Association Ltd* [1903] 2 Ch 284.

22   *Re Brightlife Ltd* [1987] Ch 200.

23   *Re Bank of Credit and Commerce International SA (No 8)* [1998] AC 214.

24   *Insolvency Act 1986* (UK), ss 40 and 175(2)(b), and, more recently, s 176A.

25   See the recent *Spectrum* litigation (*National Westminster Bank plc v Spectrum Plus Ltd* [2005] UKHL 41, overruling *Re Spectrum Plus Ltd (in liq)* [2004] Ch 337), with the House of Lords finally affirming the analysis advanced in S Worthington, "An 'Unsatisfactory Area of the Law' — Fixed and Floating Charges Yet Again" (2004) 1 *International Corporate Rescue* 175.

26   *Re Cosslett (Contractors) Ltd* [1998] Ch 495 (analysis not affected by the subsequent appeal to the House of Lords, *Smith (Administrator of Cosslett (Contractors) Ltd) v Bridgend County Borough Council* [2002] 1 AC 336).

27   *Borden (UK) Ltd v Scottish Timber Products Ltd* [1981] Ch 25.

rather dramatically, the notion that "obligations" between parties often count as "property" of one sort or another.

To summarise, this section suggests that, over time, equity made two very significant moves. It treated common law obligations as property, simply by permitting their assignment and providing some protection for the assignees. It also treated obligations to divide property rights as being in themselves new forms of property. Put bluntly, equity converted obligations into property.[28]

The previous assertion tests "property" by the twin attributes of assignability and excludability, but even measured in this simple way, there has been a radical change in what is assigned to the "obligations" box and what to the "property" box. In itself, of course, this is not sufficient to establish that the divide between obligation and property has disappeared. The divide may simply have moved to a different place. The next section seeks to advance the case for disappearance.

ATTRIBUTES SAID TO DISTINGUISH PROPERTY FROM OBLIGATION

In the previous section it was suggested that the hallmarks of property are "assignability" and "excludability"; in other words, property rights are assignable, and they entitle their holders to exclude others from their enjoyment. Neither characteristic needs to be absolute. Indeed, short reflection suggests that there are no assets that entitle their holder to *absolute* rights to enjoy, to transfer, and to exclude others. The burden of this section is to show that these two attributes, along with several other attributes commonly regarded as indicative of "property" rather than "obligation", no longer successfully serve this function. None of the attributes discussed below provides a criterion for confidently allocating an asset to either the "property box" or the "obligations box". Whatever may have been true in the past, it now seems that these attributes are, to varying degrees, apt to describe all manner of assets; there is no clear distinction between property and obligation. In this sense, the divide between property and obligation is disappearing.

The discussion proceeds in a fashion that reflects a further oddity in the orthodox property/obligation divide. Rights are either specifically categorised as "property", or they are not. If they are not, then they are merely personal — they are "obligations". From this it follows that all the standard tests focus on the attributes of "property". *Absence* of the test attributes means the asset is "not property", and so is merely an "obligation". The argument in this part is therefore that these 'property attributes' no longer provide any defensible means of distinguishing between two types of assets, one "property" and one "obligation".

---

28   This might be expected to cause problems on at least two fronts: the types of interests that are recognised as "proprietary" appear to become infinitely variable as the particular contractual terms differ, so offending the numerus clausus rule and its justifications; and third parties may seem to be treated unfairly in being expected to recognise such a vast spectrum of property rights, and facing liability for unwittingly infringing them. Both issues are addressed later in this chapter.

Property terminology

Lawyers must be careful with language, and clearly loose language does not mean that implicit inaccuracies automatically become legal doctrine. Nevertheless, some usages are instructive. When we talk of "a company's property", for example, we certainly do not mean to refer only to the tangible "things" owned by the firm, as distinct from all the other rights owed to it by third parties. In the same vein, when we say that a trust cannot be created unless there is "trust property" held by the trustee on trust for the beneficiaries, we include within the notion of "trust property" both tangible "things" owned by the trustee as well as every type of obligation owed to the trustee for the benefit of the trust. And when either a company or a trustee becomes insolvent, the assets available for division amongst the creditors include all the relevant tangible and intangible assets (that is, the entire pool of property and obligations). Recent doctrinal and functional discussion of "asset partitioning",[29] or 'divided patrimonies' (in civil law jurisdictions), involves a similar bundling of property and obligation. The "asset partitioning" does not discriminate at all between different assets, or different forms of wealth. With affirmative asset partitioning, *all* corporate wealth or trust wealth is "partitioned", segregated as a pool dedicated to service the claims of the corporate or trust creditors rather than the shareholders' or beneficiaries' creditors; conversely, with defensive asset partitioning, *all* the shareholders' or beneficiaries' wealth, in whatever form, is partitioned, preserved intact against the claims of the corporate or trust creditors. In short, our common use of language affords no help in distinguishing between property and obligation. This is so even when we appear to use the distinction technically, as in requiring identification of trust "property", or an insolvent's "property".

The ambit of property rights

Professor Honoré described ownership as "the greatest possible interest in a thing which a mature system of law recognizes".[30] Perhaps derived from this, there is increasing currency given to the notion of property as a bundle of rights which include residual incidents operating in favour of the owner once all other claims have been met. Rights are proprietary if they encompass this broad scope; otherwise they are personal. Again, however, the approach does not appear to assist in distinguishing between property and obligation.

This claim is best shown by example, and the clearest modern example comes from corporate law scholarship. There the notion of residual rights is frequently used, admittedly more often by economists rather than by lawyers. The analysis usually proceeds along the following lines: residual rights indicate ownership; the shareholders have residual rights to the company's property on insolvency, so the shareholders own this property; as owners, they have the

---

29   H Hansmann and R Kraakman, "The Essential Role of Organizational Law" (2000) 110 *Yale Law Journal* 387.

30   AM Honoré, 'Ownership' in AG Guest (ed), *Oxford Essays in Jurisprudence* (Oxford University Press, Oxford, 1961) at 107, 108.

right to control its use, and to do so by controlling the board of directors. This is clearly too crude. Either we have misconceived the meaning of residual rights (perhaps employees and creditors also have such rights?), or these rights do not invariably suggest property ownership.

By contrast, the accepted analysis, at least for lawyers, is that the shareholders do *not* own the company's assets: they do not need to, and there are significant advantages if they do not. Because of express or default rules in their share *contract*, however, they have ultimate residual rights to the company's property on its insolvency. The vulnerability of this residual claim provides the necessary motivation for shareholders to monitor the corporate managers. Other groups are at risk of poor corporate management, but their risk is not quite so great (they are further up the chain), and their co-ordination costs are much higher, especially if their interests are diverse. This analysis explains why the monitoring role might reasonably be left to shareholders. However, it does not provide automatic justification for shareholder control of corporate management or the managers' need to run the company exclusively in the shareholders' interests.[31] Some other justification is needed for that. And, finally, it delivers all this without the need to differentiate between property and obligation: the consequences follow because the shareholders, as a group, have uniform residual contract/obligation rights.

So, again, identifying residual rights may indicate "property", but equally it may indicate "obligation"; it is not a distinguishing attribute.

Property rights may take only a limited number of forms — the numerus clausus principle

It is commonly observed that most legal systems recognise only a limited (and non-expanding) number of property interests. Personal rights, by contrast, can be structured in an infinite number of ways to suit the parties' personal needs. This alleged restriction on the possible forms of property is known as the numerus clausus (closed number) rule. Civil law jurisdictions certainly have such a rule, and it is supposedly the reason why trusts do not exist in these jurisdictions. The common law rule, if there is one, is much more ambivalent. Equity's permitted subdivision of interests in assets, and the concomitant creation of new forms of property, especially forms that can be specially tailored by the parties to suit their own personal requirements, appears to offend the numerus clausus rule. In this respect, at least, equitable property rights appear much more like personal rights, and it is not at all evident that some numerus clausus rule places any real restrictions on the property/obligation divide in common law jurisdictions.

In any event, the rationale for the rule has been shown to be suspect. If the goal is simply to reduce the number of property options because of some perceived efficiency in this, then it fails. The desired variety of rights which

---

31 S Worthington, "Shares and Shareholders: Property, Power and Entitlement – Parts I and II" (2001) 22 *The Company Lawyer* 258 and 307.

might operate in relation to property can usually be achieved by contract in any event, although with greater effort and therefore greater inefficiency.[32] The principle thus serves as an ineffective (and inefficient) restraint. Indeed, jurisdictions that did not expand the variety of their property rights by incremental development have generally sought to do this later, via statute, and to do so in a manner that accords these rights proprietary status, or at least some measure of protection from interference by third parties.[33] For example, civil law jurisdictions are increasingly adopting trusts legislation;[34] the United States, which did not initially grant judicial recognition to the floating charge, now achieves the same ends via the *United States Uniform Commercial Code* Article 9; and several jurisdictions, including Hong Kong, recently legislated to ensure the validity of charge backs.

Alternatively, if the reason for the principle is to prevent the multiplication of sub-interests in assets, so as to ensure that dealings do not become difficult and inefficient, then it also fails. It controls the *types* of interests that may be created, but not the numbers of parties who may hold such (restricted) interests, and it is the latter that is likely to make dealings inefficient.[35]

Finally, if the principle is designed to protect property owners by alerting strangers to the property rights they must respect, and doing so by affording third parties easy notice[36] or easy verification[37] of these property packages, then it also fails. Once we examine the strategies the law employs to protect property owners (and, indeed, all right owners), it becomes clear that the strategy is *not* to limit the number of recognised property rights (adhering to the numerus clausus principle), but to limit the number of *risks* to which a stranger can be exposed and which might count as unauthorised interference with the rights of others.[38] A large degree of flexibility as between the originating parties, A and B, could be accommodated without increasing the information costs for C if the broad rules of liability imposed on C are few and simple. This means that there is no need to adhere to the numerus clausus principle, as long as a simple

---

32   B Rudden, 'Economic Theory v Property Law: The *Numerus Clausus* Problem' in J Eekelaar and J Bell (eds), *Oxford Essays in Jurisprudence* (3rd series, Oxford University Press, Oxford, 1987) at 239.

33   For other approaches, also see GL Gretton, "Trusts without Equity" (2000) 49 *International and Comparative Law Quarterly* 599.

34   H Hansmann and U Mattei, "The Functions of Trust Law: A Comparative Legal and Economic Approach" (1998) 73 *New York University Law Review* 434; D Hayton, 'English Trusts and Their Commercial Counterparts in Continental Europe' in D Hayton (ed), *Extending the Boundaries of Trusts and Similar Ring-Fenced Funds* (Kluwer, The Hague, 2002) at 23.

35   H Hansmann and R Kraakman, "Property, Contract, and Verification: The *Numerus Clausus* Problem and the Divisibility of Rights" (2002) 31 *Journal of Legal Studies* 373.

36   TW Merrill and HE Smith, "Optimal Standardization in the Law of Property: The *Numerus Clausus* Principle" (2000) 110 *Yale Law Journal* 1.

37   H Hansmann and R Kraakman, "Property, Contract, and Verification: The *Numerus Clausus* Problem and the Divisibility of Rights" (2002) 31 *Journal of Legal Studies* 373.

38   TW Merrill and HE Smith, "Optimal Standardization in the Law of Property: The *Numerus Clausus* Principle", above n 36, take the view that the numerus clausus principle plays an important role here.

philosophy is applied in constructing the remedial regime. The approaches usually adopted are described later in this chapter.[39]

In summary, the numerus clausus characteristic does not enable common lawyers to differentiate between property and obligation, and in any event the perceived advantages of the rule appear overrated.

"Excludability": property rights are "good against the world"

Property rights are commonly described as "rights in rem", 'good against the world' (or at least a section of it), and "multital".[40] Personal rights, by contrast, are described as "rights in personam", only good against the obligee, "paucital". This is a formal, but perhaps less informative, assertion of the idea of excludability. Restated as they are here, two ideas may be unwittingly confused in these descriptions (or maybe wittingly). First, property rights are still often described as rights *in* an asset, not simply rights *to* an asset (orthodoxy suggests the latter would be rights ad rem, and personal rather than proprietary).[41] This distinction now lacks force or accuracy. Equity has ensured that rights *to* assets are commonly accorded all the attributes of property rights.[42] The evolution was described earlier in this chapter. In truth, this now outdated notion of "rights in rem" replicates the equally outdated early idea of property as a "thing". The more modern conception of property is as a "bundle of rights", and, moreover, a bundle of rights exercisable against *people*, even if in relation to a thing.

The second theme in this labelling emerges in the "multital"/"paucital" distinction: rights in rem are good against the world; purely personal rights can usually only be enforced against mutually consenting parties. But this focus is on something other than our property/obligation divide. Under this classification, all tort claims are "in rem" since they bind all the world in relation to trespass, nuisance, negligence and such like. "Things" are protected by these general defensive claims, but so too are personal rights: we now have the tort of inducing a breach of contract (that is, interfering with obligation, rather than with property), for example.[43] This means that rights may be classified as "in rem", or good against the world, even though we would not

---

39   See 103–116 below. Here a simple example suffices. All the characterisation and recharacterisation problems associated with floating charges, especially in the context of construction contracts and retention of title agreements, are at root related to the proper treatment of certain third parties, and to determining whether they have statutory rights in the underlying asset (since the *Insolvency Act 1986* (UK) gives preferred creditors rights against assets subject to floating charges). They are not related to determining whether the charge agreement between A and B is limited to a known form of property interest.

40   This last being from WN Hohfeld, *Fundamental Legal Conceptions as Applied in Judicial Reasoning* (Yale University Press, New Haven, 1923), especially at 111-114.

41   RM Goode, "Ownership and Obligation in Commercial Transactions" (1987) 103 *Law Quarterly Review* 433.

42   See the reference to RM Goode, "Ownership and Obligation in Commercial Transactions" (1987) 103 *Law Quarterly Review* 433 at 438, in the introductory passages of this chapter.

43   *Lumley v Gye* (1853) 2 El & Bl 216; 118 ER 749. Also see D Friedmann, "Restitution of Benefits Obtained Through the Appropriation of Property or the Commission of a Wrong" (1980) 80 *Columbia Law Review* 504 at 513-529.

usually think of them as "property" in any real sense, but rather as "obligations" that are simply and similarly protected by claims that may be advanced against the whole world.

Once again, the familiar "property attribute" no longer provides a reliable distinction between property and obligation.

Property is assignable

As noted earlier, it is no longer possible to suggest that "property" is assignable, but "obligations", or contract rights, are not. The modern rule is that both are assignable, but both may have specific practical or procedural limitations on assignment imposed by common law or statute for reasons of public policy.[44] These limitations do not serve to distinguish "property" from "obligation". Indeed, greater restrictions apply to the assignment of some forms of tangible property (the clearest elements in the "property" category) than apply to the assignment of most "obligations". Consider the restrictions on assignment of certain categories of land, or certain categories of goods (such as national art treasures, or petrol in periods of national shortage). Put another way, public policy determines whether a particular bundle of rights is assignable, and it does this without regard to the property/obligation divide. And when public policy determines whether it is appropriate to sell human beings into slavery, cell lines to research laboratories, or rights to litigate to the highest bidder, it does not first decide whether these rights are property. It moves immediately to the core controversies. Once again, the attribute does not serve to define a given right as property rather than obligation.

Property is accorded superior legal protection

We commonly assume that property is better protected by the legal system than contract, or obligation. This remedial insight was articulated more formally by Calabresi and Melamed almost 30 years ago.[45] They suggested that property rights are distinguishable because they are protected through "property rules", not merely through "liability rules". Put in more familiar language, injunctions and specific performance are the norm in protecting property rights, rather than mere payment of compensation.[46] Once again, however, this preferential remedial approach no longer seems to track any meaningful property/obligation divide.

Take some obvious examples. Rights that we might classify as purely personal (that is, as "obligations", rather than "property") often seem to be protected by "property rules". For example, tort claims of all types are typically remedied by compensation, but also, quite commonly, by positive or negative injunctions. The difference in remedy does not turn on whether the damage

---

44   See, for example, RM Goode, "Inalienable Rights?" (1979) 42 *Modern Law Review* 553.

45   G Calabresi and AD Melamed, "Property Rules, Liability Rules, and Inalienability: One View of the Cathedral" (1972) 85 *Harvard Law Review* 1089.

46   See the extended discussion of this issue in R Chambers, 'The Importance of Specific Performance', at chapter 17 in this book where he discusses *Semelhago v Paramedevan* (1996) 136 DLR (4th) 1 and *Tanwar Enterprises Pty Ltd v Cauchi* (2003) 217 CLR 315.

has already been done,[47] nor, any longer, on whether the rights that have been infringed are "proprietary".[48] Contract rights, too, are enforced using the full panoply of remedies. This remains true even when the rights infringed appear to be especially "personal", rather than "proprietary", such as those requiring personal services to be performed by the defendant for the claimant.[49] Generalising, it seems that "obligations" are sufficiently commonly protected by "property rules" for this form of enhanced legal protection to be of little use in distinguishing property from obligation.[50]

The inability of this remedial attribute to provide a distinguishing test appears all the more stark when the issues are examined from the property perspective. Then we notice that our legal system does not necessarily protect some of the most uncontroversial "property" forms by means of property rules, but prefers, instead, to limit protection to liability rules. This is the approach taken by the common law in protecting goods (that is, tangible personal property). These assets are clearly property, but they are not (or not necessarily) protected by property rules: an owner whose goods have been converted by another is entitled to compensation rather than to specific recovery (unless the court exercises its statutory discretion to order the latter).[51]

Generalising, the more accurate analysis seems to be that the special protective regimes that deliver performance rather than damages (Calabresi and Melamed's "property rules") are not afforded exclusively to property rights. Rather, they are afforded to *all* scarce rights, whether those rights are classified as property or as obligation. Once again, this aspect of the law's remedial regime does not enable us to distinguish between property and obligation.

Property carries an entitlement to proceeds

Property rights are commonly associated with automatic entitlement to any proceeds derived from the property. An owner can sell her car and keep the proceeds; she can hire the car out and the income is hers. The same is equally true of assets that are more on the margins of property and obligation: owners of shares or debts may sell these assets and keep the proceeds;[52] and before such

---

47   Even if the damage is still only threatened, the claimant may be obliged to take compensation for the likely harm that will be caused, rather than be afforded an injunction: *Lord Cairns' Act (Chancery Amendment Act 1858*, 21 & 22 Vict c 27 (UK), now re-enacted in the *Supreme Court Act 1981* (UK), s 50.

48   Proprietary in the sense that the tort interferes with the claimant's rights, and those rights are proprietary rather than personal (property rather than contract). At another level, all tort "rights" are sometimes considered "proprietary", since they can be enforced against all the world—that is, they are rights in rem. See the discussion earlier in this chapter at 103.

49   *Co-operative Insurance Society Ltd v Argyll Stores (Holdings) Ltd* [1998] AC 1. But see *Lumley v Wagner* (1852) 1 De GM & G 604; 42 ER 687, where the courts were prepared to order an injunction, but not specific performance.

50   See the similar conclusion in L Smith, 'Understanding Specific Performance' in N Cohen and E McKendrick (eds), *Comparative Remedies for Breach of Contract* (Hart Publishing, Oxford, 2005) at 221 and 233.

51   *Torts (Interference with Goods) Act 1977* (UK), s 3.

52   Sometimes the sale is subject to restrictions, or even prohibitions, but this is equally true of tangible property.

sale, they are entitled to the dividends or interest payments. But the same is also true of rights we class as pure obligations. Contracts of supply, or service, or hire can all be sold, and the proceeds belong to the seller;[53] and if these personal rights are not sold, then any benefits that accrue from them belong to their owner. It seems that all assets carry with them an entitlement to proceeds, and this is equally true whether the assets are classed as property or obligation. This is not controversial.

Much more controversial, however, is whether this same entitlement to gains applies when the gains are made by third parties making unauthorised use of the rights, rather than made by the right-owner herself. In these circumstances, can the owner still insist that she is entitled to the benefits derived from *her* asset? In making this claim, the owner is asking for a "disgorgement" remedy (or "restitutionary damages" or "an account of profits"). Does *this* remedy map the property/obligation divide?

This is difficult, because there is as yet no firm consensus on the availability of disgorgement as a remedy. The possibility of such a claim can arise in a variety of circumstances, and involve a wide range of assets. Depending upon the circumstances, different analyses are possible, and none has so far attracted consistent judicial (or academic) following. In an earlier article, I discussed the paradigm case of a third party using a £1 coin to purchase what turned out to be the winning lottery ticket.[54] The lottery winnings represent the "proceeds" from the £1 coin. Must these winnings be paid over to the original owner of the £1 coin? Does it matter whether the original owner remains the legal (or equitable) owner of the money throughout (that is, has a property right), or whether she has only a personal claim for recovery of its value from the third party (in unjust enrichment, for example; that is, a personal right)? Does it matter whether the third party was, from the start, a trustee of the money, or stole it, or received it completely innocently, perhaps by way of gift? Contract law and tort law can compensate the original owner for any *harm* suffered; the law of unjust enrichment can restore *expropriated gains*. But these remedies, if they are available, will rarely deliver much more than £1 (the original asset, perhaps plus some further amount for loss of use of the money for some period of time). Is there a rule that will also restore the *third party's windfall gains* to the claimant?

If it is clear that the original owner has retained a property interest in the asset despite its transfer to the third party, then (at least in the UK) it is often assumed that she will be able to recover windfall gains from interfering third parties. A 1997 Court of Appeal decision suggests this conclusion follows naturally from the nature of property rights themselves: owners are entitled to the productive capacities of their assets, even when the gains are derived through the efforts of third parties.[55] Many academic commentators reach the

---

53 Again, the sale may be subject to restrictions, or even prohibitions, but this is no different from the earlier property examples.

54 S Worthington, 'Justifying Claims to Secondary Profits' in EJH Schrage (ed), *Unjust Enrichment and the Law of Contract* (Kluwer, The Hague, 2001) at 451.

55 *Trustee of the Property of FC Jones & Sons v Jones* [1997] Ch 159.

same conclusion, but explain it on the basis of unjust enrichment.[56] I confess to remaining sceptical. Neither approach seems to be sufficiently discriminating. Both lead to results which strip gains equally from thieves and from innocent donees who fortuitously invest the mistaken gift profitably, even though they might just as readily have invested their own funds for their own benefit and left the gift untouched. I prefer an analysis that requires third parties to disgorge gains only when they have been made in defiance of some fiduciary obligation to manage the underlying assets in the owner's interests.[57] The weight of precedent also favours a more restrictive approach: bar the Court of Appeal case already noted, and one House of Lords case,[58] other instances of true disgorgement[59] all seem to arise in fiduciary contexts.[60]

Clearly this area of the law is most unsettled. But the arguments need not be analysed in detail here. The goal here is simply to determine whether there is a difference between the legal protections delivered to property and those delivered to obligation. In the United Kingdom at least, this area of the law has prompted vehement debate. In seeking to protect obligation, commentators have advocated what amounts to analogous application of the House of Lords' property analysis. They suggest that contract rights and property rights deserve equivalent protection; that expropriation of either is inappropriate; and that interference with either should be remedied by disgorgement in appropriate circumstances.[61] The argument has been used to support both disgorgement and performance interest damages for breach of contract;[62] and disgorgement to remedy profitable torts or other wrongs. The cases do not yet go so far. Disgorgement *is* available. It is commonly awarded to remedy fiduciary and other equitable breaches of the claimant's personal right to confidential or loyal

---

56 P Birks, "Property, Unjust Enrichment and Tracing" (2001) 54 *Current Legal Problems* 231; A Burrows, *The Law of Restitution* (2nd ed, Butterworths, London, 2003).

57 The details of these approaches are described in S Worthington, *Equity* (Clarendon Law Series, Oxford, 2003) at 98-102; S Worthington, 'Justifying Claims to Secondary Profits' in EJH Schrage (ed), *Unjust Enrichment and the Law of Contract* (Kluwer, The Hague, 2001) at 451.

58 In *Foskett v McKeown* [2001] 1 AC 102, Lord Millett based his conclusions primarily on the property analysis adopted in *Trustee of the Property of FC Jones & Sons v Jones*, above n 55, but he also indicated that a fiduciary analysis (which was possible on the facts) delivers the same conclusions. See also Lord Millett, 'Proprietary Restitution' at chapter 12 in this book.

59 Rather than compensation (measured by "use value") or restitution for subtractive unjust enrichment: see S Worthington, "Reconsidering Disgorgement" (1999) 62 *Modern Law Review* 218, but contrast, for example, J Edelman, *Gain-based Damages: Contract, Tort, Equity and Intellectual Property* (Hart Publishing, Oxford, 2002).

60 Although see to the contrary *Attorney-General v Blake (Jonathan Cape Ltd Third Party)* [2001] 1 AC 268, justified as being a relationship that was very close to fiduciary. This less strict approach is criticised in S Worthington and R Goode, 'Commercial Law: Confining the Remedial Boundaries' in D Hayton (ed) *Law's Future(s): British Legal Developments in the 21st Century* (Hart Publishing, Oxford, 2000) at 281.

61 L Smith, "Disgorgement of the Profits of a Breach of Contract: Property, Contract and 'Efficient Breach'" (1994) 24 *Canadian Business Law Journal* 121; D Friedmann, "The Efficient Breach Fallacy" (1989) 18 *Journal of Legal Studies* 1.

62 IM Jackman, "Restitution for Wrongs" (1989) 48 *Cambridge Law Journal* 302; and D Friedmann, "The Performance Interest in Contract Damages" (1995) 111 *Law Quarterly Review* 628, respectively.

service, even where the fiduciary has not interfered with any property owned (in equity) by his beneficiary.[63] These breaches might be regarded as interference with the claimant's (personal) right to a particular form of service from his agent. Early cases suggested that disgorgement was limited to the initial wrongful gain made by the defaulting fiduciary, and, moreover, that the remedy was restricted to a personal claim to the value of the gain.[64] But this approach has now been radically revised. Full disgorgement of the initial gain *and* any proceeds derived from it is favoured; and the remedy is now considered to be proprietary (delivering insolvency protection to the injured claimant principal).[65] The change in approach has attracted vocal adherents and equally vocal dissentients.[66]

Disgorgement has also been advocated as the appropriate remedy for torts, especially proprietary torts. Some cases can be read as supporting this stance, but it is equally possible to interpret them as supporting either compensation or autonomous unjust enrichment claims in respect of the unauthorised use of the claimant's asset.[67] Finally, disgorgement is also available for breach of contract, although the courts insist that this remedy is available only in exceptional circumstances.[68]

What conclusion can be drawn from all of this? Even though the state of the law remains unsettled, it is clear that there is no sharp divide between property and obligation in allowing right-holders access to the proceeds of unauthorised interference with the right. A narrow reading of the authorities (and my preferred reading) is that *both* property and obligation are protected in the same way: both are typically protected from interference by either compensatory remedies (for torts or breach of contract) or by restitution (for unjust enrichment); exceptionally, *both* are also protected by disgorgement remedies,

---

63   *Boardman v Phipps* [1967] 2 AC 46.

64   *Lister & Co v Stubbs* (1890) 45 Ch D 1.

65   *Attorney-General for Hong Kong v Reid* [1994] 1 AC 324.

66   Suggesting that the remedy should not be proprietary, see RM Goode, 'Property and Unjust Enrichment' in A Burrows (ed), *Essays on the Law of Restitution* (Clarendon Press, Oxford, 1991) at 215; RM Goode, 'The Recovery of a Director's Improper Gains: Proprietary Remedies for the Infringement of Non-Proprietary Rights' in E McKendrick (ed), *Commercial Aspects of Trusts and Fiduciary Obligations* (Clarendon Press, Oxford, 1992) at 137; and that it should perhaps be subordinated to the claims of the defendant's other creditors, see P Jaffey, "Restitutionary Damages and Disgorgement" [1995] *Restitution Law Review* 30 at 44; V Finch and S Worthington, 'The *Pari Passu* Principle and Ranking Restitutionary Rights' in F Rose (ed), *Insolvency and Restitution* (Lloyds of London Press, London, 2000) at chapter 1.

67   *Wrotham Park Estate Co Ltd v Parkside Homes Ltd* [1974] 1 WLR 798; *Penarth Dock Engineering Co Ltd v Pounds* [1963] 1 Lloyd's Rep 359; *Whitwham v Westminster Brymbo Coal and Coke Co* [1896] 2 Ch 538, especially 541-2 per Lindley LJ. In *Strand Electric & Engineering Co Ltd v Brisford Entertainments Ltd* [1952] 2 QB 246 it was commented that if the defendant *had* profited from the use, then disgorgement of those profits would *not* be required (per Somervell LJ at 252) *or* might be (per Denning LJ at 255).

68   *Attorney-General v Blake (Jonathan Cape Ltd Third Party)* [2001] 1 AC 268, criticised in S Worthington and R Goode, 'Commercial Law: Confining the Remedial Boundaries' in D Hayton (ed) *Law's Future(s): British Legal Developments in the 21st Century* (Hart Publishing, Oxford, 2000) at 281. See also M McInnes, 'Account of Profits for Common Law Wrongs' at chapter 16 of this book.

but only when the infringement is the result of interference by the right-holder's own fiduciary. The more common, wider, reading of the authorities reaches quite different conclusions, but is equally strong in aligning the treatment of property and obligation: this alternative approach sees *both* property and obligation as routinely protected by disgorgement remedies. In short, this attribute of entitlement to proceeds is, like all the others, equally inadequate in differentiating between property and obligation.

Property rights "run with the asset"

Relatively recently, a further distinguishing characteristic of property rights has been suggested: a property right, unlike a personal right, "runs with the asset".[69] This sounds promising. It captures an attribute that we *do* regard as a characteristic of property. If a thief steals A's car and sells it to C, A's ownership of the car (A's property rights in the car) run with the car, and can be enforced against C. It does not matter that A and C are strangers, and have reached no agreement between themselves about A's rights.

This attribute of rights "running with the asset" is especially attractive if owners want to *divide* rights in an asset between several parties, and then allow the individual parties to deal with their respective rights independently of the other interest holders. Put generally, if A shares proprietary rights in an asset with B, and B then transfers the asset to C, will A's interests in the asset persist and be enforceable against C? The commercial attractions of this result, at least to A, are clear. This is one of the classical attractions of property rights. But the concomitant risks to C are equally evident, especially if C is ignorant of A's interests.

In the context of this chapter, two issues need to be resolved. The first is whether this idea of rights that run with the asset *is* a characteristic of property rights; the second is whether the same attribute is also evident with personal rights. To anticipate, it seems that both property and obligation are, once again, very similar.

At first sight it seems that the common law, at least, does consider property rights to run with assets. The earlier example of the theft of A's car is illustrative. Closer examination shows something different, however. Across a range of property interests, the real focus seems to be better described as one protecting A *only* to the extent that this is consistent with preserving C's rights, unless C knew or ought to have known of A's competing interests: C is really in the line of sight, not A.

Examples make this clearer. If the subject matter is tangible property, then C can often be put on notice that others have rights to the asset simply because she knows that *she* does not hold those rights: the mere fact of the property's existence is sufficient indication that other people have rights that need to be respected.[70] She does not need to know *who* has competing interests; all she

---

69   H Hansmann and R Kraakman, "Property, Contract, and Verification: The *Numerus Clausus* Problem and the Divisibility of Rights" (2002) 31 *Journal of Legal Studies* 373.

70   TW Merrill and HE Smith, "Optimal Standardization in the Law of Property: The *Numerus Clausus* Principle" (2000) 110 *Yale Law Journal* 1.

needs to know is that *she* does not. The physical reality of the property acts as its own form of notice to the world that someone has interests that merit protection. This form of public notice, or some marginal variant of it, is used quite commonly. The rule applies to real and personal tangible property. It also applies to intangible rights that are "marked" by trademarks or copyright symbols. Strangers are liable, often strictly liable, for infringements of these ownership or possessory property rights.

But this type of rule has its limits. It works tolerably well in cases of potential theft, conversion or trespass to tangible property, where C is made liable for unilaterally interfering with property rights she knows are not hers, even if she is unaware of the real owner's identity. The rule seems less apt, however, when an intermediate party, B, purports to sell or give property rights to C, and C is then visited with the same remedial consequences because B turns out to be a thief or fraudster. The physicality of tangible property, or of copyright or trademark symbols, cannot serve as adequate notice to C if C intends a legitimate acquisition rather than a unilateral invasion of the relevant rights.[71]

The law has developed further strategies to deal with this difficulty. The choice of different approaches to suit different circumstances appears designed to balance the fairness and costs of imposing the risk on one party as against the other. There are two extremes. The first confirms the merits in protecting A's interests, but recognises the difficulties for C in discovering that these interests exist. The preferred strategy is then one that enables A to give better notice to the world of his interests by filing them on a public register. It matters little, it seems, whether the registry details A's precise interests,[72] or merely provides notice that A has some sort of interest.[73] The filing system works because C can then be presumed to know of A's filed interests, whether or not she makes the effort to check the registry. C is said to have constructive notice of A's filed interests, and A's interests will then prevail over C's, if there is a conflict, even if C has acquired her interests innocently and for value. There are many illustrations of this strategy in operation: there are registries of interests in land, certain classes of security interests granted by corporate borrowers, and ownership of second hand cars.

---

71   Notwithstanding this, the common law imposes strict liability for the tort of conversion. See A Tettenborn, 'Conversion, Tort and Restitution' in N Palmer and E McKendrick (eds), *Interests in Goods* (2nd ed, Lloyds of London Press, London, 1998) at 825, for a suggestion that conversion's separate functions should be divided, and liability modified, so that there could be strict liability for recovery (a surrogate vindicatio); fault based tort liability, based on dishonesty or lack of good faith, enabling compensation for loss from misuse of the property; and strict liability enabling reversal of unjust enrichments arising from either the owner's property or its proceeds. In this way, the common law tort-style liability would be brought into line with the equitable liability for "knowing receipt".

72   As now happens in the UK when companies file charges with Companies House: *Companies Act 1985* (UK), ss 395, 396.

73   As now happens in the US when *Uniform Commercial Code* Art 9 security interests are filed. The UK Law Commission proposes adopting this strategy in a reformed UK regime: see The Law Commission, Consultation Paper No 176, *Company Security Interests: A Consultative Report* (2004).

The second approach is almost the complete reverse of the first. It favours C's interests over A's, and allows C's interests to prevail so long as she is a bona fide purchaser for value without notice of A's rights. The rule operates without a register of A's interests. The burden is thus on A to inform third parties, or, more often, to control the behaviour of his agent, B, to ensure that B does not do anything unauthorised to defeat A's interests. Put another way, where A and B choose particular organisational structures to enable them to divide property interests efficiently between them, then they, not the outsiders (that is, C), should shoulder the risk that poor internal management might enable B to deal with C in unauthorised ways. In these circumstances, A should lose his rights, not C. This protective strategy is the primary rule that operates when A is a company, B the board of directors, and C a party dealing with the company. By and large C is allowed to assume that all of B's advances in dealing with A's assets are authorised, unless C is either a donee or on notice that the transfer is in defiance of A's legitimate interests. The same rule applies when A is the beneficiary of a trust, B is a trustee, and C is a stranger dealing with the trustee over the transfer of the trust assets.

Context helps to define commercial needs, and hence the appropriate style of rule. Contrast the protection afforded to C in any dealings with currency (the second style of rule) with those applying to her dealings with goods (the first style of rule, and with very few registers to assist in improving the protection offered).

As noted earlier,[74] neither the magnitude of this problem, nor the ease of solving it, is assisted by the numerus clausus rule. As soon as parties wish to divide rights and deal with them independently, some form of verification or protection is necessary. This clearly increases the costs well beyond those necessary to operate a scheme of sole and undivided ownership, but the commercial advantages of division are overwhelming. Once this is conceded, then, as between a small and large number of possible divisions (or types) of property rights, the same verification rules are equally apt.[75] This is easily illustrated. Consider the practicalities of filing: it is expensive because a registry needs to be established and the parties will incur costs in filing and in searching; but these costs are not further increased simply because what is filed is a novel form of private arrangement between A and B.

All of this can be summarised briefly. Property rights may indeed "run with the asset", so A's rights may be enforceable against C, but only if certain specific verification or protective rules permit this. These rules aim to balance the burdens and benefits of a system that permits bundles of rights to be divided, and the divided parcels to be transferred independently of the other co-owners.

The next issue is the important one for this chapter. Can *obligations* also "run with the asset"? Can the same protective strategies be used to achieve similar ends with obligations as with property?

---

74   See 101–103 above.
75   H Hansmann and R Kraakman, "Property, Contract, and Verification: The *Numerus Clausus* Problem and the Divisibility of Rights" (2002) 31 *Journal of Legal Studies* 373.

There is no theoretical or doctrinal reason why the law should not permit this to happen. Nevertheless, the commercial attractiveness of this in relation to obligations is far more limited than it is in the case of orthodox property rights. This is because "contract bundles" are less commonly the object of unauthorised dealings in defiance of the original contract-holder's rights (as happened in our stolen car example), and they are less frequently the object of commercially attractive sub-division that gives different co-owners different interests in an asset. This is when verification and protective regimes are especially useful. Nevertheless, although the need for contract rights to run with the asset is less extreme, there are situations where this would be commercially attractive.

Does the law then allow for the possibility, and adopt the protective strategies already noted in the context of property? Consider each of the earlier approaches in turn. Since contract rights are intangible, simple physical notice to the world is difficult (although there is a sense in which copyright and trademark labels might be regarded as protecting contract rights, rather than orthodox property rights). That leaves verification and protective strategies. First consider the use of registers of intangible assets. These do exist. As with registers of orthodox property rights, there is no need for registers to record every possible interest in every possible asset. This is a cost-benefit game. Registers are worth their costs if the rights being filed are especially valuable, even if the number of filings is relatively small over time (consider registers of land, ships and aircraft engines); or if the register is used often and by large numbers of the trading community (consider registers of security interests or second hand car ownership). Are there registers of "contracts"? Registers of intellectual property interests, such as patents, can be viewed in this way. So, too, can registers of security interests, especially in the United States, where the courts had denied the proprietary possibility of floating charges, yet such contractual arrangements could be effectively enforced by filing under the *United States Uniform Commercial Code*, Article 9. Filing certainly increases the variety of rights that can be accorded "proprietary" status, in the sense that they run with the asset. For example, there have been suggestions that negative pledges could usefully be filed.[76]

The protective strategy is also used with contract rights. This strategy is the more efficient option where the contract rights are sufficiently valuable to warrant protection, but the dealings are sufficiently unique to make filing impractical. The types of contract rights that might warrant this protection are A's right to use B's assets in a particular manner (as in a contract of hire), or A's claim against B that B use his property in specified ways, as defined by negative pledge agreements or agreements to vote shares in a pre-determined manner. In these circumstances, can A prevent C from using the asset in a manner that is inconsistent with A's contractual rights? The law remains uncertain, but a line

---

76 H Hansmann and R Kraakman, "Property, Contract, and Verification: The *Numerus Clausus* Problem and the Divisibility of Rights", above n 79 at fn 79, citing BE Adler, "Financial and Political Theories of American Corporate Bankruptcy" (1993) 45 *Stanford Law Review* 311 at 336-339; and BE Adler, 'Secured Credit Contracts' in P Newman (ed), *The New Palgrave Dictionary of Economics and the Law* (Palgrave Macmillan, London, 1998), Vol 3 at 405-410.

of cases suggests that A might obtain a negative injunction against C to prevent interference, provided C had notice of A's rights when she acquired her own interests in the asset.[77]

Of course, when rights recognised by equity were regarded as operating in personam, and so were seen as personal rather than proprietary, then equity's bona fide purchaser for value without notice rules, and knowing receipt rules, could also have been regarded as major components of this protective regime to ensure that contract rights "ran with the asset" in an appropriate manner.[78]

Of course, there is a downside to all of this. Any regime that enables rights to run with the asset also enables increasing fragmentation of rights between different owners, and this is widely regarded as inefficient. It hampers advantageous dealings with the underlying asset because it leads to increased transaction costs and the risk of holdout problems, and these can soon become so large that they frustrate the efficient use of the asset.[79] The problem is minimised a little by devices like the rule against perpetuities, and limitations of actions. Moreover, registries of rights promote a market in re-bundling the rights, in much the same was as in the market for corporate control. Finally, the protective notice regime, by its very nature, is unlikely to produce significant fragmentation since A's rights will generally only persist if C has adequate notice of their existence.

Once again, there seems to be no sharp divide between the law's treatment of property and obligation in allowing rights to "run with the asset". The differences that do exist appear to be more closely related to commercial needs than to legal limitations. The risk of interference and the commercial attractiveness of divided interests are both greater with orthodox property rights than with purely personal rights, but where this generalisation does not hold, the law seems to treat both types of interests in similar ways.

Property rights attract insolvency protection

Insolvency priority is widely regarded as the lynchpin of proprietary characteristics. Property rights are accorded insolvency protection; personal rights are not. In reality, this may be the least significant characteristic in making, or losing, the argument that there is a disappearing divide between property and obligation. This is because the *logic* of the property/insolvency link is not associated in some fundamental way with an attribute that distinguishes

---

77   *De Mattos v Gibson* (1858) 4 De G & J 276; 45 ER 108. Also see S Worthington, *Proprietary Interests in Commercial Transactions* (Oxford University Press, Oxford, 1996) at chapter 5.

78   Also see the different analysis in L Smith, "Unravelling Proprietary Restitution" (2004) 40 *Canadian Business Law Journal* 317.

79   In the US, this is known as the "problem of the anticommons": see H Hansmann and R Kraakman, "Property, Contract, and Verification: The *Numerus Clausus* Problem and the Divisibility of Rights", above n 75 at fn 85, citing MA Heller, "The Tragedy of the Anticommons: Property in the Transition from Marx to Markets" (1998) 111 *Harvard Law Review* 621; FI Michelman, 'Ethics, Economics and the Law of Property' in *NOMOS XXIV: Ethics, Economics, and the Law* 3 (New York University Pres, New York, 1982).

property from obligation. Rather, the distinction depends utterly on current insolvency policy. Consider two simple examples.

First, suppose X is an individual, but is also the trustee of a trust and the sole director of a one-man company. If X becomes bankrupt, all the assets that appear to be his will have to be characterised as relating to one or other of his three different roles. Some will be personal assets, available to his creditors in his bankruptcy. Some will relate to the trust. They will not be distributable on X's bankruptcy, but will be partitioned off and preserved for the trust beneficiaries. And some will belong to the company. First claim to them will be accorded to the *company's* creditors, not to X's personal creditors: X's personal interest will be limited to the net value of his shareholding. This common form of asset partitioning is effected without any thought of distinguishing between property and obligation. X's personal assets will include both types of wealth. So, too, will the trust and corporate assets. Asset partitioning on insolvency, in this sense, is simply allocating patrimonies to their appropriate owners (X and the company), and dividing patrimonies between different roles (X's personal activities and his activities as trustee). In doing this, there is no property/obligation divide in any sense that is relevant in this chapter.

Take a second case. This tests the property/obligation divide more severely. Consider the distribution of X's personal assets amongst his own creditors. On X's insolvency, *all* his wealth (proprietary and personal) is realised for the benefit of his creditors. If no creditors have proprietary claims, the entire asset pool will simply be shared amongst the claimants pro rata. This is regarded as the fairest way to proceed. By contrast, creditors who can identify an asset as "theirs" can take it, often in full satisfaction of their claims. The more privileged property-owning creditors there are, the smaller the pool for the unprivileged personal claimants, and the smaller the proportion of their losses that will be recovered. Insolvency losses are thus shifted from the privileged to the unprivileged. If a showroom owner becomes insolvent, for example, the paid up purchaser of "the only pink car in the showroom" can take her car; the paid up purchaser of "one of the four green cars in the showroom" cannot.[80] Moreover, the latter purchaser cannot specifically recover his purchase payment, even assuming (rather unrealistically) that he can identify either it or its traceable substitutes amongst the debtor's assets.[81] Many creditors are in this unhappy unsecured position, unless they take security to preserve their interests.

Why does insolvency law permit this difference in treatment between different creditors, and, in our example, between different purchaser creditors? Elsewhere, I have called this the "musical chairs" element of insolvency law: the result for different creditors depends entirely on the timing of the debtor's insolvency (that is, on the timing of when the music stops).[82] The justification is relatively simple. The task of insolvency law is to maximise returns to *all*

---

80   *Sale of Goods Act 1979* (UK), ss 16-18.
81   *Re Goldcorp Exchange Ltd (in rec)* [1995] 1 AC 74.
82   S Worthington, 'Proprietary Remedies and Insolvency Policy: The Need for a New Approach' in J Lowry and L Mistalis, *The Dimensions of Commercial Law* (Lexis-Nexis Butterworths, London, forthcoming).

creditors by effecting an orderly distribution of the debtor's assets. This goal is best achieved by a co-ordinated distribution process. Furthermore, viable enterprises should not be tipped into insolvency; this is unnecessarily costly for all concerned. The best mechanism to ensure these twin goals are met, and that creditors have no incentive to steal a march by acting unilaterally, or to tip the debtor into early insolvency, is to insist that the pre- and post-insolvency rights of all creditors remain the same. There is then no situational advantage for anyone in moving the debtor into insolvency. This reasoning means that pre-insolvency property rights must be preserved; this, in turn, means post-insolvency priority to property owners.

The ability of creditors to take legal security (by means of proprietary interests) to preserve their priority is subjected to the same form of insolvency justification. In the end, security is seen as advantageous because it increases commercial activity. Parties who would not otherwise have access to funds for business (or domestic) expansion and development can make use of these resources. In any event, pragmatism suggests that commercial parties would make arrangements designed to achieve the same ends, at greater cost, if the law did not provide a structured mechanism. Nevertheless, parliament imposes restrictions on the availability of this form of insolvency protection, imposing registration requirements and, in some cases, timing, vulnerability and claw-back limitations.[83]

All of this makes perfect sense, and yet there is a gnawing reluctance to push this preferential proprietary analysis too far. As already noted, the *Insolvency Act 1986* (UK) itself imposes limitations on the effectiveness of security. It also accords preferential status to certain contract rights, especially employee rights, on insolvency.[84] And when property priority is delivered in the form of a proprietary *remedy* from the debtor, the courts are increasingly alert to the adverse implications for the unsecured creditors.[85] Civil law jurisdictions are much happier to insist that some of these remedial property claims are contingent, not privileged. The United States, too, is more restrictive than the United Kingdom. Indeed, the *United States Uniform Commercial Code* Article 9 filing regime, for all that it asserts that all filed rights are proprietary, has effectively replaced the common law proprietary system of security with a statutory priorities system for obligations. Priority rules have replaced property rules. This makes it easier for the legislature to amend priorities without affecting non-insolvency property rights.

This complicated common law and statutory hierarchy of insolvency rights *could* be changed. There is nothing inevitable about the insolvency protection

---

83 For example, *Companies Act 1985* (UK), ss 395, 396; *Insolvency Act 1986* (UK), s 245 and Schedule B1 para 70.

84 See *Insolvency At 1986* (UK), ss 40 and 175(2)(b), and, more recently, s 176A.

85 Recall the excitement over *A-G for Hong Kong v Reid* [1994] 1 AC 324; *Re Goldcorp Exchange Ltd (in rec)* [1995] 1 AC 74; *Westdeutsche Landesbank Girozentrale v Islington London Borough Council* [1996] AC 669; and *Agnew v Commissioner of Inland Revenue* [2001] 2 AC 710, to name only a few. But also see the analysis in *Re Polly Peck International plc (in admin) (No 4)* [1998] 3 All ER 812 at 826-7 per Mummery LJ.

accorded to property rights.[86] Theoretically, the system could deliver preferential status according to some completely different regime, perhaps according to the type of claim being advanced by the creditor. This would involve prioritising certain forms of claim over other forms, and ignoring whether or not they have traditionally been regarded as proprietary or not. This would overcome the problem that some claims, by their very nature, can never attach to any specific part of the pool of debtor's assets, and yet these claims may well be thought more worthy than others that are able to assert such an attachment. Elsewhere I have argued that this sort of analysis may suggest that unjust enrichment claims should be given insolvency privileges above those accorded to compensation claims, for example.[87] Put more generally, insolvency is all about policy, and sharing losses amongst innocent parties. As a matter of policy, it is important to consider carefully the pre- and post-insolvency goals, and decide which rights should legitimately be privileged.

In summary, insolvency priority *is* currently treated as a defining characteristic of property, distinguishing it from obligation. The implications for the respective right holders are dramatic. Those with property rights often recover in full. This leaves a disproportionately diminished pool of assets for the personal right holders to share. The result is that they often receive nothing. This result is all the more worrying when, as the rest of this chapter shows, we are becoming increasingly uncertain about how to classify rights as falling on one or the other side of this privileged dividing line.

Is Disappearance of the Divide Between Property and Obligation Significant?

The significance of the conclusion that there is no longer any sharp divide between property and obligation depends upon your perspective. If given any credence, it will end the search for the Holy Grail, and that in itself might liberate a significant amount of academic effort.

Why do we have property? It is said to be necessary for all advanced and advancing societies to ensure greater productivity and commitment to effort. Parties who own assets know that they will derive the fruits of their labour, and they are then prepared to expend greater efforts. It is immediately obvious, however, that property is surplus to this equation, other than in making the point that common or community ownership does not work. Ensuring that not all wealth or property is held in common provides an incentive. This is as true of personal rights as it is of property rights.

---

86   LA Bebchuk and JM Fried, "The Uneasy Case for the Priority of Secured Claims in Bankruptcy" (1996) 105 *Yale Law Journal* 857; S Worthington, 'Proprietary Remedies and Insolvency Policy: The Need for a New Approach' in J Lowry and L Mistalis, *The Dimensions of Commercial Law* (Lexis-Nexis Butterworths, London, forthcoming), and (a shorter version of the same argument) S Worthington, "Property, Obligation and Insolvency Policy: Cutting the Gordian Knot" (2005) *Journal of International Banking and Finance Law* (forthcoming).

87   V Finch and S Worthington, 'The *Pari Passu* Principle and Ranking Restitutionary Rights' in F Rose (ed), *Insolvency and Restitution* (Lloyds of London Press, London, 2000) at chapter 1.

On other fronts, too, the news of a merger is not dramatic. But this is not because the news itself lacks dramatic impact. Rather it is that we arrived at this position quite some time ago, and so have had time to adjust to the consequences. Centuries ago, commercial parties saw that all rights, whether contract or property, could perform as usable wealth. They then adapted their practices accordingly. Economists were next to appreciate that these rights have merged. The lawyers have lagged behind.[88] Perhaps it is time to catch up.

---

88 Although see the prescient comment in R Pound, *An Introduction to the Philosophy of Law* (Yale University Press, New Haven, 1922) at 236: "Wealth, in a commercial age, is made up largely of promises".

6

Old and New in the Law of Tracing

CHARLES RICKETT*

INTRODUCTION

It is now generally accepted that, despite earlier characterisations, tracing (properly so-called) is neither a right nor a remedy.[1] Tracing is an evidential process by which one asset is permitted to stand in the place of another asset for the purposes of whatever rights or claims the claimant may have had in respect of the first asset.[2] Where the asset in which the plaintiff holds rights is used to acquire or is exchanged for another asset ("the traceable product"), the rights in the original asset are transmitted[3] to the traceable product. Even though the claimant would otherwise have no right or claim to the traceable product, it is nevertheless treated as the subject of his rights in place of the original asset. The function, then, of the specific rules of tracing is to identify those acquisitions or exchanges which are legally relevant thereby identifying which asset may properly be said to be the traceable product of the original asset. The rules of tracing are properly characterised as part of the law of property. Outstanding issues, in particular the issue of how rights are transmitted from one asset to another, are also issues within the law of property rights. This chapter intends to prove three things. First, the law of tracing will be located within the law of property. Secondly, the rules of tracing will be identified as arbitrary evidential problem avoiders. Finally, the narrow scope of the law of tracing thus outlined will accordingly reveal that some of the most difficult issues remaining are matters of the legal rules relating to claims and are not really concerns of the law of tracing at all.

---

* I am grateful to my colleague Professor Grantham with whom I have most profitably discussed these issues for many years. I am also grateful to Annaliese Jackson, who provided assistance in the research for this chapter.
1 *Boscawen v Bajwa* [1996] 1 WLR 328 at 334; *Foskett v McKeown* [2000] 2 WLR 1299 at 1323.
2 Tracing may be used to facilitate a claim to a proprietary remedy. It may also be used to identify the correct defendant in unjust enrichment claims where the value does not pass directly from plaintiff to defendant: see R Grantham and C Rickett, *Enrichment and Restitution in New Zealand* (Hart Publishing, Oxford, 2000) at 63-65.
3 *Foskett v McKeown* [2000] 2 WLR 1299 at 1322.

LOCATING THE LAW OF TRACING

The common law (including here equity) has long taken property rights particularly seriously. The common law provides increased protection for property rights. Indeed, this is why there is increasing demand for wider recognition for rights as property rights. There has been much discussion recently of the correct analytical understanding of property rights or rights in rem. This has largely followed on from Professor Birks' work on property rights. Birks argues that rights in rem are analytically a response to some legally relevant event, such as consent, wrong or unjust enrichment, and from this concludes that rights in rem cannot be the source of their own creation. However, this does not mean that, once a right in rem is in existence, that right cannot generate further rights. Ross Grantham and I have argued that analytically this must be so.[4] The following section of this chapter reproduces that argument.

The structure of rights in rem

Rights in rem must and do arise as a response to events. The vast majority of rights in rem arise as a response to the event of consent, in particular a conveyance. A right in rem may also arise as a response to a wrong,[5] and possibly also an unjust enrichment.[6] However, once in existence, a right in rem is also itself an event.[7] Once the claimant has a property right (where that property right may date from a prior consent, wrong, unjust enrichment or other event quite unrelated to the present claim founded on the property right itself),[8] this is in itself an "event" which gives rise to rights and duties. This argument proceeds in two stages. The first is that the doctrinal nature of a right in rem is such that any interference with the asset in which the right inheres must and can be sanctioned only by the creation of a new right in personam in the claimant as against the particular individual who has so interfered. The second is that such an in personam sanctioning right arises in response to and serves to vindicate the right in rem.

---

4   "Property Rights as a Legally Significant Event" (2003) 62 *Cambridge Law Journal* 717 at 730ff.

5   As perhaps occurred in *Attorney General for Hong Kong v Reid* [1994] 1 AC 324. On one view, the Crown's equitable property rights in the assets acquired with the funds received by Reid arose because of Reid's breach of his fiduciary duties: see C Rotherham, *Proprietary Remedies in Context* (Hart Publishing, Oxford, 2002) at 17-18. Alternatively, *Reid* may be seen as a case where the court gave effect to the intention of the parties as reflected in Reid's acceptance of his fiduciary duties. On this basis, the Crown's equitable property rights arise as a legal (though not necessarily real) implication of the fiduciary duty. See R Grantham and C Rickett, *Enrichment and Restitution in New Zealand* (Hart Publishing, Oxford, 2000) at 409, and P Millett, 'Proprietary Restitution' at chapter 12 in this book.

6   See, for a potential example, *Chase Manhattan Bank NA v Israel-British Bank (London) Ltd* [1981] Ch 105.

7   The view that rights in rem are only ever a response also seems incapable of explaining how rights arise in an asset that has not previously been owned. Thus, a fisherman who catches a fish from the ocean becomes the owner of the fish, but it is difficult to see to what event (other than by yet a further addition to the rather overworked rubbish bin of Birks' miscellaneous fourth category) that right in rem is a response.

8   Once in existence, however, a right in rem may then generate further rights in rem.

The common law, and indeed most legal systems, recognises a distinction between rights in personam and rights in rem. Broadly speaking, a right in personam is a right against a particular individual, while a right in rem is a right held against an indefinite class of persons in respect of an asset (res).[9] However, while this distinction between rights in personam and rights in rem accords with our intuitive understanding of property rights as essentially thing-centred, the question whether rights in personam and rights in rem are qualitatively or analytically different is more controversial. This controversy is largely a consequence of the scholarship of Professor Wesley Hohfeld.[10] Hohfeld sought to eliminate, or at least minimise, the distinction by decon-structing rights in rem into mere bundles of rights in personam. For Hohfeld, a right in rem was to be understood merely as a vast bundle of rights in personam, held by the right-holder against each and every other member of society.[11] However, Hohfeld did recognise that rights in rem and rights in personam differ from each other. This difference lay for Hohfeld in the fact that rights in rem always exist as bundles of fundamentally similar rights in personam.[12] While Hohfeld's analysis has been highly influential, it is now widely regarded as fatally flawed.[13] One sign of this was Hohfeld's inability to explain why, in the case of rights in rem, the rights always come in bundles of rights in personam.[14] This is clearly the defining feature of property rights, yet he was unable to offer a positive explanation of this quality.

The better and prevailing view, therefore, is that rights in rem are qualita-tively distinct from rights in personam. This distinction lies primarily in the identity of the subject of the obligation that the right reflects.[15] While a right in personam embodies an entitlement against a particular person, the subject of a right in rem is not a particular person but a thing or res. The res thus stands between the right-holder and the duty-ower as the focus of both the right and the duty. The right to enjoyment of the res is one held as against every person

---

9   This distinction may also be described in terms of exigibility: from whom may the right be demanded? See P Birks, *An Introduction to the Law of Restitution* (Clarendon, Oxford, 1985) at 49-50; J Penner, *The Idea of Property in Law* (Clarendon, Oxford, 1997) at 31. Rights in personam are exigible against a specific individual, while rights in rem are exigible against an indefinite class of persons.

10   WN Hohfeld, *Fundamental Legal Conceptions as Applied in Judicial Reasoning* (Yale University Press, New Haven, 1919).

11   Generally, see J Harris, *Property and Justice* (Clarendon, Oxford, 1996) at 120-125; P Elefthe-riadis, "The Analysis of Property Rights" (1996) 16 *Oxford Journal of Legal Studies* 31.

12   Hohfeld made this distinction through the concepts of "multital" rights (rights in rem) and "paucital" rights (rights in personam): *Fundamental Legal Conceptions as Applied in Judicial Reasoning*, above n 10 at 72.

13   P Birks, 'Before We Begin: Five Keys to Land Law' in S Bright and J Dewar (eds), *Land Law: Themes and Perspectives* (Oxford University Press, Oxford, 1998), chapter 18 at 473; J Penner, "The 'Bundle of Rights' Picture of Property" (1996) 43 *University of California, Los Angeles Law Review* 711; J Harris, *Property and Justice* (Clarendon, Oxford, 1996) at 120-125.

14   Hohfeld identified the difference as being "extrinsic" to the nature of the right itself. Beyond this, however, he was not able to explain what makes a multital right multital. See P Eleftheri-adis, "The Analysis of Property Rights" (1996) 16 *Oxford Journal of Legal Studies* 31 at 46-47; A Honoré, "Rights of Exclusion and Immunities Against Divesting" (1960) 34 *Tulane Law Review* 453.

15   Generally, see J Penner, *The Idea of Property in Law* (Clarendon, Oxford, 1997) at 23-31.

subject to the particular legal system, but it is a right held as against an indefinite class of persons rather than specific individuals. The correlative duty is one owed by everyone, and everyone owes the same duty, but it is not owed directly to the individual right-holder.[16] Rather, it is a duty in respect of the res itself. Accordingly, the right-duty correlation in respect of a right in rem is both impersonal and asymmetrical.[17] It is impersonal in that there is no direct chain of obligation between the right-holder and duty-ower and the identity and personal characteristics of the right-holder are irrelevant to the articulation and understanding of the right. It is asymmetrical in that the right is held as against a class of persons, but the duty is owed to the *res*.

An important analytical consequence of the nature of rights in rem concerns the manner in which an interference with an asset is sanctioned. Although a right in rem is a right that binds all of the world, when a right in rem is infringed by interference with the relevant asset, that infringement is necessarily the activity of a particular person. Accordingly, for the right in rem to mean anything in respect of that particular person, a secondary or consequential in personam obligation must be generated, by virtue of which that person's activity is sanctioned. Thus, Salmond states:[18]

> "the reason why sanctioning rights are in personam is obvious enough. Rights in rem are negative and avail against the all the world, *ie*, an open or indefinite class of persons. Violations of such rights, therefore, must consist of positive acts, and positive acts can only be performed by specific persons; it makes no sense to talk of a positive act performed by an indefinite class of persons; in other words a violation by all the world is a logical impossibility. Consequently it is only against specific persons that sanctioning rights can be either necessary or operative: they must be, therefore, rights in personam."

To similar effect, Professor Penner states:[19]

> "We do not have to frame the duty to respect property as a duty to particular individuals, but as a duty in respect of things. This will, of course, benefit the individual right-holders, but they need not be individually enumerated in order to understand the content of the duty. When the duty is breached, and the individual owner sues the individual trespasser, only then do we have a claim which is properly in personam, against a specific individual. But we must bear in mind that this is a secondary, or remedial right which arises on the breach of the primary one."

The in personam sanctioning right thus arises on the interference with the right in rem, in order to transform the rights held by a particular individual in respect of the res, which are owed by an indefinite class of persons, into a right in that particular individual held as against another particular individual. Although this process might be described in terms of a crystallisation of the right held as against an indefinite class of person into a right held

---

16   J Penner, *The Idea of Property in Law*, above n 15 at 24. See also L Smith, *The Law of Tracing* (Clarendon, Oxford, 1997) at 50-51.
17   J Penner, *The Idea of Property in Law*, above n 15 at 29.
18   P Fitzgerald, *Salmond on Jurisprudence* (12th ed, Sweet & Maxwell, London, 1966) at 244.
19   J Penner, *The Idea of Property in Law*, above n 15 at 24.

as against a particular person,[20] the right in personam nevertheless arises not as a substitute for the right in rem, but in addition to it. The existence of the right in personam "does not turn powers and rights in rem into a different kind of power or right in personam, because these powers and right continue to exist only so long as the res itself does, and only against those who are in actual violation of the right in rem".[21]

Property rights are, therefore, in one sense, inert or superstructural rights. Although they create right-duty relationships that bind everyone as a class, in order to sanction interferences with those rights in rem it is necessary to create right-duty relationships between the particular right-holders and the particular infringers. It is only by creating these additional rights in personam that the law can sanction or remedy particular infringements. The creation of these in personam sanctioning rights does not of course necessarily imply that the rights in rem are the event that creates them. It is clear, however, from an analysis of claims that serve to protect rights in rem that the in personam sanctioning rights that arise upon an interference with rights in rem do in fact arise in response to and serve to vindicate rights in rem.

This is most obviously so in respect of claims to vindicate property rights, both at common law and in equity.

Common law protection of rights in rem

The common law recognised a remedy of self-help, whereby the holder of a right in rem in respect of a particular asset could simply recapture the asset if it had been interfered with and had moved from his control. Recaption works analytically thus:

Figure 1: Recaption of the asset itself (self-help remedy)

First event (creating the right in rem)	Consent (conveyance)
	↓
Response	Creation of a right in rem
	↓
	(An event — interference with the asset) Analytical status of the interference? — it cannot be a legal event, as no new right is generated: therefore, let us refer to it simply as a 'grievance'
	↓
	Response to the grievance of interference: recaption of the asset — this can be referred back (or justified) only to (by) the right in rem as the response to the first event

---

20   C Noyes, *The Institution of Property* (Longmans, Green & Co, New York, 1936) at 241.

21   J Penner, *The Idea of Property in Law* (Clarendon, Oxford, 1997) at 31.

This shows that it is not analytically necessary in every case for a right in rem to generate an in personam sanctioning right for the right in rem to be vindicated. Since the claimant's focus in a case of recaption is directly against the asset itself, there is no need for an in personam sanctioning obligation.

It is, however, also the case at common law that in many circumstances, a sanctioning right in personam arises in order to deal with an interference with the claimant's asset and hence his right in rem. The source of the in personam right is the right in rem itself, though this is rather less clear than in respect of equitable claims. The obfuscation of this point is due principally to the decline and eventual disappearance, as a matter of history, from the common law of an action, apart from recaption, directly to vindicate property rights. As a matter of distant history, the common law probably did vindicate property rights directly. The writ of detinue in its original form was a direct proprietary action.[22] As a praecipe writ, it sought, *not* redress for a wrong, *but* the restoration of the claimant's rights: "an ear-marked chattel belonging to the plaintiff has come, no matter how, into the possession of the defendant. The claim rests not upon any transaction but upon the ear-mark. In modern or Roman terms this is the elementary proprietary claim, the claim of owner against possessor."[23] However, with the rise of the action on the case, and its considerable procedural advantages, the writ of detinue fell into disuse and although "revived"[24] after 1833 with the abolition of wager of law, its distinct juridical nature was not thereby restored. Thus, until its abolition in the United Kingdom in 1977,[25] it was treated as a species of civil wrong. Detinue worked analytically as per Figure 2.

For at least the last 300 years, therefore, the common law has provided no direct claim to enforce and protect rights in rem. In the void left by the absence of a rei vindicatio, the common law has instead sanctioned the interference with rights in rem principally through the law of civil wrongs, and in particular through the claim in conversion.[26] Thus, rather than allowing the

---

22 J Baker, *An Introduction to English Legal History* (3rd ed, Butterworths, London, 1990) at 68-69; S Milsom, *Historical Foundations of the Common Law* (2nd ed, Butterworths, London, 1981) at 243-246, 269-275; D Ibbetson, *A Historical Introduction to the Law of Obligations* (Oxford University Press, Oxford, 1999) at 107-108; A Simpson, "The Introduction of the Action on the Case for Conversion" (1959) 75 *Law Quarterly Review* 364.

23 S Milsom, "The Introduction of the Action on the Case for Conversion", above n 22 at 270. There is a fundamental cleavage in the common law between claims demanding performance of a right and those seeking redress for a wrong. Historically, this was reflected in the distinction between action founded on a praecipe writ and those founded on a plaint. This distinction is said to be Germanic in origin: F Pollock and W Maitland, *The History of English Law* (2nd ed, Cambridge University Press, Cambridge, 1968), vol 2 at 571.

24 J Baker, *An Introduction to English Legal History*, above n 22 at 451; W Rogers, *Winfield and Jolowicz on Tort* (15th ed, Sweet & Maxwell, London, 1998) at 583-585.

25 *Torts (Interference with Goods) Act 1977* (UK), s 2, abolished detinue and extended conversion to those cases that detinue did not reach. See A Dugdale, *Clerk & Lindsell on Torts* (18th ed, Sweet & Maxwell, London, 2000) at 728.

26 While they are the most-well understood, torts are not the only form of indirect enforcement of common law property rights. In particular, the actions in money had and received and debt may serve to vindicate property rights in money (see Goff and G Jones, *The Law of Restitution* (5th ed, Sweet & Maxwell, London, 1998) at 3-4, 96-103; *Holiday v Sigil* (1826) 2 C & P 176). The English Court of Appeal decision in *Trustee of Jones v Jones* [1997] Ch 159 illustrates this.

Figure 2: Detinue

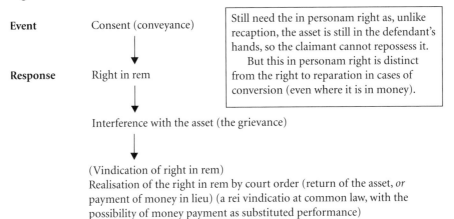

Event   Consent (conveyance)

Response   Right in rem

> Still need the in personam right as, unlike recaption, the asset is still in the defendant's hands, so the claimant cannot repossess it.
> But this in personam right is distinct from the right to reparation in cases of conversion (even where it is in money).

Interference with the asset (the grievance)

(Vindication of right in rem)
Realisation of the right in rem by court order (return of the asset, *or* payment of money in lieu) (a rei vindicatio at common law, with the possibility of money payment as substituted performance)

claimant to put rights in rem directly before the court, as occurs in equity, at common law the claimant is required to allege a wrongful interference with the asset over which he had a right in rem, which interference founded a right to monetary compensation for the loss caused by that interference. One important consequence of the role taken on by conversion was that while historically and formally it was a species of wrongdoing, it absorbed at the same time many of the features of a rei vindicatio.[27] Thus, by the mid-eighteenth Century, the allegation of wrongdoing had become a mere fiction, uncontestable by the defendant.[28] As in a classic rei vindicatio, liability became strict. Moreover, the claimant's proprietary rights in the asset misappropriated had become an indispensable foundation of the claim. Although, unlike a true rei

---

Money was transferred from the account of the plaintiff trustee to Mrs Jones, who had no right to it. Mrs Jones speculated with the money and multiplied it several times. She deposited the sum in an account specially opened for that purpose. The plaintiff sought recovery of all the funds thus deposited. The Court was clearly of the view that the plaintiff was simply seeking to protect his property rights and that the medium of this protection was the action in debt (or possibly money had and received). See also the discussion of *Jones* in P Millett, 'Proprietary Restitution' at chapter 12 in this book.

Their Lordships' emphasis in *Lipkin Gorman (a firm) v Karpnale Ltd* [1991] 2 AC 548 on the plaintiff's title to the money as the foundation of the claim in money had and received also suggests that the event in respect of which the in personam right to restitution arose was property (see W Swadling, 'Restitution and *Bona Fide* Purchase' in W Swadling (ed), *The Limits of Restitutionary Claims: A Comparative Analysis* (United Kingdom National Committee of Comparative Law, London, 1997) at 97ff; G Virgo, 'What is the Law of Restitution About?' in W Cornish et al (eds), *Restitution: Past, Present and Future* (Hart Publishing, Oxford, 1998) at 313-314; *Box v Barclays Bank plc* (1998) 5 Lloyd's Rep Banking 185.

27   Thus, conversion is often described as a proprietary action: J Baker, *An Introduction to English Legal History* (3rd ed, Butterworths, London, 1990) at 451; J Fleming, *The Law of Torts* (9th ed, LBC Information Services, Sydney, 1998) at 61.

28   *Hartop v Hoare* (1743) 2 Str 1187; 93 ER 1117; *Cooper v Chitty* (1756) 1 Burr 20; 97 ER 166; see also J Baker and S Milsom, *Sources of English Legal History* (Butterworths, London, 1986) at 533-534. The point here is that while there will always be some "wrongdoing" in the sense that the defendant has interfered with a right of the plaintiff, analytically the basis of the claim is no longer the defendant's fault or culpability.

vindicatio, liability in conversion extends beyond those who hold the res itself, the claimant's case is nevertheless founded upon an interference with an asset that is inconsistent with the claimant's right in rem to that same asset. Thus, in *Baldwin v Cole*, Holt CJ stated: "what is a conversion, but an assuming upon one's self the property and right of disposing another's goods?"[29] More recently, in *Kuwait Airways Corporation v Iraqi Airways Co (Nos 4 and 5)*,[30] Lord Hoffmann said: "the tort exists to protect proprietary or possessory rights in property; it is committed by an act inconsistent with those rights and it is a tort of strict liability. So conversion is 'a taking with the intent of exercising over the chattel an ownership inconsistent with the real owner's right of possession': per Rolfe B in *Fouldes v Willoughby*.[31] And the person who takes is treated as being under a continuing strict duty to restore the chattel to its owner".[32] The working of conversion can be presented diagrammatically as follows.

Figure 3: Conversion

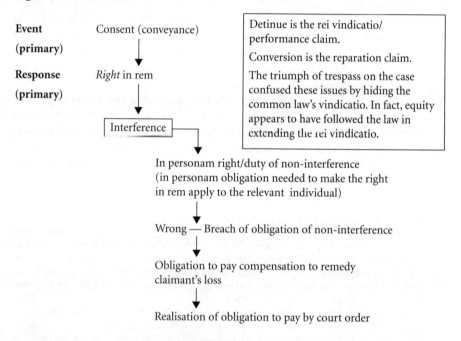

29   (1705) 6 Mod 212; 87 ER 964.
30   [2002] 2 WLR 1353. Lord Nicholls (at 1375) briefly considered the suggestion that the claim in conversion might be analysed in terms of the principle of unjust enrichment. It is clear, however, from his Lordship's characterisation of this suggestion as a "radical reappraisal" that he did not regard this as the nature of the tort at the present time.
31   (1841) 8 M & W 540 at 550; 151 ER 1153 at 1157.
32   [2002] 2 WLR 1353 at 1388. Generally, see T Weir, *Tort Law* (Oxford University Press, Oxford, 2002) at chapter 11.

The indirect nature of the common law's response to the interference with the right in rem through the law of wrongs must be acknowledged.[33] Although the so-called "proprietary torts" are atypical of civil wrongs generally, in that they impose strict liability, they have traditionally been classified as wrongs and they do give rise to a response, one of reparative compensation, that is usually associated with wrongs. However, while the formal nature of these claims is that of redress for a wrong, it is much less clear whether it is appropriate analytically to describe the law as responding here to wrongdoing or to the existence of the claimant's rights in rem. There are three factors that argue strongly in favour of the latter view.

First, the wrong of interference is intelligible only in terms of the claimant's subsisting right in rem.[34] The analytical structure of wrongs is such that they necessarily pre-suppose the existence of some prior right.[35] The wrong is the breach of that prior right, but not its source. Thus, in cases of conversion, the right that the defendant has breached is a right in personam against the particular defendant not to interfere with the claimant's right in rem.[36] The defendant's action is wrongful only because at the moment of the interference the claimant had a right to, and the defendant a duty of, non-interference. This in personam right to non-interference, however, must in turn be referable to some primary event. One has to answer the question: why should the claimant have a right to non-interference? The answer to this question is and can only be found in the claimant's persisting right in rem. The right in rem is what gives the claimant the right to undisturbed enjoyment of the asset, and it is the right to undisturbed enjoyment of the asset that justifies the law imposing liability on the defendant for infringing that right. The only complication in this is the need for the interposition of an in personam right-duty of non-interference, to which the law then, formally, responds. This, however, is the price the common law must pay for the (historical) loss of its rei vindicatio.[37]

Secondly, whatever the form of the claim in the action in conversion, its function is undoubtedly to protect the claimant's rights in rem in the asset. This is clear not only from the historical origins of conversion, but also from what counts as interference. In *Fouldes v Willoughby*,[38] the defendant asked the plaintiff to remove his horses from the defendant's ferry. The plaintiff refused

---

33   P Birks, "Personal Property: Proprietary Rights and Remedies" (2000) 11 *King's College Law Journal* 1 at 7.

34   L Smith, *The Law of Tracing* (Clarendon, Oxford, 1997) at 285.

35   P Birks, 'The Concept of a Civil Wrong' in D Owen (ed), *Philosophical Foundations of Tort Law* (Clarendon, Oxford, 1995) at chapter 1.

36   J Penner, *The Idea of Property in Law* (Clarendon, Oxford, 1997) at 128-152; A Honoré, 'Ownership' in A Guest (ed), *Oxford Essays in Jurisprudence* (Oxford University Press ,Oxford, 1961) at 119-120; J Harris, *Property and Justice* (Clarendon, Oxford, 1996) at 24, 86-90 refers to this as the non-trespass rule.

37   While somewhat convoluted, there is nothing illogical in the indirect enforcement of rights in rem. The nature of the right and the means of protecting and enforcing the right are distinct issues. See L Smith, *The Law of Tracing*, above n 34 at 59-60.

38   (1841) 8 M & W 540 at 550; 151 ER 1153 at 1157.

and the defendant led the horses from the ferry and let them loose. This was held not to be conversion because the defendant's actions were not inconsistent with the plaintiff's dominion over the horses. In contrast, in *Moorgate Mercantile Co Ltd v Finch*,[39] the defendant borrowed a car and used it for smuggling. The car was seized by and forfeited to Customs and the defendant was held liable in conversion. In the English Court of Appeal's view, it was inevitable that in using the car in that way forfeiture would result, and forfeiture was inconsistent with the plaintiff's proprietary rights.

Thirdly, the purpose of legal taxonomy is to offer a map or structure of the subject matter that enables it to be better and more clearly understood. To achieve this, however, it is not enough to be content with superficial appearances. The taxonomist "must be willing to deal in differences which really matter".[40] It is classification on the basis of essential or fundamental similarities and differences that keeps us from lumping whales together with sharks, or treating the sex of the seahorse that gives birth to its young as female.[41] In the present context, there can be no doubt that in claims such as that in conversion, the law is formally responding to a defendant's wrongdoing. However, the explanatory force of the notion of a wrong is extremely weak. As Professor Birks notes: "to say that a consequence follows certain conduct because that conduct is a breach of a primary duty is to offer a formal explanation but not a satisfying one. The real explanation has to be completed in every case from the policies and values underlying the recognition of the primary duty which is in question."[42] The real explanation of the claim in conversion is the protection of the claimant's rights in rem. If, therefore, the taxonomy of the private law is to deal in differences that really matter and thereby offer more than a simply formal explanation, it is arguably more enlightening to identify the event to which the law is responding as the claimant's right in rem.

Equity's protection of rights in rem

A claimant holding an equitable property right may seek directly to enforce that right. In substance, the claimant asks the court to declare his equitable ownership of the identified asset.[43] Thus, for example, in *Macmillan Inc v*

---

39   [1962] 1 QB 701.

40   P Birks, "Equity in the Modern Law: An Exercise in Taxonomy" (1996) 26 *University of Western Australia Law Review* 1 at 16.

41   These examples are adapted from Birks, "Equity in the Modern Law: An Exercise in Taxonomy", above n 40 at 6.

42   P Birks, 'The Concept of a Civil Wrong' in D Owen (ed), *Philosophical Foundations of Tort Law* (Clarendon, Oxford, 1997) at 51.

43   *Westdeutsche Landesbank Girozentrale v Islington London Borough Council* [1996] AC 669 at 707 per Lord Browne-Wilkinson. See also P Birks, "Property and Unjust Enrichment: Categorical Truths" [1997] *New Zealand Law Review* 623 at 650; P Birks, "Personal Property: Proprietary Rights and Remedies" (2000) 11 *King's College Law Journal* 1 at 4-5; M McInnes, "Knowing Receipt and the Protection of Trust Property: *Banton v CIBC*" (2002) 81 *Canadian Bar Review* 171 at 176-177.

Bishopsgate Investment Trust plc (No 3),[44] the claimant effectively asked the court to declare that the shares which Rupert Maxwell caused to be trans-ferred to Berlitz belonged in equity to it and that Berlitz as transferee but not bona fide purchaser thus held the shares on trust for it. Such a claim, a rei vindicatio,[45] is based upon the claimant's equitable proprietary entitlement to the asset in the defendant's hands and will succeed without proof of fault. The declaration of equitable ownership is, however, inert.[46] In order to recover the asset itself and thus fully vindicate his property right, a claimant also needs a right as against the defendant to have the defendant transfer the asset to him. This right, which is a right in personam distinct from and additional to the right in rem, is accordingly the mechanism by which the particular defendant's interference with the claimant's right in rem is sanctioned.

The important analytical question for present purposes is thus: what is the event that gives rise to the in personam sanctioning right? We can immediately reject any suggestion that the event is the order of the court. The court's order is remedial only in the weakest possible sense.[47] It reflects a pre-existing right that arose at the moment of the interference and therefore well before the litigation ever began. This would be true, moreover, even if the court were not prepared to order the transfer of the particular asset, but instead ordered the defendant to pay a sum of money.[48] The remedy, whether in specie or in pecuniary form, reflects and fulfils a pre-existing right. The in personam duty to transfer the asset is and must be a response to the claimant's right in rem. This conclusion rests upon three considerations.

First, the existence of the duty to transfer the asset is intelligible only in terms of the pre-existing right in rem. Where, as with the rei vindicatio, the claimant's case rests on his right in rem, the only justification or explanation of the claimant's right to have the asset transferred to him is that right in rem.[49] He is entitled to the asset precisely because it is his. This point can also be demonstrated in a different way. As a possessor, a defendant has a form of

---

44   [1996] 1 WLR 387.

45   B Nicholas, *An Introduction to Roman Law* (Clarendon, Oxford, 1962) at 125-128; W Buckland, *A Textbook of Roman Law from Augustus to Justinian* (3rd ed, rev by P Stein, Cambridge University Press, Cambridge, 1963) at 675; F Schulz, *Classical Roman Law* (Clarendon, Oxford, 1951) at 368-372.

46   P Birks, "Property and Unjust Enrichment: Categorical Truths", above n 43 at 656; P Birks, "Property, Unjust Enrichment, and Tracing" (2001) 54 *Current Legal Problems* 231 at 250-251.

47   P Birks, "Rights, Wrongs, Remedies" (2000) 20 Oxford Journal of Legal Studies 1 at 15.

48   It is important not to infer from the pecuniary nature of the award that the award is in response to some wrongdoing. It is perfectly rational for a system of law to convert all obliga-tions into pecuniary form at the point of judgment. In Roman law, this was referred to as the principle of condemnatio pecuniaria. See H Jolowicz, *Historical Introduction to the Study of Roman Law* (Cambridge University Press, Cambridge, 1961) at 210-212, 220-221.

49   This is manifested in the definition of those entitled to bring a claim in conversion in terms of those with either actual possession or the right to possess. Possession is central to the common law concept of title to chattels. Generally, see A Honoré, 'Ownership' in A Guest (ed), *Oxford Essays in Jurisprudence* (Oxford University Press, Oxford, 1961) at 113; C Rose, "Possession as the Origin of Property" (1985) 52 *University of Chicago Law Review* 73.

property right that is good against all except the rightful owner.[50] Thus, for example, in *Armory v Delamirie*,[51] Pratt CJ said: "the finder of a jewel, though he does not by such finding acquire an absolute property or ownership, yet he has such a property as will enable him to keep it against all but the rightful owner". The only reason, therefore, for imposing a duty on the defendant to transfer the asset, thereby overreaching his possessory right, is that the claimant is indeed the owner and thus has a superior entitlement. The claimant's right in rem is, therefore, both a necessary and sufficient explanation of the duty to transfer the asset.

However, Birks suggested that the event that gives rise to this right is "the receipt of an asset belonging to another".[52] While the description of the event as the acquisition of an asset belonging to another is not inappropriate, and may indeed be more graphic, it is nevertheless plain that such an event is not intelligible without the reference to the right in rem. The fundamental legally relevant element of this event is that the thing received is one that belongs to another. While the receipt of the asset is that which brings the claimant to court, the receipt itself is legally significant only because another person owns the asset received. The mere receipt of an asset is incapable of generating any rights to recovery and it is only where the receipt infringes the claimant's persisting right in rem that there is anything for the law to respond to. Notwithstanding this, however, Birks insisted that this event must be located in his miscellaneous fourth category. This is so, it seems, primarily because of Birks's commitment to the proposition that rights in rem cannot be a category of event.[53] While in principle one could continue to insist that the event must still be located in the miscellaneous fourth category, such is the prevalence of property rights in the legal system that this would not only greatly distend the miscellaneous category, but it would also seem to run counter to the very impetus for taxonomy: the identification from the mass of individual genera and species.

Secondly, the identification of the event as the claimant's right in rem is consistent with and gives effect to the idea that the duty to transfer the asset is consequential upon the rei vindicatio. The claimant's claim, it will be recalled, is based upon his right in rem in the asset and serves to vindicate that right. In essence, what the claimant seeks is the return of his property. The additional right in personam to a transfer of the asset is merely the perfection or realisation of his claim to recover his asset. The right in

---

50   *J A Pye (Oxford) Ltd v Graham* [2003] 1 AC 419. Indeed, in some circumstances possession becomes a property right good against all including the rightful owner.

51   (1772) 1 Str 505; 93 ER 664. Generally, see W Rogers, *Winfield and Jolowicz on Tort* (15th ed, Sweet & Maxwell, London, 1998) at 600; A Dugdale, *Clerk & Lindsell on Torts* (18th ed, Sweet & Maxwell, London, 2000) at 749.

52   P Birks, "Property and Unjust Enrichment: Categorical Truths" [1997] *New Zealand Law Review* 623 at 657; P Birks, "Property, Unjust Enrichment, and Tracing" (2001) 54 *Current Law Problems* 231 at 251; P Birks, "Unjust Enrichment and Wrongful Enrichment" (2001) 79 *Texas Law Review* 1767 at 1775.

53   P Birks, "Property, Unjust Enrichment, and Tracing", above n 52 at 245.

personam is only necessary because, as argued earlier, the right in rem is inert and can be made to bear directly on the particular defendant only through the imposition of a further personal obligation. Moreover, the claimant's right in rem is also the basis upon which the courts conceive themselves to be acting. Thus, for example, in *Macmillan Inc v Bishopsgate Investment Trust plc (No 3)*,[54] Millett J, as he then was, said: "any liability of the defendants to restore the shares or their proceeds to Macmillan or to pay compensation for their failure to do so must be based upon Macmillian's continuing equitable ownership of the shares."

Thirdly, the event that gives rise to the duty to transfer the asset must be the claimant's right in rem because there is simply no other event in play that would entitle the claimant to the delivery up of the asset. Almost by definition the event cannot be in the category of consent. The claimant's case arises as a result of a non-consensual transfer of the asset. Nor, however, is the event found in the wrong of interference with the asset. While, of course, it is the interference that brings the claimant into court,[55] the mere receipt of the asset by the defendant is not of itself wrongful.[56] It is thus not surprising that the claimant is not required to prove fault or wrongdoing as a pre-condition to establishing the defendant's duty to transfer the asset. This conclusion is, moreover, borne out by a comparison with the recaption of goods.[57] Here, the claimant does not need the court's help to recover the asset, but instead relies directly on his property right. Thus, for example, if the claimant sees his bicycle, which has been taken from him, leaning against a wall in the High Street, he is able fully to vindicate his right in rem in the bicycle by simply re-taking it. The act of re-taking, and the duty imposed on the defendant to transfer the bicycle in cases where it cannot be simply re-taken, are functionally equivalent. Both serve to fulfil the claimant's right in rem by restoring the asset to the claimant. This equivalence suggests strongly that, at an analytical level, the duty imposed to transfer the asset must arise as a consequence of the claimant's right in rem.

Locating the event in the category of unjust enrichment, rather than in consent or wrongdoing, seems more plausible, though ultimately this possibility must also be rejected. Although the event could be made to fit within the

---

54   [1995] 3 All ER 747 at 758.

55   There is an important analytical distinction between the *possibility* of analysing the claimant's case as one for redress for a wrong and the *necessity* of doing so. In cases where the law will give effect directly to the primary right, there is no need for a wrongs analysis. Perhaps the clearest example of this is the case of contract. The right to specific performance is not a response to the wrong of breach of contract, but is the fulfilment of the right to performance. Thus, specific performance is available where there is no breach: *Hasham v Zenab* [1960] AC 316. See also *Semelhago v Paramadevan* (1996) 136 DLR (4th) 1 (performance secured by an award of money as a substitute).

56   Birks, "Property and Unjust Enrichment: Categorical Truths" [1997] *New Zealand Law Review* 623 at 657; P Birks, "Property, Unjust Enrichment, and Tracing" (2001) 54 *Current Law Probems* 231 at 251.

57   *In re Eastgate* [1905] 1 KB 465; *Tilley v Bowman Ltd* [1910] 1 KB 745.

notion of unjust enrichment, principally by treating the notion of "enrichment" as satisfied by the mere factual receipt of the asset, as Birks notes, it is neither desirable nor plausible to do so.[58] One consequence of identifying the event as unjust enrichment would be to subject the claimant's rights to the defence of change of position. The consequence is that merely because of the inert nature of rights in rem, which requires the imposition of a consequential duty to transfer the asset, the rights in rem would be subjected to the inherent weakness of all rights consequent upon unjust enrichment. Not only is this not in fact the law, but it would also represent an undesirable weakening of the security and enforceability of property rights.

An analysis of the duty to transfer the asset in terms of unjust enrichment must also now be regarded as having been ruled out as a matter of precedent by the decision of the House of Lords in *Foskett v McKeown*.[59] The case concerned a claim to money stolen by a trustee to acquire, in part, an insurance policy. The House of Lords held that the beneficiaries of the trust were entitled to a beneficial interest in the proceeds of the policy in the same proportion as the trust money that had been used to acquire it. For present purposes, the importance of the case is that their Lordships treated the beneficiaries' rights in the proceeds of the policy as arising, not from unjust enrichment, but from the beneficiaries' rights in the original trust money. Lord Browne-Wilkinson's view was that: "the only trusts at issue are the express trusts of the purchasers trust deed. Under those express trusts the purchasers were entitled to the equitable interests in the original moneys ... Like any other equitable proprietary interest, those equitable proprietary interests ... now exist in any other property which, in law, now represents the original trust assets."[60] These comments leave little room for any conclusion other than that the event from which the duty to transfer arises following a successful vindicatio is the claimant's property rights.

All that has been discussed thus far in respect of equity's rei vindicatio can be represented diagrammatically.

---

58   P Birks, "Property and Unjust Enrichment: Categorical Truths", above n 56 at 657-658.

59   [2001] 1 AC 102. Professor Birks acknowledges this in "Property, Unjust Enrichment, and Tracing", above n 56 and in 'Receipt' in P Birks and A Pretto (eds), *Breach of Trust* (Hart Publishing, Oxford, 2002) at 216-217. For further discussion of *Foskett*, see P Millett, 'Proprietary Restitution' at chapter 12 in this book.

60   *Foskett v McKeown* [2001] 1 AC 102 at 108.

Figure 4: The rei vindicatio in equity

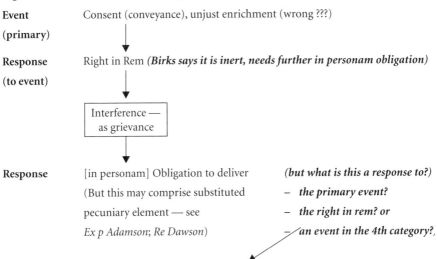

Event
(primary)

Consent (conveyance), unjust enrichment (wrong ???)

Response
(to event)

Right in Rem *(**Birks says it is inert, needs further in personam obligation**)*

Interference —
as grievance

Response

[in personam] Obligation to deliver
(But this may comprise substituted
pecuniary element — see
Ex p Adamson; *Re Dawson*)

*(**but what is this a response to?**)*
– *the primary event?*
– *the right in rem? or*
– *an event in the 4th category?,*

Thus Birks's analysis ("Property and Unjust Enrichment: Categorical Truths" [1997]
***New Zealand Law Review* 623 at 657):**

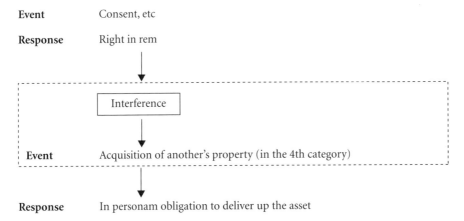

Event

Consent, etc

Response

Right in rem

Interference

Event

Acquisition of another's property (in the 4th category)

Response

In personam obligation to deliver up the asset

Birks' analysis tries to unpack the interference and treats "grievance" as "wrong" — but
there is no need to create a new event at all.

We are now in a position to compare the manner in which protection of
property rights is carried through by common law and in equity, thus:

Figure 5: Protecting rights in rem at common law and in equity

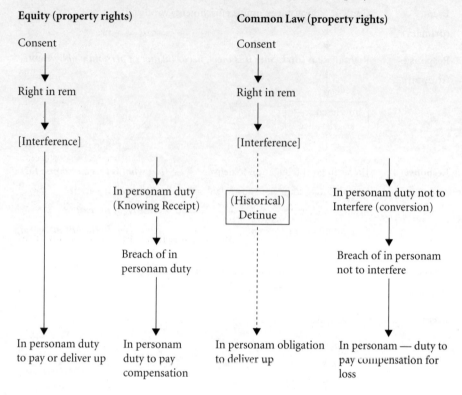

Notes:
1. At common law, the interference with a right in rem is in substance sanctioned by an in personam obligation to pay compensation. Cf the historical role of detinue.
2. However, because the common law does not know the rei vindicatio (thus the claimant cannot be heard in court to rely directly on his right in rem) (Cf the historical role of detinue), the common law has come to interpose an in personam obligation of non-interference with the claimant's right in rem. The in personam obligation to pay compensation for loss is then formally referable to that obligation (but indirectly referable to the right in rem).
2A. In the case of the historical form/role of detinue, it was a claim directly to vindicate the right in rem, which was realised by an in personam duty to deliver up the asset or to pay the money equivalent of the asset (nb: not the value of the loss to the claimant – which is what conversion does). Conversion (through trespass on the case) came to dominate the field, thus "hiding" detinue's role as a common law rei vindicatio.
3. The existence of the in personam duty of non-interference is intelligible only in terms of the right in rem:
    (i)   the in personam duty of non-interference is necessarily dependant upon the right in rem – one only has a duty not to interfere because of the claimant's ownership;
    (ii) the right in rem is an obligation mediated through the res and binds the whole world rather than individuals. The interference with the right, however, can only be by a particular individual. Thus, the sanctioning right can only be by way of an in personam obligation, and this is so for both vindication and loss claims ie detinue and conversion.

4. The right to compensation for loss is thus a response:
   — formally, to the breach of the in personam right to non-interference;
   — in substance, to the interference with the right in rem.
5. The in personam rights generated from the right in rem can be expressed in terms of the realisation or sanctioning of the right – that is: how (by what mechanism) is a right held against the world (but no-one in particular) made to apply to a particular individual? The answer depends in large measure on the nature of the available mechanisms for realisation.
   (i) Where the system of law will directly realise the right in rem, that right is made to bite on the individual by an in personam order to deliver up the asset (detinue at common law; and in equity);
   (ii) Where the system does not directly realise the right in rem, that right is made to bite on the individual by way of an in personam duty of non-interference (conversion at common law / knowing receipt in equity).

Rights in rem in substituted assets: law and equity

Turning now to the central focus of this chapter, how do common law and equity deal with rights *in rem* in respect of substituted assets?

Figure 6: The rei vindicatio (in equity and at common law) and the issue of substitution

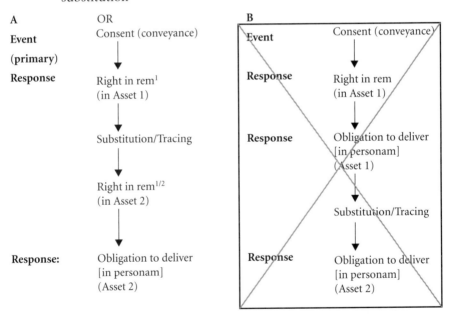

Analytically, the key question is, which right does tracing transmit from Asset 1 to Asset 2? The diagram is designed to reveal two possible answers. In part A, the answer postulated is the right in rem itself. That right in rem detaches from Asset 1 and goes to Asset 2, thus enabling the claimant to say of Asset 2 "that thing is mine!". In part B the answer postulated is the right to have the asset delivered. The claimant's in personam right to restoration of the asset

(Asset 1) is transferred to Asset 2. The analysis in part A is more consistent with the general understanding of what occurs in tracing and is consistent with the doctrine of overreaching.

Professor Birks argued, supported since by others,[61] that all rights born of tracing are responses to the legal event of unjust enrichment. This would require that, under the analysis in part A, the right in rem in Asset 2 must be a new right (right in rem^2). If, however, the right is the same right, the event generating the right in rem in Asset 2 is the same event as gave rise to the right in rem in Asset 1. The analysis in part A is of course silent on whether the right in rem in Asset 2 is the same right as in Asset 1 or whether analytically it is a new right. In fact, it is quite possible to concede that the right is a new right without having to adopt Birks's position. The crucial point, if it is a new right, is: what is the event to which it is a response? Birks says it is a new right because of the "break" in the chain – the old right is replaced with a power in rem in the claimant to vest a title in the substituted asset in himself. The event is unjust enrichment. Although the new Asset 2 never belonged to the claimant it was obtained at the claimant's expense by using his Asset 1; and the unjust factor was absence of consent.[62]

The doctrine of overreaching suggests, however, that it is the same right. Overreaching allows and explains how an authorised disposition of a trust asset by the trustee extinguishes the beneficiary's equitable interest in the asset (Asset 1), and how the beneficiary acquires an equitable interest in whatever asset (Asset 2) was acquired in substitution for the first asset. This must involve a transfer of the same right in rem in Asset 1 to Asset 2. If it does not, then this would mean that each new asset acquired by the trust in substitution for an existing asset would be held on a new separate trust. This is problematic in that:

(i)   it completely destroys the unity of the trust (this is highly counter-institutive); and,

(ii) it would fundamentally undermine the perpetuity rule — perpetuity would run differently for each new asset/trust, meaning the "trust" could go on forever.

A complete picture of equity's protection of property rights in asset substitution contexts requires further reference to the relationship between equity's rei vindicatio and its possible realisation of rights in rem by means of a lien.

---

61   A Burrows, "Proprietary Restitution: Unmasking Unjust Enrichment" (2001) 117 *Law Quarterly Review* 412; R Chambers, 'Tracing and Unjust Enrichment' in J Neyers, M McInnes and S Pitel (eds), *Understanding Unjust Enrichment* (Hart Publishing, Oxford, 2004) at chapter 11. Cf G Virgo, 'Vindicating Vindication: *Foskett v McKeown* Reviewed' in A Hudson (ed), *New Perspectives on Property Law, Obligations and Restitution* (Cavendish, London, 2004) at chapter 10. For further discussion, see L Smith, "Unravelling Proprietary Restitution" (2004) 40 *Canadian Business Law Journal* 317.

62   P Birks, "Property, Unjust Enrichment, and Tracing" (2001) 54 *Current Law Problems* 231 at 246.

Figure 7: Rei vindicatio (in equity), substitution, realisation via lien

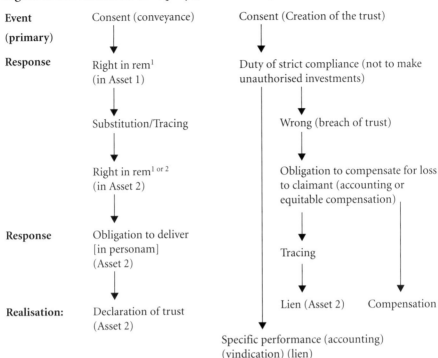

In addition to an infringement of the claimant's equitable property rights, a substitution of assets also constitutes wrongful conduct by the trustee (breach of his duty of strict compliance). This gives rise to an in personam obligation to restore the trust fund, for which a lien is the response. This is the point made forcefully by Lord Millett in *Foskett*.[63] If the claimant chooses a lien, he is affirming the unauthorised nature of the investment and is seeking a restoration of the trust fund. The claimant's claim is personal, and the lien is available to secure the trustee's personal obligation. The claimant is given the advantage of a lien because he is equity's special concern and because of the need to maintain the integrity of the trust relationship.

The alternative analysis of the option of a lien is that it is a remedy alternative to the rei vindicatio. The claimant asserts his subsisting equitable property right, but that ownership is realised not via a declaration of ownership (and re-conveyance), but by the imposition of an obligation to repay the value of Asset 1.[64] The mere fact that the claimant's claim is one based on his property right does not entail that the realisation of that right must be by way of a declaration of ownership — even in Roman law, as already seen, the rei vindicatio was subject to an alternative in the form of a condemnatio pecuniaria. That the

---

63   [2001] 1 AC 102 at 130.
64   See P Birks "Personal Property: Proprietary Rights and Remedies" (2000) 11 *King's College Law Journal* 1 at 5.

choice between the alternatives is the claimant's reflects the claimant's position as equity's special concern. This analysis is consistent with the idea of tracing as a neutral process silent as to both the claim and the remedy. However, Birks' view cannot be correct, since the rei vindicatio is concerned with the substitution of the asset, and not with the value of the asset.[65] It must also be understood that the claimant is not simply electing the remedy, but rather the claim itself (although this is not always clear in practice, conceptually it must be the case).

THE CONTENT OF THE LAW OF TRACING

Tracing is located unambiguously therefore within the law of property rights.[66] It concerns the identification of substituted assets in respect of which a claimant can assert a claim in rem, with all that that entails so far as legal protection is concerned, as discussed above. The rules of tracing are therefore properly characterised as part of the law of property. These rules are arbitrary evidential problem solvers. The common law, in its widest sense, accords holders of property rights the privilege of being able to assert rights in rem over different assets from those originally in issue. The rules of tracing provide the answer to the question: in respect of which different assets are such claims permitted? The historical division between common law and equity led to different rules being articulated depending upon whether the claimant seeking to trace had common law rights in rem or equitable rights in rem in or over the original asset. Justice Hayton[67] has rightly said that this matter of origin should no longer matter. There should be a single set of rules for tracing substitute assets, and these should be the equitable rules given their more flexible content and the advantages they therefore offer to potential claimants. The propensity for the equitable rules to produce appropriately just responses in the vast majority of cases is a major factor in choosing them over the common law rules. Once it is understood that the rules are essentially arbitrary, in the sense that their content is not forced upon us by the justificatory principles underlying why the law permits tracing and how tracing is explained doctrinally, the actual content of the rules is open for debate and choice. Once the system allows the remarkably claimant-friendly possibility of tracing, as a consequence of a strong commitment to the fundamental importance of property rights within the system, it seems somewhat incoherent and certainly rather churlish to limit in rem (and derivative in personam) claims in respect of different assets by castrating the rules of identification themselves.

The key issue in determining the content of the rules of tracing must clearly be identification of the principles upon which that content is based. Where as a matter of fact in the real world it can be established that Asset 1 has physically been exchanged for Asset 2, we have an easy case. But where it is not possible to

---

65   Ross Grantham and I made this error in our discussion of tracing in *Enrichment and Restitution in New Zealand* (Hart Publishing, Oxford, 2000) at 439.
66   See also P Millett, 'Proprietary Restitution', at chapter 12 in this book.
67   D Hayton, 'Unique Rules for the Unique Institution, the Trust', at chapter 11 in this book.

establish such matter of fact exchange, by means of a simple substitutionary equation, as is usually so in the context of mixtures, and in particular mixtures of funds in banking accounts, the rules adopted will in large measure be founded upon presumptions. What principles ought to guide the content of the presumptions which thus constitute the rules? The present debate about the appropriateness of the presumption historically derived from *Clayton's Case*,[68] wherein first debits are accounted to the first credits in mixed funds, provides some clues. There has been much anxiety whether this presumption best deals with cases of mixed funds where one or more claimants are all "innocent" victims of the mixing of their assets. How do multiple claimants trace into the mixed fund? What guides the answer? In *Commerzbank Aktiengesellschaft v IMB Morgan Plc*,[69] Lawrence Collins J discounted the *Clayton's case* presumption as "impracticable and disproportionate",[70] and adopted instead a proportionate rule of identification: the claimants were to be entitled to the mixed fund pari passu. Thus, one principle, which seems an eminently reasonable one, is not to articulate complex rules, and apparently even simple ones, which in their application are likely to deplete severely or even to exhaust the fund in question. That would be a rule designed to defeat the very objective for which it was being articulated! A second principle is that where multiple claimants are concerned, there should be a commitment to achieving a just distribution based on the proportions of the proprietary inputs into the mixed fund.[71] That again seems a reasonable principle given that tracing is about identifying asset substitutes for assets once owned by the claimants. Accordingly, applying these considerations, the new presumptive rule according to Lawrence Collins J was to be that "the fund will be shared rateably amongst the beneficiaries according to the amount of their contributions".[72] This rule reflected the best justificatory principles to be applied in deciding upon and articulating the evidential problem solver. Lawrence Collins J also rightly complimented as "valuable"[73] the discussion of the same issue in New South Wales by Campbell J in *Re Sutherland; French Caledonia Travel Service Pty Ltd*

---

68   (1816) 1 Mer 572; 35 ER 781.
69   [2004] EWHC 2771.
70   *Commerzbank Aktiengesellschaft v IMB Morgan Plc* [2004] EWHC 2771 at [39], [50].
71   In *Re Sutherland; French Caledonia Travel Service Pty Ltd (in Liq)* (2003) 59 NSWLR 361, Campbell J, after dealing with the inadequacies of the rule in *Clayton's case*, included a section in his judgment (at 417ff, [173]-[216]) expressly concerned with the question whether rateable sharing was the preferable rule. His Honour in effect announced a further principle informing the rules of tracing into mixed funds, being that rateable allocation amongst equitable claimants depended upon "the claims of the claimants being equal", in the senses, first, that all claimants had a charge over the mixed fund in issue and, second, that no claimants were entitled to equitable priority as against the other claimants (which included whether any claimants' claims might be postponed — by reason of personal equities, for example — to those of others, and whether claimants might have access to other remedies in rem). His Honour also discussed the possibility that the claimants fell into several classes, where some had charges in respect of the fund at a time before the fund fell to a level below that required to meet their claims (the lowest intermediate balance rule, another rule of tracing).
72   *Commerzbank Aktiengesellschaft v IMB Morgan Plc* [2004] EWCH 2771 at [48], [50].
73   *Commerzbank Aktiengesellschaft v IMB Morgan Plc*, above n 72 at [47].

(in Liq).[74] That case concerned a bank account in which mixed deposits belonging in equity to a number of claimants existed. A further principle to be recognised in determining the content of the rule to be applied surfaced in the analysis of Campbell J, being that since the fund in question was a bank account, and since the original assets of the claimants were deposits into that bank account, the tracing rule ought to be as consistent as possible with the legal analysis of the fund and the deposits thereinto where no issue of tracing arose. That meant that the content of banking law rules must be taken into account also. Again, this seems an eminently reasonable principle to adopt. Coherence is surely a desideratum of the private law in general? Indeed, Campbell J's determination of the inapplicability of *Clayton's case* was in large measure posited upon the nature of the banker-customer relationship.[75] A further sensible principle used by his Honour was the avoidance of fictions as to the intentions of various parties.[76]

PROBLEMS FOR THE LAW OF CLAIMS

A brief mention has already been made of the primary disagreement still bedevilling the law of tracing. This is the issue of exactly how the claimant's right in rem in respect of the identified substitute asset arises. Is it the old right in rem or is it a new right in rem? What does the new understanding of the law of tracing have to tell us about this conundrum? Ross Grantham and I have discussed this issue in our most recent foray into the structure of private law.[77]

The origin of the right in rem over the substitute asset

Until recently, the increasingly accepted view of the origin of the claimant's right in the traced substitute asset was that the right always and necessarily arises as a response to the principle of unjust enrichment.[78] Birks stated: "Proprietary interests contingent on tracing, which is as much as to say propri-etary interests in traceable substitutes for other assets in which the claimant undoubtedly did hold a proprietary interest, always arise from unjust enrichment."[79] This conclusion rests on the view that the right cannot be attrib-utable to any other event. It cannot be a response to consent because the right

---

74   (2003) 59 NSWLR 361.
75   *Re Sutherland; French Caledonia Travel Service Pty Ltd (in Liq)* (2003) 59 NSWLR 361 at 411, [151]-[153].
76   *Re Sutherland; French Caledonia Travel Service Pty Ltd (in Liq)*, above n 75 at 380-382, [61]-[65].
77   R Grantham and C Rickett, "Property Rights as a Legally Significant Event" (2003) 62 *Cambridge Law Journal* 717 at 744ff.
78   P Birks, "Property and Unjust Enrichment: Categorical Truths" [1997] *New Zealand Law Review* 623 at 661. See also P Birks, "Establishing a Proprietary Base" (1995) 3 *Restitution Law Review* 83 at 91-92; P Birks, "On Taking Seriously the Difference Between Tracing and Claiming" (1997) 11 *Trust Law International* 2 at 7-8; L Smith, *The Law of Tracing* (Clarendon, Oxford, 1997) at 299-301; C Rotherham, "The Metaphysics of Tracing: Substituted Title and Property Rhetoric" (1996) 34 *Osgoode Hall Law Journal* 321; S Worthington, 'Justifying Claims to Secondary Profits' in E Schrage (ed), *Unjust Enrichment and the Law of Contract* (Kluwer, The Hague, 2001) at 463-464. See also references cited in n 61 above.
79   P Birks, "Property and Unjust Enrichment: Categorical Truths", above n 78 at 661.

in the product arises by operation of law; it cannot be attributed to the defendant's wrongdoing, as there are cases where the defendant is wholly innocent; and it cannot, it is said, be attributed to the claimant's right in rem in the original asset because property rights are not a species of event. Thus, it is concluded, the right that arises in the substitute as a result of the tracing process must be a response to the defendant's unjust enrichment.

However, once it is recognised that, in cases where the claimant retains legal or equitable rights in rem in the original asset even after the transfer of possession to the defendant, those persisting rights in rem alone are the (and, indeed, are the only) basis for recovery, then it follows that the most likely event to which the recognition of rights in the traceable product is a response is also the property rights held in the original asset. This is most obviously so where the claim is in respect of equitable rights in rem. As *Foskett v McKeown*[80] illustrates, where the claimant's claim is one to vindicate his rights in rem in the asset, the law's response is simply to declare that the claimant's rights in the original asset are now exigible against the traceable product. Even if we need insist either that doctrinally the rights in rem in the traceable product are new rights, or that there must be imposed upon the defendant a further subsidiary obligation to transfer rights in the traceable product in order to give effect to the otherwise inert rei vindicatio,[81] these rights or obligations must arise from the claimant's rights in rem in the original asset. The persistence of the claimant's property rights is not only the most obvious source of such a response, but there will be cases, of which *Foskett* itself is an example, where there is simply no other possible basis.[82]

Although more complicated, the same conclusion must hold in respect of claims founded upon common law rights in rem. While, as we have seen earlier, the common law no longer provides a direct rei vindicatio, claims such as those in conversion do serve to vindicate legal property rights. While such claims give rise only to an in personam response, that response is nevertheless also a response to the claimant's persisting legal rights in rem. This is borne out by cases such as *Lipkin Gorman (a firm) v Karpnale Ltd*[83] and *Trustee of Jones v Jones*,[84] where the effect of tracing is conceived as being merely to permit the claimant to treat the new asset as though it were his original property. As Lord Goff said in *Lipkin Gorman*, "'tracing' or 'following' property into its product involves a decision by the owner of the original property to assert his title to the product in place of his original property".[85]

The House of Lords in *Foskett v McKeown* has confirmed that a claimant's rights in rem in the traceable product are a response to, and a means to vindicate, the claimants' rights in rem in the original asset. The plaintiffs in

---

80   [2001] 1 AC 102. See also P Millett, 'Proprietary Restitution' at chapter 12 in this book.
81   P Birks, "Property and Unjust Enrichment: Categorical Truths", above n 78 at 646-657.
82   In *Foskett*, the claimant's could not have made out a claim unjust enrichment. Their Lordships (without dissent on this point) found that the defendants were not enriched by the plaintiffs' value and, being innocent donees, there was no unjust factor that could be asserted against them.
83   [1991] 2 AC 548.
84   [1997] Ch 159.
85   [1991] 2 AC 548 at 573.

Foskett claimed a proportionate share of the proceeds of a life insurance policy. This claim arose out of the use by a trustee of money held in trust for the plaintiffs. This money had been settled upon trust to finance a real estate development. In fact the trustee misappropriated the trust money to pay three[86] of the five premiums paid under a life insurance policy. This policy was held for the benefit of the trustee's children. Their Lordships were agreed that the plaintiffs' claim was not one in unjust enrichment, but was one to vindicate their undoubted equitable property rights in the original trust money. Lord Browne-Wilkinson stressed that once the plaintiffs had successfully identified the insurance proceeds as the traceable product, "then as a matter of English property law the [plaintiffs] have an absolute interest in such moneys".[87] It is clear furthermore that his Lordship saw this "absolute interest"[88] as being a consequence of the plaintiffs' original interest in the money. Thus, the trust upon which the insurance proceeds would be held for the plaintiffs was not a constructive or resulting trust, but *the same express trust* as that upon which the original trust money had been held. In Lord Millett's view, the claim of a "continuing beneficial interest in the insurance money"[89] involved the "transmission of a claimant's property rights from one asset to its traceable proceeds".[90] This process was, in his Lordship's view, a part of the law of property, not the law of unjust enrichment.[91]

Despite the unanimous view of their Lordships in *Foskett* that the basis of the plaintiffs' claim was their rights in the original trust moneys, two contrary arguments are nevertheless made. First, it is suggested that it is incoherent to argue that the beneficial interest or property right can be detached from one res, float independently of any res, and then re-attach to a new res.[92] Property rights, it is said, simply cannot do this. Secondly, it is argued that the right in the substitute cannot be the same right as that held in the original asset because, following the identification of the substitute, the claimant is entitled to choose between claiming either a proportionate share of the substitute or a lien over it to secure the value of the original asset. As the right comprised in the lien is of a different type and extent from that held in the original asset, there cannot, it is said, merely be a transmission of rights in rem.[93] However, neither argument is persuasive.

As to the first argument, the suggestion that the right in rem can detach from one res and re-attach to another res is incoherent only if such an ability is

---

86   While it was clear that trust money was used to pay the fourth and fifth premiums, there was some doubt as the provenance of the money used to pay the third premium.

87   *Foskett v McKeown* [2001] 1 AC 102 at 109.

88   "Absolute" was used by Lord Browne-Wilkinson to indicate that no discretion was involved.

89   *Foskett v McKeown,* above n 87 at 127.

90   *Foskett v McKeown,* above n 87 at 127.

91   *Foskett v McKeown,* above n 87 at 127.

92   P Birks, "Property, Unjust Enrichment, and Tracing" (2001) 54 *Current Law Problems* 231 at 244-245; A Burrows, "Proprietary Restitution: Unmasking Unjust Enrichment" (2001) 117 *Law Quarterly Review* 412 at 418.

93   C Rotherham, *Proprietary Remedies in Context* (Hart Publishing, Oxford, 2002) at 98; S Worthington, 'Justifying Claims to Secondary Profits' in E Schrage (ed), *Unjust Enrichment and the Law of Contract* (Kluwer, The Hague, 2001) at 463-464; P Birks, "Property, Unjust Enrichment, and Tracing", above n 92 at 244.

not an attribute of the right in question. Unlike the res itself, which has immutable physical attributes, a right in rem is an intellectual construct whose attributes are malleable and are not bounded by factors beyond the intellectual construct itself.[94] It is, therefore, only incoherent to conclude that the right in rem cannot be transmitted from res to res if non-transmissibility is an attribute accorded to the concept of right in rem. In this respect, while matters may be different with respect to legal rights in rem, it would seem that the ability to transfer from res to res is indeed an attribute of equitable rights in rem. Indeed, without such transmissibility, the equitable doctrine of overreaching would not be sustainable.[95] Overreaching is the mechanism by which a trustee may transfer trust property from the trust fund and confer good title on the transferee unencumbered by the beneficiary's equitable interest. The corollary of the trustee's power effectively to transfer trust assets is that any assets received in exchange are made subject to the same equitable interests as bound the original trust assets. The important point for present purposes is that the doctrine of overreaching is clearly premised upon the notion that equitable rights in rem may be transmitted from one res to another. If this were not the case, the exchange of trust assets would entail that the beneficiary's equitable right in rem in the original asset was extinguished, and a new right in rem in his favour was created in the substitute. This would result in the original and later assets being held under what must conceptually be different (but in other ways identical) trusts. Moreover, such a change in the equitable property rights would also seem to entail that each exchange should be subject to the formalities requirements associated with dealings in such interests.[96] In fact, however, neither of these consequences follows the process of overreaching. Even where all of the assets of the trust are exchanged, there remains only the original trust and the rules on formalities do not apply.[97] This is difficult to explain unless the equitable interest in the new asset is the same interest as that which inured in the original asset.

The second argument is that because the claimant has the option of either a proportionate share in the substitute asset or a lien to secure the value of the original asset, the right in the substitute asset cannot be the same as the right in the original asset. This argument, however, rests on the mistaken premise that the lien is a remedial response to the infringement of the claimant's equitable right in rem. In fact, however, the lien is a (proprietary) response to a related but distinct *personal claim* against the trustee for a breach of the terms of the

---

94   Generally, see G Samuel, "Can Gaius Really be Compared to Darwin?" (2000) 49 *International and Comparative Law Quarterly* 297; K Gray, "Property in Thin Air" (1991) 50 *Cambridge Law Journal* 252; R Cotterrell, 'The Law of Property and Legal Theory' in W Twining (ed), *Legal Theory and Common Law* (Blackwell, Oxford, 1986) at chapter 5; C Rotherham, "Conceptions of Property in Common Law Discourse" (1998) 18 *Legal Studies* 41.

95   Generally, see C Harpum, "Overreaching, Trustees' Powers and the Reform of the 1925 Legislation" (1990) 49 *Cambridge Law Journal* 277; D Fox, 'Overreaching' in P Birks and A Pretto (eds), *Breach of Trust* (Hart Publishing, Oxford, 2002) at chapter 4; R Nolan, "*Vandervell v IRC*: A Case of Overreaching" (2002) 61 *Cambridge Law Journal* 169.

96   *Law of Property Act 1925* (UK), s 53(1)(c), requires all dealings with equitable interests to be evidenced in writing.

97   R Nolan, "*Vandervell v IRC*: A Case of Overreaching", above n 95.

trust upon which the original asset was held. Lord Millett makes this clear in *Foskett*:[98]

> "the simplest case is where a trustee wrongfully misappropriates trust property and uses it exclusively to acquire other property for his own benefit. In such a case the beneficiary is entitled *at his option* either to assert his beneficial ownership of the proceeds or to bring a personal claim against the trustee for breach of trust and enforce an equitable lien or charge on the proceeds to secure restoration of the trust fund."

The first claim involves the beneficiary electing to treat the substitution as authorised.[99] The substitution is thus binding on the trust: the original asset passes unencumbered to the third party and the asset received by the trustee is treated as an acquisition by the trust. The beneficiary's interest in the new asset is thus of the same type and extent as his interest in the original asset. This is the so-called proportionate share option. The second claim involves the beneficiary disavowing the substitution and treating it as wrongful. The substitution is thus not binding on the beneficiary and the trustee is personally liable to restore the asset improperly lost. While this claim is a personal one, the trustee's obligation is nevertheless secured by a lien or charge over the asset received by the trustee as the exchange product. The beneficiary is extended the advantage of the lien simply as a means of securing the trustee's performance of his personal duty. The choice between, on the one hand, a proportionate share in the substitute and, on the other hand, a lien over the substitute is, therefore, not a case of the claimant electing between different remedial options in respect of a proprietary claim. Rather, the election is as to the nature of the very claim itself: the *proprietary claim* alleges that the substitute is properly to be regarded as a trust asset, and the *personal claim* is that the trustee must restore the trust fund by reparative compensation. Where, therefore, the claimant elects to assert his equitable rights in rem in the original asset, there is only one response and that is to recognise the claimant as having exactly the same interest (as to type and extent) in the substitute as he held in the original.

The competing interests

There is one point which has thus far lain dormant in the discussion in this chapter. Much has been made of the importance of protecting rights in rem and the common law's claimant-friendly attitude to interference with assets belonging to the claimant. What, however, is the countervailing interest to that of extending the protection afforded to property rights, of which the law of tracing is now understood to be such a key part? That interest would appear to be the promotion of security of receipt of assets. How is this countervailing interest to be protected? Either the potential success of a claim might be limited directly, or there might be a restriction in the identification rules, away from

---

98   [2001] 1 AC 102 at 130.

99   There may be an analogy here with notions of ratification: *Re Halletts' Estate* (1879) 13 ChD 696 at 708-709; C Rotherham, *Proprietary Remedies in Context* (Hart Publishing, Oxford, 2002) at 94.

flexibility and generosity to claimants towards rigidity and miserliness. One obvious way, aimed at the issue of the claim itself, is to adopt the primary balancing technique used in the law of unjust enrichment, where similar competing interests are found, being the provision of defences against claims, in particular bona fide purchase and change of position. The first of these is present in the well-established limitation that tracing of assets based on an equitable right in rem cannot proceed if the legal title to the assets was acquired for value by a bona fide purchaser without notice of the equitable interest of the claimant. Will this defence be recognised in the case of tracing by claimants relying on their common law rights in rem? This is a live issue in the face of calls for a unitary system of tracing rules based on the present equitable rules. An understanding of its possible role in mediating the interests involved must lend weight to a positive response to this question. The defence of change of position exists in cases of claims founded in unjust enrichment, but has not as yet been recognised in claims founded on persisting property rights. Perhaps the defence needs extension to these latter claims also?[100] A further technique would be to recognise the need to protect security of receipt as itself, one of the guiding principles to be taken into account in determining the content of the rules of tracing. This might suggest the introduction of an element of knowledge or wrongdoing on the part of a defendant holder of property, being the other side of the bona fide purchaser coin. Wrongdoer claimants or claimants lacking in good faith might be disqualified from claiming, and from using tracing to identify substitute assets.

CONCLUDING COMMENTS

This chapter has argued that tracing is taxonomically located in the law of property, that the content of its rules needs to reflect that point, and that the remaining issues in the area need to be confronted as matters going to the articulation of the law of claims founded on property rights. Recent scholarship in the law of restitution has done much to clarify aspects of the law of tracing, not least freeing it from the constraints of the common law/equity divide, but there is now some need to move on from the unjust enrichment analyses to a much broader appreciation of the proprietary paradigm of the law of tracing.[101]

---

100 See discussion in L Smith, "Unravelling Proprietary Restitution" (2004) 40 *Canadian Business Law Journal* 317 at 331. See also C Rotherham, 'Property and Unjust Enrichment: a Misunderstood Relationship' in A Hudson (ed), *New Perspectives on Property Law, Obligations and Unjust Enrichment* (Cavendish, London, 2004) at 193-194.

101 Compare the critical discussion in C Rotherham, "Property and Unjust Enrichment: a Misunderstood Relationship", above n 100 at chapter 9.

7

Choice of Law for Equity

Tiong Min Yeo

INTRODUCTION

Choice of law

The subject of the conflict of laws, or private international law, deals with three large questions: when the court of the forum will assume and exercise jurisdiction in cases involving foreign elements; which legal system's substantive rules will be applied to resolve the dispute before the court; and when a foreign judgment or order will be recognised or enforced in the forum. This chapter is primarily concerned with the second question: the choice of law.

Ordinarily, when a problem which involves foreign elements is presented before a court, the first question that is addressed is whether the matter is one that should be resolved according to the law of the forum or the law indicated by the forum's choice of law rules. The primary justification for the potential reference to foreign law is justice to the parties. It is recognition by the forum of pluralism of values in different legal systems: the law of the forum may not be able to do justice to the parties where there are relevant connections with foreign legal systems.[1] Another objective of applying choice of law is to achieve, as much as possible, results that would be uniform in whichever country the case may be heard, to protect the security of transactions[2] and to prevent the undesirable effects of forum-shopping.[3] Embedded within these two objectives is the aim to protect the reasonable and legitimate expectations of the parties.[4]

---

1   L Collins et al (eds), *Dicey and Morris: The Conflict of Laws* (13th ed, Sweet & Maxwell, London, 2000) at [1-006] [hereafter *Dicey and Morris*].

2   HE Yntema, "The Objectives of Private International Law" (1957) 35 *Canadian Bar Review* 721 at 735.

3   Today, much of the control of forum-shopping lies within sophisticated jurisdictional techniques (see A Bell, *Forum Shopping and Venue in Transnational Litigation* (Oxford University Press, Oxford, 2003)). The uniformity of choice of law rules removes some of the incentive to forum shop.

4   PE Nygh, *Autonomy in International Contracts* (Oxford University Press, Oxford, 1999) explores this theme in the context of consensual relationships, but does not deal specifically with equitable principles.

In the methodology of the common law, the choice of law question is approached in a number of stages.[5]

First, is the matter one to which a mandatory rule, in the international sense, of the forum is applicable? If so, the law of the forum must apply. Such a rule must apply irrespective of any foreign elements in the case, generally because it is intended to protect some important interests or values of the forum, or sometimes simply because the legislature has said so. The common examples of such mandatory rules are statutory,[6] but in theory judge-made rules could also bear this character.

Secondly, if the issue is not one to be resolved by an international mandatory rule of the forum, then is the issue one to which no choice of law rules are applicable? This is a fuzzy area in the conflict of laws. There are a number of situations where the common law has developed no choice of law rules. Examples include: divorce; custody and guardianship of children; and the priorities of claims to limited funds in the control of the court. Some of these cases may be explicable in terms of a forum mandatory rule or principle, like the paramount consideration of the welfare of the child. In other cases, it may be the effect of the principle that where the courts are exercising a formative or creative function (as opposed to playing a declaratory role of pronouncing on the existence and content of rights), the law of the forum must apply.[7] Other situations may just be the result of under-investigation from the choice of law perspective.

Thirdly, if it is an issue that calls for choice of law analysis, then it is necessary to characterise it.[8] In general there are at least three levels at which this exercise can take place.

The first level is whether the issue is one which is substantive or procedural in the conflict of laws sense. Matters of procedure are always governed by the law of the forum. Matters of substance are governed by the law indicated by the forum's choice of law rules. Within the domestic law, the distinction between substance and procedure may be drawn in different places for different purposes.[9] In the conflict of laws the distinction may not be drawn in the same way that it is drawn in the domestic law.[10] In the conflict of laws, while the traditional common law approach towards this characterisation is to ask whether a rule of law bars the remedy or extinguishes a right for the purpose of

---

5   An important procedural rule must be mentioned: if the parties do not plead foreign law, or if the content of foreign law is not proven, then, as a general rule, the law of the forum will be applied by default. This chapter is not concerned with this situation.

6   See, for example, *The Hollandia* [1983] 1 AC 565; *Akai Pty Ltd v The People's Insurance Co Ltd* (1996) 188 CLR 418.

7   See main text to n 101 below.

8   There is an important debate whether the subject matter of characterisation is properly the issue or the rule of law, but this question is not of significance for the purpose of the arguments made in this chapter.

9   For example, for the purpose of domestic law, a time-bar provision may be procedural in the sense that it will not be applied unless it is pleaded, but substantive for the purpose of determining whether an amending legislation has the effect of retrospectively repealing a right to rely on it.

10   See *Commonwealth of Australia v Mewett* (1997) 191 CLR 471 at 507, 510-511.

characterising it as procedural or substantive, respectively,[11] there is increasing recognition that a functional approach needs to be adopted.[12] Today it is generally recognised that the distinction serves the specific function of protecting the enforcement and administrative machinery of the court of the forum from being unduly inconvenienced by the application of foreign law.

Thus, the Supreme Court of Canada has recognised that the "purpose of substantive/procedural classification is to determine which rules will make the machinery of the forum court run smoothly as distinguished from those determinative of rights of both parties".[13] The High Court of Australia has observed:[14]

> "Two guiding principles should be seen as lying behind the need to distinguish between substantive and procedural issues. First, litigants who resort to a court to obtain relief must take the court as they find it. A plaintiff cannot ask that a tribunal which does not exist in the forum (but does in the place where a wrong was committed) should be established to deal, in the forum, with the claim that the plaintiff makes. Similarly, the plaintiff cannot ask that the courts of the forum adopt procedures or give remedies of a kind which their constituting statutes do not contemplate any more than the plaintiff can ask that the court apply any adjectival law other than the laws of the forum. Secondly, matters that affect the existence, extent or enforceability of the rights or duties of the parties to an action are matters that, on their face, appear to be concerned with issues of substance, not with issues of procedure. Or to adopt the formulation put forward by Mason CJ in *McKain* [*McKain v Miller and Co (South Australia) Pty Ltd* (1991) 174 CLR 1 at 26-27], 'rules which are directed to governing or regulating the mode or conduct of court proceedings' are procedural and all other provisions or rules are to be classified as substantive [*Stevens v Head* (1993) 176 CLR 433 at 445 per Mason CJ]."

This approach has been endorsed by the English Court of Appeal.[15]

If the issue is not to be resolved by the rules of the forum as a question of procedure, then the next question is how the issue is to be characterised as a matter of substance. Characterisation is the starting point of the classical methodology in the common law approach to choice of law problems. Every legal problem calling for choice of law analysis needs to be characterised. Associated with the categories in choice of law are connecting factors which indicate to the court which legal system's substantive rules to apply to the legal problem. For example, issues characterised as contractual in the conflict of laws sense are generally governed by the law chosen by the parties, or the law with the closest connection with the contract in default of choice. In general, apart from specialised issues such as those involving family law and corporate law, one can discern two further levels of characterisations: does the issue involve a question of property or obligation? And if the issue is one of obligation, is it

---

11   See, for example, *Huber v Steiner* (1835) 2 Bing NC 202; 132 ER 80.
12   See, in the context of limitation periods: *Foreign Limitation Periods Act 1984* (UK).
13   *Tolofson v Jensen* [1994] 3 SCR 1022 at 1071-1072.
14   *John Pfeiffer Pty Ltd v Rogerson* (2000) 203 CLR 503 at [99].
15   *Harding v Wealands* [2004] EWCA Civ 1735; [2005] 1 WLR 1539 at [54] and [90]-[95].

one relating to contracts, torts, or restitution, or something sui generis within the category of obligations?

Finally, the application of foreign law indicated by the forum's choice of law rules is always subject to the fundamental public policy of the forum. If the application of the foreign law, or, more rarely, the content of the foreign law itself, is contrary to some deep moral, economic or social interest of the forum, then the forum would reject the application of the foreign law. Public policy in this context is given a narrower construction than domestic public policy, in order not to undermine the rationale for applying choice of law rules in the first place.[16]

Equity and the choice of law[17]

This chapter is concerned with the relationship between the principles of choice of law articulated above and the body of jurisprudence historically developed in the chancery court.[18] While legal systems in the civil law tradition generally take account of the functional equivalent of equitable principles within codes, or through judicial interpretation within the interstices of codes,[19] there is no doubt that in common law systems, equity represents an independent source of law. Historically, equitable principles were administered by the chancery court, while the common law was used to refer collectively to the law developed by the courts of King's/Queen's Bench, Common Pleas and Exchequer.[20] In jurisdictions where the courts have merged, the fusion has been, at least initially, one of administration only and not of the respective substantive laws. The extent of the fusion of the substantive rules of common law and equity remains a matter of great controversy today, and different legal systems in the common law tradition have adopted different approaches to this question.

There had been a number of early English authorities on the jurisdiction of the chancery court involving the inequitable conduct of parties in dealings involving foreign immovable property.[21] These tend to be inconclusive on the subject of choice of law, although they have been taken to be authoritative for the proposition that the chancery court did not concern itself with choice of

---

16   *Loucks v Standard Oil Co of New York* 120 NE 198 (NY 1918) 202; *Phrantzes v Argenti* [1960] 2 QB 19 at 33-34; *John Pfeiffer Pty Ltd v Rogerson* (2000) 203 CLR 503 at [91]; *Boardwalk Regency Corp v Maalouf* (1992) 6 OR (3d) 737.

17   The arguments in this chapter are substantially based on those proposed in the author's *Choice of Law for Equitable Doctrines* (Oxford University Press, Oxford, 2004).

18   The distinction between equitable principles applied in the court's exclusive jurisdiction and those applied in the court's auxiliary jurisdiction, while an important one in domestic law, is of little, if any, significance in choice of law discourse, except to the extent that in the auxiliary jurisdiction there is doubt as to the applicability of choice of law rules to the underlying common law issue.

19   R Newman, 'The General Principles of Equity' in R Newman (ed), *Equity in the World's Legal Systems* (Bruylant, Brussels, 1973) at 589, 590-591.

20   J Baker, *An Introduction to English Legal History* (3rd ed, Butterworths, London, 1990) at chapter 3.

21   See, for example, *Penn v Baltimore* (1750) 1 Ves Sen 444; 27 ER 1132; *Arglasse v Muschamp* (1682) 1 Vern 75; 23 ER 322; *Mercantile Investment & General Trust Co v River Plate Trust, Loan & Agency Co* [1892] 2 Ch 303.

law.[22] There had also been significant chancery contributions in the law of beneficial succession on the choice of law front.[23] But generally, until recently, the focus of choice of law analysis within the equitable jurisdiction had been on express settlements and trusts. This area, now covered largely by the Hague Convention on the Law Applicable to Trusts and on their Recognition,[24] is very important, but it falls outside the scope of this chapter.[25] More recently, courts in the common law world have had to grapple with cross-border litigation involving issues relating to breaches of fiduciary duties,[26] breaches of confidence,[27] dishonest assistance of breaches of fiduciary duties,[28] knowing or unconscionable receipt of property in breach of trust,[29] equitable duties of skill and care,[30] tracing,[31] constructive trusts,[32] resulting trusts,[33] and undue influence.[34]

---

22   See, for example, PM North and JJ Fawcett, *Cheshire and North's Private International Law* (13th ed, Butterworths, London, 1999) at 381 [hereafter *Cheshire and North*]; G Jones and W Goodhart, *Specific Performance* (2nd ed, Butterworths, London, 1996) at 139; *Paramasivam v Flynn* (1998) 160 ALR 203 at 215-216.

23   See, for example, the choice of law rules for the distinctive doctrines contributed by equity: eg, conversion (*Re Berchtold* [1923] 1 Ch 192); marshalling (*Harrison v Harrison* (1873) LR 8 Ch App 342); election (*Re Allen* [1945] 2 All ER 264, *Re Ogilvie* [1918] 1 Ch 492); ademption (*Stevenson v Masson* (1873) LR 17 Eq 78); and satisfaction (*Campbell v Campbell* (1866) LR 1 Eq 383).

24   Implemented in the United Kingdom in the *Recognition of Trusts Act 1987*, and in Australia, the *Trusts (Hague Convention) Act 1991*.

25   A comprehensive treatment on the impact of the Convention on signatory countries from a common law perspective is found in J Harris, *The Hague Trusts Convention* (Hart Publishing, Oxford, 2002).

26   See, for example, *Paramasivam v Flynn*, above n 22; *Mayo Associates SA v Cantrade Private Bank Switzerland (CI) Ltd* [1998] JLR 173; *United States Surgical Corp v Hospital Products International Pty Ltd* [1982] 2 NSWLR 766 (the issue was not resolved in the Court of Appeal ([1983] 2 NSWLR 157) and not expressly dealt with in the High Court ((1984) 156 CLR 41); *Kartika Ratna Thahir v PT Pertambangan Minyak dan Gas Bumi Negara (Pertamina)* [1994] 3 SLR 257; *National Commercial Bank v Wimborne* (1978) 5 BPR 11,958.

27   See, for example, *A-G (UK) v Heinemann Publishers Australia Pty Ltd* (1988) 165 CLR 30; *A-G (UK) v Wellington Newspapers Ltd* [1988] 1 NZLR 129.

28   See, for example, *Arab Monetary Fund v Hashim, The Times* 11 October 1994; *Dubai Aluminium Co Ltd v Salaam* [1999] 1 Lloyd's Rep 415; *Grupo Torras SA v Al-Sabah* [2001] 1 Lloyd's Rep PN 117.

29   See, for example, *Kuwait Oil Tanker Co SAK v Al Bader (No 3)* [2000] 2 All ER Comm 271; *El Ajou v Dollar Land Holdings plc* [1993] 3 All ER 717 (reversed in [1994] 2 All ER 685 on a point of domestic law); *Arab Monetary Fund v Hashim, The Times* 11 October 1994.

30   See, for example, *Base Metal Trading Ltd v Shamurin* [2003] EWHC Com 2419; [2004] 1 All ER Comm 159, affirmed: [2004] EWCA Civ 1316; [2005] 1 WLR 1157.

31   See, for example, *El Ajou v Dollar Land Holdings plc* [1993] 3 All ER 717; *Euroactivade AG v Mason Investments*, unreported, 18 April 1994).

32   See, for example, *Trustor v Smallbone* [2000] EWCA Civ 150; *Macmillan Inc v Bishopsgate Investment Trusts plc (No 3)* [1996] 1 WLR 387; *Chase Manhattan Bank NA v Israel-British Bank (London) Ltd* [1981] Ch 105.

33   *Lightning v Lightning Electrical Contractors Ltd* (unreported, 23 April 1998 (CA)), partially reported at [1998] NPC 71.

34   See, for example, *A-G for England and Wales v R* [2002] 2 NZLR 91, affirmed without reference to the choice of law issue: [2003] UKPC 22; [2004] 2 NZLR 577; *Bradley v Halsall* (unreported, 16 April 2003 (ChD)).

The approaches of the courts from various jurisdictions in these modern cases are often tentative or unclear and usually both, and may be difficult to reconcile with one another. For example, in the English conflict of laws, the question of the law applicable to a claim based on the dishonest assistance of a breach of fiduciary duty has been tentatively stated to be the law of the forum subject to some (uncertain) reference to the law of the place where the wrong occurred, but the issue has not been the subject of sustained analysis at an appellate level.[35] Also, in the English conflict of laws, it is not clear whether a claim based on the receipt of trust property obtained in breach of trust is seen as lying in restitution or wrongs,[36] and to the extent that it is restitutionary, whether it is sufficient to establish a claim under the applicable law, or whether it is necessary to go a step further to show that the defendant in the circumstances would have been regarded as, or as being in a position analogous to, a constructive trustee under English equitable principles.[37] There has been no authoritative pronouncement in English law on the choice of law rules for breaches of fiduciary duties. A Canadian court has admitted that the position in its law is unclear.[38]

More dramatic is the diametrical opposition of views expressed strongly by appellate courts in Australia and New Zealand. The Full Court of the Federal Court of Australia in *Paramasivam v Flynn* considered that, at least outside the contractual and corporate contexts, the choice of law rule for claims alleging breaches of fiduciary duties was the "general application of the lex fori", but: [39]

> "... subject, perhaps, to this: that where the circumstances giving rise to the asserted duty or the impugned conduct (or some of it) occurred outside the jurisdiction, the attitude of the law of the place where the circumstances arose or the conduct was undertaken is likely to be an important aspect of the factual circumstances in which the Court determines whether a fiduciary relationship existed and, if so, the scope and content of the duties to which it gave rise."

In contrast, in respect of the question on the law applicable to the issue of undue influence, the New Zealand Court of Appeal, in obiter,[40] stated:[41]

> "It is difficult to see the logic or overall desirability of making a distinction between legal issues and equitable issues (except possibly in terms of remedy) when deciding which legal system should govern the contract in question. The

35   The Court of Appeal did not expend much effort on this issue in *Grupo Torras SA v Al-Sabah* [2001] CLC 221 and ultimately did not resolve it. See TM Yeo, *Choice of Law for Equitable Doctrines* (Oxford University Press, Oxford, 2004) at [8.37]-[8.47].

36   See above n 28, but cf *Dexter Ltd v Harley*, *The Times*, 2 April 2001, (noted at (2001) 117 *Law Quarterly Review* 560) which treated such a claim as based on a wrong for jurisdictional purposes.

37   *Kuwait Oil Tanker Co SAK v Al Bader (No 3)* [2000] 2 All ER Comm 271.

38   *Progressive Holdings Inc v Crown Life Insurance Co* [2000] 9 WWR 79 (Manitoba) at [49].

39   (1998) 160 ALR 203, noted at (1999) 115 *Law Quarterly Review* 571.

40   The court was endorsing the common ground of counsel.

41   *A-G for England and Wales v R* [2002] 2 NZLR 91 at [29] (McGrath and Keith JJ agreeing). This statement was approved by Tomlinson J in *Base Metal Trading Ltd v Shamurin* [2003] EWHC Com 2419; [2004] 1 All ER Comm 159 (the argument for applying the law of the forum was not pressed upon appeal).

making of such a distinction can lead to quite unnecessary difficulties and potential inconsistencies."

In view of the diverse positions, the choice of law issue cries out for examination from the standpoint of principle. The first question is whether as a matter of principle, choice of law is even relevant in the equitable jurisdiction of the court.

THE RELEVANCE OF CHOICE OF LAW ANALYSIS IN THE EQUITABLE JURISDICTION

Choice of law rules are rules of municipal law.[42] Municipal rules, including choice of law rules, were administered in separate courts in England before 1873. It is theoretically possible that there may be distinctions between the courts of the common law and equity in their respective approaches to the conflict of laws. For example, in England the rules for the assumption of jurisdiction in cases involving foreign elements were different[43] until they were merged by the *Judicature Act 1873*.[44] It is theoretically possible for different choice of law rules to exist within the bodies of substantive law originating in the common law and equitable jurisdictions respectively, and to survive the merger of administration in 1873.

Choice of law from jurisdiction

There is an argument that once the chancery court has assumed jurisdiction, the equitable principles of the law of the forum were immediately applicable. Professor Graveson argued that "the only applicable law was English equity, largely because of the peculiar nature of the jurisdiction and the unique character, in an international sense, of the system of rules applied by the Court of Chancery".[45] This argument is based primarily on the line of English cases where the chancery court had assumed jurisdiction over defendants on the basis of personal equities,[46] in spite of the rule of non-justiciability of issues relating to title to foreign immovable property.[47] The effect of these authorities is summed up succinctly by Parker J:[48]

---

42   See, for example, in the common law courts: *Holman v Johnson* (1775) 1 Cowp 341 at 343; 98 ER 1120 at 1121 and *Dalrymple v Dalrymple* (1811) 2 Hag Con 54; 161 ER 665. In the chancery court: *Cookney v Anderson* (1863) 1 De GJ & S 365 at 379; 46 ER 146 at 150 and *Caldwell v Vanvlissengen* (1851) 9 Hare 415 at 425-426; 68 ER 571 at 575-576.

43   Service of the writ on the defendant was essential to constitute the court's jurisdiction in personam over the defendant at common law. In equity, jurisdiction was not founded upon service (which went instead to the issue of notice) but on the location of the defendant, the cause of action, or the subject matter of the suit, in the forum: RW White, "Equitable Obligations in Private International Law: The Choice of Law" (1986) 11 *Sydney Law Review* 91.

44   *Re Busfield* (1886) 32 Ch D 123. In Australian law, see: *Laurie v Carroll* (1958) 98 CLR 310.

45   RH Graveson, "Choice of Law and Choice of Jurisdiction in the English Conflict of Laws" (1951) 28 *British Year Book of International Law* 273 at 277.

46   See n 21 above.

47   *British South Africa Co v Companhia de Moçambique* [1893] AC 602.

48   *Deschamps v Miller* [1908] 1 Ch 856 at 863.

"[T]he general rule is that the Court will not adjudicate on questions relating to the title to or the right to the possession of immovable property out of the jurisdiction. There are, no doubt, exceptions to the rule, but, without attempting to give an exhaustive statement of those exceptions, I think it will be found that they all depend on the existence between the parties to the suit of some personal obligation arising out of contract or implied contract, fiduciary relationship or fraud, or other conduct which, in the view of a Court of Equity in this country, would be unconscionable, and do not depend for their existence on the law of the locus of the immovable property."

The modern translation of this approach to jurisdiction into a choice of law rule was made by Holland J in *National Commercial Bank v Wimborne*:[49]

"The Equity Court has long taken the view that because it is a court of conscience and acts in personam, it has jurisdiction over persons within and subject to its jurisdiction to require them to act in accordance with the principles of equity administered by the court wherever the subject matter and whether or not it is possible for the court to make orders in rem in the particular matter. In short, if the defendant is here, the equities arising from a transaction to which he is a party as ascertained by New South Wales law and the equitable remedies provided by that law will be applied to him.

The Equity Court determines according to its own law whether an equity exists, its nature and the remedy applicable."

On this view, jurisdictional rules instead would be used as a proxy for choice of law: the court would decline jurisdiction where it was an unsuitable case for the equitable principles of the forum to be applied.[50]

However, as a matter of principle, and historically, the application of the law of the forum did not necessarily follow from the assumption of jurisdiction by the chancery court. As a matter of principle, jurisdictional considerations are distinct from considerations in respect of choice of law. One is concerned with the channelling of disputes to appropriate fora, while the other is concerned with the determination of the substantive merits of the disputes.[51] While principles of natural forum may indirectly limit the instances where the forum would assume jurisdiction in cases involving foreign elements, this does not provide a principled solution to the choice of law problem, and practically the courts will still be required to deal with cases involving the invocation of equitable principles in cross-border transactions and events.[52]

It is not a sufficient reason to say that a chancery court only enforced obligations of its own creation, for it merely begs the question of the law governing

---

49   *National Commercial Bank v Wimborne* (1978) 5 BPR 11,958 at 11,982.

50   RW White, "Equitable Obligations in Private International Law: The Choice of Law" (1986) 11 *Sydney Law Review* 91.

51   A distinction emphasised in a different context in *Seaconsar Far East Ltd v Bank Markazi Jomhouri Islami Iran* [1994] 1 AC 438.

52   Arguably even more so in the Australian context where the court would stay an action only if it found itself to be a clearly inappropriate forum (*Regie National des Usines Renault SA v Zhang* (2002) 210 CLR 491), than in other Commonwealth countries that apply the test where the court would stay an action if there is a clearly more appropriate forum elsewhere unless the claimant would be denied substantial justice in the foreign jurisdiction: *The Spiliada* [1987] 1 AC 460.

the creation of that obligation.[53] Moreover, the reasoning from jurisdiction to choice of law, insofar as it is valid, was not applied universally. Historically, in respect of settlements and trusts,[54] issues of beneficial succession,[55] and agreements,[56] it is clear that choice of law considerations were regarded as different from jurisdictional ones. Further, in the modern context, choice of law is clearly recognised as distinct from jurisdiction at least where equity operates within the law of restitution.[57]

Moreover, the fact of absence of choice of law analysis in the historical cases is not necessarily the result of the inevitable application of the law of the forum. McLelland J had pointed out that there has not been any clear judicial articulation of the relationship between the assumption of jurisdiction and the application of the law of the forum.[58] It should be noted that the chancery court applied the same principle as the common law with respect to the proof of foreign law: where it is not proven, the law of the forum applies by default.[59]

The historical context of the development of the conflict of laws should also be noted. Before choice of law rules were developed in English law, jurisdiction techniques were used between the courts of the common law and admiralty effectively to control the choice of the substantive applicable law.[60] It would not be surprising to see the same phase of development in the history of equity jurisprudence.[61]

Finally, in the modern context, the merger of the administration of common law and equity has put their respective jurisdictional rules on an equal footing.[62] On one view, the breadth of the bases of modern jurisdiction, tempered to some extent by principles of appropriateness of the forum, has not affected the proposition that the equitable principles of the forum apply upon the assumption of jurisdiction over the defendant.[63] It is suggested, however, that whatever slender link that existed between jurisdiction and choice of law that had existed in equity learning had been broken by the merger of jurisdictional rules. There is nothing in the jurisdictional reasoning that justifies the invariable application of the law of the forum. The European context throws up a further

---

53   See in the context of tort: *John Pfeiffer Pty Ltd v Rogerson* (2000) 203 CLR 503 at [73].

54   See, for example, *Bunbury v Bunbury* (1839) LJ 8 Ch 297.

55   See n 23 above.

56   See, for example, *British South Africa Co v De Beers Consolidated Mines Ltd* [1910] 2 Ch 502, reversed on a point of domestic law: [1912] AC 52.

57   See, for example, *Chase Manhattan Bank NA v Israel-British Bank (London) Ltd* [1981] Ch 105, and McHugh JA in *A-G (UK) v Heinemann Publishers Australia Pty Ltd* (1987) 10 NSWLR 86 at 192.

58   *United States Surgical Corp v Hospital Products International Pty Ltd* [1982] 2 NSWLR 766 at 796-798.

59   *Bentinck v Willink* (1842) 2 Hare 1; 67 ER 1; *Henderson v Henderson* (1843) 3 Hare 100 at 115; 67 ER 313 at 319.

60   AN Sack, 'Conflict of Laws in the History of the English Law' in A Reppy (ed), *Law: A Century of Progress 1835-1935* (New York University Press, New York, 1937), Vol 3 at 342.

61   An attempt by Lord Westbury LC in *Cookney v Anderson* (1863) 1 De GJ & S 365 at 379; 46 ER 146 at 151, to link jurisdiction with choice of law was decisively repelled by Lord Selborne LC in *Ewing v Orr Ewing* (1883) 9 App Cas 34 at 39.

62   See n 44 above.

63   *OZ-US Film Productions Pty Ltd v Heath* [2001] NSWSC 298.

consideration: the Brussels I Regulation[64] has no intellectual connection with common law thinking. In England where it applies, whatever link that exists between jurisdiction and choice of law has been decisively broken.

It was argued above that the satisfaction of the jurisdiction rules of the forum does not, without more, justify the inevitable application of the principles of equity of the forum. It is arguable, though, that the proposition is a narrower one: that it is the invocation specifically of the *equitable* jurisdiction of the court, rather than the jurisdiction of the court over defendants in general, that provides the justification. However, in a world of unified jurisdictional rules, this appears to be just another way of saying that the substantive principles of equity of the forum are being sought to be applied. Equitable jurisdiction in this sense describes the reach of substantive equitable principles, not the legal authority of the courts to make a final adjudication of the dispute between the parties. It remains to consider whether there is in anything in the invocation of the equitable principles of the forum that justifies their immediate application without choice of law considerations.

This issue may be considered from two perspectives. First, is there anything in the nature of equitable principles such that they must apply to any dispute before the court without any reference to choice of law analysis? Secondly, does the law of the forum always apply anyway even within the framework for the analysis of choice of law whenever the forum's equitable jurisdiction is invoked?

The nature of equity

Equity "acts in personam"

This maxim of equity is often relied upon for applying the principles of equity of the forum upon the invocation of the equitable jurisdiction of the forum.[65] Historically, this maxim distinguished the mode of enforcement of equitable decrees from that of common law judgments: the decree did not directly interfere with common law rights, but was directed at the defendant personally. Disobedience of the decree entailed punishment for contempt; thus the order was in personam. This distinction no longer holds true today.[66]

The historical sense of this maxim continues to be relevant in a significant way in the conflict of laws. It has played a very important role in the jurisdictional context, and continues to enable the courts to bypass bar on the justiciability of issues relating directly to foreign title, because the court can make orders against the defendant even if it cannot make orders that can be executed against foreign property.[67] However, the maxim says nothing about

---

64   Council Regulation (EC) 44/2001 on *Jurisdiction and the Recognition and Enforcement of Judgments in Civil and Commercial Matters*, 2001 OJ L12/1.

65   See especially: *National Commercial Bank v Wimborne* (1978) 5 BPR 11,958 at 11,982; *United States Surgical Corp v Hospital Products International Pty Ltd* [1982] 2 NSWLR 766 at 798.

66   This has been the case since the Chancery court could make vesting orders: DEC Yale (ed), *Nottingham's 'Manual of Chancery Practice' and 'Prolegomena of chancery and equity'* (Cambridge University Press, Cambridge, 1965) at 25-39.

67   To the extent that the Brussels I Regulation applies in England, the common law bar has been replaced by a statutory one in Art 22(1)(a). It remains a contentious question to what extent

the selection of the substantive legal system to govern the dispute. From the choice of law perspective, the application of the maxim is circular: it is part of the equitable principles of the forum, but it has not yet been established that the equitable principles of the forum are applicable. Merely because the court of the forum is in a position to make a decree against the defendant within its jurisdiction does not mean that the law of the forum must apply even to transactions connected with foreign legal systems.[68]

Equity "acts on the conscience"

The argument that the principles of equity of the forum apply upon the invocation of the equitable jurisdiction of the court of the forum because equitable principles act on the conscience of the defendant, is distinct from, though often closely associated with, the argument based on equity acting in personam. The focus here is no longer on the enforcement of the equitable decree, but the basis, and the mode of operation, of the chancery court's intervention. Unconscientiousness in the exercise of legal rights provides the reason for the intervention. The intervention takes the form of an order against the defendant to refrain from the unconscientious exercise of legal rights. It is in this sense that in domestic law a bona fide purchaser of legal interest for value without notice stood outside the reach of equity.[69]

However, it does not follow from this mode of operation of the equitable principles of the forum that they must apply without choice of law analysis; this is an aspect of the internal mode of operation of the domestic law. As in the previous case, it presupposes the application of the law of the forum. The content of conscience may be regulated by foreign law in the case of an express[70] or constructive[71] trustee. By itself, this argument is an inadequate justification for the exclusive application of the equitable principles of the forum.

---

equitable claims to foreign immovable property falls outside the statutory bar. See *Webb v Webb* Case C-294/92 [1994] ECR-I 1717, A Briggs, "Trusts of Land and the Brussels Convention" (1994) 110 *Law Quarterly Review* 526 and (1994) 14 *Yearbook of European Law* 563; P Birks, "In rem or in personam?" (1994) 8 *Trust Law International* 99; C MacMillan, "The European Court of Justice Agrees with Maitland: Trusts and the Brussels Convention" [1996] *Conveyancer and Property Lawyer* 125; P Rogerson, "Equity, Rights in Rem and the Brussels Convention" [1994] *Cambridge Law Journal* 462. See also *Ashurst v Pollard* [2001] Ch 595; A Briggs, "Decisions of British Courts in 2000: Private International Law" (2000) 71 *British Year Book of International Law* 443; J Harris, "Ordering the Sale of Land Situated Overseas" [2001] *Lloyds Maritime and Commercial Law Quarterly* 205.

68 See, in a not altogether different context: *MacKinnon v Donaldson, Lufkin and Jenrette Securities Corp* [1986] 1 Ch 482 at 493: "It does not follow from the fact that a person is within the jurisdiction and liable to be served with process that there is no territorial limit to the matters upon which the court may properly apply its own rules or the things which it can order such a person to do."

69 *Pilcher v Rawlins* (1872) LR 7 Ch App 259.

70 See, for example, *Anstruther v Adair* (1834) 2 My & K 513; 39 ER 1040.

71 In the sense of a person holding property on behalf of the claimant (*Macmillan Inc v Bishopsgate Investment Trusts plc (No 3)* [1996] 1 WLR 387) or in the sense of a person alleged to be personally accountable for the receipt of trust property in breach of trust (*Kuwait Oil Tanker Co SAK v Al Bader (No 3)* [2000] 2 All ER Comm 271).

Equity as a System of Relief

Historically, the chancery court granted relief according to the circumstances of individual cases where the rules applied by the other courts proved too harsh or rigid. It could be argued the court in its equitable jurisdiction always proceeds directly from jurisdiction to the appropriate relief, thus bypassing the question of substantive right, the mainstay of choice of law analysis.[72]

While this may have been a significant point in the past, it has not prevented the court from engaging in choice of law analysis in at least some cases where equitable relief had been sought. Moreover, the argument fails to take into account the unquestionable development over many years, of substantive legal principles that have emerged from the historical system of granting relief.[73] For example, it is more accurate to see the modern law of property as a single substantive law of property that is divided into concepts of legal and equitable rights,[74] rather than a system of common law of property subject to equitable relief against unconscionability. Where a party seeks the relief of rescission, within domestic law there may be a distinction between rescission at law and in equity,[75] such that a common law right to rescind a contract works differently from an equity to rescind a contract.[76] However, either way, the issue is based on substantive principles of law, so that there is no difficulty in seeing the subject matter as amenable to choice of law analysis.

The enforcement of "personal equities"

To the extent that the early English jurisdictional cases on disputes relating to title to foreign immovable property have been taken as authoritative for the application of English law upon the assumption of jurisdiction, the substantive explanation appears to be that the court of the forum had been dealing with "personal equities" between the parties, which has been assumed to be a matter that was exclusively governed by the law of the forum.[77] In *Re Courtney*,[78] the question before the court was whether a deposit of title deeds (to foreign land) which had no effect under the law of the situs nevertheless had the effect of creating an equitable charge. Holding that it did, Lord Cottenham LC said:[79]

---

72 This argument was articulated, but not endorsed, in A Briggs, "The unrestrained reach of an anti-suit injunction: a pause for thought" [1997] *Lloyds Maritime and Commercial Law Quarterly* 90 at 92. See also A Briggs, 'Conflict of Laws and Commercial Remedies' in A Burrows and E Peel (eds), *Commercial Remedies: Current Issues and Problems* (Oxford University Press, Oxford, 2003) at 271, 281, and the comment of P Reed at 287, 288.

73 Substantive common law principles also developed through a system of relief, controlled by the forms of action: J Baker, *An Introduction to English Legal History* (3rd ed, Butterworths, London, 1990) at chapter 4.

74 *Tinsley v Milligan* [1994] 1 AC 340 at 371.

75 Rescission in equity for undue influence was discussed in the language of "rights" in *Royal Bank of Scotland plc v Etridge (No 2)* [2002] 2 AC 773.

76 R Meagher, JD Heydon, and M Leeming, *Meagher, Gummow and Lehane's Equity: Doctrines and Remedies* (4th ed, Lexis Nexis, Sydney, 2002) at [24-040]–[24-070].

77 See n 22 above.

78 (1840) Mont & Ch 239.

79 *Re Courtney* (1840) Mont & Ch 239 at 251.

"[T]he courts of this country, in the exercise of their jurisdiction over contracts made here, or in administering equities between parties residing here, act upon their own rules, and are not influenced by any consideration of what the effect of such contracts might be in the country where the lands are situate, or of the manner in which the courts of such countries might deal with such equities."

This might be taken as a statement that whenever personal equities are invoked, the law of the forum would apply. In domestic law, personal equities may be unique in the sense that the court is being asked to enforce rights which are not recognised in the common law. Thus, for example, personal equities arising out of the part performance of a contract otherwise unenforceable by statute could nevertheless be enforced on the basis that they are not regarded as contractual rights barred by the statute.[80] Even if this is right in domestic law,[81] to state that personal equities are being enforced, begs, rather than answers, the choice of law question.

The quoted statement could be more simply explained as the enforcement of rights arising from English law as the law applicable to the agreement between the parties: it was a case of choice of law for contracts. The reference to contracts made in the forum is explicable in the historical context; the law of the place where the contract was made was thought to supply the prima facie choice of law rule.[82] The reference to the parties being resident in the forum is explicable because in such cases, the prima facie reference to the law of the place where the contract was made could be readily displaced by the intention of the parties as to the law to govern the agreement,[83] and it would not be unusual for two Englishmen to enter into an agreement with reference to English law in their minds. The contractual interpretation is consistent with subsequent cases,[84] and has been the explanation preferred by academics generally.[85]

Equity as Aristotelian justice

In the domestic law of common law systems, the role of equity is Aristotelian in nature, in the sense that it polished the harsh edges of the common law. The extent to which this kind of two-tiered reasoning should remain relevant in the

---

80   *Maddison v Alderson* (1883) 8 App Cas 467. Part performance is no longer part of English law in relation to land transactions (Law *of Property (Miscellaneous Provisions) Act 1989*, s 2(8)), but it remains the law in at least some other common law countries. In any event, "equities" still survive in domestic English law in, eg, equitable estoppel: *Yaxley v Gotts* [2000] Ch 162.

81   *Contra United Bank of Kuwait plc v Sahib* [1997] Ch 107 at 140-141.

82   *Robinson v Bland* (1760) 1 Bl W 256 at 258-259; 96 ER 141 at 141-142.

83   *Robinson v Bland*, above n 82 at 258-259; 141-142.

84   *Coote v Jecks* (1872) LR 13 Eq 597; *British South Africa Co v De Beers Consolidated Mines Ltd* [1910] 1 Ch 354 at 387, affirmed in [1910] 2 Ch 502 at 514-515, 518, 524, reversed on a domestic point of law in [1912] AC 52; *Re Smith* [1916] 2 Ch 206; *Re Anchor Line (Henderson Bros) Ltd* [1937] Ch 483.

85   *Dicey and Morris*, at [33-226]; L Collins, 'Floating Charges, Receivers and Managers in the Conflict of Laws' in *Essays in International Litigation and the Conflict of Laws* (Clarendon, Oxford, 1994) at 433; EI Sykes and MC Pryles, *Australian Private International Law* (3rd ed, Law Book Company, Sydney, 1991) at 707; L Barnard, "Choice of Law in Equitable Wrongs – A Comparative Analysis" [1992] *Cambridge Law Journal* 474.

modern domestic law remains highly controversial, but theoretically, this could be confined to a problem of domestic law.

However, there have been suggestions that equity plays the same role in respect of foreign law, in ancient[86] and modern[87] authorities. Thus, it has been said that foreign elements in a case would "not preclude the engrafting of binding equitable obligations. Anyone cognizant with the history of equity in our legal system would see no difficulty with such a concept in principle".[88] With respect, although there is no difficulty in seeing *how* it works, it is not easy to see *why* it should work in all cases. The projection of the overriding nature of equity in domestic law into the sphere of the conflict of laws is merely stated, and not justified. In contrast, Lord Eldon had advised: "Natural law requires the courts of this country to give credit to those of another for the inclination and power to do justice".[89] It seems to go against modern understanding of international comity to offer to improve upon foreign laws.

Application of the law of the forum within the choice of law framework

This section considers the argument that choice of law may be irrelevant when a litigant invokes the equitable jurisdiction of the court of the forum for reasons found traditionally within the classical framework of choice of law analysis.

Forum public policy and mandatory rules

It is undeniable that the forum will have non-negotiable concerns that must be protected from the application of foreign law, whether framed as public policy or forum mandatory rules. Fraud and unconscionable conduct, the catch-phrases of equity in domestic law, easily associate themselves with such concerns. "Unconscionable conduct" is sometimes used to describe instances where the fundamental public policy of the law of the forum would apply.[90] However, fraud and unconscionability in equity describe conduct lying along a broad spectrum of moral opprobrium as justification for equitable intervention. There is no complete equivalence between equitable fraud or unconscionability with domestic public policy,[91] let alone fundamental forum public policy to override choice of law considerations. For the same reason, it would not be justifiable to describe the entire body of equitable principles as forum mandatory rules in the international sense. In any event, it cannot be

---

86   *Fryer v Bernard* (1724) 2 P Wms 261; 24 ER 722; G Spence, *The Equitable Jurisdiction of the Court of Chancery* (Stevens and Norton, London, 1849), Vol 1 at 11-12.

87   *Kavalee v Burbridge* (1998) 43 NSWLR 422.

88   *Kavalee v Burbridge*, above n 87 at 438 (Mason P in obiter). Meagher JA agreed with Mason P, but Handley JA (at 458) proceeded on the basis that foreign law had not been shown to be different.

89   *Wright v Simpson* (1802) 6 Ves Jun 714 at 730; 31 ER 1272 at 1280.

90   See, for example, *Re Fuld (No 3)* [1968] P 675 at 698; RH Graveson, *Conflict of Laws* (7th ed, Sweet & Maxwell, London, 1974) at 466; CMV Clarkson and J Hill, *Jaffey on the Conflict of Laws* (2nd ed, Butterworths, London, 2002) at 136-137, 560.

91   See, for example, *Armitage v Nurse* [1998] Ch 241.

assumed that the solutions in foreign legal systems to problems of fraud, whether actual or equitable, will always fall short of the minimum norms of the forum. While there may be important areas in equity where the court of the forum sees a fundamental forum interest to protect (and the content may differ from country to country), this argument cannot go so far as to justify the application of the entire body of equitable principles of the forum.[92] There may be regulatory interests involved in the imposition of equitable duties, but it cannot be assumed in all cases that the standards of the law of the forum must always apply.[93]

Procedure

On the modern view of the meaning of "procedure" for choice of law purposes,[94] it would appear at first blush that most principles of equity do not raise issues of procedure in this sense, even though in many cases, it is not very clear where the line is to be drawn between substantive and procedural issues. Generally, the persistent use of the language of remedy in equitable discourse within the domestic law should not detract from the point that substantive issues are raised for choice of law purposes.[95]

A broader argument arises in this way: in order for the court of the forum to grant equitable relief, its equitable jurisdiction must be invoked, and because this equitable jurisdiction is known to and defined only by the equitable principles of the forum, the jurisdictional facts (ie, facts disclosing the reason, or an "equity", to justify the intervention of equity) required to establish equitable relief must be determined by the law of the forum. Stated in this way, however, it is a reiteration of the argument that the law of the forum must apply once the equitable jurisdiction is invoked, an argument that was rejected above. The link between the jurisdiction and the remedy should be viewed as a matter of domestic law only.[96]

The argument could be stated in weaker form: that the equitable jurisdiction of the forum can be invoked only if the factual circumstances could be seen as falling within the forum's own domestic rules of what constitutes such jurisdictional facts, or as *analogous* to them. On this view, while it leaves open choice of law analysis, there is still a need to comply with certain requirements of the law of the forum. For example, the court of the forum may demand that the defendant be in a position analogous to what the forum itself would regard as a fiduciary before imposing a liability to account for profits.

92　S Lee, "Restitution, Public Policy and the Conflict of Laws" (1998) 20 *University of Queensland Law Journal* 1, while accepting that not all equitable principles reflect public policy, gives a very wide scope (in the view of the present author, too wide) to the public policy of the forum that overrides the foreign applicable law.

93　*Base Metal Trading Ltd v Shamurin* [2005] 1 WLR 1157, (regulation of directors through equitable duties of skill and care – where applicable – by the law of the place of incorporation).

94　See text surrounding n 13 above.

95　*Chase Manhattan Bank NA v Israel-British Bank (London) Ltd* [1981] Ch 105.

96　No one has seriously argued that when the court is resorting to common law damages to redress the breach of a foreign right, there must be a right to such damages under the rules of English common law.

On the other hand, the general principle that operates in the conflict of laws is that the court should apply whatever remedies of the forum that gives the best effect to the foreign right.[97] Thus, Moore-Bick J had suggested that this additional layer of applying the law of the forum is unnecessary:[98]

> "[W]hat is ultimately important is the existence and nature of the underlying obligation. If the defendant incurs an obligation to the plaintiff under the lex causae which requires him to account for property he has received, that in my judgment ought equally to provide a sufficient basis for holding him liable as a constructive trustee in proceedings in this country."

While there is some authority for the requirement that the law of the forum must see jurisdictional facts under its own rules or facts analogous to them at least in some types of claims,[99] it is suggested that the view put forward by Moore-Bick J is the better one in principle and should be applied generally. There is a false analogy between the former approach and the rejection of "fusion-fallacy" – that equitable relief can only follow from jurisdictional facts recognised in equity – in the domestic law. This rejection posits a certain correlation between the types of rights and types of remedies within the domestic law. This is not relevant to choice of law analysis, where the main concern should be with matching as best as possible the forum's own machinery of relief to the nature and scope of the substantive right sought to be given effect to under the forum's choice of law rules.[100]

Formative decisions

One area where the law of the forum may apply exclusively is where the court of the forum is not being asked to declare or enforce rights (or to declare status) as such, but is being asked to alter them. Professor Kahn-Freund has argued that the court of the forum is not in a position to exercise a creative function on behalf of foreign courts.[101] For example, this may explain why the common law courts have not developed any choice of law rules for divorce.

The scope of this exceptional category of cases where the law of the forum applies exclusively is unclear. The choice between formative and declaratory jurisdiction of a court may well lie within the choice of technique in domestic laws. Thus, for example, the functional equivalent in some civil law countries of the common law right to terminate a contract for breach is a judicial power to terminate the contract. Kahn-Freund thought that the formative elements in such cases do not have any significance in choice of law analysis.[102] He also doubted that the principles of equity as such fell within the court's formative

---

97   *Phrantzes v Argenti* [1960] 2 QB 19 at 35.

98   *Kuwait Oil Tanker Co SAK v Al Bader (No 3)*, (unreported, 16 November 1998 (QBD)), affirmed in part: [2000] 2 All ER Comm 271 , but the Court of Appeal did not comment on this point.

99   *Kuwait Oil Tanker Co SAK v Al Bader (No 3)* [2000] 2 All ER Comm 271.

100 *Phrantzes v Argenti*, above n 97 at 35.

101 O Kahn-Freund, *General Problems of Private International Law* (Alphen aan den Rijn, Sitjhoff, 1976) at 206.

102 O Kahn-Freund, *General Problems of Private International Law*, above n 101 at 210.

jurisdiction for the purpose of this exception to choice of law analysis.[103] It is suggested that this viewpoint is persuasive. From the perspective of domestic law, it could be said that equity effectively alters common law (or even statutory) rights by preventing the unconscientious exercise of such rights. However, from the perspective of choice of law analysis, the domestic law should be seen in its entirety, without being unduly preoccupied by the interaction of the different components and institutions that make up the domestic legal system. It may well be that certain (limited) aspects of equity bear this creative or formative quality;[104] it goes too far to say that the entire corpus of equitable principles bears this character.

The moral content of equity

Some conflict of laws scholars have advocated the view that when it comes to issues involving morality, the court of the forum can only apply its own rules. Professor Ehrenzweig argued that the "moral data" of a legal system cannot be subject to choice of law rules, because it is inherent in the adjudicative process that the court must apply its own moral values.[105] Professor Wortley's argument is based primarily on the moral content of the rules as such. Both authors used equitable principles as the prime examples of this kind of case. Wortley argued:[106]

> "English law imposes its own standards upon defendants amenable to its jurisdiction; it even enforces rights demanded by its conception of conscience which may be unknown to a foreign system of law. ...
>
> We believe there is nothing unfair in such equitable proceedings which, after all, merely enforce a high standard of obligation upon contractors, trustees and others *in the interest of their own consciences*."

A result of Ehrenzweig's argument is that the forum can only apply the moral standards of its own, and never a foreign, law. However, this argument lost ground on his own concession that foreign moral standards may be applied if the equivalent forum rules have no moral content.[107] This shows that there is nothing inherent in the adjudicative process that necessitates the exclusive application of the moral standards of the forum.[108] Moreover, both views are

---

103 O Kahn-Freund, *General Problems of Private International Law*, above n 101 at 219-220 and footnote 102 to the text.

104 For example, this may be the case if the concept of a remedial constructive trust lying at the general discretion of the courts is accepted within the domestic law.

105 AA Ehrenzweig, "Local and Moral Data in the Conflict of Laws: *Terra Incognita*" (1966) 16 *Buffalo Law Review* 55; AA Ehrenzweig, *Conflicts in a Nutshell* (2nd ed, West Publishing, St Paul, 1970) at 93-94; AA Ehrenzweig, 'Local and Moral Data in the Conflict of Laws' in GOZ Sundström (ed), *Three Discussions on the Conflict of Laws* (Almqvist & Wiksell, Stockholm, 1970) at 45.

106 BA Wortley, "The General Principles of Private International Law from the English Standpoint" (1947) 71 *Recueil Des Cours* 1 at 61-62 (original emphasis).

107 See AA Ehrenzweig, 'Apologia' in GOZ Sundström (ed), *Three Discussions on the Conflict of Laws*, above n 105 at 83.

108 While the process of applying law (foreign or local) to the facts is necessarily governed by the law of the forum as a matter of procedure (*National Mutual Holdings v Sentry Corp* (1989) 87 ALR 539 at 556), this has nothing to do with the content of the law as such.

subject to three difficulties. First, they do not explain the cases where the court has considered choice of law to be relevant even where the potentially applicable rule in the law of the forum is "founded on the highest principles of equity".[109] Conversely, the implication that principles of law already subject to choice of law analysis are lacking in moral content is startling. Secondly, there are difficulties in defining what constitutes moral content in this approach. Thirdly, even if the requisite moral content can be defined with sufficient clarity, there are bound to be practical difficulties in distinguishing rules that have moral content from rules which do not. These variables will lead to an unstable choice of law system.

It is suggested that the concerns of the two writers were concentrated in the wrong place. The issue is not whether the forum should apply the moral standards of its own laws or the moral standards of foreign law. Practical difficulties aside, it is impossible to justify this approach especially if we believe that some kind of morality underlies all laws. The concern should really be with the fundamental moral values and interests of the forum which cannot be compromised by the application of foreign law. The existing exceptions of fundamental public policy and international mandatory rules within the conflict of laws methodology can accommodate this concern.

Conclusion

The argument that the peculiar nature of equity necessitates its invariable application in the choice of law context proves too little because it provides no substantive justification for the exclusion of choice of law analysis. It proves too much insofar as there is evidence of choice of law analysis in at least some aspects of equity jurisprudence. On the other hand, it is an established principle in the conflict of laws that historical origins of municipal rules should have little bearing on their choice of law analysis.[110] It has also been recognised that the invariable recourse to the law of the forum in litigation involving equitable principles could invite forum-shopping,[111] and could defeat the legitimate expectations of parties to a transaction with foreign connections.[112] A forum-centric approach would also, of course, work against the goal of uniformity of results as a choice of law outcome.

It has also been argued that there is no justification for the general application of the principles of equity of the forum within the framework of choice of law analysis. It has been argued above that while some aspects of equity may be procedural in the conflict of laws sense and some aspects of it may reflect the fundamental public policies or the international mandatory rules of the forum, none of these exceptions can provide that broad justification. Moreover, for the most part, the equitable principles of the forum do not raise

---

109 *Cooper v Cooper* (1874) LR 7 HL 53 at 67, 78. This was said of the English equitable doctrine of election. Yet it is one of the issues in equity jurisprudence clearly subject to choice of law analysis.

110 M Wolff, *Private International Law* (2nd ed, Clarendon, Oxford, 1950) at [509].

111 *Macmillan Inc v Bishopsgate Investment Trusts plc (No 3)* [1996] 1 WLR 387 at 402.

112 *Base Metal Trading Ltd v Shamurin* [2003] EWHC Com 2419; [2004] 1 All ER Comm 159 at [44].

issues that form part of an inchoate category of formative issues where the law of the forum must apply. It was also argued that the existence of moral content within equitable principles is not a sufficient justification to bypass choice of law analysis.

Within the discourse in equity, Lord Macnaghten warned about the dangers of the universal imposition of the standards of the equitable principles of the forum in cases involving foreign elements.[113] More recently, Tomlinson J took note of the same danger.[114] Ironically, in his treatise on equity in 1760, Scottish judge and jurist Lord Kames criticised the common law courts of England for failing to pay sufficient attention to the considerations of the conflict of laws, commenting that in applying the law of the forum in all cases: "What can be expected ... but injustice in every instance?"[115] It was Lord Kames' thesis that the nature of equity jurisprudence itself demanded that consideration should be given to choice of law. More recently, Millett J (as he then was) was careful to distinguish between equity in domestic law and the principles of choice of law:[116]

> "It is no answer to assert that a claim which invokes the intervention of equity is a claim in personam and part of the law or [sic] remedies, and – a highly dubious proposition – as such is governed by the lex fori. The principles which I have endeavoured to state are not principles of English conflict of laws, but of equity and our domestic law of restitution."

THE RELATIONSHIP BETWEEN CHOICE OF LAW PRINCIPLES AND EQUITABLE PRINCIPLES OF THE FORUM

The conclusion of the previous section is that choice of law considerations are relevant within equity jurisprudence. The next question is the relationship between such choice of law considerations and the substantive principles of equity. In other words, how should we *approach* the study of the subject of choice of law for equitable principles?

Three approaches

Three broad approaches, lying along a spectrum of possibilities, can be discerned in the authorities and the literature on the subject. First, it could be said that the division between common law and equity is a matter of domestic law only, and any questions relating to the interaction between common law and equity are relevant only to the extent that common law and equity form part of the domestic law applicable to the substantive issue before the court, or where the law of the forum is applicable because the issue is procedural, or because of the fundamental public policy or international mandatory rules of the forum.

---

113 *Concha v Concha* [1892] AC 670 at 675.
114 *Base Metal Trading Ltd v Shamurin*, above n 112 at [43].
115 Lord Kames, *Principles of Equity* (2nd ed, Kincaid & Bell, Edinburgh, 1767) at 348.
116 *Macmillan Inc v Bishopsgate Investment Trusts plc (No 3)* [1995] 1 WLR 978 at 989. See also Staughton LJ in the CA judgment [1996] 1 WLR 387 at 402.

There are authorities in support of such an approach. For example, in one case it was held that the equitable doctrine of conversion became relevant only when English law was found to be the applicable law.[117] In another case, the law governing priorities of title was determined before the English Court of Appeal proceeded to consider whether the defendant held shares on constructive trust for the claimant.[118] A further example is the characterisation by the English Court of Appeal of a company director's liability for breach of equitable duty of skill and care as an issue falling within or relating to the constitution or internal management of a corporation.[119] This would appear to be the approach generally for claims characterised as restitutionary.[120] By far the strongest statement of this approach has come from the New Zealand Court of Appeal, quoted above.[121] Academic support comes from Dicey and Morris,[122] and others,[123] even if the proposition in Dicey and Morris is made a little awkwardly from the interstices of the chapter on Restitution.

On this first approach, equitable principles of the forum, like common law rules, are the subject of analysis of choice of law. A unitary choice of law analysis transcends the division between common law and equity. To the extent that the court is concerned with the question whether to apply its own principles of equity of the forum, there is choice of law *for* equity. Because the choice of law rules may in fact point to the corresponding principles of foreign law, it is more accurate to describe the process as choice of law for the equitable principles of the forum or the functionally equivalent principles of foreign law.

A second approach is that although choice of law is relevant within equitable discourse, a different set of choice of law rules apply within the equitable jurisdiction of the court of the forum. Where an issue that arises is one which would have been dealt with under the forum's equitable jurisdiction before the fusion of administration of common law and equity, that issue would be subject to choice of law *in* equity. The strongest support for this approach comes from the Full Court of the Federal Court of Australia in *Paramasivam v Flynn*.[124] Where the choice of law points towards the law of the forum generally, the position is practically indistinguishable from the position rejected earlier that the principles of equity of the forum apply upon the assumption of jurisdiction and the invocation of equitable jurisdiction. Nevertheless, it is still theoretically distinct in that a conscious choice of law decision

---

117 *Re Berchtold* [1923] 1 Ch 192.

118 *Macmillan Inc v Bishopsgate Investment Trusts plc (No 3)*, above n 116.

119 *Base Metal Trading Ltd v Shamurin* [2005] 1 WLR 1157 at [50]-[57], [65]-[77], [89], noted at [2005] *Lloyds Maritime and Commercial Law Quarterly* 144. This case is discussed further in chapter 8 of this book by R Stevens, 'Choice of Law for Equity: Is It Possible?'.

120 *Chase Manhattan Bank NA v Israel-British Discount Bank (London) Ltd* [1981] Ch 105; *El Ajou v Dollar Land Holdings plc* [1993] 3 All ER 717; *Kuwait Oil Tanker Co SAK v Al Bader (No 3)* [1993] 3 All ER 717 at least where the claimant is not relying on a pre-existing relationship with the defendant.

121 See n 41 above.

122 *Dicey and Morris*, at [34-032].

123 A Briggs, *The Conflict of Laws* (Clarendon, Oxford, 2002) at 203; CMV Clarkson and J Hill, *Jaffey on the Conflict of Laws* (2nd ed, Butterworths, London, 2002) at 287-290; J Hill, *The Law Relating to International Commercial Disputes* (2nd ed, LLP, London, 1998) at 553.

124 (1998) 160 ALR 203, noted at (1999) 115 *Law Quarterly Review* 571.

is made independently of the assumption of jurisdiction. The discretionary reference to foreign law emphasises the choice of law considerations operating within equitable jurisprudence. Within this approach, in some instances, the chancery court may "follow the law" and apply choice of law rules analogous to those applicable in the common law. This may be an explanation of the choice of law rules for express trusts following the choice of law rules for contract by analogy at common law, and the same approach may well apply to fiduciary duties arising in contractual or corporate contexts.[125]

A third approach is to accept that there is a unitary choice of law approach to all questions whether the putatively applicable rules originate within the historical equitable jurisdiction or not, but in the analysis of the problem, principles of equity need to be considered within unique categories of choice of law.[126] One example of this is the (tentative) approach of the English courts in the analysis of the equitable wrong of dishonest assistance of breach of fiduciary duties. The starting point is choice of law analysis, and there is a unitary methodology, but the category chosen is a unique category of equitable wrongs, with choice of law rules that are different from those applicable to common law wrongs.[127] This approach is favoured to some extent by Cheshire and North.[128] On this view, there is choice of law *for* equity, but the choice of law rules for equity may not be the same as those for other principles of law.

Which is the better approach?

It is the author's submission that the first approach is to be preferred to the other two, for the following reasons:

First, distinctions within domestic law, especially distinctions which originate from the history of the legal institutions in the country, or distinctions between concepts which do not have counterparts in other major legal systems, should be minimised for choice of law purposes.[129]

Secondly, any classification system that depends on the division between common law and equity in the forum's domestic law is confronted with significant difficulties when dealing with legal systems from legal traditions which do not recognise that distinction. Many civil law countries subsume into

---

125 *Paramasivam v Flynn*, above n 124 at 216-217.

126 The use of "equitable" categories is conceptually possible on the basis of the functional characterisation of claims or issues where foreign law in a non common law country serving equivalent functions as domestic principles of equity may be applied as a result of the use of such categories. Another view of its conceptual possibility based on the characterisation of a claim according to its applicable law is discussed in chapter 8 of this book by Robert Stevens, 'Choice of Law for Equity: Is It Possible?'.

127 See n 28 above.

128 *Cheshire and North*, at 1044 (in respect of wrongs but not in respect of restitution); L Barnard, "Choice of Law in Equitable Wrongs – A Comparative Analysis" [1992] *Cambridge Law Journal* 474. *Base Metal Trading Ltd v Shamurin* [2003] EWHC Com 2419; [2004] 1 All ER Comm 159, could be interpreted to take the same approach in employing a category of "equitable wrongs", but see n 119 above.

129 See M Wolff, *Private International Law* (2nd ed, Clarendon, Oxford, 1950) at [509]. See also, in a slightly different context, A Briggs, "Restitution Meets the Conflict of Laws" [1995] *Restitution Law Review* 94 at 97, *Macmillan Inc v Bishopsgate Investment Trusts plc (No 3)* [1996] 1 WLR 387 at 407.

substantive codes or principles affecting interpretation what English law would regard as equitable concepts. Even within the Commonwealth, the same wrong may be regarded as a common law tort in some jurisdictions but an equitable wrong in others. The reasons in domestic law for choosing common law or equity to deal with a specific social problem may have nothing to do with choice of law at all. For example, it was a matter of indifference to the English Court of Appeal whether a mortgagee's duty of care to the mortgagor was to be analysed in common law or equitable terms; the substance of the duty was more important.[130] On the other hand, the use of equity instead of common law in English law to develop a wrong to protect privacy is driven purely by considerations of domestic law.[131] The influence of such differences of domestic techniques should not be allowed to play too great a role in choice of law analysis.

Thirdly, choice of law rules should be "simple and easy to apply",[132] and of the three approaches discussed above, this is the simplest and easiest to apply. Adding the division between common law and equity into the process at this stage of the choice of law process unduly complicates the analysis.[133]

Fourthly, any distinction that is based on the historical division of the sources of law will run into serious difficulties when the particular doctrine in question has uncertain or mixed historical origins. For example, it is not clear whether the doctrine of good faith in contracts of utmost good faith originated in the common law or equity.[134] The origin of the rule against penalties in English law lies in a mixture of common law, equity and statute.[135] Choice of law analysis does not need to be fraught with such complexities.

Two further points may be noted about this approach. First, it is not undermined by the existence of the separate category of trusts within the conflict of laws. This category is not necessarily defined by the historical origin of the trust in English law, but by the concept of division of ownership and management within a legal institution.[136] Institutions bearing such characteristics, whatever their historical origins, will fall to be analysed under this category. Secondly, in the context of European law, in the event that the proposed Regulation on the Law Applicable to Non-Contractual Obligations (Rome II)[137] is adopted and comes into force, it is likely that all obligations will need to be interpreted to fall for consideration under the Rome Convention[138] (for contractual obligations) or the proposed Rome II Regulation (for non-contractual obligations), unless specifically excluded by

---

130 *Medforth v Blake* [2000] Ch 86 at 102.

131 (as affected by international instruments) *A v B plc* [2002] EWCA Civ 337; [2003] QB 195.

132 *Macmillan Inc v Bishopsgate Investment Trusts plc (No 3)* [1996] 1 WLR 387 at 392.

133 *A-G for England and Wales v R* [2002] 2 NZLR 91 at [29]; *Base Metal Trading Ltd v Shamurin*, above n 128.

134 HN Bennett, "Mapping the Doctrine of Utmost Good Faith in Insurance Contract Law" [1999] *Lloyds Maritime and Commercial Law Quarterly* 165.

135 C Harpum, 'Coming to Equity in Breach of Contract' in S Goldstein (ed), *Equity and Contemporary Legal Developments* (Harry and Michael Sacher Institute, Jerusalem, 1992) at 829.

136 The Hague Trusts Convention, n 24 above, Art 2.

137 COM(2003) 427 final - COD 2003/0168.

138 *Contracts (Applicable Law) Act 1990*, schedule.

these instruments. Unless so excluded, it is likely that equitable obligations will need to fit into one or the other of the two instruments.[139]

It may be argued against this approach that the traditional categories of the conflict of laws (apart from the category of trusts) are based on the Roman law and leaves no space for equity. However, it should be noted that the categories of choice of law serve a different purpose from the categories of domestic law. *Dicey and Morris* reminds us that:[140]

"characterisation is a process of refining English conflict rules by expressing them with greater precision. ... To believe that a term such as 'succession' has an objectively defined meaning which exists independently of the purpose for which it is used is mere conceptualism.

... The way the court should proceed is to consider the rationale of the English conflict rule and the purpose of the rule of substantive law to be characterised. On this basis, it can decide whether the conflict rule should be regarded as covering the rule of substantive law."

What is said of "succession" can be equally said of "contracts" or "torts". This approach has been endorsed by the English Court of Appeal:[141]

"The overall aim [of characterisation] is to identify the most *appropriate* law to govern a particular issue. The classes or categories of issue which the law recognises at the first stage are man-made, not natural. They have no inherent value, beyond their purpose in assisting to select the most appropriate law."

Thus, characterisation for choice of law purposes has no necessary conceptual connections with domestic classifications. Just as the characterisation of an agreement unsupported by consideration as "contractual" for choice of law purposes[142] does not detract from or undermine the significance of the doctrine of consideration in domestic contract law, the characterisation of certain types of fiduciary duties as "contractual" will not undermine their character and operation in domestic law as a unique gloss on the common law standards of conduct. Similarly, there should be no difficulty in seeing common law torts, equitable wrongs, and delict in civil law, as all belonging to the choice of law category of "torts", once we accept that "torts" here is not used as a legal term of art in the domestic law sense of wrongs recognised by the common law courts, but a category containing functionally equivalent rules (irrespective of historical origin or the specific content of the duty) for solving a particular kind of social problem. If necessary, the "torts" category could be relabelled "wrongs"[143] to remove any possible misconception of doctrinal connections

---

139 It will not, however, affect the analysis of equitable proprietary interests.
140 *Dicey and Morris*, at [2-034]-[2-035].
141 *Raiffeisen Zentralbank Österreich AG v Five Star Trading LLC* [2001] QB 825 at [27].
142 *Re Bonacina* [1912] 2 Ch 394.
143 In English law, the word "torts" has been entrenched in statute, but a private international meaning is clearly intended: *Private International Law (Miscellaneous Provisions) Act 1995*, s 9(2). In Australian law, preference has been indicated for "civil wrongs" as the basis for choice of law analysis, though it is not clear whether it was intended to comprehend wrongs in equity: see TM Yeo, *Choice of Law of Equitable Doctrines* (Oxford University Press, Oxford, 2004) at [8.62].

with "torts" in the narrow meaning in the domestic common law. The problems of characterisation for equitable principles and doctrines, while considerable, are not insurmountable.[144]

The justifications for the second approach – that there is a different choice of law methodology within equitable jurisprudence – insofar as they lie in the jurisdictional analysis of equity or in the peculiar nature of equity within the domestic law, have been rejected in the previous section. In *Paramasivam v Flynn*, the court additionally considered that, as a matter of policy, its proposed choice of law approach provided convenience and certainty, and avoided the difficulty of having to ascertain the relevant foreign law.[145] This argument goes too far as it threatens to undermine the rationale of choice of law altogether. Moreover, any certainty and convenience of the application of the law of the forum is counterbalanced by the possibility of modification by foreign law. It is not clear which foreign laws will be relevant, and in what way they will be taken into account at the discretion of the court. On the other hand, English law has denied the existence of this kind of discretion within choice of law analysis.[146]

The main points in favour of the third approach – that within a unitary choice of law methodology equitable principles require distinctive categories – lie in the argument that equitable concepts like fiduciary duties are subject to unitary analysis (ie, that fiduciary duties constitute a single analytical category in domestic law), and the argument that equitable obligations are distinct from and concurrent with common law obligations in contract and tort and restitution.[147] It may be argued that the categories in choice of law analysis reflect to a large extent the domestic categories, and for that reason, equitable principles call for separate characterisation.

It should be pointed out, however, that in the domestic law, the unitary analysis of a concept like the fiduciary duty belies the diversity of contexts and sources of the duty.[148] For the most part, fiduciary obligations can be understood as the imposition of (higher) standards of conduct in situations already within recognised categories of relationships.[149] From this perspective, fiduciary duties are amenable to analysis within existing categories of the conflict of laws. These may include contracts, torts, trusts, or the law of corporations.

It is also in this context that the concurrence argument should be appreciated. While equitable obligations may exist independently from and concurrently with common law obligations in domestic law, "concurrence"

---

144 This is the subject of *Choice of Law for Equitable Doctrines*, above n 143.

145 *Paramasivam v Flynn* (1998) 160 ALR 203 at 217.

146 Cf *Stockdale v Hansard* (1839) 9 Ad & E 1 at 216-217; 112 ER 1112 at 1193 where Coleridge J said that choice of law was not a matter of discretion for the English court.

147 L Barnard, "Choice of Law in Equitable Wrongs – A Comparative Analysis" [1992] *Cambridge Law Journal* 474, approved in *Cheshire and North*, at 1044.

148 PD Finn, 'Fiduciary Law and the Modern Commercial World' in E McKendrick (ed), *Commercial Aspects of Trusts and Fiduciary Obligations* (Clarendon, Oxford, 1992) at 7, 9; PD Finn, *Fiduciary Obligations* (Lawbook Co Sydney, 1977) at 3-4; L Sealy, "Fiduciary Relationships" [1962] *Cambridge Law Journal* 69 at 73.

149 J Hackney, 'More than a trace of the old philosophy' in P Birks (ed), *The Classification of Obligations* (Oxford University Press, Oxford, 1997) 123; GL Gretton, "Constructive Trusts: I" (1997) 1 *Edinburgh Law Review* 281 at 290.

here focuses on the separateness of the jurisdictions that formerly administered common law and equity separately. Accepting that equitable obligations may exist concurrently with common law obligations within domestic law does not detract from the fact that the full effect of the domestic legal system on a transaction or situation cannot be appreciated without considering how the equitable obligations operate to modify or to provide a gloss on the common law obligations. This type of concurrence need not have any significance at the choice of law level. It should be left to the domestic applicable law to deal with the relationship and interaction between its own internal branches of the law.

CONCLUSION

The conflict of laws positions in several significant Commonwealth jurisdictions reveal different approaches to the choice of law question for equitable doctrines. Modern Australian law has shown a clear inclination towards the second approach – a distinctive choice of law methodology within equitable discourse, with the general application of the law of the forum and discretionary reference to foreign law, and "following the law" by analogy in some cases. The modern approach in English law has been wavering between the first approach of dealing with the differences between common law and equity after the domestic applicable law has been found (and found to contain such a division), and the third approach of using a unitary choice of law approach but with differences of characterisation and choice of law rules depending on whether the equitable jurisdiction of the forum has been invoked. While it has not decisively rejected the second approach, it has not been sympathetic to it. The proposed Rome II Regulation, if and when it takes effect as law in the European Union, is likely to lead to the consequence in English law that all obligations whatever their historical domestic origins will be required to be analysed under the Rome Convention for contractual obligations or the Rome II Regulation for non-contractual obligations, unless the obligation falls outside the scope of both instruments altogether. New Zealand law has indicated a clear preference for the first approach.

Do these different attitudes to the choice of law analysis of equitable principles reflect the internal thinking on the question of fusion of common law and equity within the respective jurisdictions? The correlation is certainly striking. Given that choice of law rules are rules of municipal law, the question whether there is one or two choice of law approaches in a legal system necessarily raises a question of domestic law, and ultimately the relationship between common law and equity, but *for the purpose of choice of law*. There is no necessary correlation between the question whether there should be one or two choice of law methodologies at that level, and the question of fusion or otherwise of substantive rules at the level of domestic law. While choice of law rules are rules of domestic law, they deal with problems on a different plane. Fusion fallacy would not necessarily arise even if the Australian court were to adopt the first approach. A fusion fallacy arises if a result is obtained through the combined application of the principles of common law and equity which could not have been obtained before the fusion of the administration of the two streams of jurisprudence. But there is clear evidence of the first approach within equity jurisprudence even in respect of matters within the exclusive jurisdiction of the chancery court: the express trust and doctrines in beneficial succession from an early time, and issues relating to restitution in modern times.

It is the author's submission that whatever view is taken of the relationship between common law and equity within the domestic substantive law, there should be a common choice of law methodology,[150] and that choice of law methodology should not be unduly influenced by the internal divisions and institutional histories of the domestic law of the forum.

While equity reflects a unique methodology within the common law tradition, it should be borne in mind that foreign systems from other legal traditions are likely to have found solutions to problems dealt with by the equitable principles of the forum.[151] For example, where English law would use the resulting trust, a civil law country may use principles of restitution or contract. What the common law world sees as breaches of fiduciary duties may be seen as breaches of contract, the abuse of rights or breaches of good faith. Interference with trusts or fiduciary duties may be seen as delictual. There is likely to be correspondence of rights or claims between common law systems and systems from other legal traditions, but not necessarily correspondence of domestic categories. It is the function of choice of law rules to arbitrate between the differences of domestic characterisations in disputes involving international elements, and the forum should be cautious not to project too much of its own domestic taxonomy into the conflicts sphere. The overriding nature of equity is rooted within the specific domestic law of the forum. It is highly questionable that this overriding nature in domestic law necessarily translates into values that are universal and overriding in the sense that is represented in the fundamental public policy or international mandatory rules of the forum.

A sophisticated system of conflict of laws will distinguish clearly between rules of domestic law on one hand and the rules for the selection of the applicable domestic law. It will also provide for the application of forum rules where they matter most for the smooth functioning of the machinery of adjudication and enforcement, and also allow for the protection of fundamental values which are universal in the eyes of the forum and important social or economic interests of the forum. The traditional choice of law methodology in the common law has both these characteristics. To the extent that some equitable (or common law) principles possess this universal character in the view of the forum, they can, and must, be given effect to within the traditional choice of law methodology. Apart from this, the question of choice of law for equity must remain an open and outstanding question.

---

150 The question whether this should be the traditional methodology or some version of interest analysis is beyond the scope of this chapter.

151 See, for example, T Honoré and E Cameron, *Honoré's South African Law of Trusts* (4th ed, Juta, Cape Town, 1992) at [74], [76] and [77]

8

Choice of Law for Equity: Is it Possible?

ROBERT STEVENS

INTRODUCTION

This chapter will seek to answer one question. Is it possible to adopt a characterisation of issues which is specifically equitable for the purpose of choice of law?

Equitable doctrines are the body of rules which have their historical provenance in the Chancery division of the High Court of Justice. Equity can be "described but not defined."[1] This is because the rules are unified by their origin rather than by any contextual or conceptual coherence. Prima facie, one would no more expect to have choice of law rules which are specific to the Chancery division than one would expect them in the Common Pleas.

JURISDICTION

For jurisdictional purposes it is perfectly possible to have the rules for determining when the court has jurisdiction shaped according to whether the claim is equitable or not. For example, in England under the traditional rules of jurisdiction where permission of the court is required for service out of the jurisdiction, it is necessary for the claimant to formulate his claim as falling within one of the paragraphs of rule 6.20 of the *Civil Procedure Rules 1998*. Paragraph 14 allows service to be authorised where a claim is made against the defendant as constructive trustee and his alleged liability arises out of acts committed within the jurisdiction. Whatever the desirability of framing jurisdictional rules in this way, there is no doubt that it can be done. Although commonly not differentiated, the characterisation issues raised at the jurisdiction stage are quite different from those raised in choosing the appropriate applicable law.

---

1   R Meagher, JD Heydon, M Leeming, *Meagher Gummow and Lehane's Equity: Doctrines and Remedies* (4th ed, Butterworths, 2002, Sydney).

CHOICE OF LAW

The lex fori?

As Professor Yeo has carefully shown in the previous chapter, it is unacceptable for a court when faced with a claim which under domestic law has an equitable historical provenance simply to apply the lex fori.

If the English courts' rules on jurisdiction were very narrow, it might make sense to dispense entirely with choice of law rules. If, for example, the English court would only assume jurisdiction where no foreign element was involved or where both parties were agreed that English law applied to the dispute, there would be no need for choice of law rules. This is not the case either at law or in equity. At one time the Chancery Courts did have narrower rules on jurisdiction so that applying the lex fori appeared more defensible. In most respects the rules on jurisdiction have been merged since the *Judicature Act* of 1873. To the extent that there are differences today, the equitable jurisdictional rules are wider than those at common law.[2] Sadly, Australian courts (especially those of New South Wales) have been reluctant to accept that it is inappropriate simply to apply the equitable rules of the forum where foreign elements are present.[3] What would our attitude be to another legal system if its courts simply applied its own domestic rules when exercising a long-arm jurisdiction?

Perhaps a modern day example where it is still appropriate to apply the lex fori because of narrow jurisdictional rules is the anti-suit injunction. Generally, the English court will only exercise jurisdiction when it is the natural forum of the dispute.[4] In that context, the courts have not seen choice of law as relevant.[5]

Once it is accepted that it is as necessary to discern the appropriate applicable law in the context of equitable doctrines as it is at common law, the impossibility of a uniform choice of law rule applicable to all such doctrines becomes apparent. Traditional choice of law categories are, if not the same, very similar within both the common law and civilian traditions. The chapter headings in Dicey and Morris would be recognisable by a French lawyer: contract, tort, property etc. Equitable doctrines cut across these categories. Specific performance is an equitable contractual remedy. Dishonest assistance in a breach of trust closely resembles secondary liability in tort, for example, procuring a breach of contract or procuring a trespass. To state that "equity acts in personam" is, as Meagher, Gummow and Lehane demonstrate "for most

2   *Penn v Lord Baltimore* (1750) 1 Ves Sen 444; 27 ER 1132; *Webb v Webb* [1994] QB 696; [1994] ECR I-1717 concerning what is now Art 22(1) of Council Regulation (EC) No 44/2001.

3   For example, *National Commercial Bank v Wimborne* (1978) 5 BPR 1958; *United States Surgical Corporation v Hospital Products International Pty Ltd* [1982] 2 NSWLR 766 at 797-798 per McLelland J, affirmed [1983] 2 NSWLR 157, reversed on different grounds (1984) 156 CLR 41; *Paramasivam v Flynn* (1998) 90 FCR 489 at 500-504 per curiam. Compare the approach of Millett J and the English Court of Appeal *Macmillan Inc v Bishopsgate Investment Trust plc (No 3)* [1995] 1 WLR 978 at 989; [1996] 1 WLR 387.

4   *Airbus Industries GIE v Patel* [1999] 1 AC 119.

5   See A Briggs, "The unrestrained reach of an anti-suit injunction: a pause for thought" [1997] *Lloyds Maritime and Commercial Law Quarterly* 90.

purposes ... today wholly incorrect."[6] It is not seriously arguable today that the beneficiary under a trust does not have a right in rem just as much as the owner of a £5 note.

If a uniform equitable choice of law rule is obviously unrealistic, is there room for equitable choice of law specific to particular rules? For example, could the category of "knowing receipt of trust property" be recognised as having its own specific choice of law rules? This raises a difficult question concerning the nature of characterisation.

A straitjacket or a ladder?

The recent decision of the Court of Appeal in *Base Metal Trading Ltd v Shamurin*[7] nicely raises the issue of the correct approach to characterisation. Two Russian businessmen incorporated a company under the law of Guernsey. Both were appointed as directors and one, Shamurin, was employed to trade metals. The company alleged that the defendant had been careless in his trading and that as a result it had suffered a loss of $6 million. The claim was put in three ways. First that the defendant was in breach of his contract of employment. Second that the defendant owed the claimant a duty of care in the law of tort, which had been breached. Third that as a director the defendant owed the claimant an equitable duty of care. Each claim potentially had a different law applicable to it. The defendant argued that it was impermissible in private international law to accumulate claims in this way.[8]

In order to assess the correct approach to questions of characterisation, it is important to know what the question, which the expert on foreign law will have to answer, is. For example, let it be assumed that a category of 'equitable wrongs' exists as a separate category for the purpose of choice of law,[9] alongside torts and contract. If the claim is characterised as an equitable wrong and the choice of law rule applicable to such claims, whatever it may be, pointed to Russian law as applicable, what is the question for the expert on Russian law?

The key issue is whether the initial characterisation of the issue as one concerning equitable wrongdoing persists after a particular law has been ascertained as applicable.[10] If the initial characterisation does persist,[11] if it is a straitjacket, then the question for the Russian legal expert will be one he cannot answer. The question "Would a claim on these facts based upon an equitable wrong succeed in Russia?" would be met with a puzzled frown. Legal systems outside of the common law tradition do not have a category of equitable wrongs. The alternative is for the initial characterisation to be

---

6   R Meagher, JD Heydon, M Leeming, *Meagher Gummow and Lehane's Equity: Doctrines and Remedies*, above n 1 at 118.

7   [2005] 1 WLR 1157 (CA).

8   See A Briggs, *"Choice of choice of law"* [2003] *Lloyds Maritime and Commercial Law Quarterly* 12.

9   PM North and JJ Fawcett, *Cheshire & North's Private International Law* (13th ed, Butterworths, London, 1999) at 1044.

10   A Briggs, *The Conflict of Laws* (Clarendon Press, Oxford, 2002) at 13, 18-19.

11   *Ogden v Ogden* [1908] P 46.

abandoned. The question for the Russian legal expert would be "Would a claim on these facts succeed?"

Whether an initial characterisation necessarily persists has not been squarely addressed by the courts. The decision in *Ogden v Ogden* gives some support for the persistence of the characterisation. The English court classified the question of whether parental consent was required for a marriage as a question of form. French law characterised parental consent as going to the capacity to marriage: an issue of essential validity. English law governed the marriage's formal validity; French law its essential validity. The Frenchman who had married an Englishwoman was nineteen and had not obtained his parents' consent as required by the French Code. The Court of Appeal held the marriage to be valid, since the ceremony had been performed in accordance with the requirements of English law. If a question for a French legal expert had arisen it would have been "Was the marriage essentially invalid because of a reason English law would regard as going to essential validity?" To which the answer was "No".

However, *Ogden v Ogden* does not squarely address the question of whether the initial characterisation persists. Even if the issue of parental consent had been seen as going to capacity, the result would have been the same because of the rule of English law to the effect that an incapacity by the law of one party's domicile will be ignored if the marriage is celebrated in England and the other party is domiciled in England.[12]

The fact that that we characterise issues and not simply causes of action provides some support for the view that an initial characterisation should persist. If in a contract made between a Chinese corporation and an English corporation governed by English law, the issue arose as to whether the Chinese corporation had capacity to contract, the question for the foreign legal expert would be "Does this Chinese corporation have capacity to contract?" The court would be unconcerned with whether the contract might be invalid under Chinese domestic law for some other reason, for example the failure to comply with a requirement of form or the application of duress.

On the persistence model, if it is for the lex fori to adopt an initial characterisation this must be done in a "broad internationalist spirit."[13] Put another way, it is necessary to frame our choice of law categories in such a way that they are common to legal systems which have a tradition other than the common law. So, a claim that a gratuitous promise is enforceable by the law of another legal system may be characterised as contractual, even though a promise unsupported by consideration is not contractual in English law.[14] However, this "broad internationalist" approach need not, and should not, persist when it comes to the question for the foreign legal expert. So, if the claim is characterised by the lex fori as contractual and the applicable law is ascertained, the question for the foreign legal expert is "Would a claim characterised by your domestic law as contractual succeed on these facts?" and not "Would a claim

---

12   *Sottomayer v De Barros (No 2)* (1879) LR 5 PD 94.
13   *Raiffeisen Zentralbank Osterreich AG v Five Star General Trading LLC* [2001] QB 825 at 840 [27] per Mance LJ.
14   *Re Bonacina* [1912] 2 Ch 394.

which is characterised in a broad internationalist spirit as contractual by the lex fori, succeed on these facts?" To this extent, the claim is characterised by the applicable law.

It may be that there are legal systems with idiosyncratic categorisations which do not recognise species of claim which are common to the vast majority of legal systems. I do not know of any legal system which has no contract law, no law of tort (however labelled) and, indeed, no law of unjust enrichment.[15] If the characterisation persists, adopting a separate category of equitable wrongs will inevitably mean that where the applicable law falls outside of the common law tradition, no claim based upon an equitable characterisation can succeed.

It should not be thought that this is a problem faced solely by common law systems. German law has a category of liability for bad faith in contractual negotiations, culpa in contrahendo, unknown to other legal systems. Similarly, civilian legal systems allow a "Good Samaritan" a claim for the expenses he has incurred on behalf of the defendant within a category distinct from contract, tort and unjust enrichment: negotiorum gestio contraria. Such a separate category has yet to be recognised in the common law. If an Australian legal expert was asked in a German court whether a claim would succeed in either of these categories in New South Wales, he would have to reply that no such category existed in Australian domestic law.

On the alternative model, that the initial characterisation of the issue does not persist, characterisation is a ladder which, once it has taken you to another legal system, can be kicked away. The question for the Russian legal expert would therefore be "What would a Russian court do presented with these facts?" or if issues of renvoi were sought to be avoided, "What would a Russian court do if these facts had occurred in a wholly domestic context?" On this model, it would be possible to have a category of equitable wrongs. Indeed on this approach, wholly idiosyncratic characterisations could be adopted by a legal system for purposes of choice of law and a "broad internationalist spirit" is unnecessary.

Who gets to choose?

The difficulty with the approach of dropping the initial characterisation is that a single set of facts may give rise to claims which may be analysed in a number of alternative ways.[16] If, in *Base Metal*, it had been alleged that Mr Shamurin had diverted company funds to himself, a claim in unjust enrichment or knowing receipt could have been added to the claims based upon the agreement. The choice of law rules applicable to each category of claim are not necessarily the same and will not necessarily point to the same system of law. If four different possible characterisations pointed to four different legal systems can the claimant choose how to characterise his claim for the purposes of

---

15   Cf *Roxborourgh v Rothmans of Pall Mall Australia Ltd* (2001) 208 CLR 516 at 543-544[71], 548-551[83]-[89] per Gummow J.

16   A Briggs, "Choice of choice of law" [2003] *Lloyds Maritime and Commercial Law Quarterly* 12; TM Yeo, *Choice of Law for Equitable Doctrines* (Oxford University Press, Oxford, 2004) at 81-84.

private international law? Can it be right that the claimant is successful if any one legal system would allow recovery, regardless of the basis upon which that legal system would permit recovery? If the initial characterisation does not persist, to allow the claimant to accumulate claims in this way is clearly unfair: the claimant will succeed if he wins under any one of four legal systems, the defendant must win under all four if he is to succeed. The problem is exacerbated by the view that the characterisation of a claim for the purposes of private international law is broader than it is for the purposes of domestic law. So, a promise unsupported by consideration can be characterised as contractual for the purposes of private international law[17] even though as a matter of English or Australian domestic law there would be no contract. The possibility of overlap, or alternative analysis of the same set of facts enabling the claimant to formulate his claim in multiple different ways, is consequently greatly increased.

The court will not, of its own motion, apply a foreign law. Unless one of the parties argues for the application of a different law, the domestic law of the forum will be applied. If it is argued that a foreign law applies, is it the court or the party which raises the foreign law which characterises the issue raised?

Under English domestic law, a claimant is entitled to choose to frame his claim in the way most favourable to him.[18] The Court of Appeal in *Base Metal* was confronted with the question as to whether this choice was available to the claimant for the purposes of choice of law. They held that it was.

The alternatives to the decision of the Court of Appeal in *Base Metal* are set out by Professor Yeo.[19] First a claim could be characterised as only falling within one category.[20] On the facts of *Base Metal* this solution seems the correct one. Although the claimants sought to characterise their claim in three different ways, these alternatives were more illusory than real. The categories adopted for the purposes of choice of law within the law of obligations correspond with the event which generates the obligation: contract, tort and, probably, unjust enrichment. The duty of care imposed upon the defendant arose because of the agreement employing him to trade metal. Absent this agreement, no duty of care would have existed. However the claim is dressed up, the source of the claimant's right is always the agreement and the same result should always be reached. However, this approach will not always be appropriate. If, for example, an employee is defamed in letters of reference carelessly given by his employer, an employee has two claims with two distinct sources of right. He has a right to his reputation which is good against the whole world and he has a right against his employer that the reference will be carefully prepared, a right arising because of the contract of employment.[21] A single set of facts can give rise to two claims based upon different rights. It seems indefensible to argue that a characterisation which would have been correct if it had been the only one possible becomes incorrect because additional facts make another characterisa-

---

17   *Re Bonacina*, above n 14.
18   *Henderson v Merrett Syndicates Ltd* [1995] 2 AC 145.
19   TM Yeo, *Choice of Law for Equitable Doctrines*, above n 16 at 81-84.
20   TM Yeo, *Choice of Law for Equitable Doctrines*, above n 16 at 82.
21   *Spring v Guardian Assurance Plc* [1995] 2 AC 296.

tion possible. A second possibility is to adopt a hierarchy of possible character-isations. For example, where a claim could be characterised as contractual or tortious it will be treated as contractual. Where it could be characterised as tortious or an equitable wrong it will be treated as tortious.[22] In the choice of law context, there is no authority for such a hierarchy. How is the hierarchy to be determined? Is a tortious claim always to be subordinate to a contractual, no matter how implausible the contractual claim? Would the hierarchy approach apply only to claims or to choice of law issues generally? A third possibility is that choice of law rules are sufficiently flexible that it does not matter which characterisation is adopted. It may be doubted whether different choice of law rules will always point to the same system of law where the rights relied upon are quite distinct, as in the example of the defamed employee, and such uniformity of result is "crying for the moon".[23]

If the claimant is entitled to frame his claim in any way he sees fit, this approach can only be justified if the original characterisation persists. If the choice of law rules for contract point to Russia, tort to Guernsey, equitable wrongs to New South Wales and unjust enrichment to England, it cannot be correct that the claimant can win if any one of those four categories of claim can be made out in any one of the four legal systems. By contrast, if the characteri-sation does persist, applying Russian contract law to the contractual claim, the tort law of Guernsey to the tort claim and so on, allowing the claimant freedom to assert his claim in these different ways is no more objectionable than it would be if the matter arose in a wholly domestic context. The approach of the court in *Base Metal* implicitly supports the persistence of the characterisation.

If the characterisation persists, there is the possibility of gaps. It is possible that under Russian domestic law the claim would succeed, but not in the law of contract. Similarly, under the law of Guernsey the claim would succeed but not in the law of tort. Indeed, it is possible that the claim would succeed under all possible applicable laws, but not under the characterisation for which they are applicable. Concluding that the claim fails, although it would succeed if it had arisen in a domestic context of any of the possibly applicable laws, seems unac-ceptable.[24] If the characterisation does persist, an exception must be made in such a case and the claim should succeed.

Most importantly for the purposes of this chapter, if the court's initial characterisation does persist, is there room for a category of choice of law rules for 'equitable wrongs' or any other specifically equitable doctrine? It would only make sense to allow such equitable categories if it was also always accepted that the claim could also be characterised in other ways which are universally recognised. Adopting a single characterisation which does not approach the universal, for example the category of equitable wrongs, will increase the number of 'gaps'. Like an Englishman with a laptop computer with a three-pin plug who travels to France, asking a French lawyer whether the defendant is liable for an equitable wrong will not be productive. If however, it was accepted

---

22 Cf the subordination of claims in unjust enrichment to contractual claims in French law.
23 *Henderson v Merrett Syndicates Ltd*, above n 18 at 186 per Lord Goff.
24 Cf *re Cohn* [1945] Ch 5. See generally O Kahn-Freund, *General Problems of Private Interna-tional Law* (Alphen aan den Rijn, Sitjhoff, 1976), chapter IX at 231-236.

that all equitable wrongs could also always be characterised as tortious, specific rules could be made to work, although the inevitable duplication makes such an approach unattractive.

How free is the choice?

If *Base Metal* is right, how free is the claimant's choice to frame his claim in a particular way? One limitation is that the category of claim must be one for which the court is prepared to recognise that there are choice of law rules which apply. So, a claimant probably cannot assert in an English or Australian court:

> "I wish to bring a negotiorum gestio contraria claim. There are specific choice of law rules for such claims which indicate that German law is to apply, under which law I have a good claim."

There are probably no such choice of law rules specific to such claims in England or Australia. This is so despite their conceptual distinctiveness, at least as a matter of German law. The claimant must fit the claim, however artificially into one of the English or Australian forum's categories. If this cannot be done, such claims cannot be brought before the court and are lost in the void. Further, as already noted, if the initial characterisation persists and the applicable law does not recognise the sort of claim being asserted, the claim will fail.

The importance of the Hague Trusts Convention is that it inserts into non-common law jurisdictions a set of choice of law rules for trusts. It is possible to assert before an Italian court:

> "I wish to claim that there is an asset held on trust for me. There are specific choice of law rules applicable to trusts which indicate that English law is to apply, under which law such a trust is valid."

Trusts are not, therefore, lost in a void before the Italian court. The English implementing statute was the *Recognition of Trusts Act 1987*.[25] At first sight, this title appears a misnomer, as the legislation does not concern *recognition* of foreign court judgments but applicable law. However, the goal of the Convention is the recognition of trusts in countries which do not have such an institution, or only have it in an undeveloped form. It may be doubted whether the choice of law rules adopted under the Convention for trusts are in any way an improvement upon the common law rules as they could have developed over time, but this criticism misses the point of the Convention.

Let us assume that under the domestic law of the forum a claim based upon a tort would be unsuccessful. If a claim may only be characterised as tortious where it would succeed under the forum's domestic law, this would be to require "double actionability" of the tort both under the law of the forum and the law applicable to the tort. Such an approach closely resembles the rule in *Chaplin v Boys*[26] which has been criticised by academics and abandoned in England by legislation.

---

25   *Trusts (Hague Convention) Act 1991* (Cth) in Australia.
26   [1971] AC 356.

As stated above, it is usually argued that an "internationalist" approach allow the court to recognise claims as tortious even though not recognised as such under the court's domestic law. For example some systems may have torts of privacy or insult whilst others do not, the lex fori may characterise such claims as tortious although they do not exist as a matter of domestic law. A claim based upon a gratuitous promise may be recognised as contractual although unsupported by consideration. The category of equitable wrongs would also be potentially wider than those claims which would succeed under the domestic law of the forum. The claimant's choice would be fettered to the extent that the court would not permit the claimant to assert a characterisation outside of the limits it determines as legitimate for the purposes of private international law but this need not be the same as the limits in a domestic context.

The difficulty with the 'internationalist' approach is that it requires the answer to a potentially impossible question. The correct characterisation of claims as a matter of English domestic law can be extremely controversial. In principle, however, it should be possible to classify all forms of successful action. How are claims to be characterised in a different way for the purposes of private international law? There is not an international law of tort, still less an international law of equitable wrongs from which the question "is this claim tortious?" or "is this claim based upon an equitable wrong?" can be answered. If, say, the domestic law of Ruritania would classify a certain claim as a tort, when no other jurisdiction would do so, by what criteria are we to assess whether the Ruritanian classification is "wrong" or one which we will not allow a claimant to assert?

Using someone else's sockets

If *Base Metal* is correct that the claimant is entitled to assert his claim in anyway he chooses, it is possible that the characterisation is to be done in accordance with the applicable law, without reference to the lex fori.[27] The claimant can argue:

> "Under Ruritanian tort law, I have a good claim. English choice of law rules in tort indicate that Ruritanian law determines tortious issues. Therefore, I have a good claim. The fact that English domestic law would characterise the claim as contractual is irrelevant."

Characterising according to the applicable law is usually dismissed as unworkable. It is criticised as circular[28] but no circularity arises if the claimant is entitled to make an initial choice as to how his claim is to be asserted. Only one law will be applicable to the tortious claim as the forum's conflicts rules will point to one potentially applicable legal system for such a claim. Similarly a defendant could argue:

> "Under Ruritanian tort law, this claim fails. English choice of law rules in tort indicate that Ruritanian law determines tortious issues. Therefore, the claim

---

27 M Wolff, *Private International Law* (2nd ed, Clarendon Press, Oxford, 1950) at 138-157.
28 L Collins (ed), *Dicey and Morris on 'The Conflict of Laws'* (13th ed, Sweet & Maxwell, London, 2000) at 36.

fails. The fact that English domestic law would characterise the claim as contractual is irrelevant."

If successful, it would then be for the claimant to establish that he had a good claim characterised in some other way.

Such an approach does not require the court to characterise the claim according to a notional international standard as to when a particular characterisation of a claim is a legitimate one, even though not one which would be adopted in the domestic law of the forum. It suffices if the characterisation is one which accords with the domestic law of the applicable law and is selected by the forum's choice of law rule for that category of claim.

A mirror?

It would be possible for equity to develop an international set of choice of law rules which mirrors those at common law. So, there are equitable rules for contract, tort, property and so on, but no category of, say, equitable wrongs. However, it is difficult to see what reason there could be for different sets of rules. Nor would it be clear how, in a world where the common law and equity are administered in the same court, the court is supposed to choose between different sets of rules applicable to the same category of claim. Presumably the equitable rules would prevail and we would have one set of rules.

The dead hand of legislation

In England, the choice of law rules for contractual claims are now set out in the Rome Convention enacted by the *Contracts (Applicable Law) Act 1990*. At some point, the Convention will be replaced by a Council Regulation. For the purposes of the Convention "contractual obligations" has an autonomous meaning and is not defined by the domestic law of any country.[29] It seems highly likely that fiduciary duties which arise because of contract, as defined under the Convention, should be within the scope of the Convention.

The result under the Convention appears appropriate. Some have argued that fiduciary duties belong to a distinct category of equitable wrongs.[30] This appears to be a category error. A parallel can be drawn with duties of care, which can arise at law and in equity. The categories for the purposes of choice of law within the law of obligations correspond with the event which generates the obligation, rather than the content of the obligation: contract, tort and, probably, unjust enrichment. So, if it is alleged a duty of care arises because it has been agreed to, the governing law will be the law of the contract. If it is alleged that the duty of care arises independently of agreement, the governing law will (virtually always) be selected by the choice of law rules for tort.

Describing a duty as one of care describes the content of the obligation, not the reason for its existence. Similarly, describing a duty as a fiduciary duty describes the content of the duty not the reason for its existence. A fiduciary

---

29   Article 18.
30   L Barnard, "Choice of law in Equitable Wrongs: A Comparative Analysis" (1992) 51 *Cambridge Law Journal* 474.

duty could be described as a duty to subordinate one's own interests to the interests of someone else. Sometimes this duty arises because of agreement. Solicitors owe fiduciary duties to their clients because they have agreed to act for them. Sometimes the duty arises by operation of law. A parent who is asked by a surgeon to make a decision about the treatment of his sick child is under a fiduciary duty in the making of the decision, but such duty does not arise by agreement.

There is not, and nor should there be, a unitary choice of law rule applicable to fiduciary obligations anymore than there is for duties of care.

When (if?) the choice of law rules for non-contractual obligations are finally handed down in the form of a Regulation of the Council of the European Union, there will no longer be any room in England for arguing about the independence of equitable wrongs within private international law. If and when this Regulation comes into effect, all obligations will have to be interpreted as fitting into either the Rome Convention or the Rome II Regulation.

CONCLUSION

In the ninth edition of *Dicey and Morris' on The Conflict of Laws*, published in 1973, the editors included for the first time a chapter concerning the law applicable to trusts. As the common law authorities applicable to such claims were almost non-existent the chapter was "an exercise in the difficult art of making bricks without straw."[31] The example of a specific rule applicable to trusts makes it at least plausible that rules specific to other forms of equitable right are possible if it can be demonstrated that they are both coherent and distinct from categories for which choice of law rules already exist.

Claims for restitution, under the heading Quasi-Contract, appeared earlier in the sixth edition of *Dicey's The Conflict of Laws* in 1949.[32] In England, it seems that further innovation is about to become impossible as the verdant common law is covered in concrete by Regulations of the European Union. Fortunately, the same fate need not befall legal systems within the common law family outside of Europe.

Outside of the European Union the possibility of choice of law rules for equitable doctrines will continue to turn upon whether the court's approach to the characterisation of a claim has only one correct answer which persists for the purpose of the question for the expert in foreign law. "What would a Japanese court do in these circumstances?" will be comprehensible to a Japanese lawyer, "Is there an estoppel by convention?" will not be. If the view of the English Court of Appeal prevails and the claimant is entitled to characterise his claim in any way he sees fit, then the characterisation must persist. However, as the court also allowed the claim to be characterised in several different ways, it may be possible to formulate categories of claim which are specific to the

---

31   JHC Morris (ed), *Dicey and Morris on the Conflict of Laws* (9th ed, 1973, London, Stevens & Sons Ltd) at x.

32   JHC Morris (ed), *Dicey and Morris on the Conflict of Laws*, above n 31. The heading in the current edition is "Restitution"

common law tradition, provided that it is also always accepted that such claims can also always be characterised in more universal ways. With only *Base Metal* to work with, whether specific equitable rules are possible is unclear.

In this chapter, I have not tried to answer the question whether choice of law rules which are specific to equitable doctrines are desirable. Those who wish to know the full answer to that question should read Professor Yeo's chapter and his superb book, *Choice of Law for Equitable Doctrines*.

9

Are the Duties of Company Directors to Exercise Care and Skill Fiduciary?

J D Heydon[*]

---

[*]   I am indebted to Rachel Davis and Julie Taylor for their comments.

SOME CONTROVERSIES

Plaintiffs to whom duties are owed by fiduciaries often suffer losses as a result of the misconduct of third parties. Sometimes the losses occur contemporaneously with breach by those fiduciaries of their duties; sometimes they also occur contemporaneously with failures by the plaintiffs to protect their own interests. Where redress is barred by the insolvency of the third parties, the plaintiffs tend to search the law for avenues of recovery against the fiduciaries. Those avenues are often obstructed by the absence, or weakness, of any causal relationship between the breach by the fiduciaries and the loss suffered by the plaintiffs. These plaintiffs appeal to equitable doctrines which, they asseverate, are not encumbered by any, or any onerous, need to prove causation. As a result, the plaintiffs – immune from allegations that their own fault contributed to the loss,[1] but choosing to proceed against the less blameworthy of potential defendants, the fiduciaries – sometimes appear to be in an unmeritorious position, as between themselves and those fiduciaries. It is therefore not surprising that that endeavour has stimulated judicial scepticism. One of its manifestations concerns controversies about the characterisation of duties to exercise care and skill owed by fiduciaries as not being fiduciary.

There are examples of controversies about the duties of skill and care, prudence and diligence owed by a trustee (the "trustee's duty to exercise care and skill").[2]

(a) It has been affirmed[3] and denied[4] that the trustee's duty to exercise care and skill is not fiduciary.

(b) It has been affirmed[5] and denied[6] that the trustee's duty to exercise care and skill is not part of the "irreducible core of obligations owed by the trustees to the beneficiaries and enforceable by them which is fundamental to the concept of a trust", and is distinct from the fiduciary's "core liability" – the obligation of "single-minded loyalty".[7]

---

1 At least in Australia (*Pilmer v Duke Group Ltd (in liq)* (2001) 207 CLR 165 at 201[86] and 231[173]) and England (*Nationwide Building Society v Balmer Radmore (a firm)* [1999] PNLR 606); cf New Zealand (*Day v Mead* [1987] 2 NZLR 443).

2 *Armitage v Nurse* [1998] Ch 241 at 253. The expressions appear to be used interchangeably in relation to trustees. There are express references to "skill" in *Trustee Act 2000* (UK), s 1. See also *Trustee Act 1925* (NSW), s 14A(2); *Trustee Act 1925* (ACT), s 14A(2); *Trustee Act* (NT), s 6(1); *Trusts Act 1973* (Qld), s 22(1); *Trustee Act 1936* (SA), s 7; *Trustee Act 1898* (Tas), s 7(1); *Trustee Act 1958* (Vic), s 6(1); *Trustees Act 1962* (WA), s 18(1) and *Trustee Act 1956* (NZ), ss 13B-13C.

3 *Permanent Building Society (in liq) v Wheeler* (1994) 11 WAR 187 at 237 ("*Wheeler's* case"); *Bristol and West Building Society v Mothew* [1998] Ch 1 at 17 ("*Mothew's* case").

4 DSK Ong, *Trusts Law in Australia*, (2nd ed, Federation Press, Sydney, 2003) at 209.

5 *Armitage v Nurse* [1998] Ch 241 at 253.

6 DSK Ong, *Trusts Law in Australia*, above n 4 at 216-217.

7 *Mothew's* case, above n 3 at 18. This idea has been taken further, in the assertion that "fraud, even when committed by a trustee, is a tort, not a breach of trust": S Worthington, "Fiduciaries: When is Self-Denial Obligatory?" [1999] *Cambridge Law Journal* 500 at 502: but the authority cited, *Paragon Finance plc v Thakerar & Co (a firm)* [1999] 1 All ER 400, does not support the proposition: the Court of Appeal held only (at 406) that an amendment alleging an intentional breach of fiduciary duty introduced a properly pleaded but new cause of action, which was additional to an unsatisfactorily pleaded allegation of non-intentional breach of fiduciary duty.

(c) It has been affirmed[8] that, and questioned whether,[9] although the trustee's duty to exercise care and skill is equitable, and breach of it sounds in equitable compensation, the availability of that equitable compensation rests on common law damages rules, adopted by analogy, and not on the rules which apply to equitable compensation for breach of duties which are "fiduciary" in a narrower sense.

There are also examples of controversies about the duties of a company director to exercise reasonable care, skill and diligence ("the director's duty to exercise reasonable care and skill").[10]

(d) Thus it has been affirmed[11] and denied[12] that there is a director's duty to exercise reasonable care and skill in tort.

(e) It has also been affirmed[13] and denied[14] that although there is a director's duty to exercise reasonable care and skill in equity,[15] it is not a fiduciary duty.

There is almost unanimous support for those who affirm the propositions set out above.[16]

Yet this widespread support flies in the face of past common linguistic usage, by which the trustee's and the director's duties to exercise care and skill are referred to as "*fiduciary* duties of care". Lord Browne-Wilkinson, for example, did this in *Henderson v Merrett Syndicates Ltd* ("*Henderson's* case").[17] In that case he also referred to "any duty of care arising under the *Hedley Byrne* principle (of which *fiduciary duties of care* are merely an example)".[18] And in *White v Jones*[19] he said:

> "A trustee assumes responsibility for the management of the property of the beneficiary, a company director for the affairs of the company and an agent for those of his principal. By so assuming to act in B's affairs, A comes under fiduciary duties to B. Although the extent of *those fiduciary duties (including*

---

8   *Mothew's* case, above n 3 at 17.

9   *Youyang Pty Ltd v Minter Ellison Morris Fletcher* (2003) 212 CLR 484 at 500[38]–501[40].

10 Sometimes "care" is distinguished from "skill" in relation to directors. Statute apart, there was traditionally no objective requirement for skill in relation to directors, and statutory language referring to "reasonable diligence" has been read as excluding "skill": *Byrne v Baker* [1964] VR 443. See now *Corporations Act 2001* (Cth), s 180(1), discussed in *ASIC v Rich* (2003) 44 ACSR 341 at 348[31]–352[50]; *ASIC v Vines* (2003) 48 ACSR 322 at 323[3]–334[48]. The *Canada Business Corporations Act*, RSC 1985, c C-44, s 122(1)(b), is an example of a statutory duty on directors and officers to "exercise the care, diligence and skill that a reasonably prudent person would exercise in comparable circumstances."

11 *Daniels v Anderson* (1995) 37 NSWLR 438 at 501-505; *Wheeler's* case (1994) 11 WAR 187 at 238.

12 *Daniels v Anderson*, above n 11 at 602.

13 *Wheeler's* case, above n 11 at 238-239.

14 A Goldfinch, "Trustee's Duty to Exercise Reasonable Care: Fiduciary Duty?" (2004) 78 *Australian Law Journal* 678 at 681.

15 The duty was denied by J Glover, *Commercial Equity: Fiduciary Relationships* (Butterworths, Sydney, 1995) at [5.109], writing before *Daniels v Anderson*.

16 Below nn 77-79.

17 [1995] 2 AC 145 at 205.

18 *Henderson's* case, above n 17 at 206 (emphasis added).

19 [1995] 2 AC 207 at 271 (emphasis added).

duties of care) will vary from case to case some duties (including a duty of care) arise in each case."

Sir Robert Megarry V-C described the trustee's duty of prudent investment, among other trustee duties, as "fiduciary".[20] The accuracy of this usage has been challenged by, in particular, authorities asserting a doctrine that a director's duty to exercise care and skill is not fiduciary ("the *Wheeler* Doctrine"). This chapter is directed primarily to a discussion of the *Wheeler* Doctrine as developed in those authorities.

That narrow inquiry is narrowed further by the impact on the general law in its practical application of corresponding provisions in companies legislation. On the other hand, the statutory provisions operate on assumptions which require acquaintance with the general law, and contain silences and gaps perhaps capable of being filled by it. The inquiry is not irrelevant to a book on fusion because it is related to broader questions. For example, a commentator, in noting a "strong impetus towards confluence of the principles for assessment of compensation in equity and at common law in Canadian law", has said "the same trend is nascent in Australia[21] and, until very recently, in England."[22]

But before describing how the *Wheeler* Doctrine emerged, and then turning to the question whether it is correct, it is desirable to consider why the answer to that question might matter.

THE SIGNIFICANCE OF THE QUESTION

The significance of the question, and of related controversies, is that if a fiduciary's duty of care is a fiduciary duty, the advisers of plaintiffs conceive that there are fewer barriers in their clients' paths. Some of these potential barriers relate to causation, remoteness and limitation. Some relate to the availability of particular remedies.

---

20   *Cowan v Scargill* [1985] Ch 270 at 276 and 289. See also RR Pennington, *Directors' Personal Liability* (Collins Professional Books, London, 1987) at 81 ("a fiduciary duty ... to exercise their powers and functions as directors with proper care and appropriate skill") and p 145 ("their ... fiduciary duty to conduct the company's affairs with proper care and skill"). On the other hand, JF Corkery, *Directors' Powers and Duties* (Longman Cheshire, Melbourne, 1987) at 54 and 130 spoke of "fiduciary duties" and "duties of diligence and skill".

21   For this an "Australian High Court" case is cited. The case is *Commonwealth Bank of Australia v Smith* (1991) 42 FCR 390 at 394-396; 102 ALR 453 at 479-483. It is in fact a decision of the Full Federal Court, and it demonstrates no such trend, nascent or otherwise. The trial judge selected a figure for damages which was identical for three causes of action – breach of the *Trade Practices Act 1974* (Cth), negligence and breach of fiduciary duty. He said the measure of damages for the last breach was the same as for the other two "from a practical point of view". He specifically said that the last "was not necessarily limited by common law concepts of foreseeability and remoteness" but in the instant case damages "could be quantified" in a particular way, and there was "no difference in result" as between tort and equity. The Full Federal Court held merely that this approach was open and was not indicative of error.

22   L Hoyano, 'The Flight to the Fiduciary Haven' in P Birks (ed), *Privacy and Loyalty* (Oxford University Press, Oxford, 1997) at 215. Any suggestion there made that the trend has ceased in England because of *South Australia Asset Management Corporation v York Montague Ltd* [1997] AC 191 is difficult to follow. No equitable compensation was sought in that case.

Causation rules

At least for that type of breach of fiduciary duty which occurs when trustees holding office under an express trust have parted with the trust property in breach of trust, it is often said[23] that common law rules as to causation of loss, foreseeability of loss and remoteness of loss do not apply. That conclusion was arrived at in partial reliance on *Caffrey v Darby*, a case in which sums which ought to have been paid to the trustees were not paid. At least to that extent the type of breach of duty in question is wider than that just indicated. While in the common law tort of negligence, a novus actus interveniens can break the chain of causation between the breach of duty and the damage, *Caffrey v Darby* held that there was no such "defence" where trustees, who had sold a trust asset, negligently but non-fraudulently failed to ensure that payments of the purchase price were made and failed to take possession of the property sold. The property was lost when the purchaser became bankrupt. The trustees were liable, and it would not have mattered whether some other cause of the loss had intervened, such as a loss of the property by fire or lightning or some erroneous judicial decision.[24] Similarly, the "commonsense" test of causation at common law[25] may be more onerous than a "but-for" test in equity.[26]

Remoteness

If a personal representative, not "exercising reasonable care and diligence", invests trust property in unauthorised investments, or places it in the control of persons to whom it ought not to have been entrusted, and loss results, the personal representative must make it good "however unexpected the result, however little likely to arise from the course adopted, and however free such conduct may have been from any improper motive."[27] Common law tests of remoteness, whether based on foreseeability or directness, are irrelevant.

Limitation periods

The question can be important from the point of view of limitation. Thus one case has been read as assuming that a cause of action for common law negligence might be statute-barred, even though a cause of action on the same facts for equitable compensation for breach of fiduciary duty was not.[28]

---

23   In the many cases which have cited *Re Dawson (dec'd); Union Fidelity Trustee Co Ltd v Perpetual Trustee Co Ltd* [1966] 2 NSWR 211 at 215 ("*Re Dawson*").

24   *Caffrey v Darby* (1801) 6 Ves Jun 488 at 496-497; 31 ER 1159 at 1162-1163; *Re Dawson*, above n 23 at 215; *Bennett v Minister of Community Welfare* (1992) 176 CLR 401 at 426-427; *Maguire v Makaronis* (1997) 188 CLR 449 at 469-470.

25   *March v E & M H Stramare Pty Ltd* (1991) 171 CLR 506.

26   *Re Dawson*, above n 23 at 215.

27   *Clough v Bond* (1838) 3 My & Cr 490 at 496; 40 ER 1016 at 1018.

28   *Bennett v Minister of Community Welfare*, above n 23 at 426-427. The passage was so read in *Chittick v Maxwell* (1993) 118 ALR 728 at 741-742 on the basis that statutes of limitation are not to be applied by analogy in these circumstances (cf, for example, s 14 with s 23 of the *Limitation Act 1969* (NSW)).

Proprietary remedies

Finally, the existence of a fiduciary duty is sometimes urged with a view to obtaining a proprietary remedy.[29]

How did the *Wheeler* Doctrine evolve?

THE WHEELER DOCTRINE IS BORN: GIRARDET'S CASE

Girardet's case is a trial decision of the Supreme Court of British Columbia in 1987. The judgment of Southin J began:[30]

"Counsel for the plaintiff spoke of this case in his opening as one of breach of fiduciary duty and negligence. It became clear during his opening that no breach of fiduciary duty is in issue. What is in issue is whether the defendant was negligent in advising on the settlement of a claim for injuries suffered in an accident. The word 'fiduciary' is flung around now as if it applied to all breaches of duty by solicitors, *directors of companies* and so forth. But 'fiduciary' comes from the Latin 'fiducia' meaning 'trust'. Thus, the adjective, 'fiduciary' means of or pertaining to a trustee or trusteeship. That a lawyer can commit a breach of the special duty of a trustee, eg, by stealing his client's money, by entering into a contract with the client without full disclosure, by sending a client a bill claiming disbursements never made and so forth is clear. But to say that simple carelessness in giving advice is such a breach is a perversion of words. The obligation of a solicitor of care and skill is the same obligation of any person who undertakes for reward to carry out a task. One would not assert of an engineer or physician who had given bad advice and from whom common law damages were sought that he was guilty of a breach of fiduciary duty. Why should it be said of a solicitor? I make this point because an allegation of breach of fiduciary duty carries with it the stench of dishonesty – if not of deceit, then of constructive fraud." (Emphasis added)

THE WHEELER DOCTRINE APPROVED BY PROFESSOR FINN

In a paper delivered in 1988 to a conference held in British Columbia, Professor Finn referred to *Girardet's* case, and not merely as a gesture to local sensibilities. The paper had as its epigraph the fourth sentence of the above passage. The paper described the duty of fiduciary loyalty as follows:[31]

"A fiduciary –

(a) cannot use his position to his own or to a third party's possible advantage; or

(b) cannot, in any matter within the scope of his service, have a personal interest or an inconsistent engagement with a third party

---

29 *In re Goldcorp Exchange Ltd (in receivership)* [1995] 1 AC 74 at 97-98 (where the goal was not so much to establish that a particular duty owed by a fiduciary was itself of a fiduciary nature, but to establish that there was a fiduciary).

30 *Girardet v Crease & Co* (1987) 11 BCLR (2d) 361 at 362.

31 P Finn, 'The Fiduciary Principle' in TG Youdan (ed), *Equity, Fiduciaries and Trusts* (Carswell, Canada, 1989) at 27.

unless this is freely and informedly consented to by his beneficiary or is authorised by law . . ."

It continued:[32]

"Loyalty is thus exacted, often in a draconian way. But save in one very distinctive class of case involving 'fiduciary powers,' no more than loyalty is exacted. This warrants emphasis. It is not the case that the pure negligence of a lawyer, an agent's excess of authority, a partner's breach of the partnership contract or *a trustee's improvident investment* is, as such, a breach of fiduciary duty, no matter how harmful to the interests of the client, the principal, etc. If no issue of disloyalty is involved, such matters will be actionable through those primary bodies of law which constitute or govern the ordinary incidence of the relationship in question – negligence, breach of contract or breach of trust. What is being rejected here is the proposition that the fiduciary principle is a prescriptive one in what it exacts.[33] If a fiduciary's liability was to be determined by reference to whether or not the beneficiary's interests had in fact been served, an often impossible inquiry, more than curious consequences would follow. Much of the law of trusts, of agency *and of companies* would, for example, be rendered superfluous. The law of torts and of contract would be displaced from their now accepted roles in many relationships." [Footnotes omitted; emphasis added.]

The dictum in *Girardet's* case quoted above was the only authority cited.

THE WHEELER DOCTRINE IN THE SUPREME COURT OF CANADA

The dictum in *Girardet v Crease & Co* was then approved by Sopinka J and La Forest J in *Lac Minerals Ltd v International Corona Resources Ltd* ("the *Lac Minerals* case").[34] The approval was given in support of a proposition put thus by La Forest J: "not every legal claim arising out of a relationship with fiduciary incidents will give rise to a claim for breach of fiduciary duty." [35]

HENDERSON'S CASE

A few years later, in *Henderson's* case, Lord Browne-Wilkinson said:[36]

"The liability of a fiduciary for the negligent transaction of his duties is not a separate head of liability but the paradigm of the general duty to act with care imposed by law on those who take it upon themselves to act for or advise others. Although the historical development of the rules of law and

32 P Finn, 'The Fiduciary Principle' in TG Youdan (ed), *Equity, Fiduciaries and Trusts*, above n 31 at 28. For a contention to the same effect, see RP Austin, 'Moulding the Content of Fiduciary Duties' in AJ Oakley (ed), *Trends in Contemporary Trust Law* (Oxford University Press, Oxford, 1997) at 153.

33 From this Professor Finn exempted "fiduciary powers": see 227, text to nn 182-186 below.

34 [1989] 2 SCR 574 at 597-598 and 647.

35 *Lac Minerals* case, above n 34 at 647.

36 [1995] 2 AC 145 at 205.

equity have [sic], in the past, caused *different labels to be stuck on* different manifestations of the duty, in truth the duty of care imposed on bailees, carriers, trustees, directors, agents and others is the same duty: it arises from the circumstances in which the defendants were acting, not from their status or description. It is a fact that they have all assumed responsibility for the property or affairs of others which renders them liable for the careless performance of what they have undertaken to do, not the *description* of the trade or position which they hold." (Emphasis added)

There are points of difference between what Lord Browne-Wilkinson said and other statements in this line of cases. Unlike them, he did speak of fiduciary duties of care; unlike them, he seemed to suggest that there was only one duty for directors, not one at law and one in equity. But what he said has been much relied on to support the theory that duties of care and skill are not fiduciary.

WHEELER'S CASE

Three days after Lord Browne-Wilkinson's speech in *Henderson's* case, the Full Court of the Supreme Court of Western Australia decided *Wheeler's* case.

Preliminary propositions

The court stated four preliminary propositions.

(i) *The trustee's duty.* "It is a rule of equity that, in the management of the business of the trust, a trustee should exercise the same care and skill as an ordinary prudent man of business would exercise in conducting that business if it were his own ... ."[37] There are qualifications to what has, perhaps questionably, been called this "undemanding standard of prudence".[38] First, "[p]rudent businessmen in their dealings incur risk"[39] and hence "an ordinary prudent man" may incur "a prudent degree of risk", but must use "caution" in the sense of avoiding "hazard".[40] Secondly, "an ordinary prudent man" may commit errors of judgment without being liable.[41] Thirdly, the duty of a trustee in making an investment is to "take such care as an ordinary prudent man would take if he were minded to make an investment for the benefit of other people for whom he felt

---

37 *Wheeler's* case (1994) 11 WAR 187 at 235. See *In re Speight; Speight v Gaunt* (1883) 22 Ch D 727 at 739, 758 and 762 (and "prudent and reasonable man", approved at 754) and, in the House of Lords, sub nom *Speight v Gaunt* (1883) 9 App Cas 1 at 19. See also *Knox v Mackinnon* (1888) 13 App Cas 753 at 768 ("care and diligence"). The test was referred to in *Austin v Austin* (1906) 3 CLR 516 at 525 and *Fouche v The Superannuation Fund Board* (1952) 88 CLR 609 at 641. The origins of the requirement of reasonable diligence can be traced at least to *Charitable Corporation v Sutton* (1742) 2 Atk 400 at 406; 26 ER 642 at 645, and of the remainder of the test at least to *Massey v Banner* (1820) 1 Jac & W 241 at 247; 37 ER 367 at 369.

38 *Nestlé v National Westminster Bank Plc* [1993] 1 WLR 1260 at 1285.

39 *In re Godfrey; Godfrey v Faulkner* (1883) 23 Ch D 483 at 493.

40 *Learoyd v Whiteley* (1887) 12 App Cas 727 at 733; *Bartlett v Barclays Trust Co Ltd (No 1)* [1980] Ch 515 at 534; *ASC v AS Nominees* (1995) 62 FCR 504 at 516. This is preserved by the *Trusts Act 1973* (Qld), s 23(2)(b) and its Australasian equivalents listed above n 2.

41 *In re Chapman* [1896] 2 Ch 763 at 776 and 778; *Bartlett v Barclays Trust Co Ltd (No 1)* [1980] Ch 515 at 531.

morally bound to provide."[42] This test has been modified slightly by statute: if the trustee's profession, business or employment is not, or does not include, acting as a trustee or investing money for other persons, the duty is to exercise the care, diligence and skill a prudent person of business would exercise in managing the affairs of other persons.[43] Fourthly, the trustee cannot invest in all investments which "an ordinary prudent man" might if the trust deed or a statute confines the permissible class.[44] Fifthly, the trustee must act impartially towards beneficiaries and between different classes of beneficiaries. Hence the interests of those presently entitled to the income must be weighed with the interests of those entitled in future. Thus a power of investment must be exercised so as to yield the best return for the beneficiaries, judged in relation to the risks of the investment in question, and the prospects of the yield of income and capital appreciation both have to be considered in judging the return from the investment.[45] Finally, there was some authority that a higher test applies to persons (like trust corporations) carrying on a specialised business of trust management: they were to be liable if they neglected to exercise the special care and skill which they professed to have.[46] There is now a slightly different statutory test: if the trustee's profession, business or employment is, or includes, acting as a trustee or investing money for other persons, the duty is to exercise the care, diligence and skill a prudent person engaged in that profession, business or employment would exercise in managing the affairs of other persons.[47]

(ii) *The director's duty in equity.* "[T]he duty of directors to exercise care and skill is essentially the same as that of trustees."[48] Cases are cited in *Wheeler's* case for this proposition, but they, and others, in fact reveal it to be inaccurate.[49] In *In re Faure Electric Accumulator Co*[50] Kay J said that directors:

---

42   *In re Whiteley* (1886) 33 Ch D 347 at 355; see also at 350 and 358. This was described by AW Scott and WF Fratcher, *The Law of Trusts* (4th ed, Little Brown & Co, Boston, 1988), vol III at [227.3] as perhaps "as good a statement of the rule as any".

43   *Trusts Act 1973* (Qld), s 22(1)(b) and its Australasian equivalents referred to above n 2.

44   *Learoyd v Whiteley* (1887) 12 App Cas 727 at 733. This is preserved by the *Trusts Act 1973* (Qld), s 21 and its Australasian equivalents listed above n 2.

45   *In re Whiteley; Whiteley v Learoyd* (1886) 36 Ch D 347 at 350; *Cowan v Scargill* [1985] Ch 270 at 287; *Nestlé v National Westminster Bank plc* [1993] 1 WLR 1260 at 1282; *Re Mulligan (decd)* [1998] 1 NZLR 481 at 500 (with useful quotation from the unreported judgment of Hoffmann J at trial in the *Nestlé* case). This is preserved by s 23(2)(c) of the *Trusts Act 1973* (Qld) and its Australasian equivalents referred to above n 2.

46   *Bartlett v Barclays Trust Co Ltd (No 1)* [1980] Ch 515 at 534; *ASC v AS Nominees Ltd* (1995) 62 FCR 504 at 518; *Wilkinson v Feldworth Financial Services Pty Ltd* (1998) 29 ACSR 642 at 693.

47   *Trusts Act 1973* (Qld), s 22(1)(a) and its Australasian equivalents referred to above n 2.

48   *Wheeler's* case (1994) 11 WAR 187 at 235.

49   *Overend & Gurney Co v Gibb* (1872) LR 5 HL 480 at 486-487 ("crassa negligentia"); *Lagunas Nitrate Co v Lagunas Syndicate* [1899] 2 Ch 392 at 435; *ASC v Gallagher* (1993) 10 ACSR 43 at 53; *Re City Equitable Fire Insurance Co Ltd* [1925] Ch 407 at 428. See also *Mulkana Corp NL (in liq) v Bank of New South Wales* (1983) 8 ACLR 278 at 284; *Daniels v Anderson* (1995) 37 NSWLR 438 at 495 and 599; *ASC v AS Nominees Ltd* (1995) 62 FCR 504 at 517.

50   (1888) 40 Ch D 141 at 150-151. See also *In re Railway and General Light Improvement Co; Marzetti's Case* (1880) 28 WR 541 at 542.

"certainly are not trustees in the sense of those words as used with reference to an instrument of trust, such as a marriage settlement or a will. One obvious distinction is that the property of the company is not legally vested in them. Another and perhaps still broader difference is that they are the managing agents of a trading association, and such control as they have over its property, and such powers as by the constitution of the company are vested in them, are confided to them for purposes widely different from those which exist in the case of such ordinary trusts as I have referred to, and which require that a larger discretion should be given to them. ... [I]t is quite obvious that to apply to directors the strict rules of the Court of Chancery with respect to ordinary trustees might fetter their action to an extent which would be exceedingly disadvantageous to the companies they represent."

While the standards which directors are required to meet have tended to rise considerably over the past century,[51] at least two differences between the tests applying to directors and to trustees remain.[52] First, a trustee must meet an objective standard: the personal knowledge and experience of the particular trustee is generally irrelevant. For directors who are not engaged by contract[53] and who have not held themselves out as possessing particular skills,[54] whether pursuant to any duty undertaken[55] to the company or otherwise, while the standard of care was probably always objective,[56] the standard of skill is less objective: the question is what an ordinary person with the knowledge and experience of the particular director would have done if acting on that person's own behalf.[57] Another difference relates to the test of prudence. Thus Jacobs J said: "A trustee in

---

51   *Daniels v Anderson* (1995) 37 NSWLR 438 at 497-505.

52   If the dicta recognising an objective duty of care and skill in *Daniels v Anderson*, above n 51 at 501-505 are correct, the first difference remained until that case but not thereafter. Hoffmann J has also said that the duty to exercise skill is objective, and is the same as that created by s 214(4) of the *Insolvency Act 1986* (UK), namely, the conduct of "a reasonably diligent person having both – (a) the general knowledge, skill and experience that may reasonably be expected of a person carrying out the same functions as are carried out by that director in relation to the company, and (b) the general knowledge, skill and experience that that director has": *Norman v Theodore Goddard* [1991] BCLC 1027 at 1030-1031; *Re D'Jan of London Ltd* [1994] 1 BCLC 561 at 563.

53   A contract, particularly with a director engaged as an executive director, may contain implied terms warranting the possession of skills and promising that the director will act with reasonable care, diligence and skill.

54   RR Pennington, *Directors' Personal Liability* (Collins Professional Books, London, 1987) at 37.

55   Isaacs and Rich JJ spoke of "the duty [a director] has undertaken to the company" and "the terms upon which he has undertaken to act as a director" in *Gould v The Mount Oxide Mines Ltd (in liq)*, above n 55 at 529 and 531.

56   For example, *Dorchester Finance Co v Stebbing* [1989] BCLC 498. In *Gould v The Mount Oxide Mines Ltd (in liq)*, above n 55 at 516 Griffith CJ said: "a director is not required to use in conducting the affairs of a company any greater care than a business man of ordinary intelligence and capacity may reasonably be expected to use in the conduct of a similar transaction in his own affairs."

57   *Lagunas Nitrate Co v Lagunas Syndicate* [1899] 2 Ch 392 at 435; *In re Brazilian Rubber Plantations and Estates Ltd* [1911] 1 Ch 425 at 437; *Barnes v Andrews* 298 F 614 at 630 (1924) per Judge Learned Hand; *ASC v Gallagher* (1993) 11 WAR 105 at 116.

the ordinary way is obliged primarily to keep the trust property safe. However, a director of a company is a commercial man and any duty of his in regard to dealings with the property on its behalf must be looked at in the light of his position in commerce."[58] And Clarke and Sheller JJA said: "While the duty of a trustee is to exercise a degree of restraint and conservatism in investment judgments the duty of a director may be to display entrepreneurial flair and accept commercial risks to produce a sufficient return on the capital invested."[59]

(iii) *The director's duty at law.* "The duty of a director to exercise care and skill is owed both in equity and in law."[60] This is true for equity, but perhaps questionable for law. So learned a company lawyer as Professor Pennington knew of "no decided cases where liability for negligence has been imposed at common law on directors."[61] It is true that respectable dicta in old cases can be collected to support the existence of that liability.[62] But in *Daniels v Anderson*, Clarke and Sheller JJA pointed out that: "These references to negligence do not ... support any significant argument for holding that directors can be sued for negligence in the modern sense. The negligence spoken of was something grosser or more culpable determined by subjective rather than objective tests."[63] In that case the subject was examined, after full argument, in very lengthy and thoroughly considered dicta.[64] The minority judgment of Powell JA concluded that directors did not owe to the company any common law duty to exercise care and skill[65] unless one were owed pursuant to *Donoghue v Stevenson*,[66] and that the principles developed since that case did not compel the recognition of any common law duty of care for directors.[67] The majority (Clarke and Sheller JJA) appeared to accept the correctness of Powell JA's conclusions as a matter of history,[68] but decided that the law ought to be changed. They held that directors owed an

---

58   *Re International Vending Machines Pty Ltd and the Companies Act* [1962] NSWR 1408 at 1420.

59   *Daniels v Anderson* (1995) 37 NSWLR 438 at 494; see also at 501.

60   *Wheeler's* case (1994) 11 WAR 187 at 235-236.

61   RR Pennington, *Directors' Personal Liability* (Collins Professional Books, London, 1987) at 37.

62   For example, *Lagunas Nitrate Co v Lagunas Syndicate* [1899] 2 Ch 392 at 435.

63   (1995) 37 NSWLR 438 at 493.

64   *Daniels v Anderson*, above n 63. The majority concluded that directors owed a common law duty of care – that is, a duty in tort which caused them to fall within New South Wales legislation dealing with contribution between joint tortfeasors. As to certain non-executive directors, the reasoning consisted of dicta, in the sense of not being necessary for the outcome, because the court upheld the trial judge's conclusion that they were not negligent. As to an executive Chairman of directors, the reasoning consisted of dicta in the same sense, because although he was found negligent, it was thought wrong that the tortfeasors seeking contribution (the company's auditors) should be given contribution in view of an allowance already made in their favour as a result of the contributory negligence of the company, which included the Chairman's acts of negligence: at 579-580.

65   *Daniels v Anderson*, above n 63 at 602.

66   [1932] AC 562.

67   *Daniels v Anderson*, above n 63 at 607-608.

68   *Daniels v Anderson*, above n 63 at 492.

objective duty of care and skill in tort.[69] The truth of that proposition is not immediately material to the present inquiry, and it will be accepted for present purposes.

(iv) *Multiple duties from a single set of facts.* "[A]n equitable duty of care may arise from the same facts which give rise to a tortious duty of care."[70] Assuming that there can be a relevant tortious duty, this statement is not controversial, but its extreme generality points nowhere in particular.

The Wheeler doctrine enunciated

The Full Court then referred to *Girardet's* case, to its approval in the *Lac Minerals* case, and to Finn's paper. The Court continued:[71]

> "It is essential to bear in mind that the existence of a fiduciary relationship does not mean that every duty owed by a fiduciary to the beneficiary is a fiduciary duty. In particular, a trustee's duty to exercise reasonable care, though equitable, is not specifically a fiduciary duty … . Similarly … a director's duty to exercise reasonable care, though equitable (as well as legal) is not a fiduciary obligation. …
>
> The director's duty to exercise care and skill has nothing to do with any position of disadvantage or vulnerability on the part of the company. It is not a duty that stems from the requirements of trust and confidence imposed on a fiduciary. … [T]hat duty is not a fiduciary duty, although it is a duty actionable in the equitable jurisdiction of this court."

THE WHEELER DOCTRINE COMES TO ENGLAND

Wheeler's case was decided in the most remote and isolated city in the world, at least if one's vantage point is London, but its existence did not escape the forensic genius of Mr Jonathan Sumption QC. He made an allusion to it while arguing *Mothew's* case two years later.[72] Millett LJ's leading judgment in the English Court of Appeal thereupon quoted and approved parts of the *Wheeler* passages just set out. It stated:[73] "it is obvious that not every breach of duty by a fiduciary is a breach of fiduciary duty." After quoting from the relevant parts of the *Girardet*[74] and *Lac Minerals* cases[75] it continued:[76]

> "It is … inappropriate to apply the expression [fiduciary duty] to the obligation of a trustee or other fiduciary to use proper skill and care in the

---

69   *Daniels v Anderson* (1995) 37 NSWLR 438 at 501-505.

70   *Wheeler's* case (1994) 11 WAR 187 at 237.

71   *Wheeler's* case, above n 70 at 237-239. The trial judge had stated similar views: *Permanent Building Society (in liq) v McGee* (1993) 11 ACSR 260 at 287.

72   [1998] Ch 1 at 4.

73   *Mothew's* case, above n 72 at 17. The case is conspicuous for the stylistic distinction of that judgment and for a statement of Staughton LJ at 27, which ought to be inscribed in letters of fire and perused daily by every Australian judge. Speaking of a period of reservation of two months and two days he said: "our judgment is already long delayed".

74   (1987) 11 BCLR (2d) 361 at 362.

75   (1989) 61 DLR (4th) 14 at 28.

76   *Mothew's* case, above n 72 at 16-17.

discharge of his duties. If it is confined to cases where the fiduciary nature of a duty has special legal consequences, then the fact that the source of the duty is to be found in equity rather than the common law does not make it a fiduciary duty. The common law and equity each developed the duty of care, but they did so independently of each other and the standard of care required is not always the same. But they influenced each other, and today the substance of the resulting obligations is more significant than their particular historic origin."

The Court then agreed with the key *Henderson* and *Wheeler* passages.

Like the *Henderson* passage,[77] the *Wheeler* and *Mothew* cases have been widely approved by both judge[78] and jurist.[79]

---

77   For example, *S v G* [1995] 3 NZLR 681 at 688-689; *Prince v Attorney-General* [1996] 3 NZLR 733 at 746; *Swindle v Harrison* [1997] 4 All ER 705 at 716; *Williams v Minister, Aboriginal Land Rights Act 1983* (1999) 25 Fam LR 86 at 231[740]. It has also been held in much extra-curial esteem: see RP Austin, 'Moulding the Content of Fiduciary Duties' in AJ Oakley (ed), *Trends in Contemporary Trust Law* (Oxford University Press, Oxford, 1997) at 173 ("persuasive", "logical progression" from *Wheeler's* case); CF Rickett, 'Where are We Going with Equitable Compensation?' in AJ Oakley (ed), *Trends in Contemporary Trust Law* (Oxford University Press, Oxford, 1997) at 191 ("important ... insightful contribution towards the integration of equity into the broader scheme of civil liability") and 194 ("not ... fundamentally new and heretical", "enormous potential for the future"); P Birks, "The Content of Fiduciary Obligation" (2000) 34 *Israel Law Review* 3 at 36 ("almost precisely" correct); G Watt, *Trusts and Equity* (Oxford University Press, Oxford, 2003) at 358; S Elliott and J Edelman "*Target Holdings* Considered in Australia" (2003) 119 *Law Quarterly Review* 545 at 550; J Glover, *Equity, Restitution and Fraud* (Butterworths, Sydney, 1995) at [4.71].

78   *South Australia v Clarke* (1996) 66 SASR 199 at 223; *South Australia v Peat Marwick Mitchell & Co* (1997) 24 ACSR 231 at 266 and 270; *Beach Petroleum NL v Abbott Tout Russell Kennedy* (1997) 26 ACSR 114 at 281-282 and 285-286; *Re Moage Ltd (in liq); Moage Ltd (in liq) v Jagelman* (1998) 153 ALR 711 at 718-719; *Paragon Finance plc v D B Thakerar & Co (a firm)* [1999] 1 All ER 400 at 406; *Farrow Finance Co Ltd (in liq) v Farrow Properties Pty Ltd (in liq)* (1997) 26 ACSR 554 at 580; *A (C) v Critchley* (1998) 166 DLR (4th) 475 at 514; *Coulthard v Disco Mix Club Ltd* [1999] 2 All ER 457 at 476-477; *Satnam Investments Ltd v Dunlop Haywood & Co Ltd* [1999] 3 All ER 652 at 664-665; *Williams v Minister, Aboriginal Land Rights Act 1983* (1999) 25 Fam LR 86 at 241-242[741]; *Cia de Seguros Imperio v Heath (REBX) Ltd* [2001] 1 WLR 112 at 119; *Base Metal Trading Ltd v Shamurin* [2005] 1 WLR 1157 at 1164-1165[19].

79   It is not surprising that there is approval in conventional textbooks, which naturally tend to accept the law as it is stated in the higher courts, for example, *Lewin on Trusts* (17th ed, Sweet & Maxwell, London, 2000) at [34-01]; J McGhee (ed), *Snell's Equity* (30th ed, Sweet & Maxwell, London, 2000) at [6-05], [13-03] and [13-14]; (31st ed, Sweet & Maxwell, London, 2005) at [7-03]; JE Martin (ed), *Hanbury and Martin Modern Equity* (16th ed, Sweet & Maxwell, London, 2001) at 653-654; HAJ Ford and W Lee, *Principles of the Law of Trusts* (Looseleaf, Lawbook Co) at [22500] and [22620]; P Davies (ed), *Gower & Davies, The Principles of Modern Company Law* (7th ed, Sweet & Maxwell, London, 2003) at 432; A Boyle (ed), *Gore-Browne on Companies* (44th ed, Jordan Publishing, Bristol, 2004) at [27.1]; AJ Oakley (ed), *Parker and Mellows: The Modern Law of Trusts* (8th ed, Sweet & Maxwell, London, 2003) at 337-338, 765 and 784; D Hayton (ed), *Underhill and Hayton: Law Relating to Trusts and Trustees* (16th ed, Butterworths, London, 2003) at 701 and 858; A Hudson, *Equity & Trusts* (3rd ed, Cavendish Publishing, London, 2003) at 580; G Watt, *Trusts and Equity* (Oxford University Press, Oxford, 2003) at 355; GE dal Pont and DRC Chalmers, *Equity and Trusts in Australia* (3rd ed, Lawbook Co, Sydney, 2004) at [4.10]. The almost universal approval of other commentators, who give themselves a freer hand, is more surprising: RP Austin, 'Moulding the Content of Fiduciary Duties' in AJ Oakley (ed), *Trends in Contemporary Trust Law* (Oxford University Press, Oxford, 1997) at 155, 172 and 173, and CEF Rickett, 'Where are We Going with Equitable Compensation?' in Oakley (ed), *Trends in Contemporary Trust Law,* (Oxford University Press, Oxford, 1997) at 197-199 ("of interest and importance", "extremely instructive" and "significant"); L Griggs, "Equitable Compensation,

Mothew's case gave some non-exhaustive illustrations of fiduciary duties: duties of good faith and loyalty, duties not to make a profit out of the relationship, and duties preventing fiduciaries placing themselves in positions of conflict between duty and interest or duty and duty. It is duties of this kind which proponents of the distinction between non-fiduciary duties and fiduciary duties usually have in mind as instances of the latter.

THE WHEELER DOCTRINE REACHES NEW ZEALAND

In 1998, in *Bank of New Zealand v New Zealand Guardian Trust Co Ltd* ("the *Guardian Trust* case") the New Zealand Court of Appeal quoted relevant parts of the *Henderson, Wheeler* and *Mothew* cases. It then described these propositions as "now well established".[80]

THE PROCEDURAL BACKGROUND IN THE WHEELER LINE OF CASES

The now quite long line of cases containing statements enunciating the *Wheeler* Doctrine have no authority in that respect. The *Wheeler* Doctrine asserts a proposition about company directors, but apart from *Wheeler's* case itself, none of the cases had anything to do with company directors. The statements were not necessary for any of the decisions. They do not appear to have been made with the benefit of contrary argument.

Common Law Damages and the Directors' Duty in Tort" (1997) 10 *Corporate and Business Law Journal* 207; JK Maxton, 'Equity and the Law of Civil Wrongs' in P Rushworth (ed), *The Struggle for Simplicity in the Law: Essays for Lord Cooke of Thorndon* (Butterworths, Wellington, 1997) at 95-97; S Worthington, "Fiduciaries: When is Self-Denial Obligatory?" [1999] *Cambridge Law Journal* 500 at 502; P Birks, "The Content of Fiduciary Obligation" (2000) 34 *Israel Law Review* 3 at 30 ("indubitably correct"), 31 ("powerful" and "quite right" – although at 32-37 it becomes riddled with difficulties); P Birks (ed), *Privacy and Loyalty* (Oxford University Press, Oxford, 1997): D Hayton, 'Fiduciaries in Context: An Overview' at 289 (the controversial propositions were "usefully" stated); C Harpum, 'Fiduciary Obligations and Fiduciary Powers – Where Are We Going?' at 148; L Hoyano, 'The Flight to the Fiduciary Haven', at 201-203 and L Smith, 'Constructive Fiduciaries?', at 264; J Hackney, 'More than a trace of the old philosophy' in P Birks (ed), *The Classification of Obligations* (Oxford University Press, Oxford, 1997) at 143, 147; G Dempsey and A Greinke, "Proscriptive fiduciary duties in Australia" (2004) 25 *Australian Bar Review* 1 at 9 and 13; S Elliott, "Remoteness Criteria in Equity" (2002) 65 *Modern Law Review* 588 (retreating from "Fiduciary liability for client mortgage frauds" (1999) 13 *Trust Law International* 74); S Elliott and J Edelman, "*Target Holdings* Considered in Australia" (2003) 119 *Law Quarterly Review* 545; J Glover, *Equity, Restitution and Fraud* (Lexis Nexis, Sydney, 2003) at [4.8], [4.9] and [7.10]; RP Austin, HAJ Ford and IM Ramsay, *Company Directors: Principles of Law and Corporate Governance* (Lexis Nexis, Sydney, 2005) at [6.13], [6.15], [18.38], [18.39] and [18.41]. M Conaglen, "The Nature and Function of Fiduciary Loyalty" (2005) 121 *Law Quarterly Review* 452 at 455-456. There appears to be only one significant critic outside this country of the *Wheeler* line of cases: J Getzler, 'Equitable Compensation and the Regulation of Fiduciary Relationships' in P Birks and F Rose (eds), *Restitution and Equity: Vol I, Resulting Trusts and Equitable Compensation* (Mansfield Press, London, 2000) at 254-257 ("a questionable example of judicial creativity") and 'Duty of Care' in P Birks and A Pretto (eds), *Breach of Trust* (Hart Publishing, Oxford, 2002) at 71-72. Much of what appears below owes a considerable debt to Dr Getzler. See also his chapter titled "Am I My Beneficiary's Keeper? Fusion and Loss-Based Fiduciary Remedies" (chapter 10 in this book).

80   *Guardian Trust* case [1999] 1 NZLR 664 at 680.

THE AUTHORITY OF GIRARDET'S CASE

The passage from Southin J's judgment in *Girardet's* case[81] quoted above goes to the outermost boundaries of obiter dicta. It was not merely uttered by the way, but well off the way. The plaintiff in that case was injured in a motor accident and was treated by a doctor. An issue arose as to whether the plaintiff's injuries had been worsened by the medical treatment. The insurance company acting for the driver and owner of the motor vehicle which injured the plaintiff offered the plaintiff less than a third of what her solicitor demanded in negotiations. The plaintiff accepted that offer. A factual dispute then arose between the plaintiff and her solicitor. The solicitor said the offer had been accepted contrary to his advice that the offer was low and that it would be difficult to pursue the doctor for anything more. The plaintiff said the offer was accepted after the solicitor had said that it was a good offer and that the plaintiff would have to sue the doctor for more. Southin J resolved that factual dispute by accepting the solicitor's evidence and rejecting the plaintiff's evidence. She therefore rejected the plaintiff's contention that the solicitor had breached his duty to exercise reasonable care and skill. The passage quoted above did not assist in reaching that conclusion. It consisted merely of a protest at the unquestionably erroneous reference in the plaintiff's opening to breach of fiduciary duty. Nor does that passage appear to have been uttered in response to and as the resolution of any debate between counsel.

Southin J's observations also went beyond the necessities of the occasion in suggesting that the position of fiduciaries generally was the same as that of a solicitor. It is true that the solicitor's duty in that case was not fiduciary. Indeed, it was not equitable at all. Breach of a solicitor's duties to exercise reasonable care and skill, whether they arise in tort or contract or both, are actionable only at common law: equity has long refused relief.[82] No non-equitable duty can be fiduciary, because fiduciary duties were not developed in or enforced by courts of common law. Hence the duties of a solicitor in cases where no special fiduciary duty of the type described in *Mothew's* case arises do not differ from those of an engineer or physician. The content and source of the solicitor's duties in *Girardet's* case were identical with those of the architect in *Voli v Inglewood Shire Council*:[83]

---

81   (1987) 11 BCLR (2d) 361 at 362: see text at n 30 above.

82   *Mare v Lewis* (1869) 4 Ir R (Eq) 219 at 235; *British Mutual Investment Co v Cobbold* (1875) LR 19 Eq 627; *Nocton v Lord Ashburton* [1914] AC 932 at 956, where Viscount Haldane LC, however, rightly said that although it no longer existed, there had once been a concurrent jurisdiction. For examples of it, see *Floyd v Nangle* (1747) 3 Atk 567; 26 ER 1127; *Dixon v Wilkinson* (1859) 4 De G & J 508 at 523; 45 ER 198 at 203; *Chapman v Chapman* (1870) LR 9 Eq 276 at 294 and 296. In *Tuiara v Frost & Sutcliffe (a firm)* [2003] 2 NZLR 833 at 849[47], Baragwanath J treated *Mothew's* case as recognising that a solicitor owed an equitable duty of care and skill. *Mothew's* case referred to Viscount Haldane LC's denial of that proposition, but just before and just after that reference there are passages which were, understandably, capable of misleading Baragwanath J.

83   (1963) 110 CLR 74 at 84.

"An architect undertaking any work in the way of his profession accepts the ordinary liabilities of any man who follows a skilled calling. He is bound to exercise due care, skill and diligence. He is not required to have an extraordinary degree of skill or the highest professional attainments. But he must bring to the task he undertakes the competence and skill that is usual among architects practising their profession. And he must use due care. If he fails in these matters and the person who employed him thereby suffers damage, he is liable to that person. This liability can be said to arise either from a breach of his contract or in tort."

If the solicitor, architect, engineer or physician were in a position of conflict or in a position to make a profit at the client's expense, fiduciary duties might well arise, and if their breach led to loss, remedies of a fiduciary character would lie for those breaches. Whether the duties of a trustee to beneficiaries, or the duties of a director to the company, are all fiduciary in character, and whether all breaches of those duties attract the remedies typically available for breach of fiduciary duty, are not questions to be resolved by seeking to draw an analogy with the duties of solicitors, architects, doctors or engineers to advise considered in isolation.

THE AUTHORITY OF THE LAC MINERALS CASE

The propositions stated by Sopinka J and La Forest J in the *Lac Minerals* case[84] were dicta. The case did not turn on any question about whether a particular duty in a fiduciary relationship was itself fiduciary. Rather Sopinka J denied, and La Forest J upheld, the existence of a fiduciary relationship among prospective joint venturers, and La Forest J in consequence imposed a constructive trust.

THE AUTHORITY OF HENDERSON'S CASE

No member of the House of Lords agreed with Lord Browne-Wilkinson's statement.[85] Counsel debated whether a fiduciary obligation of due care and skill existed alongside the common law duties[86] but Lord Goff of Chieveley, with whom Lords Keith of Kinkel, Mustill and Nolan agreed, having concluded that there were duties of care owed in both contract and tort, found it unnecessary to consider the matter.[87] Lord Browne-Wilkinson's statement thus forms no part of the ratio decidendi. Further, the terms of Lord Browne-Wilkinson's remarks do not appear to reflect any precise lis between the parties. Lord Browne-Wilkinson described them as only "a few words of my own on the relationship between the claim based on liability for negligence and the alternative claim advanced by the Names founded on breach of fiduciary duty".[88] They

---

84   [1989] 2 SCR 574 at 597-598 and 647: referred to above, text at nn 34-35.
85   *Henderson's* case [1995] 2 AC 145 at 205: quoted above, text to n 36.
86   *Henderson's* case, above n 85 at 155 and 162.
87   *Henderson's* case, above n 85 at 196-197.
88   *Henderson's* case, above n 85 at 204.

were neither necessary, nor even treated by him as necessary, for his conclusion, which immediately follows them. That conclusion was:[89]

> "the duties which the managing agents have assumed to undertake in managing the insurance business of the Names brings them clearly into the category of those who are liable, whether fiduciaries or not, for any lack of care in the conduct of that management."

It cannot have been necessary for the conclusion that they were liable, "whether fiduciaries or not", to propound statements about fiduciary liability.

THE AUTHORITY OF THE WHEELER STATEMENTS

The facts in Wheeler's case

The propositions stated in *Wheeler's* case were strictly irrelevant to the problem addressed. That problem arose from the position of the fifth respondent, Hamilton. He had been the chief executive and managing director of the plaintiff building society. The building society had suffered loss by reason of its purchase of a parcel of industrial land with a view to subdivision into lots and sale of them to the public. The case against Hamilton was put in three ways.

Improper conduct?

The first depended on implicating him in the conduct of certain of the building society's other directors, who had caused it to enter the sale agreement in order to confer advantages on other entities. However, Hamilton denied knowledge of this improper conduct, and was believed.

Breach of duty at common law?

The second claim against Hamilton was a claim for damages at common law for failure to exercise a reasonable degree of care, diligence and skill in failing to oppose the board resolutions to enter the sale agreement. It was found that Hamilton was in breach of duty for various failures to make sufficient inquiry about the transaction.[90] However, he was held not liable to pay damages. That was because his failures to inquire had not caused the loss: if proper inquiry had been made, the facts learned would not have caused reasonable persons in the position of the building society directors to vote against the purchase.[91]

Equitable compensation for breach of equitable duty?

The Full Court then turned to the third way the case against Hamilton was put: that he was liable to pay equitable compensation for breach of his equitable duties to exercise care and skill as a company director.

---

89   *Henderson's* case, above n 85 at 205.
90   *Wheeler's* case (1994) 11 WAR 187 at 241.
91   *Wheeler's* case, above n 90 at 242-243.

The Full Court, having found that the facts which placed him in breach of his duty at common law also placed him in breach of his equitable duty, considered that the correct causation test to apply was that stated in *Re Dawson*.[92] Unlike the Court of Appeal in *Mothew's* case,[93] the Full Court did not see that test as limited to "the breach of a true fiduciary obligation" but as extending to "the breach of an equitable obligation to take care". The Full Court read the cases referred to by Street J in the passage it quoted from *Re Dawson*, namely *Caffrey v Darby*[94] and *Clough v Bond*,[95] as being cases of the latter kind.[96] This was a sound approach, with which Brennan CJ, Gaudron, McHugh and Gummow JJ agreed in *Maguire v Makaronis*.[97] The Full Court did not see the *Re Dawson* test as wholly annihilating causation requirements, because while Street J said it was not necessary to inquire "as to whether the loss was caused by or flowed from the breach", it was necessary to inquire "whether the loss would have happened if there had been no breach."[98] As the Full Court put it, "a court of equity ... should not require an honest but careless trustee to compensate a beneficiary for losses without proof that but for the breach of duty those losses would not have occurred."[99] The Full Court then endeavoured to negate the possibility, which would have been fatal for Hamilton, that the case before it fell into a category prohibiting any causal inquiry at all. It referred to two such categories.

Did Brickenden's case apply?

The first was the category described thus in *Brickenden v London Loan & Savings Co*:[100]

"When a party, holding a fiduciary relationship, commits a breach of his duty by non-disclosure of material facts ... he cannot be heard to maintain that disclosure would not have altered the decision to proceed with the transaction ... ."

The Full Court said that this did not apply, because it only applied:

"where there has been a breach of a true fiduciary obligation, carrying with it, ordinarily, in the words of Southin J in [*Girardet's* case]: 'the stench of dishonesty – if not of deceit then of constructive fraud'. The principle applies because the fiduciary has abused the control of the trust, there is a substantial potential for gain through such wrongdoing, the fiduciary has superior information concerning his or her acts, and there is a need to 'keep persons in a

---

92   [1966] 2 NSWR 211 at 215.
93   [1998] Ch 1 at 17.
94   (1801) 6 Ves 488; 31 ER 1159.
95   (1838) 3 My & Cr 490; 40 ER 1016.
96   *Wheeler's* case (1994) 11 WAR 187 at 243.
97   (1997) 188 CLR 449 at 473.
98   *Re Dawson*, above n 92 at 215.
99   *Wheeler's* case, above n 96 at 247.
100 [1934] 3 DLR 465 at 469.

fiduciary capacity up to their duty' ... .[101] These factors do not apply to a breach of duty of care."[102]

However, it was not necessary to make these points in order to rule out the *Brickenden* principle, because it was incapable of applying in any event. The plaintiff was not arguing that Hamilton was liable because of his "non-disclosure of material facts". Rather the plaintiff was arguing that he was liable because he had failed to find out material facts.

Account of profits?

The other category to which the Full Court referred exists "where an account is ordered by reason of a breach of the fiduciary obligation to avoid a conflict of interest." The Full Court set out a statement[103] by Burt CJ that the party claiming an account of profits made by a fiduciary in a position of conflict between duty and interest did not have to prove that the fiduciary used the information or opportunity which came to the fiduciary, or that their use caused the profits. The Full Court held that the category described by Burt CJ rested on a conflict of duty and interest and on difficulties of proof, and neither feature existed in relation to breaches of an equitable duty to exercise reasonable care and skill. A more direct reason for excluding Burt CJ's category as irrelevant to Hamilton's breach of equitable duty is that he gained no information or opportunity to make a profit, he made no profits, and no account of profits was sought from him.

The Full Court's conclusion

By these means the Full Court succeeded in its endeavour to negate the possibility that the case fell within a category having no causation requirement at all. The Full Court then applied *Re Dawson*, and concluded that the plaintiff had failed to prove that but for Hamilton's breach, the loss would not have occurred. Neither the Full Court's decision that the case fell outside categories having no causation test, nor its decision that the applicable test was that stated in *Re Dawson*, called for a denial of any fiduciary character to the director's equitable duty to exercise reasonable care and skill. Even if that duty had been held to be fiduciary, it would not have fallen within the categories having no causal requirement at all, and the Full Court would still have held *Re Dawson* applicable. Hence it did not matter one way or another whether the equitable duty was fiduciary or not. It follows that all the reasoning leading to the conclusion that the duties owed by fiduciaries are not all fiduciary, and in particular that the equitable duty of directors to exercise reasonable care and

---

101 The phrase comes from *Nocton v Lord Ashburton* [1914] AC 932 at 963 per Lord Dunedin.

102 *Wheeler's* case (1994) 11 WAR 187 at 246. It is highly questionable whether all breaches of fiduciary obligation carry the stench of dishonesty. The conduct of Boardman in *Phipps v Boardman* [1967] 2 AC 46 was not of that character, but it still led to liability. Other aspects of the reasoning in this passage are discussed at 222–225, text to nn 169-178 below.

103 *Green & Clara Pty Ltd v Bestobell Industries Pty Ltd* [1982] WAR 1 at 5-6.

skill is not fiduciary, was entirely unnecessary to the decision that Hamilton was not liable.

Further, while it is not clear from the report whether the Full Court's denial of a fiduciary character to the equitable duty of directors to exercise reasonable care and skill responded to and resolved any debate between the parties on that point, it seems unlikely. Substantial parts of the judgment comprise summaries of particular arguments of counsel and detailed consideration of them: no counsel is recorded as advancing, or controverting, those parts of the judgment which enunciate the *Wheeler* Doctrine.[104]

THE AUTHORITY OF THE MOTHEW STATEMENTS

The English Court of Appeal said in *Mothew's* case that the *Wheeler* distinction between breaches of a non-fiduciary duty to exercise care and skill and breaches of a fiduciary duty properly so called "is sound in principle and is decisive of the present case".[105] It has been seen that whether or not the distinction is sound in principle, it was not decisive of *Wheeler's* case. It was not in truth decisive of *Mothew's* case either.

The facts

The defendant was a solicitor who acted both for the purchasers of a house and for the building society which was to finance their purchase. The price was £73,000 and the loan was £59,000. It was a condition of the advance that the balance of the purchase price, £14,000, was to be provided by the purchasers personally without recourse to further borrowing and that no second mortgage or other loan was being arranged or contemplated in connection with the purchase. The solicitor was obliged to report to the building society that this was so. The purchasers intended to fund the difference between the purchase price and the building society loan from the net proceeds of sale of their existing residence. They owed money to a bank on the security of that property. They arranged for a small part of the debt (£3,350) to remain outstanding and to be secured by a second charge on the property to be purchased. The solicitor was advised of this, but did not refer to it in his report, which incorrectly said that there was no further borrowing. The solicitor admitted that he had acted negligently and in breach of his contract with the building society. Soon after the transaction was completed the purchasers defaulted. The building society sold the property purchased at a loss, which it sought to recover from the solicitor.

The stands of the parties

The solicitor's far from implausible position was that his failure to disclose the £3,350 loan secured by the second charge was not causative of the loss, because even if he had disclosed it the building society would have proceeded and

---

104 *Wheeler's* case, above n 102 at 235-249.
105 [1998] Ch 1 at 22.

suffered precisely the same loss: the indebtedness was relatively trivial and did not represent a fresh borrowing.

The competing stands at trial were as follows:[106]

"It was common ground ... that no damages would be recoverable at common law for breach of contract or tort unless the society could show that it would not have proceeded with the transaction if it had been informed of the facts. The society, however, submitted that the position was different in equity. It alleged that the defendant had committed a breach of trust or fiduciary duty, and submitted that common law principles of causation and remoteness of damage have no application in such a case so that it was not necessary for the society to show that it would not have proceeded with the transaction if it had been informed of the facts."

The courts below

The trial judge accepted the building society's arguments. On the common law claims for breach of contract and negligence, she gave summary judgment for damages to be assessed (thus leaving it open to the solicitor to contend that the breach caused no loss on the basis that the society would have proceeded with the transaction even if it had been informed of the facts). She also gave summary judgment for the society for breach of trust for £59,000 less what it received on selling the property (but without leaving open a possible causation escape hatch). Chadwick J dismissed an appeal. The Court of Appeal reversed him and the trial judge in relation to the equitable claim.

Breach of trust?

The Court of Appeal, for reasons that are irrelevant to the present debate, held that the solicitor had not acted in breach of trust. The relevant part of the Court's reasoning deals with the question whether the solicitor was otherwise in breach of fiduciary duty.

No breach of "fiduciary" duty

As was noted above,[107] the Court of Appeal was of opinion that the expression "fiduciary duty" comprised the duty of the solicitor to be loyal to the building society, and thus to act in good faith, not to make a profit out of the relationship, not to put himself in a position where his duty and his interest might conflict, not to act for the benefit of himself or a third person without the building society's consent, and not to allow the performance of his duties to the building society to be affected by his duties to the borrowers. The Court of Appeal said that it was no part of the solicitor's "fiduciary duty" to take care in making an accurate report.

The Court of Appeal held that the solicitor had not been shown to be in breach of the duty to act in good faith: it had not been shown that he knew the

---

106   *Mothew's* case, above n 105 at 8.
107   See 199 above.

report to be incorrect. He had not knowingly preferred the interests of the borrowers to those of the building society. He had not knowingly refused to disclose a material fact. His duties did not conflict: the duty to make a correct report was owed to each of the two principals and the content of each duty was identical. The fact that he was acting for both lender and borrowers did not contribute to his failure to report the second charge.

Conclusion

These favourable conclusions about the solicitor's conduct meant that the plaintiff building society could not succeed against the solicitor unless it proved that the solicitor caused it loss. In distinguishing between equitable duties which are fiduciary and those which are not, the Court of Appeal referred to Viscount Haldane LC's statement[108] that solicitors owe no equitable duty to exercise reasonable care and skill. But the significance of that statement appears to have been overlooked when the Court of Appeal said that the distinction drawn in *Wheeler's* case was decisive of *Mothew's* case. Its significance is that, taken with the court's favourable findings about the solicitor, no question arose about any distinction between equitable duties which are fiduciary and those which are not. The question of what the relevant causation and damages tests were in relation to the defendant solicitor was a narrow one: he owed no equitable duty to exercise reasonable care and skill, only a legal one. The solicitor's breach of that legal duty to exercise reasonable care and skill could not attract equitable remedies, since equity does not grant additional or different damages from the common law in its auxiliary jurisdiction, and in relation to the duty of solicitors to exercise reasonable care and skill equity does not have any exclusive jurisdiction. Since the only relevant wrong was breach of a common law duty, only common law causation tests applied. The plaintiff's rights in that respect were safeguarded by the trial judge's grant of summary judgment with damages to be assessed. No question whether more favourable equitable tests applied was capable of arising.

It follows that the Court of Appeal's approval of the *Wheeler* Doctrine was not an essential part of its reasoning. The Court's quotation and reiteration of very general statements about the equitable duties to exercise care and skill owed by fiduciaries cannot have been decisive of a case about a solicitor who was not relevantly a fiduciary and owed no equitable duties to exercise care and skill.

Further, since *Mothew's* case dealt only with a solicitor, its general statements about solicitor-fiduciaries have no binding force in relation to trustees or directors. The fact that a solicitor owes no equitable duty to exercise care and skill cannot support the proposition that the equitable duties of a trustee or director to exercise care and skill are not fiduciary. It is true that the solicitor's liability in *Nocton v Lord Ashburton* depended on his having placed himself in a position of conflict. He "had financial transactions with his client, and ... handled his money to the extent of using it to pay off a mortgage made to himself, [and] getting the client to release from his mortgage a property over which the solicitor by such release ... obtained further security for a mortgage

---

108 *Nocton v Lord Ashburton* [1914] AC 932 at 956.

of his own ... ."[109] Hence it is true that, for solicitors, there is a "distinction ultimately to be drawn from Viscount Haldane's speech between the fiduciary duty and the fiduciary's duty of care."[110] But *Wheeler's* case and *Mothew's* case extended that distinction beyond the position of solicitors into quite different fields when this was not necessary for their resolution.

Further, there is an even more fundamental sense in which the statements in *Mothew's* case were lacking authority. It was common ground that "if the defendant had been acting for the society alone, his admitted negligence would not have exposed him to a charge of fiduciary duty", since "counsel for the society accepted as much".[111] The society argued that the fact that the solicitor acted for the purchasers made a difference, and this was the point, and the only point, at which the Court of Appeal disagreed. A proposition of law incorporated into the reasoning of a particular court, even if it forms part of the ratio decidendi (which it did not in *Mothew's* case), is not binding on later courts if the particular court merely assumed its correctness without argument.[111A]

Finally, the brief summaries of counsel's argument make it impossible to conclude positively that counsel were at issue on the question whether the duties of a fiduciary to take reasonable care are fiduciary: counsel for the solicitor cited the *Girardet*, *Lac Minerals* and *Wheeler* cases, but nothing is attributed to counsel for the society in that regard. The court does not express its approbation of the *Wheeler* Doctrine as being necessary to still a controversy between counsel.

THE AUTHORITY OF THE GUARDIAN TRUST CASE

The statement in the *Guardian Trust* case that the *Wheeler* Doctrine is "now well established"[112] is surprising in view of the fact that the relevant propositions rest on, and consist themselves only of, statements unnecessary for the outcome in the cases in which they were made. However, the *Guardian Trust* case itself joined that tradition.

The facts

Guardian was trustee under a debenture deed securing advances from five banks to a property investment company, Comsec. One of the banks was NAB. Clause 7.05(e) of the deed provided that the trustee:

> "shall exercise reasonable diligence to ascertain whether or not [Comsec] or any of the charging subsidiaries has committed any breach of the provisions of this deed ... ."

This duty was equivalent to the trustee's general law duty. Clause 5.03(d) of the deed provided that Comsec was not to make advances to its subsidiaries.

---

109   [1914] AC 932 at 956; see also 943-944.
110   RP Austin, 'Moulding the Content of Fiduciary Duties' in AJ Oakley (ed), *Trends in Contemporary Trust Law* (Oxford University Press, Oxford, 1997) at 173.
111   *Mothew's* case [1998] Ch 1 at 18.
111A *Baker v R* [1975] AC 774 at 787-789.
112   *Guardian Trust* case [1999] 1 NZLR 664 at 680.

The July 1987 accounts of Comsec revealed that Comsec had made advances to its subsidiaries. The trustee admitted that it had failed to exercise reasonable diligence to detect this. Comsec reported its breach to the trustee in May 1988, and the trustee informed the banks in July 1988. In 1989 Comsec went into receivership. Had NAB been able to opt out of the facility in 1987, when the trustee ought to have detected Comsec's breach in 1987, by using its commercial position to persuade the other banks to take up its share of the facility, it would have suffered no loss. But the New Zealand Court of Appeal declined (unlike the trial judge) to find that NAB could have procured the other banks to buy out its share.[113]

NAB's unattractive case

NAB's case was that by reason of the trustee's failure, in breach of an express term of the trust deed, to exercise reasonable diligence, it was entitled to recover equitable compensation, being the difference between what it had advanced and the much smaller sum it received on sale of the securities for the loan to Comsec when Comsec failed. This was said to be the value of the opportunity which NAB had lost by reason of the trustee's failure to notify NAB of the unsecured loans in 1987.

NAB's case, morally speaking, lacked charm. It was unattractive to complain of the trustee's failure to appreciate the significance of a note in Comsec's annual accounts in the light of other suspicious circumstances, for NAB had received the same accounts, NAB had an agent who knew of the note, NAB knew of the suspicious circumstances, NAB had equal opportunities to monitor Comsec's activities, and NAB had expertise equal to that of Comsec.[114] It was also unattractive to contend that the correct valuation of the loss of a chance to avoid a financial loss was 100 percent of that financial loss.[115]

The four judges (Richardson P, Gault, Henry and Blanchard JJ) who joined in the leading judgment of the New Zealand Court of Appeal rejected NAB's case for the following reasons.

No loss of trust estate

First, the Court said that the trust estate consisted of the securities for the loans and associated rights and powers. These were the same both before and after Comsec's unsecured advances. It said that the claim was "for personal losses extraneous to the trust estate":[116]

---

113 *Guardian Trust* case, above n 112.

114 *Guardian Trust* case [1999] 1 NZLR 213 at 255 per Fisher J, the trial judge, whose language was in the circumstances very moderate (the trustee's "conduct was not the most heinous example of negligence" and hence it had only moderate relative culpability). The Court of Appeal noted but did not comment on this: *Guardian Trust* case, above n 112 at 674. The reference to the "relative culpability" doctrine, like the Court's reliance at 682 on authority asserting the proposition that contributory negligence is relevant to breach of fiduciary duty (*Day v Mead* [1987] 2 NZLR 443) is a reminder of the extreme care which must be employed in handling modern New Zealand cases (cf *Nationwide Building Society v Balmer Radmore (a firm)* [1999] PNLR 606; *Pilmer v Duke Group Ltd (in liq)* (2001) 207 CLR 165 at 201[86] and 231[173]).

115 *Guardian Trust* case, above n 1124 at 679.

116 *Guardian Trust* case, above n 112 at 679-680.

"The loss … was the loss to NAB of an opportunity to exit. That opportunity was not part of the trust estate entrusted to Guardian. … The claim is not founded on any loss or diminution in value of the trust estate."

No right to restitutionary compensation

Secondly, the Court said it had not been referred to any authority supporting the proposition that a breach of trust causing loss to a beneficiary personally but not to the trust estate may be remedied by awarding the beneficiary equitable compensation on a restitutionary basis as if the loss were of trust property.

Approval of Wheeler's and Mothew's cases

Thirdly, the Court then relied on *Wheeler's* and *Mothew's* cases for the proposition that not every breach of duty by a fiduciary is a breach of fiduciary duty and, in particular, not the breach of a trustee's duty to exercise reasonable care.[117]

No need for deterrence

Fourthly, the Court said, in a key passage:[118]

"The issue then is whether the breach of duty by Guardian to act with reasonable diligence is to attract liability on a restitutionary basis by analogy with breaches of trust causing loss to the trust estate or breaches of fiduciary duties of loyalty and fidelity. The rationale for a restitutionary approach in those situations is the need to deter breaches of trust and confidence by those in a position to take advantage of the vulnerable by using powers to be exercised solely for their benefit. Where that is not present as where a person, though under some fiduciary obligations, merely fails to exercise reasonable skill and care, there is no reason in principle for the law to treat that person any differently than those who breach duties of care imposed by contract or tort. That the liability arises in equity is no sufficient reason. Surely the stage has been reached in the development of the law where something *more substantial than historical origin* is needed to justify disparate treatment in the law of those in breach of the obligation to exercise reasonable care. The proper focus ought to be on the scope of the duty in the circumstances, with a consistent approach to compensating for breach. Only where good reasons exist is differentiation warranted. They do exist where breaches of trust dissipate trust property, where there is abuse of fiduciary duties of fidelity and loyalty or where there is dishonesty in the commission of certain intentional torts such as fraudulent misrepresentation… ."

The Court then said that while a "but for" causation test might suffice for breaches of trust causing loss to the trust estate or breaches of fiduciary duties of loyalty and fidelity, it had been consistently rejected in contract and tort. "No

---

117 It has been followed on this point: *S v Attorney-General* [2003] 3 NZLR 450 at 471[77]—472[79].
118 *Guardian Trust* case [1999] 1 NZLR 664 at 681 (emphasis added).

good reason has been advanced to show it should be sufficient for breach of a duty in equity of equivalent scope. On the contrary, recent authority favours the equivalent approach to causation and remoteness."

Passages in authorities relied on

The Court then quoted a series of passages in ostensible support of its conclusions. One was the *Henderson* passage. Another was a passage from *Mothew's* case stating that the common law rules of causation, remoteness and measure of damages should be applied by analogy to breaches of the equitable duty of care and skill.[119]

Common law causation test applied

The Court concluded its discussion of causation tests by applying that *Mothew* passage.[120]

> "There being no suggestion of fraud, impropriety, or breach of duties of fidelity or loyalty on the part of Guardian, there is no reason to approach its breach of its duty to act diligently in any different manner as regards causation and remoteness than would be the case if the cause of action were in contract or tort rather than in equity."

Scope of trustee's duty defined

The Court then said it was necessary to consider the scope of the trustee's duty, and inquire as to the risks against which the trustee had a duty to protect the plaintiff. The Court said:[121]

> "[T]he failure to inform left NAB continuing as a lender on a false basis (that there were no unsecured loans). Even if that had been true, the loss to NAB would have been the same. If the scope of the duty to inform extends only to protect against the consequences of leaving a false understanding it cannot assist NAB."

The Court held that the duty extended no more widely, and hence rejected the NAB case.

Unforeseeability of loss

The Court then set out an alternative path leading to the rejection of NAB's claim as follows. The recovery of damages for the trustee's failure to exercise diligence depends on common law tests of remoteness; common law tests of remoteness require loss to be foreseeable; it was not foreseeable to the trustee that from July 1987 NAB might desire to withdraw as a stockholder as distinct

---

119 [1998] Ch 1 at 17, discussed at 221–223 below, text to nn 166-173.
120 *Guardian Trust* case, above n 118 at 682.
121 *Guardian Trust* case, above n 118 at 683.

from working with the other stockholders to rectify Comsec's default. Even if it were foreseeable that NAB desired or might desire to withdraw, NAB was not entitled under the deed to determine its lending, and hence its withdrawal was unforeseeable on that ground. The claimed "opportunity" to withdraw which had been lost was in truth of no value because of NAB's inability to insist on it.[122]

If so, the case could have been decided not on questions of definition of duty, nor on foreseeability, nor on any distinction between equitable compensation assessed by reference to a common law remoteness test and equitable compensation assessed on a more favourable equitable test, but simply on the basis that there was no loss. Even if the *Re Dawson* test for assessing equitable compensation is invoked, it still calls for proof that there was a loss which would not have been suffered but for the breach by the fiduciary. Here, on the Court of Appeal's reasoning, even if the trustee had noticed the reference to Comsec's loans to its subsidiaries and had told NAB, NAB could not have withdrawn, and it would have suffered the loss caused by the later deterioration in value of the securities in any event.

Thus the *Guardian Trust* case, like its predecessors, contains numerous pronouncements which were entirely unnecessary for the result. Nothing in the report suggests that those pronouncements were offered in response to a specific debate between the parties about their merits.

Tipping J

The fifth judge, Tipping J, who agreed with the majority in the result, divided trustee breaches into three. He said that in the case of the first two, questions of foreseeability and remoteness did not arise, and causation depended on a "but for" test; while in the case of the third, common law tests applied. The first class comprised breaches which "directly caused loss of or damage to the trust property". The second class comprised breaches which involve "an element of infidelity or disloyalty engaging the fiduciary's conscience". The third class comprised breaches where "the relationship of trustee (or fiduciary) and beneficiary is, in a sense, accidental". The third class:[123]

> "provides the setting in which the breach of duty occurs, and with it such tortious proximity or contractual privity as may be necessary. The duty to take care is one which arises as an incident of the relationship, but for the purpose of determining the proper approach to causation and remoteness, it is the failure to take care which is the material dimension, not the fact that the relationship also creates duties of a fiduciary kind. Those duties are not relevantly engaged.
>
> ... [W]here the wrong amounts in substance to carelessness or breach of contract, the policy considerations underpinning the stricter approach are absent."

These remarks are as unnecessary for the outcome as those of the majority.

---

122 *Guardian Trust* case, above n 118 at 685-686.
123 *Guardian Trust* case, above n 118 at 687-688.

THE WHEELER DOCTRINE: A NECESSARY SOLUTION TO LIVE CONTROVERSIES?

Where a court gives two sets of reasons for reaching a conclusion, in many circumstances it is not possible to treat one as the ratio decidendi and the other as obiter dicta, and the case is to be regarded as one with two rationes decidendi.[124] What is the test?

At one extreme there is Vaughan CJ: "An opinion given in Court, if not necessary to the judgment given of record, but that it might have been as well given if no such, or a contrary, opinion had been broach'd is no judicial opinion, nor more than a gratis dictum."[125] After three centuries, there remains power both in the thought and in the manner of its expression.

On the other hand, MacCormick said:[126]

"The *ratio decidendi* is the ruling expressly or impliedly given by a judge which is sufficient to settle a point of law put in issue by the parties' arguments in a case, being a point on which a ruling was necessary to his justification (or one of his alternative justifications) of the decision in the case."

Cross and Harris said:[127]

"The *ratio decidendi* of a case is any rule of law expressly or impliedly treated by a judge as a necessary step in reaching his conclusion, having regard to the line of reasoning adopted by him ... ."

That formulation was a crisper version of Schreiner JA's statement:[128]

"where a single judgment is in question, the reasons given in the judgment, properly interpreted, do constitute the *ratio decidendi,* originating or following a legal rule, provided (*a*) that they do not appear from the judgment itself to have been merely subsidiary reasons for following the main principle or principles, (*b*) that they were not merely a course of reasoning on the facts ... and (*c*) (which may cover (*a*)) that they were necessary for the decision, not in the sense that it could not have been reached along other lines, but in the sense that along the lines actually followed in the judgment the result would have been different but for the reasons."

Each of these formulations has a potential difficulty avoided by Vaughan CJ, namely that since the law is to be found in the rationes decidendi of cases decided in superior courts not contradicted by higher or co-ordinate authority, undue preponderance cannot be given to what the particular judge irrationally regards as necessary, as distinct from what is necessary. That vice is removed in a formulation advanced by Kirby J:[129]

---

124 *Jacobs v London County Council* [1950] AC 361 at 369-370.

125 *Bole v Horton* (1673) Vaughan 360 at 382; 124 ER 1113 at 1124.

126 N MacCormick, *Legal Reasoning and Legal Theory* (Oxford University Press, Oxford, 1978) at 215.

127 R Cross and JW Harris, *Precedent in English Law* (4th ed, Oxford University Press, Oxford, 1991) at 72.

128 *Pretoria City Council v Levinson* 1949 (3) SA 305 at 317.

129 *Garcia v National Australia Bank Ltd* (1998) 194 CLR 395 at 417[56].

"It is fundamental to the ascertainment of the binding rule of a judicial decision that it should be derived from (1) the reasons of the judges agreeing in the order disposing of the proceedings; (2) upon a matter in issue in the proceedings; (3) upon which a decision is necessary to arrive at that order."

The reference by MacCormick and Kirby J to matters in issue is important. If controversial legal propositions on a particular point are to be accepted as the law, it is even more important that they not be enunciated without the benefit of forensic argument from legal representatives who regard the point as crucial. Legal statements by a judge not controverted by the parties are not binding; legal statements by a judge which the losing party had no opportunity to controvert cannot be binding either.

Leading cases involve grim, harrowing and painful human dramas. For the Court the question is: Is it necessary to ruin Mr Hamilton? Must Mr Mothew's reputation be destroyed? Our law has developed out of intense contests. In them the reputation, the property, the liberty, or, once upon a time, the life, of a particular citizen is at stake. In them all parties are represented by skilful and forceful advocates. In them the outcome turns on the decision, one way or the other, of a specific issue which is perceived by all to be, and which is, crucial. The conflict between informed advocates on that crucial point takes place in public before their professional peers, unaccustomed to emotions of mercy. When the conflict is sharpened by judicial testing, an intense friction can build up. That in turn generates a terrible energy capable of illuminating the law. Then the judge, with that aid, must resolve the conflict – must retire, to use Sir Owen Dixon's famous but perhaps blasphemous words, into some private Gethsemane of his own. Those who have not endured the stress of those hard and bitter struggles are unable to understand how greatly their stern discipline can purify thought – by burning away the dross of error, irrelevance, loose reasoning and facile analysis – by sharpening focus, clarifying perception and strengthening grip. This entire process is directed to quelling genuine and bitter controversy, not pursuing abstract inquiries. It does so by searching for answers which it is necessary to give to live questions having a direct impact on the interests of the parties, rather than offering theoretical, abstract or hypothetical advice merely. The process, as a method of revealing the law, has safeguards and advantages wholly absent from its exposition by reference to propositions not essential to the resolution of the particular concrete human drama before the court. The *Wheeler* Doctrine did not evolve through a process of that salutary kind. Its correctness has never been crucial to the success or failure of a particular litigant. More importantly, it is not apparent that any counsel has seen it to be so. These considerations create significant barriers to its immediate acceptance.

Despite that, a question remains. Have the supporters of the *Wheeler* Doctrine demonstrated its correctness?

A DEFINITIONAL EXPLANATION?

One explanation offered for the *Wheeler* Doctrine is definitional – at least in the sense that the relevant part of the reasoning in *Mothew's* case commences: "It is … necessary to begin by defining one's terms". It continues:[130]

---

130 *Mothew's* case [1998] Ch 1 at 16.

"The expression 'fiduciary duty' is properly confined to [(a)] those duties which are peculiar to fiduciaries and [(b)] the breach of which attracts legal consequences differing from those consequent upon the breach of other duties."

By reason of this it was said to be "obvious that not every breach of duty by a fiduciary is a breach of fiduciary duty".

The duty of a trustee to exercise care and skill is "peculiar" to the trustee as a fiduciary, because there is no equivalent common law duty. Hence the trustee's duty would appear to meet element (a) of the definition. If so, it is not explained why the director's equitable duty, which is derived from that of the trustee, does not meet it as well, even though it may have an attenuated common law counterpart which no judge or jurist has ever been able to illustrate by any reported case.

Element (b) of the definition appears to be circular. The question is – "Does some particular legal consequence flow from the breach of duty proved?" The answer is: "Only if it is a fiduciary duty which has been breached." That provokes the question: "What is a fiduciary duty?" The answer is: "That which attracts the particular legal consequence differing from those consequent on the breach of non-fiduciary duties."

Hence the *Wheeler* Doctrine cannot be shown to follow from the postulated definition of "fiduciary duty".

AN EXPLANATION DERIVED FROM EXAMPLES OF FIDUCIARY DUTIES?

The list of examples of fiduciary duties[131] which *Mothew's* case contrasted with the duty of a fiduciary to exercise care and skill does not by itself explain the non-inclusion in that list of the duty of care and skill. The list is avowedly non-exhaustive.[132] On what ground are some duties in it, but not others?

THE IN RE COOMBER EXPLANATION?

In re Coomber; Coomber v Coomber[133] was cited in *Mothew's* case as containing a warning against an "unthinking resort to formulae" which had "bedevilled" this branch of the law.[134] In that case the English Court of Appeal rejected a challenge to the gift by a mother to her son of a business he was conducting on her behalf. The reasoning in Fletcher Moulton LJ's celebrated ex tempore judgment did not establish that the duty of care and skill owed by the son (as his mother's agent to conduct the business) was not fiduciary. Nor did it establish that a trustee's or director's duty of care and skill is not fiduciary. All it established was that the gift made by mother to son had no connection with the fiduciary relationship – "nothing in the fiduciary relationship ... affected this

---

131 See above 199.
132 *Mothew's* case, above n 130 at 18.
133 [1911] 1 Ch 723 at 728-729.
134 *Mothew's* case, above n 130 at 16.

transaction." She meant to give it, and there was no evidence of undue influence, or indeed any influence at all.

The Company's Position of Disadvantage or Vulnerability

In *Wheeler's* case the Full Court quoted the following observation of Dawson J:[135]

"There is ... the notion underlying all the cases of fiduciary obligation that inherent in the nature of the relationship itself is a position of disadvantage or vulnerability on the part of one of the parties which causes him to place reliance upon the other and requires the protection of equity acting upon the conscience of that other."

The Full Court then said:[136]

"The director's duty to exercise care and skill has nothing to do with any position of disadvantage or vulnerability on the part of the company. It is not a duty that stems from the requirements of trust and confidence imposed on a fiduciary."

Later it explained the significance of "vulnerability" thus:[137]

"There is a fundamental distinction between breaches of fiduciary obligations which involve dishonesty and abuse of the trustee's advantages and the vulnerable position of beneficiaries, on the one hand, and, honest but careless dealings which breach mere equitable obligations, on the other. There is ample justification on policy grounds for more stringent rules in the case of breaches of fiduciary obligations, but not where there [have] been honest but careless dealings."

The suggestion appears to be that companies, for example, are not "vulnerable" to honest but careless dealings by directors.

Later authorities suggest that vulnerability may be neither necessary nor sufficient for the recognition of fiduciary obligations.[138] However that may be, it can be acknowledged that some companies, some of the time, are not vulnerable to misconduct by particular directors – because of the alertness of other directors, or of senior managers, or creditors, or shareholders (including large institutional shareholders with access to expert skills and advice), or regulatory authorities, or trade unions, or a vigilant financial press. Further, the members of a company are less likely trustingly to rely on the directors than, for example, a young ward is on a guardian. But most companies at some times are vulnerable to the misconduct of their directors – particularly their day-to-day controllers, the executive directors.

135 *Hospital Products Ltd v United States Surgical Corporation* (1984) 156 CLR 41 at 142.
136 *Wheeler's* case (1994) 11 WAR 187 at 239.
137 *Wheeler's* case, above n 136 at 247.
138 *Breen v Williams* (1996) 186 CLR 71 at 107; *News Ltd v Australian Rugby Football League Ltd* (1996) 64 FCR 410 at 541.
139 HAJ Ford, *Ford's Principles of Corporations Law* (12th ed, LexisNexis Butterworths, Chatswood, 2005) at para 8.010; approved in *Duke Group Ltd (in liq) v Pilmer* (1998) 27 ACSR 1 at 296.

Speaking of the power which directors have to control the management of the company, *Ford's Principles of Corporations Law* says:[139]

> "With this power comes the opportunity for fraud and *mismanagement*. Anyone who entrusts their property or affairs to another person is at risk of suffering loss by the other person's wrongdoing. The shareholders of companies are often especially vulnerable, because they are frequently passive investors who do not follow the company's progress on a day-to-day basis. Their vulnerability is all the more acute if they are numerous and not organised.
>
> The law responds to the directors' position of temptation and the vulnerability of shareholders by subjecting the directors to strict fiduciary and *statutory* duties." (Emphasis added.)

The statutory duties of care and diligence are of course closely related to the common law and equitable duties of care and skill. Ford thus appears to find in the vulnerability of the company a source of the duty to exercise care and skill.

Further, in *O'Halloran v R T Thomas & Family Pty Ltd*[140] Spigelman CJ said:

> "The strict standard applicable to a trustee of a traditional trust with respect to improper application of trust property is based on the vulnerability of beneficiaries with respect to the disposition of property by a trustee who has control over such disposition. This policy applies equally to the case of a director of a company, such as a managing director, (or a group of directors) who has (or have) the power to dispose of company property and who does (or do) dispose of such property for an improper purpose. ... Such a director (or directors) is (are) subject to the same stringent test with respect to the exercise of the fiduciary power to dispose of property, as is the trustee of a traditional trust. ...
>
> ... It is the vulnerability of a company which places its property in the power of directors, that makes it appropriate to adopt the approach to causation applicable to the trustee of a traditional trust in deciding issues of causation for the contravention by a company director of his or her duty not to exercise the power to dispose of property for an improper purpose."

If companies (and trust beneficiaries) are vulnerable to directors (and trustees) who dispose of trust or company property for an improper purpose, the companies (and the trust beneficiaries) are equally vulnerable to directors (and trustees) who fall below their duties to exercise reasonable care and skill. Spigelman CJ said that directors who misappropriate or misapply property fraudulently, in the equitable sense, are under duties equivalent to those of a trustee and should be liable to the same equitable compensation remedies and causation tests.[141] The purposes served by the rules requiring directors and trustees to exercise care and skill are consistent with the purposes of the rules against improper conduct. While the duties of directors and trustees to exercise care and skill are not identical, they are sufficiently close, given the similarity of the underlying purposes, to suggest that the same remedies apply. The director's duty of care and skill was derived from the duty of trustees. The duty of trustees in turn derived from the trust and confidence reposed in them as fiduciaries. The director's duty of care and skill is thus historically and functionally related

---

140 (1998) 45 NSWLR 262 at 277.
141 *O'Halloran v R T Thomas & Family Pty Ltd*, above n 140 at 277-278.

to the disadvantage and vulnerability of the company, and breaches of that duty are capable of being dealt with by the same kinds of remedy as breaches of the duty of fidelity – in particular, compensation calculated by reference to the tests stated in *Re Dawson*.

The director's duty is further reflected in the commercial position of directors as regulated by modern company legislation. It is difficult for those who wish to conduct business to do so without using companies and without becoming a company director. In practice the role of directors is vital to the life of a company. Directors are office holders. "An office holder is in law someone who is appointed to fulfil a function which is continuing in character, and for which a succession of appointees will be appointed so long as the function remains to be fulfilled. The office is the personification of the function."[142] The office held by directors is a statutory office. Appointment to it, and conduct in it, are subject to very detailed statutory regulation. Directors are usually appointed with some formality, or elected by members at meetings to which detailed procedural requirements apply. Every proprietary company must have at least one director, and every public company must have at least three.[143] The signed consent of directors is a necessary precondition of taking up office.[144] These signed consents must be retained by the company.[145] There are strict conditions of eligibility. Once directors are appointed their conduct must conform not only with common law and equitable duties, but with statutory norms backed by criminal and penal sanctions, some heavy. One of those sanctions is disqualification from office, and exposure to that risk is exposure to a penalty.[146]

The primary duty of persons who hold this centrally important office of director is to advance the interests of the company and prevent it suffering loss. Loss can be caused to a company as much by a failure to exercise care and skill as by deliberate wrongdoing, or conduct carried out while in a position of conflict.[147]

The *Wheeler* Doctrine has the peculiar outcome of narrowing the remedies available against directors who have failed fully to vindicate the interests of their company. It would be less surprising if many of the duties affecting the conduct by directors of their office were infused by its inherently and intensely fiduciary character, and it would not be surprising at all if the duty to exercise care and skill were one of them.

THE IDENTITY OF DUTIES?

Another justification for the *Wheeler* Doctrine advanced by the Full Court employed the language of "policy". However, if sound, the reasoning appears to bear an orthodox conceptual character.[148]

---

142 RR Pennington, *Directors' Personal Liability*, (Collins Professional Books, London, 1987) at 20.

143 *Corporations Act 2001* (Cth), s 201A.

144 *Corporations Act 2001* (Cth), ss 117(2) and 201D.

145 *Corporations Act 2001* (Cth), ss 117(5) and 201D(2).

146 *Rich v ASIC* (2004) 209 ALR 271.

147 RR Pennington, *Directors' Personal Liability*, above n 142 at 207.

148 *Wheeler's* case (1994) 11 WAR 187 at 247-248. The Full Court then quoted some general remarks of McLachlan J and La Forest J in *Canson Enterprises Ltd v Boughton & Co* [1991] 3 SCR 534 at 545 and 586-587 (the latter in turn quoting Somers J in *Day v Mead* [1987] 2

"It is also significant, as regards matters of policy, that the tortious duty not to be negligent, and the equitable obligation on the part of a trustee to exercise reasonable care and skill are, in content, the same. There is every reason ... , in such circumstances, to apply the maxim that 'equity follows the law'."

This passage assumes that there are two wrongs with the same content.[149] The assumption must be wrong. "Since the common law did not recognise equitable ownership a legal owner could not owe a common law duty to the equitable owner as such."[150] A similar fallacy appears in *Mothew's* case in the passage set out above dealing generally with the inappropriateness of applying the expression "fiduciary duty" to obligations of skill and care said to have been developed both at law and in equity.[151] The passage, which refers specifically to trustees, is incorrect. It is incorrect in so far as it suggests that the common law and equity each developed the trustee's duty of care: the common law knew nothing of it.

Is the tortious duty on a company director not to be negligent the same as the equitable obligation to exercise reasonable care and skill?[152] So far as that passage from *Mothew's* case was referring to company directors (and it immediately precedes quotations from *Henderson's* case[153] and *Wheeler's* case[154] which refer to directors), it suggests that the duties are different. It does not say how they are different, and perhaps the differences contemplated are not great. In *Daniels v Anderson* the majority of the New South Wales Court of Appeal, in turn, were of opinion that the equitable duty was different from the common law duty – historically, having been recognised over a century ago, and conceptually, for the common law duty was, but the equitable duty was not, sourced in the principles expounded in *Donoghue v Stevenson*.[155] That conclusion[156] corresponds with the more briefly stated views of Hoffmann J in England.[157] Because the modern common law tort of negligence has moved close to strict liability, it imports a radically higher standard than that recognised in equity.

If so, the view stated in *Wheeler's* case that the measure of duty for directors at common law and in equity is the same is wrong. Hence the Full Court had no

---

NZLR 443 at 457-458) and the endorsement of McLachlan J's remarks by A Mason "The Place of Equity and Equitable Remedies in the Contemporary Common Law World" (1994) 110 *Law Quarterly Review* 238 at 244. The proposition that the duties are the same also appears at 238.

149 It is contradicted by an earlier statement, apparently denying that "there exists an equitable 'wrong' analogous to and co-terminous with the common law tort of negligence": *Wheeler's* case, above n 148 at 237. At that point reliance is placed on *Wickstead v Browne* (1992) 30 NSWLR 1 at 16; for the Full Court's handling of that case, see R Meagher, JD Heydon and M Leeming (eds), *Meagher, Gummow & Lehane's Equity—Doctrines and Remedies* (4th ed, LexisNexis Butterworths, Sydney, 2002) at [5-315].

150 *Wickstead v Browne* (1992) 30 NSWLR 1 at 17 per Handley and Cripps JJA.

151 Above 197–198, text to n 76 above.

152 It will be recollected that for the purposes of this chapter it is being assumed that both duties exist.

153 [1995] 2 AC 145 at 205.

154 (1994) 11 WAR 187 at 237 and 239.

155 [1932] AC 562.

156 *Daniels v Anderson* (1995) 37 NSWLR 438 at 505.

157 See above n 52.

reason to apply the maxim that equity follows the law. The question whether the equitable duty is fiduciary remains open. It would not however be surprising if the plaintiff-friendly hurdles called for by the tort of negligence at common law attracted relatively onerous causation tests, normally now called "common sense" tests, while the hurdles of the equitable duty, if overcome, were accompanied by the more generous causation test set out in *Re Dawson*.

The proposition that common law and equitable duties are not identical is also supported by certain remarks of McLachlin J which have been approved by the High Court and which point against a justification for the *Wheeler* Doctrine advanced particularly in the *Guardian Trust* case. It is convenient to refer to them a little later, since they are relevant to another explanation advanced for the *Wheeler* Doctrine. [158]

DO DETERRENCE CONSIDERATIONS UNDERPIN THE WHEELER DOCTRINE?

The *Guardian Trust* case referred to policy considerations as justifying the *Wheeler* Doctrine. These policy considerations, in the reasoning of the majority,[159] appear to boil down to the idea that a stricter approach is called for where there has been dissipation of trust property in breach of trust, breaches of duties of fidelity and loyalty, or conduct equivalent to deceit at common law, and that that stricter approach rests on the need to deter breaches of trust and confidence. It was said that the stricter approach – that deterrent function – is absent where only breaches of a duty of care and skill are concerned.

In *Maguire v Makaronis* the High Court pointed out that where profits had been made by a fiduciary out of that fiduciary's position as fiduciary, where they had been made by reason of that fiduciary having taken advantage of an opportunity or knowledge derived from his or her fiduciary position, where a fiduciary mixes his or her moneys with moneys subject to fiduciary duties, and where trustees have wrongly parted with trust property, the relevant "principles" and "presumptions, some elevated to rules" express "the policy of the law in holding fiduciaries to their duty".[160] The New Zealand judges did not explain why, as distinct from asserting that, the same policy of the law should not be pursued in relation to holding trustees to their duty to exercise care and skill and holding company directors to their related duty. Why is it not important to deter breaches of these duties as much as of other duties? It is notable that one of the cases relied on by the High Court in *Maguire v Makaronis* to illustrate the strictness of a trustee's duty to restore lost trust property was *Clough v Bond*, in which the liability of a personal representative who had invested the property in unauthorised investments or placed the property "within the control of persons who ought not to be entrusted with it" was described as not "exercising reasonable care and diligence".[161]

158　See below 223, text to nn 172-173.
159　*Guardian Trust* case [1999] 1 NZLR 664 at 681.
160　(1997) 188 CLR 449 at 468, 470 and 474.
161　*Clough v Bond* (1838) 3 My & Cr 490 at 496; 40 ER 1016 at 1018.

In *Maguire v Makaronis* the High Court also pointed to the close link between a trustee's duty to exercise skill and care in administering the trust, and the duty to maintain the trust fund.[162]

> "Whilst the trustee is the archetype of the fiduciary, the trust has distinct characteristics. In particular, where a trust is created by will or settlement in traditional form, the trustee holds title to property on behalf of beneficiaries or for charitable purposes. If the trust be still subsisting, the objective of an action to recover loss upon breach of trust is the restoration of the trust fund. The right of the beneficiaries is to have the trust fund reconstituted and duly administered, rather than to recover a specific sum for the sole use and benefit of any beneficiary. Indeed, no one particular beneficiary may have sustained a present and individual loss. This may be so if the trust is a discretionary trust or no interest vests, either in interest or possession, before the termination of a prior interest.
>
> Further, the particular breach of which complaint is made may be consequent upon failure in observance of one or other of the duties which attend trust administration, such as those to make only authorised investments, and to use due diligence and care in the administration of the trust. Nineteenth century authorities such as *Caffrey v Darby*[163] and *Clough v Bond*[164] concerned failure to observe these rules for due administration rather than that disloyalty and conflict between interest and duty which was considered in *Nocton v Lord Ashburton*."

In short, the law relating to trustees focuses primarily on their obligation to act in the interests of the beneficiaries.[165] Those interests are vindicated as much by the trustee's duty to exercise reasonable care and skill as they are by the duty to act in good faith and avoid conflicts. Why is there not an equal focus on the duty of directors to act in the interests of the company? Why are not those interests vindicated as much by the director's duty to exercise reasonable care and skill as they are by the duty to act in good faith and avoid conflicts?

An important statement in *Youyang Pty Ltd v Minter Ellison Morris Fletcher*[166] casts doubt on one aspect of *Mothew's* case.

Mothew's case, without fanfare, broke radically from the view stated in *Wheeler's* case that the assessment of equitable compensation for breach of the director's duty to exercise reasonable care and skill depended on the test stated in *Re Dawson*.

> "Although the remedy which equity makes available for breach of the equitable duty of skill and care is equitable compensation rather than damages, *this is merely the product of history* and in this context is ... a distinction without a difference. Equitable compensation for breach of the duty of skill and care resembles common law damages in that it is awarded by way of compensation for the plaintiff for his loss. There is no reason in principle why the common law rules of causation, remoteness of damage and measure of

---

162 *Maguire v Makaronis*, above n 160 at 473 (various footnotes omitted).
163 (1801) 6 Ves Jun 488; 31 ER 1159. The Full Court in *Wheeler's* case took the same view of this case and *Clough v Bond*: see above 203, text to nn 94-96.
164 (1838) 3 My & Cr 490; 40 ER 1016.
165 *Pilmer v Duke Group Ltd (in liq)* (2001) 207 CLR 165 at 201[86].
166 (2003) 212 CLR 484 at 500[39].

damages should not be applied by analogy in such a case. It should not be confused with equitable compensation for breach of fiduciary duty, which may be awarded in lieu of rescission or specific restitution." [167]

It is not clear:

(a) why it was thought appropriate to discuss the measure of damages for equitable compensation for breach of an equitable duty to exercise reasonable skill and care in a case in which the defendant was a solicitor who did not owe any equitable duty of that kind, only a legal duty;

(b) what was meant by "the common law rules of causation, remoteness of damage and measure of damages" which are to be applied to equitable compensation "by analogy": the common law rules differ as between deceit, negligence, trespass and case, for example,[168] and they have tended in the last century to fluctuate bewilderingly, sometimes over quite short time periods; and

(c) why the *Re Dawson* test should be departed from in assessing equitable compensation for breach of an equitable duty to exercise reasonable care and skill.

Whatever the answers to these questions, the statement just quoted must be read by Australian lawyers in the light of a comment made by the High Court about the New Zealand Court of Appeal's approval of that statement in the *Guardian Trust* case.[169] The High Court alluded to Lord Dunedin's celebrated statement that "there was a jurisdiction in equity to keep persons in a fiduciary capacity up to their duty."[170] The High Court continued:[171]

---

167 *Mothew's* case [1998] Ch 1 at 17 (emphasis added). RP Austin, 'Moulding the Content of Fiduciary Duties' in Oakley (ed), *Trends in Contemporary Trust Law* (Oxford University Press, Oxford, 1997) at 173-174 says this is what Lord Browne-Wilkinson meant in the *Henderson* passage. That view is supported by the fact that the passage is quoted in *Mothew's* case at 16-17, just above the remarks in *Wheeler's* case quoted in the text above at the reference to n 71. The passage is accepted by A Burrows, *Remedies for Torts and Breach of Contract* (3rd ed, Oxford University Press, Oxford, 2004) at 603-604.

168 In deceit there is a direct consequence test: *Smith New Court Securities Ltd v Citibank NA* [1997] AC 254; *Palmer Bruyn & Parker Pty Ltd v Parsons* (2001) 208 CLR 388 at 408 [64]-[65] per Gummow J. In negligence the kind of damage must be reasonably foreseeable: *Overseas Steamship (UK) Ltd v Morts Dock & Engineering Co Ltd (The Wagon Mound (No 1))* [1961] AC 388. The same is true in public nuisance: *Overseas Steamship (UK) Ltd v Morts Dock & Engineering Co Ltd (The Wagon Mound) (No 2))* [1967] 1 AC 617. In injurious falsehood recovery is limited to losses which were intended, or were the natural and probable consequence, of a tort: *Palmer Bruyn & Parker Pty Ltd v Parsons* (2001) 208 CLR 388. For trespass, see RP Balkin and JRL Davis, *Law of Torts* (3rd ed, Butterworths, Sydney, 2004) at [5.15]-[5.19] and [27.15].

169 [1999] 1 NZLR 664 at 681.

170 *Nocton v Lord Ashburton* [1914] AC 932 at 963.

171 *Youyang Pty Ltd v Minter Ellison Morris Fletcher*, above n 166 at 500[39]. The passage is criticised by two supporters of the *Wheeler* Doctrine, S Elliott and J Edelman "*Target Holdings* Considered in Australia" (2003) 119 *Law Quarterly Review* 545 at 550 – question-beggingly, but their opposition makes clear the inconsistency between what the High Court said and the *Wheeler* Doctrine. Justice Hayton has politely said that the High Court is wrong in his chapter in this book: "Unique Rules for the Unique Institution, The Trust", 291–292 of this book.

"there must be a real question whether the unique foundation and goals of equity, which has the institution of the trust at its heart, warrant any assimilation even in this limited way with the measure of compensatory damages in tort and contract. It may be thought strange to decide that the precept that trustees are to be kept by courts of equity up to their duty has an application limited to the observance by trustees of some only of their duties to beneficiaries in dealing with trust funds."

That is, the *Re Dawson* test operates to keep trustees up to their duties – their duties to exercise care and skill as much as other duties.

The High Court also cited with approval the following statement of McLachlin J:[172]

"The basis of the fiduciary obligation and the rationale for equitable compensation are distinct from the tort of negligence and contract. In negligence and contract the parties are taken to be independent and equal actors, concerned primarily with their own self-interest. Consequently, the law seeks a balance between enforcing obligations by awarding compensation and preserving optimum freedom for those involved in the relationship in question ... . The essence of a fiduciary relationship, by contrast, is that one party pledges itself to act in the best interest of the other. The fiduciary relationship has trust, not self-interest, at its core, and when breach occurs, the balance favours the person wronged."

And in *Pilmer v Duke Group Ltd (in liq)*[173] the High Court cited the following passage of McLachlin J with approval:[174]

"The foundation and ambit of the fiduciary obligation are conceptually distinct from the foundation and ambit of contract and tort. Sometimes the doctrines may overlap in their application, but that does not destroy their conceptual and functional uniqueness. In negligence and contract the parties are taken to be independent and equal actors, concerned primarily with their own self-interest. Consequently, the law seeks a balance between enforcing obligations by awarding compensation when those obligations are breached, and preserving optimum freedom for those involved in the relationship in question. The essence of a fiduciary relationship, by contrast, is that one party exercises power on behalf of another and pledges himself or herself to act in the best interests of the other."

These passages sit ill with any idea that the equitable obligations of a trustee or director are to undergo a process of filleting, by which although in all cases breach sounds in equitable compensation, some obligations are fiduciary and some not, some obligations core and some not, and the compensation recoverable for breach of some obligations is subject to different causation and remoteness tests from those which apply to others.

There is a very close relationship between the duties of a trustee to get property in, to invest it with care and skill and not to pay it out wrongly. The

---

172 *Canson Enterprises Ltd v Boughton & Co* [1991] 3 SCR 534 at 543.
173 (2001) 207 CLR 165 at 196-197[71].
174 *Norberg v Wynrib* [1992] 2 SCR 226 at 272.

economic value of the property can be lost to the trust as much by unsatisfactory decisions about investing it as by failing to get it in, or failing to keep it in. These duties are linked by more than just a duty to act in good faith and avoid conflicts. The basal link is that the role of a trustee is to advance the interests of the beneficiaries in a manner more effective than that of an honest and disinterested fool. The office calls not only for honesty, and an avoidance of conflicts, but for the exercise of care and skill as well. The obligations on and remedies against trustees recognised by the law of trusts fulfil a unitary function – to keep trustees up to their duty to protect the beneficiaries.

Whether or not the same is true of all other fiduciaries in relation to other principals, it has not been shown not to be true of directors in relation to their companies. The pledge of company directors to exercise power on behalf of, and in the best interests of, the company is not to be fragmented. It calls not only for good faith and an avoidance of conflicts, but for the exercise of reasonable care and skill. The function of equitable compensation calculated on *Re Dawson* principles was identified in the *Guardian Trust* case[175] as being "to deter breaches of trust and confidence by those in a position to take advantage of the vulnerable by using powers to be exercised solely for their benefit." If that is so, why does it not have an identical function of deterring trustees from breaches of their duty to exercise care and skill? And why does it not have the same function of deterring directors from breaches of their duty to exercise care and skill?

Getzler has pointedly asked two questions:[176] "How can a fiduciary trustee be said to be loyal to his beneficiary if he takes no care for the running of the trust? ... What use is a trust obligation if the obligee is protected from liability for lack of diligence?" He has also drawn attention to the words of Sir William Grant MR in *Caffrey v Darby*:[177]

> "It would be very dangerous, though no fraud could be imputed to the trustees, and no kind of interest or benefit to themselves was looked to, to lay down this principle; that trustees might without any responsibility act, as these did: in eight years, within which time the whole money ought to have been paid, receiving only £250; and taking no step as to the remainder. It would be an encouragement to bad motives; and it may be impossible to detect undue [sic; scil bad] motives."

Sir William Grant MR was speaking of conduct which could have been analysed as failure to get trust property in, or failure to invest it soundly, or as a general lack of care and skill. Whichever way it is analysed, his reasoning rests

---

175 [1999] 1 NZLR 664 at 681: quoted above 210–211, text to n 118. Similar reasoning appears in *Wheeler's* case (1994) 11 WAR 187 at 246: see 204, text to n 102.

176 J Getzler, "Equitable Compensation and the Regulation of Fiduciary Relationships" in P Birks and F Rose (eds), *Restitution and Equity: Vol I, Resulting Trusts and Equitable Compensation* (Mansfield Press, London, 2000) at 255.

177 (1801) 6 Ves Jun 488 at 495-496; 31 ER 1159 at 1162 (the attribution in the English Reports to "Lord Eldon MR" is a mistake: see *Compact Edition of the Dictionary of National Biography* (Oxford University Press, Oxford, 1975) at 825 and 1872 and *Oxford Dictionary of National Biography* (Oxford University Press, Oxford, 2004), Vol 23 at 345 and Vol 49 at 421).

on the same deterrent ideas as underlie remedies for breaches of duties of loyalty. Or, as Getzler puts it:[178]

"The prophylactic pressures of equitable procedure and remedy as applied to the loyalty duties may have point even in the sphere of duty of care; the stringent rules of causation, for example, are designed to put deterrent pressure on the fiduciary to reach a high standard where proof of misfeasance may be difficult to gather."

IMBALANCE OF REMEDIES AND WRONGS

Under the *Wheeler* Doctrine, a fiduciary's duties of good faith are fiduciary; equitable duties of care and skill are not fiduciary; duties not to profit from a fiduciary position, or not to get into a position of conflict, are fiduciary. Duties of good faith are only breached if the fiduciary has a culpable mental state; duties not to profit or get into a position of conflict can be breached however non-culpable the fiduciary's mental state; equitable duties of care and skill are in an intermediate position, depending on a form of culpability. Why is it that duties, breach of which rests on a culpable mental state, and duties, breach of which requires no culpable mental state, are fiduciary, but duties breach of which rests on an intermediate level of fault, are not? Why do the remedial consequences differ?

ARE THE COMMON LAW AND THE EQUITABLE DUTIES OF FIDUCIARIES ALWAYS IDENTICAL?

The approval by the High Court of the passages from judgments of McLachlin J quoted above suggests a further reason why the equitable duty of care and skill owed by fiduciaries is distinct from any common law duty, and in particular from any duty that exists in the tort of negligence. It is of the essence of the duties which a fiduciary is to perform that, subject to the principal's consent, the self-interest of the fiduciary is to be suppressed. In contrast, in assessing whether there has been a breach of a common law duty of care in the tort of negligence, the self-interest of the defendant is a relevant consideration and not something that the defendant is under a duty to suppress.[179]

"[If] a reasonable man in the defendant's position would have foreseen that his conduct involved a risk of injury to the plaintiff or to a class of persons including the plaintiff ... it is ... for the tribunal of fact to determine what a reasonable man would do by way of response to the risk. The perception of the

---

178 'Duty of Care' in P Birks and A Pretto (eds), *Breach of Trust* (Hart Publishing, Oxford, 2002) at 72.

179 *Wyong Shire Council v Shirt* (1980) 146 CLR 40 at 47-48. If this test applies to negligent directors, within "conflicting responsibilities" could be accommodated the need for directors to seek profits, take risks and trust other officers: *Daniels v Anderson* (1995) 37 NSWLR 438 at 501-505.

reasonable man's response calls for a consideration of the magnitude of the risk and the degree of the probability of its occurrence, along with the expense, difficulty and inconvenience of taking alleviating action and any other conflicting responsibilities which the defendant may have."

The reference to "expense, difficulty and inconvenience" is a reference to expense to the defendant, difficulty for the defendant, and inconvenience to the defendant. Up to a certain point defendants at risk of being sued at common law for the tort of negligence are entitled to prefer their interests in saving money, pursuing easy paths instead of difficult ones and taking the more personally convenient course. And they are entitled to give weight to responsibilities which conflict with their duty to the plaintiff. Fiduciaries are different: subject to the consent of their principals, they must suppress both self-interest and responsibilities arising out of duties to other persons. Fiduciaries could not excuse what would otherwise be breaches of the duty to exercise care and skill by contending that any other course would have been unduly damaging to their self-interest in avoiding expense, difficulty and inconvenience.

Can "Fiduciary" and "Non-Fiduciary" Duties be Readily Distinguished?

The *Wheeler* Doctrine depends on a sharp distinction between the "fiduciary duties" of fiduciaries and the "non-fiduciary" duties of fiduciaries. In practice this is difficult to draw.

Thus the duties breached by the trustees in *Cowan v Scargill*,[180] which Sir Robert Megarry V-C described as "fiduciary", included not only the duty to invest carefully, but also the duty to put the beneficiaries first, the duty to put aside the trustees' personal interests and views, the duty not to act for ulterior purposes and the (statutory) duty to diversify investments. The pointlessness of limiting the characterisation "fiduciary" to only some of these duties is suggested by the fact that a breach of even the duties which could be called "fiduciary" in a narrow sense can be characterised as a failure to take the care an ordinary prudent person would take if investing for the benefit of other persons for whom that person felt morally bound to provide. Persons acting with ordinary prudence on behalf of those for whom they feel morally bound to provide will not advance their own interests or act for ulterior purposes.

Similarly, Pennington said that breaches of the companies legislation:[181]

"which may cause [the company] loss, may ... be treated either as being acts in excess of the company's powers or in excess of the directors' own powers conferred by the company's articles ... . Alternatively, they may be treated as acts or omissions involving the directors in breaches of their other *fiduciary* duty to conduct the company's affairs with proper care and skill ... . The court would then use the directors' disregard of the relevant prescription of the ... Act ... as the basis for concluding that the directors had exceeded their powers or

---

180   [1985] Ch 270 at 276.
181   RR Pennington, *Directors' Personal Liability* (Collins Professional Books, London, 1987) at 145 (emphasis added).

had acted negligently, and the resulting breach of their fiduciary duties would justify the award of appropriate remedies against them."

Further, some duties which are fiduciary in their practical operation overlap with duties of care and skill. It will be remembered[182] that Finn exempted "fiduciary powers" from his denial that fiduciaries had prescriptive duties. He analysed "fiduciary powers" thus: [183]

"... there is a class of persons who, having been entrusted with powers for another's benefit, are under a general equitable obligation when dealing with those powers, to act honestly in what they consider to be that other's interests. The powers so given are themselves commonly described as being 'fiduciary powers'."

He described fiduciaries of this class as "the holders of fiduciary offices", and said that company directors and trustees were the two most notable members of it.[184] He explained the recognition of "fiduciary" powers in the holders of fiduciary offices as follows:[185]

"The feature which distinguishes these fiduciaries is that while they are entrusted with discretions to be exercised for another's benefit, they are not subject to the immediate control and supervision of that other in their exercise. Because of this autonomy, this freedom of the office holder within his discretions, Equity has intervened and not simply to prevent self-interested action. It has imposed a general obligation on the fiduciary controlling the manner in which he deals with and exercises his discretions. He is positively required in his decision making to act honestly in what he alone considers to be the interests of those for whose benefit his position exists – his beneficiaries."

Finn identified three defining characteristics of fiduciary office holders:[186]

"First, the position held by each of them exists, not for his own, but for another's benefit – in the case of the director, for example, for the company ... Secondly the duties imposed on, and the powers exercised by, each have a source *other than* in an agreement between him and the person(s) for whose benefit he is required to act – with the receiver, for example, they stem from the order of the court; with the executor, from the will, legislation and the general law. Thirdly, as a general rule, each alone is ultimately responsible for determining how those duties are to be discharged, how those powers are to be exercised."

Finn's inclusion of duties of loyalty and duties to act honestly in what directors alone consider to be interests of the company within the class of "fiduciary duties", but his exclusion of duties of care and skill, is not explained. For the latter duties, the first criterion of recognition is met: Finn says so in terms. The second is met, because even if there is no contract the company

---

182 See 192, text at n 32 above.
183 PD Finn, *Fiduciary Obligations* (Law Book Company, Sydney, 1977) at 3.
184 PD Finn, *Fiduciary Obligations,* above n 183 at 8.
185 PD Finn, *Fiduciary Obligations,* above n 183 at 8.
186 PD Finn, *Fiduciary Obligations,* above n 183 at 9 (emphasis in original).

director's duty of care and skill is one imposed by equity (with another duty of care, it has been assumed above, imposed by the common law). As to the third, while the duties of care owed by directors are objective, the duties of skill have, at least traditionally, been tied to the level of knowledge and experience which the particular directors in question have. And even if the duties of care and skill rested on wholly objective standards, there remains an immense range of ways in which directors can carry out their duties: that is, they alone are responsible for determining how their duties are to be discharged and how their powers are to be exercised within that range.

It has been said[187] that one illustration of a fiduciary power is what Sir Robert Megarry V-C described as "the duty of trustees to exercise their powers in the best interests of present and future beneficiaries of the trust, holding the scales impartially between different classes of beneficiaries."[188] That is a process which could call for the exercise of both care and skill. The process was explicitly linked by Sir Robert Megarry V-C with the trustee's duty of care and skill affecting investments: "the power must be exercised so as to yield the best return for the beneficiaries, judged in relation to the risks of the investments in question; and the prospects of the yield of income and capital appreciation both have to be considered in judging the return from the investment."[189] Although Sir Robert Megarry V-C went on to discuss the duty of care in exercising a power of investment separately,[190] in fact the level of care is inevitably linked to the goal of achieving the best return bearing in mind income yield and capital appreciation.

Similarly, in *Harries v Church Commissioners for England*[191] Sir Donald Nicholls V-C said:

"… trustees … are concerned to further the purposes of the trust of which they have accepted the office of trustee. That is their duty. To enable them the better to discharge that duty, trustees have powers vested in them. Those powers must be exercised for the purpose for which they have been given: to further the purposes of the trust. … Everything which follows is no more than the reasoned application of that principle in particular contexts.

… Where property is … held [as an investment], prima facie the purposes of the trust will be best served by the trustees seeking to obtain therefrom the maximum return, whether by way of income or capital growth, which is consistent with commercial prudence."

It will be seen that the learned Vice-Chancellor started by stating a "fiduciary power" test and moved to a "care and skill" test ("commercial prudence"). He saw the latter as no more than the reasoned application of the former.

There is authority, not disapproved by Finn,[192] that the fiduciary duty of directors to act bona fide in the best interests of the company calls for an

---

187　C Harpum, 'Fiduciary Obligations and Fiduciary Powers – Where Are We Going?' in P Birks (ed), *Privacy and Loyalty* (Oxford University Press, Oxford, 1997) at 160.
188　*Cowan v Scargill* [1985] Ch 270 at 286-287.
189　*Cowan v Scargill*, above n 188 at 287.
190　*Cowan v Scargill*, above n 188 at 289.
191　[1993] 2 All ER 300 at 304.
192　PD Finn, *Fiduciary Obligations* (Law Book Company, Sydney, 1977) at 53.

inquiry into whether intelligent and honest persons in the position of the directors could in all the circumstances reasonably have believed that particular transactions were for the benefit of the company.[193] That inquiry at least overlaps with the inquiry whether ordinary persons in the position of the directors, with their knowledge and experience, behaving prudently but with entrepreneurial flair, would enter those transactions.[194] Yet according to the distinctions propounded in the *Wheeler* Doctrine, the former duty is fiduciary[195] and the latter is not.

The latter duty cuts across Finn's contention[196] that although fiduciaries have specific duties not to delegate discretions, not to act under another's dictation, not to place fetters on discretions, to consider whether a discretion should be exercised, not to act for their own benefit or that of any third party, to treat beneficiaries with similar rights equally, to treat beneficiaries with differing rights fairly, and not to act capriciously, the law leaves it to fiduciaries to determine how their duties are to be discharged and their powers exercised for the benefit of the beneficiaries.[197]

> "As a general rule, it is the province of the fiduciary to determine what actions *are in the interests of his beneficiaries.* The courts are not entrusted with this decision. On the other hand, it is the province of the courts to determine what actions *are not in the beneficiaries' interest,* and an action will not be in the beneficiaries' interest if it constitutes a breach of any of the specific duties."

If the scheme has to be qualified in this way, why is it not also to be qualified by the recognition as a fiduciary duty of another duty which calls on the courts to some extent to determine what actions are or are not in the interests of the beneficiaries, namely the duty to exercise care and skill?

ARE "NEGLIGENCE" AND "DISHONESTY" ALWAYS DISTINCT?

The *Wheeler* Doctrine distinguishes negligence from conduct in bad faith.[198] But it can be difficult to distinguish negligence from dishonesty; and some kinds of negligence are in one sense dishonest. Thus Kekewich J acquitted a negligent trustee of a building society's deed of dissolution of "dishonesty in the usual sense of the word", but said that "in another sense he is not honest. It seems to me that a man who accepts such a trusteeship, and does nothing,

---

193 *Charterbridge Corp Ltd v Lloyds Bank Ltd* [1970] Ch 62 at 74-75; *Reid Murray Holdings Ltd (in liq) v David Murray Holdings Pty Ltd* (1972) 5 SASR 386 at 402; *Extrasure Travel Insurances Ltd v Scattergood* [2003] 1 BCLC 598 at 619[91].

194 *Farrow Finance Co Ltd (in liq) v Farrow Properties Pty Ltd (in liq)* (1997) 26 ACSR 544 at 580-581.

195 RP Austin 'Moulding the Content of Fiduciary Duties' in AJ Oakley (ed), *Trends in Contemporary Trust Law* (Oxford University Press, Oxford, 1997) at 159-161 acknowledges that it "is commonly described as 'fiduciary'", but leaves open the possibility that it either is not or should not be.

196 PD Finn, *Fiduciary Obligations,* (Lawbook Company, Sydney, 1977) at 15-17.

197 PD Finn, *Fiduciary Obligations,* above n 196 at 16 (emphasis in original).

198 For example, the *Guardian Trust* case [1999] 1 NZLR 664 at 681.

swallows wholesale what is said by his co-trustee, never asks for explanation, and accepts flimsy explanations, is dishonest."[199]

IS THERE DISHARMONY BETWEEN THE PURPOSE OF THE WHEELER DOCTRINE AND ITS OUTCOME?

One of the concerns underlying the development of the *Wheeler* Doctrine is a fear that existing areas of law would become obsolete.[200]

Sometimes it is feared that "fiduciary obligation could swallow whole much of the law of torts and a considerable portion of contractual obligation."[201] These fears are misplaced in relation to company directors. The law relating to them does not rest primarily on contract and their duties have only recently been analysed as coming within the law of tort.[202] In any event, to treat a director's duty of care and skill as fiduciary does not swallow anything: at most it widens the range of remedies.

Another image to which appeal has been made is that where tortious and contractual duties exist, there is no "room" for fiduciary obligations.[203] But different duties having different historical sources and different functions can co-exist without uncomfortable squeezing. It is not the case that a given set of facts can generate one, and only one, cause of action.

It has also been suggested[204] that *Mothew's* case is supported by the proposition, asserted by the Privy Council, that a fiduciary duty "cannot be prayed in aid to enlarge the scope of contractual duties".[205] That support does not exist. The question is not whether the particular duty of a particular fiduciary is to be *enlarged*. The particular duty is constant – to be careful. The question relates to what compensation remedy is to be available for breach of that duty and what causation/remoteness tests are to govern it.

Similar fears are sometimes expressed where a plaintiff has attempted to claim an advantage by contending that a particular person is a fiduciary. Thus,

---

199   *Re Second East Dulwich 745th Starr-Bowkett Building Society* (1889) 68 LJ Ch 196 at 198, discussed by J Getzler, 'Duty of Care', in P Birks and A Pretto (eds), *Breach of Trust* (Hart Publishing, Oxford, 2002) at 72.

200   PD Finn, 'The Fiduciary Principle' in TG Youdan (ed), *Equity, Fiduciaries and Trusts* (Carswell, Canada, 1989) at 28. In *Breen v Williams* (1996) 186 CLR 71 at 113, Gaudron and McHugh JJ referred to p 26, where Professor Finn said that the "prescriptive" view of fiduciary duties had "the potential if unrestrained to outflank the law of professional negligence". Gaudron and McHugh JJ said that many Canadian cases paid "insufficient regard to the effect that the imposition of fiduciary duties on particular relationships has on the law of negligence, contract, agency, trusts and companies in their application to those relationships" – a different, but perhaps related, point.

201   JD McCamus "Prometheus Unbound: Fiduciary Obligation in the Supreme Court of Canada" (1997) 28 *Canadian Business Law Journal* 107 at 115.

202   *Daniels v Anderson* (1995) 37 NSWLR 438.

203   *Breen v Williams* (1996) 186 CLR 71 at 93 per Dawson and Toohey JJ.

204   D Hayton, 'Fiduciaries in Context: An Overview' in P Birks (ed), *Privacy and Loyalty* (Oxford University Press, Oxford, 1997) at 289 n 30.

205   *Clark Boyce v Mouat* [1994] 1 AC 428 at 437.

in *In re Goldcorp Exchange Ltd (in receivership)*, the Privy Council refused to find that a bailment contract created fiduciary duties.[206]

> "No doubt the fact that one person is placed in a particular position vis-à-vis another through the medium of a contract does not necessarily mean that he does not also owe fiduciary duties to that other by virtue of being in that position. But the essence of a fiduciary relationship is that it creates obligations of a different character from those deriving from the contract itself. Their Lordships have not heard in argument any submission which went beyond suggesting that by virtue of being a fiduciary the company was obliged honestly and conscientiously to do what it had by contract promised to do. Many commercial relationships involve just such a reliance by one party on the other, and to introduce the whole new dimension into such relationships which would flow from giving them a fiduciary character would (as it seems to their Lordships) have adverse consequences far exceeding those foreseen by Atkin LJ in *In re Wait*[207] ... ."

Mothew's case has been seen as expressing a view which "echoes" that of the Privy Council.[208] This is not so for two reasons. First, *In re Goldcorp Exchange Ltd* did not concern the question whether a particular duty of a person concededly a fiduciary was fiduciary, but whether the relevant person was a fiduciary at all. Secondly, problems about proprietary rights and remedies, which were central in *In re Goldcorp Exchange Ltd*, do not commonly arise where the only issue is whether a company director's duty to exercise care and skill is fiduciary.

In *Mothew's* case Staughton LJ said that it was wrong "that a breach of contract or tort should become a breach of fiduciary duty".[209] In general that is so, just as "[f]iduciary duties should not be superimposed on ... common law duties simply to improve the nature or extent of the remedy."[210] But this injunction is not contravened by characterising a fiduciary's equitable duties of care and skill as fiduciary: they are not "superimposed" on "common law duties" – they are in truth co-existing equitable duties. And while not all breaches of contract or tort are breaches of fiduciary duty, received principles indicate that some are. It is neither unusual nor troubling that a particular course of conduct can result in several causes of action, each with different remedies. The majority of the New South Wales Court of Appeal in *Daniels v Anderson*,[211] for example, did not see it as an obstacle to recognising a common law duty of care and skill owed by directors in tort that there already existed an equitable duty of care and skill as well as a statutory duty of care.

The *Wheeler* Doctrine has been defended as consistent with the caution of the courts in recognising fiduciary relationships too freely (for example, the

---

206 [1995] 1 AC 74 at 98.
207 [1927] 1 Ch 606: see 639-640.
208 D Hayton, 'Fiduciaries in Context: An Overview' in P Birks (ed), *Privacy and Loyalty*, above n 204 at 289.
209 [1998] Ch 1 at 26.
210 *Norberg v Wynrib* [1992] 2 SCR 226 at 312, approved in *Breen v Williams* (1996) 186 CLR 71 at 110; *Pilmer v Duke Group Ltd (in liq)* (2001) 207 CLR 165 at 197[71].
211 (1995) 37 NSWLR 438 at 505.

doctor-patient relationship)[212] and with their reluctance to treat the perpetrators of sexual abuse as fiduciaries.[213] However, it is one thing to oppose extensions of fiduciary relationships into new areas to remedy what are perceived to be weaknesses in the common law. It is another thing to fasten on an already recognised equitable duty owed by a person who is unquestionably in a fiduciary relationship and deny it the character "fiduciary". In *Maguire v Makaronis*, the majority thought it wiser to restrict the recognition of new fiduciary relationships than to deny the applicability of received doctrines, rigorous though they might be, to persons in existing fiduciary relationships.[214] The recognition as fiduciary of duties owed in the trustee-beneficiary relationship and the director-company relationship, which are relationships which are incontestably fiduciary, does not offend any inhibition against excessive recognition of fiduciary relations.

The recognition that within these fiduciary relationships the duty of care and skill is fiduciary does not prevent the protection otherwise afforded by the common law of contract and tort from continuing, and does not prevent contractual remedies and tortious remedies from remaining available.

IS THE PROSCRIPTIVE/PRESCRIPTIVE DISTINCTION RELEVANT?

Another suggestion[215] is that the *Wheeler* Doctrine is supported by the High Court's view in *Breen v Williams*[216] that fiduciary duties are proscriptive, not prescriptive.

> "Equity does not go beyond these proscriptive rules to lay down particular positive obligations which go beyond exacting loyalty in relationships. It leaves it to the law of contract or the law of tort or the law of trusts to govern their traditional areas and determine the extent of a defendant's liability for negligence or misrepresentation or non-disclosure or wrongfully giving property away."

Further, it is said that in the light of *Mothew's* case and *Breen v Williams*:

> "it cannot be long before the House of Lords spells out the exclusively proscriptive nature of fiduciary duties established in the 'no profit' and 'no conflict' rules. Positive prescriptive obligations such as those to distribute trust property to the right beneficiaries, to manage trust property with due care and skill, to observe a contractual or tortious duty of care and skill and to perform the terms of a bailment properly, arise from particular characteristics of trusts, contracts, torts and bailments and not from any fiduciary obligation."

---

212 *Breen v Williams* (1996) 186 CLR 71 at 83, 94-95, 110-114 and 136-137.

213 D Hayton, 'Fiduciaries in Context: An Overview' in Birks (ed), *Privacy and Loyalty* (Oxford University Press, Oxford, 1997) at 291-292.

214 (1997) 188 CLR 449 at 474, speaking of *Brickenden v London Loan & Savings Co* [1934] 3 DLR 465 at 469.

215 D Hayton, 'Fiduciaries in Context: An Overview' in P Birks (ed), *Privacy and Loyalty,* above n 213 at 290-291.

216 *Breen v Williams*, above n 212 at 92-93, 113 and 137-138 per Dawson and Toohey JJ, Gaudron and McHugh JJ and Gummow J respectively.

A similar reading of the relevant passages in *Breen v Williams* has been propounded in *Aequitas v AEFC*:[217]

> "In the High Court's view, the essential fiduciary obligations were to avoid conflicts between interest and duty or between duty and duty, and profits arising out of the fiduciary office, in the absence of fully informed consent. Obligations to act in the interests of another, or to act prudently, are not fiduciary obligations. According to Dawson and Toohey JJ ... , what the law extracts from a fiduciary relationship is loyalty, often of an uncompromising kind, but no more than that. Gaudron and McHugh JJ ... held that a fiduciary is obliged not to obtain any unauthorised benefit from the relationship and not to be in a position of conflict, but 'the law of this country does not otherwise impose positive legal duties on the fiduciary to act in the interests of the person to whom the duty is owed'. Gummow J ... said that the special position of the trustee does not provide a proper foundation for 'the imposition upon fiduciaries in general of a quasi-tortious duty to act solely in the best interests of their principals'. Fiduciary obligations often arise in cases where one person is under an obligation to act in the interests of another, but that does not mean that the obligation to act in the interests of another is a fiduciary obligation."

It would be dangerous to conclude that the passages from *Breen v Williams* referred to in the above quotations support the *Wheeler* Doctrine. The passages must be read in the context of the question being decided in that case – whether a doctor owed a duty to the plaintiff, his patient, to grant her access to her medical records. The court excluded various avenues to relief based on contract, property and other bodies of law. Opinions differed on whether, and how far, the doctor-patient relationship was fiduciary; even those justices who thought that it was, or could be, fiduciary for certain purposes, did not conclude that it created an obligation to give access to medical records. Nor did the doctor's duty to advise and treat the patient with reasonable care and skill encompass that obligation. This was to say no more than that, in the absence of special facts, doctors are in the same position as solicitors, engineers or architects: they owe duties in tort, and if there is a contract, in contract, of care and skill, but these are not equitable duties and not fiduciary duties.

When Gaudron and McHugh JJ said that apart from the proscriptive obligations imposed on fiduciaries, "the law of this country does not otherwise impose positive legal duties on the fiduciary to act in the interests of the person to whom the duty is owned",[218] they cannot have been referring to directors or trustees because that statement is not true for directors or trustees: those persons owe positive legal duties, independently of tort or contract, to act bona fide in the best interests of the company or the beneficiaries, and to do so with care and skill. Dawson and Toohey JJ said: "The concern of the law in a fiduciary relationship is not negligence or breach of contract. Yet it is the law of negligence and contract which governs the duty of a doctor towards a patient.

---

217   (2001) 19 ACLC 1,006 at 1,058-1,059[284]. The passage was not necessary for the decision: although the court criticised a pleading treating various contractual duties as fiduciary, the pleaded facts did reveal a breach of fiduciary duty.

218   *Breen v Williams* (1996) 186 CLR 71 at 113.

This leaves no need, or even room, for the imposition of fiduciary obligations."[219] But that passage appears in the middle of a passage dealing entirely with doctors, and does not purport to address the question whether the duty of a company director can be described exhaustively in terms of "negligence or breach of contract". While fiduciaries in general may not have a quasi-tortious duty to act solely in the best interests of their principals, it does not follow that directors do not have a fiduciary duty of care and skill any more than that trustees do not.

It cannot be said that equity does not lay down prescriptive rules and leaves it to "company law" to do so: the prescriptive duty to act in the best interests of the company is imposed on directors because of equity, not because of some aspect of "company law" which is outside equity. "Company law" is a body of law whose manifold sources include equity.

In the course of argument in *Breen v Williams*, Brennan CJ asked the solicitor representing the plaintiff: "Is there any instance where a fiduciary duty has been held to impose an obligation to act where the obligation does not arise also pursuant to contract or express trust?"[220] He received no answer, but one would be: "Whenever a company director engaged otherwise than by contract is called on to act bona fide in the best interests of the company as a whole". Another would be: "Wherever a company director engaged otherwise than by contract has been held subject to an obligation to act carefully and skilfully – for example, the non-executive directors and the Chairman of directors in *Daniels v Anderson*.[221]"

The Fiduciary Character of Some Powers of Management

Apart from the general duty of a trustee to exercise reasonable care and skill, trustees have related powers, which are often described as fiduciary powers. This suggests that the trustee's general duty of care and skill is also fiduciary.

For example, s 15(e) of the *Trustee Act 1958* (Vic) gave trustees a discretion to delay in pursuing a debtor to the trust and provided that trustees were not liable for loss if they acted in good faith. Starke J in *National Trustees Executors and Agency Co of Australasia Ltd v Dwyer*[222] held that good faith involved the exercise of an active discretion, not loss caused by supineness or carelessness, and that the statutory powers of trustees "are fiduciary powers and must be exercised for the benefit of their beneficiaries and for them alone." It would be strange if a statutory power to delay recovering debts were fiduciary but the trustee's duty to exercise reasonable care and skill were not.

Similar reasoning was employed in the case of a testamentary power to delay pressing for a debt. In *Partridge v Equity Trustees and Agency Co Ltd* the High Court had to consider the following clause in a will:

---

219 *Breen v Williams*, above n 218 at 93.
220 *Breen v Williams*, above n 218 at 75.
221 (1995) 37 NSWLR 438.
222 (1940) 63 CLR 1 at 23.

"I desire that my trustee shall not press for payment of any debt which may be owing to me by William Hartley and Company Proprietary Limited but will grant the said company such reasonable time as it may require at such rate of interest as my trustees may deem fit."

The testator died in 1926. In 1929 the trustee agreed with the company on a schedule for repayment of the debt. The last two instalments due on 1 January and 1 July 1932, totalling £2150, were not paid. Interest was paid, and on 29 January 1936 the trustee agreed to let the debt remain outstanding for five years. A receiver was then appointed, and the whole debt, with some interest, was found not to be capable of payment. Starke, Dixon and Williams JJ said:[223]

"we are of opinion that the power was a fiduciary power to be exercised with due care and diligence and solely in the interests of the beneficiaries. It was the duty of the defendant to examine the financial position of the company and only to grant further time if it was satisfied that the company reasonably required such time to pay the debt and that it could be granted without detriment to the estate."

Thus a power calling for the use of care and diligence was seen as a fiduciary power.

LIABILITY FOR KNOWING PARTICIPATION BY THIRD PARTIES IN A BREACH OF DUTY TO EXERCISE CARE AND SKILL

In Australian law, perhaps unlike English law, under the second limb of the rule in *Barnes v Addy*,[224] "a person who knowingly participates in a breach of fiduciary duty is liable to account to the person to whom the duty was owed for any benefit he has received as a result of such participation".[225] If the trustee's and the director's duties to exercise reasonable care and skill are not fiduciary, a defendant who persuades a trustee or director to behave without care or skill will not be liable unless the tort of conspiracy, or interference with any contract which exists, is established. That would be a very surprising result.

AWAKENING FROM THE NIGHTMARE OF HISTORY

Cases enunciating the *Wheeler* Doctrine have sought to invalidate or discount the worth of particular propositions by treating them as of only historical significance – musty and obscurantist relics of a benighted past which should not fetter enlightened progress in future. Thus *Mothew's* case discounted the "particular historic origin" of common law and equitable duties of care, and said that to distinguish the award of equitable compensation for breach of an equitable duty of skill and care, in contrast to the award of damages for breach of the common law duty, is "merely the product of history" and is "a distinction

---

223 *Partridge v Equity Trustees and Agency Co Ltd* (1947) 75 CLR 149 at 163.
224 (1874) LR 9 Ch App 244.
225 *Consul Development Pty Ltd v DPC Estates Pty Ltd* (1975) 132 CLR 373 at 397.

without a difference".[226] Similar language was used in the italicised part of a passage from the *Guardian Trust* case quoted above.[227]

Sometimes the denigration of history is coupled with other disparaging language. An example is Lord Browne-Wilkinson's italicised references in the passage from *Henderson's* case quoted above to the sticking on of labels and to the need to avoid being misled by mere description.[228] A similar distinction between labels and contents, and between descriptions and reality, was drawn in *AWA Ltd v Daniels (t/as Deloitte Haskell & Sells)*.[229] Rogers CJ Comm Div said that as well as the equitable duty of a director to exercise care and skill, there was a duty at common law, but that the duties were identical: "The legal label may change but the contents of the bottle will remain the same."

A primary difficulty with this language is the fact, frequently and extensively overlooked though it is, that our law depends on the doctrine of stare decisis. The doctrine of stare decisis compels close attention to what existing authorities, some of which might be quite old, have actually decided. Admittedly early authorities may have been decided in a milieu of structures and principles which have changed. The history of a legal rule is not necessarily the equivalent of the rule itself. But they can have a close relationship. As Sir Victor Windeyer said: "a full understanding of a doctrine of the living law is often only got by looking at its history ... ."[230] This is not mere antiquarianism. "The only reason for going back into the past is to come forward to the present, to help us to see more clearly the shape of the law of today by seeing how it took shape."[231] But having gone back into the past for assistance in vision, it is wrong wantonly to abandon those ocular aids on returning to the present.

Another difficulty is that the language in question seeks to renew the law, or to restate the law in an elegant and lapidary way, without full acquaintance with the details of what is being renewed or restated. Wells J advocated a sounder approach: "I hope that this Court will never shrink from the task of making new law, but before committing itself to such a task in a particular case we ought, I think, to attempt to state as carefully and as comprehensively as we can, the present law with respect to the topic being explored so that we can perceive clearly where an advance will be, if it must be, made."[232] That advice can only be followed if the court is assisted by detailed argument from counsel specifically directed to the relevant point, and counsel, not surprisingly, are unlikely to offer this assistance unless the point is one which is crucial to the dispute between the parties. Without it conclusions of the type making up the *Wheeler* Doctrine cannot command an intellectual assent.

In various respects the duties of directors, including their duties to exercise care and skill, are derived from those of trustees in the sense that they are

---

226 *Mothew's* case [1998] 1 Ch at 16-17.
227 See 210, text to n 117.
228 See 192–193, text to n 36.
229 (1992) 7 ACSR 759 at 873.
230 "Learning the Law" (1961) 35 *Australian Law Journal* 102 at 109.
231 *Attorney-General (Vic) v Commonwealth* (1962) 107 CLR 529 at 595
232 *Lietzke (Installations) Pty Ltd v EMJ Morgan Pty Ltd* (1973) 5 SASR 88 at 119.

"equitable extensions" of them.[233] Not all the duties of trustees of express trusts can apply to directors: for example, trustees own the trust property at law, company directors merely control the company's property.[234] And for other reasons the duties to exercise care and skill owed by trustees are not identical with those of company directors.[235] But an historical inquiry would reveal that one source from which the equitable duties of trustees and of directors to exercise care and skill do not derive is the common law, if only because before 1873 the courts of common law had very little opportunity to develop any such doctrines, and because after 1873 the development of these duties, if it ever happened, would have performed the unlikely feat of antedating the 20th century development of negligence law. Nor can the duties of a director to exercise care and skill be seen as having developed analogously with those of professionals who follow a "skilled calling" and are "bound to exercise due care, skill and diligence" towards the person who "employed" them.[236] Is a director-ship "a skilled calling"? Does the company "employ" the director? It was probably doubts of these kinds which caused Griffith CJ to say: "The question of the degree of care required under an implied contract to use reasonable care in the performance of an act requiring personal skill is obviously quite a different question from that of the reasonable prudence required by law from persons in a fiduciary position."[237]

It is also necessary to bear in mind limits on the extent to which even ultimate appellate courts are at liberty to change the law. Apart from dicta in the Supreme Court of Canada and by one member of the House of Lords in *Henderson's* case, none of the statements in the *Wheeler* line of cases were made in ultimate appellate courts until, regrettably, so distinguished a lawyer as Lord Walker of Gestingthorpe recently made an approving, although unnecessary, reference to *Mothew's* case.[238] Thus, although this is perhaps not a field into which a foreigner should trespass, when the New Zealand Court of Appeal in the *Guardian Trust* case spoke of stages in the development of the law, it was speaking as a court not well positioned to develop the law in any significant way, for it was not the ultimate appellate court for New Zealand. Its proper role was only to apply the law.

CONCLUSION

The *Wheeler* Doctrine may be sound. It cannot, however, yet be said that its soundness has been demonstrated.

---

233 *Swindle v Harrison* [1997] 4 All ER 705 at 734.
234 *Breen v Williams* (1996) 186 CLR 71 at 137.
235 See 194–196 text to nn 48-59 above.
236 *Voli v Inglewood Shire Council* (1963) 110 CLR 74 at 84.
237 *Austin v Austin* (1906) 3 CLR 516 at 525.
238 *Hilton v Barker Booth and Eastwood (a firm)* [2005] 1 All ER 651 at 660[29]. Lords Hoffmann, Hope of Craighead, Scott of Foscote and Brown of Eaton-under-Heywood concurred.

10

Am I My Beneficiary's Keeper? Fusion and Loss-Based Fiduciary Remedies

Joshua Getzler[*]

INTRODUCTION

Should the content of fiduciary duties be determined through experimentation with remedies for breach of fiduciary obligation? This question raises in turn the problem of how in a post-Judicature system courts ought to apply legal remedies to uphold rights and duties associated with equity, or vice versa. This chapter commences with some observations on the historical course of the fusion debate which still informs so much law-making. It then turns to modern debates concerning fiduciary duties of care and the nature of accounting and compensatory remedies for breach of fiduciary obligations. The next few pages offer a summary of the main themes and arguments.

There can be no doubt that lawyers today are increasingly applying common law categories to classical fiduciary law. Lord Millett's influential judgment in *Mothew*[1] has provided a foundation for much of this trend. In the wake of *Mothew*, courts and commentators have sought to inject common-law devices controlling the extent of liability into the remedy of compensation for breach of fiduciary and other equitable duties. Those control devices include rules of remoteness in calibrating causation (rather than the simple but-for test); rules of contributory negligence applied by analogy from legislation and case-law governing tort claims, and rules of mitigation controlling the factual measure of damages. These various interlocking rules can be conceived as methods of mitigating or apportioning the defendant's liability for causing loss by comparing it with (i) causation of harm by the plaintiff or by third parties or

---

*   I thank Andrew Burrows, James Edelman, Steven Elliott, Lionel Smith, Robert Stevens, and especially Mike Macnair for discussing some of the themes of this chapter with me. They are free of any responsibility for the result.
1   *Bristol and West Building Society v Mothew* [1998] Ch 1.

by general circumstances viewed ex ante to breach, or (ii) causation of loss by the same actors viewed ex post initial breach. However in all areas of law the correct causal rules are set by reference to the nature of the duty in question, and unless the duty is correctly specified the framing of the causal tests risks going astray.

The post-*Mothew* theorists have proposed three main distinctions between types of fiduciary duty: between custodial and non-custodial fiduciary duties, between fiduciary duties of loyalty and allegedly non-fiduciary duties of skill and care, and between subjectively dishonest breaches and less serious breaches. The argument is then made that consistency between common-law and equitable categories of duty should confine the most generous pro-plaintiff causal rules of compensatory recovery to breaches of loyalty or breaches involving dishonesty. Cases of custodial breach are placed in a separate category of restoration of a fund rather than compensation, where simple causal rules ought to favour the plaintiff but a cap on recovery is set to the level of the fund as it would have been without degradation, and without permitting recovery for further consequential loss. The distinction between account and compensation allows causal control mechanisms to be applied readily to loss to trusts or beneficiaries caused by breaches of duty of care. At the same time it insulates "substitutive" orders for reconstitution of assets from such controls as this merely involves direct enforcement of the primary duty to account for trust property.

Much of this energy spent in distinguishing cases of account from equitable compensation and developing control mechanisms for the latter remedy modelled on the common law is suspect. It relies on a difficult distinction between custodial trusts and fiduciary law, it ignores the equitable policies of objectifying fraud and requiring prudence as a dimension of good faith, and moreover it does not take into account the contexts shaping common law apportionment and mitigation doctrines within contract and tort, which differ from fiduciary contexts. The account model is nonetheless attractive if it prevents common-law controls infiltrating the core duty of the trustee to execute his or her trust through due custodianship of the entrusted res.

Clarity in this area of law is not helped by the difficult reasoning contained in leading opinions such as *Target* per Lord Browne-Wilkinson in England and *Canson* per McLachlin J in Canada,[2] which use the classical equitable language of but-for causation in cases of breach of custody in the one case and negligence in the other, in order to justify a result seemingly departing from the but-for causal model. The High Court of Australia in cases such as *Maguire*, *Pilmer* and *Youyang*[3] has been more sceptical of common-law control mechanisms in the causal sphere as threats to the policy objectives of fiduciary law but has not embraced the account-compensation distinction to reach such a position. The High Court has instead indicated that analysis should focus on the policy content of the duty in question in order to decide appropriate controls. This might lead analysts to review the current balance of concurrent

---

2   *Target Holdings Ltd v Redferns (A Firm)* [1996] 1 AC 421; *Canson Enterprises Ltd v Boughton & Co* [1991] 3 SCR 534.

3   *Maguire v Makaronis* (1997) 188 CLR 449; *Pilmer v Duke Group Ltd (In Liq)* (2001) 207 CLR 165; *Youyang Pty Ltd v Minter Ellison Morris Fletcher* (2003) 212 CLR 484.

liabilities for duties of care and doubt the modern rise of tort law packaging of such duties.

The deterrent policies undergirding this area of law are of key importance, and could conceivably be emphasised through recognition of punitive damages in equity. Should that shift in the remedial armoury occur, the path might then be opened to a more thoroughgoing fusion of legal and equitable rules, with deterrent damages rather than variegated causal rules being used in order to uphold the community's independent interest in fiduciaries offering high levels of loyalty, skill and care to clients who are vulnerable to fiduciary default. However, traditional fiduciary policy might prefer a "broken windows" approach, setting deterrent incentives at a low threshold by sanctioning even the smallest infractions of bright-line fiduciary rules, and not simply reacting in force to major breakdowns in honesty and loyalty. The combination of bright-line rules with discretionary excuse may amount to the best-judged deterrent and regulatory system available for maintaining trust in commercial relationships.

THE GENERAL HISTORICAL PROBLEM OF FUSION

The subject of personal remedies for loss caused by breach of trust or other equitable obligation has become one of the fiercest battlegrounds in the law-equity fusion wars. Let us momentarily stand back from the fray and ask why there are fusion wars in the first place.

So much has been said about the general problem of fusion of law and equity in the past few years (or centuries) that perhaps one ought to hesitate before adding yet another statement to a growing heap.[4] Yet the debate has urgent practical implications as well as theoretical fascination. In *Harris v Digital Pulse Pty Ltd*[5] the New South Wales Court of Appeal had to consider the availability of exemplary damages in equity; Heydon JA considered that the jurisdictional history, and not merely the legal policies of the present, was of the highest importance in considering the law's correct remedial approach. Heydon JA conceded that the egregious behaviour by the defendants in that

---

4   Cf J Getzler, 'Patterns of Fusion' in P Birks (ed), *The Classification of Obligations* (Clarendon Press, Oxford, 1997) at 157. Significant recent additions to the fusion debate may be found in AS Burrows, 'We Do This At Common Law But That In Equity' (2002) 22 *Oxford Journal of Legal Studies* 1; AS Burrows, *Fusing Common Law and Equity: Remedies, Restitution and Reform* (Hochelaga Lectures 2001, Sweet & Maxwell, Hong Kong, 2002); AS Burrows, 'Limitations on Compensation' in AS Burrows and E Peel (eds), *Commercial Remedies: Current Issues and Problems* (Oxford University Press, Oxford, 2003) at chapter 4. For a rejoinder to Burrows' calls for accelerated doctrinal fusion see R Meagher, JD Heydon and M Leeming (eds), *Meagher, Gummow and Lehane's Equity: Doctrines and Remedies* (4th ed, Butterworths, Sydney, 2002) at [2-320], [23-020]. Burrows tackles fusion of legal and equitable obligations and does not address the main territory of distinctive equitable rights and duties being the trust. This is a virtually unexplored frontier for fusion theory: how to conceive of trusts without a separate body of equity jurisprudence. An initial foray is made by T Honoré in 'Trusts: The Inessentials', in J Getzler (ed), *Rationalizing Property, Equity and Trusts: Essays in Honour of Edward Burn* (LexisNexis, London, 2003) at 7.

5   (2003) 56 NSWLR 298. The anti-fusion sentiments in this case have attracted some academic ire; see J Edelman, "A 'Fusion Fallacy' Fallacy?" (2003) 119 *Law Quarterly Review* 375.

case would have warranted exemplary damages had they been jurisdictionally available; hence it was not a question of the merits (or demerits) of the parties driving his decision.[6] We can compare this with the approach of the English court in *Attorney General v Blake*,[7] where the call to sanction especially infamous behaviour led to the court stretching its remedial jurisdiction, allowing the novel remedy of disgorgement damages for contract yet without formally describing the breached relationship as one of fiduciary quality.

Examples of fusion questions such as these driving curial debates could be multiplied across the common law world. Even in modern American jurisprudence, which today has no significant theoretical debates over fusion at all, problems can arise where, for example, the constitutional right to civil jury trial or the availability of equitable remedies auxiliary to statutory jurisdictions demands an answer about the jurisdictional pedigree of one doctrine or another.[8] We seem to be condemned to fusion debates without end.

Possibly much of it comes down to timing. To take one example, it is well known that the Judicature Act system came late to New South Wales in 1970, nearly a century after the English reforms, and the New South Wales bar's professional evolution within a split jurisdiction has therefore been very different from that of Lincoln's Inn. A late date of administrative fusion might have encouraged a separatist equity consciousness, a professional identity mandating rejection of many of the fusionist reforms of the English courts. But this is only a partial answer and it raises further questions. Why did South Australia have a fused jurisdiction (from 1853) early, and New South Wales such a late one, and did this make for any doctrinal or procedural differences? Does the date of administrative fusion help explain the approaches taken by the Queensland courts (fused from 1876) or those in Victoria (from 1883) or Tasmania (beginning in 1903, completed in 1932), or by courts in New Zealand or Ontario, or Massachusetts or New York?[9]

Some judges and commentators have suggested that a strong modern equity represents the present-minded laws of a social democracy, contrasted with the

---

6   *Harris v Digital Pulse Pty Ltd* (2003) 56 NSWLR 298 at 422.

7   [2001] 1 AC 268.

8   See for example, *Grupo Mexicano de Desarrollo, SA v Alliance Bond Fund, Inc* 527 US 308 (1999) where Chancery jurisdiction before 1789 was said to set the boundaries for federal court insolvency jurisdiction; or *Mertens v Hewitt Associates* 508 US 248 at 257-58 (1993) where "equitable" relief under ERISA was held to exclude compensatory damages on the basis that historically this was a legal and not an equitable remedy. See further JH Langbein, "What ERISA Means By 'Equitable': The Supreme Court's Trail of Error in *Russell, Mertens*, and *Great-West*" (2003) 103 *Columbia Law Review* 1317; P Devlin, "Jury Trial of Complex Cases: English Practice at the Time of the Seventh Amendment" (1980) 80 *Columbia Law Review* 43; MS Arnold, "A Historical Inquiry into the Right to Trial by Jury in Complex Civil Litigation" (1980) 128 *University of Pennsylvania Law Review* 829 (1980); J Oldham, 'The Seventh Amendment Right to Jury Trial: Late-Eighteenth-Century Practice Reconsidered', in GR Rubin and K O'Donovan (eds), *Human Rights and Legal History: Essays for Brian Simpson* (Oxford University Press, Oxford, 2000) at 225.

9   G Taylor, "South Australia's Judicature Act Reforms of 1853: The First Attempt to Fuse Law and Equity in the British Empire" (2001) 22 *Journal of Legal History* 55, arguing that early administrative fusion had little impact on legal and equitable doctrine. The history of separatism in New South Wales is broached in ML Smith, "The Early Years of Equity in the Supreme Court of New South Wales" (1998) 72 *Australian Law Journal* 799; Sir Frederick

more conservative common law whose classical period, and hence its ethos, lies in the later nineteenth century. Associated with this approach are claims that equity represents codified ethical standards and thickly written legal normativity, as opposed to a favouring of informal commercial trust allied to legal laissez faire. Or putting the same point another way, equity is said to have roots in natural law and communitarianism as opposed to worldly asceticism and individualism.[10] The political and institutional context of different court systems may also be significant. The language of equity suits the style of activist, governmental courts within a federal system of dispersed and limited legislatures, contrasting with restrained, technocratic courts within a unitary system of unlimited parliamentary sovereignty.[11] Pursuing the theme of political justification, Heydon JA has suggested from the bench that the craft of equitable adjudication has changed since the late nineteenth century when single judges such as Jessel MR could confidently mould the rules governing the fortunes of the dominant propertied classes to which the judges themselves belonged:[12]

> "Sir George Jessel MR's judicial life coincided with the time when democracy in a modern form was beginning and the responsiveness of Parliament to social or legal ills was starting to develop. It was a time when the judiciary was small, highly skilled and united. It is now large, less skilled, and far from entirely united. For courts below the High Court to act in the manner of the single judges sitting in Chancery who made modern equity is to invite the spread of a wilderness of single instances, a proliferation of discordant and idiosyncratic opinions, and ultimately an anarchic 'system' operating according to the forms, but not the realities, of law."

Heydon JA is here advancing a normative rather than an historical or positive claim.[13] Other interpretations are possible; Sir Anthony Mason has

---

Jordan, 'Chapters on Equity in New South Wales' in *Select Legal Papers* (Legal Books, Sydney, 1983); cf PM Perell, "A Legal History of the Fusion of Law and Equity in the Supreme Court of Ontario" (1988) 9 *The Advocates' Quarterly* 472; R Meagher, JD Heydon and M Leeming (eds), *Meagher, Gummow and Lehane's Equity: Doctrines and Remedies* (4th ed, Butterworths LexisNexis, Sydney, 2002) at chapter 2 generally.

10   P Parkinson, 'The Conscience of Equity' in P Parkinson (ed), *The Principles of Equity* (2nd ed, LawBook Co., Sydney, 2003) at 29; Sir Anthony Mason, "The Place of Equity and Equitable Remedies in the Contemporary Common Law World" (1994) 110 *Law Quarterly Review* 238; Sir Anthony Mason, "Contract, Good Faith and Equitable Standards in Fair Dealing" (2000) 116 *Law Quarterly Review* 66; cf AJ Duggan, "Is Equity Efficient?" (1997) 113 *Law Quarterly Review* 601, and AJ Duggan, 'The Profits of Conscience: Commercial Equity in the High Court of Australia', in P Cane (ed), *Centenary Essays for the High Court of Australia* (LexisNexis Butterworths, Sydney, 2004) at 256, also in (2003) 24 *Australian Bar Review* 150. Duggan seeks to describe equity doctrines and especially fiduciary law using simple price incentive models, tending to confuse his efficiency model with the normative values of the law he describes.

11   Equitable Australia and Canada would go on the federal side of the line and fusionary England on the unitary state side. New Zealand and the Unites States somewhat disrupt this explanatory model; note however the strong equity of James Kent and Joseph Story in the early American federal republic.

12   *Harris v Digital Pulse Pty Ltd* (2003) 56 NSWLR 298 at 419.

13   See further JD Heydon, "Judicial Activism and the Death of the Rule of Law" (Jan-Feb 2003) *Quadrant* 9.

argued that activist equitable adjudication can be an essential and complementary adjunct to the most lively political democracy.[14]

It is also likely that quirks of personality are at work in the fortunes of fusion in the courts. English judges and jurists of the 1980s expressed a horror of broad equitable discretion,[15] perhaps in flight from the later career of Lord Denning. Now the English courts are far more prepared to acknowledge the role of judicial creativity.[16] Australian judges have as an exemplar Sir Owen Dixon, whose traditional equity learning was as rigorous as the strict legalism of his common law.[17] Another countervailing example is the Mason High Court of the 1980s, which used equity doctrine to provide much of the vocabulary for its modernising restatements of private and commercial law.[18] The devotion to a distinctive equity, whether traditional or radical, in the modern Australian judiciary and profession has doubtless been reinforced by the fact that so many respected judges have also been active teachers and writers of equity jurisprudence.

From a historian's vantage point looking backwards, the movement to fuse law and equity leading to the Judicature system in England was partly an attempt to bridge sharp ideological differences in the adjudication of rights and duties, differences that deepened in the later nineteenth century and were perceived to interfere with the administration of civil justice.[19] By contrast, in the period of Lord Mansfield co-operation was rife and hence formal fusion was otiose. To give just one example, in a case on breach of lease covenant Wilmot CJ stated:[20]

"If the equity and the law can be mixed together, and made to flow in the same channel, it must be the inclination of every Court of Law to give a complete relief, without sending the parties to another Court to obtain it at a great expence. If the law be settled, we will not disturb it."

---

14   See references above at n 10.
15   See generally D Robertson, *Judicial Discretion in the House of Lords* (Clarendon Press, Oxford, 1998).
16   *Kleinwort Benson Ltd v Lincoln CC* [1999] 2 AC 349 at 377-389, per Lord Goff.
17   K Hayne, 'Owen Dixon', in T Blackshield, M Coper and G Williams (eds), *The Oxford Companion to the High Court of Australia* (Oxford University Press, Oxford, 2001) at 218; P Ayres, *Owen Dixon* (Miegunyah Press, Melbourne, 2003).
18   P Parkinson, 'Equity', in *Oxford Companion*, above n 17 at 243; cf, AJ Duggan, 'The Profits of Conscience: Commercial Equity in the High Court of Australia', in P Cane (ed), *Centenary Essays for the High Court of Australia* (LexisNexis Butterworths, Sydney, 2004) at 256.
19   For recent historical work on fusion and reform of the civil jurisdictions see P Polden, "Mingling the Waters: Personalities, Politics and the Making of the Supreme Court of Judicature" [2002] *Cambridge Law Journal* 575; P Polden, *A History of the County Court, 1846-1971* (Cambridge University Press, Cambridge, 1999); M Lobban, "Preparing for Fusion: Reforming the Chancery, 1810-1860" (2004) 22 *Law and History Review* 389 at 565, 615; J Getzler, "Chancery Reform and Law Reform" (2004) 22 *Law and History Review* 601; J Oldham, "A Profusion of Chancery Reform" (2004) 22 *Law and History Review* 609; M Lobban, "Henry Brougham and Law Reform" (2000) 115 *English Historical Review* 1184; M Lobban, "'Old wine in new bottles": The Concept and Practice of Law Reform, c. 1780–1830', in A Burns and J Innes (eds), *Rethinking the Age of Reform: Britain 1780–1850* (Cambridge University Press, Cambridge, 2003) at chapter 4.
20   *Bally v Wells* (1769) Wilmot 341 at 344; 97 ER 130 at 131.

This judgment was delivered in 1769, not 1869 or 1969. Note also that this was an opinion from the Chief Justice of the supposedly conservative Common Pleas; King's Bench was still more ready to integrate equity learning into its procedure.[21]

Professor Polden's recent historical studies of fusion show how the long-standing co-operation between Chancery and common law judges diminished, especially from the time of Baron Parke's domination of the law courts. Many of the common law judges were plainly ignorantly hostile towards equitable doctrine. We learn from Polden the story of how a certain common lawyer, Mr Justice Grove, when hearing at an assize sermon a reading from the bible promising the people equity, whispered loudly: "poor people".[22] Breakdown of the comity between jurisdictions set up by the Common Law Procedure Acts called for a remedy. The Judicature Acts of 1873-1875 therefore initiated a close administrative fusion, but in inauspicious circumstances. So, paradoxically, administrative fusion was a product of a decline in the common law-equity partnership of English law.

After 1875 the common lawyers, who greatly outnumbered the Chancery judges in the Supreme Court and appellate jurisdictions, were able to put their stamp on equitable doctrine. If equitable rights prevailed over legal,[23] it was nonetheless often a common lawyer in the new Judicature system who stated what the equities should be. The string of major decisions after 1875 including

---

21 See for example, *Moses v Macferlan* (1760) 2 Burr 1005; 97 ER 676; *Taylor v Plumer* (1815) 3 M & S 562; 105 ER 721. Gummow J lays claim to the unjust enrichment concepts in *Moses v Macferlan* as a common-law adaptation of equitable rather than civilian concepts: *Roxborough v Rothmans of Pall Mall Australia Limited* (2001) 208 CLR 516 at 539-51.

22 P Polden, "Mingling the Waters", above n 19 at 581-82. Sir William Grove was a famous scientist and natural philosopher who invented the nitric acid battery and the gas fuel cell, and who helped create the theory of energy conservation. He was also an early supporter of Darwinian natural selection. He nearly became professor of chemistry at Oxford but developed his law practice instead, joining the court of Common Pleas in 1871 and Queen's Bench in 1880. His was a curious case of fusing law and science, though he leaves little trace in the law reports. See IR Morus, 'Sir William Robert Grove', *New Dictionary of National Biography* (web edition, Oxford University Press, Oxford, 2004).

23 Under s 25 of the *Judicature Act 1873* various conflicts between law and equity were resolved, and s 25(11) dealt with the residuum by enacting that "generally in all matters not herein-before particularly mentioned, in which there is any conflict or variance between the Rules of Equity and the Rules of the Common Law with reference to the same matter, the Rules of Equity shall prevail". In R Meagher, JD Heydon and M Leeming (eds), *Meagher, Gummow and Lehane's Equity: Doctrines and Remedies* (4th ed, Butterworths, Sydney, 2002) at [2-070] it is argued that this clause impliedly saves the separate bodies of equity and law doctrine for the future, since an intention to effect full merger would have left nothing to resolve. This may have been the intent of Lord Selborne C and the draftsman, as *Meagher, Gummow and Lehane* suggests at [2-085] and [2-095]; but the plain meaning of the clause might just as well indicate that equitable norms should be given priority within a fused body of doctrine that would develop over time: cf Getzler, 'Patterns of Fusion' in P Birks (ed), *The Classification of Obligations* (Clarendon Press, Oxford, 1997); P Polden, "Mingling the Waters: Personalities, Politics and the Making of the Supreme Court of Judicature", above n 22.

Derry v Peek,[24] *Nocton v Lord Ashburton*,[25] *Sinclair v Brougham*,[26] *Bray v Ford*,[27] and *Speight v Gaunt*,[28] must be read in the light of this culture war.[29]

Yet if substantive doctrine was important, then even more so was adjectival law embracing mesne process, evidence and remedies. As Justice Gummow reminds us in his Clarendon lectures, on the procedural plane of fusion at least, "Equity won".[30] This was not necessarily all gain. One might follow Sir Owen Dixon and PV Baker QC in suggesting that Chancery's open probative approach to suits worked well as an auxiliary jurisdiction, but that after 1875 the infusion of the Chancery approach (including the practice of appealing decisions in toto rather than simply reviewing the doctrinal decision on its face) might have corrupted the operation of the common law actions.[31] It is surely significant that, without design, the Judicature system proved inhospitable to civil jury trial, which had been a hallmark of the ancient common law and which was still going strong at the turn of the century, but which had all but died out by 1930.[32] This was yet another pressure converting the moral economy of mixed law and fact assessment in the older common law into the political economy of modern doctrinally-driven adjudication.[33]

Thus the post-1875 fused system emerged as a welding together of common law styles of reasoning with equitable procedures. Without realising it, without purposing it, the reformers had created the conditions for a new jurisprudence. This view of fusion history suggests that we should finally put away the Ashburner metaphor of legal and equitable waters running side by side;[34] the fluvial metaphor was never accurate or informative. Dr Macnair

---

24   (1889) 14 App Cas 337.

25   [1914] AC 932.

26   [1914] AC 398.

27   [1896] AC 44.

28   (1883) 9 App Cas 1.

29   Cf W Gummow, 'Compensation for Breach of Fiduciary Duty', in TG Youdan (ed), *Equity, Fiduciaries and Trusts* (Carswell, Toronto, 1989) at 57.

30   W Gummow, *Change and Continuity: Statute, Equity, and Federalism* (Oxford University Press, Oxford, 1999) at 38-42, quoting Laycock, "The Triumph of Equity" (1993) 56 *Law and Contemporary Problems* 53 at 53.

31   For references see Getzler, 'Patterns of Fusion', in P Birks (ed), *The Classification of Obligations* (Clarendon Press, Oxford, 1997) at 185-192; R Meagher, JD Heydon and M Leeming (eds), *Meagher, Gummow and Lehane's Equity: Doctrines and Remedies*, (4th ed, Butterworths, Sydney, 2002) at [2-270]-[2-320].

32   J Getzler, 'The Fate of the Civil Jury in Late Victorian England: Malicious Prosecution as a Test Case' in Rubin and O'Donovan (eds), *Human Rights and Legal History* (Oxford University Press, Oxford, 2000) at 205, reprinted in JW Cairns and G McLeod (eds), *'The Dearest Birth Right of the People of England': The Jury in the History of the Common Law* (Hart Publishing, Oxford, 2002) at 217; M Lobban, 'The Strange Life of the English Civil Jury, 1837–1914', in *Dearest Birth Right*, at 173.

33   AV Dicey's hostility to the jury in civil trial may be read as an example of the political economy mood of the time: *An Introduction to the Study of the Law of the Constitution* (1st ed, Macmillan, London, 1885; 10th ed, Palgrave Macmillan, London, 1959) at 394, 398.

34   "The two streams of jurisdiction, though they run in the same channel, run side by side and do not mingle their waters": W Ashburner, *Principles of Equity* (London, Butterworths, London, 1902) at 23.

suggests a fresh metaphor of the wall of the common law overgrown by the ivy of equity, where the ivy finally holds up the structure of the wall itself. To play with this metaphor: neither stone nor plant can stand without the other, but mineral and vegetable do not combine completely into a new amalgam.[35]

The history of jurisdictions is relevant to fusion debates today, as *Digital Pulse* so powerfully demonstrates. But legal history is important not just as a source of positive authorities that condition judgments, but as a spur to reflection on the basic concepts of the law. Professor Maitland argued that the only way to break with the past and take conscious control of the law is to know the history so deeply that one can transcend it. Maitland himself could study the English proprietary actions with tremendous care and erudition, and at the same time call for liberal-minded lawyers to consign the historical complexity of English land law to the dustbin. He had a like attitude to equity: analyse it carefully in order to escape it. In a letter to MM Bigelow in 1906, written some thirty years after the putative union of legal and equitable jurisdictions under the Judicature Acts, Maitland wrote:[36]

> "Do you ever regret the whole equitable development? I sometimes do ... at times I hate Equity and think of her as a short sighted busybody. Yet I was bred in Equity chambers and used to despise the common lawyer as an inferior person."

Striking as that quote may be, Maitland should not too quickly be turned into a common lawyer's fusionist hero. Those who like to quote Maitland's famous lines about looking forward to the day when lawyers would not inquire into the legal or equitable provenance of a right[37] should also be aware that Maitland tilted towards wholesale replacing of the common law as well. He broached codification in emulation of the German Civil Code as the ideal example of legal reform, and indeed the German historical jurisprudence that led to Pandecticism and codification was Maitland's truest inspiration. Statute, not fusion, was the future.[38] By contrast the father of the Pandectist school,

---

35   M Macnair, "Judicial Reasoning in Seventeenth Century England" (forthcoming) at 2; and see also M Macnair, "'Conscientia' / "Conscience", "Epieikeia" / "Equity", and the Nature of the Early Modern Equity Jurisdictions' (MS, 2004, forthcoming); M Macnair, 'The Conceptual Basis of Trusts in the Later 17th and Early 18th Centuries', in R Helmholz and R Zimmermann (eds), *Itinera Fiduciae: Trust and Treuhand in Historical Perspective* (Duncker & Humblot, Berlin, 1998) at 207.

36   FW Maitland, 'Letter to MM Bigelow of 19 April 1906', in CHS Fifoot (ed), *The Letters of Frederic William Maitland* (Harvard University Press, Cambridge, Massachusetts, 1965) at 372. Hostility to Chancery jurisdiction can be seen scattered across Maitland's work: 'A Historical Sketch of Liberty and Equality' (1875) in HAL Fisher (ed), *Collected Papers of Frederic William Maitland*, 3 Vols (Cambridge University Press, Cambridge, 1910) Vol I at 1, 24–25; more muted in *Equity: A Course of Lectures* (AH Chaytor and WJ Whittaker (eds)); 2nd ed rev by J Brunyate, Cambridge University Press, Cambridge, 1936) at 1–23ff; and 'Trust and Corporation', in *Collected Papers*, in Vol III at 335. The general anti-equity drive in Maitland's writings merits a fuller study.

37   FW Maitland, *Equity: A Course of Lectures,* above n 36 at 20.

Friedrich von Savigny, warned his reform-minded students that rapid modernisation of the law, including codification, if pursued without the deepest study of legal doctrine, would risk mistaking or misunderstanding the evolved policies of the law.[39] Yet here was another paradox: if jurists understood the law well enough to codify it, there would then be no need of radical restructuring in order to make the law work effectively.

RELATIVE FAULT, CAUSATION AND DUTY

The writings of the late Professor Birks, our most Savigny-like modern figure, provide an essential reference point in the fusion debates. Birks believed that legal rationality and orderly taxonomy demanded that equity be fused into law through a process of juristic and judicial reform. Not legislation, but the fruitful partnership of rationalising jurist and scholarly judge was the way forward. Even if one remains an unjust enrichment sceptic,[40] it is hard to resist Birks' claim that no informed policy debate about the law can take place if we are not sure what the law comprises due to its undisciplined, irrational, non-juristic, evolutionary growth. More controversially, Birks claimed that the jurist must, through taxonomic analysis, seek consistency of principle throughout the law. Here the line between positive description and normative reform rapidly breaks down.[41]

In his note for the *Law Quarterly Review* of July 2004, dealing with change of position, Birks wrote that in cases where one person negligently enriched another and that other negligently received the enrichment,

---

38   See Maitland's unsigned Westminster Review essay of 1879, 'The Law of Real Property', in *Collected Papers,* above n 36, Vol I at 162, reiterated 22 years later in 'A Survey of the Century', *Collected Papers,* above n 36, Vol III at 431, 437–438; also FW Maitland, 'The Making of the German Civil Code' (1906), in *Collected Papers,* above n 36, Vol III at 475; see further J Getzler, 'Law, History and the Social Sciences: Intellectual Traditions of Late Nineteenth- and Early Twentieth-Century Europe', in M Lobban and A Lewis (eds), *Law and History: Current Legal Issues, Vol 6* (Oxford University Press, Oxford, 2004) at 215, 242-249.

It is worth noting that the first serious programme for fusion was that of the radical parliamentarians of 1651, who sought to abolish Chancery via codification. They were effortlessly defeated by the legal faction in the Commons: B Worden, *The Rump Parliament, 1648-1653* (Cambridge University Press, Cambridge, 1974) at 105-118.

39   HU Kantorowicz, "Savigny and the Historical School of Law" (1937) 53 *Law Quarterly Review* 326.

40   Or simply puzzled as to the focus of unjust enrichment theory as analysis of unjustified retention or unjust transfer of value — see P Birks, *Unjust Enrichment* (2nd ed, Oxford University Press, Oxford, 2005) at 101-160; P Jaffey, "Classification and Unjust Enrichment" (2004) 67 *Modern Law Review* 1012. Samuel Stoljar's seminal proprietary theory of restitution may here be recalled: SJ Stoljar, *The Law of Quasi-Contract* (Lawbook Company, Sydney, 1964; 2nd ed, Lawbook Company, Sydney, 1988); SJ Stoljar, "Unjust Enrichment and Unjust Sacrifice" (1987) 50 *Modern Law Review* 603.

41   Compare how the civilian commentators of the sixteenth century moved from the method of *inventio,* or finding the law through categorisation of *loci* (topics, classifications), to *iudicium,* whereby the *loci* point the way to truth in judgment: see HJ Berman, *Law and Revolution II: The Impact of the Protestant Reformations on the Western Legal Tradition* (Harvard University Press, Cambridge, Massachusetts, 2003) at 108-113ff.

"experience showed that, these episodes being different and often separated in time, attempts to quantify the relative fault of the parties were likely to produce arbitrary and inscrutable allocations of the loss."

Birks then wrote of "the need for a bulwark against inquiries into relative fault".[42] We might generalise his approach regarding change of position and claim that the measurement of relative fault is inherently a problematic method for civil adjudication — especially where the faults of the parties are separated in time and place, and hence not comparable as corresponding causal and moral factors that can be weighed and balanced in order to apportion liability for loss.

Relative fault may be intellectually unsatisfying, but it permeates much of the modern common law's reasoning.[43] Traditionally the common law took an all-or-nothing approach, whereby the evidential balance of probabilities rule allowed the slightest superiority of causal proof of harm to prevail.[44] The discretions involved in relative fault judgments were thereby concealed within the jurisdiction of the civil trial jury, but now in a judge-dominated common law such judgments surface as codified doctrine. Historically in the jury-free Chancery it was a common technique to evaluate relative fault or risk assumption, and thereby strike a balance between the equities; but such determinations being factual did not necessarily set strong precedents. It is therefore no surprise that many of the guiding maxims of equity concern the judgment of relative fault: clean hands, he who seeks equity must do equity, no assistance to a volunteer, first in time, and so on.

---

42 P Birks, "Change of Position: The Two Central Questions" (2004) 120 *Law Quarterly Review* 373 at 376. See also P Birks and Chin Nyuk Yin, 'On the Nature of Undue Influence' in J Beatson and D Friedmann, *Good Faith and Fault in Contract Law* (Clarendon Press, Oxford, 1995) at chapter 3.

43 The literature on relative fault, contributory negligence and mitigation in tort is immense and spills over into causation and efficiency debates; see for example, T-Y Cheung, 'Comparative Negligence', in P Newman (ed), *The New Palgrave Dictionary of Economics and the Law* (Macmillan, London, 1998) Vol I at 352; and MJ White, 'Contributory and Comparative Negligence: Empirical Comparison', in the same text, Vol I at 449. The doctrinal issues surrounding contributory negligence in contract are only beginning to be developed; see *Astley v Austrust Ltd* (1999) 197 CLR 1, discussed further below in the text accompanying n 66. Contributory fault is also emerging as an analytical framework in criminal law: see A Harel, "Efficiency and Fairness in Criminal Law: The Case for a Criminal Law Principle of Comparative Fault" (1994) 82 *California Law Review* 1181. Where the issue concerns the relative fault of parties not including the victim of breach, the applicable principles embrace joint and several liability, contribution and apportionment, rather than contributory fault. The auditing industry in Britain has recently sought apportionment reform in order to limit its exposure to liability for corporate misfeasances: see Department of Trade and Industry, *Feasibility Investigation of Joint and Several Liability* (HMSO, London, 1996); AS Burrows, 'Should one reform joint and several liability?' in NJ Mullany and AM Linden (eds), *Torts Tomorrow: A Tribute to John Fleming* (LawBook Company, Sydney, 1998) at 101; C Mitchell, *The Law of Contribution and Reimbursement* (Oxford University Press, Oxford, 2003). Australia's sharp break with the common-law commitment to solidary liability is discussed below at n 127.

44 As noted by D Daube, "The Scales of Justice" (1951) 63 *Juridical Review* 109. See further A Rodger, "Law for All Times: The Contribution of David Daube" (2004) 2 *Roman Legal Tradition* 3 at 9-11.

Relative fault analysis continues to ignite controversy in the modern common law. The all-or-nothing principle has been described as a rule being swallowed by a myriad of exceptions. Mr Weir has recently argued that relative fault has so seeped into the common law through piecemeal judicial and legislative reforms that the whole nature of civil litigation has been transformed from adjudication through trial to arbitration and administration by courts, a turn for the worse.[45] A suspicion of adjudication conceived as the fact-based balancing of fault drove the important recent House of Lords decision of *Shogun Finance Ltd v Hudson* on common mistake. Lord Hobhouse insisted that we must ask the lawyer's question: was there an event that according to legal rule triggered a contractual shift of title? And he held further that we must resist the question posed by the minority: who was most culpable in creating or realising the risk of the transaction going awry, and how can the risk be divided?[46]

Relative fault inquiry expresses itself through a plethora of devices in obligational law. These include causal rules based on sufficient and historical contribution, adding the discretions of practical reason to the untrammeled application of the basic but-for test; and also through policy-governed controls such as remoteness and proximity of causation.[47] Further controls are added with the rules of contributory negligence apportioning liability between wrongdoer and victim; and rules of mitigation controlling the factual measure of damages in light of reasonable reduction of loss by the victim. These various interlocking rules can be conceived as methods of mitigating or apportioning the defendant's liability for causing loss by comparing the causal potency of the defendant's actions to (i) causation of harm by the plaintiff or by third parties or by general circumstances viewed ex ante breach, and (ii) causation of loss by those same actors viewed ex post initial breach.

Courts in Australia and Canada tend to argue that the law ought to resist the wholesale importation of relative fault inquiry into the sphere of compensation for breach of equitable duties. In practice what this means is that relative fault assessment is hidden within the causal calculus ascribing initial liability, and not overtly expressed in remoteness, contributory negligence and mitigation rules. Courts in New Zealand and England are now beginning to tilt the other way and increasingly recognise these explicit control devices in the equitable sphere. Perhaps the really interesting question is not which side of the debate over causative technique is right, but what should be the content of duties and the goal of remedies, for these are the upstream issues of legal policy that ought to govern the choice and application of causal rules. We should be suspicious of all attempts to foreclose this debate by claiming that equity cannot use common law analogies, or that it ought to do so wherever possible. Both fundamentalist positions are not only historically false, but amount to a refusal to debate the deeper policy issues of fusion.

---

45   See T Weir, "ALL or Nothing?" (2004) 78 *Tulane Law Review* 511.

46   *Shogun Finance Ltd v Hudson* [2004] 1 AC 919.

47   See *South Australia Asset Management Corporation v York Montague Ltd* [1997] AC 191; J Stapleton, "Cause-in-Fact and the Scope of Liability for Consequences" (2003) 119 *Law Quarterly Review* 388.

Any inquiry into causation of loss involving two or more parties will necessarily bring with it a scrutiny of relevant fault. How that relativity is assessed will depend upon which duties are held to bind the parties in the first place, since actionable fault emerges from breach of a prior duty.[48] A parent causes both factual and legal harm to a child by not feeding it, whilst a stranger who has no extant relationship or duty to the child does not cause harm by non-feeding, at least in the eyes of the law. This simple point — that the characterisation of duty helps frame the relevant causal rules for establishing liability for loss upon breach — is the reason why one cannot exaggerate the impact of Lord Millett's celebrated judgments in *Bristol and West Building Society v Mothew*[49] and *Armitage v Nurse*.[50] Those judgments offered nothing less than a reconceptualisation of the nature of a fiduciary's duties. Lord Millett laid down that duties of skill and care generated by trust and fiduciary relationships are not in themselves fiduciary duties, and are not subject to the special rules protecting the "irreducible core" of loyalty duties that are of the essence of fiduciary relationships. This approach, heralded in earlier commentary and cases[51] but given their most forceful expression by Lord Millett, has now become close to orthodoxy in England. It is the first and essential doctrinal step in opening the way to common law control mechanisms within equitable compensation, for if certain duties owed by a fiduciary have no qualities distinguishing them from like duties of contract and tort, then this invites the application of like rules for gauging causation and measure of damages.

The second, minor theme in this development is the idea that when remedying fiduciary default the law deploys not only *compensation* or pecuniary repair of loss caused by breach of duty where other remedies (for example, tracing or specific restitution, or rescission) are inadequate, but perhaps more commonly the action of *account* (particularly the account of administration in common form), following which an order for payment might be made to directly enforce a primary duty of custody or stewardship. There is an implicit methodological argument built in to this approach, which is that identification of the historically appropriate remedy can reveal the true contours of different fiduciary duties. This idea was developed first in writings

---

48   The locus classicus for this approach is HLA Hart and T Honoré, *Causation in the Law* (2nd ed, Clarendon Press, Oxford, 1985) especially at 205-307. For a fresh appraisal of the impact of this book on common-law thought, see N Lacey, *A Life of HLA Hart: The Nightmare and the Noble Dream* (Oxford University Press, Oxford, 2004) at 209-219.

49   [1998] Ch 1.

50   [1998] Ch 241.

51   Notably in three articles: PD Finn, 'The Fiduciary Principle', in TG Youdan (ed), *Equity, Fiduciaries and Trusts* (Carswell, Toronto, 1989) at 1; R Austin, 'Moulding the Content of Fiduciary Duties', in AJ Oakley (ed), *Trends in Contemporary Trust Law* (Oxford University Press, Oxford, 1996) at 164, DJ Hayton, 'The Irreducible Core Content of Trusteeship', in AJ Oakley (ed), *Trends in Contemporary Trust Law*, at 47; and in two cases: *Girardet v Crease & Co* (1987) 11 BCLR (2d) 361 at 361-362, per Southin J; *Permanent Building Society v Wheeler* (1994) 14 ACSR 109 at 157, per Ipp J.

of Lord Millett and Professor Birks,[52] and has now been given extensive attention in Dr Elliott's work.[53] Though there are variations between different writers, I shall call the view splitting duties of care from core trust obligations, and looking to payments following a common accounting for remedy of the latter, the "post-*Mothew*" model of breach of trust.[54]

THE "POST-MOTHEW" MODEL

Three main distinctions governing remedies for loss caused by breach of fiduciary duty are propounded within the post-*Mothew* model.[55] I shall describe these in turn, indicating judicial support and opposition regarding these positions.

---

52   See P Birks, "Equity in the Modern Law: An Exercise in Taxonomy" (1996) 26 *University of Western Australia Law Review* 1 at 45-48; P Millett, "Equity's Place in the Law of Commerce" (1998) 114 *Law Quarterly Review* 214 at 225-27. Though Birks may have retreated from his surmise that account had explanatory or normative import in his later work: *Unjust Enrichment* (2nd ed, Oxford University Press, Oxford, 2005) at 293-95 ("accountability is dying and there is no point in trying to turn the clock back").

53   SB Elliott, *Compensation Claims Against Trustees* (Oxford DPhil thesis, 2002); SB Elliott, "Fiduciary liability for client mortgage frauds" (1999) 13 *Trust Law International* 74; SB Elliott, "Remoteness Criteria in Equity" (2002) 65 *Modern Law Review* 588; SB Elliott, "Restitutionary Compensatory Damages for Breach of Fiduciary Duty?" (1998) 6 *Restitution Law Review* 135; SB Elliott, "Rethinking Interest on Withheld and Misapplied Trust Money" [2001] *Conveyancer* 313; SB Elliott and J Edelman, "*Target Holdings* Considered in Australia" (2003) 119 *Law Quarterly Review* 545; J Edelman and SB Elliott, "Money remedies against trustees" (2004) 18 *Trust Law International* 116; SB Elliott and C Mitchell, "Remedies for Dishonest Assistance" (2004) 67 *Modern Law Review* 16 especially at 23-34. The last reference is the most considered statement of the account theory to date.

54   See further R Chambers, 'Liability', in P Birks and A Pretto (eds), *Breach of Trust* (Hart Publishing, Oxford, 2002) at 1, which gives an especially valuable critical discussion of the account and compensation remedies. For other recent contributions see MDJ Conaglen, "The Nature and Function of Fiduciary Loyalty" (2005) 121 *Law Quarterly Review* 452; MDJ Conaglen, "Equitable Compensation for Breach of Fiduciary Dealing Rules" (2003) 119 *Law Quarterly Review* 246; MDJ Conaglen, "Fiduciary Liability and Contribution to Loss" [2001] *Cambridge Law Journal* 480; WA Gregory, "The Fiduciary Duty of Care: A Perversion of Words" (2005) 38 *Akron Law Review* 181; C Rickett, "Equitable Compensation: Towards a Blueprint?" (2003) 25 *Sydney Law Review* 31; and C Rickett, 'Compensating for Loss in Equity' in P Birks and FD Rose (eds), *Restitution and Equity Vol 1: Resulting Trusts and Equitable Compensation* (Lloyds of London Press, London, 2000) at 173, 176-179; J Berryman, "Equitable Compensation for Breach by Fact-Based Fiduciaries: Tentative Thoughts on Clarifying Remedial Goals" (1999) 37 *Alberta Law Review* 95; S Worthington, *Equity* (Oxford University Press, Oxford, 2003) at 144-164; D Hayton in chapter 11 of this book. AS Burrows expresses doubts about the utility of the account model in *Remedies for Torts and Breach of Contract* (3rd ed, Oxford University Press, Oxford, 2004) at 600-606; see also J Getzler, 'Equitable Compensation and the Regulation of Fiduciary Relationships' in P Birks and F Rose, *Resulting Trusts and Equitable Compensation*, at 248-251; and R Chambers, 'Liability', in in P Birks and A Pretto (eds), *Breach of Trust*, at 9-10.

55   Note that account of profits made in breach of fiduciary obligation form a separate if adjacent subject; here a key issue is how disgorgement is best to be effected, whether by in rem remedies such as constructive trust, lien or charge, or by personal account remedies.

The first distinction is that between custodial and non-custodial fiduciary duties. A custodial fiduciary duty — more plainly, a trust — is typically enforced by account, such that information about the property receipts and outgoings can be demanded and any shortfalls caused by improper failure to take in property or improper payment out must be made up from the trustee's own pocket. By requiring a report of the handling of the trust, and then surcharging items received but not accounted for and falsifying accountable items that should not have been paid out, the primary trust obligation of due custody is directly enforced, in the manner of specific performance of a primary duty. No wilful default or other breach of trust need be shown in order to enforce this primary duty and hence no issues of controlling the extent of remediable loss flowing from breach enter into the exercise. By contrast wilful default in failing to get in trust assets or invest for a reasonable return leads to a secondary compensatory remedy for loss caused by breach. This model explains why in *Target*[56] it was correct for the court to exclude remoteness and foreseeability as controls curbing but-for causal liability, yet at the same time find that a solicitor who had wilfully released funds in breach of trust in order to clinch a sale was not liable when the sale proved to be fraud on the part of the vendor, causing steep losses to the purchaser. The solicitor had succeeded in bringing the security and title for the property back into the trust assets notwithstanding his technical breach, and so an account of the trust property would assess the fund as having been replenished notwithstanding the breach in paying out the purchase money. The losses that followed on the sale were not therefore caused by the paying out of funds, because substitute property was put back into the trust satisfying the primary duty to account, before any loss occurred.

The High Court may have given some credence to the account theory of trustee liability in the recent case of *Youyang*.[57] However not all commentators are happy with the deployment of account language. Some find the idea that where a trustee effectively reconstitutes a trust fund after wilful default involving misapplication of assets, and so breaks any chain of causation between the original misapplication and consequential losses, then this amounts to nothing more than saying that the trustee need only compensate for losses flowing from the original breach where those losses are a natural or foreseeable consequence of the breach; and that the chain of causation where the fund was reconstituted may have been broken by a sufficiently remote cause such as third-party fraud or a market fall independent of unauthorised investment.[58] But the account model is not merely a semantic variation or exercise in jurisprudential antiquity. The account model has a more practical implication of raising the strictness of the trustee's liability whilst at the same time capping it to the level of the existing asset, as it should have been at time

---

56 *Target Holdings Ltd v Redferns (A Firm)* [1996] 1 AC 421.
57 *Youyang Pty Ltd v Minter Ellison Morris Fletcher* (2003) 212 CLR 484; SB Elliott and J Edelman, "*Target Holdings* Considered in Australia" (2003) 119 *Law Quarterly Review* 545.
58 See for examples, A Burrows, *Remedies for Torts and Breach of Contract* (3rd ed, Oxford University Press, Oxford, 2004) at 604-606; R Chambers, 'Liability' in P Birks and A Pretto (eds), *Breach of Trust* (Hart Publishing, Oxford, 2002) at 1.

of judgment. It thus prevents common-law controls infiltrating the core territory of the trust, being the trustee's duties to execute his or her trust and perform a due custodianship of the res.

The second main distinction drawn by the post-*Mothew* model is between fiduciary duties of loyalty and allegedly non-fiduciary duties of skill and care. Since a fiduciary's duty to manage the affairs of another with skill and care are said to be indistinguishable from duties of care arising in tort and contract, there is seen to be no good reason to treat the secondary liabilities flowing from breach of such equitable duties any differently from those duties of care sounding in the common law causes of action. As Millett LJ puts it:[59]

> "Equitable compensation for breach of the duty of skill and care resembles common law damages in that it is awarded by way of compensation to the plaintiff for his loss. There is no reason in principle why the common law rules of causation, remoteness of damage and measure of damages should not be applied by analogy in such a case. It should not be confused with equitable compensation for breach of fiduciary duty, which may be awarded in lieu of rescission or specific restitution."

The reference here to true equitable compensation as a pecuniary substitute for rescission or restitution can be seen as a modern expression of the remedies available to enforce the duty to account for an asset in fiduciary custody. It should be noted however that debate has now deepened over what "rescission" of a transaction at law or equity means and how remedial responses should best be formulated where a transaction is voidable.[60] In this chapter it will be assumed that surcharge and falsification of account on the one hand, and rescission, restitution or pecuniary substitutes on the other, are different nomenclatures or methods for similar remedial objectives;[61] and further that, of itself, the classificatory language chosen does not determine the correct causal policies to be applied in identifying loss and effecting remedy.

The High Court majority in *Youyang*, which as we have seen gave some credibility to the strict account theory for breach of primary duty, went out of its way to doubt the concomitant theory that causal control mechanisms applied to duties of skill and diligence within fiduciary relationships. The majority noted that according to the *Mothew* model,[62]

---

59   *Bristol and West Building Society v Mothew* [1998] Ch 1 at 17.

60   D O'Sullivan, *The Evolving Structure of Equitable Rescission with particular reference to Rescission for Fraud and Breach of Fiduciary Duty* (Oxford DPhil thesis, 2000); T Akkouh, "Equitable compensation where rescission is impossible" (2002) 16 *Trust Law International* 151; VJ Vann, "Equitable compensation when rescission is impossible: a response" (2003) 17 *Trust Law International* 66; WS Swadling, "Rescission, Property, and the Common Law" (2005) 121 *Law Quarterly Review* 123.

61   See for example, *Nocton v Lord Ashburton* [1914] AC 932 at 956-58, per Viscount Haldane LC.

62   (2003) 196 ALR 482 at 491. To similar effect was *Maguire v Makaronis* (1997) 188 CLR 449 at 473; see J Getzler, 'Equitable Compensation and the Regulation of Fiduciary Relationships' in P Birks and FD Rose (eds), *Restitution and Equity Vol 1: Resulting Trusts and Equitable Compensation* (Lloyds of London Press, London, 2000) at 254-255.

"the stricter view of liability for breaches of trust causing loss to the trust estate and for breaches of the fiduciary duties of loyalty and fidelity is not required where the complaint concerns failure to exercise the necessary degree of care and diligence....

However, there must be a real question whether the unique foundation and goals of equity, which has the institution of the trust at its heart, warrant any assimilation even in this limited way with the measure of compensatory damages in tort and contract. It may be thought strange to decide that the precept that trustees are to be kept by courts of equity up to their duty has an application limited to the observance by trustees of some only of their duties to beneficiaries in dealing with trust funds."

It is not surprising that post-*Mothew* theorists have been very hostile to this part of the judgment. Dr Elliott and Dr Edelman in the *Law Quarterly Review* blankly call for this "unfortunate suggestion" to be rejected by the Australian courts, claiming that rhetorical appeals to the sanctity of trust relationships are misplaced when it is merely duties of care that are at stake. They commend the emerging New Zealand and English approach, and put forward the claim that the prevailing concurrent liability theory expressed in *Henderson v Merrett Syndicates Ltd*[63] demands that "careless misconduct should provoke the same measure of recovery whether the defendant is a trustee or bailee or anyone else charged with the affairs of another".[64] This interpretation of the nature and implications of concurrent liability for carelessness is a central — perhaps the central — issue of the debate, and will be addressed at length later in the argument.

In the earlier case of *Pilmer*[65] the majority of the High Court reiterated the view put in *Astley*[66] that contributory negligence applied to tort law solely by force of legislation, and was alien to contract at common law. Building from this premise, the *Pilmer* court stated that a fortiori the doctrine of contributory negligence was out of place in a fiduciary context. The majority gave little substantive reasoning beyond the claim that "contributory negligence focuses on the conduct of the plaintiff, fiduciary law upon the obligation by the defendant to act in the interests of the plaintiff". This explanation had some tinge of circularity since the very question being examined was whether the conduct of the plaintiff had any legal implications for the defendant's liability.[67] Kirby J in *Pilmer* noted the conventional arguments that fiduciary law with its emphasis on trust, confidence and loyalty could not expect a beneficiary to be on guard against his fiduciary's negligence, and so contributory negligence

---

63   [1995] 2 AC 145 at 205.

64   SB Elliott and J Edelman, '*Target Holdings* Considered in Australia' (2003) 119 *Law Quarterly Review* 545, 550; cf A Goldfinch, "Trustee's duty to exercise reasonable care: Fiduciary duty?" (2004) 78 *Australian Law Journal* 678, and Dr Elliott's earlier views in "Fiduciary liability for client mortgage frauds" (1999) 13 *Trust Law International* 74.

65   *Pilmer v Duke Group Ltd (In Liq)* (2001) 207 CLR 165.

66   *Astley v Austrust Ltd* (1999) 197 CLR 1.

67   See further MDJ Conaglen, "Fiduciary Liability and Contribution to Loss" [2001] *Cambridge Law Journal* 480; A Lynch, "Equitable compensation for breach of fiduciary duty: Causation and contribution – The High Court dodges a fusion fallacy in *Pilmer*" (2001) 22 *Australian Bar Review* 173.

would weaken the pressure on the fiduciary to perform.[68] The source of this idea lies in the judgment in *Brickenden v London Loan and Savings Co* where Lord Thankerton said "once the court has determined that the non-disclosed facts were material, speculation as to what course the constituent, on disclosure, would have taken is not relevant".[69] Kirby J appeared to accept the *Brickenden* approach in his insightful judgment in the earlier fiduciary breach case of *Maguire*.[70] In *Pilmer* he noted that discretions to adjust equitable awards in effect amounted to an apportionment mechanism between fiduciary and beneficiary;[71] but Kirby J acknowledged that Australian legal opinion did not permit a more overt doctrinal apportionment technique to be developed. The High Court has not developed its stance regarding contributory negligence for fiduciaries any further since its forthright obiter in *Pilmer* and *Youyang*. Heydon JA in *Digital Pulse* reviewed the state of the authorities and indicated that Australian courts were now unlikely to follow New Zealand decisions[72] and embrace contributory negligence in fiduciary law by analogy with tort statutes.[73] The impact of contributory negligence now being applied by statute directly to contract *pace Astley* may still keep the issue alive in Australian law.[74]

The third distinction in the post-*Mothew* model is between subjectively dishonest breaches and less serious breaches. Here equity follows the model of the pro-plaintiff rules for common-law deceit where a subjective mens rea is present, and denies the defendant the benefit of remoteness, contributory

---

68   An idea expressed forcefully by Gummow J and Handley JA in extra-curial writings — see W Gummow, 'Compensation for Breach of Fiduciary Duty', in TG Youdan (ed), *Equity, Fiduciaries and Trusts* (Carswell, Toronto, 1989) at 82-91; K Handley, 'Reduction of Damages Awards' in PD Finn (ed), *Essays on Damages* (LawBook Company, Sydney, 1992) at 113, 127. English law has so far kept to a like policy, largely on the basis of the learned but hesitant decision of Blackburne J in *Nationwide Building Society v Balmer Radmore* [1999] Lloyds Rep PN 241 at 270-82; 558, 564-5, also *The Times* 1 March 1999 (Lexis Transcript) (Ch D). Blackburne J's approach has now been reinforced by the House of Lords decision in *Hilton v Barker Booth & Eastwood* [2005] 1 WLR 567, where a vendor was not held responsible for failing to be on his guard against his solicitors' failure to disclose the patent unreliability of a purchaser.

69   [1934] 3 DLR 465 at 469. This statement has generated considerable scrutiny in courts and by commentators, and has been criticised as both vague and draconian, yet its authority has not directly been attacked: see below, n 76. See also, JD Heydon, in chapter 9 of this book; JD Heydon, "Causal Relationships between a Fiduciary's Default and the Principal's Loss" (1994) 110 *Law Quarterly Review* 328; JD Heydon, "The Negligent Fiduciary" (1995) 111 *Law Quarterly Review* 1; D Hodge, "Professionals as Fiduciaries: The Remedial Consequences" (Speech to Chancery and Professional Negligence Bar Associations, London, 10 February 2003): www.maitlandchambers.com/articles (last visited 11 July 2005).

70   *Maguire v Makaronis* (1997) 188 CLR 449 at 492-499. For more detailed analysis see J Getzler, 'Equitable Compensation and the Regulation of Fiduciary Relationships' in P Birks and F Rose, *Resulting Trusts and Equitable Compensation* (Lloyds of London Press, London, 2000) at 237-244.

71   *Pilmer v Duke Group Ltd (In Liq)* (2001) 207 CLR 165 at 224-26, 228-32, [149]-[154], [165]-[176].

72   The leading case is now *Bank of New Zealand v New Zealand Guardian Trust Co Ltd* [1999] 1 NZLR 664 and [1999] 1 NZLR 213 (Fisher J), reinforcing the decision of the NZCA in *Day v Mead* [1987] 2 NZLR 443. See further SB Elliott, "Remoteness Criteria in Equity" (2002) 65 *Modern Law Review* 588.

73   *Harris v Digital Pulse Pty Ltd* (2003) 56 NSWLR 298 at 391-394, 413-417.

74   See references at n 127.

negligence and perhaps mitigation rules,[75] as a fraudulent person cannot complain when his victim is propelled by that fraud into possibly avoidable losses. The argument is then made that consistency between common-law and equitable categories of duty should confine the most generous pro-plaintiff but-for causal rules of compensatory recovery largely to breaches of loyalty involving dishonesty. Honest breach of the loyalty rules, such as inadvertent drift into conflicts of interest, may be sanctioned, but not to the same extent as fraudulent breaches, as one would wish to protect the honest but breaching fiduciary from liability for non-remote losses.[76]

Let us recap the "post-*Mothew* model" as it is presently emerging. Cases of custodial breach are placed in a separate category of restoration of a fund by an account process, rather than reparation by compensation. The simple causal rules of account favour the plaintiff's recovery by barring remoteness controls,

---

75 Though note that in the analogous area of tortious deceit, the House of Lords in *Smith New Court Securities Ltd v Citibank NA* [1997] AC 254 decided that whilst remoteness criteria do not apply there remains a duty to mitigate. Canadian case law suggests that there is no overt duty upon the victim of a fiduciary breach to mitigate, but that unreasonable behaviour may snap the chain of common-sense causation: see *Canson Enterprises Ltd v Boughton & Co* [1991] 3 SCR 534 at 542-556, per McLachlin J; *Hodgkinson v Simms* [1994] 3 SCR 377; *Hunt v TD Securities Inc* [2003] C37797; 2003 CanLII 3649.

76 See for example, *Swindle v Harrison* [1997] 4 All ER 705, where the court held that remoteness controls would be applied for loss flowing from a breach of fiduciary obligation, unless something "equivalent to fraud" appeared. However in all cases, including fraud cases where remoteness criteria did not apply, there still had to be some common-sense causal link between the breach and the loss. Hence if it were possible to say that a beneficiary would have gone ahead with a loss-making venture in any event, then a material and fraudulent breach by the fiduciary will not be causally potent and so damage is not proved. To like effect is *Gwembe Valley Development Company Ltd v Koshy* [2003] EWCA Civ 1048 at [142]-[147], where the Court of Appeal found that even where there was a dishonest fiduciary breach of loyalty, the court could speculate that a loss materially flowing from the breach might still have been suffered in the absence of breach and so exclude liability. This would seem to be a narrow reading of the *Brickenden* doctrine, see above text accompanying nn 65-74. Australian cases tilting in this direction include *Greater Pacific Investments Pty Ltd v Australian National Industries Ltd* (1996) 39 NSWLR 143; *Beach Petroleum NL v Abbott Tout Russell Kennedy* (1999) 33 ACSR 1; [1999] NSWCA 408; *Karam v ANZ Banking Group Ltd* [2001] NSWSC 709; and especially *Aequitas v AEFC* (2001) 19 ACLC 1006 per Austin J, and *WA Fork Truck Distributors Pty Ltd v Jones* [2003] WASC 102 per Pullin J. These cases can be seen as attempts to give meaning to the elusive *Target* doctrine applying but-for tests for causation, adding a requirement of common-sense causation even where there is no remoteness inquiry. However other courts have refused to make a distinction between different remoteness rules for honest and dishonest breach of trust: see for example, *Collins v Brebner* [2000] Lloyds Rep PN 587; and also do not see the but-for test as permitting factual speculation as to whether a material breach was causative or not: see for example, *Collins v Brebner*; *Bairstow & Ors v Queens Moat Houses Plc* [2001] EWCA Civ 712 (where the dishonesty of the fiduciary led the court to apply but-for causation stringently). To like effect in Australia: *Wan v McDonald* (1991) 33 FCR 491; *Stewart v Layton* [1992] 111 ALR 687; *Maguire v Makaronis* (1997) 188 CLR 449; *O'Halloran v R T Thomas & Family Pty Limited* (1998) 45 NSWLR 262. The unsettled case law suggests that no consistent approach has yet evolved in either England or Australia. It is perhaps a pity that the High Court on 14 April 2000 refused leave to appeal in *Beach Petroleum*, since Gleeson CJ acknowledged that one of the grounds of appeal was "with respect to the recovery of equitable compensation, the authority to be accorded in Australia to the decision of the Privy Council in *Brickenden v London Loan & Savings Co* (1934) 3 DLR 465".

but a cap on recovery is set to the level of the fund as it would have been without degradation, and so without permitting recovery for further consequential loss. Account is used as a kind of *in personam* vindication of the asset, a strict personal enforcement of the primary duty to hold the asset safely and return it when the entrustment is ended. Outside personal vindication of funds and repression of actual fraud, where the common law itself takes a stringent causal line against malfeasant parties, the full gamut of causal controls including remoteness, contributory negligence and mitigation, ought to be applied for breaches of equitable duties. This means that "honest" breaches of the stringent loyalty requirements and any form of fiduciary negligence fall to be governed by the common-law control mechanisms listed earlier (remoteness and so on). Only truly "fraudulent" fiduciary disloyalties attract the strictest causal liability.

I have noted en passant the Australian courts' traditionalist rejection of at least the second and third parts of the post-*Mothew* theory. Building beyond the High Court's briefly stated positions, I will next try to develop a more radical set of criticisms. My contrary case may be stated briefly. First, the distinction between custodial trusts and fiduciary management of another's affairs is important in some areas of equity but ought not to be here. Secondly, there are good reasons to regard prudence as a dimension of good faith in close fiduciary relationships, so that duties of skill and care cannot be divorced from the requirements of loyalty. But if fiduciary duties of care are different, then this means that the nature of concurrent liabilities of care across contract, tort and equity must rationally be thought through. Next, there are longstanding equitable policies of objectifying fraud; subjective dishonesty is not a good yardstick for parsing fiduciary liability and applying differential causal rules. And finally, relative fault doctrines must be tailored carefully to their doctrinal environment. Apportionment and mitigation doctrines in contract are predicated on the policy of permitting or even encouraging efficient breach within markets for fungibles; equivalent tort doctrines are predicated on liability being based on fault and foresight. Fiduciary liability by contrast is predicated on control and deterrence of those with a dominant position over persons vulnerable to their power, and regulation through deterrence is not here served by strong apportionment and mitigation regimes. Equity has instead developed its own language of excuse and relief that maintains deterrence but does not harshly treat a well-meaning and reasonable trustee who loses the value of a fund or asset in breach of obligation yet in a manner that seems non-culpable. To replace this deterrent system with the common law causal rules risks degrading the prophylactic impulses within equity. Finally, it is not clear that repression of egregious cases of fiduciary breach by exemplary damages, rather than achieving constant deterrent pressure through stringent causal rules in each and every case, would yield a superior method of enforcing fiduciary duties.

This whole area of law is not helped by the difficult reasoning of the leading appellate decisions of *Target* in England and *Canson* in Canada, where judges used the classical equitable language of but-for causation to justify results that clearly departed from the but-for model. But-for causal language often seems like a shell covering what is substantially an approach based on relative fault, and arguably the fiction of "but-for" should here be dropped and replaced with more discriminating use of causal concepts such as sufficient contribution and historical involvement, and further allowing rules of remoteness and proximity overtly to control the legal reach of findings of causation. The call for reform of equitable compensation and account through introduction of common law causal concepts is driven in part by justifiable frustration with a causal approach in equity that can seem both inscrutable and draconian. The concomitant danger is that the proposed solution of applying common-law control mechanisms may itself undermine the policy objectives of fiduciary law; the proposed cure may be too costly.

Equitable compensation is difficult because it straddles so many categories of private law — contract, tort, trusts, fiduciary obligations, property, principles of remedies. With so many potential flashpoints of controversy, so many dependent variables, it is a challenge to isolate the key problems. An initial methodological problem is that the "post-*Mothew*" model uses the technical packaging of remedy to make steep policy decisions about the correct content of the primary fiduciary duties, decisions that would better be made by explicitly discussing the policies of the law across contract, tort and fiduciary duties.

CUSTODIAL AND NON-CUSTODIAL FIDUCIARY DUTIES

Modern lawyers need to delineate sharply the line between rights in personam and rights in rem for a variety of purposes: determining priorities in insolvency, tracing and accounting for profits in substitutes and mixed funds; deciding due levels of interest; deciding jurisdiction where there is conflict of laws, and so on. A looming issue is whether interests under trusts subsist as custodial property in the period before a breach of duty or whether the breach creates the interest; this may have implications for when a limitation period starts to run.[77] It is more doubtful, however, whether there is any relevant distinction to be drawn between a trust involving fiduciary custody of some asset, and a fiduciary obligation mandating selfless management of another's affairs. Kirby J in *Pilmer* noted that "fiduciary obligations were never limited to disputes about property interests",[78] and further it is not clear that those fiduciary obligations concerned with property should be treated as more intense than those that are not. The principle of *Re Coomber*[79] amply explains how a fiduciary obligation has a certain scope of operation or subject matter, and this can be property custody or management of a sphere of activities or any

---

77   *Paragon Finance plc v DB Thakerar & Co* [1999] 1 All ER 400; *Gwembe Valley Development Company Ltd v Koshy* [2003] EWCA Civ 1048; W Swadling, 'Limitation', in Birks and Pretto, *Breach of Trust* (Hart Publishing, Oxford, 2002) at 319. The limitation implications of classifying damages sought against a fraudulent agent or other non-custodial fiduciary relations are analysed in *Companhia de Seguros Imperio v Heath (REBX) Ltd* [2000] Lloyd's Rep PN 795; [2001] Lloyd's Rep IR 109 per Waller LJ.

78   *Pilmer v Duke Group Pty Ltd (in liq)* (2001) 207 CLR 165 at 213[126], citing D DeMott, "Fiduciary Obligation Under Intellectual Siege: Contemporary Challenges to the Duty to be Loyal" (1992) 30 *Osgoode Hall Law Journal* 471 at 473-75; *Breen v Williams* (1994) 35 NSWLR 522 at 543-544.

79   (1911) 1 Ch 723 at 728-729, per Fletcher Moulton LJ, and sees *Warman v Dwyer* (1995) 182 CLR 544.

blend of the two spheres such as managing property in order to promote a charitable purpose or to benefit a person.

It is possible to identify duties of a fiduciary nature where the law requires not management of another's interests or property in any meaningful way, but something more akin to self-denial in relation to that person's interest. Presumptive undue influence relationships are one example. But even if self-denial is a key aspect of fiduciary obligations, there is arguably little analytical purchase in the High Court's statements in *Breen v Williams*[80] and *Pilmer*[81] characterising the fiduciary relationship as purely proscriptive of certain forms of self-interested conduct, as opposed to prescriptive of certain forms of loyalty or altruistic service or performance. Kirby J's broader view of fiduciary duty expressed in *Pilmer* is here to be preferred against the notions of proscription expressed in obiter by the majorities in *Breen* and *Pilmer*.[82]

An expanded denotation of the fiduciary relationship, employing a mix of prescriptive and proscriptive terms, would stipulate a strong set of powers of one person over another, hedged by certain restrictions mandating self-denial.[83] Here the equitable and Hohfeldian meaning of power coincides, denoting a capacity unilaterally to change the rights of another person. The examples of non-fiduciary powers in contract are plentiful (for example, options, or a decision to terminate) and in equity (mere powers, decisions to rescind voidable transactions or to execute security interests), but these powers will typically involve an absence of the requirements of self-denial, sometimes described as altruism or loyalty. One must further explain why fiduciary duties are imposed in some relationships involving powers and not in others. A "mere power" is coloured with fiduciary loyalty and denial when vested in a trustee or fiduciary proper — sometimes called a "power coupled with a trust", and sometimes simply lumped together with trust powers.[84] Here it is the relational status of the persons, their being in or coming into a relationship of dependency and control, confidence and trust, that is the key factor in colouring

---

80   (1996) 186 CLR 71 at 113.

81   (2001) 207 CLR 165 at 197-199.

82   See *Pilmer v Duke Group Ltd (In Liq)*, above n 81 at 212-220 [123]-[136] per Kirby J, which consciously moves away from PD Finn's influential account whereby fiduciary powers and competencies and other prescriptive duties are excluded from the core fiduciary injunction to avoid self-serving conduct: cf PD Finn, 'The Fiduciary Principle', in Youdan, *Equity, Fiduciaries and Trusts* (Carswell, Canada,1989) at 1, 24-31. The High Court's earlier decision in *Daly v Sydney Stock Exchange Ltd* (1986) 160 CLR 371 at 377, 385 would seem to recognise a positive fiduciary duty to disclose material information, in tension with the *Breen* decision. Criticism of the proscription theory of fiduciary duty in *Breen* is given in MDJ Conaglen, "Fiduciary Liability and Contribution to Loss" [2001] *Cambridge Law Journal* 480 at 481-82; D DeMott, 'Fiduciary Obligation in the High Court of Australia', in *Centenary Essays for the High Court of Australia* (LexisNexis Butterworths, Sydney, 2004) at 277. In chapter 9 of this book, Justice Heydon suggests that the *Breen* doctrine be read narrowly; see text accompanying nn 235-241.

83   For a locus classicus see Mason J's judgment in *Hospital Products Ltd v US Surgical Corp* (1984) 156 CLR 41 at 96-97, discussed in R Meagher, JD Heydon, M Leeming, *Meagher Gummow and Lehane's Equity: Doctrines and Remedies* (4th ed, Butterworths, Sydney, 2002) at [5-005].

84   *Mettoy Pension Trustees Ltd v Evans* [1990] 1 WLR 1587; S Gardner, *An Introduction to the Law of Trusts* (2nd ed, Oxford University Press, Oxford, 2003) at chapter 11.

a power as fiduciary. Fiduciary custody of property is simply a special case of the wider genus. Fiduciary duty is not merely the obligational aspect of a trust floated free of the core custodial trust institution; the reverse is at least as true.

It is nonetheless sometimes suggested that fiduciary obligations outside custodial trust relations are a late addition to the categories of our law, a lifting of the in personam duties of trustees from their natural custodial context and their transplantation into obligational law.[85] It all depends what one is looking for — the fiduciary label or the phenomenon itself. In Roman law fiduciary obligations did not fit neatly into the classical institutional series of obligations comprising contract, delict and the residuum of quasi-contract (largely unjust enrichment) and quasi-delict. But there was a strong body of fiduciary law dispersed throughout the law, impacting on contract, property, and persons.[86] These fragmented sources offered a foundation for a workable fiduciary law in civilian Europe, which is only just coming into view.[87] In England fiduciary powers reach a recognisably modern form in Sugden's youthful treatise of 1808,[88] but these powers stretch back through the classical era of Nottingham and Hardwicke into the formative period of Chancery in the sixteenth and early seventeenth centuries.

An important point emerging from the history (or prehistory) of fiduciaries is that there can be trusts of incorporeals; in particular, one can have fiduciary management of a contractual power such as agency or partnership. One can if one likes describe these relationships in trust terms as holding the *custody* of a contractual power; you stand as trustee of an incorporeal res, and

---

85 Cf J Hackney, 'More Than a Trace of The Old Philosophy', in Birks (ed), *Classification of Obligations* (Oxford University Press, Oxford, 1997) at 123; PD Finn, *Fiduciary Obligations* (Sydney, Lawbook Company, 1977) at 1, citing LS Sealy, "Fiduciary Relationships" [1962] *Cambridge Law Journal* 69 and "Some Principles of Fiduciary Obligation" [1963] *Cambridge Law Journal* 119. The trust itself has been moving steadily in an in personam direction, especially since *McPhail v Doulton* [1971] AC 424; see *Schmidt v Rosewood Trust Ltd* [2003] 2 AC 709; DJ Hayton, "Developing the Obligation Characteristic of the Trust" (2001) 117 *Law Quarterly Review* 96; recent debate is summarised in J Hilliard, "On the irreducible core content of trusteeship – a reply to Professor Matthews and Parkinson" (2003) 17 *Trust Law International* 144.

86 D Johnston, *The Roman Law of Trusts* (Oxford University Press, Oxford, 1988).

87 For historical and modern treatments of the Civilian trust see R Helmholz and R Zimmermann (eds), *Itinera Fiduciae: Trust and Treuhand in Historical Perspective* (Duncker & Humblot, Berlin, 1998); WA Wilson (ed), *Trusts and Trust-like Devices* (UK National Committee on Comparative Law, London, 1981); M Lupoi, *Trusts: A Comparative Study* (translated by Simon Dix, Cambridge University Press, Cambridge, 2000); M Graziadei, U Mattei and L Smith (eds), *Commercial Trusts in European Private Law* (Cambridge University Press, Cambridge, 2005). To this corpus of law must be added the rise of international recognition of cross-border trusts: see DJ Hayton (ed), *Modern International Developments in Trusts Law* (Aspen, London, 1999); DJ Hayton (ed), *Extending the Boundaries of Trusts and Similar Ring-fenced Funds in the Twenty-first Century* (Aspen, London, 2002); J Harris, *The Hague Trusts Convention: Scope, Application and Preliminary Issues* (Hart Publishing, Oxford, 2002).

88 EB Sugden (later Lord St Leonards), *Practical Treatise on Powers* (London, 1808). Sugden was most proud of this work, which also proved to be a durable classic, exerting influence on American as well as English law. The last edition under Sugden's authorship was the eighth edition of 1861.

as a fiduciary you must account for your handling of the res. Because what is held is incorporeal and cannot be possessed, "custody" slightly strains our semantics unless we remember the key insight of Gaius — that all rights are incorporeal and yet may exist in the mind of lawyers as entities of value that may be moved, harmed, borrowed, misappropriated and so on. Dematerialisation of property happened in the second century AD, not in the era of late capitalism.[89]

The phenomenon of trusts of incorporeals is rife. We see it in the body of law on trusts of contracts;[90] in the institutions of partnership;[91] in agency.[92] To give just one historical example: in the 1713 case of *Dawson v Franklyn*[93] partners were fiduciaries of an expectation of a naval contract being awarded. They were liable to account for the expectation interest inhering in this asset to each other, even though the thing hardly counted as custodial property. The elaborate law of covenants to trust gives another example of this phenomenon. Yet another example is the trust of money without earmark, which is difficult to distinguish from more recognisable types of contractual account.[94] All of this suggests that the modernists' attempts to sharply distinguish custodial from non-custodial fiduciary responsibilities may run into trouble both conceptually and in practice.

What must be rendered up in accounting for a trust asset will commonly be decided by assessing where a business venture ought to have been at the time of accounting had it been managed properly. It will often be hard to describe a remedy for shortfall of the "asset" in terms distinguished from compensating for loss to an expectation interest, for the court of equity assesses the value the asset should have had at the time of judgment with the benefit of hindsight;[95] it can therefore embrace calculation of loss of chance.[96] This expectation interest can conceivably be more generous than contractual measures – though in

---

89   Cf MJ Horwitz, *The Transformation of American Law 1870-1960: The Crisis of Legal Orthodoxy* (Oxford University Press, New York, 1992) at 145-167; T Grey, 'The Disintegration of Property', in JR Pennock and JW Chapman (eds), *Property* (Nomos xxii, New New York University Press, York, 1980) at 69.

90   *Fletcher v Fletcher* (1844) 4 Hare 67; 67 ER 564, and the law emanating from that case, summarised in *Jacobs Law of Trusts in Australia* (6th ed by R Meagher and W Gummow, Butterworths, Sydney, 1997) at 99-103; HAJ Ford and W Lee, *Principles of the Law of Trusts* (3rd ed, Lawbook Company, Sydney, 1996, rev 2004) at [3270]-[3340].

91   See J Getzler and M Macnair, 'The Firm as an Entity before the Companies Acts', in P Brand, K Costello and WN Osborough (eds), *Adventures in the Law: Proceedings of the British Legal History Conference, Dublin 2003* (Dublin, 2005) at 263, 274-84.

92   SJ Stoljar, *The Law of Agency: Its History and Present Principles* (Sweet & Maxwell, London, 1961).

93   (1713) 4 Brown PC 626; 2 ER 427.

94   See JH Baker, *The Oxford History of the Laws of England Volume VI* (Oxford University Press, Oxford, 2003) at 875-878.

95   *Canson Enterprises Ltd v Boughton & Co* [1991] 3 SCR 534 at 556, per McLachlin J, cf La Forest J at 580-88; W Gummow, 'Compensation for Breach of Fiduciary Duty', in TG Youdan (ed), *Equity, Fiduciaries and Trusts* (Carswell, Toronto, 1989) at 69-73.

96   See for example, *Ferrari v Ferrari Invest (T'ville) P/L (in liq)* [2000] 2 Qd R 359; *Tavistock Holdings Pty Ltd v Saulsman* (1991) 9 ACLC 450; *Bristol & West v May May & Merrimans* [1996] 2 All ER 801 at 823, per Chadwick J.

much of the case-law the courts have set quite low the standard of managerial care and investment prowess expected of fiduciaries, so that mismanagement without clear breach of authority rarely leads to an accounting for loss.[97] This leads us to the next battleground in fiduciary law.

DUTIES OF LOYALTY, DUTIES OF SKILL AND CARE

In *Mothew* Lord Millett divided a fiduciary's duties between the core fiduciary duties of loyalty, and the duties of care and skill in management that are generated by the fiduciary office but which are not themselves "fiduciary" and which are therefore not protected with the full gamut of equitable procedures and remedies.[98] Some important results flow from this position: an honest but incompetent fiduciary is not in breach of fiduciary obligation; gross negligence does not convert fiduciary misfeasance into equitable fraud; incompetence can be indemnified by exemption clause; and common-law causal control mechanisms do apply to limit recovery.

I have given my reasons for disagreeing with this approach elsewhere, on the grounds that it is against voluminous authority ancient and modern, against basic equitable principle, and has unattractive policy implications.[99] Here I will reiterate just three points. The first is that gross negligence is not merely "negligence with a vituperative epithet", but shades into fraud as presumptive dishonesty, a type of objective fraud. This point is well made in a characteristic dictum in a late nineteenth-century company case. Writing of a grossly negligent company director, Kekewich J stated:

---

97   See for example, *Speight v Gaunt* (1883) 9 App Cas 1; *Nestle v National Westminster Bank plc* [1993] 1 WLR 1260.

98   *Bristol and West Building Society v Mothew* [1998] Ch 1 at 16-22. Millett LJ drew from Canadian and Australian authorities in formulating this doctrine, including *Girardet v Crease & Co* (1987) 11 BCLR (2d) 361 at 361-362, per Southin J; *LAC Minerals Ltd v International Corona Resources Ltd* (1989) 61 DLR (4th) 14 at 28 per La Forest J; and *Permanent Building Society v Wheeler* (1994) 14 ACSR 109 at 157, per Ipp J. Southin J's judgment in *Girardet* at 362 is perhaps the first significant statement of the modern doctrine and the key passage bears repetition:

"The word "fiduciary" is flung around now as if it applied to all breaches of duty by solicitors, directors of companies and so forth. But "fiduciary" comes from the Latin "fiducia" meaning "trust". Thus, the adjective, "fiduciary" means of or pertaining to a trustee or trusteeship. That a lawyer can commit a breach of the special duty of a trustee, eg, by stealing his client's money, by entering into a contract with the client without full disclosure, by sending a client a bill claiming disbursements never made and so forth is clear. But to say that simple carelessness in giving advice is such a breach is a perversion of words. The obligation of a solicitor of care and skill is the same obligation of any person who undertakes for reward to carry out a task. One would not assert of an engineer or physician who had given bad advice and from whom common law damages were sought that he was guilty of a breach of fiduciary duty. Why should it be said of a solicitor? I make this point because an allegation of breach of fiduciary duty carries with it the stench of dishonesty – if not deceit, then of constructive fraud".

99   J Getzler, 'Duty of Care' in Birks and Pretto (eds), *Breach of Trust* (Hart Publishing, Oxford, 2002) at 41.

"He is acquitted of dishonesty in the usual sense of the word. But in another sense he is not honest. It seems to me that a man who accepts such a trusteeship, and does nothing, ... never asks for explanation, and accepts flimsy explanations, is dishonest."[100]

In the sphere of modern company law, directors face sanctions enforcing due levels of care and skill that can be seen as core to their duties of fiduciary loyalty.[101] Commercial trustees at least should face similar pressures.

The second point is that unreasonably bad management leading to loss of investment has often been described as a breach of fiduciary obligation. It often seems a lesser duty than the intense loyalty requirements because the courts after 1875 set the standard of care so low. The leading case of the post-Judicature Act period is *Speight v Gaunt*,[102] where a family will trustee foolishly paid over a testamentary fund to a rogue believing that he was buying investments for the trust in local company shares. No account was ordered as there was no breach of the usual standards of local Yorkshire investment. The case showed that judges at that time, especially those from the common law side such as Lord Blackburn, were anxious to keep the standard of care very low in order to indemnify and protect trustees who were often mere volunteers, unremunerated managers acting in family and other intimate relationships as players in an elaborate gift economy. With the modern shift to professional remuneration of trustees who now act within impersonal markets, courts have moved towards raising and objectifiying the standard of care, and legislation in England has mirrored and accelerated that policy. This legislative trend returns the duty of care to the core of fiduciary duties — just as *Mothew* tries to expel it to the periphery.

The third point is that it is not only the courts who set standards of fiduciary care in today's financial markets. The law, setting levels of fiduciary care, has increasingly been subjected to contract through the device of building exemption clauses into settlements, which are held to bind beneficiaries as a condition for their accepting benefits under the trust.[103] So general are these clauses that the normal fiduciary level of care sometimes seems to be a superseded and nugatory default position. But this outburst of contractarian-

---

100   *Re Second East Dulwich 745th Starr-Bowkett Building Society* (1889) 68 LJ Ch 196 at 198 per Kekewich J. The same judge showed similar severity in *Glaiser v Rolls* (1889) 42 Ch D 436 (I am grateful to Nicola Murphy for this reference). For modern articulations of the idea of culpable negligence and recklessness by a fiduciary, see DM Phillips, "The Commercial Culpability Scale" (1982) 92 *Yale Law Journal* 228; T Frankel, "Fiduciary Law" (1983) 71 *California Law Review* 795; T Frankel, "Fiduciary Duties as Default Rules" (1995) 74 *Oregon Law Review* 1209; and see n 53 above.

101   As demonstrated by Heydon in chapter 9 of this book; and see generally E Ferran, *Company Law and Corporate Finance* (Oxford University Press, Oxford, 2000) at 206-38, The fact that nexus-of-contracts economic analysts of the corporation dislike this aspect of company law is a telling sign: cf E Rock and M Wachter, "Dangerous Liaisons: Corporate Law, Trust Law, and Interdoctrinal Legal Transplants" (2002) 96 *Northwestern University Law Review* 651; WA Gregory, "The Fiduciary Duty of Care: A Perversion of Words" (2005) 38 *Akron Law Review* 181.

102   (1883) 22 Ch D 727; (1883) 9 App Cas 1.

103   M Bryan, 'Contractual Modification of the Duties of Trustees', in S Worthington (ed), *Commercial Law and Commercial Practice* (Hart Publishing, Oxford, 2003) at 513.

ism in fiduciary law, fuelled by John Langbein's writings, may possibly have reached an apogee.[104] It is significant that in the volatile field of exemption clauses, the Law Commission has proposed expanding the irreducible core of trustee obligation to protect duties of care from contractual diminution.[105] The tightening of standards in New York and other key United States jurisdictions is an important part of this story. It may be that market forces are the driving power here, with investors not wishing to favour managerial interests with slack legal standards, but rather seeking heightened investor protection of beneficiary clients. Such a shift of market sentiment is demonstrated by Delaware's failure to attract trusts business by offering a stripped down pro-manager vehicle.[106] It is always possible that the law could tilt the other way; it has been suggested that the irreducible core be shrunk rather than expanded, allowing managers exemption even from the demands of exclusive loyalty.[107] The City of London seems genuinely divided as to whether financial markets would do better with a shrunken or expanded fiduciary core, and it will be fascinating to see how, in our post-Enron era, the debate will run. Arguably if capital market actors in the United States had enjoyed a rigorously enforced fiduciary law with a large core embracing loyalty and due performance, they would not now be enduring Eliot Spitzer's prosecutions and the pressures applied by Sarbanes-Oxley and other regulatory statutes.[108]

---

104 JH Langbein, "The Contractarian Basis of the Law of Trusts" (1995) 105 *Yale Law Journal* 625; JH Langbein, "Questioning the Trust Law Duty of Loyalty: Sole Interest or Best Interest?" (2005) 114 *Yale Law Journal* 929. For a sharp normative attack on Langbein's contractarian trust theories, and on Easterbrook and Fischel's reduction of fiduciary law to contract, see S FitzGibbon, "Fiduciary Relationships Are Not Contracts" (1999) 82 *Marquette Law Review* 303; see further references in n 129, below.

105 Law Commission, *Trustee Exemption Clauses* (Law Com CP 171, London, 2002) at 45-73. The City has launched a (predictable) campaign against this attempt to tighten legal regulation, arguing that trustees in capital markets should be free to negotiate exemptions in order to maintain London's attractiveness to capital market managers: see Financial Markets Law Committee, *Trustee Exemption Clauses* (Issue No 62, London, May 2004). Of greatest interest is the Scottish Law Commission's recent contribution, *Breach of Trust* (Discussion Paper No 123, Edinburgh, September 2003), which suggests an indemnity for personal liability for ultra vires investments made in good faith, but no other relaxation of intensity of duties; professional trustees' duties of care are expressly made non-excludable, and *Armitage v Nurse* [1998] Ch 241, allowing sweeping exemption of negligence liability for trustees in English law, is rejected: [3.43], [3.46].

106 See T Frankel, "The Delaware Business Trust Act Failure as the New Corporate Law" (2001) 23 *Cardozo Law Review* 325.

107 J Penner, 'Exemptions', in Birks and Pretto, *Breach of Trust* (Hart Publishing, Oxford, 2002) at 241; Langbein, "Questioning the Trust Law Duty of Loyalty: Sole Interest or Best Interest?", above n 104. The recent House of Lords decision in *Hilton v Barker Booth & Eastwood* [2005] 1 WLR 567 by contrast pushes against the relaxation of exclusive loyalty in cases such as *Kelly v Cooper* [1993] AC 205.

108 On the startling career of the New York Attorney-General in prosecuting corporate and financial fraud, see BA Masters, "Eliot Spitzer Spoils for a Fight" (*Washington Post* May 31, 2004) at A01. Spitzer's extraordinarily successful legal campaigns can be seen as a backlash not only against corrupt managers and financiers but also a reaction to the lacklustre record of the SEC, the NYSE and other regulatory agencies who are perceived to have failed to supply effective oversight of capital markets.

CONCURRENT LIABILITY

Whatever one's policy commitments (whether for strong, non-excludable, mandatory fiduciary law, or a weak, excludable, contractarian fiduciary law), does it make any real difference whether duties of care emanating from a fiduciary relationship are held to be within the core of fiduciary obligation or not? The answer is that it does matter for many practical reasons — limitation, exemption, causation, and so on. But it is also a basic conceptual question regarding the architecture of private law, a challenge to taxonomic rationality, to use Birksian language. If there is nothing unique about the duties of care and skill emanating from fiduciary relationships, then why would one want to open up a third form of concurrent liability, having equitable fiduciary care added to contractual and tortious duties of care?[109] The law already has a method, albeit "untidy" to add ex lege tort primary duties to supplement or articulate consensual contractual duties.[110] One who assumes responsibility by contract can today be liable concurrently for more onerous tort duties of care than one who assumes responsibility without contract. It seems more than untidy — simply otiose and confusing – to permit a raft of fiduciary ex lege obligations to arise as a third stream of primary liability where one person assumes responsibility for the affairs of another under a contract or trust. And in the same way it seems otiose to allow a concurrent remedial regime of equitable compensation as secondary obligations to arise alongside account for trust property and compensatory damages for breach of non-fiduciary duties of care emanating from trusting relationships. The use of tort actions as a second-tier of remedial devices defending primary obligations of property and contract is well known; we should not necessarily allow some new-fangled mirroring remedy of equitable compensation admission into the last category of the classical trilogy of persons, things and actions.

In *Henderson v Merrett Syndicates* Lord Browne-Wilkinson proposed a radical solution to the concurrency problem — to lump all duties of care from whichever source together into a single undifferentiated mass:[111]

> "The liability of a fiduciary for the negligent transaction of his duties is not a separate head of liability but the paradigm of the general duty to act with care imposed by law on those who take it upon themselves to act for or advise others. Although the historical development of the rules of law and equity have in the past caused different labels to be stuck on different manifestations of the duty, in truth the duty of care imposed on bailees, carriers, trustees, directors, agents, and others is the same duty: it arises from the circumstances in which the defendants were acting, not from their status or description. It is the fact that they have all assumed responsibility for the property or affairs of others which renders them liable for the careless performance of what they have undertaken to do."

---

109 P Birks poses this problem forcefully in "The Content of Fiduciary Obligation" (2000) 34 *Israel Law Review* 3; also (2002) 16 *Trust Law International* 34.

110 *Henderson v Merrett* [1995] 2 AC 145 at 184-194, per Lord Goff.

111 [1995] 2 AC 145 at 205.

Birks reacted to this rather indiscriminate approach by suggesting that fiduciary care is distinct from other forms of care because it is overlaid or infected by the fiduciary's overriding duty to act in a disinterested manner. He acknowledged that it is a fine line between his position that the status or office of the duty-holder influences the quality of the duty, and the overt recognition of a specific and distinct fiduciary duty of care. Overall he praised the *Henderson* approach for repressing the risk of full tripartite concurrent liability; a fiduciary may owe a heightened standard of care within the common-law spectrum, but not a different sort of duty of care sourced in equity.[112]

---

112 P Birks, "The Content of Fiduciary Obligation", above n 109 at 30-38. The key passages in Birks' analysis (at 33-34) are as follows:

> "There is not and there must not be a metatort of fiduciary negligence. But, at the same time, we cannot treat the obligation of disinterestedness as capable of having a separate existence. It can only exist parasitically upon an obligation to act in the interests of another with care and skill. The core trust obligation – synonymously, the core fiduciary obligation – is that inseverably compound obligation. And, even so, there is no distinct wrong of 'fiduciary negligence'.... Contentually, the trustee's obligation to show care and skill would be distinct from that of a mere contracting party or one who assumed a responsibility if the standard to be applied were different. But it cannot be said that the standard set by the prudent person from the world of business is different from that of the passenger on the Clapham bus. Reasonableness is always fine-tuned to context....
> [C]ontentually, carelessness in the promotion and preservation of the interests of the beneficiary is not a distinct wrong. That is, the primary duty is a duty of care according to a given standard, and the standard, though fine tuned, is the same standard as is set by the common duty of care."

Professor Birks' argument was presaged by SB Elliott, "Fiduciary liability for client mortgage frauds" (1999) 13 *Trust Law International* 74 at 79-81, 84-85, suggesting that the fiduciary status of an agent can "aggravate" a breach of duty to take care. Building on *Nocton*, Dr Elliott argues that negligence by itself cannot be disloyal, but that where a fiduciary is negligent and there is evidence of possible conflicts of interest to boot, the court can readily presume a breach of loyalty from the fact of negligence. He, therefore, sees *Mothew* as going too far in denying that fiduciary negligence has an identity separate from common negligence. Elliott has moved away from this position in his later analyses; see references at n 53 above. A distinct characterisation of fiduciary obligations is advanced by LD Smith, 'The Motive, Not the Deed', in Getzler (ed), *Rationalizing Property, Equity and Trusts* (LexisNexis, London, 2003) at 53, arguing that it is the motive brought to performance of duties rather than the content of those duties that is the decisive factor in analysing correct behaviour of a fiduciary. MDJ Conaglen, in *Locating Loyalty: Fiduciary Protection of Non-Fiduciary Duties* (Cambridge PhD thesis, 2003) at 137-152, and "The Nature and Function of Fiduciary Loyalty" (2005) 121 *Law Quarterly Review* 452, offers a framework where the fiduciary duties are objective in content and designed to uphold other duties. He argues that the duties of care of a fiduciary, unlike the duties to avoid conflicts of interest and self-dealing, are not factually distinct from normal tort and contract duties and do not warrant the special deterrent protection of fiduciary law. The obvious counter-argument is that heightened prophylactic pressure is appropriate in order to enforce the fiduciary's duties of competence and diligence, just as for any other core fiduciary duties: see J Getzler, 'Equitable Compensation and the Regulation of Fiduciary Relationships' in P Birks and F Rose, *Resulting Trusts and Equitable Compensation* (Lloyds of London Press, London, 2000); J Getzler, 'Duty of Care' in Birks and Pretto (eds), *Breach of Trust* (Hart Publishing, Oxford, 2002); and Justice Heydon in chapter 9 of this book, text accompanying nn 120-193. Heydon suggests, *pace* Birks, that equitable duties of care might in some contexts involve a lower standard than common-law counterparts, counterbalanced by more stringent causal rules and extensive remedies; on this view the contexts and traditions of the various duties of care in law and equity are too varied to be combined into a monotonic duty (chapter 9 of this book, text accompanying nn 166-173).

Other reactions to the new dispensation in *Henderson* are possible. If we were to take a serious anti-concurrency position, we might want the razor of conceptual parsimony to fall elsewhere. It is not clear why one would cut away fiduciary care alone at the primary obligational level, or equitable compensation alone at the secondary tier. Conceivably one could cut away tort duties of care and tort remedies as well wherever these are concurrent with contract or consensual trusts. Let us focus first on the contract-tort interface.

The judicial analyses welcoming concurrent tort-contract liability into the law offered in *Hawkins v Clayton*[113] in Australia and in *Henderson v Merrett* in England represent a change in the mood of the law and cannot be taken as uncontroversial.[114] In French law, for example, where there is a contractual relationship then contract must be the exclusive institution regulating the relationship. The law then discriminates between different intensities of contractual duty in order to articulate the correct standards in each contractual context.[115] The way in which our law has developed has been to convert the kind of demanding standards of care expected from a consensual fiduciary assumption of responsibility and to redescribe these as stand-alone tort duties — *Hedley Byrne & Co Ltd v Heller*.[116] With hindsight it may have been better for the ex lege duties of care necessary or desirable for close contract and trusting relationships to have been dealt with not by the broad brush of *Donoghue v Stevenson*-derived duties of care sounding as negligence actions in tort, but rather by implied terms of due care or good faith performance internal to contract, or due standards of prudent management internal to fiduciary law.[117] Thus there is a plausible sense in which *Hedley Byrne v Heller* was itself an unfortunate fusion experiment,[118] an unruly tort-based "equity" distorting adjacent categories of the law, quite apart from any jurisdictional reservations about the potential for courts to cross-blend categories of law and equity.

The rise of general tort duties may also dull our awareness that negligence or fault standards are not, and ought not become, a common or default position for all species of private obligation. Where one person invades without consent the interests of another, be it person or possessions or assets, the

---

113 (1988) 164 CLR 539.

114 The debate and relevant literature is summarised in A Burrows, *Remedies for Torts and Breach of Contract* (3rd ed, Oxford University Press, Oxford, 2004) at 5-9, adducing reasons for not collapsing contract into tort but (reservedly) accepting concurrent liability. The English courts were hostile to concurrent contract-tort liabilities as recently as 1986: see *Tai Hing Cotton Mill Ltd v Liu Chong Hing Bank Ltd* [1986] AC 80 at 107, per Lord Scarman.

115 M Bridge, "Mitigation of Damages in Contract and the Meaning of Avoidable Loss" (1989) 105 *Law Quarterly Review* 398 at 406-408; LD Smith, 'The Motive, Not the Deed', in Getzler (ed), *Rationalizing Property, Equity and Trusts* (LexisNexis, London, 2003) at 65-66; B Nicholas, *French Law of Contract* (2nd ed, Clarendon Press, Oxford, 1992) at 38-58.

116 [1964] AC 465.

117 A like argument is advanced in N McBride and A Hughes, "*Hedley Byrne* in the House of Lords: an interpretation" (1995) 15 *Legal Studies* 376 especially at 387-389; cf NJ McBride, "Duties of Care – Do They Really Exist?" (2004) 24 *Oxford Journal of Legal Studies* 417.

118 Cf R Meagher, JD Heydon, M Leeming, *Meagher Gummow and Lehane's Equity: Doctrines and Remedies* (4th ed, Butterworths, Sydney, 2002) at [2-145].

common law historically reached for a strict liability standard, wrapped in the envelopes of trespass actions vi et armis and contra pacem regis.[119] Direct force or transgression of boundaries destroying a claimant's interests without any prior risk-allocating relationship ought to lead to a prima facie strict responsibility simply for causing such loss; it is tantamount to theft or destruction of someone's property.[120] Some element of comparative assessment of fault creeps into the assessment of cause, but in the historical common law that judgment would have been hidden in the jury's discretion. Even when the law, driven by road accident cases involving reciprocal cause, moved over to fault liability at the doctrinal duty level, the strict liability instinct remained through probative devices such as res ipsa loquitur, and through measure of damages principles such as the eggshell skull rule. By contrast where there is a contractual or other consensual relationship, fault liability seems more appropriate for by the very act of choosing a particular contractual partner, a claimant is accepting a certain risk of the quality of performance likely to be received. This is a contractual version of the maxim volenti non fit injuria. This idea stretches back to the classical Roman rule that one cannot complain about the quality of one's partner or agent that one has selected.[121] Just as tort uses fault liability with streams of strict liability below the immediate surface, so contract uses a formal idea of strict liability — pacta sunt servanda — subject to underlying fault ideas such as the so-called duty to mitigate loss and the rule limiting damages to non-remote or reasonably foreseeable loss. Frustration and mistake doctrines also serve to shift contractual liability from a strict to fault liability basis. An historical surmise is that despite the fault-based, loss-oriented packaging of the secondary liability for breach of contract through the use of the assumpsit action on the case, the law still deployed a concept of the primary contract claim as a res, an asset or debt, which is protected as patrimony of the promisee.[122] Professor Smith has recently argued that even within this proprietary manner of thinking, contract remedies are always fault-based as they involve either a payment for wrongful breach or the enforcement of an agreed secondary remedy, such as an agreed sum where the money payment is

---

119 DJ Ibbetson, *A Historical Introduction to the Law of Obligations* (Oxford University Press, Oxford, 1999) at 58-70; JH Baker, *An Introduction to English Legal History* (4th ed, Butterworths, London, 2002) at 391-400 (personal property), and at 401-421 (negligent harm).

120 Cf RA Epstein, "A Theory of Strict Liability" (1973) 2 *Journal of Legal Studies* 151.

121 See for example, *Justinian's Institutes* (translated by P Birks and G McLeod, Duckworth, London, 1987) at 3.25.9:

"Does the liability of one partner to another in the action on partnership extend only to malice, as with a person who accepts a deposit? Or does it run to unintentional fault such as laziness and negligence? The opinion which has prevailed makes a partner liable for fault as well. But the measure is not the very highest standard of care. It is enough of the partner shows in the partnership affairs the same care as he usually displays in his own. *Someone who chooses a careless partner has only himself to blame.* [emphasis added]"

122 This is an abstract recasting of what possibly was at stake in *Slade's Case* (1602) 4 Co Rep 91a; 76 ER 1072; see further D Ibbetson, *A Historical Introduction to the Law of Obligations* (Oxford University Press, Oxford, 1999) at 135-40; J Baker, *An Introduction to English Legal History* (4th ed, Butterworths, London, 2002) at 333-346.

equivalent to specific performance; in the latter case there is no "breach" and hence no question of strict liability arises.[123]

Contributory negligence changes the landscape by applying apportionment at the stage of causal attribution of liability. It once operated in tort law directly as an all-or-nothing defence that in effect denied the causative potency of the defendant's conduct; it was only converted into a relative fault partial defence by legislation, driven by the social policy of improving the position of injured workers.[124] It has proved difficult to engraft the doctrine into contract. It is understandable that the High Court of Australia in *Astley* might choose to resist applying the tort contributory negligence statutes by analogy to contract and so maintain the surface of strict liability of promisors to achieve the result contracted for; but also understandable that in England *Vesta* is taken to open contract liability to possible contributory negligence controls by direct analogy from tort.[125] However the matter is not settled even in the English courts where *Astley* and *Pilmer* have recently been cited in order to resist the entry of contributory negligence into contract.[126] In Australia, by contrast, legislation has been passed in order to reverse the blunt exclusion of apportionment of contractual liability between claimant and defendant expressed in *Astley* and apply contributory negligence doctrines to contract as well as tort.[127] The separate doctrine that a version of relative fault applies in the assessment of both contract and

---

123 Cf SA Smith, *Contract Theory* (Oxford University Press, Oxford, 2004) at 376-386; and see GH Treitel, 'Fault in the Common Law of Contract', in M Bos and I Brownlie (eds), *Liber Amicorum for the Rt Hon Lord Wilberforce* (Clarendon Press, Oxford, 1987) at 185; M Bridge, "Mitigation of Damages in Contract and the Meaning of Avoidable Loss" (1989) 105 *Law Quarterly Review* 398.

124 See JG Fleming, *The Law of Torts* (9th ed, Lawbook Co, Sydney, 1998) at 302-305 on the historical operation of contributory negligence.

125 *Forsikringsaktielskapet Vesta v Butcher* [1989] AC 879; see E McKendrick, *Contract Law* (2nd ed, Oxford University Press, Oxford, 2005) at 1101-1108.

126 *Barings Plc & Anor v Coopers & Lybrand (a firm) & Ors* [2002] EWHC 461 at [155] and [2003] EWHC 1319 at [953]-[957], per Evans-Lombe J. It is significant that English law reformers have been guarded in advising that a contributory negligence element be applied explicitly to assessment of contract damages: see *Contributory Negligence as a Defence in Contract* (Law Com No 219, London, 1993).

127 See for example *Law Reform (Contributory Negligence and Apportionment of Liability) Act 2001* (South Australia). Section 4 of the Act applies a contributory negligence rule to limit damages arising from tort, breach of a contractual duty of care, or statute, but not trusts or fiduciary duty. Similar acts were passed in the other Australian States, but with still broader effect, for example, *Wrongs Amendment Act 2000* (Vic) and the *Law Reform (Miscellaneous Provisions) Amendment Act 2000*, applying to damages arising from any cause. These amendments have now been superseded by the radical reforms brought in by the "Civil Liability Acts" which were brought in at the time of the *Report of the Negligence Review Panel* (the "Ipp Report") (Canberra, 2002), following intense pressure from governments and the insurance industry to reduce their exposure to civil recovery. The States, Territories and Federal Government have now brought in non-standard statutes eliminating or cutting back on duties of care and capping liabilities. Joint and several or solidary liability has been replaced by apportionment, and the language of some of the legislation suggests that all civil heads of liability including fiduciary law are caught. Commentators have rightly expressed concern over the policies and principles of these statues, which failed to observe key principles of the Ipp Report and which have shattered the unity and coherence of Australian civil law. From a growing exegetical and critical literature, see J Dietrich, "Duty of Care under

tort damages (through the duty of mitigation) makes it more difficult to resist a like approach to causative ascription of liability (through contributory negligence), especially since courts have found it notoriously difficult to separate mitigation, contributory negligence, and remoteness in practice.

The area of primary, assumed fiduciary relationships (to be marked off from secondary, remedial fiduciary obligations) might have been thought to resemble contract more than tort. It has often been noticed that fiduciary relationships are commonly consensual and can be conceived as a layer superimposed on contractual relations, such as agency, joint ventures and so on.[128] American law and economics scholarship takes this one step further, seeing fiduciary relations simply as open-ended contracts with high levels of discretion arising as implied terms where the parties cannot specify "complete contracts".[129] Taking my earlier model associating tort with strict liability and contract with fault liability, the volenti aspects of fiduciary law would then plausibly lead to a fault-flavoured liability regime and contributory negligence and mitigation would then apply by strong natural affinity. But this is a false trail. Despite the volenti qualities of fiduciary law a more strict liability independent of relative fault is justifiable, as a separate stream to either invasive tort or consensual contractual relations, predicated on the dependency of the beneficiary on the fiduciary agent. The dependency takes two main forms: the difficulty of monitoring and controlling the fiduciary, and the vulnerability of the former to the latter's open-ended powers.[130] The quality of dependency is present in commercial as well as familial fiduciary relations. These vulnerabilities require greater legal sanctions than contract and tort in order to check the fiduciary's self-interest and keep the fiduciary to the mark of due performance. Hence it possibly was a wrong-turn for fiduciary care emerging from consensual fiduciary relations (involving "assumption of responsibility") to be expressed in *Hedley Byrne* in a fault-based tort packaging. Tort was used in *Hedley Byrne* because of the absence of orthodox "consideration" allowing the enforcement of a normal contract, but a more direct path would have been to declare a fiduciary responsibility in cases of professional advice and dependency, with a narrow scope set on the duty by the terms of the assumption of responsibility.

---

the Civil Liability Acts" (2005) 13 *Torts Law Journal* 17; J Watson, "From contribution to apportioned contribution to proportionate liability" (2004) 78 *Australian Law Journal* 126. For the purposes of this chapter, it need only be noted that there is a deep discordance between the stringent approach to fiduciary loss in the Australian courts and the policies restricting liability stated in the new legislation.

128 R Meagher, JD Heydon, M Leeming, *Meagher Gummow and Lehane's Equity: Doctrines and Remedies* (4th ed, Butterworths, Sydney, 2002) at [5-010].

129 FH Easterbrook and DR Fischel, "Contract and Fiduciary Duty" (1993) 36 *Journal of Law and Economics* 425; and see JH Langbein, "The Contractarian Basis of the Law of Trusts" (1995) 105 *Yale Law Journal* 625, arguing that custodial trusts operate as contract-like devices for the benefit of third parties.

130 This much is conceded even by those in a law-and-economics position: see for example, LE Ribstein, "Are Partners Fiduciaries?" (2004) *University of Illinois Legal Working Paper* 10. JD Heydon analyses vulnerability as a hallmark of fiduciary relationships in the corporate context in chapter 9 of this book, text accompanying nn 149-161.

The above analysis suggests some mild modification of the celebrated identification by McLachlin J (as she then was) in *Canson* of the "trust at the heart" of consensual fiduciary relationships, supposedly marking them off from egoistic contract and tort relations.[131] It is not that actors are more egoistic when they contract into responsibility, or when they have tort responsibilities imposed upon them; nor are they less egoistic when they stand as fiduciaries. Rather it is the quality of vulnerability to power, including difficulties of monitoring and controlling the managerial party, that distinguishes the fiduciary relationship from the paradigm cases of contracts-as-deals or torts-as-invasions.

The mixture of vulnerability and difficulty of monitoring and control is the key policy reason why the law requires parties in that status to act differently, to take a more strict responsibility for the affairs of another. Thinking in a classical Roman fashion, if one puts oneself into a stereotypical relationship one triggers a stereotyped menu of legal responses. Hence fiduciary relationships ought not be collapsed into contract or tort, and tripartite concurrent liability for duties of care makes sense. If simplification is called for, it is plausible that we should curb concurrent contract-tort and fiduciary-tort liability — that is, roll back tort duties and expand both contract and fiduciary law to cover the necessary space.

The analysis presented here suggests a response to the challenges laid down by Lord Millett in *Mothew* and Lord Browne-Wilkinson in *Henderson*. In deciding the correct lines between contractual, fiduciary and tort-based duties of care, the demotion of fiduciary-based duties — which represents a major shift in our law — involves the complete acceptance of the architecture left by *Hedley Byrne*. But *Hedley Byrne* may well have been a mistake; civil obligations should not generally be overlaid or dominated by ex lege duties to take reasonable care sounding in tort. Such territory could instead be better covered by doctrines internal to contractual and fiduciary law.

"DISHONEST" BREACH

In *Armitage v Nurse* Millett LJ (as he then was) suggested that a fiduciary breaching an obligation dishonestly would be subjected to the gamut of fiduciary remedies, but in a case of honest breach of duties of care would not.[132] Later courts and commentators have developed this thought, seeming to move the law of fiduciary breach almost to a requirement of dishonest mens rea.[133] The "post-*Mothew*" model proposes that outside primary custody duties, only subjectively dishonest breaches of the loyalty requirements, which may include advertent decisions to act imprudently in reliance on trust indemnity

---

131 (1991) 85 DLR (4th) 129 at 163. Mason J's formulation in *Hospital Products Ltd v US Surgical Corp* (1984) 156 CLR 41 at 96-97 may be preferred; see references in n 83 above.

132 *Armitage v Nurse* [1998] Ch 241 at 251-56.

133 See for example, *Swindle v Harrison* [1997] 4 All ER 705 at 715-18 per Evans LJ; *Bank of New Zealand v New Zealand Guardian Trust Co Ltd* [1999] 1 NZLR 664 and [1999] 1 NZLR 213 (Fisher J); G Vos, "Linking Chains of Causation: An Examination of New Approaches to Causation in Equity and the Common Law" [2001] *Cambridge Law Journal* 337.

clauses,[134] should be treated with causal rules disfavouring the misfeasant fiduciary; absent such a level of mens rea, all control mechanisms should apply to losses flowing from fiduciary breach. This brings the causal rules for fraudulent or dishonest breach into line with the pro-plaintiff causal rules found in the tort of common-law deceit.[135]

Should the mind-state of a fiduciary who breaches an obligation be a significant factor in setting remedy? Such a position might be described as an exaggeration of the original *Mothew* theory. There Millett LJ suggested that the only type of fiduciary fraud is disloyalty, but it is not clear that disloyalty requires advertent betrayal; "wilful default" did not connote a subjective mens rea in historical equity. In the new mens rea gloss the only type of fiduciary disloyalty outside custodial duties which are to be subjected to full remedial discipline is actual fraud. If there is a policy idea here it is perhaps that strongly deterrent rules only make sense against the strongly culpable; and just as negligent fiduciaries are not very culpable, so are those who accidentally fall into conflicts of interest or other technical breaches.

This development is particularly novel and questionable. Equity has long allowed a ready use of objective evidence in order to presume fraud or other conduct binding the conscience, expressed in classic judgments of Lord Hardwicke,[136] Lord Nottingham,[137] Lord Eldon[138] and Sir William Grant MR.[139] This approach has raised constant controversy in the post-Judicature system. Lawyers have vehemently disagreed over whether the law should treat as an actionable fraud conduct which is not necessarily tainted by a proven subjective intention to deceive. Common lawyers after 1875 in the fused courts

---

134 *Armitage v Nurse* [1998] Ch 241 at 251-259.

135 As per *Doyle v Olby (Ironmongers) Ltd* [1969] 2 QB 158; *Smith New Court Securities Ltd v Citibank NA* [1997] AC 254 (remoteness criteria not applied where losses flow from deceit, though there remains a duty to mitigate); *Kuwait Airways Corp v Iraqi Airways Co & Anor (Nos 4 and 5)* [2002] 2 AC 883 (deceit rules displacing remoteness criteria apply also to dishonest conversion but semble but-for causal rule not applied so rigorously to innocent conversion); *Standard Chartered Bank v Pakistan National Shipping Corporation* [2001] QB 167; [2003] 1 AC 959 (contributory negligence is no defence in cases of deceit).

136 *Earl of Chesterfield v Janssen* (1751) 2 Ves Sen 125; 28 ER 82; R Meagher, JD Heydon, M Leeming, *Meagher Gummow and Lehane's Equity: Doctrines and Remedies* (4th ed, Butterworths, Sydney, 2002) at [12-050]. The use of presumptions to combat fraud goes deep into equity history; see for example, *Wiseman v Beak & Tyson* (1689) 2 Freem, 111; 22 ER 1092 at [112], per Keck Lord Cssr: "and it was said per Keck, as fortifications of fraud do increase, so the courts of equity must invent new batteries against them". More briefly, "fraud is infinite": *Natal Land and Colonization Co v Good and Bowes* (1868) LR 2 PC 121; 5 Moo PC NS 132; 16 ER 465; *Reddaway v Banham* [1896] AC 199 at 221, per Lord Macnaghten.

137 *Cook v Fountain* (1676) 3 Swans 585; 36 ER 984, per Lord Nottingham C; and note objectivist gloss put on this case in Isaacs J's great dissenting speech in *Commissioner of Stamp Duties (Queensland) v Jolliffe* (1920) 28 CLR 178 at 187-194; cf *T Choithram International SA v Pagarani* [2001] 2 All ER 492 .

138 *Bulkley v Wilford* (1834) 2 Cl & Fin 102 at 177; 6 ER 1094 at 1122; SC 8 Bligh NS 111 at 143; 5 ER 888 at 899-900, cited in SB Elliott, "Fiduciary liability for client mortgage frauds" (1999) 13 *Trust Law International* 74 at 80, and see references collected by Dr Elliott at 79, n 31.

139 *Caffrey v Darby* (1801) 6 Ves Jun 488 at 495-496; 31 ER 1159 at 1162, discussed in J Getzler, 'Equitable Compensation and the Regulation of Fiduciary Relationships' in P Birks and F Rose (eds), *Resulting Trusts and Equitable Compensation* (Lloyds of London Press, London, 2000) at 256.

charged Chancery lawyers with being swayed by the facts and equities of each case and holding to no principles; and equity lawyers hit back claiming that common lawyers misunderstood the policies of equity which was apt to find actionable misconduct proven by presumptions.[140] The controversy reached a climax in *Derry v Peek*, and since then the basic issues have hardly gone away, viz, how to measure actionable fraud and whether subjective dishonesty must be proved.[141]

Recently the Court of Appeal in *Walker v Stones*[142] indicated that it saw the formulations in *Armitage* on breach of express trust as creating a degree of tension with the Privy Council's *Royal Brunei* tests for accessory liability. In *Royal Brunei* Lord Nicholl elaborated a theory of dishonesty akin to recklessness:[143]

"acting dishonestly, or with a lack of probity, which is synonymous, means simply not acting as an honest person would in the circumstances. This is an objective standard. At first sight this may seem surprising. Honesty has a connotation of subjectivity, as distinct from the objectivity of negligence. Honesty, indeed, does have a strong subjective element in that it is a description of a type of conduct assessed in the light of what a person actually knew at the time, as distinct from what a reasonable person would have known or appreciated. Further, honesty and its counterpart dishonesty are mostly concerned with advertent conduct, not inadvertent conduct. Carelessness is not dishonesty. Thus for the most part dishonesty is to be equated with conscious impropriety. However, these subjective characteristics of honesty do not mean that individuals are free to set their own standards of honesty in particular circumstances. The standard of what constitutes honest conduct is not subjective. Honesty is not an optional scale, with higher or lower values according to the moral standards of each individual. If a person knowingly appropriates another's property, he will not escape a finding of dishonesty simply because he sees nothing wrong in such behaviour. In most situations there is little difficulty in identifying how an honest person would behave. Honest people do not intentionally deceive others to their detriment. Honest people do not knowingly take others' property. Unless there is a very good and compelling reason, an honest person does not participate in a transaction if he knows it involves a misapplication of trust assets to the detriment of the beneficiaries. Nor does an honest person in such a case deliberately close his eyes and ears, or deliberately not ask questions, lest he learn something he would rather not know, and then proceed regardless."

In *Walker v Stones* Sir Christopher Slade after reviewing *Armitage* suggested that different formulations of the concepts of fraud and dishonesty might be

---

140 M Macnair, *The Law of Proof in Early Modern Equity* (Duncker & Humblot, Berlin, 1999) at 267-275. The heightened availability of evidence in modern litigation is not necessarily a reason to discard the historical objective presumptions of culpability, as wrongdoers not keeping up to their fiduciary duties are more likely than not to conceal than reveal their delinquent activities; cf JH Langbein, "Questioning the Trust Law Duty of Loyalty: Sole Interest or Best Interest?" (2005) 114 *Yale Law Journal* 929.

141 CM Reed, "*Derry v Peek* and Negligence" (1987) 8 *Journal of Legal History* 64.

142 [2001] QB 902 at 937-942.

143 *Royal Brunei Airlines Sdn Bhd v Tan* [1995] 2 AC 378 at 389.

used in different pockets of equity doctrine, but he was disquieted by tension between the authorities:[144]

"There is an obvious difference of emphasis between the judgments in *Royal Brunei Airlines Sdn Bhd v Tan* [1995] 2 AC 378 and *Armitage v Nurse* [1998] Ch 241 so far as they relate to the concept of dishonesty and it has been suggested that they may be irreconcilable. I do not think they are. The decision in *Royal Brunei Airlines Sdn Bhd v Tan* [1995] 2 AC 378 was cited to the Court of Appeal in *Armitage v Nurse* [1998] Ch 241. Millett LJ did not purport to distinguish *Royal Brunei Airlines Sdn Bhd v Tan* [1995] 2 AC 378, either on the grounds that it related to the liability of accessories or on any other grounds. As already stated, I can see no grounds for applying a different test of honesty in the context of a trustee exemption clause ... from that applicable to the liability of an accessory in a breach of trust. It would be surprising if the court in *Armitage v Nurse* [1998] Ch 241 had regarded itself as differing from *Royal Brunei Airlines Sdn Bhd v Tan* [1995] 2 AC 378 without saying so or explaining why. I think that in the relevant passage from his judgment quoted above [1998] Ch 241 at 250-251 — and in particular in saying that if trustees deliberately commit a breach of trust they are not dishonest provided that 'they do so in good faith and in the honest belief that they are acting in the interests of the beneficiaries' — Millett LJ was directing his mind to the not uncommon case of what Selwyn LJ had once described as 'judicious breaches of trust'. I think it most unlikely that he would have intended this dictum to apply in a case where a solicitor-trustee's perception of the interests of the beneficiaries was so unreasonable that no reasonable solicitor-trustee could have held such belief. Indeed in my opinion such a construction of the clause could well render it inconsistent with the very existence of an effective trust."

Walker v Stones was appealed to the House of Lords but settled before hearing, and so we must wait for a reasoned Lords decision clarifying the status of subjectivist theories of fiduciary duty and duty of care under the express trust.[145] In the interim we have the House of Lords decision in *Twinsectra Ltd v Yardley*[146] exploring how far objective measures should be used in determining the presence of dishonesty in third party intermeddling or dishonest assistance in breach of trust. Lord Hutton who gave the leading majority speech tended to emphasise subjective aspects of dishonesty, writing: "dishonesty requires knowledge by the defendant that what he was doing would be regarded as dishonest by honest people, although he should not escape a finding of dishonesty because he sets his own standards of honesty and does not regard as dishonest what he knows would offend the normally accepted standards of honest conduct." Lord Millett's dissenting speech in *Twinsectra* interestingly expressed a more objective view of dishonesty than that of the majority; he reinterpreted *Royal Brunei* to mean a wilful act that objectively falls below standards of honesty. This approach would increase the strictness of liability in

---

144 *Walker v Stones* [2001] QB 902 at 941.
145 In *Hilton v Barker Booth and Eastwood* [2005] 1 WLR 567 at 575, Lord Walker issued a casual obiter dictum adopting the reasoning in *Mothew* concerning fiduciary duty and negligence, but since the point was neither argued nor relevant to the facts of the case this statement has uncertain authoritative or persuasive force.
146 [2002] 2 AC 164.

the area of breach of trusts and fiduciary duties, and may represent a shift from the judge's positions in *Mothew* and in *Armitage*.[147]

If honesty in modern equity has strong objective elements, as Lord Millett latterly argued, then the "post-*Mothew*" requirement of mens rea or some intention "equivalent to fraud" as a precondition of full fiduciary liability seems either minimal or redundant. Fraud here plausibly means nothing more than wilful, conscious default of due standards that the party ought to have known about — what traditional equity judges were wont to call simply "unconscionability" not so very long ago.[148] If a more intensely subjective mens rea is required as a component of fiduciary breach then it collides with basic equity jurisprudence setting standards in other areas of doctrine.[149]

Coda: Prophylaxis and Excuse in Equity

It is commonly observed that a major source of fiduciary law and of the distinct equitable causal rules attached to that law is a policy of prophylaxis or deterrence. It is tempting to argue that if the deterrent policies underpinning this area of law were to be explicitly recognised and emphasised through awards of exemplary or punitive damages in equity, then the path might be opened to a more thoroughgoing fusion of legal and equitable rules. Special damages awards to repress wrongdoing rather than variegated causal rules could be a useful direct method to uphold the community's independent interest in

---

147 *Twinsectra Ltd v Yardley*, above n 146 at 194-202. Lord Millett wrote (at 200):

"The question for your Lordships is not whether Lord Nicholls was using the word dishonesty in a subjective or objective sense in *Royal Brunei Airlines Sdn Bhd v Tan* [1995] 2 AC 378. The question is whether a plaintiff should be required to establish that an accessory to a breach of trust had a dishonest state of mind (so that he was subjectively dishonest in the *R v Ghosh* sense); or whether it should be sufficient to establish that he acted with the requisite knowledge (so that his conduct was objectively dishonest). This question is at large for us, and we are free to resolve it either way.

I would resolve it by adopting the objective approach. I would do so because:

(1) Consciousness of wrongdoing is an aspect of mens rea and an appropriate condition of criminal liability: it is not an appropriate condition of civil liability. This generally results from negligent or intentional conduct. For the purpose of civil liability, it should not be necessary that the defendant realised that his conduct was dishonest; it should be sufficient that it constituted intentional wrongdoing.

(2) The objective test is in accordance with Lord Selborne C's statement in *Barnes v Addy* (1874) LR 9 Ch App 244 and traditional doctrine. This taught that a person who knowingly participates in the misdirection of money is liable to compensate the injured party. While negligence is not a sufficient condition of liability, intentional wrongdoing is. Such conduct is culpable and falls below the objective standards of honesty adopted by ordinary people".

148 See for example, Nourse LJ's judgment in *BCCI v Akindele* [2001] Ch 437 at 455. The opacity of the concept of unconscionability need not matter if judges and legal advisers to parties have some communal sense for what it means; in a similar fashion the opaque probative standard of "beyond reasonable doubt" is held to resist definition yet may guide even a lay jury.

149 Contra LD Smith, 'The Motive, Not the Deed', in J Getzler (ed), *Rationalizing Property, Equity and Trusts* (LexisNexis, London, 2003), who argues for a radically subjective test for fiduciary breach. See further I Greenstreet, "Trustees, exoneration clauses and dishonesty in occupational pension schemes" (2004) 18 *Trust Law International* 132.

fiduciaries offering high levels of loyalty, skill and care to clients who are vulnerable to fiduciary default. Here Canadian and United States experience offers important lessons and warnings. Parties are led by the availability of large damages awards to seek the fiduciary label in order to open the gate to exemplary damages seeking to punish and deter, rather than damages calculated simply to vindicate rights and enforce duties.

We can make a distinction here between ex ante and ex post deterrence. Traditional fiduciary policy favours the former policy, which we may call (borrowing from criminology) a "broken windows" approach. This involves having deterrent incentives that are triggered at a low threshold of wrongdoing, sanctioning even the smallest infractions of bright-line fiduciary rules, and not simply reacting in force to major breakdowns in honesty and loyalty. The discretionary relief afforded to breaching fiduciaries through the inherent jurisdiction of the court or the statutory jurisdiction to reduce damages or give relief on terms represents a prerogative of mercy that does not disturb the basic and constant prospective deterrence of the fiduciary causal rules.[150] Hence the decision of the majority in *Digital Pulse* may be defended on policy and principle; the rejection of deterrent damages in equity is not simply a case of jurisdictional denial. Vigorously repress small breaches and the large breaches will be less likely. Indeed, by constant practice at being trustworthy and trusting, cultivated by the law and ethos of fiduciary duties and remedies, it may be that true trust has more of a chance to emerge.[151]

I have suggested that the way forward in the equitable compensation debate does not lie in scrutiny of the correct historical taxonomy of the various genres of account and compensation and the permissible limits of fusion. The history must be known, but it does not yield determinate answers to the really important questions concerning the content of duties and the correct approach to causation and remedy. History and precedent can help reveal the extent of our policy choices but it cannot make those choices for us.

---

150 J Getzler, 'Equitable Compensation and the Regulation of Fiduciary Relationships' in P Birks and F Rose (eds), *Restitution and Equity: Vol I, Resulting Trusts and Equitable Compensation* (Lloyds of London Press, London, 2000) at 251ff; cf J Lowry and R Edmunds, 'Excuses', in P Birks and A Pretto (eds), *Breach of Trust* (Hart Publishing, Oxford, 2002) at 269.

151 D Gambetta, 'Can We Trust Trust?', in D Gambetta (ed), *Trust: Making and Breaking Cooperative Relations* (Basil Blackwell, Oxford and New York, 1988) at 213.

11

Unique Rules for the Unique Institution, the Trust

DAVID HAYTON

Maitland[1] made us very aware that equity is merely a "gloss" on the common law and is not a self-sufficient system like the common law. However, equity's greatest invention, the trust, has developed its own unique free-standing rules. The question is whether in the 21st Century such rules should be subsumed within some broader scheme as part of a process of fusion of law and equity flowing from the fusion of the administration of law and equity in the courts, and whether these rules should be modified or extended in the light of developments at common law.

THE UNIQUENESS OF THE TRUST CONCEPT AS A PROPRIETARY CONCEPT

Historically, the trust was developed by the Court of Equity in respect of property which the Common Law Court treated simply as fully owned by its apparent owner. Equity, however, regarded this legal owner as a trustee subject to obligations, whether expressly created or implied by equity, in favour of the beneficiaries intended to receive the full economic benefits provided by the trustee's management of the assets from time to time comprised within the trust fund. This trust fund includes, through the equitable doctrine of over-reaching, assets substituted for other assets within the fund where the trustee acted rightfully, and, at the beneficiaries' option, can extend to substituted assets wrongfully acquired by the trustee, whether on behalf of himself or the trust.[2] The equitable obligations came to extend beyond personal obligations of

---

1   FW Maitland, *Equity* (2nd ed, Cambridge University Press, Cambridge, 1936) at 18-19.
2   The trustee's expressly or impliedly agreed primary obligation is not to do anything that is not authorised, so if he does something that is actually unauthorised he cannot deny the beneficiaries' claim that this was a rightful authorised substituted performance of his primary obligation; see 315–317 of P Millett, 'Proprietary Restitution' at chapter 12 in this book and P Birks and A Pretto (eds), *Breach of Trust* (Hart Publishing, Oxford, 2002) at chapter 4, 'Overreaching' by D Fox, and chapter 13, 'Overview' by D Hayton at 390-391, and n 23 below.

the trustee relating to such property so that the beneficiaries also came to acquire equitable proprietary interests in that property, capable of binding everyone except a bona fide purchaser of the property for value without notice of the beneficiaries' interests.

In contrast, legal proprietary interests, which are normally much more discoverable for purchasers than equitable proprietary interests, bind everyone. This basic difference has been confused by legislation[3] requiring certain interests in land, whether legal or equitable, to be registered if they are to bind purchasers. However, the rules governing priority of legal and equitable propri- etary interests are very well-established so that, as Professor Burrows has accepted,[4] it would seem to be a futile task to use different terminology to replicate the effect of such rules without distinguishing between legal and equitable interests. Nevertheless, assimilation of law and equity to the extent of making the equitable tracing rules available as evidential rules to support legal, as well as equitable, proprietary interests does make very good sense where the rules at law in support of legal proprietary interests happen to be inadequate for the task of protecting the claimant's original proprietary interest. Lords Steyn and Millett justifiably made this clear in forceful obiter dicta in *Foskett v McKeown* [5] which should be taken up by judges in all common law jurisdic- tions.[6] However, the "cherry-picking" possibilities[7] available to beneficiaries against a wrongdoing trustee withdrawing moneys from a bank account (and who cannot deny or disprove whatever the beneficiaries claim) should probably not be available in support of a legal claimant suing a thief or receiver of his stolen property, who knowingly did him wrong but who did not undertake any primary obligations to him.

It is a truism that like claims should be treated alike and different claims treated differently in ways appropriate to the differences, taking account of the nature of the relevant obligations and policy considerations. If two valuable paintings are stolen from one house, but one painting is owned by the house- owner while the other painting is owned by a trustee but in the authorised custody of the house-owner as a beneficiary, the tracing process available to the trustee and his beneficiaries should be equally available to the house-owner in respect of his own painting if his legal remedies are inadequate. If the "fence", who sold the paintings to an undiscoverable person, is insolvent, but the proceeds of sale can be traced into a flat purchased with the proceeds of sale of the two paintings, it makes no sense for such flat to be available to satisfy the

---

3   For example, *English Land Charges Act 1925* (UK) and *English Land Charges Act 1972* (UK), *Land Registration Act 2002* (UK).

4   A Burrows, "We Do This At Common Law But That In Equity"(2002) 22 *Oxford Journal of Legal Studies* 1 at 5.

5   [2001] 1 AC 102 at 113 and 129-130.

6   Accepted in *Bracken Parners Ltd v Gutteridge* [2003] WTLR 1241 at 31 and by Mantell LJ on appeal in [2004] WTLR 599; [2004] 1 BCLC 377 at [29], though in *Shalson v Russo* [2003] WTLR 1165 at [104], Rimer J held a first instance judge should follow the traditional view. This is supported by the restrictive approach to precedent of the Court of Appeal in *National Westminster Bank plc v Spectrum Plus Ltd* [2004] 3 WLR 503, so that a leapfrog appeal to the House of Lords is strictly necessary.

7   *Shalson v Russo* [2003] WTLR 1165 at [144].

equitable claim relating to the trust painting but not to satisfy the house-owner's legal claim to his absolutely owned painting. If the flat had been purchased for £1 million as to 60% with the proceeds of sale of the trust painting and 40% with the proceeds of the house-owner's painting, then the flat should be treated as beneficially owned 60:40 by the trust and the house-owner, so that it can then be sold and the proceeds paid in 60:40 proportions to the trustee and the house-owner.

Whether law and equity are administered in separate courts or in the one court, there is clearly scope for each to learn from the other in striving to produce an appropriately just response to the relevant events. However, this is much more likely when the one court is accustomed to dealing with law and equity and so is more aware of any inappropriate discrepancies between them. Lords Steyn and Millett, one a common lawyer and one an equity lawyer, have in administering law and equity in the House of Lords, made clear a most inappropriate tracing discrepancy that needs to be removed. Are there other discrepancies when examining the unique personal obligations of trustees?

THE UNIQUENESS OF TRUSTEES' PERSONAL OBLIGATIONS

Introduction

At law in negligence and in contract, McLachlin J (as she then was) in a passage[8] endorsed by the High Court of Australia,[9] stated that "the parties are to be taken to be independent and equal actors, concerned primarily with their own self-interest", so "the law seeks a balance between enforcing obligations by awarding compensation and preserving optimum freedom for those involved in the relationship." In the case of a trust, while the wealthy settlor (advised by her lawyer) and the trustee (advised by its lawyer) are usually independent and equal actors, the settlor drops out of the picture and has no enforcement rights,[10] leaving the beneficiaries very exposed and vulnerable to the conduct of the trustee managing the trust property over a lengthy period for the benefit of the beneficiaries. Thus, equity drastically diminishes the trustee's freedom of action by insisting that the trustee is not only confined to what is authorised by the trust instrument but must act with undivided loyalty so as exclusively to further the interests of the beneficiaries, being obliged to insulate himself from conflict of interest situations which might affect his judgment. Equity imposes strict liability for the consequences of any breach of these primary obligations as a positive incentive for the trustee to properly carry out his duties in the best interests of the beneficiaries.

---

8   *Canson Enterprises Ltd v Boughton & Co* [1991] 3 SCR 534 at 543 (and to similar effect in *Norberg v Wynrib* [1992] 2 SCR 226 at 272 quoted in *Pilmer v Duke Group Ltd (In Liq)* (2001) 207 CLR 165 at 196-197).

9   *Youyang Pty Ltd v Minter Ellison* (2003) 212 CLR 484 at 501.

10   *Re Astor's ST* [1952] Ch 534 at 542; *Bradshaw v University College of Wales* [1987] 3 All ER 200 at 203. He may, however, have express powers within the trust structure exercisable by him as power-holder (not as settlor).

As Megarry V-C stated in *Cowan v Scargill*,[11] "the starting point is the duty of trustees to exercise their powers in the best interests of the present and future beneficiaries of the trust, holding the scales impartially between different classes of beneficiaries. This duty of the trustees towards their beneficiaries is paramount. They must, of course, obey the law; but subject to that, they must put the interests of their beneficiaries first." Furthermore, Lord Browne-Wilkinson has emphasised[12] that "the basic right of a beneficiary is to have the trust duly administered in accordance with the provisions of the trust instrument, if any, and the general law."

Thus, the primary obligations of the trustee are faithfully to perform the trust provisions in authorised fashion and with altruistic loyalty in the best interests of the beneficiaries. He is not authorised to act otherwise,[13] though it is open to the beneficiaries to treat unauthorised acts as substitute performance of this primary obligation. While at law a person is permitted to be a "bad" person so long as reimbursing losses caused by bad conduct, equity, at the behest of the beneficiaries, compels a trustee to be a "good" person who cannot deny the beneficiaries allegations that the trustee must be treated as having acted as a good person where this is to their advantage.[14] The trustee must then account to the beneficiaries for this substituted performance of his primary obligations which exist whether or not there is any breach,[15] though sought to be enforced only after a breach.[16] No question arises of reparation for losses (as where a secondary obligation to replace losses arises for negligent intra vires conduct), so rules of causation and remoteness are irrelevant as Dr Elliott and Professor Mitchell have pointed out.[17]

The proscriptive primary obligation of altruistic loyalty and liability for unauthorised conduct in breach

In order to try to ensure full compliance with the trustee's paramount duty to exercise his powers in the best interests of the beneficiaries by removing the trustee from temptation, it is trite law[18] that a trustee (unless authorised by the

---

11   [1985] Ch 270 at 286-287.

12   *Target Holdings Ltd v Redferns* [1996] 1 AC 421 at 433.

13   *Re Smith* [1896] 1 Ch 71 at 77.

14   See Lord Millett when Millett J in "Bribes and Secret Commissions" [1993] *Restitution Law Review* 7 at 19-20 (approved by *Attorney-General of Hong Kong v Reid* [1994] 1 AC 324 at 337) and in 'Proprietary Restitution' in chapter 12 of this book.

15   See R Chambers, 'Liability' in P Birks and A Pretto (eds) *Breach of Trust* (Hart Publishing, Oxford, 2002), chapter 1 at 6.

16   However, it is not necessary to plead and prove a breach of trust in order to have the trustee account for any misapplied property: *Ahmed Angullia bin Hadjee v Estate & Trust Agencies (1927) Ltd* [1938] AC 624 at 636-637.

17   C Mitchell and S Elliott, "Remedies for Dishonest Assistance" (2004) 67 *Modern Law Review* 16 at 23-31 dealing with the nature of a trustee's liability before that of the facilitator of a breach of trust. This is further developed in J Edelman and S Elliott, "Money remedies against trustees" (2004) *Trust Law International* 116. Also see P Millett on 'Proprietary Restitution' in chapter 12 of this book.

18   D Hayton, *Underhill and Hayton, Law of Trusts and Trustees* (16th ed, Butterworths, London, 2003) at Articles 33 and 59.

trust instrument) must not place himself in a position where there is a sensible possibility of a conflict between his self-interest and his paramount duty to further the beneficiaries' best interests — or if such a conflict arises he must further the beneficiaries' interests — and he must not make a profit out of the trust property or his office as trustee. If such duty is broken, the trustee has acted in an unauthorised fashion and so is strictly required to disgorge all profits as a substituted performance of his primary obligation without any time-barring of claims.[19] It is immaterial that such profits could not otherwise have been obtained, that the trustee acted with subjective honesty and in what he perceived to be the beneficiaries' best interests or that the trustee made the profits from using his own assets and skills. He undertook to be loyal but was disloyal, whether subjectively or objectively, and so must be put in the position he was in before his disloyal conduct, thereby making it futile to be disloyal.

In the special case where a trustee receives a present as a secret commission or bribe then, as Sir George Jessel MR stated,[20] he is bound at the beneficiaries' option "to account either for the value at the time of the present he was receiving, or to account for the thing itself and its proceeds if it had increased in value." Thus, if the gift comprised shares each worth £80 at the time of the gift but only £1 at the date of trial the defendant trustee is liable at £80 a share. He should have sold the assets forthwith and treated the proceeds as trust property, equity looking on as done that which ought to have been done.

If his breach of the primary duty to act with undivided loyalty in further-ance of the interests of the beneficiaries, and not in his own interests, leads to a loss instead of a profit, then because the trustee undertook to be loyal but was not, he is strictly liable (by way of substituted performance of his primary obligation) to restore the value of the trust fund to what it would have been worth but for his breach of duty[21] — unless he can prove that the loss would have occurred in any event, that is, without any breach on his part. Common law notions of remoteness of damage and causation, including novus actus interveniens do not apply: the position is as if at common law a person had contracted that he guaranteed he would not breach a specific duty but, if he did, then he would restore the position to what it would have been if he had never broken the duty and so be liable for all loss, except for any loss that would have been incurred even if he had not broken that duty.

While there is extensive strict liability for breach of the duty of undivided loyalty, whether causing a loss to the trust fund or making a profit for the

---

19   *Limitation Act 1980* (UK), s 21(1)(b); *Gwembe Valley Development Co Ltd v Koshy (No 3)* [2003] EWCA Civ 1048; [2004] WTLR 97.

20   *Re Caerphilly Colliery Company* (1877) LR 5 Ch D 336 at 341, endorsed in *Attorney-General of Hong Kong v Reid* [1994] 1 AC 324 at 334.

21   As La Forest J stated in *Canson Enterprises Ltd v Boughton* [1991] 3 SCR 534 at 578, "In the case of a trust relationship, the trustee's obligation is to hold the res or object of the trust for his cestui que trust and on breach the concern of equity is that it be restored to the cestui que trust or if that cannot be done to afford compensation for what the object would be worth." Thus, if trust assets were worth 100,000 before the trustee's disloyal conduct and only 60,000 thereafter (or were sold for 100,000 due to disloyalty, but can now be acquired for 60,000), the trustee needs to restore 40,000 to the trust fund: *Re Smith* [1896] 1 Ch 71 at 77.

trustee, in the case of a profit there is not just a personal claim but also a proprietary claim. The beneficiaries under an express trust necessarily have a proprietary interest in a trust "fund" consisting of the original trust property, property subsequently added to such trust property and substituted property from time to time that is the product of such property,[22] whether by virtue of the rightful or wrongful conduct of the trustee.[23] After all, the protection of a ring-fenced fund exclusively for the beneficiaries is illusory if the protection can be lost simply by the trustee taking trust property over the ring-fence into the outside world and using the property or the proceeds of sale thereof to purchase assets for himself as his private property, discharged and freed from all proprietary claims of the beneficiaries. Thus, to vindicate the beneficiaries' proprietary interests in the property transferred to the trustee as part of a ring-fenced trust fund, such assets wrongfully purchased purportedly on behalf of the trustee in his private capacity must be held by him in his capacity as trustee of an express trust[24] for the beneficiaries: as trustee he cannot deny their claim that such property must feature in the trust accounts.

However, where the trustee's profit is not made out of the trust property but out of an opportunity that arises to him in his office as trustee (for example, to take a bribe or a secret commission and invest such profitably for himself), many have questioned whether it is equitable or fair that the trust beneficiaries should have a proprietary interest in that profit (rather than a mere personal claim), so that they have priority over the trustee's private creditors if he is insolvent. While equity's strict prophylactic approach justifiably prevents the trustee from retaining any profit, might it not be more appropriate and equitable as held by the Court of Appeal in *Lister v Stubbs*[25] (favoured by Professors Goode[26] and Worthington[27]) to treat the beneficiaries' claim as only a personal claim, so that the profit is available for division rateably between the insolvent trustee's creditors and the beneficiaries? Indeed, Worthington has further suggested that if it so happens that the beneficiaries have suffered no loss, while the trustee's private creditors have suffered a loss, it would surely be fairer to defer the beneficiaries' claims to those of the private creditors.

As matters currently stand according to the decision of the Privy Council in *Attorney General of Hong Kong v Reid*,[28] because the trustee's profit would not have arisen but for his office as trustee for the beneficiaries, so that he cannot deny their claim that as a "good person" he obtained the profit on their behalf,[29] it is the beneficiaries who have a proprietary claim to the profit in

---

22 Trust deeds normally make explicit what would otherwise be implicit by defining the "Trust Fund" along the lines of "property transferred to the Trustees to hold on the terms of this Settlement and all property from time to time representing such property".

23 *Attorney-General for Hong Kong v Reid* [1994] 1 AC 324 at 338; *Re Halletts' Estate* (1879) LR 13 Ch D 696 at 708-709; *Foskett v McKeown* [2001] AC 102 at 108, 127.

24 See P Millett, 315–317 of 'Proprietary Restitution' at chapter 12 of this book.

25 (1890) 45 Ch D 1.

26 R Goode, 'Proprietary Restitution Claims' in W Cornish et al (eds), *Restitution: Past, Present and Future* (Hart Publishing, Oxford, 1998) at 69.

27 S Worthington, *Equity* (Clarendon, Oxford, 2003) at 125-126.

28 [1994] 1 AC 324.

29 *Re Smith* [1896] 1 Ch 71 at 77.

priority to the claims of the trustee's private creditors.[30] After all, as the Privy Council pointed out, in *Boardman v Phipps*[31] the majority of their Lordships had held that because the profit-making information and opportunity had been obtained by Boardman in the course of his fiduciary office, the shares acquired by Boardman for himself were held on trust for the beneficiaries (subject to Boardman's lien for reimbursement of his expenditure on the shares) so that the wealthy Boardman had personally to account for the amount of the profit.

This fully accords with good equitable principles. The beneficiaries expect the trustee to perform his primary obligations or be unable to deny their claim that conduct in breach thereof is to be regarded as substituted performance, so that property acquired in breach of such obligations is held on trust for them, they not having voluntarily undertaken to be at risk from the trustee's bankruptcy. There is no justification to distinguish between misuse of property and misuse of office (whether honestly[32] or dishonestly[33]), while distinguishing them may well be capricious.[34] In the vernacular, "beneficiaries are entitled to expect not to be ripped off by their trustee, or if he tries to rip them off, then they are entitled to expect that his profits become part of the trust fund". Whether or not the trustee is insolvent is immaterial. Equity's strict rules which incidentally deter trustees' misconduct, are not founded on such deterrence (which has no impact on an insolvent trustee personally), but on the beneficiaries' expectations that the trustee must fulfil his primary obligations or be unable to deny that what he has done is by way of substituted performance of those obligations.

In contrast, in actions at law in contract and in tort the general rule, of course, is that wrongdoers only have to compensate for the loss or harm they cause because their relationship to the claimants is not one requiring them to act altruistically to make profits only for the claimants. They can take an economically efficient line in their own self-interest if they consider they can profit from breaking a common law obligation and paying compensation for the defendant's loss.

In exceptional cases, the law can follow equity's lead and make a defendant liable for profits he made. Thus, if a defendant is liable in conversion for misappropriating the claimant's property, it may be that the claimant has suffered no loss because the defendant replaces the property, but the defendant had sold the property for £2x and then reacquired the property for £x so as to be able to

---

30   *Attorney-General for Hong Kong v Reid* is to prevail over *Lister v Stubbs* according to Lawrence Collins J in *Daraydan Holdings Ltd v Solland International Ltd* [2005] Ch 119 at 138-140, though contrast the restrictive approach of the Court of Appeal with Privy Council precedents in *National Westminster Bank v Spectrum Plus Ltd* [2004] 3 WLR 503.

31   [1967] 2 AC 46.

32   As in *Boardman v Phipps* [1967] 2 AC 46.

33   As in *Attorney-General of Hong Kong v Reid* [1994] 1 AC 324.

34   Where a well-known senior soldier receives a bribe from a smuggler to sit in a vehicle to go through a checkpoint does it matter if the vehicle is a private one or if the soldier is in uniform or civilian clothes (but then what if wearing army underpants?); cf *Reading v Attorney-General* [1951] AC 507.

return it to the claimant and make a profit of £x. The defendant should then have to pay £x to the claimant.[35] Indeed, if no loss is suffered from a breach of contract in circumstances where the defendant is not quite in a fiduciary relationship with the claimant but has exploited his contractual position to make a profit for himself by breaking the contract, there can, according to the House of Lords, be exceptional circumstances[36] where the claimant's positive legitimate interest in the defendant not breaking the contract, as undertaken by the defendant, justifies making the defendant pay over the profit to the claimant, so that trying to make any profit is futile.

The proscriptive primary obligation of fidelity to the terms of the trust and liability for unauthorised conduct in breach

As Randerson J has stated,[37] "it is fundamental to the law of trusts that the trustee's overriding duty is to obey the terms of the trust." Thus, there is also strict liability imposed on a trustee where he has failed to do what he undertook to do under the terms of the trust, as where he has done something he was not authorised to do. The beneficiaries are entitled to delete the relevant entry as unauthorised and so falsify the up-to-date trust accounts that the trustee must provide of his trusteeship of the trust property. The beneficiaries can insist on the trustee being treated as if he had been a good trustee acting in their best interests so as to produce a substituted performance of his obligation: hence issues of causation and remoteness are irrelevant.

Take the case where T sold an authorised investment in X Ltd and invested the £1 million proceeds in an unauthorised investment in Z Ltd.

If, fortunately for all concerned, the Z Ltd shares are now worth more than the X Ltd shares are worth, and are worth more than £1 million, the beneficiaries can accept the trust accounts featuring the Z Ltd shares, but can require those shares be sold and the proceeds re-invested in authorised investments.[38] Otherwise, the entry of the Z Ltd shares is falsified, that is, deleted, so that the accounts can record the position as if the trustee had acted in the best interests of the beneficiaries which he is not permitted to deny. If replacement of the X Ltd shares is the best course of action, because such shares are now worth more than the Z Ltd shares and more than £1 million, then the beneficiaries will falsify the accounts by deletion of the sale of the X Ltd shares and the purchase of the Z Ltd shares, leaving the X Ltd shares featuring in the accounts. The trustee must re-acquire the X Ltd Shares, using the proceeds of sale of the Z Ltd

---

35   See dicta of Lord Nicholls in *Attorney-General v Blake* [2001] 1 AC 268 at 280 and *Kuwait Airways Corporation v Iraqi Airways Co (Nos 4 and 5)* [2002] 2 AC 883 at [88] in explaining *Solloway v McLaughlin* [1938] AC 247.

36   *Attorney-General v Blake* [2001] 1 AC 268; *Lane v O'Brien Homes Ltd* [2004] All ER (D) 61 trenchantly criticised by D Campbell in, "The Extinguishing of Contract" (2004) 67 *Modern Law Review* 818. One cannot help but think that it would have been better not to have opened up this can of worms, so restricting profits claims to fiduciary situations.

37   *Smith v Hugh Ward Society Inc* [2004] 1 NZLR 537 at [62].

38   *Target Holdings Ltd v Redferns* [1996] 1 AC 421 at 433.

shares and such additional money of his own as is necessary, so that the X Ltd Shares accurately appear in the trust accounts.[39]

If, sadly, the X Ltd and the Z Ltd shareholdings are each now worth less than the £1 million proceeds of sale of the X Ltd shares, then the accounts are falsified only as to the purchase of the Z Ltd shares so that the £1 million proceeds feature in the accounts[40] and in respect of which compound interest will be payable at 1% above the clearing banks' base rate.[41] The trustee must restore this value to the trust fund.

The trustee can only escape from this stringent liability if the breach was ratified by all the beneficiaries or if he remedied his breach of trust.[42] Thus, if he happened to sell the Z Ltd shares for an amount in excess of the higher of £1 million plus interest and the then value of the X Ltd shares, and invested the proceeds in an authorised investment worth only £900,000 in the end of year accounts examined by the beneficiaries, there is nothing that the beneficiaries can do, assuming that the authorised investment was not made negligently.

In all the above cases it will be seen that the justification for the strict equitable rules is equity upholding the trust by regarding the trustee as a good man who has specifically performed his duty to act in the beneficiaries' best interests and who cannot deny this. He is held to his voluntarily incurred undertaking to perform the terms of the trust so as to promote the beneficiaries' best interests.

As Lord Browne-Wilkinson stated in *Target Holdings v Redferns*:[43]

"If specific restitution of the trust property is not possible then the liability of the trustee is to pay sufficient compensation to the trust estate to put it back to what it would have been had the breach not been committed (see *Caffrey v Darby*[44] and *Clough v Bond*[45]). Even if the immediate cause of the loss is the dishonesty or failure of a third party, the trustee is liable to make good that loss to the trust estate if, but for the breach, such loss would not have occurred. Thus, the common law rules of remoteness of damage and causation do not apply. However there does have to be some causal connection between the breach of trust and the loss to the trust estate for which compensation is recoverable, viz the fact that the loss would not have occurred but for the breach."

In *Clough v Bond* Lord Cottenham LC concluded that if:[46]

"any part of the property be invested by any such [trustees] in funds or upon securities not authorised, or be put within the control of persons who ought not to be entrusted with it, and a loss be thereby eventually sustained, such [trustees] will be liable to make it good, however unexpected the result,

---

39 Specific restoration (sometimes confusingly referred to as restitution) is required: *Target Holdings Ltd v Redferns* [1996] 1 AC 421 at 434.

40 *Knott v Cottee* (1852) 16 Beav 77; 51 ER 705; *Re Duckwari plc* [1999] Ch 253 at 262-263.

41 *Wallersteiner v Moir (No 2)* [1975] QB 373 at 397.

42 As he did in *Target Holdings Ltd v Redferns* [1996] 1 AC 421, as was pointed out in *Youyang Pty Ltd v Minter Ellison* (2003) 212 CLR 484 at 502 where the breach was not remedied (as emphasised at [48]) nor was the breach ratified.

43 [1996] 1 AC 421 at 434.

44 (1801) 6 Ves Jun 488; 31 ER 1159.

45 (1838) 3 My & Cr 490; 40 ER 1016.

46 (1838) 3 My & Cr 490 at 496; 40 ER 1016 at 1018.

however little likely to arise from the course adopted, and however free such conduct may have been from any improper motive".

Thus, the trustee's failure to retain personal control of money led to strict liability of the trustee when the money was lost through another person's dishonesty.

The High Court of Australia,[47] the Supreme Court of Canada[48] and the Court of Appeal of New Zealand[49] have endorsed this strict approach requiring a trustee strictly to comply with the obligation he has undertaken. Equity requires of a trustee fidelity to such obligations. As Lord Haldane LC stated:[50]

"a man may misconceive the extent of the obligation which a Court of Equity imposes on him. His fault is that he has violated, however innocently because of his ignorance, an obligation which he must be taken by the Court to have known and his conduct has in that sense always been called fraudulent...What it really means is not moral fraud in the ordinary sense, but breach of the sort of obligation which is reinforced by a Court that from the beginning regarded itself as a Court of conscience".

It is against conscience to allow a trustee to escape liability for all losses that would not have occurred but for him failing to comply with the primary obligations undertaken by him, for example, only to distribute income and capital to beneficiaries interested therein, only to invest in authorised investments, only to act personally and retain title and possession of trust property unless otherwise authorised. Any breach of these obligations is regarded as a "knowing" breach. There is no scope for the common law distinction[51] between "knowing" converters of others' goods strictly liable for all consequences directly flowing from the conversion and "innocent" converters liable only for the foreseeable losses which can be expected to arise from the conversion. A trustee in breach of a primary obligation cannot be "innocent".

What then of the situation where the trustee faithfully invests only in authorised investments or employs an agent as authorised but does not perform these tasks diligently because of a failure to use the requisite degree of care so as to be negligent? Old case law indicates that the courts readily presumed that the trustee had obtained the trusteeship by undertaking at his own risk the primary obligation to act diligently and not negligently, so that any negligent conduct can then be regarded as unauthorised and equitably fraudulent, so that there is strict liability for all losses flowing from the negligence — though this is not as harsh as first appears because up to the 1870's trustees had fairly straightforward management responsibilities in respect of a limited range of investments.

As Holt CJ said in *Coggs v Bernard*:[52]

---

47   *Maguire v Makaronis* (1997) 188 CLR 449 at 473-474.
48   *Canson Enterprises Ltd v Boughton* [1991] 3 SCR 534.
49   *Bank of New Zealand v New Zealand Guardian Trust Co Ltd* [1999] 1 NZLR 664.
50   *Nocton v Lord Ashburton* [1914] AC 932 at 954.
51   *Kuwait Airways Corporation v Iraqi Airways Co (Nos 4 and 5)* [2002] 2 AC 883 at [102]-[104] per Lord Nicholls.
52   (1703) 2 Ld Raym 909 at 919; 92 ER 107 at 113.

"This undertaking [of a bailee to manage the goods] obliges the undertaker to a diligent management…The reasons are first, because in such a case, a neglect is a deceit to the bailor. For when he instructs the bailee upon his undertaking to be careful, he has put a fraud upon the plaintiff to trust him. And a breach of trust undertaken voluntarily will be a good ground for an action."

This approach can justify the following statement in 1801 of the Master of the Rolls in *Caffrey v Darby*[53] (relied on by Lord Browne-Wilkinson):

"if they [the trustees] have been guilty of negligence they must be responsible for any loss in any way to that [trust] property: for whatever may be the immediate cause, the property would not have been in a situation to sustain that loss, if it had not been for the negligence … If the loss had happened by fire, lightning or any other accident, that would not be an excuse for them if guilty of previous negligence. That was their fault."

In that case, a widow on marrying P assigned to trustees a 25 year lease at £80 pa of a public house inherited from her late husband with 22 years unexpired. She authorised the trustees to allow P to occupy and run the pub so long as P paid £100 pa for eight years to the trustees for investing in Government and other good securities on trust for her for life remainder for her four children, the whole family living in the pub which was their livelihood. The trustees let P get away with paying only £250 in the first three years and then nothing until he became insolvent around the time the eight years expired. The lease was then sold, and an arbitrator held P's assignee in bankruptcy was entitled to the proceeds, not the trustees whose appeal to the courts failed. The trustees argued they could not be liable for the strange unforeseen act of the arbitrator (who had regarded the lease as having been purchased by P so that it and its proceeds belonged to P's creditors).

The Master of the Rolls held the trustees strictly liable for all consequences of their negligence. It appears that he was treating their negligent failure to collect the £550 as unauthorised conduct so they had to be treated as if they had received the £550:[54] one assumes that the accounts entry of the sale proceeds going to P's assignee in bankruptcy would be deleted and replaced by £550 plus interest. Alternatively, P's total failure to pay any of the yearly instalments for over four years resulted in his possession becoming unauthorised,[55] so that the trustees became obliged to repossess the wasting leasehold premises and sell them with vacant possession. Failure to comply with this obligation therefore led to strict liability to account for the whole unforeseen deficiency, there not being fidelity to the trustees' duties under the trust.

Cases like this (where the trustees felt they had done their best for the family) led to an apprehension that liability was too severe and extensive, so as to deter persons from acting as trustees. As a result of the report of the Select Committee on Trusts Administration (1895) the *Judicial Trustees Act 1896* was passed.[56] By

---

53 (1801) 6 Ves Jun 488 at 496; 31 ER 1159 at 1162.
54 *Caffrey v Darby*, above n 53 at 497; 1163, the trustees "dealing as if he had paid them".
55 *Caffrey v Darby*, above n 53 at 495; 1161 "…they ought not to have given great latitude. They were hardly justifiable in permitting two instalments to become due; still less three; still less four."
56 See further J Lowry and R Edmunds, 'Excuses' in P Birks and A Pretto (eds), *Breach of Trust* (Hart Publishing, Oxford, 2002) at chapter 9.

section 3, where a trustee has acted honestly and *reasonably* and ought fairly to be excused for the breach of trust and for omitting to obtain the directions of the court in the matter in which he committed such breach, the court may relieve him either wholly or partly from personal liability for the breach.

Failure to perform authorised management duties with requisite degree of care

There is a world of difference between a trustee's failure to do only what he is authorised and obliged to do (when there is an unauthorised entry in the accounts that can be falsified) and his failure to exercise the requisite degree of care in performing his undertaken functions (so the relevant entry in the accounts cannot be deleted, the accounts, instead, having to be surcharged with the amount needed to make reparation for the relevant loss). In the former case the trustee is justifiably regarded as having deliberately flouted his primary obligation of fidelity requiring him only to perform his authorised functions in furthering the interests of the beneficiaries. A trustee is taken to know and understand his functions and to have undertaken only to perform those functions. The nature of this undertaken obligation means that he is strictly liable to make "substitutive compensation"[57] if he does break this obligation, unless the relevant loss would have occurred in any event without any breach on his part – so that any need to investigate this latter possibility will oust any suit for summary judgment based on a prima facie strict liability as in *Target Holdings Ltd v Redferns*.[58]

When the trustee is managing the trust assets within the parameters authorised under the trust, the issue of whether or not a secondary obligation has arisen to make reparation for wrongful losses resulting from the requisite degree of care not having been exercised, is very often a difficult question of degree and so not as clear as the issue whether an act was authorised or was not authorised.

More significantly, the trustee-beneficiaries relationship is the key dimension to the proscriptive primary obligation of fidelity to the terms of the trust, so that breaches are unauthorised conduct. In modern times, however, when the management role of trustees is very complex and extensive, it is surely time to accept that a trustee is not under a primary proscriptive obligation not to exercise care and skill below the requisite degree of care and skill, so that breaches thereof are unauthorised conduct and he is thus strictly liable to make substitutive performance. Equity should accept the normal, natural understanding of a trustee that he is under a duty to exercise the requisite degree of care and skill to avoid losses foreseeably flowing from breaking that duty, and that this duty will be enforced by the award of compensation for breach of this duty after taking up-to-date accounts. The trustee-beneficiaries relationship is then only an incidental factor when the trustee is charged with negligence, in

---

57   See J Edelman and S Elliott, "Money remedies against trustees" (2004) 18 *Trust Law International* 116.
58   [1996] 1 AC 421.

which event it is the alleged negligence requiring reparation[59] of the relevant loss that should become the key dimension, as in cases where a common law negligence claim is brought.[60]

At law a defendant is only liable for the proximate losses caused by his own negligence and not for losses arising from some intervening or extraneous cause, for example, a sudden drop in value of the relevant market for houses or stocks and shares. As Lord Millett made clear in obiter dicta in *Bristol & West Building Society v Mothew*,[61] equity should take the same approach as the law to such intervening or extraneous causes when surcharging a trustee's accounts so as to make reparation to the trust fund of the amount lost by virtue of the trustee's negligence.

As Millett LJ there stated (adopting obiter dicta[62] of the Western Australian Full Court in *Permanent Building Society (in liquidation) v Wheeler*[63]) , "there is no reason in principle why the common law rules of causation, remoteness of damage and measure of damages should not be applied by analogy in such a case" of negligence. Obiter dicta of the New Zealand Court of Appeal[64] are to the same effect.

However, the High Court of Australia in *Youyang Pty Ltd v Minter Ellison* reserved its position:[65]

> "there must be a real question whether the unique foundation and goals of equity, which has the institution of the trust at its heart, warrant any assimilation even in this limited way with the measure of compensatory damages in tort and contract. It may be thought strange to decide that the precept that trustees are to be kept by courts of equity up to their duty has an application limited to the observance by trustees of some only of their duties to beneficiaries in dealing with trust funds."

No doubt, it had in mind its dicta in *Maguire v Makaronis*[66] which assumed that there will be strict liability "upon failure in observance of one or other of the duties which attend trust administration, such as those to make only authorised investments and to use due diligence and care in the administration of the trust. Nineteenth century authorities such as *Caffrey v Darby* and *Clough v Bond* [imposing strict liability for all consequences] concerned failure to observe these rules for due administration".

---

59   See S Elliott C Mitchell, "Remedies for Dishonest Assistance" (2004) 67 *Modern Law Review* 16 at 24-31.

60   *Bank of New Zealand v New Zealand Guardian Trust Co Ltd* [1999] 1 NZLR 664 at 687.

61   [1998] Ch 1 at 16-17. Lord Walker in obiter in *Hilton v Barker Booth and Eastwood* [2005] 1 WLR 567 at 575 accepted Millett LJ's distinction between breach of proscriptive fiduciary obligation and breach of a prescriptive duty of care.

62   See the forceful chapter of Heydon J in chapter 9 of this book entitled 'Are the Duties of Company Directors to exercise care and skill fiduciary?'

63   (1994) 14 ACSR 109.

64   *Bank of New Zealand v New Zealand Guardian Trust Co Ltd* [1999] 1 NZLR 664.

65   (2003) 212 CLR 484 at 500. After all, the greater the saving of all losses by a trustee the greater should be the efforts put in by the trustee as pointed out by Cooter R and Freedman BJ, "The Fiduciary Relationship: Its Economic Character and Legal Consequences" (1991) 66 *New York University Law Review* 1045.

66   (1997) 188 CLR 449 at 473.

When the point is fully argued before the High Court and the nineteenth century cases put in context, it is hoped that, despite the contrary views of Heydon J and Dr Getzler in the preceding two chapters of this book, it should be persuaded of the practical logic of not treating negligent conduct as unauthorised conduct and of the merits of distinguishing between strict liability for doing what is not authorised to be done (with substitutive performance for enforcement of a primary obligation) and liability for negligently doing what is authorised to be done (with reparation of losses for breach of obligation). It would, of course, be possible to retain strict liability for negligence of trustees of traditional trusts (as if they had strictly undertaken not to be negligent and so to act at their peril if acting in such unauthorised fashion) but not for trustees of trusts for absolutely entitled beneficiaries, as commonly arises in the commercial context when it is also appropriate to raise issues of contributory negligence which are not at all apt for traditional trusts. However, in the modern context it is submitted that there is no justification at all for imposing the same stringent liability for negligent conduct as for unauthorised conduct. Liability for all the consequences of negligent conduct should only be strict if the defendant has clearly undertaken not to do anything negligent so as to be strictly liable for doing what is not authorised, namely being negligent. This reflects the position for a similar contractually undertaken liability.

Due performance of undertaken distributive duties and discretions

In modern discretionary trusts there are very extensive discretionary powers of appointment of income and capital in favour of broad classes of objects (whether to benefit individuals or charities or to create sub-trusts or new independent trusts) followed by discretionary trusts in favour of a broad class of beneficiaries.

As already seen as crucial to the trustee-beneficiaries dimension, the trustee in exercising discretions must comply with the duty of loyalty and must not benefit persons not authorised to be benefited under the terms of his discretion. Neither must he act within the apparent parameters of his powers so as to achieve a corrupt or ulterior purpose[67] or a purpose that is arbitrary, capricious or perverse to any sensible expectation of the settlor.[68] His decisions must be his own independent conscious decisions,[69] so that he must not automatically do what he is told by the settlor or life tenant or anyone else, while he must make his decisions fairly and disinterestedly when discriminating between discretionary beneficiaries.[70] Unless authorised, he must not delegate his powers[71] nor fetter their future exercise.[72] Breach of these prohibitions will prevent the trustee's action being valid.

---

67   *Hillsdown Holdings plc v Pensions Ombudsman* [1997] 1 All ER 862; *Wong v Burt* [2005] 1 NZLR 91.
68   *Re Manisty's ST* [1974] Ch 17.
69   *Turner v Turner* [1984] Ch 100.
70   *Edge v Pensions Ombudsman* [2000] Ch 602.
71   *Speight v Gaunt* (1883) 9 App Cas 1.
72   *Re Vestey's Settlement* [1950] 2 All ER 891.

The trustee must consider from time to time (as appropriate) the exercise of his distributive discretions[73] or he will be replaced by the court at the behest of any disgruntled beneficiaries. In this consideration process he must take steps to enable him adequately to ascertain for himself the relevant considerations[74] (taking particular account of the settlor's requests or letter of wishes)[75] and then ensure that he does not reach a decision that he would not have reached but for ignoring those relevant considerations or taking account of an irrelevant consideration.[76] If his decision is reached without such a real and genuine consideration of those relevant matters then the decision will not be valid.[77]

It is noteworthy that the focus is on the mental processes of the trustee[78] to see if they properly enabled him to reach his decision as to which he has much autonomous leeway, so that he may properly reach a poor decision that many trustees or the court might consider unreasonable, although not irrational in the sense of a decision that no rational trustee could possibly reach.[79] Unless the decision is an irrational one that could not possibly have been reached if the proper mental processes had been followed — and necessarily perverse to any sensible expectation of the settlor — the court does not focus on the decision to see if it is the sort of objective reasonable decision that the court would have reached if it had been the decision-maker.

The discretionary subjective decision-making of the trustee (as intended by the settlor) is at the heart of the trustee-beneficiaries relationship: it is the central mechanism for distributions of income and capital and cannot be replaced by the court substituting its own objective decision (except as a last resort in very odd rare cases).[80] It cannot even be struck down by the court, unless it is proved that there was a crucial deficiency in the processes by which the trustee reached his decision.

In the case of negligent management decisions of the trustee, there is no question of striking down the decisions which are faits accomplis in favour of third party purchasers. After establishing that the relevant decision was not one

---

73 *Re Hay's ST* [1981] 3 All ER 786.

74 *R v Charity Commissioners for England and Wales ex p Baldwin* [2001] WTLR 137.

75 *Re Barr's ST* [2003] Ch 409; *Re Esteem Settlement* [2004] WTLR 12; *Shalson v Russo* [2003] WTLR 1165.

76 *Re Hastings-Bass* [1975] Ch 25, applied to a decision of company directors to forfeit a shareholder's shares in *Hunter v Senate Support Services* [2004] EWHC (Ch) 1085; [2005] 1 BCLC 175. "Might" rather than "would" in the case of pension trusts. Further see D Hayton, "Pension trusts and traditional trusts: drastically different species of trusts" [2005] *Conveyancer* 259 and *Sieff v Fox* [2005] WTLR 891 at [77].

77 But void in the case of pension trusts (*Hearn v Younger* [2002] WTLR 1317) though only voidable in the case of family trusts (*Re Barr's ST* [2003] Ch 409) unless, it seems, that overlooking the relevant consideration prevents exercise of a power for "the benefit of" someone actually being for that person's benefit, so that there is a void ultra vires act as alleged but rejected in *Re Hastings-Bass* [1975] Ch 25.

78 Note L Smith, 'The Motive not the Deed' in J Getzler (ed), *Rationalising Property, Equity and Trusts: Essays in Honour of Edward Burn* (Lexis Nexis, London, 2003) particularly at 67-73.

79 *Edge v Pensions Ombudsman* [2000] Ch 602.

80 *McPhail v Doulton* [1971] AC 424 at 457; *Schmidt v Rosewood Trust Ltd* [2003] 2 AC 709 at [42] and [51]; *Mettoy Pension Trustees Ltd v Evans* [1990] 1 WLR 1587 at 1617-1618.

that a trustee exercising the appropriate degree of care could have reached,[81] the focus is on comparing what resulted from the negligent decision with what would have resulted if the decision had been the objective decision of the trustee if he had exercised the appropriate degree of care.[82] The beneficiaries will claim expectation losses unless reliance losses would be higher as at common law where a claimant's negligence claim is based in contract and in tort.[83]

Liability to restore trust fund's value without regard to tax liabilities

As Brightman LJ stated in *Bartlett v Barclays Trust Co Ltd (No 2)*,[84] when rejecting the trustee's contention that the tax liabilities the beneficiaries would have faced should reduce the amount of the trustee's liability to them:

> "The obligation of a trustee who is held liable for a breach of trust is funda-mentally different from the obligation of a contractual or tortious wrongdoer. The trustee's obligation is to restore to the trust estate the assets of which he has deprived it. The tax liability of individual beneficiaries, who have claims qua beneficiaries to the capital and income of the trust estate, do not enter into the picture because they arise not at the point of restitution to the trust estate but at the point of distribution of capital or income out of the trust estate."

Liability to compound interest

As notoriously established by the House of Lords in *Westdeutsche Landesbank Girozentrale v Islington London Borough Council*,[85] in England only simple interest is allowed at law, while equity in appropriate circumstances can award compound interest with yearly or half-yearly rests. These are circumstances[86] where the defendant trustee has received compound interest or ought to have received it, or can fairly be presumed to have received it so that he is estopped from denying it (for example, where he has made — or is deemed to have made[87] — an unauthorised use of trust money for his own purposes and any actual profits made by him are unascertainable).

Here it seems that the law can benefit from adopting the flexibility available in equity and should certainly award a commercial rate of compound interest where this is the true measure of the claimant's loss.

---

81   *Wight v Olswang* (No 2) [2000] WTLR 783 (applying the common law approach of *Saif Ali v Sydney Mitchell & Co* [1980] AC 198 at 218 to the negligence of professional persons) reversed on appeal where this approach was accepted [2001] WTLR 291.

82   *Nestle v National Westminster Bank* [1994] 1 All ER 118, *Re Mulligan* [1998] 1 NZLR 481.

83   *Midland Bank Trust Co Ltd v Hett Stubbs & Kemp* [1979] Ch 384; *White v Jones* [1995] 2 AC 207; *South Australian Asset Management Corporation v York Montague Ltd* [1997] AC 191.

84   [1980] Ch 515 at 545.

85   [1996] AC 669. The English Law Commission Report No 287 on Pre-judgment Interest on Debts and Damages now recommends compound interest be payable at law. Further see *Bank of America v Mutual Trust Co* (2002) 211 DLR (4th) 385 awarding compound interest.

86   Examined by Heydon JA in *Harris v Digital Pulse Pty Ltd* (2003) 56 NSWLR 298 at 365-369.

87   *Wallersteiner v Moir (No 2)* [1975] QB 373 at 397.

ESCAPING FROM PERSONAL LIABILITY

General statutory relief

It seems all trust law jurisdictions have a statutory provision very like the *English Trustee Act 1925*, section 61. "If it appears to the court that a trustee is or may be personally liable for any breach of trust but has acted honestly and reasonably and ought fairly to be excused for the breach of trust and for omitting to obtain the directions of the court in the matter in which he committed such a breach, then the court may relieve him either wholly or partly from personal liability for the same."

This enables relief to be given against any strict personal liability for unauthorised conduct or against liability for the full extent of consequential losses, and contemplates a trustee "reasonably" committing a negligent breach of trust.[88] Accordingly, as in the case of the similarly worded section 727 of the *Companies Act 1985*, "it follows that conduct may be reasonable despite amounting to lack of reasonable care", as made clear by Hoffmann LJ in *Re D'Jan of London Ltd*.[89] It has thus been appreciated that liability in Equity can be too rigorous, particularly for unpaid lay persons acting as trustees.[90]

Exemption or ouster of duty clauses

Indeed, the liability of trustees may be expressly prevented by the use of clauses in trust instruments that exempt trustees from any liability for "loss or damage happening to the trust fund" arising from a breach of duty unless arising from personal dishonesty or recklessness,[91] or in some jurisdictions also from gross negligence[92] or even from ordinary negligence.[93] In England it has become established[94] that the irreducible core content of the trust obligation only requires a trustee to act honestly and not recklessly, but his assertion that he believed he acted honestly will not avail him if no reasonable trustee of his type could have held such belief.[95] It would appear, however, that if a trustee does what he is not authorised to do, so that by way of substituted performance his accounts are falsified so that he is obliged to restore the value of the fund to what it would have been but for the unauthorised conduct, then he will not be protected by a clause construed as only covering reparation for loss or damage

---

88 As seems to have been the case in *Re Smith* (1902) 86 LT 401.

89 [1994] 1 BCLC 561.

90 Further see J Lowry and R Edmunds, 'Excuses' in P Birks and A Pretto, *Breach of Trust* (Hart Publishing, Oxford, 2002).

91 *Armitage v Nurse* [1998] Ch 241.

92 Scotland under the general law (*Lutea Trustees Ltd v Orbis Trustees Guernsey Ltd* [1988] SLT 471), Jersey and Guernsey under legislation.

93 Legislation in Turks & Caicos Islands and the provisional proposal of the English Law Commission in Consultation Paper No 171 for professional trustees.

94 *Armitage v Nurse*, above n 91; *Bogg v Raper* (1998) 1 ITELR 267; *Walker v Stones* [2001] QB 902.

95 *Walker v Stones*, above n 94 (solicitor-trustee).

arising from authorised but negligent conduct.[96] No loss or damage has happened to the trust fund where the account is falsified, so that £X paid out in unauthorised fashion is deleted from the account, so that the trustee still has the £X in the trust account and cannot deny this.

If a clause expressly purported to exclude a trustee of a discretionary trust for S's descendants from any liability for distributing income or capital to persons other than such descendants or for any other unauthorised conduct, then it would seem that this would only be effective to the extent that the trustee acted honestly and not recklessly. Thus, any claim by a trustee to retain property acquired for himself, in unauthorised breach of his primary obligation of undivided loyalty, instead of for the beneficiaries as part of their interest in the trust fund, would fail as dishonest.[97]

Going beyond an exemption clause, a clause may, indeed, oust a particular duty that would otherwise automatically be imposed on the trustee by trust law. Ouster of a duty then prevents any breach of duty arising in respect of which there can be a liability.[98] Of course, the duty to act honestly and not recklessly cannot be ousted, while "if the beneficiaries have no rights enforceable against the trustees there are no trusts".[99] Furthermore, ouster of the trustee's independent role will lead to the so-called trustee being a nominee or bare trustee of a ring-fenced fund held to the order of another.

Instances of strict liability

As already seen, breaches of the undertaken proscriptive duties of loyalty to the beneficiaries and of fidelity to the terms of the trust, so as positively to further the beneficiaries' interests and not put them at any risk, occasion strict liability for breach of primary obligations. The trustees are in the same position as if contractually undertaking to fulfil those proscriptive duties and to be liable for all losses flowing from any breach of such duties unless the losses would have occurred in the absence of such breach.

As emphasised by the English House of Lords,[100] the High Court of Australia[101] and the New Zealand Court of Appeal,[102] questions of foreseeability and remoteness do not arise: there is[103] "only a narrow escape route from liability based on proof that loss or damage would have occurred even if there

---

96   For example, *Alexander v Perpetual Trustees WA Ltd* [2001] NSWCA 240. Further see text to n 112 below.

97   For example, *Reader v Fried* [2001] VSC 495.

98   *Hayim v Citibank NA* [1987] AC 730. Trust law (like contract law, as emphasised in *Kelly v Cooper* [1993] AC 205 at 215) facilitates settlors' intentions unless unlawful or against public policy. For example, a trustee may be expressly enabled (a) to speculate with the trust fund as if an absolute beneficial owner speculating on his own behalf and who can afford to lose the whole fund without this affecting his standard of living one iota; (b) to retain assets without diversifying the trust fund; (c) to distribute to a specific beneficiary on a request therefrom without any duty to consider the claims of any other beneficiaries.

99   *Armitage v Nurse*, above n 94 at 253; *Foreman v Kingstone* [2005] WTLR 823 at [85]-[88].

100   *Target Holdings Ltd v Redferns* [1996] 1 AC 421.

101   *Maguire v Makaronis* (1979) 188 CLR 449.

102   *Bank of New Zealand v New Zealand Guardian Trust Co Ltd* [1999] 1 NZLR 664.

103   *Bank of New Zealand v New Zealand Guardian Trust Co Ltd*, above n 102 at 687.

had been no breach". There is no duty on a beneficiary to mitigate loss or to safeguard his interests against the trustee because this would subvert the trustee's fundamental overriding primary obligation of loyalty and fidelity to safeguard and further the beneficiary's interests. Indeed, the traditional approach is to regard the trustee as guilty of equitable fraud if he breaks the proscriptive duties of loyalty and fidelity, so that questions of relative causation and contributory negligence do not arise, just as they do not arise in the case of common law deceit.[104] The modern approach is that if the trustee does not perform its primary obligations it is still to be treated as if it had performed these obligations, with the money for which the trustee must account being regarded as awarded by way of substitute performance, so issues of causation and remoteness are irrelevant.[105]

Moreover, in the vast majority of cases there is a trust for a wide range of beneficiaries with the duty of the trustee being to account to any one of them to restore the value of the trust fund to what it would have been but for the breach of trust. Thus, the negligence of one beneficiary will not affect that duty, except that if one beneficiary instigates or gives a fully informed consent to a breach of trust, then he cannot sue in respect of the breach nor can he benefit from the trustee remedying the breach.[106]

In the exceptional case of a trustee holding on trust for one beneficiary absolutely, then in the rare event of the beneficiary becoming aware of the trustee's breach and having the opportunity to remedy it but unreasonably failing to take remedial steps, losses flowing from such clearly unreasonable behaviour will be adjudged to flow from that behaviour and not from the breach.[107]

The High Court of Australia recently dealt with issues of contributory negligence in the context of a claim under a statute very similar to the English *Civil Liability Contribution Act 1978*. In *Alexander v Perpetual Trustees WA Ltd*[108] the background was that in an earlier case investors (whether as individuals or as trustees) had successfully sued PTWA in respect of millions of dollars given to PTWA on trust only to invest them in EC Consolidated Capital Ltd if receiving the security of bearer deposit certificates. PTWA did not obtain such security and so had done what it was not authorised to do and so was strictly liable for losses arising on the insolvency of Consolidated Capital — as were the defendants in *Youyang Pty Ltd v Minter Ellison*[109] in similar circumstances. It so happened that PTWA had invested those investors' moneys (and its own moneys) by giving them to Minters on trust only to invest them in Consolidated Capital if receiving the security of bearer deposit certificates. Minters, solicitors to Consolidated Capital, in a "blatant, deliberate breach of trust"[110] invested the moneys without receiving any security.

---

104 *Standard Chartered Bank v Pakistan National Shipping Corp (No 2)* [2003] 1 AC 959.
105 See n 17 above.
106 *Fletcher v Collis* [1905] 2 Ch 24.
107 *Lipkin Gorman v Karpnale* [1992] 4 All ER 331 at 361; *Canson Enterprises Ltd v Boughton* [1991] 3 SCR 534 at 556.
108 (2004) 216 CLR 109.
109 (2003) 212 CLR 484.
110 Per Davies AJA in the Court of Appeal [2002] WTLR 937 at [128].

Minters were clearly liable to PTWA but had the audacity to claim that the investors were "entitled to recover compensation" from both PTWA and Minters who were both "liable in respect of the same damage" or harm: thus Minters could claim a contribution from PTWA to take account of PTWA's contributory negligence in failing to check whether the documents it received were proper bearer certificates of deposit.

The trial judge, Rolfe J, held that if the case turned on the negligence of Minters, then PTWA's contributory negligence would be relevant and they would be regarded as contributorily negligent as to 40%. However, Minters were strictly liable for doing what they were not entitled to do, so that contributory negligence was then not material. "That was correct" stated Gleeson CJ, Gummow and Hayne JJ in the High Court.[111]

One would then have expected them to analyse the investors' claim as one to falsify the outgoing entries of their moneys in PTWA's accounts, so that the investors' moneys remained with PTWA, which must be regarded as having invested its own moneys and not the investors' moneys. Thus, PTWA was personally liable to account to the investors for the investors' moneys regarded as retained in the trust account by way of performance of PTWA's primary obligation: their money had not been lost so no "compensation" or reparation was due for any loss as the House of Lords had pointed out in *Royal Brompton Hospital NHS Trust v Hammond*[112] when endorsing R Goff and G Jones, *The Law of Restitution* (5th ed at 396) "a claim for restitution cannot be said to be a claim to recover compensation" (and disapproving the contrary view of the Court of Appeal in *Friends Provident Life Office v Hillier Parker*).[113]

PTWA would then falsify the outgoing entries in Minter's accounts relating to the moneys given by PTWA on trust to Minters, so that PTWA's moneys remained in Minters' accounts as held for PTWA, with Minters regarded as having invested its own moneys, not PTWA's moneys. Thus, Minters were personally liable to account to PTWA for PTWA's moneys regarded as retained in the trust account by way of performance of Minters' primary obligation.

Leaving aside the meaning of "compensation" as only covering reparation for a loss, Minters were liable to PTWA for the harm or damage caused by Minters not returning PTWA's moneys, while PTWA was liable to the investors for the harm or damage caused by it not returning the investors' moneys. Thus, the harm or damage caused exclusively by PTWA to the investors was wholly different from the harm or damage caused exclusively by Minters to PTWA, so they could not be liable in respect of the same harm or damage.

However, Gleeson CJ, Gummow and Hayne JJ dismissed Minters' appeal on the basis that, while beneficiaries in exceptional circumstances can directly sue a third party if joining a recalcitrant trustee as co-defendant, the investor-beneficiaries never had an entitlement to sue Minters as third party, having successfully recovered their money from PTWA. Thus, Minters and PTWA were not liable to the investors in respect of the same damage.

---

111   *Alexander v Perpetual Trustees WA Ltd*, above n 108 at 127[44].
112   [2002] 2 All ER 801 at 816.
113   [1997] QB 85.

The three other judges would have allowed the appeal, McHugh and Callinan JJ on the basis of a liability for the same damage under the *Fair Trading Act 1985* (NSW), with Kirby J agreeing with them but also basing himself on a more flexible interpretation of the "same damage" concept so as to cover the breach of trust liabilities.

Leaving aside the *Fair Trading Act*, Minters' claim to contribution from PTWA would clearly have been rejected if Minter's obligation to PTWA had been regarded like a strict contractual obligation to indemnify PTWA from all loss flowing from Minters' failure to obtain secured investments as it had undertaken to do. The substance of Minters' strict obligation in trust law can be regarded as the same as such contractual obligation. Intriguingly, in tort law where a principal had wholly delegated a task to an agent and both had been found liable in negligence to an injured person, the principal has been held entitled to recover from the agent the whole sum payable by the principal to the injured person.[114] This seems analogous to PTWA delegating to Minters the task of investing solely in secured assets.

Reparation for negligent losses

As already apparent, in the case of a trust for one or more beneficiaries absolutely entitled against the trustee, especially in the commercial context, there is justifiably scope for a defendant trustee to allege that some, or even all, of the loss for which the claimant seeks reparation was caused by the claimant's contributory negligence or failure to mitigate his loss. Indeed, as Millett LJ stated in *Bristol and West Building Society v Mothew*[115] "there is no reason in principle why the common law rules of causation, remoteness of damage and measure of damages should not be applied by analogy in such a case", while, as stated by Gault J in *Bank of New Zealand v New Zealand Guardian Trust Co Ltd*,[116] "surely the stage has been reached where something more substantial than historical origin is needed to justify disparate treatment of those in breach of the obligation to exercise reasonable care".

Thus, as at law,[117] these issues in equity should require answering the question "from what kind of harm was it the defendant's duty to guard the claimant?" Usually the negligence will be innocent (not dishonest) so that it would appear that, as in the case of an innocent converter of goods,[118] there should only be a duty to avoid foreseeable losses which can be expected to flow from the negligence. In the case of a trustee responsible to one beneficiary in a commercial contractual context, this duty may very well be a limited one where the beneficiary might be expected to take some steps himself rather than put 100% trust in the trustee, so as to be guilty of contributory negligence, or might

---

114 For example, *Florida Hotels Pty Ltd v Mayo* (1965) 113 CLR 588; *Oxley CC v MacDonald* [1999] NSWCA 126; *Redken Laboratories (Aust) Pty Ltd v Docker* [2000] NSWCA 100.

115 [1998] Ch 1 at 17.

116 [1999] 1 NZLR 664 at 681.

117 *Rahman v Arearose Ltd* [2001] QB 351 at 367-368, per Laws LJ, endorsed in *Fairchild v Glenhaven Funeral Services Ltd* [2003] 1 AC 32 at [12] per Lord Bingham; *South Australia Asset Management Corporation v York Montague Ltd* [1997] AC 191.

118 *Kuwait Airways Corporation v Iraqi Airways Co (Nos 4 and 5)* [2002] 2 AC 883 at [103].

be expected to take steps to mitigate an obviously looming loss.[119] A proper construction of the contract in all the circumstances could well lead to a dilution or ouster of trust law principles by way of necessary implication.[120]

In traditional trusts the beneficiaries are entitled to expect the trustee, in performing his fundamental duty to further their best interests, to be under a duty to safeguard the beneficiaries against everyone, including himself. The beneficiaries are entitled to trust their trustee and are not expected to guard their own backs[121] and, of course, will not be in a position to do so if they are minors or mental patients or unborn or otherwise unascertained. Any beneficiary who has not instigated or consented to a breach of trust can require the trustee to produce up-to-date accounts restoring to the account any value lost by reason of the breach, though the instigating or consenting beneficiaries are, of course, excluded from benefiting from this restoration. Thus, suggestions that a trustee of a traditional trust should have the defence of the contributory negligence of the beneficiaries available to him are wholly misconceived, with one reservation. If it so happened that the trustee held on trust for A for life, remainder to B absolutely, A and B each being of full capacity, then if the two beneficiaries did not intervene to replace the trustee[122] once fully aware of his misconduct, they should not be able to sue him for future losses resulting from his continuing misconduct, having themselves really caused such losses which they could easily have prevented.[123]

EXEMPLARY DAMAGES AND DISTRESS AND INCONVENIENCE DAMAGES

As emphasised in *Armitage v Nurse* [124] and *Foreman v Kingstone,*[125] at the heart of the trust concept is the accountability of the trustee for his ownership and management of the trust property. Such accountability is enforced by the drawing up of paper accounts[126] (in common form or on the footing of wilful default or an account of profits) which involve accounting principles calculat-

---

119 *Canson Enterprises Ltd v Boughton* [1991] 3 SCR 534 at 556.

120 *Kelly v Cooper* [1993] AC 205, just as obligations in tort may not be greater than those found expressly or by necessary implication from the relevant contract: *Tai Hing Cotton Mill v Liu Chong Hing Bank* [1986] AC 80.

121 "The whole point of having a trustee is to look after the [beneficiaries]" as emphasised in R Meagher, JD Heydon, M Leeming, *Meagher Gummow and Lehane's Equity: Doctrines and Remedies* (4th ed, Butterworths, Sydney, 2002) at 840. The costs efficiency of trusts (brought out in H Hansmann and U Mattei, "The functions of Trust Law: A Comparative Legal and Economic Analysis" (1998) 73 *New York University Law Review* 434) is wholly undermined if the beneficiaries have to keep up with what the trustees are doing with a view to intervening when appropriate.

122 Under *Trusts of Land and Appointment of Trustees Act 1996* (UK), s 19 or utilising *Saunders v Vautier* rights as collective beneficial owner.

123 See cases cited in n 107 above.

124 [1998] Ch 241.

125 [2004] 1 NZLR 841.

126 See R Chambers, 'Liability' in P Birks and A Pretto (eds), *Breach of Trust* (Hart Publishing, Oxford, 2002) at chapter 1, particularly at 16-20.

ing losses or profits that are real or that the trustee cannot deny are real, being based upon actual figures or figures that cannot be denied to be actual. In this arithmetical exercise there is no room for adding huge extra amounts for exemplary damages or small extra amounts for distress and inconvenience.

The settlor's intention at the core of the trust concept is that the beneficiaries are interested in a trust fund as ascertained by drawing up accounts. The beneficiaries receive windfall benefits from the settlor's bounty as implemented by the trustees: the settlor does not intend them to receive further windfall benefits in the form of exemplary damagers or damages for distress and inconvenience. Indeed, the settlor assumes that the strict proscriptive duties of trustees will ensure that the trustees' duties are fully performed with any profits automatically belonging beneficially to the beneficiaries by way of substituted performance of the trustee's obligations,[127] so that there cannot be an occasion for such extraordinary extra damages, the criminal law providing the extra sanctions sufficing to ensure that trustees honestly perform their duties and do not misappropriate property belonging to the beneficiaries.[128] The award of compensation beyond that contemplated by the settlor and sanctioned by the criminal law should not be awarded.

Thus for the above reasons, coupled with those given by Heydon JA in *Harris v Digital Pulse Pty Ltd*,[129] exemplary damages and damages for distress and inconvenience[130] cannot be awarded where beneficiaries make a trustee liable to account in equity. However, outside accountability of trustees there is scope for equity to make trustees liable to pay compensation to beneficiaries, so might there then be scope for exemplary damages or damages for distress and inconvenience?

EQUITABLE COMPENSATION OUTSIDE THE ACCOUNTABILITY OF TRUSTEES

It is possible that the actual drawing up of correct accounts will not compensate a beneficiary for actual loss suffered by that beneficiary. Take the case of an accumulation and maintenance settlement for the settlor's only son, adopted just before he made the settlement, and his three nephews contingent upon each attaining 25 years to take his equal share, where the trustee has a power before the eldest reaches 25 years to appoint the capital to one or more of the beneficiaries exclusive of the other beneficiaries and to delete one or more of the beneficiaries from the class of four beneficiaries, even if leaving only one

---

127 See nn 19 and 23 above and the text relating to them.

128 *R v Clowes (No 2)* [1994] 2 All ER 316. This should oust the need for exemplary damages (proposed by R Cooter and BJ Freedman, "The Fiduciary Relationship: Its Economic Character and Legal Consequence" (1991) *New York University Law Review* 1045) to deter trustees from trying to get away with benefiting themselves, on the basis that 100% detection is unlikely so more than capture of profits is needed.

129 (2003) 56 NSWLR 298.

130 See the antipathy towards such damages in *West v Lazard Bros Jersey Ltd* (1993) JLR 165 and *Miller v Stapleton* [1996] 2 All ER 449, though the Pensions Ombudsman can award damages for distressing, inconvenient "maladministration": *Westminster CC v Heywood* [1998] Ch 377.

beneficiary. The settlor has made it clear to his trustee that he expects the power to be exercised to appoint all to his adopted son and to delete the nephews from being beneficiaries if, just before the eldest nephew reaches 25, the son is a bright, hard-working, ambitious young man. This clearly is the case, so the trustee decides to appoint all to the son and to delete the nephews from being beneficiaries. The trustee has her solicitor prepare the appropriate deed for the trustee to execute. The trustee attends the 21st birthday party of the son which coincides with the birthday of the eldest nephews who are twins. At the party the trustee executes the deed and hands it to the son appointing all to him contingent upon attaining 25 but deleting the nephews as beneficiaries forthwith, so the son alone will be entitled to the intermediate income. The nephews correctly allege the deed is a nullity because the power expired the day before the deed was executed and so falsify the accounts that show the son as entitled to the income and then the capital at 25.[131]

The son sues the trustee for negligently having failed to execute the deed of appointment in due time, so the son will not forthwith receive all the income nor all the capital at age 25, only one quarter, so the trustee will have to make up the lost three quarters of income and capital. There seems no justification for compensation for distress and inconvenience nor for exemplary damages even if the trustee had been bribed by the nephews' father to delay executing the deed and had tried to manufacture a (failed) defence of contributory negligence by getting the son to reply to a letter from the trustee saying she would be happy to turn up at the son's party with an executed deed, but would the son not prefer to take a digital film recording of the trustee's signature at the party, leading the son to write back accepting this "great idea." In my view, equity will be satisfied with the existing liability of the trustee to compensate the son for his loss[132] and to account to the son for the bribe,[133] with the nephew's father having concurrent liability for instigating the breach.[134]

Further, take the case of B who tells T that she is £100,000 in debt and crippled with 15% interest so that she is desperately looking forward to receiving from T £100,000 to which she becomes entitled under the trust on attaining 30 years in three months' time. Despite this, T does not get round to paying B till three months after her 30th birthday because T was taking a four months round-the-world trip of a lifetime during which he kept his where-abouts secret. While T must account to B for the £100,000 plus three months interest thereon at a commercial rate presumed from him being deemed wrongfully to have used the money for his own benefit, it seems clear that equity will require T to compensate B for the amount of the 15% interest she would not have had to pay if he had promptly paid the £100,000 when due.

What if the situation was one where B's debt was in respect of a mortgage and the mortgagee had already commenced legal proceedings with a view to obtaining vacant possession of B's house so as to sell it and recoup the debt out of the proceeds of sale. Three months before attaining 30, when B was to

---

131 As in *Breadner v Granville-Grossman* [2001] Ch 523.
132 *Swindle v Harrison* [1997] 4 All ER 705.
133 *Att-Gen for Hong Kong v Reid* [1994] 1 AC 324.
134 *Eaves v Hickson* (1861) 30 Beav 136; 54 ER 840; *Twinsectra Ltd v Yardley* [2002] 2 AC 164.

become entitled to trust capital of £100,000, B had approached T for T to advance her half the capital under a power in that behalf and, in any event, to provide her with copies of the trust deed which she could show the mortgagee to try to stop the mortgagee pursuing its legal proceedings. T simply refused to do either, due to his malice towards her for breaking off her engagement to his son which had so unsettled his son for many months that the son was dismissed from his accountancy job and remained unemployed.

T refused to change his mind when B told him that she was entitled under another trust to £1million if at the age of 31 years she had "settled down" by then, such to be proved only by proof that she had continuously resided within the previous 12 months in a house owned by her alone or equally with another person, whether or not her spouse, and she would lose this if she were evicted from her house and the house sold by her mortgagee.

T went off on a six month round-the-world trip of a lifetime commencing one month before B attained 30 years, having deliberately made no arrangements for paying B her capital on the due date before he left England and without leaving any contact details for the duration of his trip. Finding it impossible to contact him, B fell into a clinical depression and the mortgagee obtained vacant possession and sold the property to a purchaser. When T returned he eventually gave B a signed cheque in her favour to cover the £100,000 plus only five per cent simple interest but only when she succumbed to him acting in an outrageously abusive sexual fashion. She then sued for equitable compensation for the extra interest and for exemplary damages and damages for distress and inconvenience

These are very extreme circumstances to try the patience even of an equity judge in pre-fusion days. The settlor's trust had run its course so that T held on trust for B absolutely, yet T had monstrously failed to obey B's instruction to pay the capital to her (though fully knowing the grave implications of this) and had exploited his position to abuse her in a dreadfully demeaning fashion, both causing her grave distress and inconvenience. I see no reason why equity should not learn from the availability at law in restricted circumstances of damages for distress and inconvenience, so as to regard the special circumstances affecting B as justifying the award of compensation against T for the distress and inconvenience suffered by B in the period after she had attained 30 years. Indeed, the conduct of T is such that, in my opinion, it should be open for equity to follow the law and award exemplary damages against T for monstrously abusing his office of trustee.[135]

On B's 30th birthday the settlor's trust had run its course so that T held the £100,000 absolutely for B. Thus, T became B's nominee just as if B had transferred her £100,000 to T on trust for B absolutely. T's failure to do what B directed him to do was a breach of his proscriptive duty of fidelity to the terms

---

135 As suggested by Spigelman CJ and Mason P in *Harris v Digital Pulse Pty Ltd* (2003) 56 NSWLR 298 and C Mitchell and S Elliott in "Remedies for Dishonest Assistance" (2004) 67 *Modern Law Review* 16. Query whether nowadays an action might succeed in England for breach of human rights under Articles 3 and 8 of the Convention implemented by the *Human Rights Act 1998* (UK): see *Wainwright v Home Office* [2004] 2 AC 406 at 429[62]-[63].

of his trust obligation, so that he became strictly liable for all the consequences of his actions covering the loss of B's house and the loss of B's £1million.

POSSIBLE EXPLOITATION OF STRICT TRUST LIABILITY IN THE COMMERCIAL CONTEXT?

In *Target Holdings v Redferns*[136] there was no occasion for strict liability where a bare trust was used in the commercial loan contract context and a breach of trust action was brought. As Lord Millett has pointed out,[137] on trust accounting principles the entry of £1,500,000 paid out by the defendant in breach of trust, because without obtaining the security for an intended mortgage loan of that amount by the plaintiff, was a false payment: the proper account of the defendant's holding of the claimant's money therefore needed to reveal that the defendant still retained the £1,500,000 on trust for the claimant. Two weeks later, when the defendant obtained the relevant documents as security there could be entered the payment out of the money in return for the security so the transaction had become an authorised one.

It followed that for the claimant to succeed the plaintiff had to prove that the authorised transaction had been carried out negligently: that, but for the defendant's negligence, the prospective mortgagor would not have been able to carry out his mortgage fraud through having the use of £1,500,000 for two weeks without having needed to provide the required security for the loan of that money. Such proof needed a trial, so that summary judgment for £1 million (£1,500,000 less the £500,000 received on sale of the mortgaged property) could not be granted.

Alternatively, as the House of Lords held, because a defendant trustee can never be liable for a loss which the claimant beneficiary would, in any event, have suffered even if there had been no breach of trust, the plaintiff had to prove that the loss suffered from the breach of trust would not have happened but for the premature payment of the money without having obtained the required security. This required a trial so that summary judgment could not be granted.

Thus, in this breach of trust action, the same result flowed from applying trust accounting rules (the historically justified approach favoured by Lord Millett)[138] or equitable compensation rules.

However, could the position in equity be exploited to provide greater protection in the commercial contracts sphere than is provided at law?

Take X Ltd which wants to sell smoke alarms to the public and so, in consideration of paying Y Ltd a £20,000 commission, delivers £1 million to Y Ltd on trust to be used only for the purpose of purchasing efficient smoke alarms. Y Ltd spends this £1 million on smoke alarms which it delivers to X Ltd. It transpires that the alarms have a design defect making them inefficient so that X Ltd's warehouse is burnt down, as is the house of C who had purchased these inefficient smoke alarms and installed them in his house.

---

136 [1996] 1 AC 421.

137 P Millett, "Equity's Place in the Law of Commerce" (1998) 114 *Law Quarterly Review* 214 at 226-227.

138 Further see P Millett, 'Proprietary Restitution' in chapter 12 of this book.

It so happens that X Ltd's warehouseman had been asked to store a trunk in the warehouse by an acquaintance, who was a terrorist who had secreted powerful explosives in the trunk, but the warehouseman had not asked to see what was inside the trunk. The combination of the fire with these explosives destroys twelve buildings and twelve people (including a billionaire financier) in the vicinity of the warehouse, as well as the warehouse itself.

C's house is destroyed, including within it C's stamp collection worth £1 million, which that evening he had taken from a bank vault to show his friend, F, who was staying with him that night. As it happens, F is an art dealer who had a £1 million painting in his car which he had moved into the house overnight for safe keeping, but it is destroyed in the fire.

X Ltd first has a straightforward claim to falsify Y Ltd's account so as to delete the unauthorised payment out of £1million, so that Y Ltd is regarded as still having X Ltd's £1million and has to account to X Ltd for it. Because the purchase had been unauthorised equity regards Y Ltd as having purchased the alarms with its own money, but because the inefficient alarms are worthless (with any sold alarms having to be recalled), Y Ltd cannot offset any reasonable price for any unreturned alarms against the £1million due to X Ltd which it must pay.

When it turns out that the smoke alarm manufacturer is insolvent, X Ltd claims to be fully reimbursed by Y Ltd for all of X Ltd's personal losses in respect of the warehouse and its contents and to be indemnified against any claims against X Ltd in respect of the fire and explosion at its premises and, also, for claims against X Ltd by C and F for all their losses.

As already explained, under traditional trust law principles where the trustee Y Ltd does what it is not authorised to do, then it acts at its peril, being liable for all consequential loss that would not have occurred but for the original unauthorised act: issues of foreseeability, causation, novus actus interveniens, and contributory negligence all being irrelevant.

At law the same strict situation can be achieved if a contract makes it plain that if one party breaks the contract in fundamental fashion, then he acts at his peril and is strictly liable for all consequential losses that would not have occurred but for his fundamental breach.

However, where a bare trust is mere incidental machinery in the furtherance of a contractual agreement it seems that there are sufficient policy reasons to oust traditional trust law principles as to consequential losses. After all, traditional trusts govern the ownership-management of property for a group of vulnerable beneficiaries over a lengthy duration of 100 years or so in circumstances where the trustee will normally be a trust corporation well-knowing its extensive liabilities or, exceptionally, an individual knowing that attached to her trusteeship are special responsibilities of which she should make herself aware.

In contrast, where Y Ltd happens to hold money on a bare trust for X Ltd over a brief period in the furtherance of a contract, X Ltd and Y Ltd consider themselves to be in a commercial relationship where the parties are of full capacity dealing with each other to further their commercial interests and are in a position to take steps to avoid or mitigate loss. In the case of the smoke alarms, it seems reasonable for X Ltd and Y Ltd to consider that Y Ltd is to use X Ltd's money only to purchase efficient alarms so as not to cause losses to X Ltd that on a common sense view of causation are caused by Y Ltd's failure to purchase efficient alarms[139] — rather than the activities of a terrorist which could well have been prevented by the warehouseman.

If X Ltd claims that by sharp practice in using a temporary bare trust it intended to make Y Ltd as strictly liable for consequential losses as if Y Ltd had been a traditional trustee, its claim to enforce such strict liability should fail because it is surely reasonable for Y Ltd, in the over-arching contractual context, to believe that there will be no such strict liability unless spelled out in the contract.

The extent of equitable compensation for a breach of trust in these contractual circumstances should thus be the same as if damages for breach of contract were sought at law. In *Target Holdings Ltd v Redferns*[140] it so happened that the action was commenced in the Chancery division as if it were an ordinary breach of trust action. There seems no reason in these days with the fusion of the administration of law and equity why such an action should not be regarded as an over-arching breach of contract action in which the bare trust is merely an incidental feature introduced by "independent and equal actors concerned primarily with their own interests",[141] so that the measure of damages should depend on contractual common law principles.

CONCLUSIONS

There should be no unique rules for consequential losses where there is an incidental trust element of a contract, but, as earlier indicated, there does need to be uniquely stringent rules for the traditional trust concerned with the trustee's continuing management of assets for individuals exposed to the trustee's controlling functions,[142] and often also vulnerable through being weak-minded or minors or, as yet, unborn.

Liability for consequential losses needs to be strict for breach of the proscriptive primary obligations of undivided loyalty and of fidelity to the terms of the trust: such breaches amount to unauthorised conduct to which is attached liability for substitutive performance. However, it should be appreciated nowadays that there is no proscriptive primary obligation not to fall below the requisite degree of care and skill so as to cause negligent conduct to be treated as unauthorised. Thus, there should be no such strict liability once there has been a breach of the requisite degree of care and skill in the course of authorised conduct: there should be no liability for intervening or extraneous causes, it being necessary to restrict liability to whatever was the foreseeable kind of harm that it was the trustee's duty to guard against. Whether the

---

139 See *Canson Enterprises Ltd v Boughton* [1991] 3 SCR 534 at 556 per McLachlin J, endorsed in *Target Holdings Ltd v Redferns* [1996] 1 AC 421, and the need to focus on the kind of harm against which it was the defendant's duty to guard the claimant as in the cases in n 117 above.

140 [1996] 1 AC 421.

141 See nn 8 and 9 above.

142 Company directors are subject to the same stringent liability if disposing of company property for unauthorised purposes: *Bishopsgate Investment Management v Maxwell (No 2)* [1994] 1 All ER 261; *O'Halloran v R T Thomas & Family Pty Ltd* (1998) 45 NSWLR 262; *Re Duckwari plc* [1999] Ch 253.

trustee's wrongful conduct was unauthorised or authorised, questions of contributory negligence and mitigation of loss are irrelevant and there cannot be an award of compensation for distress and inconvenience nor the award of an exemplary sum.

However, in the case of a trustee holding property for a beneficiary absolutely entitled to income or capital or both, there is scope for contributory negligence and mitigation of loss to be relevant and there should be scope in special circumstances for the award of compensation for distress and inconvenience, while in monstrous circumstances there should even be scope for the award of an exemplary sum. These possibilities should also arise where a claimant sues someone over a fiduciary aspect of their relationship not covering the continuing proper management of property, although the strength of the scope of the fiduciary obligation may oust any questions concerning contributory negligence and mitigation of loss and also give rise to strict liability for all consequential issues, especially if deceit is involved[143] — but these wider issues fall outside the scope of this investigation into the rules of trusts law.

Finally, common law judges when dealing with trust issues must not allow themselves to be taken in by a superficial view of the merits of a party, but should clearly analyse the trust issues and not take a shallow, broad-brush approach like that taken by the majority of the Ontario Court of Appeal in *Froese v Montreal Trust Co*:[144] they readily allowed the tort of negligence to be too pervasive and extend beyond its scope so as to override the position in equity. They held pension trust beneficiaries entitled to common law damages against a custodian trustee (a "deep-pocket" defendant) where it had failed to chase up and collect contributions that should have been paid to it by the beneficiaries' employer, which was trustee of the trust and had gone into liquidation without paying many months of contributions as if it was entitled to a "holiday" from such payments.

In the trust deed, the employer-trustee had expressly arranged for the custodian trustee to be custodian of moneys paid to it and investments purchased by it in accordance with directions given by the employer-trustee's portfolio manager. Crucially, under the terms of the deed the custodian trustee was to restrict itself to its custodianship functions and not be under any duty to chase up the employer-trustee over payment of contributions. Thus, in Equity, under the trust deed the beneficiaries took their benefits subject to the burden or risk of the above arrangements, so making it unnecessary for the custodian trustee to consider further the beneficiaries' interests. The beneficiaries could not have made the custodian trustee account in equity for the contributions that the employer-trustee in breach of trust had failed to pay.

It is then not at all justifiable to take the broad-brush approach that the custodian should have appreciated that the beneficiaries were its "neighbours", who could be adversely affected if the employer-trustee were allowed to get away with not paying overdue contributions, and therefore the custodian came under a common law duty to check whether or not payments had been duly

---

143 *Standard Chartered Bank v Pakistan National Shipping Corp* [2003] 1 AC 959.
144 (1996) 137 DLR (4th) 725.

paid and, if they had not been paid, a duty promptly to stimulate the beneficiaries to take steps to enforce their rights against the employer-trustee. Before fusion of the administration of law and equity the common law courts had no jurisdiction to hear a dispute within the exclusive jurisdiction of equity, and a court of equity would have issued an injunction to prevent a claimant proceeding in a common law court with any "dressed-up" claim that essentially was within equity's exclusive jurisdiction. Fusion of administration of law and equity should not have increased the burdens of custodian trusteeship.

We should all heed the warning of Stevenson J in *Canson Enterprises Ltd v Boughton*[145] when he said, "I greatly fear that talk of fusing law and equity results in confusing and confounding the law."

---

145 [1991] 3 SCR 534 at 590.

12

Proprietary Restitution

PETER MILLETT

FUSION

I shall begin with a question of those who organised this conference, from which the chapters in this book derive. Why choose this subject? It excites some academic lawyers, but it is of little interest to the judiciary and none to practitioners. 130 years have passed since the *Judicature Acts*, and this issue, if it was ever truly alive, is surely dead by now. I thought it had been killed off by the preface to the second edition of *Meagher, Gummow & Lehane*.

Those who favour the fusion of law and equity might perhaps reflect that the three greatest systems of jurisprudence in the Western world have all been dual systems. Jewish law had its written and oral law; Roman law its civil and praetorian or bonitary law; English law common law and equity. In each case the duality served a similar function. One system provided certainty; the other the necessary flexibility and adaptability to enable justice to be done. But the common law and equity are not two separate and parallel systems of law. The common law is a complete system of law which could stand alone, but which if not tempered by equity would often be productive of injustice; while equity is not a complete and independent system of law and could not stand alone. In the words of that fine Australian judge Kitto J it is "the saving supplement and complement of the Common Law."[1]

Is it true to say that the division between law and equity is, as Professor Burrows puts it, "a purely historical and not a rational division"?[2] This assertion is based on the premise that "similar functions are performed by the remedies available for equitable wrongs as by the remedies for torts and breach of contract;... there is therefore a coherence in remedial function for civil wrongs which transcends the common law/equity divide."[3]

---

1 FW Kitto, 'Foreword' to R Meagher, WMC Gummow and J Lehane, *Equity: Doctrines and Remedies* (1st ed, Butterworths, Sydney, 1975) at vii.

2 A Burrows, *Remedies for Torts and Breach of Contract* (3rd ed, Oxford University Press, Oxford, 2004) at 636.

3 A Burrows, *Remedies for Torts and Breach of Contract*, above n 2 at 637.

I do not accept this. Those who would extend the common law, and particularly the law of contract into those areas which have hitherto been the province of equity's exclusive jurisdiction ignore the fundamental difference between the remedies awarded in the two jurisdictions. The entire concept of equitable proprietary interests rests upon the fact that equity, unlike the common law, can order the defendant to transfer property in specie to the claimant. The primary remedy for breach of contract is damages, and common lawyers tend to describe all monetary remedies for breach of an obligation, whether legal or equitable, as damages or compensation. But it is misleading, and potentially dangerous, to equate a breach of trust or fiduciary obligation as if it were the equitable counterpart of breach of contract at common law, or to think of equitable compensation for breach of an equitable obligation as if it were common law damages masquerading under a fancy name.

The common law treats a breach of contract as a wrong and awards damages as compensation for loss suffered in consequence. A contracting party is under a primary obligation to perform his part of the bargain and a secondary obligation to pay damages if he does not.[4] Equity, in the exercise of its exclusive jurisdiction over trustees and fiduciaries, that is to say persons who are obliged to act in the interests of others, does not award compensation for loss. Trustees are stewards of other persons' property. Their primary obligation is to account for their stewardship. The primary remedy of a beneficiary is to have the account taken, to surcharge or falsify the account, and to make the trustee to make good any deficiency which appears when the account is taken. The liability is strict. The account must be taken down to the date of the account.

If a trustee or fiduciary has committed a breach of trust or fiduciary duty, Equity makes him account as if he had not done so,[5] and allows his beneficiary to surcharge or falsify the account accordingly. This is a radically different approach; indeed it is the converse approach. It does not treat the defendant as a wrongdoer; it disregards his wrongdoing, makes him account as if he has acted properly throughout, and does not permit him to deny that he has done so. By this means it not only requires him to make good any loss suffered by the beneficiary, but makes him disgorge his gain

If the beneficiary complains that the trustees have misapplied trust money, he falsifies the account; that is to say, he asks the court to disallow the disbursement. If he complains that the trustees have failed to obtain all that they should have done for the benefit of the trust estate, he surcharges the account. The trustees are made to account, not only for what they have in fact received, but also for what they would have received if they had acted with due diligence or proper skill and care.

---

4   *Moschi v Lep Air Services Ltd* [1973] AC 331.
5   He is not allowed to say that he acted in breach of duty: see *Fawcett v Whitehouse* (1829) 1 Russ & M 132; 39 ER 51; *Re Biss* [1903] 2 Ch 40; *Re Smith* [1896] 1 Ch 71 at 77 per Kekewich J; J Story, *Story's Equity Jurisprudence* (3rd ed, Charles C Little & James Brown, Boston, 1843) at [1210]-[1211a]; PD Finn, *Fiduciary Obligations* (Sydney, Law Book Co, 1977) at 221; and see *Attorney-General for Hong Kong v Reid* [1994] 1 AC 324 at 337 citing with apparent approval my own article, "Bribes and Secret Commissions" [1993] *Restitution Law Review* 7.

A firm grasp of these principles would have provided a simple solution in the unsatisfactory case of *Target Holdings Ltd v Redfern*.[6] It would only be right to observe that Burrows does not agree with me on this; but then as an ardent fusionist he could not. In fact my analysis is entirely orthodox, supported by centuries of case law. Only *Target Holdings Ltd v Redfern* is inconsistent with it. It also explains the difficult case of *Attorney-General for Hong Kong v Reid*,[7] of which I thoroughly approve and to which I must return later.

This is not to say that we should stay as we are. We should not integrate equity and the common law by fusing them; but we should seek to harmonise them wherever possible. There is no justification for requiring dishonesty for liability for procuring a beach of trust but not for procuring a breach of contract.[8] There is no justification for retaining different rules to deal with the same factual situation, which may happen where the case falls within equity's concurrent jurisdiction. We have far too many causes of action for recovering the proceeds of fraud, each with different rules. We do not need three personal claims to recover the proceeds of fraud: (a) the claim at law for money had and received (b) the claim in equity for "knowing receipt" and (c) the claim in restitution. They should be replaced by a single personal claim for restitution with a single set of rules. We do not need three defences: (a) the common law defence of ministerial receipt (b) the equitable defence that the money was not received for the defendant's own use and benefit and (c) the restitutionary defence of innocent change of position. As long ago as 1989 when sitting at first instance I called for the development of a single unified restitutionary remedy for such cases.[9]

I was dealing with a personal claim against a defendant who had parted with the property in question, and was concerned by the difference between the common law claim for money had and received, where liability is strict and determined at the date of receipt, and the equitable claim for knowing receipt, which was thought to require proof that the defendant had constructive notice of the claim before parting with the property. There is no justification for two different rules. I have always agreed with the late Professor Birks,[10] whom I gratefully acknowledge as my mentor, guide and friend through the thickets of the law of restitution, and whose presence we sorely miss today, that we should

---

6   [1996] 1 AC 421. The breach of trust consisted of the release by a solicitor of money in his client account in payment of the purchase price of land without receiving the title deeds in exchange. This put the trust fund at risk, but the risk did not eventuate; completion took place a few days later. After discussing the appropriate test of causation, the House of Lords refused to "stop the clock" and award damages for a loss which had not been sustained. But it is surely better to say that, on taking a full account of the trustee's dealings, the unauthorised disbursement of the money should be disallowed and the solicitor treated as accountable as if the money were still in his client account and available to be laid out in the manner authorised by the trust. The subsequent acquisition of the title deeds and any disbursement necessary to obtain them were so authorised. In taking the account the solicitor should be treated as having made an authorised disbursement of money notionally restored to the trust. No question of causation would arise.

7   [1994] 1 AC 324.

8   *Twinsectra Ltd v Yardley* [2002] 2 AC 164.

9   *Agip (Africa) Ltd v Jackson* [1990] Ch 265 at 289.

10 P Birks, *Unjust Enrichment* (2nd ed, Oxford University Press, Oxford, 2005) at 156-158.

simplify the law and subject the equitable claim for knowing receipt to the common law rule. Restitution is receipt based, not fault based, and liability should be strict whether the claim is brought at law or in equity. Equity made liability depend on notice only because it would be unjust to make an innocent recipient disgorge the value of property after he has consumed or parted with it on the faith of the receipt and without notice of the claimant's interest. But such considerations should provide a defence; they should not go to liability. The development of a change of position defence has made it possible to simplify and rationalise the law of restitution by dispensing with the need for the claimant to prove notice on the part of the recipient in equity as at common law: the way is clear for harmonisation.[11]

THE PROPRIETARY RESTITUTIONARY REMEDY

The question to which I now turn is one of the most difficult in the law of restitution: in what circumstances may a claimant be awarded a proprietary remedy, and when is he confined to a personal remedy?

Property or unjust enrichment?

I would like to begin by asking you to consider the question: What branch of the law are we discussing? Will we find our answer in the law of property or in the law of unjust enrichment? The relationship between them is obscure and controversial. This is partly at least because the taxonomy and terminology of restitution are still unsettled, with consequent semantic and conceptual confusion. Scholars are not agreed on the ambit of the law of restitution or the relationship of restitution and unjust enrichment. To my mind restitution is both a cause of action and a remedy; unjust enrichment is its unifying jurisprudential basis. But, leaving aside restitution for wrongs (the existence of which is highly problematic), do restitution and unjust enrichment quadrate? Burrows adheres to Birks' original view that they do. But Birks changed his mind. In his latest and, alas! last, book he acknowledges that restitution is wider than unjust enrichment. He describes the law of unjust enrichment as "the law of gain-based recovery ... a right to a gain received by the defendant";[12] refers to "restitution outside unjust enrichment";[13] and says that "restitution ... is a category of response ... [t]he causative event is not always unjust enrichment."[14] I respectfully agree, and shall adopt the same terminology today.[15]

We derive our legal architecture from the Romans. They divided the civil law into (1) the law of property and (2) the law of obligations. They insisted that every action must fall into one or the other; it could not fall simultaneously into both. They would have liked to subdivide the law of obligations into

---

11   See my own judgment in *Boscawen v Bajwa* [1996] 1 WLR 328 at 341.
12   P Birks, *Unjust Enrichment,* above n 10 at 3.
13   P Birks, *Unjust Enrichment,* above n 10 at 11.
14   P Birks, *Unjust Enrichment,* above n 10 at 17.
15   He would not, however, agree with much that follows!

(i) contract and (ii) delict, but the law is untidy and whatever classification is adopted there is always a bit left over.[16] So the Romans added (iii) actions quasi ex contractu and (iv) actions quasi ex delicto. English judges misunderstood the word "quasi" (which they though meant that the action was "sort of contractual" when it really signified that it was not actually contractual at all) and based their law of quasi-contract on an implied promise on the part of the recipient to repay. This theory has long been exploded; the law does not imply a fictitious promise to repay but imposes a personal obligation to make restitution in order to reverse unjust enrichment. Civilian systems confine unjust enrichment to the law of obligations. So, I suggest, should we.

But where does equity fit in? It is impossible to fit it neatly into the legal structure bequeathed to us by the Romans. It straddles both the law of property and the law of obligations. It gives rise to a paradox which civilian lawyers find incomprehensible. The common law, which acts in rem, has virtually no proprietary remedies; equity, which acts in personam, has a full range of proprietary remedies.

The common law of restitution was developed as an appendage to the law of contract; and in its concurrent jurisdiction, when it was concerned to reverse unjust enrichment, equity took the same view. But in its exclusive jurisdiction, when it was concerned with trustees who absconded with the trust property, equity regarded the law of restitution as part of the law of trusts, that is to say, part of the law of property. This distinction is critical; we must not disregard it even as we try to develop a unified law of restitution.

The majority academic view, expounded in particular by Birks and Burrows, is that the law of property governs the claimant's original property, while the law of unjust enrichment governs its traceable proceeds. As Birks puts it:[17]

"Proprietary interests contingent on tracing, which is as much to say proprietary interests in traceable substitutes for other assets in which the claimant undoubtedly did hold a proprietary interest, always arise from unjust enrichment."

They claim that the recipient is invariably enriched by having the use of the traceable proceeds of claimant's property (though not, apparently, of his original property), and the law responds to the unjust enrichment by creating a new proprietary right which it then carries back to the claimant. This convoluted analysis is not based on anything in any reported case, is not universally accepted by commentators, and is inconsistent with the analysis adopted by the House of Lords in *Foskett v McKeown*.[18] I reject it. I prefer to say with Lord Ellenborough in *Taylor v Plumer* that:[19]

---

16 Even in Birks' world of event and response, he is compelled to have a category of events which he describes as "a residual miscellany of events". There is always need for a dustbin.

17 P Birks, "Property and Unjust Enrichment: Categorical Truths" [1997] *New Zealand Law Review* 623 at 661. See other articles by him and A Burrows, "Proprietary Restitution: Unmasking Unjust Enrichment" [2001] 117 *Law Quarterly Review* 412 (explaining why the House of Lords was wrong on this point in *Foskett v McKeown* [2001] 1 AC 102).

18 [2001] 1 AC 102 at 119.

19 (1815) 3 M & S 562 at 575; 105 ER 721 at 726.

"[T]he product of or substitute for the original thing still follows the nature of the thing itself[.]"

Admittedly Lord Ellenborough did not explain why the product or substitute belongs to the person who owned the original thing; but he obviously thought, as I do, that it belongs to him *because* he owned the original thing. In other words, the consequence is an ordinary incidence of the English law of property; what Birks, begging the question, dismisses as "the fiction of persistence".[20]

There is a difference, of course, between owning a thing and owning its exchange product. Suppose you steal my antique silver candlesticks, sell them and give the proceeds to a friend, who uses them to buy a picture. If it is worth less than the candlesticks, I can follow them into the purchaser's hands and demand them back. If I can identify them I can say: "Give them back to me because they are mine". I can prove they are mine by showing that I bought them, or was given them, or inherited them.[21] I succeed by invoking two principles: (i) that a thief does not acquire title to the goods he has stolen; and (ii) the principle nemo dat quod non habet. Both rules form part of the law of property. They tell us who owns the candlesticks.

Now suppose the picture is worth more than the candlesticks. I can trace my proprietary interest in the candlesticks into their substitute, first into the proceeds of sale and then into the picture. I can demand that the picture be handed over to me "because it is mine". It is no use your friend saying: "Nonsense: it is mine. I bought it from a reputable dealer. It never belonged to you at all and does not belong to you now". She is speaking as a layman, who thinks of property as a physical thing. But as Jeremy Bentham observed, property is not a thing but a legal concept, like possession. It is a relationship between a person and a thing. If the law says that something is mine, it means that I have title to it. And title is a legal concept.

So far Birks and Burrows agree with me: they acknowledge that the picture belongs to me. The difference between us is that they say that I have an entirely new proprietary right created by the law of restitution at the point of the substitution in order to reverse unjust enrichment, whereas I say that I own the picture because the law of property says that I do. It says that I can assert title to anything bought with my money, whether I authorised the purchase or not.

Why bring unjust enrichment into it? It is the law of property which deals with the creation, acquisition, disposal and transmission of property rights. It protects pre-existing rights of property. It tells us who owns disputed property. One of the rules of our law of property, common to both equity and the common law, is that the owner of a thing can claim ownership of its traceable proceeds. The rule is not a rule of natural law. It is not universal. We do not have to have such a rule. We choose to have it. Most civilian systems do not.

---

20   P Birks, *Unjust Enrichment* (2nd ed, Oxford University Press, Oxford, 2003) at 198.
21   In fact I do not have to do this: it is enough to show that I was in possession.

The basis of the rule

How did we arrive at the rule? Not by way of unjust enrichment. Equity took the authorised disposition of trust property by the trustee as its starting point. A trust fund is not a res. The beneficiaries' interests in a trust fund are proprietary interests in the assets from time to time comprised in the fund subject to the trustees' overriding powers of managing and alienating the trust assets and substituting others. On an authorised sale of a trust investment, the beneficiaries' proprietary interests in the investment are overreached; that is to say, they are automatically transferred from the investment which is sold to the proceeds of sale and any new investment acquired with them. This is "the fiction of persistence", except that it is not a fiction. The beneficiaries' interests in the new investment are exactly the same as their interest in the old. They have a continuing beneficial interest which persists in the substitute.

Now suppose that the disposal is unauthorised. The trustee sells a trust investment in breach of trust and uses the proceeds to buy shares for himself. The beneficiaries have a continuing proprietary interest in the original investment but they cannot recover it from the purchaser if he is a bona fide purchaser of the legal title without notice of the breach. But they can instead claim a proprietary interest in the shares which the trustee bought for himself. He bought them with trust money, and the beneficiaries are not bound to challenge sale of the trust shares or the purchase of the new shares as a breach of trust. That is a matter for them. They can have the trust account taken on the footing that the sale and purchase were authorised transactions, and the trustee cannot be heard to say that they were not.[22] The beneficiaries do not thereby ratify or authorise the trustee's conduct. They simply require the trustee to account for all his dealings with the trust property whether authorised or not; and then decide whether to falsify the account by disallowing the disposal of the trust investments (in which case the trustee must restore them or their value to the trust) or to let the account stand, in which case the new shares are treated as if they were an authorised investment made for the beneficiaries' account. The trustee cannot resist the claim by saying: "You have got it wrong. I acted in breach of trust. I stole the trust property and used it to buy shares for myself."

The only difference between an unauthorised substitution of trust property and an authorised one is one of timing. If the substitution is authorised the beneficiaries' interest in the substituted property is automatically and fully vested at the moment of acquisition. If the substitution is unauthorised, their interest is inchoate, for they may reject it. Their interest in the substitute does not crystallise fully until they elect to accept it. Their right to accept it is a right given to them by the law of property. It is an incident of their property rights in the original asset. Unjust enrichment does not come into it.[23]

It is often said that wrongfully substituted assets are held on a constructive trust. I do not think they are. I think that they continue to be held on the same

---

22 *Re Biss* [1903] 2 Ch 40.
23 For a fuller discussion see D Fox, 'Overreaching' in P Birks and A Pretto (eds), *Breach of Trust* (2nd ed, Hart Publishing, Oxford, 2002), chapter 4.

trusts throughout. If the claimant was the beneficiary under an express trust, the substituted assets are held on the same express trusts. If he was an absolute beneficial owner, they are held on a resulting trust for him. It is sometimes said that the resulting trust is a response to unjust enrichment. In this context it is a response to the disposal of property without the owner's consent. This gives us a principled basis for proprietary restitution. I have long argued that the resulting trust provides a sound basis, indeed the only basis, for proprietary restitution.

Birks and Burrows are troubled by what they call "the geometric multiplication of claims". In the example I have given, the claimant can, in theory at least, lay claim to own the candlesticks, the proceeds of sale, and the picture. He must elect between them, of course; and usually the facts will dictate the choice he has to make. I do not see a problem; but, if there is, it is not solved by invoking the law of unjust enrichment instead of the law of property. Whichever theory is adopted, the result is the same; the claimant can lay claim to the original asset or its traceable proceeds at his option. There is no problem unless you treat property as meaning the physical thing rather than the title.

There is a serious problem with proprietary restitution, though: it may give the claimant an undeserved windfall. In the example I have given, I can claim ownership of the picture even though its value far exceeds the value of the candlesticks.[24] Where the defendant is or claims through a wrongdoer, we need not worry. In the extreme case where A misappropriates B's money and uses it to buy a winning ticket in the lottery, B is entitled to the winnings. Since A is a wrongdoer, it is irrelevant that he could have used his own money if in fact he used B's. This may seem to give B an undeserved windfall, but the result is not unjust. Had B discovered the fraud before the draw, he could have decided whether to keep the ticket or demand his money back. He alone has the right to decide whether to gamble with his own money. If A fraudulently keeps him in ignorance until after the draw, he suffers the consequence. He cannot deprive B of his right to choose what to do with his own money; but he can give him an informed choice.

But suppose the defendant or his predecessor in title is innocent? Suppose A did not realise that the money belongs to B, that he had sufficient resources of his own to buy the ticket, and being an honest man would have used his own money if he had appreciated that the money he did use did not belong to him? In such a case it is mere chance that he used the claimant's money and not his own. It is an affront to our notions of justice that the claimant should recover the winnings if he used the claimant's money but not if he used his own. It makes the law itself a lottery.

The problem is well known, and still unsolved. There several possible solutions: (i) we could entitle the innocent recipient to all just allowances for his input, whether labour, skill or luck; in the extreme case of the lottery ticket bought for a nominal sum, that arguably amounts to the whole of the winnings, for the contribution made by the money is negligible; or (ii) we

---

24 In *Trustee of the Property of FC Jones & Sons v Jones* [1997] Ch 159 the property which the claimant recovered was worth five times the value of the property of which he had been deprived.

could confine the claimant an equitable lien on the winnings to recover his stake. But, as Professor Worthington has observed,[25] abandoning the property analysis and substituting unjust enrichment does not solve the problem. The unjust element in unjust enrichment has nothing to do with fault. It is either always unjust to use another's property without his consent or it is not. I prefer to recognise the flexibility with which equity is capable of manipulating our concepts of property. When determining the nature and extent of the proprietary remedy which it will make available, equity can easily distinguish between wrongful and innocent misapplication of funds.[26]

In what circumstances is a proprietary restitutionary remedy available?

So I hold firmly to the view (i) that the answer to this question is to be found in the law of property, not in the law of unjust enrichment; and (ii) that the answer must be the same whether we are dealing with the original property or its traceable proceeds. But what is the answer?

There are two views in play. One is propounded by most though by no means all of the most distinguished academic restitutionary lawyers, particularly Professors Goode (who first propounded it), Burrows, and Birks (who was a late convert to it), but has no firm support in authority and none in principle; while the other has less academic support but is at least principled and accords better with traditional taxonomy.

The majority draw the line between those cases where the right to restitution arises at the outset, eo instanti with the impugned payment or transfer, and those cases where the payment or transfer is unassailable when made but becomes reversible subsequently when an unjust factor occurs. I prefer to draw the line in a different place; between those cases which depend on unjust enrichment and those where it depends on title.

While completely different the two approaches would in fact reach the same result in most cases, which may explain why the question remains unresolved in English law. They agree on four matters:

(1) A proprietary claim cannot succeed unless (and except to the extent that) the claimant can locate the property in question or its traceable proceeds in the hands of the defendant. This is not, of course, a sufficient condition of proprietary relief; but it is a necessary one.

(2) Whether a proprietary remedy is or is not available depends upon the particular ground on which restitution is claimed (the so-called "unjust factor"). This is one reason why the decision of the House of Lords in *Westdeutsche Landesbank Girozentrale v Islington LBC*[27] is unsatisfactory. The Court of Appeal held that the ground of restitution was either "absence of consideration" – which is not a ground at all – or total failure of consideration – which is; and there was no appeal from this part of their decision. In fact the true ground of restitution was mistake.

---

25 S Worthington, *Equity* (Oxford University Press, Oxford, 2003) at 100-101.

26 In *Foskett v McKeown* the defendants were innocent but claimed through a wrongdoer.

27 [1996] AC 669.

(3) A proprietary remedy is not available where the ground of restitution is failure of consideration.

(4) A proprietary remedy is available where the ground of restitution is (as I would say) want of title rather than unjust enrichment; or (as Birks would say) where the ground of restitution is unauthorised substitution.

The difference between the two approaches arises in those cases where the payment or transfer is voidable for mistake, duress, legal compulsion, and so on. The paradigm case, of course, is mistaken payment. The majority say that in principle a proprietary remedy is available in such a case. They can pray in aid the decision of Goulding J in *Chase Manhattan Bank NA v Israel-British Bank (London) Ltd.*[28] But no one supports the actual reasoning in the case; and the decision is highly doubtful. I regard it as wrongly decided.

I shall in due course ask you to consider, not what the law is – for it is undecided – but what it should be. Does justice require the innocent recipient of a mistaken payment to disgorge the money in specie together with any profits made by its use and (if insolvent) in priority to his other creditors? Or is it sufficient that he repay a sum equal to the amount he received and if insolvent pari passu with his other creditors?

The property based personal claim

The advantages of claiming a proprietary remedy are well known: (i) unless the claimant is confined to a lien, he recovers the asset in specie, even if it is worth far more than the original asset which was taken; (ii) the claim can be brought not only against the immediate recipient but against a successor in title; (iii) it is not subject to the change of position defence; and (iv) it prevails in an insolvency. But there are important drawbacks: (i) a proprietary claim is subject to the bona fide purchaser defence; (ii) it may be subject to all just allowances in favour of an innocent defendant; and (iii) the claimant must identify an asset in the defendant's hands in which he claims a proprietary interest. If the substituted asset is worth more than the original the claimant gets a windfall. If is worth less he suffers a loss. He can assert a proprietary interest in the substitute, but he is too late to assert a proprietary interest in the more valuable asset which the defendant has disposed of. If the defendant has consumed the original or given it away without receiving anything in exchange, there is nothing to which claimant can lay claim at all. This has nothing to do with the change of position defence, though it has much the same effect; a proprietary claim is confined to the asset remaining in the defendant's hands.

But the claimant is not without a remedy in these circumstances; he may have a personal remedy, for property generates personal as well as proprietary claims. There are two kinds of personal restitutionary claim; the purely personal claim which is brought to reverse unjust enrichment, and the property based personal claim which is brought to recover the value of the claimant's property. A property based personal claim to restitution is

---

28   [1981] Ch 105.

available whether the defendant has parted with the property or not. At law the claimant had an action for money had and received, which lay not only where the defendant was personally indebted to him but also where he had had the claimant's money in his possession. In equity he has a claim for knowing receipt.

Property based personal claims share some of the advantages of a proprietary claim; as Mansfield CJ made clear, even at law they can be brought against a successor in title of the original recipient. But in other respects they share most of the disadvantages of purely personal claims which lack a property base and are brought to reverse unjust enrichment. Purely personal claims (i) do not (normally) allow recovery in specie; (ii) are confined to the value originally received, so no windfall and no loss; (iii) lie against the original recipient only; (iv) do not (normally) prevail in a bankruptcy; and (v) are subject to the change of position defence; but (vi) do not permit just allowances. Some of this may be controversial; but in general it holds good.

But what of the change of position defence? As I have explained, this is not needed as a defence to a proprietary claim. It is available as a defence to a purely personal claim to reverse unjust enrichment, where it reflects the fact that the defendant has become disenriched. Is it available to the property based restitutionary claim? This question is not yet resolved. It is not, *pace* many commentators, excluded by the decision of the House of Lords in *Foskett v McKeown*,[29] a case to which I shall return.

Different categories of case

So I come at last to the question: in what circumstances is a proprietary restitutionary remedy available? There are three main categories of case to be considered.

(1) At one extreme there is the case where the claimant intends to part with both legal and beneficial interest in the property. There is no resulting trust and so no proprietary remedy. An example is a claim for money paid on a total failure of consideration. The claimant makes a valid payment which passes title both at law and in equity, fully intending to part with the beneficial interest and never expecting to see his money again. He clearly has no proprietary claim. The buyer who pays in advance for goods which he never receives because the supplier goes into liquidation must enforce his claim to restitution by proving in the liquidation. The seller who supplies goods on credit must prove in the buyer's liquidation. It will not help him that he may be able to identify the goods in the liquidator's possession. Goode and others agree; the payment or transfer itself was unassailable when made; the unjust factor supervened afterwards. But there is a better reason than this for denying the claimant a proprietary claim. He relinquished all beneficial interest in the goods when he supplied them. Title both at law and equity passed to the buyer (and probably to its bank under a floating charge). The claimant has a

---

29 [2001] 1 AC 102.

personal claim; but it is a purely personal claim which lacks any kind of proprietary base.

(2) At the other extreme there are those cases where the beneficial interest (or a fortiori the legal title) does not pass. Here the claimant clearly has a proprietary remedy, either to give effect to his legal title or (if this has passed) to his beneficial title under a resulting trust. There are two situations. One, very rare, where there is a defect in the payment or transfer itself. Where this is void, no title passes to the recipient. The other, far more common, is the three-party case where a fiduciary, in breach of his fiduciary duty and without the knowledge or authority of his principal, pays away his principal's money. The rule of equity is that the principal's beneficial interest is not extinguished by a disposal in breach of trust or fiduciary duty unless the recipient is a bona fide purchaser for value without notice. The legal title will pass but the beneficial interest will not. There is no need for the principal to rescind the transaction in order to revest the property; in the eyes of equity the beneficial interest never left him, for it never accompanied the legal title.[30] The ground of specific restitution is want of title.

(3) The large, intermediate class comprises all those two-party cases of unjust enrichment where the claimant makes a valid payment or transfer, fully intending to part with the beneficial interest to the recipient but his consent is vitiated by some unjust factor such as fraud, mistake, misrepresentation and so on. In these cases the beneficial interest passes and there is no resulting trust for the claimant to enforce. He does, however, have the right to elect whether to affirm the transaction or rescind it. If he rescinds it, it is often assumed[31] that the beneficial title automatically revests in the claimant, and the authorities suggest that it does so retrospectively. But the recipient cannot anticipate his decision. Pending the

---

30 Technically an absolute owner does not possess an equitable interest. He has the full legal and beneficial interest. His equitable interest under the resulting trust arises for the first time on the disposition, when the equitable interest became separated from and did not accompany the legal title: see *Westdeutsche Landesbank Girozentrale v Islington LBC* [1996] AC 669. But nothing turns on this. It would be absurd to distinguish between the case of the absolute owner whose property is misappropriated by a fiduciary and the beneficiary under a bare trust whose property is misappropriated by the trustee.

31 When I delivered this paper in Sydney in December 2004 I accepted the traditional view that rescission for fraud revested the legal title in the transferor: see *Carr & Universal Finance Co Ltd v Caldwell* [1965] 1 QB 525. The proposition can be traced back to the judgment of Parke B in *Load v Green* (1846) 15 M & W 216; 153 ER 828. Since then, however, Mr Swadling has convincingly demonstrated that Parke B invented the rule, which is difficult to justify in principle and is based on previous authority which does not support it: W Swadling, "Rescission, Property, and the Common Law" (2005) 121 *Law Quarterly Review* 122. The better view, which he espouses and which is supported by authority before and since, is that a defrauded vendor should be able to rescind his contract of sale but this should not carry with it any revesting of title, at least in the case where title passed by delivery pursuant to the rescinded contract and not by the contract itself: see *Singh v Ali* [1960] AC 167. If this is right, then equity must follow the law by denying any revesting of title merely because the underlying transaction is set aside.

claimant's decision to rescind, the recipient is entitled and may be bound to treat the payment as effective.[32] It is well established that the claimant's subsequent rescission does not invalidate or render wrongful transactions which have taken place in the meantime on the faith of the receipt. Pending rescission, therefore, the recipient has the whole legal and beneficial interest, but (or so it is assumed) his title is defeasible. There is no fiduciary relationship, and so no basis for a resulting trust. If the recipient's title is defeasible, this ought not to inhibit his use of the property pending rescission. In these circumstances any right which the claimant may have to a retransfer in specie after rescission is best regarded, not as a consequence of a constructive or resulting trust, nor as a response to unjust enrichment, but as part of the working out of the equitable remedy of rescission, which is tightly controlled and subject to its own defences. I have suggested elsewhere that the right to a retransfer *in specie* might be treated, by analogy with the remedy of specific performance, as available where, in the particular circumstances of the case, a monetary payment would be inadequate. If so, then proprietary restitution in this third category of case should be confined to cases of land or other property of special value to the claimant.

What distinguishes this third category of case from the second is not the absence of a fiduciary relationship. It may be present. It is the distinction between property obtained, whether by a fiduciary or not, by means of a voidable transaction, and property obtained by a fiduciary in breach of fiduciary duty. Put another way, the distinction is between property obtained with the knowledge and consent of the beneficial owner, but whose consent is vitiated by some unjust factor; and property obtained without his knowledge or authority by a fiduciary exploiting his position for his own benefit.

This results in the perpetuation of the much criticised distinction between breach of trust or fiduciary duty and other cases, but for a new purpose. It has nothing to do with tracing; but it is a real distinction which is relevant to the nature of the remedy. The existence of a breach of trust or fiduciary duty should not be a precondition of the application of the equitable tracing rules, which may be necessary to establish a claim (whether to a proprietary or personal remedy) to traceable proceeds. But in the absence of a right to specific reconveyance after rescission, which may depend on the nature of the property, it should be a necessary precondition for proprietary restitution.

Of course there are other cases – a bit left over – where the obligation to make restitution arises from "other varied causes". An example would be the right to recover money paid in anticipation of a contract which does not materialise. If the claimant can overcome the main obstacle which faces him, of showing that he did not knowingly take the risk that the contract would not materialise, he may have a personal claim to restitution. But there is no basis on which he can have a proprietary remedy unless he can establish a *Quistclose* trust. It is not sufficient to show that he paid the money for a purpose which failed; he must go further and show that he paid it to the intent that it should

---

32   See *Bristol and West Building Society v Mothew* [1998] Ch 1.

be used for the stated purpose and for no other purpose. This creates a resulting trust in favour of the claimant and entitles him to a proprietary remedy.[33]

The merits of the rival views.

As I have indicated, there is no difference in outcome between the two approaches except in the third or intermediate class of case, of which mistaken payment is the paradigm example. Which should we adopt? The question is at large. What does justice require?

Let us assume that I pay you £1 million by mistake. I mistakenly thought that I owed you the money. Or perhaps I did owe you the money, but forgot that I had already repaid you. You did nothing to induce my mistake, and are unaware of it. You pay the money into your bank account; and it is still there. When I wake up and realise my mistake, I naturally demand that you repay me £1 million. I am plainly entitled to that. But suppose you have become insolvent in the meantime. Can I claim a lien on the bank account to ensure my repayment ahead of your other creditors? Or must I prove in the liquidation alongside them? Goode would give you a lien. But justice does not demand that my claim should rank in priority to theirs. I paid the money voluntarily just as they did. They gave you credit, thinking that you were good for the money, and voluntarily took the risk of insolvency. They have only themselves to blame if their faith in your ability to repay was mistaken. I did not intend to give you credit; but I did intend you to have the money. I too took the risk that if for any reason you came under an obligation to repay it, you might be unable to do so.

Or take another case. Take the case of Warwick Reid, the defendant in *Attorney-General for Hong Kong v Reid*,[34] a case which, interestingly enough, Goode and Birks consider to have been wrongly decided. You will remember that he was head of the HK anti-corruption force who took bribes and invested them profitably in landed property in New Zealand. The Privy Council held that the Crown was entitled to the property in specie, and not merely to the value of the bribes. But suppose that Mr Reid had been an honest man and had not taken bribes, but had retired full of honour and with a full pension. Suppose that the HK government had miscalculated the amount of his pension, and that it had paid him double his true entitlement. Suppose he was entirely innocent and had not contributed to the government's mistake at all? Of course he must reimburse the Government to the extent of the excess payment; otherwise he will have been unjustly enriched. But does justice require more? Does it require that he disgorge his profits? The government intended him to have the money and to invest it as he saw fit. It should be satisfied to negate the overpayment. It does seem strange that Goode and Birks should think that the corrupt employee should be entitled to keep the profits and the innocent but overpaid employee should disgorge them. I think the reverse.

---

33 See *Twinsectra v Yardley* [2002] 2 AC 164.
34 [1994] 1 AC 324.

THREE MISUNDERSTOOD CASES OF PROPRIETARY RESTITUTION

Trustee of the Property of FC Jones & Sons v Jones[35]

This is the first case in which a claimant has recovered at common law the profit made by the use of his money. Mr Jones was a partner in a firm of potato growers. The partners committed an act of bankruptcy and in due course were adjudicated bankrupt. After the act of bankruptcy but before adjudication Mr Jones drew cheques totalling £11,700 on the partnership account and gave them to his wife, who paid them into an account in her own name with a firm of commodity dealers in order to deal in the London potato futures market. Her dealings proved highly profitable, and she turned the £11,700 into £50,000, which she paid into a call deposit account at a different bank. The trustee demanded payment from the bank, which interpleaded and paid the money into court. Issue was joined between the trustee and Mrs Jones.

The trustee's case was simple. On adjudication the trustee's title to Mr Jones' assets related back to the act of bankruptcy. Accordingly Mrs Jones never acquired any title at all to the money. The money which she obtained from her husband was in her possession but belonged at law to the trustee, and the money in court represented the proceeds of her successful speculation with his money.

Birks has described the case as a paradigm example of unjust enrichment. Yet the Court of Appeal went out of its way to say that the trustee was not suing Mrs Jones for money had and received. In fact he was not suing her at all. He was suing the bank for the balance due to her on her deposit account, and his cause of action was in debt. The dispute between the trustee and Mrs Jones was a property dispute: who owned the disputed property, that is, the right to claim payment from the bank: a chose in action. It had nothing to do with unjust enrichment.

Critics of the decision have exclaimed at the injustice that the trustee should have obtained the whole of the profit that Mrs Jones made by her skill in investing the trustee's money, observing that it was a profit which the trustee could not have made himself. There is much force in this; but the Court could not award Mrs Jones a just allowance for her skill which produced the profit because she never claimed one. Had she done so, she might have succeeded; though she would have had to show that she was an innocent party, which might well have been difficult. Interestingly, however, any claim to a just allowance would depend on classifying the dispute as a property dispute, not as unjust enrichment.

Attorney-General for Hong Kong v Reid[36]

This is a well known case where the claimant obtained a proprietary remedy against a corrupt employee to recover a bribe and the property which the

---

35   [1997] Ch 159.
36   Above n 34.

defendant had bought with the money. Goode and others consider that the case was wrongly decided. They argue that it was a case of restitution for wrong and not a case of unjust enrichment; and that there should have been no proprietary remedy because the claimant did not own the bribe before the defendant received it.

I do not agree. The case does not belong in the laws of wrongs at all. Lord Templeman held that the claimant was entitled to a proprietary remedy because the defendant was bound to pay the bribe to him in specie as soon as he received it. This can only be because it belonged to the claimant the moment it was received.

The question is: why did the bribe belong to the claimant? It cannot be because the defendant was bound to hand it over the moment he received it. You cannot say that the defendant was bound to hand it over because it belonged to the claimant and that it belonged to the claimant because the defendant was bound to hand it over to him. Nor can you say that the bribe belong to the claimant because it was wrong for the defendant to receive it. The claimant did not complain of the receipt, without which his claim must have failed! He complained of the defendant's failure to pay it over. In other words, he sought to take advantage of the defendant's wrong by treating it as an authorised receipt for his own account and not for that of the defendant.

This is an entirely orthodox application of equitable principles. The defendant was a fiduciary. As Lord Templeman explained,[37] a fiduciary must not make a profit for himself out of his fiduciary position. If he does, equity insists on treating him as having obtained it for his principal; he is not allowed to say that he obtained it for himself. He must not accept a bribe. If he does so, equity insists on treating it as a legitimate payment intended for the benefit of the principal; he is not allowed to say that it was a bribe intended for himself.

Strictly speaking, this is not quite an end of the matter. Some agents, though fiduciaries, are authorised to receive money for the account of their principal, keep it and use it as part of their cash flow, and account periodically to their principal for what they have received. But the defendant could not bring himself within this category. He had no authority to receive the payments at all, and could not say that he was authorised to retain them on terms that he should account for them in due course.[38]

Foskett v McKeown[39]

This was a successful claim to the beneficial ownership of the traceable proceeds of trust moneys misappropriated by a trustee. The case was conducted on the questionable assumption that the defendant had not been enriched.

I distinguished between such actions to recover the claimant's property or its traceable proceeds and actions to reverse unjust enrichment. Actions to

---

37   *Attorney-General for Hong Kong v Reid*, above n 34 at 337.

38   It is one thing to say that the principal need not challenge the receipt; it is quite another to say that, if he does not challenge it, he must be taken to authorise the agent to keep the money and account for it in due course.

39   [2001] 1 AC 102.

reverse unjust enrichment, I said, are subject to the change of position defence, which "usually operates by reducing or extinguishing the element of enrichment".[40] A claimant who brings "an action like the present", however, must show that the defendant is in receipt of property which belongs beneficially to him or its traceable proceeds, but he need not show that the defendant has been enriched.

I chose my words with great care; and it is very irritating to see how widely they have been misunderstood. A recent commentator[41] has written that I said that it followed from the fact that tracing was part of the law of property that the change of position defence was not available in the context of actions contingent on this process. I said no such thing. I drew no distinction between the misappropriated asset and its traceable proceeds. On the contrary, I was concerned to say that a claimant has the same interest in the proceeds as he had in the property which they represent.

Nor did I say that a property based action for a personal remedy (eg, a claim for knowing receipt) was not subject to the change of position defence. I said that "an action like the present" (ie, a claim to a *proprietary* remedy) did not depend on showing that the defendant had been enriched, and (inferentially) was not subject to the defence. And I did not say that the change of position defence invariably operates by reducing or extinguishing the element of enrichment. I said that it *usually* does so.

In my opinion, there are only two kinds of case where the change of position defence is not available: (i) where the claimant seeks a proprietary remedy (where it is not needed); and (ii) where the defendant is the original wrongdoer (who is an accounting party and in any case could hardly plead an innocent change of position). But it is available where the claimant seeks a personal remedy against a successor in title, whether the defendant parted with the original asset or its traceable proceeds; and whether the action is brought to reverse unjust enrichment, when it reflects the fact that the defendant is no longer enriched, or to recover the value of the claimant's property, when it has a different rationale, viz to mitigate the harshness of the rule that all restitutionary liability restitution is strict.

Summary

(1) The tracing rules form part of our law of property, not of the law of unjust enrichment. They dictate that the owner of an asset may assert ownership of its traceable proceeds whether the substitution was authorised or not. They identify the subject-matter of the claim; they do not establish the claim or identify the remedy. The claimant has the same interest in the proceeds as he had in the property which they represent.

(2) Property generates personal as well as proprietary claims, which lie in respect of traceable proceeds as they lay in respect of the original asset .

---

40 *Foskett v McKeown*, above n 39 at 129.

41 C Rotherham, "Tracing Misconceptions in *Foskett v McKeown*" [2003] 11 *Restitution Law Review* 57 at 71.

(3) There are two situations, and two situations only, in which proprietary restitutionary remedies are available. The first is where the claimant can establish a continuing beneficial interest in the asset to which he lays claim. Such an interest usually arises under a resulting trust. The second is where the original transfer is rescinded and specific restitution is ordered because monetary compensation would not be an adequate remedy.

(4) Personal liability in restitution, whether based on unjust enrichment or property, is always strict but subject to the change of position defence. The change of position defence is not available where the claim is for a proprietary remedy or where it is brought against the original wrongdoer. But it is available where the action is for a personal remedy and is brought against a successor in title, whether he parted with the original asset or its traceable proceeds; and whether the action is brought in unjust enrichment, when it operates by reducing or extinguishing the enrichment, or to recover the value of the claimant's property, when it has a different rationale.

FUSION (AGAIN)

With some reluctance I return to the subject of the conference, from which the chapters in this book derive: fusion. I quote a celebrated passage from the Book of Deuteronomy: "Justice, justice shalt thou pursue".[42] The rabbis applied the presumption against redundancy. They said that no word in the Bible was superfluous. So the word "Justice" meant two different things. The first meant law and the second compassion, or as we would say, equity.

It is the same word; but it is repeated twice.

---

42 Chapter 16, verse 20.

13

The Liability of the Recipient: Restitution at Common Law or Wrongdoing in Equity?

MICHAEL BRYAN

INTRODUCTION

Lord Selborne's judgment in *Barnes v Addy* belongs to an era in which brevity in the exposition of legal principle was not so much a virtue as an unspoken assumption of judgment writing.[1] Four and a half pages of an unreserved judgment, containing no citation of authority were all that were thought necessary to establish the conceptual structure of accessory liability. This display of Victorian self-confidence has been little shaken in over a century of *Barnes v Addy* jurisprudence. Most of the principles so succinctly enunciated by the Chancellor have been confirmed and applied in numerous later decisions, involving fiduciary defaults far removed from the fortuitous involvement of the two solicitors in the misfortunes of a mid-nineteenth century family trust.[2] In particular, the distinction drawn in *Barnes v Addy* between liability for

---

1   (1874) LR 9 Ch App 244. The judgment was very nearly not handed down by Lord Selborne as Lord Chancellor. Little more than a month after *Barnes v Addy* had been decided in February 1874 a general election was held. The defeat of Gladstone's Liberal government by Disraeli's Tories resulted in Lord Cairns succeeding Selborne on the woolsack. The succinctness of the judgment might have been due to Lord Selborne's wish to clear the decks before the general election was held, though it could just as easily have been due to the unmeritorious nature of the plaintiff's claim. In spite of their political differences, Lord Selborne and Lord Cairns had similar judicial philosophies. A judgment delivered by Lord Cairns on accessory liability might have contained a more extensive review of the authorities but the outcome of the case is likely to have been the same.

2   An exception is Lord Selborne's requirement that liability for assistance is imposed on the basis of "knowledge in a dishonest and fraudulent design on the part of the trustees": *Barnes v Addy*, above n 1 at 251. The dishonesty of the trustee or other fiduciary is not a prerequisite for the imposition of liability under Anglo–Australian law: *Consul Developments Pty Ltd v DPC Estates Pty Ltd* (1975) 132 CLR 373 at 386 (McTiernan J), 398 (Gibbs J), and at 412 (Stephen J); *Royal Brunei Airlines Sdn Bhd v Tan* [1995] 2 AC 378 at 385. In contrast, Canadian law has remained faithful to Lord Selborne's formulation: *Air Canada v M & L Travel Ltd* [1993] 3 SCR 787 at 813–826 per Iacobucci J.

"knowing receipt" and for "knowing assistance" has endured because it recognises crucial differences in the aims of awarding equitable relief.[3]

Twenty-first century judges cannot reasonably be expected to be as succinct as Lord Selborne. The authorities on accessory liability have multiplied in recent years. It is hard to say whether the increase is attributable to an increased incidence in fiduciary wrongdoing or to greater ingenuity in the identification of solvent defendants who can be fixed with equitable accessory liability. The multiplication of concepts has ineluctably followed the multiplication of precedents. In a typical *Barnes v Addy* claim a judge will undertake three distinct inquiries into the state of the defendant's knowledge.[4] The aim of the first inquiry will be to determine the level of knowledge required to hold the defendant liable. As likely as not, the inquiry will adopt the typology of knowledge identified by Peter Gibson J in the *Baden Delvaux* decision.[5] The second inquiry will determine exactly what it is, on the facts found, that the defendant must know. And both inquiries are separate from the evidential inquiry into the knowledge that the defendant actually possessed.

A final difference between Lord Selborne and his successors in the administration of this head of equity is that the Chancellor did not have to consider academic writing on accessory liability. This is an unremarkable proposition as legal scholarship, in the sense that it is understood today, did not exist in Lord Selborne's time. In the case of "knowing receipt", much of the recent literature either applies or reacts against insights derived from unjust enrichment scholarship. This chapter belongs to this genre: it provides qualified support for analysing this head of liability as an application of the principle of reversing unjust enrichment. In the case of assistance-based liability, in which the reversal of unjust enrichment plays no part, a focus of recent writing has been to determine the rationale for holding assisters accountable. Specifically, is it correct to classify this head of liability as a species of "equitable tort"?[6]

This chapter is concerned only with the liability, under the first limb of *Barnes v Addy*, of recipients of property from a fiduciary who has acted in breach of obligation. As a contribution to the exploration of fusion issues it examines the argument that this head of equitable liability can be analysed as an application of the principle of reversing unjust enrichment. The case for locating recipient liability within the law of unjust enrichment has been argued in a strong and a weak version. The strong version asserts that a

---

3   The rationale for the distinction has occasionally been queried or challenged: see *Consul Developments Pty Ltd v DPC Estates Pty Ltd* (1975) 132 CLR 373 at 410-411 per Stephen J. Liability in most American jurisdictions is not predicated on the distinction. W Fratcher, *Scott on Trusts* (4th ed, Little, Brown & Co, Boston, 1989) at [506], 'Liability of Third Parties'. For a sceptical view of its utility see PD Finn, 'The Liability of Third Parties for Knowing Receipt or Assistance' in DM Waters (ed), *Equity, Fiduciaries and Trusts* (Carswell, Toronto, 1993) at 195.

4   *Koorootang Nominees Pty Ltd v ANZ Banking Group Ltd* [1998] 3 VR 16 at 77.

5   *Baden v Societe Generale pour Favoriser le Developpement du Commerce et de l'Industrie en France SA* [1992] 4 All ER 161 at 235-248.

6   C Mitchell, 'Assistance' in P Birks and A Pretto (eds), *Breach of Trust* (2nd ed, Hart Publishing, Oxford, 2002) at 139; S Elliott and C Mitchell, "Remedies for Dishonest Assistance" (2004) 67 *Modern Law Review* 16.

"knowing receipt" claim is analytically always a claim in unjust enrichment.[7] The weak version accepts that recipient liability is a form of equitable wrongdoing, but argues that, in some cases and on appropriate facts, a plaintiff will be entitled to restitution for unjust enrichment.[8] It follows from acceptance of the strong version that the word "knowing" in "knowing receipt" should be discarded and that, conformably with other applications of the unjust enrichment principle, recipient liability ought to be strict. The weak version accepts that fault-based liability is established in the authorities — even if the degree of fault required for its imposition has not been authoritatively settled — but it insists that a strict liability claim in unjust enrichment is sometimes available as an alternative.

The chapter argues, first, that Australian law has adopted the weak version of the unjust enrichment theory, though the adoption has been little noticed, and that it may well eventually come round to recognising the strong version. The argument cannot be substantiated by reference to the equitable "knowing receipt" cases, where fault-based liability is firmly entrenched. It relies instead on a series of common law decisions holding recipients of the proceeds of fiduciary wrongdoing strictly accountable to make personal restitution of the proceeds they have received, subject to the application of recognised restitutionary defences such as change of position. Even if the arguments from principle and precedent for fault-based liability appear strong, some place has to be found for this line of common law authority unless it can be shown to be unsound or irrelevant. Its precise relationship to the equity cases has to be worked out.

The second, more theoretical section of the chapter examines some of the implications of the common law line of authority for the principled development of recipient liability. Specifically, it considers whether the liability of recipients can be explained in terms of the principle of reversing unjust enrichment on either the strong or weak versions of the theory. Opponents of such an explanation have argued that recipient liability in equity cannot be stretched on the procrustean bed of the unjust enrichment formula. The common law cases suggest that the bed might not in fact be uncomfortable. The thesis of this part of the chapter is that, while the paradigmatic example of recipient liability (that of the recipient who receives the proceeds of a breach of trust, the beneficiary of the trust being a volunteer) may not be able to be

---

7   The argument was most fully developed by the late Professor Birks in "Misdirected funds: restitution from the recipient" [1989] *Lloyds Maritime and Commercial Law Quarterly* 296, in a form from which he later resiled. See also P Birks, "Persistent problems in misdirected money: a quintet" [1993] *Lloyds Maritime and Commercial Law Quarterly* 218; P Creighton and E Bant, "Recipient Liability in Western Australia" (2000) 29 *University of Western Australia Law Review* 205.

8   P Birks, 'Receipt' in P Birks and A Pretto (eds), *Breach of Trust* (2nd ed, Hart Publishing, Oxford, 2002) at 213, 223-224. See also Lord Nicholls of Birkenhead, 'Knowing Receipt: The Need for a New Landmark' in WR Cornish et al (eds), *Restitution, Past, Present and Future: Essays in Honour of Gareth Jones* (Hart Publishing, Oxford, 1998) at 231. Lord Walker, "Dishonesty and Unconscionable Conduct in Commercial Life: Some Reflections on Accessory Liability and Knowing Receipt" (2005) 27 *Sydney Law Review* 187.

analysed as an application of the unjust enrichment principle, other examples of recipient liability are explicable on this basis. They include some cases of breach of trust where the beneficiary is not a volunteer but has paid valuable consideration. Where trust property has been transferred by a trustee to a recipient in breach of trust, the trustee and recipient will be held accountable in equity, but the relief will not usually include a claim in unjust enrichment (or in an action for money had and received, if that is the preferred label). But some beneficiaries will be able to establish a ground of restitution, such as failure of consideration, in addition to equitable and statutory remedies for wrongdoing.

But before the issue of personal liability at common law can be addressed some ground clearing is necessary. What is meant by a "knowing receipt" claim, or recipient liability? Like many innocent-seeming definitional questions it turns out to be surprisingly hard to answer.

THE PROPRIETARY LIABILITY OF RECIPIENTS

What is a "knowing receipt" claim under *Barnes v Addy*?[9] They are claims to hold a recipient of property from a fiduciary, who has acted in breach of obligation, personally liable to make restitution for the value of the property received. The personal accountability of the constructive trustee in "knowing assistance" cases is easy to understand because the assistance involves no beneficial receipt of property. But the position is no different in "knowing receipt" cases. The recipient will have beneficially received property, directly or indirectly, from the fiduciary but will not have title to the property by the time the claim has been brought. As likely as not, the money or other property will have been dissipated, or passed on to yet another recipient "down the line", who might variously be a good faith purchaser, a recipient who can claim the benefit of a change of position defence, or one who has applied the money to the discharge of the fiduciary's indebtedness to the recipient (as will often be the case where the recipient is a bank). All these situations can only give rise to personal claims against the first recipient.

Can a proprietary remedy be awarded against a recipient under *Barnes v Addy*? Take a simple example. Suppose that T, a trustee, who holds property on trust for B, the beneficiary, conveys the property in breach of trust to R, the recipient. Is a claim brought by B (or by a new trustee who has replaced the delinquent T) to recover the misappropriated property a recipient claim under *Barnes v Addy*? The claim can be analysed in one of three ways:[10]

(1) R holds the property on express trust for B, being "bound" by the trust that originally bound T, provided that R has actual or constructive notice of the existence of the trust affecting the property.

---

9   Or a "receipt-based" claim in equity, or "recipient liability in equity". The terminology is unstable.

10 See L Smith, 'Transfers' in P Birks and A Pretto (eds), *Breach of Trust* (2nd ed, Hart Publishing, Oxford, 2002) at 111 for a detailed analysis, showing that equitable protection against wrongful interference does not inevitably, or indeed generally, entail the conferral of a proprietary interest on the party entitled to that protection.

(2) R holds the property as trustee for B, as in (1), on the basis of having actual or constructive notice of the trust, but the trust is constructive, being confined to an obligation to reconvey the property to T (or to a replacement T), with an ancillary obligation to preserve the property pending retransfer.

(3) R holds the property on trust for B, as constructive trustee as in (2), but the trust is a *Barnes v Addy* recipient trust, imposed only if B (or the replacement T) establishes that R has the requisite degree of knowledge (whatever that might be) to justify the imposition of a constructive trust over the property for the benefit of B.

Of the three analyses (1) is the least convincing.[11] It is inaccurate to characterise R as a substitute trustee for the original T. If the trust is not a bare trust, when R will be under an obligation to hold the property to the order of B,[12] R's duty, pending transfer, is only to hold the property to the order of T or the replacement T. R will not be subject to the management obligations which the original T was required to perform. The reference to R being "bound" by the trust is misleading, at least if it implies that the personal obligations of the trustee persist after transfer, because the equitable obligations imposed on R are different in nature from the obligations imposed on T.

The choice between the constructive trust solutions in (2) and (3) is more finely balanced. The difference between them is, however, significant. Under (2) the onus will rest on R to show that he does not have actual or constructive notice of the trust.[13] But under (3) the burden of proof will rest on B (or the replacement T) to prove that R has the requisite degree of knowledge (again, whatever that might be). Deciding between these alternatives is not made easier by the use of the term "constructive trust", which, as Professor Smith appositely remarks, "is a smokescreen between the legal analyst and the law".[14] To hold that R is a constructive trustee still leaves us with the question: what kind of constructive trust is it?

Most authority favours (2).[15] Indeed, the application of the doctrine of notice to these facts would not be seriously questioned if the problem were to be presented as a priority dispute.[16] But in the recent New South Wales Court of Appeal decision of *Robins and Others v Incentive Dynamics Pty Ltd (in liq)*[17] it was assumed, in the absence of argument to the contrary, that the correct

---

11 But see R Meagher and WMC Gummow, *Jacobs' Law of Trusts in Australia* (6th ed, Butterworths, Sydney, 1997) at [1304] stating that "[w]hile the third party is often called a constructive trustee, he is more properly treated as one against whom the beneficial interest under the primary trust persists because he cannot set up a title as bona fide purchaser of the legal title without notice".

12 See L Smith, 'Transfers' in P Birks and A Pretto (eds), *Breach of Trust*, above n 10 at 136.

13 *Re Nisbet and Potts' Contract* [1906] 1 Ch 386 at 404.

14 See L Smith, 'Transfers' in P Birks and A Pretto (eds), *Breach of Trust,* above n 10 at 137.

15 *Re Nisbet and Potts' Contract* [1906] 1 Ch 386; *Re Diplock* [1948] 1 Ch 465, affirmed sub nom *Minister of Health v Simpson* [1951] AC 251; *Barclays Bank Ltd v Quistclose Investments Ltd* [1970] AC 567.

16 *Jared v Clements* [1902] 2 Ch 399.

17 (2003) 175 FLR 286.

analysis was (3). The case concerned a company, Incentive Dynamics, formed for the purpose of marketing "incentive schemes" for employees of large companies. The directors of Incentive Dynamics established another company, Coldwick, which bought properties in South Melbourne and Crows Nest. Most of the purchase price for the properties was provided by Incentive Dynamics. Their acquisition conferred no benefit on Incentive Dynamics, and the directors of that company were held to have acted in breach of s 232(6) of the Corporations Law in using company money for this purpose.[18] The New South Wales Court of Appeal held that the liquidator of Incentive Dynamics was entitled to the benefit of a proprietary constructive trust over the properties acquired by Coldwick. The trust was imposed on the basis that the directors of Coldwick had received the purchase money for the properties with knowledge of the breaches of statutory duty committed by the directors of Incentive Dynamics.

The award of a proprietary remedy in a "knowing receipt" case was said to be an application of a "remedial" constructive trust.[19] The difficulty in accepting this proposition has less to do with the problematic status of the remedial constructive trust in Australian law than with the assumption that *Robins* is a decision on the "knowing receipt" constructive trust. The enforceability of an equitable interest against a transferee of a legal estate or interest in property depends on whether the transferee can show that he is a good faith purchaser for value of the legal estate or interest without notice of the trust. It is in this proprietary sense that the trust "persists" against a transferee who has notice (even though, as suggested above, it is misleading to characterise the transferee as the new express trustee of the property). So in *Barclays Bank Ltd v Quistclose Investments Ltd*[20] the trust created by Quistclose Investments[21] was held to be enforceable against Barclays Bank on the basis that the bank had notice of the facts giving rise to the trust. Quistclose was not required to show that the bank had "knowingly received" the money lent to Rolls Razor for the purpose of paying the dividend to the shareholders which it had declared. A defendant who has wrongly obtained another's property must either give it back or pay compensation if unable to give it back. If the property is equitable it will be subject to the infirmity of the application of the doctrine of notice applied in favour of a later purchaser. But recovery of the property should not be subject to the additional condition of requiring the plaintiff to establish the defendant's cognition of the wrongdoing.

---

18   This provision forbids officers of a company from making improper use of their position to gain, directly or indirectly, an advantage for themselves or others or to cause detriment to the company. It has since been replaced by s 182 of the *Corporations Act 2001* (Cth). The Court held that it was "unnecessary to consider the exact scope of the non-statutory fiduciary duty that probably corresponds with s 232(6)" ((2003) 175 FLR 286 at 297 per Mason P).

19   (2003) 175 FLR 286 at 297 per Mason P, citing *Bathurst City Council v PWC Properties Pty Ltd* (1998) 195 CLR 566 at 585.

20   [1970] AC 567.

21   The classification of the *Quistclose* trust is controversial. See *Twinsectra Ltd v Yardley* [2002] 2 AC 164 at 187 per Lord Millett, and the various analyses canvassed in W Swadling (ed), *The Quistclose Trust: Critical Essays* (Hart Publishing, Oxford, 2004). The controversy does not, however, affect the nature of the bank's liability in that case.

Whether the distinction currently drawn by equity between the notice-based proprietary claim and the knowledge-based personal claim[22] is defensible is a separate and important question. Some unjust enrichment theorists argue that on this point there is no good reason for distinguishing between personal and proprietary liability. If a recipient is strictly liable to return misappropriated property that is still traceable,[23] personal liability, imposed in cases where the property is no longer traceable, should also be strict. The recognition of strict liability proprietary remedies clearly reinforces the argument for recognising strict liability personal remedies for restitution of the value of the property.[24] But this, in Holmesian terms, is to argue from the "logic" and not from the "life" of the law. For the time being, the distinction between notice–based proprietary remedies and knowledge–based equitable personal accountability manifestly exists. What is important, however, is that the two should not be confused.

STRICT PERSONAL LIABILITY AT COMMON LAW

It is not hard to find cases where personal restitution has been ordered against recipients of the proceeds of fiduciary wrongdoing who were unaware of the wrongdoing. But the examples come from the common law, not equity. This part of the chapter examines three recent Australian examples of strict liability before going on to explore the implications of the decisions for the analysis of recipient liability.[25]

State Bank of New South Wales v Swiss Bank[26]

A "trusted senior employee" of the plaintiff bank fraudulently inserted a false document into the bank's payment system, causing it to pay over US$20 million to the defendant bank. The plaintiff, relying on the false document, thought it was repaying an overnight loan made by the defendant. The defendant, for its part, thought that the payment represented the proceeds of a loan to one of its customers and disbursed most of the funds at the customer's direction. Neither the customer nor the proceeds could be traced. It turned out that the "trusted" employee of the plaintiff had been acting in collusion with the defendant's customer. The plaintiff bank claimed the US$20 million from the defendant in a personal claim for unjust enrichment.

The principal issue at trial and before the Court of Appeal was whether the defendant bank could avail itself of the defence of change of position. Both

---

22   Or a strict liability personal claim in unjust enrichment, if that is the preferred analysis.

23   Subject to the application of defences such as good faith purchase and change of position.

24   P Birks, 'Receipt' in P Birks and A Pretto (eds), *Breach of Trust* (2nd ed, Hart Publishing, Oxford, 2002) at 215-220.

25   For a recent English example see *Barros Mattos Junior v General Securities & Finance Ltd* [2004] 2 Lloyd's Rep 475; [2004] EWHC 1188.

26   (1995) 39 NSWLR 350.

courts gave a negative answer to this question.[27] But for present purposes the relevance of the case lies in the formulation of the plaintiff's claim. The fraud on the plaintiff bank constituted a breach of fiduciary obligation committed by the bank's own employee. The claim against the defendant bank, as recipient of the proceeds of the fraud, could have been conceptualised as a claim in "knowing receipt". The plaintiff preferred, however, to bring a common law claim for unjust enrichment, being a claim for money had and received, with the result that upon proof of the enrichment the onus passed to the defendant to show that it had changed its position in good faith. Upon failure to establish the defence the plaintiff was entitled to personal restitution from the defendant of the funds of which it had been defrauded. At no stage was the plaintiff required to establish that the defendant was aware of the breach of fiduciary duty that had caused the fraudulent transmission of funds.

Port of Brisbane Corp v ANZ Securities (No 2)[28]

Peter Hinterdorfer was a financial officer employed by the plaintiff who had authority to invest funds not required for the plaintiff's immediate operating purposes. Having incorporated a company, Windermere Investments, of which he was the only shareholder and director, in the Turks and Caicos Islands Hinterdorfer appointed the defendant to be the custodian trustee of any funds received. The defendant was to act as trustee at the direction of Windermere Investments. Hinterdorfer then withdrew $4.5 million from the plaintiff's account and, by changing the identity of the payee on the cheque, credited it to the defendant. By the time the fraud was exposed he had withdrawn (using his Windermere alter ego) and lost through gambling about half the money misappropriated. The plaintiff claimed restitution from the defendant custodian trustee of the money dissipated by Hinterdorfer.[29] The Queensland Court of Appeal held that the defendant had in good faith changed its position and that therefore the claim failed.[30]

The plaintiff brought, in the alternative, an equitable personal claim for the return of its money. It was not based on "knowing receipt", but was a claim to personal restitution based on a resulting trust arising from the voluntary transfer of the money to the defendant. Insofar as the money had been withdrawn from the defendant's account and spent on gambling, the plaintiff unsuccessfully claimed equitable compensation for its loss. The Court of Appeal held that there was no duty on the recipient to pay compensation for

---

27   This aspect of the decision is controversial. See R Chambers, "Change of Position on the Faith of the Receipt" [1996] *Restitution Law Review* 103.

28   [2003] 2 Qd R 661; [2002] QCA 158 (10 May 2002). Leave to appeal to the High Court was granted but the case was later settled: HC B32/2002 (14 March 2003).

29   An obstacle to the success of the plaintiff's claim, noticed by McPherson JA (*Port of Brisbane Corp v ANZ Securities (No 2)*, above n 28 at 670) was that the defendant, as trustee for Windermere, had not beneficially received the misappropriated money. The point was, however, not pursued in the Court of Appeal.

30   The defendant was agent, as well as trustee, for Windermere Investments and, as McPherson JA noted (*Port of Brisbane Corp v ANZ Securities (No 2)*, above n 28 at 667), the defence was in substance that of an agent's payment over at the direction of the principal.

failure to perform duties which had not been voluntarily undertaken, and of which it was unaware.[31] Moreover, the defendant could not be made a resulting trustee of assets it had not beneficially received.[32] Whatever might be said about the merits of this attempt to claim equitable compensation by way of a resulting trust, it does at least illustrate the lengths plaintiffs are prepared go in order to avoid becoming embroiled in the intricacies of a "knowing receipt" claim.

Spangaro v Corporate Investment Australia Funds Management Ltd[33]

The plaintiff subscribed to a managed investment scheme. He paid money to a custodian trustee, Cardinal, on terms which required Cardinal to hold the money on trust for individual investors until a "minimum subscription" amount had been raised. If the figure was reached by a specified date the subscriptions were to be paid to the defendant, which was the "responsible entity" administering the scheme. In the event that Cardinal received insufficient money to allow the scheme to go ahead it was obliged to refund to investors the money actually subscribed. Cardinal, acting in breach of trust, paid out the plaintiff's money to the defendant even though it had not received sufficient subscriptions by the due date to enable the scheme to proceed. The plaintiff was awarded restitution of part of his investment[34] against the defendant on the ground of failure of consideration. The basis upon which the payment had been made, namely that the scheme would only go ahead if the minimum subscription amount had been raised, had failed.[35]

In *Spangaro*, in contrast to *Swiss Bank* and *Port of Brisbane Corporation*, the concurrency of the common law money had and received and equitable "knowing receipt" claims was noticed. Finkelstein J reviewed the state of the authorities on the cognition requirement, concluding that the defendant could also have been held accountable in equity for having received the plaintiff's money with knowledge of the breach of trust.[36] But, as in the other cases discussed in this part of the chapter, the plaintiff was disinclined to explore the

---

31 *Port of Brisbane Corp v ANZ Securities (No 2)*, above n 28 at 681. The reasoning on this point is unsatisfactory. The law of unjust enrichment does require restitution of payments, for example mistaken payments, even though the recipient is unaware that a mistake has been made.

32 *Port of Brisbane Corp v ANZ Securities (No 2)*, above n 28. This underlines the point that the defendant's real defence to all the claims was that, as agent, it had paid over the plaintiff's money at the direction of its principal.

33 [2003] FCA 1025; (2003) 47 ACSR 285.

34 No restitution was sought of money paid for shares in the company managing the project, or money loaned to the plaintiff in order to enable him to participate in the scheme.

35 The definition of failure of consideration as "failure of basis", adopted in *Roxborough v Rothmans of Pall Mall Australia Ltd* (2001) 208 CLR 516 at 525, was applied. See *Spangaro v Corporate Investment Australia Funds Management Ltd*, above n 33 at [51], 301.

36 Knowledge for this purpose was said to include "knowledge of circumstances which would indicate to an honest and reasonable person that the property received is trust property transferred in breach of trust", *Spangaro v Corporate Investment Australia Funds Management Ltd*, above n 33 at [60], 305. This is usually taken to be the 4th point of the *Baden Delvaux* scale and, as the judgment of Finkelstein J shows, is consistent with most previous Australian authority.

gradations of equitable knowledge. Moreover, restitution was straightforward, there being no suggestion that the defendant had changed its position to its detriment as a result of having received the money.

LIPKIN GORMAN CLAIMS

In all three cases discussed the House of Lords decision in *Lipkin Gorman v Karpnale*[37] was relied on in order to establish the availability of the common law claim. *Lipkin Gorman* has within a relatively short time become an analytical battleground within (and indeed outside) the scholarship of unjust enrichment. As is well-known, a firm of solicitors successfully obtained restitution of money from the defendant casino after a partner of the firm had taken money from the client account in order to feed his gambling habit at the casino. At first instance the firm had brought an equitable "knowing receipt" claim, as well as a common law claim for money had and received.[38] But by the time the case reached the House of Lords the case had resolved itself into a common claim to restitution. The firm recovered from the casino the amount of client money that the solicitor had gambled, minus his occasional winnings, payment of which was held to constitute a change of position by the casino.

Lipkin Gorman has a justified reputation as being one of the most difficult cases in the modern law of restitution. Some writers argue that it is not an example of unjust enrichment at all but of vindicating the plaintiff's property rights.[39] But if it is a decision on unjust enrichment, the precise ground of restitution, or "unjust factor", was never clearly identified in the judgments. Candidates include ignorance (in the sense of the plaintiff being unaware that it was being deprived of its property), property (in the sense of the defendant's interference with the plaintiff's property rights) and the absence of a legal basis for the defendant's enrichment.[40] Moreover, it is not easy to explain why the defendant's enrichment was held to have been at the expense of the law firm, as opposed to being at the expense of the solicitor who was held to have acquired a valid legal title to the money misappropriated from the client account.[41] Finally, it is not yet settled whether the model of the defence of change of

---

37   [1991] 2 AC 548. In *Swiss Bank* the *Lipkin Gorman* decision was discussed in the context of the defence of change of position. In the other two cases it was treated as authority for the existence of the common law unjust enrichment claim against the recipient.

38   Before Alliott J claims against the casino included knowing receipt, knowing assistance, as well as a *Re Diplock* personal claim: *Lipkin Gorman v Karpnale Ltd* [1987] 1 WLR 987. It was conceded before the CA that, in the event of the failure of the common law claim, the equitable claims could not succeed: *Lipkin Gorman v Karpnale Ltd* [1989] 1 WLR 1340.

39   G Virgo, *Principles of the Law of Restitution* (Oxford University Press, Oxford, 1999) at 11-17. Cf P Birks, *Unjust Enrichment* (2nd ed, Oxford University Press, Oxford, 2005) at 66-67.

40   E McKendrick, "Tracing Misdirected Funds" [1991] *Lloyds Commercial and Maritime Law Quarterly* 378; R Grantham and CF Rickett, *Enrichment and Restitution in New Zealand* (Hart Publishing, Oxford, 2000) at 34; RB Grantham and CF Rickett, "Property Rights as a Legally Significant Event" (2003) 62 *Cambridge Law Journal* 717; P Birks, *Unjust Enrichment*, above n 39 at chapter 6.

41   P Birks, 'Trusts in the Recovery of Misapplied Assets: Tracing, Trusts, and Restitution' in E McKendrick (ed), *Commercial Aspects of Trusts and Fiduciary Obligations* (Clarendon, Oxford, 1992) at 149, 163.

position proposed by Lord Goff in *Lipkin Gorman* will be the model adopted by English or Australian law.[42]

In summary, every point determined by the House of Lords, or implicit in the decision, is controversial. What has escaped controversy, however, is the actual outcome of the case. The "three party" case, in which X takes P's property without his consent and gives it to D has always been recognised as giving rise to a personal claim to restitution from D of the value of the property received. The availability of such a claim was established long before the House of Lords decision in *Lipkin Gorman*.[43] The claim does not require proof of any "privity" between plaintiff and defendant. It is therefore potentially available, as an alternative to the equitable "knowing receipt" claim, to victims of fraud who are understandably reluctant to explore the subtleties of knowledge in equity. Liability in a *Lipkin Gorman* claim is strict, save to the extent that the recipient can establish change of position or other recognised defence. It is also immaterial how many intermediaries have acquired title to the proceeds of the fraud before (or, indeed, after) the defendant obtained title, provided that the requisite transactional links between the plaintiff's property and the defendant's acquisition of title can be established.[44] In Professor Birks's words: "[i]f I find your wallet it makes no difference whether I am the first recipient or the second or the twenty-second".[45]

The three cases discussed show that Australian law has applied the *Lipkin Gorman* decision in order to hold some recipients of the proceeds of fiduciary wrongdoing strictly liable at common law. This is a development of which practitioners, particularly those practising in the area of commercial fraud, should be aware.[46] It is not necessary to subscribe to an analysis of the strict liability claim *in terms of unjust enrichment* in order to recognise the significance of this development; but it is necessary to take note of the fact that strict liability is well established at common law, and that increasing reliance on common law strict liability by plaintiffs and their lawyers has made reconciliation of the common law cases with the equitable "knowing receipt" line of

---

42 E Bant and P Creighton, "The Australian Change of Position Defence" (2002) 30 *University of Western Australia Law Review* 208.

43 See for example *March v Keating* (1834) 2 Cl & Fin 250; 6 ER 1149; *Banque Belge v Hambrouck* [1921] 1 KB 321 at 335-336 per Atkin LJ.

44 Bona fide purchase will be a defence to a personal claim for the restitution of money or negotiable instruments, although in *Lipkin Gorman* the defence failed since the solicitor's gambling contracts with the casino were void and therefore did not constitute a purchase. See R Grantham and CF Rickett, *Enrichment and Restitution in New Zealand* (Hart Publishing, Oxford, 2000) at 327-328.

45 P Birks, *Unjust Enrichment* (2nd ed, Oxford University Press, Oxford, 2005) at 87. For Birks, *Lipkin Gorman* is a decision on unjust enrichment, but a property characterisation does not affect the argument on this point.

46 They should also be aware of the possibility of a common law claim in conversion. Where available it provides even stronger protection of the plaintiff's property rights since it cannot be defeated by an application of the change of position defence. But equitable property will only be protected by the action of conversion if it confers a right to possession: *Healey v Healey* [1915] 1 KB 938, as explained in *Leigh & Sillavan Ltd v Aliakmon Shipping Co Ltd (The Aliakmon)* [1986] AC 785 at 812; *MCC Proceeds Inc v Lehman Bros International (Europe)* [1998] 4 All ER 675 at 689, 700-701. The potential of a claim in conversion was noted in *Port of Brisbane Corp v ANZ Securities(No 2)* [2003] 2 Qd R 661 at 669 at [8].

authority more urgent. The reconceptualisation of *Barnes v Addy* claims as *Lipkin Gorman* claims is by now well established.

Unjust enrichment has not been judicially accepted as the basis of the personal liability of recipients, in either the strong or weak senses described above.[47] But it remains the most convincing explanation of the cases even where alternative reasoning is employed. Restitution on the basis of strict liability is only tolerable if the law also respects a recipient's interest in security of receipt.[48] Recipients of money and other property should be able to enjoy it, and to dispose of it, as their own unless an established legal basis for recognising that the enrichment is unjust exists. Change of position, applied as a defence to an unjust enrichment claim, is the most sensitive method of balancing a claimant's right of restitution with a recipient's interest in security of receipt. It would no doubt be possible to adjust these interests within other legal frameworks, such as property law, but it would come at the cost of distorting important objectives of those other areas of law. The protection of property interests, for example, does not involve the same balancing of interests, particularly the interests of innocent donees of property, as is in practice secured by the law of unjust enrichment. And a property law which distinguished not only between legal and equitable interests, but also between interests defeasible by an application of the change of position defence, and those that are not, would certainly be more complex and, arguably, less coherent in its techniques for protecting different forms of wealth.

But before a strict liability model of recipient liability – whether predicated on the reversal of unjust enrichment or on some other basis – can be accepted, some important objections to the model require consideration.

RECIPIENT LIABILITY AND UNJUST ENRICHMENT THEORY

In his article "Unjust Enrichment, Property and the Structure of Trusts"[49] Professor Smith takes issue with the argument that a *Barnes v Addy* "knowing receipt" action is in substance a claim in unjust enrichment. He distinguishes between two types of unjust enrichment claim. One is a claim to restitution based on a defective transfer of wealth, such as a claim to restitution of a mistaken payment, or of property transferred under the exercise of undue influence. The other is a title-based claim, where the plaintiff claims that he has been deprived of property without his consent. *Lipkin Gorman* exemplifies the title-based claim. A plaintiff will want to recover the property taken if it is traceable, but if tracing is no longer possible a title-based claim to personal restitution of the value of the property will be awarded. A plaintiff making a title-based claim must be able to establish a "proprietary base" to the property being claimed, in other words that he had an interest in the property to which the claim, either personal or proprietary, is now being made.

The basic objection to analysing "knowing receipt" liability as a common law title-based unjust enrichment claim can be illustrated by returning to the

---

47   See text to nn 7-8 above.

48   P Birks, *An Introduction to the Law of Restitution* (Clarendon, Oxford, 1989) at 148.

49   (2000) 116 *Law Quarterly Review* 412.

paradigm example of T, holding property on trust for B, who in breach of trust transfers that property to a recipient, R. Suppose, further, that R dissipates the property so that B is limited to a personal claim against him. Smith argues that B cannot establish a title-based claim in unjust enrichment because B and R hold different titles to the property in respect of which the personal claim is being asserted. B's interest is equitable, whereas R has received the legal title to the property. Notwithstanding T's breach of trust, the transfer confers a valid legal title on R, being a title B never had. How can it be said that R has been unjustly enriched at the expense of B when R has received a title to property which B never enjoyed?

Smith later modified the approach taken in this article, preferring a proprietary analysis of *Lipkin Gorman* claims.[50] But the argument based on the incompatibility of the beneficiary's title with the recipient's interest is logically compelling. As an argument for rejecting an unjust enrichment analysis of "knowing receipt" liability it cannot be rejected as mere formalism (and analytical arguments are, anyway, no less cogent for being formal). Moreover, it is an argument which has been accepted as being essentially correct by other writers on recipient liability.[51] As Smith states, "the argument for strict liability consistently ignores the essential fact that there is a trust, and seeks to treat the trust beneficiary like a legal owner".[52] In his view the "knowing receipt" claim should be conceptualised as a species of equitable wrongdoing. As he notes, this is in fact how almost all the authorities characterise it.

It will be suggested later that defective transfers and title-based claims are not conceptually watertight categories, and that some title-based claims are also examples of defective transfers of property. But even if the distinction is too sharply drawn the underlying argument cannot easily be discounted. The beneficiary and recipient of trust property from the trustee hold different interests in the property, the former being more fragile by reason of its potential for destruction by a good faith purchaser.[53] R has not been unjustly enriched at the expense of B if he has received, not B's title, but a title from T whose legal incidents are materially different from B's.

Some of the objections to Smith's argument miss the point he is making. In his last major contribution to the debate on the nature of recipient liability — a debate which he originated, and the terms of which he largely shaped — the late Peter Birks took as "a commitment of principle" the proposition that:[54]

> "…except so far as differences are inescapably dictated by authority or demanded by reason, wealth should be protected to precisely the same extent

---

50   L Smith, "Restitution: The Heart of Corrective Justice" (2001) 79 *Texas Law Review* 2115 at 2163-2174.

51   See below n 53.

52   L Smith, "Unjust Enrichment, Property and the Structure of Trusts", above n 49 at 433.

53   For similar analysis see S Barkehall Thomas, "'Goodbye' Knowing Receipt, 'Hello' Unconscientious Receipt" (2001) 21 *Oxford Journal of Legal Studies* 239; S Worthington, *Equity* (Clarendon Law Series, Oxford, 2003) at 170-173. J Glover, *Equity, Restitution and Fraud* (Lexis Nexis, Sydney, 2004) at [8.39].

54   P Birks, 'Receipt' in P Birks and A Pretto (eds), *Breach of Trust* (Hart Publishing, Oxford, 2002) at 214-215.

whether it is held at law or in equity behind the curtain of a trust… The new market mechanisms which take advantage of computer technology mean that ever more investors in shares and other company securities acquire only equitable interests. The reason is that the legal title is likely to be consolidated in some bank acting as custodian for many clients. Since the choice of the mode of holding – directly or behind the curtain of a trust – will often be largely fortuitous, it seems right in principle that it should make as little as possible difference."

The proposition on which this commitment of principle rests is attractive but it does not take the argument very far. This is not because it threatens the rationale for, the integrity of, the trust. There is no necessary doctrinal inconsistency involved in supporting the integration of the common law and equitable doctrine along functional lines while simultaneously recognising that the basis of the trust is to be found in the separation of legal and equitable title to property. What is problematic with Birks's proposition is that it assumes the answer to the very question Lionel Smith has posed, namely whether an equitable owner *can* bring an unjust enrichment claim against a later recipient of the legal title of the trust property. The argument is that such a claim would entitle the equitable owner to restitution of an interest he had never previously enjoyed, namely the legal title to the property.[55] To respond, as Birks does, that the law should *presume*, for policy reasons, that legal and equitable titleholders ought to be entitled to the same remedies in this situation is not a direct response to the argument that, unlike a legal titleholder, an equitable titleholder cannot logically bring an unjust enrichment claim against a later recipient of the legal title to the property.

Smith's analysis on this point cannot be disproved by drawing attention to the policy consequences of his argument. It can be refuted by showing that the law of unjust enrichment already recognises circumstances in which an equitable titleholder can establish a claim in restitution against a legal titleholder.[56] But for present purposes it suffices to accept the basic proposition that beneficiaries of trusts cannot be treated, for the purposes of the law of unjust enrichment, like the legal owners of property. It does not, however, follow from acceptance of the argument that a "knowing receipt" claim can *never* be analysed in terms of the reversal of unjust enrichment, thereby attracting strict liability and the potential application of the change of position defence. The cases discussed in the previous section suggest that, at least in some situations, an equitable "knowing receipt" claim can be metamorphosed into a strict liability common law claim for money had and received based on unjust

---

55   Strictly speaking, the claim is for the value of this interest, as it is personal. He also shows that no equitable owner has ever succeeded in bringing a title-based unjust enrichment claim: L Smith, "Unjust Enrichment, Property and the Structure of Trusts" (2000) 116 *Law Quarterly Review* 412 at 430, 435.

56   If the resulting trust is correctly characterised as a response to unjust enrichment, the enforcement of such trusts against trustees and later recipients from trustees, upon the "event" of a voluntary transfer or purchase in the name of another, supplies an example of an unjust enrichment claim by an equitable titleholder against a legal titleholder. See R Chambers, *Resulting Trusts* (Clarendon, Oxford, 1997).

enrichment.[57] In the light of Lionel Smith's argument, we have to choose between the following alternative responses. First, the judges in these cases were wrong to allow a *Barnes v Addy* "knowing receipt" claim to be pleaded as a common law action for money had and received.[58] The second is that there may be some "knowing receipt" cases which can be analysed in terms of the "unifying legal concept" of "unjust enrichment", justifying the imposition of strict liability.[59] It is the second alternative that this chapter explores.

The respective merits of strict liability "unjust enrichment" or fault-based "equitable wrong" analyses of the "knowing receipt" claim have been debated in the context of the traditional model of the express trust created for volunteer beneficiaries. The model is appropriate for a number of reasons. The express trust is generally considered to be the paradigm fiduciary relationship. Moreover, the separation of legal and equitable title under the express trust raises in its purest form the question of whether an equitable owner can bring an unjust enrichment claim against a recipient of the legal interest from the trustee. Lionel Smith's arguments against the conceptualisation of the claim against the recipient as the reversal of unjust enrichment are most convincing when applied to this central case.

But the express trust, though paradigmatic, is a far from typical fiduciary relationship.[60] Not all fiduciary relationships are premised on the separation of legal and equitable title to property. Fiduciary agents will often have authority to transfer property, legal title to which is vested in the principal, to a third party. If the agent, acting in breach of fiduciary duty, makes a transfer of the property to another, the latter will receive the self-same title to the property previously enjoyed by the principal. In this situation the third party can accurately be described as having been unjustly enriched at the expense of the principal.[61] Lionel Smith's objection to the application of the unjust enrichment principle to permit recovery of property, or of its value, to which the claimant never had the legal title is not directed at these decisions.[62] *Swiss Bank* and *Port of Brisbane Corp* belong to this category. In both cases the honest recipients of the proceeds of fraud acquired the same title to the proceeds as that enjoyed by the victims of the fraud. Subject to the application of the defence of change of position, the recipients really had been unjustly enriched at the expense of the victims of the fraud.

---

57 Whether the action for money had received is premised on the reversal of unjust enrichment is controversial, as noted above, but both *Lipkin Gorman* and *Port of Brisbane Corp v ANZ Securities (No 2)* [2003] 2 Qd R 661 at [10] assume that it is.

58 *Port of Brisbane Corp v ANZ Securities(No 2)* and *Spangaro v Corporate Investment Australia Funds Management Ltd* were both decided after Lionel Smith's article had been published. The article seems not to have been cited in either case, and its arguments were not considered in the judgments.

59 *Pavey & Matthews Pty Ltd v Paul* (1987) 162 CLR 221 at 256-257 per Deane J.

60 *Breen v Williams* (1996) 186 CLR 71 at 137 per Gummow J.

61 There may in some cases be an issue as to whether the third party beneficially received the property: *Robb Evans of Robb Evans & Associates v European Bank Ltd* [2004] NSWCA 82 (25 March 2004).

62 As his article acknowledges. See L Smith, "Unjust Enrichment, Property and the Structure of Trusts" (2000) 116 *Law Quarterly Review* 412 at 429, n 71, citing *Jyske Bank (Gibraltar) Ltd v Spejldnaes* [1999] 1 Lloyds Rep Bank 511.

Other "knowing receipt" cases which can be predicated on the reversal of unjust enrichment include at least some instances of trusts constituted for non-volunteer beneficiaries. A characteristic of many trusts created for commercial objectives is that the beneficiaries have provided valuable consideration for their equitable interests, as well as for the proper administration of the trust.[63] Superannuation trusts and managed investments are just two examples. Under these trusts the beneficiaries enjoy contractual rights against the trustee as well as their equitable rights as beneficiaries.[64] Misapplication of money paid by a beneficiary to the trustee can in some circumstances entitle the beneficiary to common law restitution from either the trustee or a later recipient of the payment (or both, provided that the rules relating to the cumulation of remedies are observed). The claim will be based on a legally recognised ground of restitution, the most likely being failure of consideration (or basis) of the payment. *Spangaro* illustrates this kind of unjust enrichment claim.

Between them the two classes of case demonstrate that many equitable claims against recipients can be reconceived as common law unjust enrichment claims. Precisely how the law of unjust enrichment applies to the cases discussed earlier in the chapter is the subject of the next section.

WHEN IS "KNOWING RECEIPT" A CLAIM IN UNJUST ENRICHMENT?

The agency fraud cases

We have noticed that until it reached the House of Lords *Lipkin Gorman* was argued in equity, as well as at common law.[65] Although the casino could not, on the evidence, be fixed with knowledge of the solicitor's wrongdoing in gambling client money both the trial judge and the Court of Appeal were in no doubt that the facts had been properly configured as a "knowing receipt" claim. It was only in the House of Lords that the claim was analysed exclusively as an action for money had and received. The facts were amenable to both common law and equitable analyses, although the common law claim was always the more promising in view of the obvious difficulties involved in proving that a casino knew (in any sense of that word) of the solicitor's breach of fiduciary duty.

Swiss Bank v State Bank of New South Wales is also a "knowing receipt" case which can, without conceptual distortion, be analysed as a *Lipkin Gorman* decision on common law liability. The dishonest fiduciary had no authority to make the inter-bank payment to the defendant bank. The plaintiff bank had legal title to the money transferred to the defendant bank as a result of the fiduciary fraud. As in *Lipkin Gorman*, the precise ground of restitution, or "unjust factor", in *Swiss Bank* is disputed. But for present purposes the point is that, whatever the difficulties in identifying the precise ground of restitution, a

---

63   JH Langbein, "The Secret Life of the Trust: the Trust as an Instrument of Commerce" (1997) 107 *Yale Law Journal* 165.

64   The beneficiaries will usually also have statutory rights and remedies but they are not the concern of this chapter.

65   See above n 38.

common law strict liability claim can be brought on facts which also support an equitable fault-based analysis. This was not a case in which an equitable owner was claiming the legal title to property from the recipient. The principal was claiming restitution of money to which it enjoyed the full beneficial title before that title passed as currency to the defendant bank, which, on the facts, could not establish that it had changed its position in good faith.

Port of Brisbane Corporation v ANZ Securities (No 2) is slightly more complex because the plaintiff's lax employment and compliance practices conferred authority on Hinterdorfer, the dishonest fiduciary, to disburse the plaintiff's funds, though the actual fraudulent alteration of a cheque in favour of the defendant was, of course, not authorised. But, as the Queensland Court of Appeal recognised, the fiduciary fraud was an example of the *Lipkin Gorman* factual configuration. The fiduciary relationship did not involve any separation of legal and equitable title to the money paid out by Hinterdorfer, to which the plaintiff, as principal, held legal title until payment had been made to the defendant bank, which received the cheque, and changed its position, in good faith.[66] Again, there was no question here of the unjust enrichment claim ignoring or conflating the distinction between legal and equitable ownership.

In *Swiss Bank* and *Port of Brisbane Corp* restitution in a common law claim for money had and received was permitted where the facts also admitted of an equitable "knowing receipt" claim. This kind of concurrency very often occurs in the law, the best known example being the concurrent liability of professional advisers in negligence and for breach of contract. The cases do not go as far as establishing that all "knowing receipt" cases can be configured as unjust enrichment claims, though the "agent's fraud" cases are not uncommon. A dictum of Lord Nicholls suggests that the reasoning of this line of authority is capable of rational extension. In the recent House of Lords decision of *Criterion Properties plc v Stratford UK Properties LLC* Lord Nicholls analysed the recipient's liability in the following terms:[67]

> "If a company (A) enters into an agreement with B under which B acquires benefits from A, A's ability to recover these benefits from B depends essentially on whether the agreement is binding on A. If the directors of A were acting for an improper purpose when they entered into the agreement, A's ability to have the agreement set aside depends on the application of familiar principles of agency and company law. If, applying these principles, the agreement is found to be valid and is therefore *not* set aside, questions of 'knowing receipt' by B do not arise. So far as B is concerned there can be no question of A's assets having been misapplied... If, however, the agreement *is* set aside, B will be accountable for any benefits he may have received from A under the agreement. A will have a proprietary claim, if B still has the assets. Additionally, and irrespective of whether B still has the assets in question, A will have a personal claim against B for unjust enrichment, subject always to a defence of change of position. B's personal accountability will not be dependent upon proof of fault or 'unconscionable' conduct on his part. B's accountability in this regard will be 'strict.'"

---

66   As McPherson JA noted, *Port of Brisbane Corp v ANZ Securities (No 2)* [2003] 2 Qd R 661 at 669, the plaintiff's title could have supported an action for conversion of the misdirected cheque.

67   [2004] 1 WLR 1846; [2004] UKHL 28 at [4].

In Lord Nicholls's example B will have acquired A's title to the assets, and Lionel Smith's title-based objection to unjust enrichment analysis will not apply. The practical importance of a remedy in unjust enrichment may be reduced by the availability of statutory remedies on these facts, but, statute apart, the imposition of strict liability is consistent with the principles discussed in this chapter.

The restitution of payments made by beneficiaries to trustees

Spangaro is harder to explain in terms of strict liability unjust enrichment than the agency fraud cases. In contrast to those cases, a trust, separating legal and equitable title to the trust property, had been created. Lionel Smith's analysis suggests the unauthorised payment of the beneficiary's money made by the custodian trustee to the third party recipient "responsible entity" should not have been characterised as an unjust enrichment, and therefore was not recoverable in a strict liability claim. The "responsible entity", as recipient of the legal title to the money from the custodian trustee, was not enriched at the expense of the plaintiff beneficiary whose title was equitable. The only question should have been whether an equitable wrong, necessitating proof of fault of some kind, had been committed.[68]

But, accepting for our purposes the validity of Lionel Smith's title-based argument, there are features of *Spangaro* which suggest that the case is an example of the imposition of strict liability on the basis of unjust enrichment. The starting point is to recall that the plaintiff was entitled to exercise contractual rights against the custodian trustee, as well as the personal and proprietary rights of a beneficiary under the trust. A trustee's failure to comply with the terms of the investment contract can, if the breach is sufficiently serious and the contract has been terminated, provide the investor with a ground of restitution of money paid under the contract.[69] These conditions were satisfied in *Spangaro.* The plaintiff's payment was to be handed over by the custodian trustee to the defendant "responsible entity" only if sufficient funds had been subscribed to enable the investment scheme to go ahead. In breach of this provision, the custodian trustee had paid over the plaintiff's subscription to the defendant before the appropriate funding level required to activate the scheme had been reached. The plaintiff was, as Finkelstein J found, entitled to personal restitution of the payment on the ground of failure of consideration. The basis of the plaintiff's payment to the trustee had failed.[70]

---

68   As the defendant was characterised as an equitable wrongdoer by Finkelstein J, the outcome of the case would have been exactly the same on this analysis.

69   It has been doubted whether the termination requirement has survived the High Court decision in *Roxborough v Rothmans of Pall Mall Australia (Ltd)* (2001) 208 CLR 516. See J Beatson and G Virgo , "Contract, Unjust Enrichment and Unconscionability" (2002) 118 *Law Quarterly Review* 352 at 356.

70   "The concept [of failure of consideration] embraces payment for a purpose which has failed as, for example, where a condition has not been fulfilled, or a contemplated state of affairs has disappeared", *Roxborough v Rothmans of Pall Mall Australia Ltd*, above n 69 at 525 per Gleeson CJ, Gaudron and Hayne JJ.

So far, so straightforward. The plaintiff was clearly entitled to restitution of the money he had invested from the custodian trustee on the ground of failure of consideration. But a custodian trustee is unlikely to have free assets at its disposal to satisfy a judgment in restitution obtained by the beneficiary. Can the personal claim to restitution for failure of consideration be additionally brought against the "responsible entity" to which the unauthorised payment had been made? Finkelstein J, relying on *Lipkin Gorman* as authority, held that it could. But *Lipkin Gorman* is doubtful authority for this conclusion. It was not a decision on restitution for failure of consideration. Moreover, it does not follow that just because a *Lipkin Gorman* title-based claim can be brought against parties other than the immediate recipient of the plaintiff's money that a similar claim can be brought for failure of consideration. The policy of protecting a recipient's interest in security of receipt applies with special intensity to cases of failure of consideration.

In most cases of failure of consideration the immediate recipient of the payer's money will usually have obtained full beneficial title to the money at the moment of receipt. As beneficial owner that recipient can confer a good title to the money on a later recipient. That title will defeat any personal or proprietary claim in unjust enrichment brought against the later recipient.[71] So if A pays money in advance to B for the delivery of goods, and the goods are not delivered but B pays A's money to C, A will not ordinarily be entitled to restitution from C, even though she would be entitled to personal restitution of the money paid, on the ground of failure of consideration, from B.[72] There is good reason for limiting the consequences for failure of contractual reciprocation to the parties to the original contract. Third parties, who have received money on the basis that they can dispose of it as absolute owners, should not be placed at risk of an action of unjust enrichment. This is an application of the policy of protecting a recipient's interest in security of receipt which, as we have seen, informs the application of the defence of change of position.

But *Spangaro* was not the ordinary case of a payee receiving full beneficial title to a payment. By virtue of the fact that the investment scheme was structured as a trust the investor was entitled to a proprietary interest in the managed investment fund. It is at this point that the plaintiff's title becomes relevant. The subsequent release of the money to the "responsible entity" was traceable. Had the money been preserved by the entity, which was neither a good faith purchaser nor entitled to the benefit of the change of position defence, it could have been traced and impressed with a constructive or resulting trust in favour of the plaintiff.[73] Since it had been spent, and there being no residuum to which a proprietary remedy could be attached, the plaintiff was rightly awarded a personal remedy against the entity for unjust

---

71 For an analysis of the circumstances in which a failure of consideration confers beneficial title on a recipient at the time of receipt see R Chambers, *Resulting Trusts* (Clarendon, Oxford, 1997) at 144-153.

72 *Re Goldcorp Exchange Ltd* [1995] 1 AC 74; *Westdeutsche Landesbank Girozentrale v Islington LBC* [1996] AC 669.

73 That many constructive trusts are really resulting in form has been judicially noticed. See *Deabel v V'Landys* [2002] NSWSC 438 at [5] (21 May 2002).

enrichment. It was the plaintiff's ability to show a continuing proprietary interest in the investment, preventing full beneficial title to the money passing to the responsible entity, that distinguished his position from the general run of plaintiffs claiming restitution for failure of consideration. In the absence of the traceable proceeds of his investment to which title could be asserted, he was entitled to personal restitution, not only against the custodian trustee but also against a recipient from the trustee.[74]

CONCLUSION

The aim of this chapter has been to show that Australian law recognises the existence of a common law strict liability claim in unjust enrichment against a recipient of property from a delinquent fiduciary. It is a limited claim, though it is likely to be broadened when Australian law recognises the full implications, for equity as well as for common law, of recognising unjust enrichment as an organising principle. The chapter has shown that some recipients of the proceeds of fiduciary wrongdoing are already strictly liable to make personal restitution of those proceeds. The development has so far proceeded without any clear statement of the basis – in unjust enrichment, property or equitable wrongdoing – on which liability has been imposed. Moreover, if not all recipients are to be held strictly liable to make restitution, *Spangaro* illustrates the necessity for a closer definition of the class of recipient to whom the principles of strict liability will apply. Finally, and most important of all, the growing body of common law authority on strict liability restitution has yet to be reconciled with the fault-based equitable liability. On the present state of the authorities it may be prudent to recognise a "weak" version of strict liability existing alongside fault-based liability, but in the longer term litigant pressure is likely to compel recognition of the "strong" version. The preference of plaintiffs for strict liability, as evidenced by the cases discussed in this chapter, may ultimately prove irresistible.

One can only speculate what Lord Selborne would have made of developments in recipient liability since his day. Much of the evolution of the *Barnes v Addy* jurisprudence has gone against the grain of his seminal judgment. Lord Selborne wanted to limit strictly the circumstances in which participants other than the fiduciary could be held accountable for involvement in a breach of duty.[75] The trend of recent decisions has been to cast the equitable net ever wider so as to extend the reach of accessory accountability. His judgment was in terms limited to participation in a breach of trust.[76] It is nowadays accepted that *Barnes v Addy* applies generally to breaches of fiduciary obligation.[77]

---

74 Provided, of course, that no question of double recovery arises.

75 "I apprehend that those who create trusts do expressly intend, in the absence of fraud and dishonesty, to exonerate such agents of all classes from the responsibilities which are expressly incumbent, by reason of the fiduciary relation, upon the trustees": *Barnes v Addy* (1874) LR 9 Ch App 244 at 252.

76 Though he recognised that liability could be imposed, for example on a trustee de son tort, outside the trust relationship: *Barnes v Addy*, above n 75 at 251.

77 *Warman International Ltd v Dwyer* (1995) 182 CLR 544.

Finally, his judgment adopted a robust common sense definition of knowledge.[78] The trend of modern decisions has been to favour exquisitely differentiated degrees of cognition. It seems improbable that the last Chancellor whose practising experience was derived predominantly from the pre-*Judicature Act* Court of Chancery[79] would have welcomed the incursion of the common law into the field of fiduciary wrongdoing, but the decisions discussed in this chapter suggest that, to a limited extent at least, the common law may indeed have arrived.

---

78 The solicitor, Duffield, who advised against the substitution of Barnes for Addy as trustee, "not at all apprehending, and having no reason to apprehend, any dishonest purpose on the part of either Addy or Barnes…"*Barnes v Addy*, above n 75 at 253.

79 Lord Selborne's preference for equity in his own practice at the Bar is not concealed in the *Dictionary of National Biography* entry for Roundell Palmer, first Earl of Selborne: "Before becoming a law officer of the crown Palmer had little or no experience of common law practice, and he never found it possible to acquire the needful dexterity in cross-examination, and the peculiar tact indispensable for addressing juries. Finding the work extremely irksome, he protected himself as far as possible from retainer in such cases by charging unusually heavy fees. When retained, however, he spared no pains to fit himself for the discharge of his duty"

14

The Equitable Basis of the Law of Restitution

ROSS GRANTHAM

The law of restitution is in many respects unique. As a coherent body of law it is of remarkably recent origin and, unlike many other areas of law, it is largely uncorrupted by statutory intervention.[1] These two factors perhaps explain why the modern law of restitution has emerged in a form that was, initially at least, consistent across virtually the entire common law world, if not in all its finer detail, then certainly in respect of the basic conception of the law. Thus, the superior courts of most common law jurisdictions have accepted that the principle that underlies and gives coherence to the law of restitution is that of unjust enrichment.[2] Notwithstanding this rationalisation, however, there has always been a lingering perception that the law of restitution and the principle of unjust enrichment reflects or is ultimately based upon broader notions of equity, conscience and natural justice.[3] Thus, in the fons et origo of the modern

---

1   This is less true in New Zealand. Prior to the emergence of a coherent law of restitution, there were legislative reforms of aspects of contract law that also purported to deal with aspects of the law of restitution (eg, *Contractual Mistakes Act 1977*, *Contractual Remedies Act 1979*). These statutory intrusions represent two major obstacles to the development in New Zealand of a coherent law of restitution. First, they rest on a contextual view of contract that cuts across conceptual boundaries. Secondly, they vest in the courts wide and unprincipled discretions that are inimical to coherence and rationality in the law.

2   *Lipkin Gorman (a firm) v Karpnale Ltd* [1991] 2 AC 548; *Woolwich Equitable Building Society v IRC (No 2)* [1993] AC 70; *Pavey and Matthews Pty Ltd v Paul* (1987) 162 CLR 221; *David Securities Pty Ltd v Commonwealth Bank of Australia* (1992) 175 CLR 353; *Delgman v Guaranty Trust Co of Canada* [1954] SCR 725; *Goss v Chilcott* [1996] AC 788; *National Bank of New Zealand Ltd v Waitaki International Processing (NI) Ltd* [1999] 2 NZLR 211; *Credit Agricole Indosuez v Banque Nationale de Paris (No 2)* [2001] 2 SLR 301; *Management Corporation Strata Title No 473 v De Beers Jewellery Ptd Ltd* [2002] 2 SLR 1. In the United States, this is made explicit in the *Restatement of the Law of Restitution* (American Law Institute, Minnesota, 1937) at chapter 1. In the Republic of Ireland, see *East Cork Foods Ltd v O'Dwyer Steel Co* [1978] IR 103.

3   G Virgo, 'Restitution Through the Looking Glass: Restitution Within Equity and Equity Within Restitution' in J Getzler (ed), *Rationalizing Property, Equity and Trusts* (LexisNexis, London, 2003) at 87; M Bryan, 'Unjust Enrichment and Unconscionability in Australia: A False Dichotomy' in J Neyers, M McInnes and S Pitel (eds), *Understanding Unjust Enrichment* (Hart Publishing, Oxford, 2004) at 66; E Sherwin, "Restitution and Equity: An Analysis of the Principle of Unjust Enrichment" (2001) 79 *Texas Law Review* 2083 at 2085.

law of restitution, *Moses v Macferlan*, Lord Mansfield said of the action for money had and received: "This kind of equitable action, to recover back money, which ought not in justice to be kept, is very beneficial, and therefore much encouraged. It lies only for money which, ex æquo et bono, the defendant ought to refund".[4]

More recently, in *Banque Financière de la Cité v Parc (Battersea) Ltd*, Lord Clyde described the principle of unjust enrichment as "equitable in the sense that it seeks to secure a fair and just determination of the rights of the parties concerned in the case."[5] This view was echoed recently by the Supreme Court of Canada in *Pacific National Investments Ltd v Victoria (City)*: "The doctrine of unjust enrichment provides an equitable cause of action that retains a large measure of remedial flexibility to deal with different circumstances according to principles rooted in fairness and good conscience."[6]

In Australia, despite earlier acceptance of the principle of unjust enrichment,[7] Gummow J in the High Court of Australia in *Roxborough v Rothmans of Pall Mall Australia Ltd*[8] recently emphasised the equitable nature of the action in money had and received in particular, and of restitutionary recovery in general. His Honour stated: "in deciding cases such as the present which question the boundaries of the established categories, recourse should be had to the general considerations referred to in *Moses v Macferlan*. As in the United States, there is a long tradition in the Supreme Court of New South Wales of proceeding in this manner. If those general considerations resonate with equitable notions, then in a system in which equity prevails that cannot be a source of surprise."[9]

In the common law world, with its historic formal jurisdictional separation of "law" and "equity", the development of a coherent law of restitution has led to tension between the aims and perceptions of "restitution lawyers" and "equity lawyers".[10] On the one hand, restitution lawyers have sought to ratio-

---

4   (1760) 2 Burr 1005 at 1012; 97 ER 676 at 680.

5   [1999] 1 AC 221 at 237. See also *Peter v Beblow* [1993] 1 SCR 980 at 987-990, where McLachlin J said: "There is a tendency on the part of some to view the action for unjust enrichment as a device for doing whatever may seem fair between the parties. In the rush to substantive justice, the principles are sometimes forgotten."

6   [2004] 3 SCR 575 at 586. In *Vedatech Corporation v Crystal Decisions (UK) Ltd* [2002] EWHC 818 at [74], Jacob J stated: "The principle of unjust enrichment is in large part founded on conscience. Can the receiver of a benefit in all conscience hang on to it without paying? If he cannot, then he is unjustly enriched."

7   *Pavey and Matthews Pty Ltd v Paul* (1987) 162 CLR 221 at 256-261, 227 per *David Securities Pty Ltd v Commonwealth Bank of Australia* (1992) 175 CLR 353.

8   (2001) 208 CLR 516, noted by R Grantham, "Restitutionary Recovery Ex Æquo Et Bono" [2002] *Singapore Journal of Legal Studies* 388. B Kremer, "Restitution and Unconscientious-ness: Another View" (2003) 119 *Law Quarterly Review* 188, suggests that the whole of the High Court has set its face against the principle of unjust enrichment. This is not, however, evident in the judgments themselves.

9   (2001) 208 CLR 516 at 553. This echoes the Roman jurist Pomponious: "this by nature is equitable, that no one be made richer by another's loss", quoted in J Dawson, *Unjust Enrichment: A Comparative Analysis* (Little Brown, Boston, 1951) at 3.

10 *Westdeutsche Landesbank Girozentrale v Islington London Borough Council* [1996] AC 669 at 685 per Lord Goff. See also *Brambles Holdings Ltd v Bathurst City Council* (2001) 53 NSWLR

nalise a large body of apparently disparate common law and equitable rules and doctrines into a principled and coherent body of law, in which discretion and appeal to justice in the round has no place.[11] On the other hand, equity lawyers have been concerned to preserve the distinctive flavour and methodology of equitable doctrines and the reliance on open-textured principles.[12] One important aspect of this debate is the extent to which the various restitutionary actions, such as that of money had and received, and the principle of unjust enrichment in general are inherently "equitable".[13]

How this question is answered has important implications for our understanding of the nature and methodology of the law of restitution. First, this question bears upon the structure and focus of the law of restitution. In English law, the focus of unjust enrichment is very much on the plaintiff and her or his state of mind.[14] Thus, the various "factors" that justify a finding that the defendant's enrichment is "unjust", such as mistake and failure of consideration, are concerned with matters that vitiate or qualify the plaintiff's consent.[15] Restitutionary recovery is thus premised fundamentally on the idea that no-one is to be deprived or her or his property except by consent.[16] In contrast, an approach concerned with "conscientiousness" seems to direct the focus onto the state of the defendant's mind and whether the defendant is acting properly

153 at 155; K Mason, "Where has Australian Restitution Law Got to and Where is it Going" (2003) 77 *Australian Law Journal* 358 at 365; J McConvill and M Bagaric, "The Yoking of Unconscionability and Unjust Enrichment in Australia" [2002] *Deakin Law Review* 13; PD Finn, 'Equitable Doctrine and Discretion in Remedies' in W Cornish et al (eds), *Restitution Past, Present and Future* (Hart Publishing, Oxford, 1998) at 251.

11 P Birks, *An Introduction to the Law of Restitution* (Clarendon, Oxford, 1989) at 19.

12 J Glover, *Equity, Restitution and Fraud* (LexisNexis, Sydney, 2003) at 8; S Hedley and M Halliwell, *The Law of Restitution* (Butterworths, London, 2002) at 19; M Halliwell, *Equity and Good Conscience in a Contemporary Context* (Old Bailey Press, London, 1997) at 1-3 and 146-147.

13 Generally, see G Virgo, 'Restitution Through the Looking Glass: Restitution Within Equity and Equity Within Restitution' in J Getzler (ed), *Rationalizing Property, Equity and Trusts* (LexisNexis, London, 2003) at chapter 5; M Bryan, 'Unjust Enrichment and Unconscionability in Australia: A False Dichotomy' in J Neyers, M McInnes and S Pitel (eds), *Understanding Unjust Enrichment* (Hart Publishing, Oxford, 2004) at chapter 4.

14 E O'Dell, 'Incapacity' in P Birks and F Rose (eds), *Lessons of the Swaps Litigation* (Mansfield, London, 2000) at 116-117; P Birks, *Unjust Enrichment* (2nd ed, Clarendon, Oxford, 2005) at 105-106; R Grantham and CF Rickett, "On the Subsidiarity of Unjust Enrichment" (2001) 117 *Law Quarterly Review* 273.

15 In the last major work before his untimely death, (*Unjust Enrichment*) Professor Birks appeared to recant this view in favour of a Civilian-like approach based on the absence of a legal basis for the transfer of the enrichment. However, it appears from this book that Birks remained content to express the reasons why there may be an absence of legal basis for the transfer in terms of "unjust factors", P Birks, *Unjust Enrichment*, above n 14 at 104 and 116.

16 Liberal western society generally privileges individual autonomy and freedom. This in turn justifies both the privilege accorded by the law to the allocation of wealth at the moment before the impugned transaction, and why insufficiently voluntary transactions must be reversed. This may also explain why the law of restitution should be regarded as a manifestation of corrective rather than distributive justice. Cf D Klimchuck, 'Unjust Enrichment and Corrective Justice' in J Neyers, M McInnes and S Pitel (eds), *Understanding Unjust Enrichment* (Hart Publishing, Oxford, 2004) at chapter 6.

in seeking to retain the enrichment.[17] Secondly, it bears upon what might be called the methodology of the law of restitution. On the one hand, the common law is associated with a rule-oriented approach, which privileges certainty in the application of the law and a conception of formal justice. Equity, in contrast, is commonly associated with open-textured principles, flexibility, and recourse to broad notions of conscience and justice.[18] In the context of the law of restitution, it is thus a choice between the articulation of a set of nominate grounds justifying restitutionary recovery and an approach, typified by that of Gummow J in *Roxborough*, whereby direct recourse may be had in deciding cases to such broad notions as unconscientiousness.[19] Thirdly, the issue of an "equitable" law of restitution has important implications for what can properly be seen as justified or rationalised by the principle of unjust enrichment. It bears directly upon the issue of the extent to which equitable doctrines such as undue influence and unconscionable bargain can be regarded as restitutionary in any sense beyond the bare effect or pattern of the remedy in restoring the status quo ante between the parties.[20] Fourthly, the proper characterisation of the principle of unjust enrichment has implications for the place of the law of restitution in the wider taxonomy of the private law. It has been suggested that the principle of unjust enrichment is a third pillar of the private law, alongside the law of contract and of tort.[21] An "equitable" characterisation may, however, suggest a different and subsidiary role for the law of restitution as a mechanism to relieve the parties from the common law consequences of their transactions.

The aim of this chapter is to consider the extent to which the modern law of restitution may properly be regarded as "equitable". In exploring this question it is hoped a better understanding of the essential nature, function, and character of the law of restitution is gained, and that some way is made towards resolving the "restitution lawyer"–"equity lawyer" dispute. Before embarking on a consideration of this question, however, it is important briefly to clarify the two central concepts under consideration in this chapter.

---

17 P Birks, *Unjust Enrichment*, above n 14 at 5; Lord Walker, "Dishonesty and Unconscionable Conduct in Commercial Life: Some Reflections on Accessory Liability and Knowing Receipt" (2005) 27 *Sydney Law Review* 187 at 202.

18 J Glover, *Equity, Restitution and Fraud* (LexisNexis, Sydney, 2003) at 8; M Halliwell, *Equity and Good Conscience in a Contemporary Context* (Old Bailey Press, London, 1997) at 3.

19 Superficially, Gummow J's approach in *Roxborough* bears a similarity to Birks' "absence of legal basis approach" (see, P Birks, *Unjust Enrichment* (2nd ed, Clarendon, Oxford, 2005) at 117. On this approach, Birks also may be understood as advocating an appeal to a broader notion beyond the establish categories as a means of deciding actual cases. Read in light of Civilian, especially German, unjust enrichment jurisprudence, upon which this approach is based, the similarity is less clear. As T Krebs, *Restitution at the Crossroads: A Comparative Study* (Cavendish, London, 2001), has demonstrated, the absence of legal basis approach in fact employs, and is limited in its operation to, clearly defined circumstances (see also P Birks, *Unjust Enrichment*, at 104 and 116). This approach differs from the unjust factors approach of English law in that the identification and definition of the circumstances in which the legal basis of the transfer will be avoided is undertaken outside of the law of unjust enrichment.

20 S Hedley and M Halliwell, *The Law of Restitution* (Butterworths, London, 2002) at chapter 2.

21 *Banque Financière de la Cité v Parc (Battersea) Ltd* [1991] AC 221 at 227.

The first is the meaning of "restitution". At its broadest, this refers to that body of law concerned with remedies assessed with respect to the defendant's gain rather than the loss suffered by the plaintiff. The notion of restitution has, however, been given a more restricted technical meaning, and it is this restricted meaning that is used in this chapter. Restitution as used here refers to the law's response to the enrichment of the defendant through a transfer of wealth from the plaintiff to the defendant, where that enrichment is identified as unjust.[22] Thus, "restitution" is properly limited to cases where the aim is to restore the status quo ante between plaintiff and defendant, where the reason for that restoration (the cause of action) lies outside of the law of contract, wrongs and property.[23] The terms restitution and unjust enrichment will, therefore, be used interchangeably.

The second concept is that of "equity". The notion of "equity" has many meanings,[24] and as applied to the law of restitution or unjust enrichment it may denote at least five things. First, it may mean that the jurisdictional origins of the principle of unjust enrichment, or at least the historic actions that are now seen as part of, or rationalised by, the principle of unjust enrichment, arose in the Court of Chancery prior to the *Judicature Act 1873* (UK).[25] In so far as one is concerned with the action in money had and received this meaning can be quickly dismissed. The action for money had and received as a matter of its historical origins is indisputably a common law *action*.[26] While in some early cases, such as *Straton v Rastall*,[27] it was suggested that success in the action for money had and received was dependent upon the plaintiff showing that he or she could have succeeded in Chancery, the view that the action for money had and received was an equitable *action* has long since been shown to be false. Thus, in *Miller v Atlee*,[28] Pollock CB described the action as a "perfectly legal

---

22 The abandonment of the "perfect quadration" thesis, which held that restitution was only ever a response to unjust enrichment, in favour of a multi-causal analysis, makes it necessary to distinguish restitution as a response to unjust enrichment and gain-based responses (disgorgement) that arise in response to other causes of action. See M McInnes, "Restitution, Unjust Enrichment and the Perfect Quadration Thesis" [1999] *Restitution Law Review* 118; P Birks, "The Law of Unjust Enrichment: A Millennial Resolution" [1999] *Singapore Journal of Legal Studies* 318 at 319-320.

23 R Grantham and CF Rickett, "Disgorgement for Unjust Enrichment" [2003] *Cambridge Law Journal* 159.

24 E Sherwin, "Restitution and Equity: An Analysis of the Principle of Unjust Enrichment" (2001) 79 *Texas Law Review* 2083 at 2088-2089; G Virgo, 'Restitution Through the Looking Glass: Restitution Within Equity and Equity Within Restitution' in J Getzler (ed), *Rationalizing Property, Equity and Trusts* (LexisNexis, London, 2003) at 85.

25 FW Maitland, *Equity* (2nd ed, Cambridge University Press, Cambridge, 1936) at 1; R Meagher, JD Heydon and M Leeming, *Meagher, Gummow and Lehane's Equity: Doctrines and Remedies* (4th ed, LexisNexis, Sydney, 2002) at 3; CF Rickett, 'Equity' in R Cooke (ed), *Laws of New Zealand* (Butterworths, Wellington, 2003) at [1].

26 W Evans, "An Essay on the Action for Money Had and Received" [1998] *Restitution Law Review* 1; P Birks, "Failure of Consideration and its Place on the Map" (2002) 2(1) *Oxford University Commonwealth Law Journal* 1; *Roxborough v Rothmans of Pall Mall Australia Ltd* (2001) 208 CLR 516 at 589-590.

27 (1788) 2 Term Rep 366 at 370; 100 ER 197 at 199.

28 (1849) 3 Ex 799; 13 Jur 431. See also, *Roxborough v Rothmans of Pall Mall Australia Ltd* (2001) 208 CLR 516 at 590.

action". However, it is equally clear that there are actions that are now understood as being based on, or a manifestation of, the principle of unjust enrichment that are "equitable" in this jurisdictional sense. Thus, for example, most orthodox accounts of the law of unjust enrichment include the doctrines of undue influence, unconscionable bargain, account and subrogation as being explicable in terms of the principle of unjust enrichment.[29]

Secondly, the characterisation of the law of restitution as "equitable" may refer to a methodology that involves the use of more flexible, discretionary principles rather than fixed rules and bright-line standards.[30] Equitable doctrines are historically associated with a more open-textured formulation than the common law. Thus, for example, in *National Australia Bank Ltd v Nobile*, Davies J stated in respect of a claim in unconscionability: "The grounds for intervention by a court of equity cannot be circumscribed by definition".[31] Similarly, in *National Westminster Bank v Morgan*, Lord Scarman eschewed any attempt to reduce the principle of undue influence to a definitive statement: "This is a world of doctrine, not of neat and tidy rules".[32] On this basis, the particular unjust factors that have been articulated would be regarded merely as illustrations of a more abstract and necessarily wider principle of "unjust enrichment". A court might, therefore, find restitutionary liability beyond the established cases through a direct application of the principle of unjust enrichment to the particular facts of the case.

Thirdly, and closely related to the second meaning, the label "equitable" may indicate a direct appeal to broad and overarching notions of fairness, conscience and justice in the disposition of individual cases.[33] Thus, while it may be possible to identify a set of categories where restitutionary recovery will be granted as a matter of course, the court may nevertheless impose a restitutionary response in novel situations to meet the demands of justice of that particular case. As will be discussed below, such an approach gives rise to important questions about the basis of adjudication and the tension between a conception of the law as a body of settled principles and "law" as the pursuit of the "Holy Grail of individualised justice".[34]

---

29   R Goff and G Jones, *The Law of Restitution* (6th ed, Sweet & Maxwell, London, 2002) at chapters 11 and 12; A Burrows, *The Law of Restitution* (2nd ed, Butterworths, London, 2002) at chapters 6 and 7; R Grantham and CF Rickett, *Enrichment and Restitution in New Zealand* (Hart Publishing, Oxford, 2000) at chapter 7.

30   J Glover, *Equity, Restitution and Fraud* (LexisNexis, Sydney, 2003) at 8-12; S Hedley and M Halliwell, *The Law of Restitution* (Butterworths, London, 2002) at 19.

31   (1988) 100 ALR 227 at 229. Lord Hardwicke said: "As to relief against frauds, no invariable rules can be established. Fraud is infinite" (Letter to Lord Kames, quoted in L Sheridan, *Fraud in Equity: A Study in English and Irish Law* (Pitman, London, 1957) at 2).

32   [1985] AC 686 at 709.

33   E Sherwin, "Restitution and Equity: An Analysis of the Principle of Unjust Enrichment" (2001) 79 *Texas Law Review* 2083 at 2091; G Virgo, 'Restitution Through the Looking Glass: Restitution Within Equity and Equity Within Restitution' in J Getzler (ed), *Rationalizing Property, Equity and Trusts* (LexisNexis, London, 2003) at 85; DR Klinck, "The Unexamined 'Conscience' of Contemporary Canadian Equity" (2001) 46 *McGill Law Journal* 571.

34   KM Hayne, "Australian Law in the Twentieth Century" (2000) 74 *Australian Law Journal* 373 at 375.

Fourthly, "equity" may indicate a concern with the state of the defendant's conscience.[35] Thus, in *Westdeutsche Landesbank Girozentrale v Islington London Borough Council*, Lord Browne-Wilkinson stated "[e]quity operates on the conscience of the owner of the legal interest. In the case of a trust, the conscience of the legal owner requires him to carry out the purpose for which the property was vested in him".[36] A focus on the defendant's conscience in the law of restitution suggests that the concern is with the quality of the defendant's conduct rather that the state of the plaintiff's consent to the transfer.[37]

Finally, "equity" may refer to the historic role of the Court of Chancery in supplementing or ameliorating the effect of common law rules.[38] Thus, to describe the principle of unjust enrichment as equitable may be to denote that its function, like those rules deriving from the Court of Chancery, is to relieve the plaintiff from a transaction that, but for the principle of unjust enrichment, would be regarded as valid by the law of contract, tort, and property.

These various attributes or meanings of "equitable" can be, for present purposes, organised under three principal headings. The law of restitution as a whole, and the principle of unjust enrichment in particular, may be "equitable" in the sense that:

1. it is concerned with the quality of the defendant's conduct;

2. that it serves a supplementary or ameliorative role, modifying the common law; and

3. that it proceeds by way of general, open-ended principles rather than more precise rules.[39]

The conclusions that will be reached in this chapter may be explained as follows. The law of restitution, and the principle of unjust enrichment, may be

---

35 J Story, *Commentaries on Equity Jurisprudence as Administered in England and America* (13th ed, Rothman, Litttleton, Colorado, 1988), Vol I at 17; G Virgo, 'Restitution Through the Looking Glass: Restitution Within Equity and Equity Within Restitution' in J Getzler (ed), *Rationalizing Property, Equity and Trusts*, above n 33 at 85; P Parkinson (ed), *The Principles of Equity* (2nd ed, Lawbook Co, Sydney, 2003) at 29; DR Klinck, "The Unexamined 'Conscience' of Contemporary Canadian Equity" (2001) 46 *McGill Law Journal* 571 at 577.

36 [1996] AC 669 at 705.

37 Lord Walker, "Dishonesty and Unconscionable Conduct in Commercial Life: Some Reflections on Accessory Liability and Knowing Receipt" (2005) 27 *Sydney Law Review* 187 at 202; P Birks, *Unjust Enrichment* (2nd ed, Clarendon, Oxford, 2005) at 5.

38 J Baker, *An Introduction to English Legal History* (4th ed, Butterworths, London, 2002) at 105; *Roxborough v Rothmans of Pall Mall Australia Ltd* (2001) 208 CLR 516 at 545 per Gummow J, 579 per Kirby J.

39 It is interesting to note that the Canadian notion of unjust enrichment is also described as "equitable" in character: G Fridman, "The Reach of Restitution" (1991) 11 *Legal Studies* 304. In Canadian law, the label "equitable" has three possible interpretations: (i) it may reflect the Civilian influence, particularly French, on Canadian law, where unjust enrichment is "equitable" in the sense that it is a doctrine that exists outside of the relevant Code; (ii) that there is a background notion, or even further element, of "unjustness" such that even where unjust enrichment is made out, the availability of a remedial response might still be conditioned on such a remedy being just in the circumstances; and (iii) that "equitable" may refer to a direct appeal to notions of fairness and justice.

properly regarded as "equitable" in the second sense only. While sometimes hidden within the incomplete taxonomy of the private law, the law of restitution is supplementary in a way similar to that in which equity has traditionally been understood to be supplementary. Both equity and the law of restitution serve to modify or undo the effects of other (common law) rules.[40] The operation of the principle of unjust enrichment necessarily begins only when the law of contract, the law of wrongs and the law of property have finished their work. Unjust enrichment operates to reverse or undo a transfer of wealth that would, but for its intervention, remain valid and effective. In contrast, it is not appropriate to regard the law of restitution as "equitable" within the first or third senses. To regard restitutionary liability as a species of wrongdoing, where the focus is on the quality of the defendant's conduct in refusing to make restitution voluntarily, is to beg the essential question: why is the defendant obligated to make restitution such that his refusal is wrongful or unconscientious? Nor is it appropriate to regard the law of restitution as "equitable" in the sense that it proceeds by way of flexible rules and a direct appeal to broad notions of conscience. As will be discussed at some length below, it is far from clear that equitable doctrines and principles are as *ad hoc* as is sometimes suggested and that, even if they are, there are serious questions about the political legitimacy of such an approach.

CONSCIENCE, WRONGDOING AND CONSENT

As it is conceived within the dominant model,[41] the justification for restitutionary liability is that the plaintiff did not subjectively consent to the enrichment of the defendant.[42] Whether manifested in the denial of legal capacity to minors and juristic persons, or the presence of mistake, coercion, or morbid dependence on the defendant, it is the defect in the plaintiff's subjective consent that identifies the transfer of wealth as one that, if not reversed, would unjustly enrich the defendant.

---

40 For this purpose, "equity" is used in its jurisdictional sense. Viewed from a modern perspective, this feature can often be difficult to discern. Thus, for example, the modern "law of contract" is a mixture of rules having their origins in the common law courts and in the Court of Chancery. Equity's role here, through doctrines such as estoppel, undue influence and unconscionable bargain, is so longstanding and fundamental that, quite appropriately, we no longer see the law of contract as being just the common law rules, "occasionally" supplemented by equitable principles.

41 This refers to the conceptualisation of the law of restitution developed by R Goff and G Jones, *The Law of Restitution* (6th ed, Sweet & Maxwell, London, 2002); P Birks, *An Introduction to the Law of Restitution* (Clarendon, Oxford, 1985) and A Burrows, *The Law of Restitution* (2nd ed, Butterworths, London, 2002).

42 E O'Dell suggests that the linking thread of the unjust factors is "that ... the plaintiff had no real intention to enrich the defendant, so the payment was unintended, non-consensual or involuntary": see 'Incapacity' in P Birks and F Rose (eds), *Lessons of the Swaps Litigation* (Mansfield Press, London, 2000) at 116.

In *Roxborough v Rothmans of Pall Mall Australia Ltd*,[43] however, Gummow J rejected the unjust enrichment-based view of the law of restitution.[44] In his Honour's view, the claim in money had and received, and by implication all restitutionary claims,[45] were "equitable" rather than common law in nature.[46] While acknowledging that in purely jurisdictional terms the claim in money had and received, as with the majority of restitutionary claims, arose in the courts of common law, Gummow J nevertheless considered that such claims were "equitable" in their character and mode of operation.[47] Thus, while the claim in money had and received was properly a common law *action*, it nevertheless represented the absorption into common law, in determining the nature and scope of liability, of what were fundamentally equitable concepts. This, in Gummow J's view, is what Lord Mansfield meant in *Moses v Macferlan* when he characterised the claim as "equitable".[48]

---

43 (2001) 208 CLR 516.

44 Gummow J was alone in expressly rejecting unjust enrichment. Gleeson CJ, Gaudron and Hayne JJ (*Roxborough v Rothmans of Pall Mall Australia Ltd*, above n 43 at 528) seemed to agree that the action in money had and received was equitable, although this was not decisive in their reasoning. Callinan J (at 589-590) rejected any suggestion money had and received was an equitable claim but did not suggest that it was equitable in character. Kirby J, dissenting on the result, continued to use the language of unjust enrichment (at 579).

45 G Virgo, 'Restitution Through the Looking Glass: Restitution Within Equity and Equity Within Restitution' in J Getzler (ed), *Rationalizing Property, Equity and Trusts* (LexisNexis, London, 2003) at 88-89.

46 Gummow J, *Roxborough v Rothmans of Pall Mall Australia Ltd*, above n 43 at 543, adopted a passage from PD Finn, 'Equitable Doctrine and Discretion in Remedies' in W Cornish et al (eds), *Restitution Past, Present and Future* (Hart Publishing, Oxford, 1998) at 252, in which Finn rejected the principle of unjust enrichment on the basis that it concealed rather than revealed the basis of legal intervention. That may or may not be the case. However, Finn's further suggestion that "unconscionability" does not suffer from the same obfuscating tendency is much less acceptable. As is clear from the confusion in the case law, "unconscionability" embraces a range of reasons for intervention that range from a cognitive defect in the plaintiff to active wrongdoing by the defendant: see G Dal Pont, "The Varying Shades of 'Unconscionable' Conduct – Same Term, Different Meaning" (2000) 19(2) *Australian Bar Review* 135; P Wilson, "Unconscionability and Fairness in Australian Equitable Jurisprudence" (2004) 11(1) *Australian Property Law Journal* 1; KM Hayne, "Australian Law in the Twentieth Century" (2000) 74 *Australian Law Journal* 373 at 375; R Grantham and CF Rickett, *Enrichment and Restitution in New Zealand* (Hart Publishing, Oxford, 2000) at chapter 7.

47 (2001) 208 CLR 516 at 554. The general attachment in Australian law to notions of unconscionability is well known. The reasons for this attachment are more speculative. It has, however, been suggested that it may lie in the "…importance which Australians attach to straightforwardness and fair play" and in the use of unconscionability in statutes such as ss 51AA-51AC of the *Trade Practices Act 1974* (Cth): Lord Walker, "Dishonesty and Unconscionable Conduct in Commercial Life – Some Reflections on Accessory Liability and Knowing Receipt" (2005) 27 *Sydney Law Review* 187 at 199.

48 As a matter of history, this conclusion is not convincing. See, P Birks, "Failure of Consideration and its Place on the Map" (2002) 2(1) *Oxford University Commonwealth Law Journal* 1 at 13, who suggests that Lord Mansfield's reference to "equity" was to the Roman notion of aequitas and not to Chancery; G Virgo, 'Restitution Through the Looking Glass: Restitution Within Equity and Equity Within Restitution' in J Getzler (ed), *Rationalizing Property, Equity and Trusts*, above n 45 at 94.

This characterisation of restitutionary claims as equitable in turn led Gummow J to identify as the basis of restitutionary recovery[49] the defendant's unconscientious refusal to account to the plaintiff.[50] Thus, unlike the dominant account of restitutionary liability developed in the works of Lord Goff and Professor Jones,[51] and Professor Birks,[52] which is based on the principle of unjust enrichment and which focuses on the quality of the plaintiff's consent to the transfer in question, Gummow J focused on the position of the defendant, in particular on the question whether the defendant could in good conscience refuse to make restitution of the enrichment.

This conception of restitutionary liability has a number of important doctrinal and theoretical implications. First, the characterisation of the right to restitution as arising from the defendant's unconscionable *refusal to account* for the enrichment suggests that liability is not strict, but rather is dependant upon the quality of the defendant's conduct, or of his response to the plaintiff's claim. Indeed, implicit in the very idea of "unconscientiousness" is the require-ment that the defendant's conscience be bound. This in turn suggests that liability does not arise at the moment of receipt, but only at some later point. Logically, one can be said to have retained an enrichment only after the moment of receipt,[53] while a refusal to account for the enrichment implies at the very least being aware of the plaintiff's claim.

In terms of the overall quantum of restitutionary liability in any given case, such an analysis is probably not inconsistent with the orthodox unjust enrichment-based understanding. There is, however, a substantial difference in the doctrinal explanation of that liability. On the unjust enrichment analysis, liability arises at the moment of receipt, but is offset or reduced by defences such as change of position (which takes account of good faith).[54] Thus, a defendant who receives $100 by mistake is liable at the point of receipt to repay $100. However, where he or she has changed his or her position with respect to $20 of the money received, the effective liability is reduced to $80. On

---

49   Gummow J (*Roxborough v Rothmans of Pall Mall Australia Ltd* (2001) 208 CLR 516 at 543-544), in particular, also seemed influenced in his rejection of unjust enrichment by a mistrust of the taxonomy of the private law championed by Peter Birks. In doing so, his Honour evinced a remarkably conservative view of the private law, in which the stability of historical categories is preferred to rationality. See P Birks, "Failure of Consideration and its Place on the Map" (2002) 2(1) *Oxford University Commonwealth Law Journal* 1, 12.

50   *Roxborough v Rothmans of Pall Mall Australia Ltd*, above n 49 at 542-543. It is important to note that Gummow J was alone in expressly rejecting the principle of unjust enrichment. Accordingly, *Pavey and Matthews Pty Ltd v Paul* (1987) 162 CLR 221 and *David Securities Pty Ltd v Commonwealth Bank of Australia* (1992) 175 CLR 353, must still be regarded as stating the law in Australia. These cases adopt the principle of unjust enrichment as the basis of resti-tutionary recovery.

51   R Goff and G Jones, *The Law of Restitution* (6th ed, Sweet & Maxwell, London, 2002).

52   P Birks, *An Introduction to the Law of Restitution* (Clarendon, Oxford, 1985).

53   The literal meaning of "retain" is to "keep hold or possession of; to continue having or keeping, in various senses": *Oxford English Dictionary* (2nd ed, Clarendon, Oxford, 1989), Vol XIII.

54   On the defence of change of position generally, see G Virgo, *The Principles of the Law of Resti-tution* (Clarendon, Oxford, 1999) at chapter 25; R Grantham and CF Rickett, *Enrichment and Restitution in New Zealand* (Hart Publishing, Oxford, 2000) at chapters 14 and 15.

Gummow J's analysis in *Roxborough*, the defendant's liability on these facts is also $80. However, this is because the defendant's liability is necessarily dependent upon the quality of the defendant's conduct in refusing to account to the plaintiff. Logically, however, such liability cannot extend to the $20 spent prior to the justification of the liability by a refusal to account.[55]

Secondly and more fundamentally, the emphasis placed by Gummow J on the defendant's refusal to account for the enrichment suggests that restitutionary liability is a species of wrongdoing.[56] This is implicit not only in the very notion of "unconscientious", but also in the analytical structure of unconscientious retention. As articulated in the judgments in *Roxborough*, the unconscientiousness lies in the defendant's refusal to account for the enrichment in circumstances where the defendant had "no title" or right to retain it.[57] The defendant's lack of title to retain the enrichment seems to be consequence of the vitiation of the transfer by factors such as mistake or failure of consideration. However, the restitutionary liability imposed on the defendant is not directly a response to the vitiation of the plaintiff's consent, but rather to the defendant's refusal to make restoration of the enrichment to the plaintiff at the moment of receipt. This is perhaps most clearly stated in the context of the rejection of the passing off defence.[58] In Gummow J's view, "[t]he doctrinal reason which points against the 'passing-on' defence is the unconscientious conduct of the defendant in refusing to account to the plaintiff",[59] while for Gleeson CJ, Gaudron and Hayne JJ, the passing on defence rested on the false premise that "in the circumstances of a case such as the present, it would only be unconscionable of the respondent to withhold repayment of the amounts

---

55 It might be argued that the differences between the unjust enrichment-receipt model and the refusal to account model are overstated in that the refusal to account model might equally start at the point of receipt, but only crystallize in terms of quantum at the point of refusal to make restitution. On this basis, liability in the present example would start as being $100 but be reduced by expenditure by the plaintiff prior to demand and refusal. The difficulty with such an analysis is that, as articulated by Gummow J in *Roxborough*, the trigger for liability is the refusal itself.

56 Lord Walker, "Dishonesty and Unconscionable Conduct in Commercial Life: Some Reflections on Accessory Liability and Knowing Receipt" (2005) 27 *Sydney Law Review* 187 at 202; R Grantham, "Restitutionary Recovery Ex Æquo Et Bono" [2002] *Singapore Journal of Legal Studies* 388.

57 In *Unjust Enrichment* (2nd ed, Clarendon, Oxford, 2005), Birks adopts a Civilian-like model of unjust enrichment that bases restitutionary liability on an absence of legal basis for the defendant's enrichment. At one level this suggests that, if the basis of the transfer is avoided, the defendant's title to the subject matter of the enrichment is impeached and the plaintiff can simply be left to assert his or her (now) pre-existing title. Birks, however, draws a distinction between initial and subsequent invalidity (at 110). This enables him to continue to insist that in the core case of a mistaken payment, the plaintiff's action is in unjust enrichment, which in turn is not about the passive vindication of pre-existing property rights.

58 Generally, see W Woodward, "Passing on the Right to Restitution" (1985) 39 *University of Miami Law Review* 873; G Jones, *Restitution in Public and Private Law* (Sweet & Maxwell, London, 1991) at 28-37 and 46-47; B Rudden and W Bishop, "Gritz and Quellmehl: Pass it On" (1981) 6 *European Law Review* 243.

59 *Roxborough v Rothmans of Pall Mall Australia Ltd* (2001) 208 CLR 516 at 542.

referable to the tax if the appellants, for their part, were ultimately left impoverished to that extent".[60]

Put in analytical terms, the High Court's approach is one that imposes liability for a breach of a defendant's obligation not to refuse to make restitution, rather than being the enforcement of an obligation to make restitution. There is of course nothing objectionable per se in the notion that the law will not directly enforce a primary duty (in this case the duty to make restitution), but will instead enforce it indirectly through the recognition of a wrong resulting from a breach of the primary duty.[61] The common law is full of illustrations of such an approach. Thus, in the law of contract, the contract gives rise to a primary obligation to perform. However, exceptional cases aside, that primary obligation is not enforced directly. Rather, it is enforced indirectly through an action for (wrongful) breach of contract. In a similar fashion, the common law does not directly vindicate property rights, but instead mediates its protection through actions such as conversion which analytically involve the allegation of a wrongful interference with the plaintiff's (primary) right of property.[62] The tendency of the law to seek to rectify wrongs rather than enforce rights has been apparent in the common law since the 14th century.[63] Why the law should have moved in this direction is far from clear, though the historical procedural advantages of claims brought at *plaints* over those brought pursuant to praecipe writs,[64] and a perception that the law is on stronger moral ground when it requires the defendant to make good wrongs for which the defendant is by definition responsible,[65] undoubtedly had some bearing on this movement. However, while the strategy of indirect enforcement of primary rights via the notion of wrongdoing is now well established in the

---

60   *Roxborough v Rothmans of Pall Mall Australia Ltd*, above n 59 at 527-528. For an analysis of the Court's treatment of the defence see, P Birks, "Failure of Consideration and its Place on the Map" (2002) 2(1) *Oxford University Commonwealth Law Journal* 1; R Grantham, "Restitutionary Recovery Ex Æquo Et Bono" [2002] *Singapore Journal of Legal Studies* 388.

61   P Birks, "The Content of the Fiduciary Obligation" (2002) 16 *Trust Law International* 34, 39; P Birks, 'The Concept of a Civil Wrong' in D Owen (ed), *Philosophical Foundations of Tort Law* (Clarendon, Oxford, 1995) at 29-51.

62   R Grantham and CF Rickett, "Property Rights: A Legally Significant Event" [2003] *Cambridge Law Journal* 417.

63   J Baker, *An Introduction to English Legal History* (3rd ed, Butterworths, London, 1990) at 67-69.

64   There is a fundamental cleavage in the common law between claims demanding performance of a right and those seeking redress for a wrong. Historically, this was reflected in the distinction between actions founded on a praecipe writ and those founded on a plaint. This distinction is said to be Germanic in origin: F Pollock and F Maitland, *The History of English Law* (2nd ed, Cambridge University Press, Cambridge, 1968), Vol 2 at 571.

65   More analytically, this might be couched in terms of Mill's "harm principle", which limits the scope for the imposition of positive duties: J Mill, *Utilitarianism, On Liberty and Considerations on Representative Government* (Acton (ed), Dent, London, 1987) at 78. A concern with enforcing positive obligations also underlies Fuller's and Perdue's critique of classical contract: L Fuller and R Perdue, "The Reliance Interest in Contract Damages" (1936-1937) 46 *Yale Law Journal* 52. See also S Smith, "Justifying the Law of Unjust Enrichment" (2001) 79 *Texas Law Review* 2177 at 2189-2191.

common law,[66] the characterisation of restitutionary liability in *Roxborough* as a species of wrongdoing is nevertheless problematic in three important aspects.

The first concerns the appropriate remedy for the defendant's unconscientious retention. The majority in *Roxborough* regarded the liability imposed as being restitutionary.[67] As Gummow J noted, restitution differs from compensation in that the focus is the defendant's gain not the plaintiff's loss. However, if the cause of action is properly regarded as one founded on the defendant's wrongdoing, the presumptive and appropriate remedy would seem to be compensation for the loss caused by the wrong.[68] While in many cases the defendant's gain and the plaintiff's loss will be merely opposite sides of the same coin, the analytical nature of the remedy is nevertheless important. The nature of the remedy as restitution or compensation has important consequences for the scope of recovery. On the one hand, compensation is measured by the plaintiff's loss, both direct and consequential,[69] rather than the defendant's gain from the wrong.[70] On the other hand, restitution is logically limited to the defendant's gain, but as the High Court held in *Roxborough*, the gain is not necessarily limited to the extent of the plaintiff's loss. Moreover, the issue is one of doctrinal importance. Although many Commonwealth courts have shown a willingness to sever the link between right and remedy,[71] it is nevertheless essential to the coherence of the law that the objectives of the cause of action and the remedial response align.[72] The alternative is an unprincipled

---

66 As a matter of principle, however, there remains the issue of whether such a strategy is rational. If the law is to recognize, for example, a right to contractual performance, why does it not enforce that right directly, as seems to be the case in Civilian jurisdictions? See T Krebs, *Restitution at the Crossroads: A comparative study* (Cavendish, London, 2001) at 22.

67 (2001) 208 CLR 516 at 542.

68 P Birks, 'The Concept of a Civil Wrong' in D Owen (ed), *Philosophical Foundations of Tort Law* (Clarendon, Oxford, 1995) at 47; M Tilbury, 'Remedies and the Classification of Obligations' in A Robertson (ed), *The Law of Obligations: Connections and Boundaries* (UCL Press, London, 2004) at 15. This is not to say that compensation is the necessary or only response to a wrong, merely that it is the most common response and one that is well attuned to remedying the harm caused by a breach of the plaintiff's primary right.

69 S Smith, "Justifying the Law of Unjust Enrichment", above n 65 at 2184.

70 *Attorney-General v Blake* [2001] 1 AC 268 at 278.

71 See, for example, *Bathurst City Council v PWC Properties Pty Ltd* (1998) 195 CLR 566 at 585: "before the court imposes a constructive trust as a remedy, it should first decide whether, having regard to the issues in the litigation, there are other means available to quell the controversy. An equitable remedy which falls short of the imposition of a trust may assist in avoiding a result whereby the plaintiff gains a beneficial proprietary interest which gives an unfair priority over other equally deserving creditors of the defendant." See also, *Giumelli v Giumelli* (1999) 196 CLR 101 at 125. Generally, see DM Waters, "Liability and Remedy: An Adjustable Relationship" (2001) 64 *Saskatchewan Law Reports* 429; DM Waters, "The Role of the Trust Treatise in the 1990s" (1994) 59 *Missouri Law Review* 121 at 137; CF Rickett, 'Where Are We Going With Equitable Compensation' in AJ Oakley (ed), *Trends in Contemporary Trust Law* (Oxford, Clarendon, 1996) at 178-183; E Thomas, "An Endorsement of a More Flexible Law of Civil Remedies" (1999) 7 *Waikato Law Review* 23.

72 M McInnes, "Disgorgement for Wrongs: An Experiment in Alignment" [2001] *Restitution Law Review* 516; R Grantham and CF Rickett, "Disgorgement for Unjust Enrichment" [2003] *Cambridge Law Journal* 159.

palette of remedies where the choice rests on the court's perception of the relative colours of the parties. [73]

The second concern is that it is far from clear how the wrong of unconscientious refusal to make restitution relates to or is justified by the primary right/duty that arises from a vitiation of the transfer of wealth by factors such as a failure of consideration or a mistake.[74] The existence of a wrong is logically dependent upon the existence of a prior right/duty: one cannot infringe a right that has yet to come into existence. Moreover, the content of the wrong is dependent upon and justified by the nature of the prior right: the wrong consists of the breach of the primary duty.[75]

Despite recent academic attempts at expansion, the range of circumstances giving rise to restitutionary liability have not changed greatly from the list proposed by Lord Mansfield in *Moses v Macferlan*: "money paid by mistake… (express or implied); or extortion, or oppression, or an undue advantage taken of the plaintiff's situation, contrary to laws made for the protection of persons under those circumstances."[76] What each of these factors articulates is a reason why the plaintiff should not be held to the diminution of her or his wealth effected by the transfer. The concern is thus with the quality of the plaintiff's consent to the transfer and whether the plaintiff's wealth position should be restored to the status quo ante.[77] The emphasis in the majority judgments in *Roxborough*, especially that of Gummow J, however, is on the refusal of the defendant to make restoration and not merely the fact of non-restitution. The concern is thus with the quality of the defendant's conduct in refusing, not the plaintiff's wealth position. This is clear from the facts that Rothmans was held liable to repay the money even though Roxborough had already recouped its loss.[78] The analytical concern, therefore, must be that, as formulated by Gummow J in particular, the wrongdoing is both unrelated to and cannot be justified by the primary right: the primary right focuses on restoration of the plaintiff's wealth, yet the wrongdoing (breach of a primary right) focuses on the defendant's conduct in refusing. If, therefore, the duty not unconscientiously to refuse to make restitution is to be doctrinally coherent, a different primary right must be articulated. Conceptualising exactly what this right might be is,

---

73   M Tilbury, 'Remedies and the Classification of Obligations' in A Robertson (ed), *The Law of Obligations: Connections and Boundaries* (UCL Press, London, 2004) at 17ff.

74   At an abstract level, the concern must be why, given that in the core case (P Birks, *Unjust Enrichment* (2nd ed, Clarendon, Oxford, 2005) at 3) the defendant is in no way responsible for the plaintiff's actions, the defendant should be regarded as having done anything wrong. See D Klimchuk, 'Unjust Enrichment and Corrective Justice' in J Neyers, M McInnes and S Pitel (eds), *Understanding Unjust Enrichment* (Hart Publishing, Oxford, 2004) at chapter 6.

75   P Birks, "The Content of the Fiduciary Obligation" (2002) 16 *Trust Law International* 34 at 39.

76   (1760) 2 Burr 1005 at 1012; 97 ER 676 at 681.

77   R Grantham and CF Rickett, "On the Subsidiarity of Unjust Enrichment" (2001) 117 *Law Quarterly Review* 273.

78   This was accepted as matter of fact by the High Court: *Roxborough v Rothmans of Pall Mall Australia Ltd* (2001) 208 CLR 516 at 543-544.

however, extraordinarily difficult.[79] Yet, without a clearly defined right the likelihood is that the law of restitution as articulated in *Roxborough* will amount to little more than the application of a general abstract principle, extending to many contexts *to justify relief* for a "deserving" plaintiff.

The High Court of Australia in *Roxborough* may have been correct in its conclusion that as a matter of history the common law restitutionary actions absorbed something of equity's preference for more open-textured principles rather than hard rules. This conclusion does not, however, warrant the further conclusion that restitutionary recovery is properly to be understood as a response to a species of wrongdoing, in that the fundamental justification for restitutionary liability is the defendant's refusal voluntarily to make restitution. As a matter of descriptive analysis, the grounds that justify restitutionary liability, which have been largely stable since *Moses v Macferlan*, are all concerned with the quality of the plaintiff's consent, and not the defendant's refusal to make restitution.[80] Although it may not be possible as a matter of formal logic to conclude that a descriptive analysis of the law of restitution as concerned with defective subjective consent holds true at a normative level,[81] the pervasiveness of this concern and the remarkable historical stability of the range of factors justifying restitution must suggest strongly that a defect in consent is not merely a sufficient condition but also *the* necessary one.

Thirdly, and closely related to the second point, the notion of unconscionability is superfluous to the analysis of the reasons for legal intervention.[82] The presence of a mistake or a failure of consideration acts to deny the voluntariness of the plaintiff's transfer of wealth. The mistake or failure of consideration demonstrates that the plaintiff's apparently voluntary decision to transfer the enrichment in fact lacks the qualities of true voluntariness that are necessary to support any notion that he or she must bear responsibility for the decision to transfer away the wealth.[83] Once, therefore, it is accepted that a plaintiff is subject

---

79   The unjust factors identified in the cases suggest that the plaintiff's primary right is to restitution of his wealth. Any wrongdoing (ie, breach of the primary/duty to restitution) arising from that would thus lie in the fact of the defendant's failure to make restitution. The wrongdoing identified in *Roxborough*, in contrast, lies in the defendant's *refusal* to make restitution and implies that the plaintiff's primary right is to have the defendant not refuse to make restitution.

80   E O'Dell, 'Incapacity' in P Birks and F Rose (eds), *Lessons of the Swaps Litigation* (Mansfield Press, London, 2000) at 116; P Birks, *Unjust Enrichment* (2nd ed, Clarendon, Oxford, 2005) at 105; R Grantham and CF Rickett, "On the Subsidiarity of Unjust Enrichment", above n 77.

81   As a matter of strict logic, a deduction from a necessarily incomplete set of premises can only ever indicate a probable conclusion (generally, see J Hospers, *An Introduction to Philosophical Analysis* (2nd ed rev, Routledge & Kegan Paul, London, 1981) at 131-133). However, since virtually all legal reasoning is inductive, the strength of that "probable" outcome is greatly enhanced by the consistency of the known premises.

82   The unconscientious refusal analysis is thus a candidate for Occam's razor (Non sunt multi-plicanda entia praeter necessitatem (Entities are not to be multiplied beyond necessity)).

83   Aristotle, *Nichomachean Ethics* (Thomson Translation, Penguin, London, 1976), Book III at [1109b]-[1111b]; R Nozick, *Philosophical Explanations* (Harvard University Press, Cambridge, 1981) at 49; HLA Hart, 'Legal Responsibility and Excuses' in *Punishment and Responsibility: Essays in the Philosophy of Law* (Clarendon, Oxford, 1968) at chapter 2; C Fried, *Contract as Promise* (Harvard University Press, Cambridge, Mass, 1981) at 20; M Dan-Cohen, "Responsibility and the Boundaries of the Self" (1992) 105 *Harvard Law Review* 959;

to a vitiating factor there is no need to invoke the wrongfulness of the defendant's conduct in order to justify recovery. The involuntary nature of the plaintiff's action is itself sufficient to justify setting the transfer aside and restoring the status quo ante. The focus on the quality of the defendant's conduct in retaining the enrichment, or refusing to make restitution, thus adds nothing to the justification for the law's intervention.

To the above analysis can quite properly be raised the objection that if the law of restitution is concerned entirely with the vitiation of the plaintiff's consent to the transfer of wealth, then equitable doctrines such as undue influence and unconscionable bargain cannot properly be part of the law of restitution.[84] From an historical perspective, it is clear that these doctrines derive from the ancient jurisdiction of equity over "fraud".[85] However, what is less clear is that these doctrines are actually concerned with wrongdoing, at least in the same sense in which those equitable doctrines such as a breach of fiduciary duty or breach of (a duty of) confidence are concerned with wrongdoing.

Although there are occasional statements labelling a person with influence or who deals with a person with a special disadvantage as a wrongdoer,[86] active wrongdoing is a requirement of neither equitable doctrine. Thus, for example, in the context of undue influence, in *Niersmans v Pesticcio*[87] the English Court of Appeal recently stated, "[a]lthough undue influence is sometimes described as an 'equitable wrong' or even as a species of equitable fraud, the basis of the court's intervention is not the commission of a dishonest or wrongful act by the defendant, but that, as a matter of public policy, the presumed influence arising from the relationship of trust and confidence should not operate to the disadvantage of the victim, if the transaction is not satisfactorily explained by ordinary motives". In the context of the doctrine of unconscionable bargain, in *Nichols v Jessup*[88] the New Zealand Court of Appeal similarly rejected the need for the presence of improper conduct: "unconscionability is not confined to deceit; it need not consist in an act of extortion of a benefit. Indeed the passage just cited [from the decision of the Privy Council in *O'Connor v Hart*] would suggest that a bargain may be unconscionable if made by a poor or ignorant

---

J Manwaring, "Unconscionability: Contested Values, Competing Theories and Choice of Rule in Contract Law" (1993) 25 *Ottawa Law Review* 235 at 284; A Wertheimer, *Coercion* (Princeton University Press, New Jersey, 1987) at 21.

84   Most orthodox accounts of the law of restitution include these: R Goff and G Jones, *The Law of Restitution* (6th ed, Sweet & Maxwell, London, 2002) at chapters 11 and 12; A Burrows, *The Law of Restitution* (2nd ed, Butterworths, London, 2002) at chapters 6 and 7; R Grantham and CF Rickett, *Enrichment and Restitution in New Zealand* (Hart Publishing, Oxford, 2000) at chapter 7.

85   *Earl of Chesterfield v Janssen* (1751) 2 Ves Sen 125; 28 ER 82 at 95-100; *Symons v Williams* (1875) 1 VLR(E) 199; R Meagher, JD Heydon and M Leeming, *Meagher, Gummow and Lehane's Equity: Doctrines and Remedies* (4th ed, LexisNexis, Sydney, 2002) at 452-453.

86   *Barclays Bank plc v O'Brien* [1994] AC 180 at 191; *National Westminster Bank v Morgan* [1985] AC 686 at 707; *Contractors Bonding Ltd v Snee* [1992] 2 NZLR 157 at 165; *Boustany v Piggot* (1993) 69 P & CR 298 at 303; *Hart v O'Connor* [1985] AC 1000.

87   [2004] EWCA Civ 372 at [20]. See also *Hammond v Osborn* [2002] EWCA Civ 885, noted by P Birks, "Undue Influence as Wrongful Exploitation" (2004) 120 *Law Quarterly Review* 34 at 37.

88   [1986] 1 NZLR 226 at 233. See also, *Bridgewater v Leahy* (1998) 194 CLR 457 at 479 and 493.

person without advice because of its inherent unfairness and without any element of overreaching by one party."

What these doctrines are concerned with is the quality of the plaintiff's consent in those cases where because of excessive trust or intellectual incapacity the plaintiff cannot be assumed to have acted voluntarily in her or his own best interests. Equity may well describe the defendant who takes the benefit of such a transaction as fraudulent. However, it is difficult to attach to that epithet the degree of culpability necessary to justify the conclusion that in these cases the law is responding to the quality of the defendant's conduct rather than the lack of voluntariness of the plaintiff's actions.

THE SUBSIDIARY ROLE OF RESTITUTION

Historically, the role of equity in the private law has been a supplementary one. That is, the rationale and function of equitable doctrines and principles was always to mitigate and ameliorate the unjustness that would be caused by the supposed rigidity and rule-bound nature of the common law.[89] To this end, equity's involvement began only where the common law left off. This is most obviously so in the law of trusts, where equity accepted the trustee as the legal title holder, but engrafted onto that title obligations in respect of the benefit of the title and the scope for the legal title holder to deal that title.[90] The law of restitution, while comprising mostly common law actions, is properly regarded as "equitable" in this sense.[91] Thus, like the function historically ascribed to equitable doctrines, analytically the function of the principle of unjust enrichment is to modify and ameliorate other parts of the private law, most notably the law of contract and the law of property, and to undo transfers of wealth that would, but for the law of restitution, remain valid and efficacious.

At a doctrinal level, the province or area of operation of the law of restitution is defined by two factors.[92] First, there must be a defect in the plaintiff's subjective consent. The principle of unjust enrichment is triggered where an apparently consensual transfer of wealth which is accompanied by defective subjective consent on the plaintiff's part. It is this defect that marks out those transfers of wealth where the plaintiff's interest in restoration outweighs the defendant's interest in the security of receipt. Secondly, there must be a transfer of wealth effective to vest in the defendant not merely factual possession of, but also a right to, the enrichment. Such a transfer represents a necessary doctrinal boundary of the law of restitution for two reasons. The first is that such a transfer is necessary to support the conclusion that the defendant is enriched. While there have been suggestions that mere factual receipt of an enrichment is sufficient to establish

---

89   *Earl of Oxford's Case* (1615) 1 Ch Rep 1 at 7; 21 ER 485 at 486 per Lord Ellesmere.

90   K Gray, "Equitable Property" (1994) 47 *Current Legal Problems* 157 at 163; *Commissioner of Stamp Duties (Queensland) v Livingstone* [1965] AC 694.

91   *Roxborough v Rothmans of Pall Mall Australia Ltd* (2001) 208 CLR 516 at 545 per Gummow J, 579 per Kirby J.

92   R Grantham and CF Rickett, "On the Subsidiarity of Unjust Enrichment" (2001) 117 *Law Quarterly Review* 273.

the defendant's enrichment,[93] this is not supported by the authorities.[94] In order to be enriched, therefore, the defendant must have acquired a right to the wealth transferred. The second is that as a matter of principle, the objective of the law of unjust enrichment, to restore the status quo ante, can only be understood against the background of a transaction that is prima facie effective. Almost by definition, a doctrine that is concerned with the restoration or reversal of a transfer of wealth can operate only where there is a relevant transfer of wealth to be reversed. The law of restitution must, therefore, presuppose that there is a transfer of wealth that *but for* the intervention of the law of restitution will be valid and effective to pass rights in the enrichment. These two doctrinal requirements combine to suggest that the role and function of the law of restitution is necessarily both supplementary and subsidiary.

A supplementary doctrine

Although unjust enrichment is a source of rights and not merely a remedial response to other rules,[95] its sphere of operation is nevertheless defined by and dependent upon the operation of other rules of law. It is necessarily supplementary of other doctrines of the private law, particularly contract and property.[96] Its concern with transfers of wealth vitiated by a defect in the plaintiff's subjective consent means that it is, and can only be, relevant where there has been an expression of objective consent and a transfer of wealth that is consequently prima facie effective. It is only where the *doctrinal* elements of the law of contract and the law of property are satisfied, so that, unless modified by a rule external to the rules of contract and property, the defendant would be entitled to retain that wealth, that the law of unjust enrichment can have any role.[97] Moreover, this is not merely to say that a defendant is not enriched without the acquisition of rights. While enrichment is obviously a functional prerequisite to an unjust enrichment claim, the point is one of more fundamental doctrine and policy. The objective is to reverse transfers of wealth that, ex aequo et bono, cannot be allowed to stand. The notion ex aequo et bono is given concrete expression by the concern with defects in the plaintiff's subjective consent. Therefore, unjust enrichment can be invoked only where a

---

93 P Birks, "On Taking Seriously the Difference Between Tracing and Claiming" (1997) 11 *Trust Law International* 2 at 7-8.

94 *Ilich v R* (1987) 162 CLR 110; *Trustee of Jones v Jones* [1997] Ch 159 at 168 per Millett LJ; *Portman Building Society v Hamlyn Taylor Neck (a firm)* [1998] 4 All ER 202; *Macmillan Inc v Bishopsgate Investment Trusts plc (No 3)* [1996] 1 All ER 585 at 596; *Foskett v McKeown* [2001] 1 AC 102.

95 *Banque Financière de la Cité v Parc (Battersea) Ltd* [1999] AC 221 at 227 per Lord Steyn: "After all, unjust enrichment ranks next to contract and tort as part of the law of obligations. It is an independent source of rights and obligations."

96 D Laycock, "The Scope and Significance of Restitution" (1989) 67 *Texas Law Review* 1277 at 1278; G Rinker, "Quasi-Contracts—Concept of Benefit" (1948) 46 *Michigan Law Review* 543 at 551; B Nicholas, 'Modern Developments in the French Law of Unjustified Enrichment' in PL Russell (ed), *Unjustified Enrichment: A Comparative Study of the Law of Restitution* (University of Amsterdam Press, Amsterdam, 1996) at 92; J Dietrich, *Restitution: A New Perspective* (Federation Press, Sydney, 1998) at 29.

97 See Lord Wright of Durley, *Legal Essays and Addresses* (Cambridge University Press, Cambridge, 1939) at 36.

transfer of wealth is accompanied by at least some manifestation of (objective) consent, because, doctrinally, unjust enrichment is concerned with manifestations of consent that are subjectively defective. Quite simply, if there is no manifestation of (objective) consent at all, or no defect in subjective consent, and no *prima facie* effective transfer of wealth, there is nothing calling into play the objectives of unjust enrichment: there is neither an apparent consent to correct, nor a status quo ante to restore. This means that the law of unjust enrichment is, therefore, essentially modificatory in nature. It modifies the normal consequences that would flow from the manifestation of (objective) consent by the plaintiff to the transfer of the enrichment.

As a doctrine supplementing or modifying the law of contract and the law of property, unjust enrichment fulfils a function similar to that historically attributed to equity.[98] Like equity, unjust enrichment operates to mitigate the rigidities and objective focus of other doctrines, and to "reverse" transactions that on closer inspection cannot be allowed to stand.[99] For most purposes, the law is and can only be concerned with objective manifestations of consent. An inquiry into subjective intention imposes problems of proof, does little to promote security of receipt, and is time-consuming to administer. If, for example, every contractual dispute required a "tour through [the plaintiff's] cranium"[100] the institution of contracting would cease to have utility.[101] The law thus provides straightforward mechanisms that promote certainty and deal with the vast majority of cases. This means that the law in general will not admit considerations relating to a party's genuine subjective intention to contradict appearances.[102] However, while such an approach efficiently

---

98 R Meagher, JD Heydon and M Leeming, *Meagher, Gummow and Lehane's Equity: Doctrines and Remedies* (4th ed, LexisNexis, Sydney, 2002) at 3; FW Maitland, *Equity* (2nd ed, Cambridge University Press, Cambridge, 1936) at 18-19; T Plucknett and J Barton (eds), *St German's Doctor and Student* (91 Selden Society, London, 1974) at 97: "and to that intent equytie is ordeyned that is to say to tempre and myttygate of the lawe." See also D Laycock, "The Scope and Significance of Restitution" (1989) 67 *Texas Law Review* 1277 at 1278, and J Story, *Commentaries on Equity Jurisprudence as Administered in England and America* (13th ed, Rothman, Litttleton, Colorado, 1988), Vol I at 24. Generally, see R Newman, *Equity and Law: A Comparative Study* (Oceana, New York, 1961) at chapters 1 and 2.

99 It is no surprise that unjust enrichment and equity have a similar function. The renewed interest in unjust enrichment has revealed that, although it is traditionally conceived of as a product of the common law, many equitable doctrines fulfil a restitutionary function. The doctrines of undue influence and unconscionable bargain, for example, are now seen as offering reasons why an otherwise effective transfer of wealth or an apparently valid contract should be set aside in much the same way as in the circumstances of mistake or duress. As equitable doctrines, however, there was never any doubt that they were supplementary to the other rules.

100 *Skycom Corporation v Telstra Corporation*, 813 F 2d 810 at 814 (7th Cir 1987).

101 *Anon* (1478) YB 17 Edw IV, Pasch fI 1 pl 2 per Brian CJ: "the intent of a man cannot be tried, for the Devil himself knows not the intent of a man." See also R Barnett, "A Consent Theory of Contract" (1986) 86 *Columbia Law Review* 269 at 302 (objective manifestation of consent is an informational and boundary-defining requirement); and discussion in R Bigwood, "Conscience and the Liberal Conception of Contract: Observing Basic Distinctions" (2000) 16 *Journal of Contract Law* 1 and 191

102 This is also manifested in the parol evidence rule: G Treitel, *The Law of Contract* (11th ed, Sweet & Maxwell, London, 2003) at 176ff; D McLauchlan, *The Parol Evidence Rule* (Professional, Wellington, 1976).

regulates the rights and duties of the parties in the vast majority of cases, the focus is necessarily objective and as such may work injustice. Moreover, where this objective focus takes the form of a failure to respond to a defect in the plaintiff's subjective consent, that failure undermines the philosophical and theoretical basis for holding the plaintiff responsible for the consequences of his actions. Responsibility is predicated upon *voluntary* choices,[103] and decisions made under the influence of factors such as mistake and coercion are not voluntary. While, therefore, in most cases the law may safely infer voluntariness from the outward manifestation of consent,[104] it must nevertheless respond to those cases where that inference is not on the facts justified. That supplementary response is the province of the law of unjust enrichment.

A subsidiary doctrine

A further and important implication of the doctrinal elements of the law of unjust enrichment is that it has no role to play where the consequences of a defect in subjective consent are already regulated, and the restoration of the status quo ante is already provided for.[105] This is most obviously the case where the parties have dealt with the matter by express agreement.[106] Thus, for example, where the parties have agreed that if, in making payment, the assumptions upon which the plaintiff paid later turn out to have been mistaken, the defendant will return the payment, the doctrinal basis for restoration of the payment to the plaintiff is the express agreement, not the law of unjust enrichment. Thus, in *The Trident Beauty*,[107] it was held that ship charterers

---

103   HLA Hart, 'Negligence, Mens Rea and Criminal Responsibility' in *Punishment and Responsibility: Essays in the Philosophy of Law* (Clarendon, Oxford, 1968) at 152: "What is crucial is that those whom we punish [ie, hold legally responsible] should have had, when they acted, the normal capacities, physical and mental". See also J Kleinig, "The Ethics of Consent" (1982) *Canadian Journal of Philosophy* (Supp Vol VIII) 91 at 99-100.

104   Aristotle, Book III at [1109b]-[1111b]; M Dan-Cohen, "Responsibility and the Boundaries of the Self" (1992) 105 *Harvard Law Review* 959; J Manwaring, "Unconscionability: Contested Values, Competing Theories and Choice of Rule in Contract Law" (1993) 25 *Ottawa Law Review* 235 at 284; R Bigwood, "Undue Influence: 'Impaired Consent' or 'Wicked Exploitation'?" (1996) 16 *Oxford Journal of Legal Studies* 503 at 504.

105   B Nicholas, 'Modern Developments in the French Law of Unjustified Enrichment' in PL Russell (ed), *Unjustified Enrichment: A Comparative Study of the Law of Restitution* (University of Amsterdam Press, Amsterdam, 1996) at 94, speaking in the context of French law, says: "Windscheid's formulation does, however, point to the fundamental limit on any enrichment remedy – that it must not circumvent an existing rule or law which envisages the relevant aspect of the matter in issue. It must not perpetrate a fraud on the law."

106   G Virgo, *Principles of the Law of Restitution* (Clarendon, Oxford, 1999) at 41. This is also true of the German law of unjustified enrichment: see BS Markesinis, W Lorenz and G Dannemann, *The German Law of Obligations* (Clarendon, Oxford, 1997), Vol 1 at 43; T Krebs, *Restitution at the Crossroads: A comparative study* (Cavendish, London, 2001) at 104ff.

107   *Pan Ocean Shipping Ltd v Creditcorp Ltd (The 'Trident Beauty')* [1994] 1 All ER 470; 1 WLR 161 at 164 per Lord Goff. See also *Stocznia Gdanska SA v Latvian Shipping Co* [1998] 1 All ER 883; 1 WLR 574, where it was held that the contract itself dealt with the consequences of rescission of the contract; *Concrete Constructions Group v Litevale Pty Ltd* [2003] NSWSC 411 at [16].

could not recover advance hire payments from the vessel's owners in unjust enrichment, since the charter-party provided expressly for repayment and that was thus the basis for restitution. This conclusion, furthermore, does not turn merely on some ill-defined hierarchical notion of the primacy of contract, but rather on the simple fact that, since the parties have already provided for the possibility of restoration if the plaintiff's subjective consent was defective, there is no longer any call for the intervention of the law of unjust enrichment. The "active creation of new rights to undo enrichment … is the business of the law of unjust enrichment".[108] The agreement, however, means that it is no longer the case that, but for the "active creation" of a restitutionary obligation, the defendant would be able to retain an enrichment in circumstances that make it unjust to do so.

A right to restoration of the enrichment, quite apart from the law of unjust enrichment, may also be implicit in the nature of the particular rights held by the plaintiff. This is importantly so in the case of property rights. The right to protection from interference and the right to exclusive benefit of the asset are central rights that in large measure define property.[109] Where, therefore, the plaintiff retains rights in rem in the assets transferred, the plaintiff's right to recover the value of the asset, and any incidental benefits obtained from the use of the asset, are, therefore, already present at the moment of interference by virtue of that claimant's right in rem.[110] The presence of such a right of recovery also means that it is not possible to say that the defendant will be improperly enriched but for the creation of an obligation to make restoration. An obligation already exists, by virtue of the claimant's right in rem, in the defendant to restore the value received, and that obligation necessarily has its origins in an occurrence prior to the fact of the defendant's receipt. While it may be possible in lay terms to describe the defendant as enriched, as a matter of legal science and doctrine there is no enrichment.[111] The defendant's receipt was always encumbered with an obligation, arising from the plaintiff's right in rem, to return the property. There is, therefore, nothing for the principle of unjust enrichment to do.[112]

Instances of the provision of restoration outside of the law of unjust enrichment are, however, relatively rare. In many cases, the law may nod in the direction of the quality of the plaintiff's consent but leave the consequences to

---

108 P Birks, *Unjust Enrichment* (2nd ed, Clarendon, Oxford, 2005) at 37.

109 AM Honore, 'Ownership' in R Guest (ed), *Oxford Essays in Jurisprudence* (Oxford University Press, Oxford, 1961) at chapter V.

110 See *Foskett v McKeown* [2001] 1 AC 102. See further, EJ Weinrib, "Restitutionary Damages as Corrective Justice" (2000) 1 *Theoretical Inquiries in Law* 1; R Grantham and CF Rickett, *Enrichment and Restitution in New Zealand* (Hart Publishing, Oxford, 2000) at chapter 3. The sufficiency of claims based on the plaintiff's persisting property rights is also recognised in German law: Art 985, *Burgerliches Gesetzbuch*. See further, R Grantham and CF Rickett, "Property Rights: A Legally Significant Event" [2003] *Cambridge Law Journal* 417.

111 In *Portman Building Society v Hamlyn Taylor Neck (a firm)* [1998] 4 All ER 202, the Court of Appeal expressly rejected the notion that a purely factual enrichment would suffice for this purpose.

112 *Foskett v McKeown* [2001] 1 AC 102.

be regulated by the law of unjust enrichment.[113] The law of contract, for example, grants limited recognition of the effects of mistake by allowing the parties to avoid their obligations. It does not, however, provide for restoration of the status quo ante.[114] These instances do, however, serve to highlight the wider issue of the inherent subsidiarity of the law of unjust enrichment. The objective of the law of unjust enrichment is to restore to the plaintiff wealth where the transfer of the asset representing that wealth cannot be permitted to stand.[115] This objective is achieved through the active creation of a *new* obligation that carries the wealth back to the plaintiff, thus restoring the status quo ante between the parties. Logically, however, that response is called for only where, *but for* the intervention of the law of unjust enrichment, the defendant would be able to retain the enrichment. Indeed, quite to the contrary, a transfer that is prima facie effective to convey rights to the asset to the defendant is a necessary condition for the operation of the principle of unjust enrichment.[116] It follows that, if at the moment of transfer, the law, or indeed the parties,[117] have already provided for restitution in the event that the transfer of the asset representing the wealth cannot be permitted to stand, the conditions which would otherwise call unjust enrichment into action to create a *new* right to restitution simply do not arise. In such cases, the presence of a mechanism to restore the status quo ante, which encumbers the enrichment from the moment of receipt, denies the possibility both that the defendant is enriched and that such enrichment is unjust. There can be no enrichment because the defendant already bears a liability to return the asset or its value. The receipt is not unjust because, in being compellable to restore the value inherent in the enrichment, the defendant "buys" an entitlement, in much the same way as a converter does,[118] to what he has received.

Further support for the "equitable" or subsidiary nature of the law of restitution can be gleaned from the ordering of, and basic values inherent in, the private law. One feature of the more recent history of the Anglo-American

---

113   This is to be contrasted with Civilian systems where invalidation of the putative obligation pursuant to which the transfer was made necessarily entails restitution. The ambiguity that is inherent in the common law's use of concepts such as "void", "voidable", and "unenforceable" is a serious obstacle to the adoption in the common law of the Civilian "absence of legal basis" approach to unjust enrichment.

114   A further example is the statutory denial of contractual capacity to minors. For example, the *Minors' Contracts Act 1987* (UK) denies contractual capacity, but does not provide for restoration of the *status quo ante*. It is, however, quite possible for the relevant statute also to provide for restoration, as is the case with the *Minor's Contracts Act 1969* (NZ) (see R Grantham and CF Rickett, *Enrichment and Restitution in New Zealand*, above n 110 at chapter 6): restoration is then by provision of the Act, not by the law of unjust enrichment.

115   *Moses v Macferlan* (1760) 2 Burr 1005 at 1012; 97 ER 676 at 680-681; *Fibrosa Spolka Akcyjna v Fairbairn Lawson Combe Barbour Ltd* [1943] AC 32 at 61; *Dollar Land (Cumbernauld) Ltd v CIN Properties Ltd* [1998] 3 EGLR 79; *Banque Financière de la Cité v Parc (Battersea) Ltd* [1999] AC 221 at 231.

116   P Birks, *Unjust Enrichment* (2nd ed, Clarendon, Oxford, 2005) at 66.

117   *Pan Ocean Shipping Ltd v Creditcorp Ltd (The 'Trident Beauty')* [1994] 1 WLR 161 at 164.

118   JG Fleming, *The Law of Torts* (9th ed, LBC Information Services, Sydney, 1998) at 61; W Prosser, "The Nature of Conversion" (1956-1957) 42 *Cornell Law Quarterly* 168; E Warren, "Qualifying as Plaintiff in an Action for a Conversion" (1936) 49 *Harvard Law Review* 1084.

common law tradition has been a fundamental commitment to according primacy to and maximising the individual autonomy of citizens. The traditional basic classification of private common law is the juridical expression of this commitment.[119] Thus, the law of contract facilitates individual choice, the law of tort protects individuals from the consequences of other's choices, and the law of property secures individual wealth.

Unjust enrichment, while certainly a player, does not have a leading role along side contract, torts, and property. Rather, unjust enrichment has an understudy role – one that sees it take centre stage only when the stars themselves fall silent. It protects a person from losing wealth where, because accompanied by the required objective consent, there has been an effective transfer of assets, but where a closer look reveals that the transferor's subjective consent was defective.[120] The transaction should not be taken at face value. Historically, the common law (including equity) was willing in defined situations to respect the lack of effective subjective consent over the existence of effective objective consent. The subsidiarity of unjust enrichment appears to have been "understood" in the practice of the common law,[121] and may in part explain why unjust enrichment remained "hidden" and was not developed conceptually until recently. Today, it is possible to understand those defined situations as cases of unjust enrichment founded on defective subjective consent, but the subsidiary nature of unjust enrichment as a justiciable principle remains "one of the basic building blocks of nature".[122]

RULES, PRINCIPLES AND JUSTICE

The view is sometimes put by "equity lawyers" that equity is distinguishable not merely by its historical origins in the Chancellor's court, but that it is qualita-

---

119 In large measure, as private law, the common law "protects private interests by empowering private parties to facilitate their private decisions" (P Smith (ed), *The Nature and Process of Law: An Introduction to Legal Philosophy* (Oxford University Press, New York, 1993) at 285). A Chloros, "Common Law, Civil Law and Socialist Law: Three Leading Systems of the World, Three Kinds of Legal Thought" (1978) 9 *Cambrian Law Review* 11 at 14-15, identifies individualism and liberty (autonomy), as two of the most obvious characteristics of the common law. Thus, it has, not surprisingly, developed a categorisation of private interests which is testimony to, and which then further promotes, the notion of individual autonomy.

120 R Sutton, "FW Guest Memorial Lecture: Unjust Enrichment" (1983) 5 *Otago Law Review* 187 at 199.

121 One challenge presented by the "absence of legal basis" approach to unjust enrichment is how to constrain the scope of restitutionary liability. In some Civilian jurisdictions, such as Germany (BS Markesinis, W Lorenz and G Dannemann, *The German Law of Obligations* (Clarendon, Oxford, 1997) at 43) and France (K Zweigert and H Kotz, *An Introduction to Comparative Law* (3rd ed, Clarendon, Oxford, 1998) at 584-590), this has been achieved through elaborate interpretative devices. In other Civilian jurisdictions, such as Italy, it is achieved by express provision in the code (Italian Civil Code, by Article 2042). Generally, see B Dickson, "Unjust Enrichment Claims: A Comparative Overview" (1995) 54 *Cambridge Law Journal* 100.

122 R Epstein, "The Ubiquity of the Benefit Principle" (1994) 67 *Southern California Law Review* 1369. See also R Epstein, *Simple Rules for a Complex World* (Harvard University Press, Cambridge, Mass, 1995).

tively different in its modus operandi.[123] Accordingly, it is said, that, whereas the common law is rule-bound, equity proceeds by way of more abstract, flexible standards that are more closely attuned to individualised as opposed to formal justice.[124] Thus, for example, Glover says: "Equity must be maintained as a separate system, with its own concepts and doctrines, if it is to continue to function as the law's corrective. The purity of equity will be lost if its doctrines are applied as rules, rather than as the expression of underlying principles."[125]

In order properly to evaluate a characterisation of the law of restitution as equitable in this sense, it is necessary to distinguish between a weak and a strong form of this claim. The weak form contends merely that whereas the common law proceeds on the basis of rules stated in more or less precise terms and intended to apply generally regardless of the particular facts, equity proceeds on the basis of principles stated at a more abstract level and which, by virtue of that fact, tend to be more open-textured when applied to the disposition of individual cases. A characterisation of unjust enrichment in this way is apparent in *Roxborough v Rothmans*. In Gummow J's view, the common law action in money had and received is "equitable" in that the specific grounds of restitutionary recovery, such as mistake and failure of consideration, are merely examples of the "general considerations referred to in *Moses v Macferlan*"[126] which could justify the imposition of restitutionary liability in situations outside of the previously recognised categories. This also seems to be what the Binnie J meant in *Pacific National Investments Ltd v Victoria (City)* when he said that while a "court is to follow an established approach to unjust enrichment

---

123 J Glover, *Equity, Restitution and Fraud* (LexisNexis, Sydney, 2003) at 8-10; S Hedley and M Halliwell, *The Law of Restitution* (Butterworths, London, 2002) at 19; P Parkinson (ed), *The Principles of Equity* (2nd ed, Lawbook Co, Sydney, 2003) at 9; M Halliwell, *Equity and Good Conscience in a Contemporary Context* (Old Bailey Press, London, 1997) at 2-3.

124 R Meagher, JD Heydon, M Leeming, *Meager, Gummow and Lehane's Equity* (4th ed, LexisNexis, Sydney, 2002) at 8; P Wilson, "Unconscionability and Fairness in Australian Equitable Jurisprudence?" (2004) 11 *Australian Property Law Journal* 1; A Mason, 'The Place of Equity and Equitable Doctrines in the Contemporary Common Law World: An Australian Perspective' in DM Waters (ed), *Equity, Fiduciaries and Trusts* (Carswell, Toronto, 1993) at 23; A Mason, "The Place of Equity and Equitable Remedies in the Contemporary Common Law World (1994) 110 *Law Quarterly Review* 238 at 239; R Meagher and WMC Gummow, *Jacobs' Law of Trusts in Australia* (6th ed, Butterworths, Sydney, 1997) at lxxxvii; *Winkworth v Edward Barons Development Co Ltd* [1986] 1 WLR 1512 at 1516 per Lord Templeman: "Equity is not a computer"; *Amalgamated Investment & Property Co Ltd v Texas Commerce International Bank Ltd* [1982] QB 84 at 103 per Goff J; *Pacific National Investments Ltd v Victoria (City)* [2004] 3 SCR 575 at 586; R Newman, *Equity and Law: A comparative study* (Oceana, New York, 1961) at 42; WMC Gummow, *Change and Continuity: Statute, Equity, and Federalism* (Oxford University Press, Oxford, 1999) at 53-54.

125 J Glover, *Equity, Restitution and Fraud* (LexisNexis, Sydney, 2003) at 12; S Hedley and M Halliwell, *The Law of Restitution* (Butterworths, London, 2002) at 19. The "Jesuitical fervour" (P Wilson, "Unconscionability and Fairness in Australian Equitable Jurisprudence" (2004) 11 *Australian Property Law Journal* 1 at 3) apparent in some recent equity scholarship makes that the criticisms levelled at the "proselytising members of the restitution industry (academic division)" (R Meagher, JD Heydon, M Leeming, *Meagher, Gummow and Lehane's Equity*, above n 123 at xi) seem somewhat hypocritical.

126 (2001) 208 CLR 516 at 553.

predicated on clearly defined principles ... their application should not be mechanical."[127]

The strong form of this claim suggests that an equitable approach is one that seeks to achieve individualised justice and thus proceeds on the basis of direct recourse to highly abstract notions of fairness, justice and conscience.[128] This type of approach is apparent, for example, in the comment of Jacob J in *Vedatech Corporation v Crystal Decisions (UK) Ltd*, that the "principle of unjust enrichment is in large part founded on conscience".[129] It is also apparent in the judgments of the New Zealand Court of Appeal in *National Bank of New Zealand Ltd v Waitaki International Processing (NI) Ltd*.[130] In the context of discussing the change of position defence, Thomas J said: "Principles of fairness and justice have always been at the heart of actions for restitution. ... This eternal desire to do justice, and with it a significant degree of judicial discretion, is necessarily inherent in the concept of unjust enrichment".[131]

The implications of the weak and strong form versions of the claims made about the methodology of "equity" are very different. While the weak form remains consistent with a notion of adjudication constrained by settled principles and objective standards, the strong form asserts a highly individualised notion of justice and adjudication. Therefore, in assessing the extent to which the law of restitution is equitable, in the sense that it shares with the principles developed in the Court of Chancery a more open-ended and flexible formulation, the weak and strong forms of this claim will be dealt with separately.

Equity as principle

The doctrines and principles developed in the Court of Chancery have traditionally been associated with a greater degree of flexibility and discretion than is apparent in the formulation of common law rules.[132] Indeed, this was part and parcel of the original explanation of and justification for the development of equity. The Chancellor, in right of the King, dispensed justice according to the King's conscience in order to deal with individual cases in which the operation of the common law was seen to work an injustice.[133] The discretion

---

127 [2004] 3 SCR 575 at 586. The Court's statement that, "The doctrine of unjust enrichment provides an equitable cause of action that retains a large measure of remedial flexibility to deal with different circumstances according to principles rooted in fairness and good conscience" suggests a strong form pf this claim. However, the Court also expressly rejects an appeal to "a free-floating conscience that may risk being overly subjective." ([23])

128 KM Hayne, "Australian Law in the Twentieth Century" (2000) 74 *Australian Law Journal* 373 at 375: "the Holy Grail of individualized justice". See also, E Sherwin, "Restitution and Equity: An Analysis of the Principle of Unjust Enrichment" (2001) 79 *Texas Law Review* 2083 at 2091.

129 [2002] EWHC 818 at [74].

130 [1999] 2 NZLR 211.

131 *National Bank of New Zealand Ltd v Waitaki International Processing (NI) Ltd*, above n 130 at 229.

132 P Parkinson (ed), *The Principles of Equity* (2nd ed, Lawbook Co, Sydney, 2003) at 5.

133 As Parkinson ((ed), *The Principles of Equity*, above n 132 at 10), notes, "conscience" may refer to both that of the King and to that of the individual defendant. See also, D Klinck, "The Unexamined 'Conscience' of Contemporary Canadian Equity" (2001) 46 *McGill Law Journal* 571 at 577.

that was inherent in the equitable jurisdiction from the very first often led to the assertion that this discretion was also unbounded by settled principles and rules.[134] Equity has, however, long since ceased to be a synonym for broad brush discretions or appeals to the individual conscience of the Chancellor. During the 17th and 18th centuries, equity matured from a system of ad hoc relief granted by the Chancellor into a full-blown system of law. Thus, by 1818, Lord Eldon was able to say: "[I]t is not the duty of a judge in equity to vary rules, or to say that rules are not to be considered as fully settled here as in a Court of Law. The doctrines of this Court ought to be as well settled and made as uniform almost as those of the common law."[135] More recently, in *Muschinki v Dodds*, Deane J said: "Long before Lord Seldon's anachronism identifying the Chancellor's foot as the measure of Chancery relief, undefined notions of 'justice' and what was 'fair' had given way in the law of equity to the rule of ordered principle which is the essence of any coherent system of rational law."[136]

The systemisation of equity that occurred under the Chancellorships of Nottingham,[137] Hardwicke,[138] Thurlow,[139] and Eldon,[140] and as inherited into the 19th and 20th centuries, did not remove discretion altogether from equitable principles or indicate that equity was no longer concerned with conscience. The continuing vital role of conscience in equity underpins recent attempts, particularly in Australia, to articulate as the fundamental organising principle of all equitable doctrines a principle of unconscionability.[141] Rather, what systemisation meant was that equity's conscience and the discretions inherent in its rules were no longer practised as an ad hoc assessment on the particular facts of the case. Equity's conscience thus changed from being that of an individual Chancellor's to a public and objective one exercised on

---

134 *Earl of Oxford's Case* (1615) 1 Ch Rep 1 at 6: "The cause why there is a Chancery is for that men's actions are so diverse and indefinite that it is impossible to make any general law which may aptly meet every particular act and not fail in some circumstances." See also, P Vinogradoff, "Reason and Conscience in Sixteenth-Century Jurisprudence" (1908) 24 *Law Quarterly Review* 373.

135 *Davis v Duke of Marlborough* (1819) 2 Swanst 108 at 163. Generally, see D Klinck, "The Unexamined 'Conscience' of Contemporary Canadian Equity", above n 133 at 577.

136 In *Australian Broadcasting Corporation v Lenah Game Meats Pty Ltd* (2001) 208 CLR 199 at 259, Gummow and Hayne JJ rejected an ad hoc conception of unconscionability, saying: "Decisions of equity courts are not a wilderness of single instances determined by idiosyncratic exercises of discretion." See also *Tanwar Enterprises Pty Ltd v Cauchi* (2003) 201 ALR 359 at 364-365.

137 1673-1682.

138 1736-1756.

139 1778-1792.

140 1801-1806 and 1807-1827.

141 P Parkinson (ed), *The Principles of Equity* (2nd ed, Lawbook Co., Sydney, 2003) at 29-31; CF Rickett, 'Equity' in R Cooke (ed), *Laws of New Zealand* (Butterworths, Wellington, 2003) at [2]; A Mason, 'Themes and Prospects' in PD Finn (ed), *Essays in Equity* (LBC, Sydney, 1985) at 244; PD Finn, 'The Fiduciary Principle' in TG Youdan (ed), *Equity, Fiduciaries and Trusts* (Carswell, Toronto, 1980) at 6.

established grounds.[142] The discretion vested in courts by equitable doctrines thus changed from being one exercisable on the basis of the length of the Chancellor's foot,[143] to one exercised according to "fixed rules and settled principles."[144] At an analytical level, these discretionary considerations are functionally equivalent to Dworkin's "principles".[145] Although not dictating a particular result, these factors nevertheless state a "a consideration inclining in one direction or another",[146] and offer a mechanism to resolve a conflict in the absence of clear rules without the need to resort to extra-legal considerations.[147]

To characterise the law of restitution as equitable in this sense, therefore, is to suggest that in determining the scope of restitutionary liability the courts may have regard directly to the principle of unjust enrichment or unconscientious retention in deciding actual cases.[148] These principles, which are abstract but which nevertheless have an established content, constrain and inform judicial decision making.[149] Thus, while a court may find that a defendant was unjustly enriched or unconscientiously retained an enrichment in circumstances not hitherto recognised, the court is nevertheless constrained in that there is an accepted range of meaning or content to notions of "unjust" and "unconscientious". This content is derived from an analogy both with existing case law and the standards of behaviour required of the law in cognate areas.

This analysis does not, however, accord with the conventional understanding of the law of restitution and the role within it of the principle of unjust

---

142 *Cook v Fountain* (1676) 3 Swanst 585 at 600 per Lord Nottingham: "With such a conscience as is only naturalis et interna this court has noting to do: the conscience by which I am to proceed is merely civilis et politica and it is infinitely better for the public that a trust, security or agreement should miscarry than that men should lose their estate by the mere fancy and imagination of a Chancellor." See also *National City Bank v Gelfert* 29 NE (2d) 449 at 452 (1940); D Klinck, "The Unexamined 'Conscience' of Contemporary Canadian Equity" (2001) 46 *McGill Law Journal* 571 at 577.

143 *Gee v Pritchard* (1818) 2 Swan 402 at 409 per Lord Eldon.

144 *Lamare v Dixon* (1873) LR 6 HL 414 at 423. See also *White v Damon* (1802) 7 Ves 30 at 35 per Lord Eldon LC: the discretion is not "arbitrary or capricious"; *Doherty v Allman* (1878) 3 AC 709 at 728-729 per Lord Blackburn: "rules which have been established by precedent".

145 R Dworkin, *Taking Rights Seriously* (Duckworth, London, 1977) at 26. See also M Tilbury, *Civil Remedies* (Butterworths, Sydney, 1990), Vol 1 at 288; P Loughlan, "No Right to the Remedy?: An Analysis of Judicial Discretion in the Imposition of Equitable Remedies" (1989) 17 *Melbourne University Law Review* 132 at 137.

146 R Dworkin, *Taking Rights Seriously* (Duckworth, London, 1977) at 26.

147 If the equitable maxims have any role at all in the adjudicative process, then they are perhaps best understood in this sense also. That is, they are not intended for literal application to the facts of individual cases (*Corin v Patton* (1990) 169 CLR 540 at 557; J McGhee, *Snell's Equity* (30th ed, Sweet & Maxwell, London, 2000) at 27) but they do have some explanatory power (P Loughlan, 'The Historical Role of the Equitable Jurisdiction' in P Parkinson (ed), *The Principles of Equity* (2nd ed, Lawbook Co, Sydney, 2003) at 26.

148 This, it is argued, is also how the doctrine of "unconscientious dealing" operates: J Glover, *Equity, Restitution and Fraud* (LexisNexis, Sydney, 2003) at 281: "The doctrine makes a direct appeal to the unconscionability norm".

149 E Sherwin, "Restitution and Equity: An Analysis of the Principle of Unjust Enrichment" (2001) 79 *Texas Law Review* 2083 at 2106.

enrichment. While there are occasional signs in both the commentaries[150] and the authorities[151] of a more normative conception, the concept of unjust enrichment as articulated within the dominant model does not of itself establish a rule able to be applied directly to decide the outcome of actual cases.[152] Rather, "unjust enrichment" merely expresses the generic conception of those circumstances in which the law will impose a restitutionary obligation. Accordingly, "unjust enrichment" does not seek to articulate an independent basis for restitution, one that appeals to some overriding conception of fairness or the like, but rather offers merely a descriptive label that looks downward to the cases to divine its content.[153] As Birks noted: "The generic conception of the event which triggers restitution adds nothing to the existing understanding of what is there already."[154] Therefore, while the prevailing analysis of the law of unjust enrichment now asserts that in order to justify a restitutionary remedy, outside of the law of contract, the law of torts and the law of property, the plaintiff must prove that it is unjust for her or him to be deprived of the wealth transferred to the defendant,[155] the content of "unjust" is determined not by the virtually unconstrained import of that concept, but by rules of a much lower level of abstraction.

This general approach to restitutionary liability is, moreover, equally apparent in the so-called absence of consideration basis of restitutionary

---

150 While most academic treatments of unjust enrichment ostensibly assert a formulaic approach (G Virgo, *The Principles of the Law of Restitution* (Clarendon, Oxford, 1999) at 52), a normative version is never far away. This is evident in the expansion of the range of unjust factors to include "ignorance", free acceptance and an interference with the plaintiff's property rights: see A Burrows, *The Law of Restitution* (2nd ed, Butterworths, London, 2003) at chapters 4, 10 and 15). It is also evident in the tendency to infer the presence of unjust enrichment simply from the nature of the response as "restitutionary": see J Dietrich, *Restitution: A New Perspective* (Federation Press, Sydney, 1998) at 41-42.

151 This is particularly evident in the rather open-ended concept of unjust enrichment developed in Canada (see generally R Grantham and CF Rickett, *Enrichment and Restitution in New Zealand* (Hart Publishing, Oxford, 2000) at 9-12). There are, however, signs of a similar approach elsewhere in the Commonwealth. See, for example: *Banque Financiere de la Cite v Parc (Battersea) Ltd* [1999] AC 221 at 237: "The principle [of unjust enrichment] seeks to secure a fair and just determination of the rights of the parties"; *Westdeutsche Landesbank Girozentrale v Islington LBC* [1996] AC 669 at 697: "An action of restitution appears to provide an almost classic case in which the jurisdiction should be available to enable the courts to do full justice"; *Hillsdown plc v Pensions Ombudsman* [1997] 1 All ER 862 at 903: "As to its being unjust ... one only has to compare the position of Hillsdown who successfully wielded a big but misguided stick"; *National Bank of New Zealand Ltd v Waitaki International Processing (NI) Ltd* [1999] 2 NZLR 211 at 230: "This 'eternal' desire to do justice, and with it a significant degree of judicial discretion, is necessarily inherent in the concept of unjust enrichment".

152 The principle of unjust enrichment is not a cause of action: *Rod Milner Motors Ltd v Attorney General* [1999] 2 NZLR 568 at 576.

153 P Birks, *An Introduction to the Law of Restitution* (Clarendon, Oxford, 1985) at 17; G Virgo, *The Principles of the Law of Restitution* (Clarendon, Oxford, 1999) at 52; P Birks, *Unjust Enrichment*, (2nd ed, Clarendon, Oxford, 2005) at 105.

154 P Birks, *An Introduction to the Law of Restitution*, above n 153 at 29.

155 G Virgo, *The Principles of the Law of Restitution*, above n 153 at 56.

liability.[156] While this approach formally dispenses with the nominate grounds of recovery such as mistake and failure of consideration,[157] liability is nevertheless not determined directly by an abstract principle of unjustified enrichment. What the sine causa approach does is to ask whether there is a recognised legal basis for the transfer of wealth. This question, to which "there is a finite number of known explanations",[158] is answered outside of the law of restitution by other bodies of law. Where the answer is no, restitution follows automatically.[159]

It does not, therefore, seem appropriate to characterise the law of restitution as equitable in the present sense. As it is currently understood in both English and Australian law,[160] the principle of unjust enrichment is not of itself a rule directly applicable to the disposition of individual cases. Consistently with the historical preference of the common law for more precisely formulated rules, restitutionary liability is determined by rules of a lower level of abstraction. This is not, of course, to say that those restitutionary doctrines that were developed in Chancery must, therefore, be reformulated in more precise, common law-like terms. The formulation of any rule is also influenced by the subject matter that it seeks to regulate. Where, therefore, the subject matter of the rule is those more subtle forms of cognitive impairment, the rule will invariably be more open textured. Accordingly, as equitable restitutionary doctrines, such as undue influence and unconscionable bargain, tend to deal with such matters, their open texture can be justified as a matter of principle quite apart from any historical considerations.[161]

Equity as the private conscience of the judge

There is, however, a much stronger claim made about the methodology of equity. This claim is that "equity" is to be understood in a direct Aristotelian sense: a correction of the law in individual cases when it produces harsh outcomes as consequences of its generality. Sherwin describes equity in this sense as "individualized justice, adjusting the outcomes of general rules when the application to particular cases produces results that are too harsh or are

---

156 P Birks, *Unjust Enrichment*, above n 153; T Krebs, *Restitution at the Crossroads: A Comparative Study* (Cavendish, London, 2001). In *Pacific National Investments Ltd v Victoria (City)* [2004] 3 SCR 575 at 589 the Supreme Court of Canada made this point in respect of the not dissimilar "absence of juristic reason" approach present in Canada.

157 S Meier, 'Unjust Factors and Legal Grounds' in D Johnston and R Zimmerman (eds), *Unjustified Enrichment: Key Issues in Comparative Perspective* (Cambridge University Press, Cambridge, 2002); S Meier, 'Restitution after Executed Void Contracts' in P Birks and F Rose (eds), *Lessons from the Swaps Litigation* (Mansfield Press, London, 2000).

158 P Birks, *Unjust Enrichment*, above n 153 at 102.

159 T Krebs, *Restitution at the Crossroads: A comparative study,* above n 156 at 4; P Birks, *The Foundations of Unjust Enrichment: Six Centennial Lectures* (Victoria University Press, Wellington, 2002) at 73, and *Unjust Enrichment* (2nd ed, Clarendon, Oxford, 2005) at 102, 127.

160 *Pavey and Matthews Pty Ltd v Paul* (1987) 162 CLR 221; *David Securities Pty Ltd v Commonwealth Bank of Australia* (1992) 175 CLR 353.

161 M Bryan, 'Unjust Enrichment and Unconscionability in Australia: A False Dichotomy?' in J Neyers, M McInnes and S Pitel (eds), *Understanding Unjust Enrichment* (Hart Publishing, Oxford, 2004) at 60.

contrary to the underlying objectives of the rules. The function of equity in this sense is not to overrule unjust rules, but to correct unjust applications of rules that may, as a general matter be just and desirable rules."[162]

The view of equity as licensing the individual judge to have direct recourse to broad and, therefore, private notions of justice, conscience and fairness to do what is "right" in individual cases is particularly apparent in much of New Zealand's equity jurisprudence. Thus, for example, Lord Cooke described his approach to equity cases as involving "a thorough analysis of the facts followed by the application of broad principles of conscience, fairness and reason."[163] To similar effect is Justice EW Thomas' extrajudicial dismissal of the general distrust of wide judicial discretion as "adolescent dogmas which the judiciary has outgrown and discarded as the decision-making process has assumed greater maturity".[164] This view is also apparent in the debate over discretionary remedialism: the extent to which it is desirable for the courts to select the remedy purely on the basis of the particular court's assessment of appropriateness of the remedy on particular facts of the case under consideration.[165] The question posed for present purposes by this view of equity is whether a law of restitution that relies on direct recourse to notions of fairness is appropriate.

The proper role of judicial discretion in adjudication generally, and the role of the private views of the judge in giving content to the notion of conscience in particular, are large issues that go far beyond the scope of this chapter. With that caveat in mind, however, it does seem clear that the onus in the debate must lie upon those seeking to establish the legitimacy of an approach which advocates judicial discretion in a strong sense. Prima facie, an approach to adjudication and the promulgation of norms based on the individual ad hoc and ad hominem intuition of judges is inconsistent with the rule of law and the democratic basis of the State.[166] These norms require public, not private, reasons for decision. That is, they require both that adjudication is based on rational reasons, not merely on a psychological prediction of judicial behaviour, and that these reasons be capable of public scrutiny and thereby are

---

162 E Sherwin, "Restitution and Equity: An Analysis of the Principle of Unjust Enrichment" (2001) 79 *Texas Law Review* 2083 at 2091.

163 R Cooke, 'The Place of Equity and Equitable Doctrines in the Contemporary Common Law World: A New Zealand Perspective' in DM Waters (ed), *Equity, Fiduciaries and Trusts* (Carswell, Toronto, 1980) at 29. More generally, see R Cooke, "Fairness" (1989) 19 *Victoria University of Wellington Law Review* 421.

164 E Thomas, "Judging in the Twenty-First Century" [2000] *New Zealand Law Journal* 228 at 228. Cases such as *LAC Minerals v International Corona Resources*, (1989) 61 DLR (4th) 14 at 51, *Gillies v Keogh* [1989] 2 NZLR 327 at 330-331, and *Lincoln Hunt Australia Pty Ltd v Willesee* (1986) 4 NSWLR 457 at 463, all seem to invoke a broad notion of conscience as a mechanism for deciding individual cases.

165 D Jensen, "The Rights and Wrongs of Discretionary Remedialism" [2003] *Singapore Journal of Legal Studies* 178; S Evans, "Defending Discretionary Remedialism" (2001) 23 *Sydney Law Review* 463; P Birks, "Three Kinds of Objection to Discretionary Remedialism" (2000) 29 *Western Australian Law Review* 1.

166 As Hayne J, "Australian Law in the Twentieth Century" (2000) 74 *Austalian Law Journal* 373 at 375, noted extra-judicially, "unless we are to treat judges as philosopher kings, our search must always be for the principles that guide the making of decisions".

subjected to the democratic process.[167] The law's moral and political authority to command respect from its subjects depends upon the intelligibility and knowability of the law in this public sense.

The fundamental objection to the characterisation of the law of restitution as "equitable" in this sense, therefore, lies not in the choice of formulatory language per se, but in the invitation apparently held out by concepts such as "equity" and "fairness" to judges, scholars, and claimants to substitute their own intuitions for reasons and principles. A formulation of the law of restitution that relies upon the individual discretion of individual judges thus offers no *legally* relevant basis, other than the raw coercive power of the state, upon which the judicial determination that the defendant's retention of the wealth in question is unconscientious should be privileged over the defendant's determination that he or she is entitled to keep it.

CONCLUSION

The rise of the law of restitution has been perceived as a threat to traditional equity scholarship. This is in part because the principle of unjust enrichment has sought to absorb and re-characterise doctrines historically associated with equity.[168] In part also, restitution has posed a threat because it has necessitated a rethinking of the organisation of the private law.[169] The Victorian division of the private law into contract, tort, and equity has had to make room for restitution. In so doing, the emergence of a law of restitution presented both the need and the opportunity to reorganise the law on the basis of function, principle, and rationality. In such a taxonomy, there is no room for a category whose only claim to existence is that it arose in a court that ceased to exist 130 years ago.

One response to this threat has been the "reverse takeover" seen in *Roxborough*. In emphasising the equitable nature of specific restitutionary rules, it was sought to absorb the embryonic law of restitution within equity and by doing so restore the Victorian tripartite taxonomy of contract, tort, and equity. This, however, will not do. While the principle of unjust enrichment shares with equity a supplementary or modificatory function, unjust enrichment is equitable neither in a jurisdictional sense nor in the sense that it is concerned with fairness in the round.

In *Westdeutsche Landesbank Girozentrale v Islington London Borough Council*,[170] Lord Goff spoke of the tension between restitution and equity lawyers. With respect, his Lordship may have mischaracterised what is actually at stake. The tension, which the emergence of a law of restitution has spawned, is not one between the restitution and the equity scholar per se. Rather, the tension is between the historical arch conservatism of those who want to retain equity as a meaningful category within the private law and the radical

---

167 *Cowcher v Cowcher* [1972] 1 All ER 934; 1 WLR 425 at 430: "the only justice that can be attained by mortals … is justice according to law; the justice that flows from the application of sure and settled principles to proved or admitted facts."

168 S Hedley and M Halliwell, *The Law of Restitution* (Butterworths, London, 2002) at chapter 2.

169 K Mason and JW Carter, *Restitution Law in Australia* (Butterworths, Sydney, 1995) at 4-5.

170 [1996] AC 669 at 685

rationality of those who seek to reform the private law on the basis of deductions from general principles. While both views represent extreme positions that are never likely to fully capture the content of the private law, the fact that the principle of unjust enrichment is a feature of virtually all western legal systems, common law and civilian alike, suggests that the however much notions of "equity" and "conscience" may strike a chord in the Australian legal psyche, the conservative cause, at least as it applies to the law of restitution, is lost.

15

Remedial Coherence and Punitive Damages in Equity

ANDREW BURROWS[*]

INTRODUCTION

Meagher, Gummow and Lehane (and, by succession, Meagher, Heydon and Leeming) are famous across the common law world for the vehemence of their views against the fusion of common law and equity.[1] Those who embrace, consciously or subconsciously, the "fusion fallacy" are, we are told, committing an evil offence.[2]

Donning the cloak of the Dark Lord or, as others might see it, the white robes of Gandalf,[3] I plucked up the courage to argue against the views of the famous Trinity in my inaugural lecture at Oxford. In "We Do This at Common Law but That in Equity"[4] I tried to set out as clearly as I could what the two sides of the fusion debate were saying. Then, holding aloft the flag for fusion, I argued that there are numerous inconsistencies between common law and equity: that if we are to take fusion seriously these inconsistencies should be removed so as to produce a coherent or harmonised law: and that in developing the law it is legitimate for the courts to reason from common law to equity and

---

* I would like to thank Michael Rush for his research assistance with this chapter. I would also like to thank Simone Degeling and James Edelman for inviting me to the fusion conference in Sydney where this chapter was first presented, thereby allowing me to change seasons for one glorious week in December.

1 R Meagher, JD Heydon and M Leeming, *Meagher, Gummow and Lehane's Equity: Doctrines and Remedies* (4th ed, Butterworths, Sydney, 2002) (hereinafter referred to as *Meagher, Gummow and Lehane's Equity*).

2 *Meagher, Gummow and Lehane's Equity*, at [2–105]. See generally [2–100]–[2–125], [2–270]–[2–320].

3 With apologies to JRR Tolkien, *Lord of the Rings*.

4 A Burrows, (2002) 22 *Oxford Journal of Legal Studies* 1. See also A Burrows, *Fusing Common Law and Equity: Remedies, Restitution and Reform* (Hochelaga Lecture, Sweet & Maxwell Asia, Hong Kong, 2002).

vice versa. To my way of thinking, supporting fusion at root rests on not being slaves to history and on recognising the importance of coherence in the law and of like cases being treated alike.

In this chapter I ultimately want to focus the fusion debate on one very specific issue which came up for decision before the Court of Appeal of New South Wales in *Harris v Digital Pulse Pty Ltd*.[5] Can punitive damages (otherwise referred to as "exemplary" damages)[6] be awarded for equitable wrongs? That relatively narrow issue neatly encapsulates the whole fusion debate. As David Morgan has expressed it, "the [*Digital Pulse*] case is the site of a showdown between the old-school orthodoxy of the New South Wales equity bar and the more flexible approach of the 'fusion fallacy' heretics".[7] Before coming to that, I would like to deal briefly with the reply to my inaugural lecture given in the fourth edition of *Meagher, Gummow and Lehane's Equity*. I also want to set the scene for the punitive damages issue by looking more generally at remedial coherence for common law and equitable wrongs.

MEAGHER, HEYDON AND LEEMING'S REPLY

I was honoured to discover that Meagher, Heydon and Leeming had read my inaugural lecture and deemed it worthy of comment in the fourth edition of *Meagher, Gummow and Lehane's Equity*. Given the location and theme of this conference and my overriding desire to get to the bottom of the dispute between us, I make no apology for citing in full the most relevant passage.[8]

> "A more vehement statement of Lord Millett's position has been made by Professor Burrows in his Oxford Inaugural Lecture … in which he seems to argue that in all respects common law damages are the same as equitable compensation, the same principles apply to each, and such concepts as remoteness, intervening causes, contributory negligence and penal damages apply indifferently to each concept. He does not seem to notice that it would be odd to hold that a cestui qui trust has a duty to look after his own property, so that he could be contributorily negligent if he did not do so, when the whole point of having a trustee is to look after the cestui qui trust. Nor does he explain why it is that a court may impose conditions on a plaintiff in awarding him equitable compensation but cannot do so in awarding him common law damages. Why is it that the Professor imagines such a union apparently takes place? The *Judicature Act*, apparently, has 'fused' law and equity. If that be so, by what words? And what does 'fused' mean? Moreover, why not explain how the *Judicature Act* did not abolish trusts, but did apparently 'fuse' damages and

---

5   (2003) 56 NSWLR 298.

6   Although the term exemplary damages has been preferred by English and Australian judges, led by Lord Hailsham in *Broome v Cassell* [1972] AC 1027 at 1073, the terminology of punitive damages has been preferred in the United States and Canada and is adopted throughout this chapter as being marginally clearer and more straightforward. The English Law Commission in *Aggravated, Exemplary and Restitutionary Damages*, Report No 247 (1997) at [5.39] also preferred "punitive damages". Nothing of substance should turn on the label adopted.

7   D Morgan, "Harris v Digital Pulse: the Availability of Exemplary Damages in Equity" (2003) 29 *Monash University Law Review* 377 at 377.

8   *Meagher, Gummow and Lehane's Equity*, at [23–020]. See also [2–320].

compensation? He endeavours to deal with the fact that defences such as laches, unclean hands … and hardship … are available in answer to claims for equitable remedies but not common law damages in two ways. The first is to say that the common law has doctrines, for example, illegality in public policy, 'which mirror in nature, if not in scope, the so-called 'discretionary' defences in equity', so that 'it is simply false to imagine that there are irreconcilable differences between common law and equitable defences'. That contention is utterly wrong. The second contention of the Professor is to deny 'in general terms' that there are equitable defences to 'equitable monetary remedies' that would not apply to rule out 'common law monetary remedies', and to say that so far as there are, the distinctions between the common law defences and the equitable defences are 'small'. These are highly controversial propositions, and confidence in their correctness is not increased by the sole example given, namely the 'notoriously unclear, complex and unsatisfactory' character of the law on the interrelation of limitation statutes and the doctrine of laches."

There may be said to be five distinct points made in this passage and I shall deal briefly with each of them, although not in the order in which they appear.

1. What does "fused" mean and which (statutory) words justify it?

This point mirrors other passages in the book[9] where the authors refer with approval to Justice Lehane's comment in a book review in the *Cambridge Law Journal*,[10] that those who assert that law and equity are fused rarely (if ever) explain what they mean and how it happened. With respect, I too was puzzled by what fusion means and by the meaning of the "fusion fallacy" and precisely for that reason and, with Lehane's words very much in mind, I took some time to set out the essence of the fusion, and anti-fusion, schools of thought. I would, therefore, simply refer Meagher, Heydon and Leeming back to what I said there (which for convenience is set out as an Appendix to this chapter).

As to "how it happened", the fusion school of thought argues that "the fusion of the administration of the courts brought about by the Judicature Acts 1873–5, while not dictating the fusion of the substantive law, rendered this, for the first time, a realistic possibility."[11] With that possibility opened up, there is no mystery as to how subsequently common law and equity have, in some but not all respects, merged or borrowed from each other. This has been through nothing more than ordinary incremental development by the judges applying reasoning by analogy: that is, we have witnessed nothing more than the standard development of principle through decision-making in cases. To use the terminology of Dr Edelman, the fusion that has occurred, and continues to occur, is not "automatic fusion" but "fusion by analogy".[12]

---

9   *Meagher, Gummow and Lehane's Equity,* at [2–310].

10   J Lehane, "Book Review" [1987] *Cambridge Law Journal* 165 at 175.

11   A Burrows, "We Do This at Common Law but That in Equity" (2002) *Oxford Journal of Legal Studies* 1 at 4.

12   J Edelman, "A 'Fusion Fallacy' Fallacy?" (2003) 119 *Law Quarterly Review* 375 at 377.

2. Contributory negligence by a beneficiary?

Given the discretion and flexibility open to the courts in applying limitations on compensatory damages (such as remoteness, intervening cause and contributory negligence), I argued that there is no good reason for a different approach to limitations on equitable compensation.[13] As regards contributory negligence, the argument is that it is irrational to insist that, simply because equitable compensation is an equitable rather than a common law remedy, contributory negligence can *never* be available to reduce equitable compensation (for, for example, breach of fiduciary duty).[14] That, of course, is not the same as saying that, in a particular context, contributory negligence must be applied to reduce equitable compensation. On the contrary, in examining the factual context of the contributory negligence and the content of the defendant's duty, we are embarking on a rational and sensible investigation. It may very well be that where one has a true trust, it would be extremely rare to hold the beneficiary contributorily negligent. This is because the content of the trustee's duty – to look after the trust property for the benefit of the beneficiary – means that a beneficiary could rarely, if ever, be regarded as "at fault", compared with the trustee, in relation to that property. But this is no different from saying, for example, that, if D is required under a contract with C to look after C's property (whether owing strict or reasonable care duties) C will rarely be held contributorily negligent in relation to the loss of that property. Similarly, to refer to an example I have used elsewhere,[15] if C takes his car to D's garage for work to be done on the brakes and in breach of D's duty of reasonable care in performing the work, the brakes are improperly repaired, C should not be regarded as being contributorily negligent if he fails to check that the work has been properly done and, as a consequence, has an accident. The content of D's duty, in the factual context, means that C is not at fault compared with D. But, crucially, that is not the same as saying that contributory

---

13   A Burrows, "We Do This at Common Law but That in Equity", above n 11 at 9–12. An important aspect of this flexibility at common law is that, for example, contributory negligence does not apply to a dishonestly committed tort, like deceit: see *Standard Chartered Bank v Pakistan National Shipping Corporation (No 2)* [2002] UKHL 43; [2003] 1 AC 959. For the same approach – of denying contributory negligence, because of the defendant's dishonesty – being applied to equitable as well as common law wrongs, see *Corporacion Nacional de Cobre de Chile v Sogemin Metals Ltd* [1997] 1 WLR 1396 (a bribes case).

14   But in obiter dicta in *Pilmer v Duke Group Ltd* (2001) 207 CLR 165 the High Court of Australia has said that contributory negligence is inapplicable to equitable compensation for breach of fiduciary duty. For the High Court of Australia favouring a different approach generally to equitable compensation from that taken to common law damages, see *Youyang Pty Ltd v Minter Ellison Morris Fletcher* (2003) 212 CLR 484 at 500-501. Heenan J in *Fico v O'Leary* [2004] WASC 215 at [160] cited the *Youyang* case as the basis for saying that, "[w]hile the door is still not absolutely closed to this possibility of assimilating the remedies and measure of damages at law, in contract or in tort, with those available for breach of trust or breach of fiduciary duty there is little encouragement for any Judge at first instance to cross that threshold".

15   A Burrows, 'Limitations on Compensation' in A Burrows and E Peel (eds), *Commercial Remedies: Current Issues and Problems* (Oxford University Press, Oxford, 2003) at 40, n 45.

negligence can never apply to a claim for the tort of negligence or for breach of contract.[16]

Certainly, where one moves out from the core breach of trust case to claims for breach of fiduciary duty against, for example, solicitors, one would expect contributory negligence to be as readily available as for equivalent claims for tort and breach of contract. Take the facts of the New Zealand case of *Day v Mead*.[17] The claimant's solicitor in breach of fiduciary duty advised the claimant, without taking independent advice, to invest in a company in which the solicitor had a substantial interest. The claimant invested $20,000 and then, subsequently, when knowing of the company's difficult financial position, invested a further $80,000. It was held that while the claimant could recover equitable compensation in full for the first $20,000 loss, he was equally at fault with the solicitor for the second investment loss, so that applying a reduction of 50% for contributory negligence, he should merely recover $40,000 in relation to that. That seems a correct decision. But whether one agrees with it or not, the crucial point is that rational and not historical reasons must be given for why it is incorrect. To say that it is incorrect because contributory negligence cannot apply to an equitable remedy is, unacceptably, to rely on historical dogma and not reason.

3. Why have trusts not been abolished by fusion?

It is not entirely clear to me what point is being made here by Meagher, Heydon and Leeming. In my inaugural lecture I suggested that inconsistency between common law and equity did not occur in all areas; and I gave the trust, with its split between bare legal title and beneficial equitable title, as an example of where common law and equity co-exist coherently and satisfactorily. In contrast, it is where there is inconsistency between common law and equity – where, on close examination, like cases are not being treated alike (as with, for example, equitable and common law monetary remedies for civil wrongs) – that fusion of common law and equity is required so as to eradicate that inconsistency.

4. Why is it that conditions can be imposed on a claimant awarded equitable compensation but not common law damages?

This is an excellent question but merely serves to support my argument. The answer is that there is no rational, as opposed to historical, reason why

---

16 In contrast to the position in England, the High Court of Australia in *Astley v Austrust Ltd* (1999) 197 CLR 1 decided that contributory negligence can never apply to an action for breach of contract. That decision, however, triggered legislative reform in the States and Territories so that contributory negligence does apply to a contractual duty of care provided, in some States, that there is concurrent tort liability: see, for example, *Wrongs Act 1958* (Vic), s 25; *Law Reform (Contributory Negligence and Apportionment of Liability) Act 2001* (SA), ss 3, 4 and 7. See also *Civil Law (Wrongs) Act 2002* (ACT); *Civil Liability Act 2002* (NSW); *Personal Injuries (Liabilities and Damages) Act* (NT); *Civil Liability Act 2003* (Qld); *Civil Liability Act 2002* (Tas); and the *Civil Liability Act 2002* (WA).

17 [1987] 2 NZLR 443.

conditions can be imposed in relation to equitable and not common law remedies. If the courts are willing to do this for equitable compensation it is inconsistent not to be able to do it for compensatory damages: common law and equity should therefore be fused by either allowing conditional awards of compensatory damages or by barring conditional awards of equitable compensation. The former seems the preferable way forward. In fact, for two reasons, only a small step would be needed to achieve this. First, it appears to be rare in practice for conditions to be imposed in relation to equitable compensation.[18] That is, the imposition of terms is primarily used in relation to equitable non-monetary remedies, like specific performance and injunctions,[19] rather than for equitable monetary remedies. Secondly, even for common law damages, there have been cases where the normal bar on unconditional awards has, exceptionally, been departed from. That is, in some personal injury cases involving gratuitous nursing services rendered or expenses incurred by a relative, or gratuitous payments made by an employer, damages have been made conditional on the claimant paying them over to,[20] or holding them on trust for,[21] the relative or employer.

5. Defences

Meagher, Heydon and Leeming assert that I was "utterly wrong" to contend that there are common law doctrines that mirror in nature, if not in scope, equitable defences such as laches, unclean hands and hardship; and that it was a "highly controversial proposition" to submit that the distinctions between the common law and equitable defences are small.

I make no apology for reiterating that, in my opinion, there are common law counterparts to the famous equitable defences. The defence of illegality equates to the clean hands principle; limitation of actions equates with laches; and, at least in contract, hardship is dealt with by doctrines such as mistake and frustration. One must also beware of not comparing like with like. The main operation, for example, of the hardship bar is in relation to equitable non-monetary remedies such as specific performance and injunctions, not equitable monetary remedies.[22] It may be perfectly rational for the law to take the view that hardship should operate so as to negate a non-monetary remedy, while at the same time accepting that it should not negate a monetary remedy.

---

18   An example is *McKenzie v McDonald* [1927] VLR 134 (D to pay equitable compensation to C but on terms that, if D elected to take over C's shop and dwelling for $2000, most of the compensation paid would be deducted from the $2000).

19   For examples of specific performance on terms, see A Burrows, *Remedies for Torts and Breach of Contract* (3rd ed, Oxford University Press, Oxford, 2004) at 507–508. For a discussion of a "compensated injunction" see the same at 525, 629. For rescission on terms see, for example, *Cooper v Phibbs* (1867) LR 2 HL 149; *Solle v Butcher* [1950] 1 KB 671.

20   For example *Dennis v London Passenger Transport Board* [1948] 1 All ER 779; *Schneider v Eisovitch* [1960] 2 QB 430.

21   For example *Cunningham v Harrison* [1973] QB 942; *Hunt v Severs* [1994] 2 AC 350. Cf *Kars v Kars* (1996) 71 AJLR 107.

22   See, for example, *Patel v Ali* [1984] Ch 283.

I was at pains to emphasise that I was not suggesting that one could say here and now that the scope of equity's defences is identical to those at common law. And while it may have been controversial to suggest that the differences are small, the most important point made, which Meagher, Heydon and Leeming did not seek to answer in their reply, is that "rationally [the differences] should be eliminated altogether".

REMEDIAL COHERENCE FOR COMMON LAW AND EQUITABLE WRONGS

In order to understand the significance of whether punitive damages can be awarded for equitable wrongs, it is helpful initially to look more broadly at all remedies for common law and equitable wrongs. This reveals that, contrary to what anti-fusionists may wish us to believe, there is a very large measure of consistency between remedies for common law wrongs and remedies for equitable wrongs.

One first needs to isolate what one means by a common law or equitable "wrong". Professor Birks' work is of central importance here. He argued that there is a distinction in our civil law between causes of action that are not wrongs (for example, unjust enrichment) and causes of action that are wrongs. According to Birks, the definition of a (civil) wrong is "conduct ... whose effect in creating legal consequences is attributable to its being characterised as a breach of duty".[23] Moreover, it appears that, with the conceivable exception of some statutory duties, a sure test for whether that definition is satisfied (ie, whether the law is characterising particular conduct as constituting a breach of duty) is that compensation must be an available remedial measure for the conduct in question if loss is caused to the claimant by that conduct. Applying that test, torts and breach of contract are civil wrongs. In contrast, unjust enrichment triggering the restitution of money (or non-monetary benefits) rendered by mistake, or for a failed consideration, or under duress or undue influence,[24] is a cause of action that is not a wrong. Restitution of the value of the enrichment subtracted from the claimant is the only available remedial measure; compensation for loss is not available for the unjust enrichment.

It also then becomes clear that, alongside torts and breach of contract, which are common law wrongs (because they were developed in the common law courts), there are equitable wrongs (developed in the Court of Chancery). Applying the above test, the equitable civil wrongs are breach of fiduciary duty, breach of confidence, dishonestly procuring or assisting a breach of fiduciary duty and those forms of estoppel that constitute causes of action, in particular

---

23 P Birks, *An Introduction to the Law of Restitution* (Oxford University Press, Oxford, 1989) at 313.

24 See P Birks, "Unjust Factors and Wrongs: Pecuniary Rescission for Undue Influence" [1997] *Restitution Law Review* 72 discussing *Mahoney v Purnell* [1996] 3 All ER 61; J Edelman, "Equitable Torts" (2002) 10 *Torts Law Journal* 64.

proprietary estoppel. So what we need to compare are the remedies for torts and breach of contract on the one hand, and the remedies for breach of fiduciary duty, breach of confidence, dishonestly procuring or assisting a breach of fiduciary duty and proprietary estoppel on the other.

In making that comparison it can be seen that both common law and equitable remedies[25] (for example, damages and injunctions) are available for common law wrongs; but, much more importantly, we discover that behind the differently labelled common law and equitable remedies, *essentially the same functions are being performed by the remedies for both common law and equitable wrongs.* This central, and often unappreciated point, can be most clearly seen by setting out in tabular form the primary remedial functions and particular remedies for first, the common law wrongs and, secondly, the equitable wrongs.

Table 1: Remedies for Torts and Breach of Contract

Primary function	*Remedies*
Compensation	Compensatory damages
Restitution	Restitutionary damages Account of profits Award of money had and received
Punishment	Punitive damages
Compelling performance (of positive obligations)	Specific Performance Award of an agreed sum Mandatory enforcing injunction Appointment of a receiver
Preventing a wrong	Prohibitory injunction Delivery up for destruction or destruction on oath
Compelling the undoing of a wrong	Mandatory restorative injunction Delivery up of goods
Declaring rights	Declaration Nominal damages Contemptuous damages

---

25   Common law remedies are those developed in the common law courts; equitable remedies are those developed in the Court of Chancery.

Table 2: Remedies for Equitable Wrongs

Primary Function	Remedies
Compensation	Equitable compensation (Equitable) compensatory damages
Restitution	(Equitable) restitutionary damages Account of profits Award of money had and received Constructive trust
Punishment?	Punitive damages?
Compelling performance (of positive obligations)	Mandatory enforcing injunction Appointment of a receiver
Preventing a wrong	Prohibitory injunction Delivery up for destruction or destruction on oath
Compelling the undoing of a wrong	Mandatory restorative injunction Delivery up of material containing confidential information
Declaring rights	Declaration

It would not be feasible in this chapter to fill out the details that lie behind those two tables. But just to give a flavour, compensatory damages for torts and breach of contract are concerned to compensate the claimant's loss. Subject to limitations (such as remoteness and legal causation) they aim to put the victim of the wrong into as good a position, so far as money can do it, as if the wrong had not been committed. Note also that equitable compensatory damages (awarded in lieu of an injunction under the successor to *Lord Cairns' Act*)[26] aim to compensate in respect of anticipated common law wrongs. When we switch to remedies for equitable wrongs, we find exactly the same primary function of compensation being performed by the remedies of equitable compensation (which is a standard remedy for breach of fiduciary duty)[27] and/or equitable compensatory damages awarded in addition to, or in lieu of, an injunction (which is a standard remedy for breach of confidence).[28] It may be debated whether the limitations on equitable compensation are at present identical, or merely similar, to those on compensatory damages for the common law wrongs.[29] However, once one realises that the functions are identical it is hard to see, rationally, why the limitations should differ.

---

26 *Supreme Court Act 1981* (UK), s 50.

27 *Fry v Fry* (1859) 27 Beav 144; 54 ER 56; *Re Dawson* [1966] 2 NSWLR 211.

28 *Saltman Engineering Co Ltd v Campbell Engineering Ltd* [1948] 65 RPC 203; [1963] 3 All ER 413; *Seager v Copydex* [1967] 1 WLR 923.

29 For that debate, see A Burrows, "We Do This at Common Law but That in Equity" (2002) 22 *Oxford Journal of Legal Studies* 1 at 9–12; A Burrows, *Remedies for Torts and Breach of Contract* (3rd ed, Oxford University Press, Oxford, 2004), at 601–606.

Again, if we look at restitutionary (ie, gain-based) remedies, it is clear that a number of different remedies, both common law and equitable, are available to effect restitution for a tort or breach of contract.[30] Restitutionary damages (awarded, for example, for trespass to land),[31] an award of money had and received (for example, for the tort of conversion),[32] and an account of profits (for example, for the intellectual property torts[33] or, exceptionally, for breach of contract)[34] all seek to remove some or all of the gains made by the commission of a common law wrong. When we switch to remedies for equitable wrongs, we find exactly the same primary function of restitution being performed by the remedies of an account of profits (which is a standard remedy for a breach of fiduciary duty[35] or breach of confidence),[36] by restitutionary damages awarded in lieu of, or in addition to, an injunction (which has been awarded for breach of confidence[37]), by a constructive trust (for breach of fiduciary duty[38] and possibly breach of confidence)[39] and even by an award of money had and received (which was awarded to remove a bribe acquired in breach of fiduciary duty in one of the leading cases).[40] It can, of course, be debated whether propri-etary restitution (through a constructive trust) is justified but, if it is, it is hard to see, rationally, why it should not be available for common law, as well as equitable, wrongs.

The central point being made is that, behind the detail, essentially the same functions are being performed by the remedies for both common law and equitable wrongs. Any differences in detail are, rationally, difficult to defend. It would take merely a small step to the position whereby it makes no difference whether one labels the civil wrong in question, common law or equitable. Of course, the content of the duties may differ as between the different wrongs (so that, for example, what is needed to compensate – to put the claimant into as good a position as if no wrong had occurred – may differ). In essence, as would be expected, essentially the same remedial functions are being performed for what is in essence, the same legal phenomenon, namely a civil wrong.

Tables 1 and 2 highlight clearly the importance of the question whether punitive damages are available for equitable damages. That issue has been left open by the insertion of question-marks in the second table. It can be plainly

---

30 See M McInnes, 'Account of Profits for Common Law Wrongs', below at chapter 16.

31 *Penarth Dock Engineering Co Ltd v Pounds* [1963] 1 Lloyd's Rep 359.

32 *Lamine v Dorrell* (1705) 2 Ld Raym 1216; 92 ER 303; *Chesworth v Farrar* [1967] 1 QB 407.

33 *Patents Act 1977* (UK), s 61(1)(d); *Copyright, Designs and Patents Act 1988* (UK), s 96(2); *Colbeam Palmer Ltd v Stock Affiliates Pty Ltd* (1968) 122 CLR 25.

34 *Attorney-General v Blake* [2001] 1 AC 268. Cf *Hospitality Group Pty Ltd v Australian Rugby Union Ltd* (2001) 110 FCR 157.

35 *Regal Hastings Ltd v Gulliver* [1967] 2 AC 134; *Keith Henry & Co Pty Ltd v Stuart Walker & Co Pty Ltd* (1958) 100 CLR 342.

36 *Peter Pan Manufacturing Corpn v Corsets Silhouette Ltd* [1964] 1 WLR 96; *Attorney-General v Guardian Newspapers (No 2) ('Spycatcher')* [1990] 1 AC 109.

37 *Seager v Copydex (No 2)* [1969] 1 WLR 809.

38 *Boardman v Phipps* [1967] 2 AC 46; *Attorney-General of Hong Kong v Reid* [1994] 1 AC 324.

39 *LAC Minerals Ltd v International Corona Resources Ltd* (1989) 61 DLR (4th) 14.

40 *Reading v Attorney-General* [1951] AC 507.

seen that, if punishment is not available as a remedial function for equitable wrongs, that would constitute a significant difference from the position for common law wrongs (although, as we shall see, there is some internal incoherence even at common law as punitive damages have been awarded traditionally only for torts and not for breach of contract). If punishment is not a remedial function pursued for equitable wrongs, it would be the only remedial function pursued for torts but never for equitable wrongs. Considerable light is thrown on the fusion debate in deciding whether those question-marks can be deleted from the second table. In Australia the issue of whether punitive damages are available for equitable wrongs – and, specifically, for breach of fiduciary duty – came up for decision in *Harris v Digital Pulse Pty Ltd*.[41]

HARRIS V DIGITAL PULSE PTY LTD

Before turning to the facts of this case, it is important to see that (even leaving to one side the United States) there is support from New Zealand and Canada for punitive damages being available for equitable wrongs.[42] In the well-known decision of the New Zealand Court of Appeal in *Aquaculture Corpn v New Zealand Green Mussel Co Ltd*,[43] the majority held that, in addition to compensation, punitive damages could be awarded for breach of confidence albeit that, on the facts, they were not merited. Cooke P, giving the majority's decision said:[44]

> "Whether the obligation of confidence in a case of the present kind should be classified as purely an equitable one is debatable, but we do not think that the question matters for any purpose material to this appeal. For all purposes now material, equity and common law are mingled or merged. The practicality of the matter is that in the circumstances of the dealings between the parties the law imposes a duty of confidence. For its breach a full range of remedies should be available as appropriate, no matter whether they originated in common law, equity or statute ... [A]pplying the foregoing approach as to the available range of remedies, we see no reason in principle why exemplary damages should not be awarded for actionable breach of confidence in a case where a compensatory award would not adequately reflect the gravity of the defendant's conduct."

---

41 (2003) 56 NSWLR 298.

42 For academic consideration in Australia, pre-*Digital Pulse*, of whether punitive damages are available for equitable wrongs see, for example, PM McDermott, "Exemplary Damages in Equity" (1995) 69 *Australian Law Journal* 773 at 774 (leaving the position open); L Aitken, "Developments in Equitable Compensation: Opportunity or Danger?" (1993) 67 *Australian Law Journal* 596 at 599–600 (against); ICF Spry, *The Principles of Equitable Remedies: Specific Performance, Injunctions and Equitable Damages* (6th ed, Lawbook Co., Sydney, 2001) at 636–637 (in favour); M Tilbury, *Civil Remedies* (Butterworths, Sydney, 1990) at [1014]–[1020] (in favour).

43 [1990] 3 NZLR 299.

44 [1990] 3 NZLR 299 at 301–302. In contrast, Somers J dissented on this aspect of the reasoning saying (at 302) "equity and penalty are strangers."

Following on from this in *Cook v Evatt (No 2)*,[45] Fisher J in the New Zealand High Court added punitive damages of NZ$5,000 to an account of profits of over NZ$20,000 for breach of fiduciary duty. Citing *Acquaculture*, he said, "[e]xemplary damages may be awarded whether the cause of action is founded in law or equity".[46]

In Canada in *Norberg v Wynrib*,[47] punitive damages were awarded for the tort of trespass to the person or, in the opinion of McLachlin J, for breach of fiduciary duty, where the claimant sued her defendant doctor for sexual assaults on her that she permitted in return for being prescribed drugs to which she was addicted.

As far as I am aware, the only consideration of this question by the English courts was by Lindsay J in *Douglas v Hello! Ltd (No 3)*.[48] While refusing punitive damages for breach of confidence on the facts – because the defendants' wrongful conduct had not been sufficiently outrageous – he said, after considering the House of Lords' decision in *Kuddus v Chief Constable of Leicestershire Constabulary*,[49] "I am content to assume, without deciding, that exemplary damages (or equity's equivalent) are available in respect of breach of confidence."[50]

Now to Australia and the facts of *Harris v Digital Pulse Pty Ltd*. The first and second defendants, Harris and Eden, were employees of the claimant company, Digital. They had secretly been carrying out marketing and web design work for various of Digital's clients in order to make profit for themselves and for the company they had set up called "Juice". They had, in other words, used their position to divert business away from the claimant so as to reap profit for themselves. This had been carefully planned and dishonestly carried out. What they had done constituted a clear breach of fiduciary duty in that they had allowed their self-interest to conflict with their duty of loyalty to Digital. Concurrently, and by reason of the same conduct, they had committed a breach of implied terms in their contract of employment. In addition, in more limited respects, Harris had committed a breach of confidence in misappropriating his employer's confidential information.

In an excellent judgment, Palmer J in the Supreme Court of New South Wales[51] held that, in respect of the breach of fiduciary duty, the claimant was entitled, at its election, to equitable compensation (of some $10,000) or an account of profits (of $13,119.51). The claimant elected for the latter. In

---

45 [1992] 1 NZLR 676.

46 *Cook v Evatt (No 2)*, above n 45 at 705.

47 (1992) 92 DLR (4th) 449. See also, for example: *Re MacDonald Estate* (1994) 95 Man R (2d) 123 (where the defendant was a lawyer); *Gerula v Flores* (1995) 126 DLR (4th) 506 (where the defendant was a doctor).

48 [2003] EWHC 786; [2003] 3 All ER 996. But English courts have looked at whether punitive damages can be given in respect of undertakings given to the court in seeking interim injunctions (see, for example, *Smith v Day* (1882) 21 Ch D 421 at 427–428): as the English Law Commission, Report No 247, *Aggravated, Exemplary and Restitutionary Damages* (1997) at [5.74] – [5.77] explained, this issue has been clouded by a lack of clear analysis.

49 [2001] UKHL 29; [2002] 2 AC 122. For the importance of this case see below 401.

50 *Douglas v Hello! Ltd (No 3)*, above n 48 at [273].

51 *Digital Pulse Pty Ltd v Harris* [2002] NSWSC 33; (2002) 40 ACSR 487.

addition, Palmer J held that Harris and Eden should each pay $10,000 punitive damages to Digital for their breach of fiduciary duty.

Palmer J's essential reasoning on punitive damages was that there was no precedent forbidding punitive damages for an equitable wrong; that it was unprincipled to deny such damages when they would be available for torts;[52] and that such damages were merited in the circumstances of the present case. He summarised the factual position as follows, "all of these circumstances, taken together, demonstrate deliberate wrongdoing for profit, in contumelious disregard of Digital's rights, deserving of special condemnation and punishment. To call a spade a spade, what Messrs Harris and Eden did was to defraud their employer of its valuable business opportunities".[53] His conclusion on the law was as follows:[54]

> "Consistency in the law requires that the availability of exemplary damages should be coextensive with its rationale. Where wrongful and reprehensible conduct calls for the manifest disapprobation of the community, where a punishment is called for to deter the wrongdoer and others of like mind from similar conduct and where something more than compensation is felt necessary to ameliorate the plaintiff's sense of outrage, then it should make no difference in the availability of exemplary damages that the court to which the plaintiff comes is a court of equity rather than a court of common law."

There was an appeal purely on the punitive damages issue. The Court of Appeal of New South Wales by a majority (Spigelman CJ and Heydon JA, Mason P dissenting) overturned the award of punitive damages. The judgments of Heydon JA and Mason P were very full and contained an admirable and scholarly examination of decisions in Australia and elsewhere and of the views of commentators.

In looking at the appellate judges' reasoning, an important initial point is that, despite the ongoing debate as to whether punitive damages are justified,[55]

---

52 *Digital Pulse Pty Ltd v Harris*, above n 51 at [29]–[31], [129], [137], [172], Palmer J also drew in aid that, under the *Corporations Act 2001* (Cth), the defendants could have been held liable, in an application by the Australian Securities & Investments Commission, to a civil penalty (recoverable for the benefit of the State) for breach of their statutory duty of loyalty to the company.

53 *Digital Pulse Pty Ltd v Harris*, above n 51 at [128].

54 *Digital Pulse Pty Ltd v Harris*, above n 51 at [170].

55 In *Digital Pulse Pty Ltd v Harris*, above n 51 at [141], Palmer J at first instance said, "[t]he question whether a court should be entitled to punish a defendant in any civil proceeding by the award of exemplary damages has, for more than two centuries, fuelled incessant and excoriating disputation among the jurisprudes". The modern literature on whether punitive damages are justified is extensive. See, for example, H Street, *Principles of the Law of Damages* (Sweet & Maxwell, London, 1962) at 34–36 (arguing that an empirical study of the effectiveness of punitive damages in attaining their stated goals is a necessity in order to decide whether they should be retained or abolished); A Ogus, *The Law of Damages* (Butterworths, London, 1973) at 32–34; SM Waddams, *The Law of Damages* (3rd ed, Canada Law Book, Toronto, 1997) at [11.10]–[11.100]; R Posner, *Economic Analysis of Law* (6th ed, Aspen, New York, 2003) at 192; H Collins, *The Law of Contract* (4th ed, LexisNexis, London, 2003) at 422–427; J Stone, "Double Count and Double Talk: The End of Exemplary Damages?" (1972) 46 *Australian Law Journal* 311; TJ Sullivan, "Punitive Damages in the Law of Contract: The Reality and the Illusion of Legal Change" (1977) 61 *Minnesota Law Review* 207; J Mallor and B Roberts, "Punitive Damages: Towards a Principled Approach"

the judges accepted that in Australia such damages are a valid and useful remedy. In other words, it was no part of the judges' reasoning to question the wisdom of having punitive damages. Off the agenda, therefore, was any conceivable argument that, in integrating common law and equity, it is the common law that has gone awry in ever allowing punitive damages.

The essence of Heydon JA's reasoning was that, while there was no binding precedent forbidding punitive damages for equitable wrongs, no past decisions have awarded such damages in equity. Nor has there been any equivalent notion of punishment operating under other labels or concepts in equity. The high rate of interest awarded against a defaulting fiduciary, the standard remedy of an account of profits, and the refusal in some cases of an allowance for work and skill are not independently designed to punish in the same way as punitive damages are. It would be a major change to the law for such damages to be awarded and such a major change should be implemented, if at all, by the Legislature or by the High Court of Australia. Indeed, to extend the ambit of punitive damages would be equivalent to, and would run into the same objections as, the creation of new crimes or criminal sanctions by the courts. It was not anomalous or irrational for punitive damages to be denied for breach of fiduciary duty, while being allowed for closely connected torts, such as deceit, because it is acceptable to have different remedies for different causes of action. In any event, to allow punitive damages would create a new anomaly because punitive damages are not available for breach of contract in Australia.[56]

(1980) 31 *Hastings Law Journal* 639; D Owen, "The Moral Foundations of Punitive Damages" (1989) 40 *Alabama Law Review* 705; B Chapman and M Trebilcock, "Punitive Damages: Divergence in Search of a Rationale" (1989) 40 *Alabama Law Review* 741; B Perlstein, "Crossing the Contract-Tort Boundary: An Economic Argument for the Imposition of Extra-compensatory Damages for Opportunistic Breach of Contract" (1992) 58 *Brooklyn Law Review* 877; NJ McBride, "A Case for Awarding Punitive Damages in Response to Deliberate Breaches of Contract" (1995) 24 *Anglo-American Law Review* 369; NJ McBride, 'Punitive Damages' in P Birks (ed), *Wrongs and Remedies in the Twenty-First Century* (Oxford University Press, Oxford, 1996) at 175–202; A Ogus, 'Exemplary Damages and Economic Analysis' in K Hawkins (ed), *The Human Face of Law: Essays in Honour of Donald Harris* (Oxford University Press, Oxford, 1997) at 85-102; J Edelman, *Gain-Based Damages* (Oxford University Press, Oxford, 2002) at chapter 1; A Beever, "The Structure of Aggravated and Exemplary Damages" (2003) 23 *Oxford Journal of Legal Studies* 87; EJ Weinrib, "Punishment and Disgorgement as Contract Remedies" (2003) 78 *Chicago-Kent Law Review* 55; S Smith, *Contract Theory* (Oxford University Press, Oxford, 2004) at 417–420; S Todd, "A New Zealand Perspective on Exemplary Damages" (2004) *Common Law World Review* 255. For a detailed examination of the arguments, see English Law Commission, Report No 247, *Aggravated, Exemplary and Restitutionary Damages* (1997) at part V.

56   This was apparently accepted by counsel in the New South Wales Court of Appeal: see *Harris v Digital Pulse Pty Ltd* (2003) 56 NSWLR 298 at [28], [294] (but cf [267]). It must be doubted, however, whether there is binding High Court of Australia authority for that proposition. Griffith CJ's comments in *Butler v Fairclough* (1917) 23 CLR 78 at 89 were obiter dicta; and in *Gray v Motor Accident Commission* (1998) 196 CLR 1 at 6–7 the High Court talked of no punitive damages for breach of contract as an "apparent rule". In *Hospitality Group Pty Ltd v Australian Rugby Union Ltd* (2001) 110 FCR 157 at [142] the Federal Court relied on the House of Lords in *Addis v Gramophone Co* [1909] AC 488 but that is not binding in Australia especially since the High Court in *Uren v John Fairfax & Sons Pty Limited* (1966) 117 CLR 118 established that Australian law should go its own way on punitive damages from that in England.

Punitive damages should not be available for a breach of fiduciary duty when they are not available for a breach of contract comprising the same conduct.

Spigelman CJ agreed with Heydon JA's reasons and conclusion, apart from the latter's reliance on the argument that punitive damages were a criminal sanction. He preferred to express his conclusion more narrowly and cautiously by saying that, on these facts, there was a closer analogy between breach of fiduciary duty and breach of contract than between breach of fiduciary duty and tort. "[T]he refusal to develop the law should be confined to cases of the character now before the Court ... There may be other cases in equity in which a tort analogy is more appropriate."[57] Earlier he had said, "it is, in my opinion, unnecessary and undesirable to decide this case on the basis that a punitive monetary award can never be awarded in equity. Remedial flexibility is a characteristic of equity jurisprudence".[58]

Mason P, in his dissenting judgment, largely supported Palmer J's reasoning. The crux of his judgment was that there is no precedent laying down that punitive damages cannot be awarded for breach of fiduciary duty and that consistency and coherence in the law dictates that they should be so available. There is a close analogy between tort and breach of fiduciary duty and it is far closer than that between contractual and fiduciary duties. As punitive damages can be awarded in tort, there is no good reason to deny them in equity in a situation where there would otherwise be remedial inadequacy.

The most important point to emerge from the *Digital Pulse* case for this chapter is that none of the three judges took the anti-fusion view embodied in the explanation in *Meagher, Gummow and Lehane's Equity* of the "fusion fallacy". That reads as follows:[59]

> "The fusion fallacy involves the administration of a remedy, for example common law damages for breach of fiduciary duty, not previously available either at law or in equity, or the modification of principles in one branch of the jurisdiction by concepts which are imported from the other and thus are foreign, for example by holding that the existence of a duty of care in tort may be tested by asking whether the parties concerned are in fiduciary relations. Those who commit the fusion fallacy announce or assume the creation by the Judicature system of a new body of law containing elements of law and equity but in character quite different from its components."

Applying that anti-fusion view, the answer to the question in *Harris v Digital Pulse Pty Ltd* should have been simple and straightforward. Punitive damages are a common law remedy. Breach of fiduciary duty is an equitable wrong. Pre-1873 the courts could not have awarded punitive damages (or their equivalent) for a breach of fiduciary duty. Therefore they cannot award them post-1873. To do so would involve "the administration of a remedy, for example common law damages for breach of fiduciary duty, not previously available either at law or in equity."

---

57   *Harris v Digital Pulse Pty Ltd*, above n 56 at [44].
58   *Harris v Digital Pulse Pty Ltd*, above n 56 at [4].
59   *Meagher, Gummow and Lehane's Equity*, at [2–105].

Despite his extra-judicial authorship, even Heydon JA did not seek to rely on that anti-fusion view. It is true that most of his judgment was concerned to show that no equivalent to punitive damages has been awarded for equitable wrongs and that to allow this would involve an unwarranted major change to the law. But if one is to take *Meagher, Gummow and Lehane's Equity* at face value, Heydon JA did enter "forbidden territory" by carefully considering, rather than dismissing out of hand, the argument that, as punitive damages can be awarded for the tort of deceit and as deceit and breach of fiduciary duty are closely analogous, so it would be anomalous to deny that punitive damages can be available for breach of fiduciary duty. His answer to this argument was not to say that one cannot reason from common law to equity. Rather he said that there was no anomaly in relation to – or, as one might otherwise put it, no suffi-ciently close analogy between – the tort of deceit and breach of fiduciary duty. He pointed to differences between the two causes of action in terms of burden of proof, tests of breach and causation and remoteness, stigma, and the effect on insurance. He concluded, "it is not irrational to maintain the existence of different remedies for different causes of action having different threshold requirements and different purposes. The resulting differences are not neces-sarily 'anomalous'."[60]

While I would disagree with the details of that comparison and the conclusion drawn, I would applaud the methodology. Taking fusion seriously involves careful analysis of whether there is, or is not, inconsistency between the remedies for common law and equitable wrongs. It would be unacceptable and irrational to rule out that investigation by reliance on the dogma that to allow punitive damages for an equitable wrong is a fusion fallacy.

At the other extreme – and as clarified by Mason P – no one, as far as I am aware, is suggesting that there must be an automatic and unthinking applica-tion of common law concepts to equitable wrongs and vice versa. Such an unthinking merger has not been dictated by the fusion of the courts. Rather, reasoning by analogy across the jurisdictional divide has been rendered possible and desirable by the reform of the court structure. Taking fusion seriously requires nothing more than the eradication of inconsistencies between law and equity. If, on careful analysis, what at first sight may appear to be inconsistencies can be rationally defended, then there is no inconsistency to be eradicated. In Dr Edelman's words, the compelling case is for "fusion by analogy" not "automatic fusion".[61]

It is submitted, therefore, that even Heydon JA did not adopt Meagher, Gummow and Lehane's anti-fusion view. As Edelman has expressed it, "although Heydon JA did not explicitly discuss ... fusion by analogy, he proceeded on the basis that development of equity by analogy with the common law was clearly possible."[62]

It should be added here that Mason P's judgment contains a powerful and judicious explanation, with which I would entirely agree, of why Meagher, Gummow and Lehane's "fusion fallacy" is itself "fallacious and historically

---

60   *Harris v Digital Pulse Pty Ltd*, above n 56 at [398].
61   J Edelman, "A 'Fusion Fallacy' Fallacy?" (2003) 119 *Law Quarterly Review* 375 at 377.
62   J Edelman, "A 'Fusion Fallacy' Fallacy?", above n 61 at 377.

unsound".[63] Putting to one side the view that no one adheres to – that the Judicature Acts 1873–75 by their statutory wording dictated the substantive merger of common law and equity – Mason P clarified that the essence of Meagher, Gummow and Lehane's view is that equity cannot borrow from the common law and vice versa. Mason P then continued, "in terms [Meagher, Gummow and Lehane's view] condemns law and equity to the eternal separation of two parallel lines, ignoring the history of the two 'systems' both before and after the passing of the *Judicature Act 1873*. And it treats the *permission* of the statute to fuse administration as if it were an enacted *prohibition* against a judge exercising the fused administration from applying doctrines and remedies found historically in one 'system' in a case whose roots may be found in the other 'system'."[64] And later he said, "since fusion of administration, judges have tended to use similar forms of judicial method whether administering law, equity or both ... Inevitably and appropriately, *unnecessary* barriers of separation have been broken down. Analogies have been drawn between rules operating in the two systems in the interests of coherence and simplicity. Distinctions with nothing but history to support them have, at times, been deliberately ironed out or conveniently overlooked as doctrines are passed from generation to generation."[65]

Turning from the most important general point on fusion to the details of the judges' reasoning – and, in particular, to whether fusion by analogy should here have resulted in an award of punitive damages – I would agree with Palmer J and Mason P that there is a close analogy between dishonestly committed torts, such as deceit, and the type of dishonestly committed breach of fiduciary duty in issue in this case. Both concern the dishonestly committed breach of an imposed duty and, as in many typical cases triggering punitive damages, the defendants had cynically committed the breach of fiduciary duty in order to reap a profit. The analogy is reflected in the fact that one might loosely describe what the defendants had done as an equitable fraud[66] which matches up with common law fraud embodied in the tort of deceit. If punitive damages are a useful weapon in the armoury of judges to punish and deter dishonestly committed torts, they must surely also be a useful weapon to punish and deter dishonestly committed equitable wrongs.

As the English Law Commission said, in passages cited with approval by Palmer J and Mason P:[67]

---

63   *Harris v Digital Pulse Pty Ltd* (2003) 56 NSWLR 298 at [136]. Mason P expressed himself as in entire agreement with a passage from M Tilbury, *Civil Remedies* (Butterworths, Sydney, 1990) at [1019], which includes the following illuminating remarks, "[b]ut the further conclusion ... explicit in the 'fusion fallacy', that in a fused jurisdiction it is impossible, for all time, to have a 'fused law' is both a non-sequitur and hard to justify in principle and policy. It is a non-sequitur because the proposition that the Judicature Acts do not *authorize* fusion of principles, cannot lead to the conclusion that such a fusion is *prohibited*. In short, there is no fallacy." Cf M Tilbury, "Fallacy or Fusion? Fusion in a Judicature World" (2003) 26 *University of New South Wales Law Journal* 357.

64   *Harris v Digital Pulse Pty Ltd*, above n 63 at [140] (my italics).

65   *Harris v Digital Pulse Pty Ltd*, above n 63 at [148].

66   *Meagher, Gummow and Lehane's Equity*, at chapter 12, esp [12–050].

67   English Law Commission, Report No 247, *Aggravated, Exemplary and Restitutionary Damages* (1997) at [5.55].

"We consider it unsatisfactory to perpetuate the historical divide between common law and equity, unless there is very good reason to do so ... Indeed, we can see good reason for allowing punitive damages to be recovered against, for example, the dishonest trustee who acts in breach of his fiduciary duty or the person who dishonestly abuses another's confidence. Thus if, as we propose, punitive damages are awardable in respect of the (common law) tort of deceit, it would be anomalous if analogously wrongful conduct could not also give rise to an award, just because the cause of action originated in equity."

Part of Heydon JA's reasoning against this was based on precedent: that it would be a very major and radical step forward to permit such damages for breach of fiduciary duty so that this should be implemented only by the High Court of Australia or by legislation. This was to take a narrow view of how reasoning by analogy can move judge-made law forward, which is further reflected in Spigelman CJ's argument that the analogical reasoning advocated would involve using "high level"[68] principle which is contrary to the common law judicial method. With respect, the majority judges were here adopting a needlessly stunted view of principled development of judge-made law. Once one accepts that there is a clear analogy between dishonestly committed torts and dishonestly committed equitable wrongs, the step forward does not seem such a radical one and, with no precedent directly forbidding it, would seem within the interpretative reach, by the normal development and application of principle, of the lower courts.

One should also note that Heydon JA's description of the distinctions between the tort of deceit and breach of fiduciary duty[69] does not rationalise why punishment is available for one but not the other. Moreover, as the tort of deceit might be regarded as having special rules based on the inevitable dishonesty involved, Heydon JA should have gone on to compare other torts (all of which can trigger punitive damages) with breach of fiduciary duty. For example, the facts of *Digital Pulse* might be regarded as close to the tort of conversion (where, for example, money or goods are stolen) or one of the economic torts, such as inducing breach of contract or conspiracy. And what about the tort of negligence causing pure economic loss, which again, if committed outrageously, can trigger punitive damages?[70] Had the defendants in the *Digital Pulse* case outrageously failed to comply with their fiduciary duties of care and skill, it would have been very odd for punitive damages to be available for the tort of negligence but not for the equivalent breach of fiduciary duty.

It is interesting to speculate whether Heydon JA would find objections, in respect of precedent, if the same question were to face him now that he has

---

68   *Harris v Digital Pulse Pty Ltd*, above n 63 at [12]–[13].

69   See above 397–398.

70   *Lamb v Cotogno* (1987) 164 CLR 1; *Coloca v BP Australia Ltd* [1992] 2 VR 441; *Ali v Hartley Poynton Ltd* (2002) 20 ACLC 1006; *A v Bottrill* [2002] UKPC 44; [2003] 1 AC 449. Heydon JA did consider, at [395], the argument that as the employer could be sued in the tort of negligence for which punitive damages could be awarded, so the employer should be able to recover punitive damages against an employee. However, as it was so framed he was able to dismiss the argument as lacking logic.

been promoted to the High Court of Australia. Certainly to push such a development off to the Legislature would represent a very narrow view of what is permissible judicial development of Australian law.[71]

With respect, a much more substantial objection than that of precedent (or the similar objection that analogical reasoning should be narrowly confined) was Heydon JA's argument that to allow punitive damages for equitable wrongs would create a new anomaly because precedent forbids punitive damages for breach of contract. This was also at the very heart of Spigelman CJ's judgment. That is, he thought that there was a closer analogy on these facts between breach of fiduciary duty and breach of contract than between breach of fiduciary duty and tort.[72]

In taking fusion seriously, it is precisely this type of argument that is central and must be carefully considered. It is an argument for coherence in the law, across the common law and equity divide, but one which sees the coherent position as one denying punitive damages rather than permitting them. That is, it puts breach of contract and breach of fiduciary duty on one side of the line and torts on the other.

One answer to this, as forcefully adopted by Mason P, is to meet the objection head on by arguing that the closer analogy is between tort and equitable wrongs, essentially because the basis of the fiduciary obligation is imposed rather than promise-based. In Mason P's words:[73]

"The contract analogy is ... a weak one... There are some similarities between fiduciary duties and contractual relationships, but the differences predominate. Most notably, fiduciary obligations are imposed by law (like torts) and they arise out of a relationship and/or conduct, as distinct from merely giving

---

71 For his extra-judicial views on the role of judges in developing the law, see "Judicial Activism and the Death of the Rule of Law" (2003) *Quadrant* 9.

72 Spigelman CJ, *Harris v Digital Pulse Pty Ltd* (2003) 56 NSWLR 298 at [57]–[61], raised the interesting question of the link between the unenforceability of contractual penalty clauses and the refusal to award punitive damages for breach of contract. In the context of *Digital Pulse* his argument (linked to his view that it would be anomalous to award punitive damages for breach of fiduciary duty given their unavailability for breach of contract) was that it would be incompatible to allow punitive damages for breach of fiduciary duty when a clause in the employment contract, imposing a penalty for the breach in question, would be unenforceable. Mason P replied, at [187], that this was already tolerated, and therefore irrelevant to the argument, in respect of a contractual penalty clause for a breach that concurrently constituted a tort for which punitive damages could be awarded. In the long-term, however, it is submitted that coherence does dictate that if one were to allow punitive damages for breach of contract one ought also to uphold some penalty clauses. See A Burrows, *Remedies for Torts and Breach of Contract* (3rd ed, Oxford University Press, Oxford, 2004) at 444–445, 451. For the contrary view that there is no good reason to link the purpose of an award of damages with agreed damages, see TA Downes, 'Rethinking Penalty Clauses' in P Birks (ed), *Wrongs and Remedies in the Twenty-First Century* (Oxford University Press, Oxford, 1996) at 249, 265–266.

73 *Harris v Digital Pulse Pty Ltd*, above n 72 at [182]–[184]. See somewhat similarly the views on fiduciary law of the New Zealand Court of Appeal in *Chirnside v Fay* [2004] NZCA 111 at [51]. "Fiduciary law is not concerned with private ordering. That is, it is not the function of fiduciary law to mediate between the various interests of parties who are dealing with each other. That is for contract law. Fiduciary law serves to support the integrity and utility of relationships in which the role of one party is perceived to be the service of the interests of the other. It does so by imposing a specific duty of loyalty."

effect to the negotiated private arrangement that is a contract. And there is no principle of efficient breach underpinning remedies for breach of fiduciary relationship: indeed the deterrent function of remedies like account of profits shows that equity repudiates the type of efficiency encompassed in the contractual notion of efficient breach."

In support of Mason P, it can be added that, even if one says, as Spigelman CJ does, that an undertaking by the fiduciary to act in another's interests lies at the heart of a fiduciary relationship, and even if one equates such an undertaking with a contractual promise or agreement so that both could be regarded as voluntary or consent-based, the basis of the precise fiduciary duty in question would still have to be explained. And it is strongly arguable that the no conflict duty (one must not allow self-interest to conflict with duty to act in another's interests) is better viewed as imposed rather than voluntary.[74]

Moreover, Mason P is surely correct to indicate that the deterring of a breach of duty would always be regarded as a good policy in relation to fiduciary relationships whereas, with arm's length commercial parties – who can go into the market to minimise their losses – deterrence of breach may be regarded as bad in cutting across the duty to mitigate.

In the long-term, however, it is submitted that the real answer to the majority's "new anomaly" argument is that the law ought to move to the position whereby, albeit exceptionally, punitive damages are available for breach of contract. In so far as punitive damages are regarded as a valid and useful remedy, there is no good reason why they should be excluded from the realm of contract. At least in English law, two recent developments support this and suggest that the denial of punitive damages in *Addis v Gramophone Co*[75] must be revisited.

The first was the decision of the House of Lords in *Attorney-General v Blake*[76] to the effect that restitution, through an account of profits, can be awarded, albeit exceptionally, for breach of contract. Although punishment is a more extreme remedial response to a wrong than restitution, the

---

74   There is an extensive literature on fiduciary duties. See for example PD Finn, *Fiduciary Obligations* (Law Book Company, Sydney, 1977); JC Shepherd, *The Law of Fiduciaries* (Carswell, Toronto, 1981); JC Shepherd, "Towards a Unifying Concept of Fiduciary Relationships" (1981) 97 *Law Quarterly Review* 51; PD Finn, 'The Fiduciary Principle' in TG Youdan (ed), *Equity, Fiduciaries and Trusts* (Oxford University Press, Oxford, 1989) at chapter 1; R Flannigan, 'The Fiduciary in Context: An Overview' in P Birks (ed), *Privacy and Loyalty* (Oxford University Press, Oxford, 1997) at chapter 11; L Hoyano, 'The Flight to Fiduciary Haven' in P Birks (ed), *Privacy and Loyalty,* at chapter 8; P Birks, "The Content of Fiduciary Obligation" (2002) 16 *Trust Law International* 34. Some of these writings deal with, or touch on, the basis of the fiduciary duties, for example Finn's classic 1989 article talks of duties "*imposed* on a person in his voluntary or consensual relationships with another" (my italics); and P Birks (2002) 16 *Trust Law International* 34 at 51, writes, "[t]he events which create the compound fiduciary obligation are always going to be a sub-set of those which create any special duty of positive care. The event will be either, or both, a contract or an entry into a relationship of peculiar proximity, for instance by the voluntary assumption of responsibility."

75   [1909] AC 488. For the position in Australia, see above n 56.

76   [2001] 1 AC 268.

importance of *Blake* for punitive damages is its recognition that (exceptionally) a substantial monetary remedy that is non-compensatory is appropriate for a breach of contract.

The second was the decision of the House of Lords in *Kuddus v Chief Constable of Leicestershire Constabulary.*[77] This removed the former "cause of action" restriction on punitive damages for torts. Although their Lordships did not mention breach of contract, the removal of the "cause of action" test for torts clearly leads on to the question whether it is satisfactory to rule out punitive damages just because the cause of action is breach of contract rather than tort. As Lord Nicholls said in the *Kuddus* case, "the availability of exemplary damages should be co-extensive with its rationale".[78] The rationale is the desire to punish and deter conduct that constitutes an outrageous disregard of the claimant's rights. The source of those rights whether in contract or tort should not be decisive.

While it may be more difficult to envisage cases of breach of contract, rather than torts, in which an award of punitive damages would be merited, the same considerations which support the award of punitive damages in a tort case – deterrence, for example – may equally apply in an exceptional case of breach of contract. This may be illustrated by reference to the facts of *Whiten v Pilot Insurance Co,*[79] which was the case clearly establishing that in Canada punitive damages may in certain circumstances be awarded for a breach of contract even where no tortious conduct is involved. An accidental fire destroyed the claimant's home, and she claimed under the insurance policy issued to her by the defendant company. However, the defendant alleged that the claimant had started the fire deliberately and paid hardly any of the sum due under the policy. The allegation of arson was contradicted by the local fire chief and by the company's own expert investigator and initial expert; it was made in bad faith (and pursued through an 8 week trial) in order to try to force the claimant, who was in a very poor financial position, into an unfairly low settlement. This was held by the Supreme Court of Canada to justify an award of $1 million punitive damages. Although there had been no tort in addition to the breach of contract, the defendant had committed an "actionable wrong" in breaching the contractual duty to act in good faith which, as the other party to an insurance contract, it owed to the claimant. In such a case, punitive damages are an appropriate response, and it appears unduly restrictive to allow them only if a tort has also been committed.

On the face of it, the question of whether punitive damages should be permitted for breach of contract has nothing to do with the fusion of common law and equity. This is a battle purely within the common law. However, beneath the surface, its importance to the issue in *Digital v Harris Pulse Pty Ltd* must not be underestimated. For once it is accepted that punitive damages should be available for all common law wrongs, there appears to be no rational

---

77 [2001] UKHL 29; [2002] 2 AC 122.

78 *Kuddus v Chief Constable of Leicestershire Constabulary* [2001] UKHL 29; [2002] 2 AC 122 at [65].

79 (2002) 209 DLR (4th) 257. For a useful casenote, see G Fridman "Punitive Damages for Breach of Contract – A Canadian Innovation" (2003) 119 *Law Quarterly Review* 20.

counter-argument left for denying punitive damages for equitable wrongs. In other words, fusion by analogy would, at that point, indisputably mean that punitive damages should be available for equitable wrongs. All that would be left to resist that development would be either an assertion, not borne out by careful analysis, that breach of fiduciary duty is so fundamentally different from *both* torts and breach of contract as to merit different remedies, including a denial of punishment;[80] or the anti-fusion view expressed in *Meagher, Gummow and Lehane's Equity* which none of the judges in *Digital Pulse*, including Heydon JA, were willing to apply.

CONCLUSION

Standing back from the detail, there were three main arguments against the availability of punitive damages in *Harris v Digital Pulse*: fusion fallacy, precedent, and the creation of a new anomaly. While the majority disagreed with Mason P on the second and third arguments, the major importance of the decision for the theme of this chapter is that none of the judges, including Heydon JA, applied the anti-fusion view embodied in Meagher, Gummow and Lehane's "fusion fallacy". Acceptance of that argument would have rendered careful consideration of the second and third arguments unnecessary, and Mason P expressly subjected the fusion fallacy to a withering attack as itself being a fallacy.

The lifeblood of judicial law-making is reasoning by analogy: the development of principle by treating like cases alike. There is no good reason to restrict the flow of that lifeblood by restricting analogical development to the separate limbs of equity and common law as if they do not belong to the same body of general law.

---

80   Speaking for the minority in *Canson Enterprises Ltd v Boughton & Co* (1991) 85 DLR (4th) 129, McLachlin J said at 154, in a passage approved in *Youyang Pty Ltd v Minter Ellison Morris Fletcher* (2003) 212 CLR 484, "[m]y first concern with proceeding by analogy with tort is that it overlooks the unique foundation and goals of equity. The basis of the fiduciary obligation and the rationale for equitable compensation are distinct from the tort of negligence and contract. In negligence and contract the parties are taken to be independent and equal actors, concerned primarily with their own self-interest ... The essence of a fiduciary relationship, by contrast, is that one party pledges herself to act in the best interest of the other. The fiduciary relationship has trust, not self-interest, at its core, and when breach occurs, the balance favours the person wronged ... In short, equity is concerned, not only to compensate the plaintiff, but to enforce the trust which is at its heart." With respect, this is an over simplification. The essence of many contractual and some tortious duties arising out of relationships, is that one party should act in the best interests of the other. For example, on the facts of *Harris v Digital Pulse Pty Ltd* there were contractual, as well as fiduciary, duties of loyalty. But even if one were to accept McLachlin J's distinction, it would not justify different remedies and certainly it provides no justification for punishment being available at common law but not in equity (indeed McLachlin J herself accepted that there can be punitive damages for breach of fiduciary duty in *Norberg v Wynrib* (1992) 92 DLR (4th) 449).

Appendix

EXTRACT FROM "WE DO THIS AT COMMON LAW BUT THAT IN EQUITY" (2002) 22 OXFORD JOURNAL OF LEGAL STUDIES 1 AT 4

According to the anti-fusion school of thought, the Supreme Court of Judicature Acts 1873–5 fused the administration of the courts but did not fuse the substantive law. Common law and equity sit alongside one another. Moreover, they can happily sit alongside one another. Clashes or conflicts or inconsistencies between them are very rare. Where they exist, and, in so far as they are not resolved by the more specific provisions of the 1873–5 Acts, they are resolved by the general provision in section 11 of the 1873 Act which lays down that "equity shall prevail".[81] This is not to say that common law or equity is frozen in the position it was in before 1873. Rather common law and equity can independently develop incrementally. But one should not develop the law by reasoning from common law to equity or vice versa. To do so would cut across the historical underpinnings of the two areas; and a harmonised rule or principle that has features of both common law and equity, but cannot be said clearly to be one or the other, would be unacceptable.

In contrast, the fusion school of thought argues that the fusion of the administration of the courts brought about by the 1873–5 Acts, while not dictating the fusion of the substantive law, rendered this, for the first time, a realistic possibility. While there are areas where common law and equity can happily sit alongside one another, there are many examples of inconsistencies between them. It is important to remove the inconsistencies thereby producing a coherent or harmonised law. In developing the law it is legitimate for the courts to reason from common law to equity and vice versa. A harmonised rule or principle that has features of both common law and equity is at the very least acceptable and, depending on the rule or principle in question, may represent the best way for the law to develop.

---

81   This is now contained in *Supreme Court Act 1981* (UK), s 49 (1) which reads as follows:
"Subject to the provisions of this or any other Act, every court exercising jurisdiction in England or Wales in any civil cause or matter shall continue to administer law and equity on the basis that, wherever there is any conflict or variance between the rules of equity and the rules of the common law with reference to the same matter, the rules of equity shall prevail."

16

Account of Profits for Common Law Wrongs

MITCHELL MCINNES

"Considered as a matter of principle, it is difficult to see why equity required the wrongdoer to account for all his profits … whereas the common law's response was to require a wrongdoer merely to pay a reasonable fee for the use of another's land or goods. In all these cases rights of property were infringed. This difference in remedial response appears to have arisen simply as an accident of history."[1]

Like much of *Attorney General v Blake*, the preceding quotation is controversial. Lord Nicholls conveys two propositions. First, as a matter of *description*, he asserts that while equity may compel a wrongdoer to "account for all of his profits," the common law merely requires the payment of "a reasonable fee". And second, by way of *explanation*, he attributes that difference to a simple "accident of history", rather than to the operation of any principle.

The purpose of this chapter is to assess those propositions. The exercise begins in Part I with a brief overview of accounting. Part II then defines various measures of relief with a view to isolating awards that entitle the claimant to either a reasonable hiring fee or an account of profits. Part III considers the extent to which such awards are in fact available in response to legal wrongs. And finally, Part IV critically examines several theories as to why victims of wrongdoing traditionally were treated more generously in equity than in law.

The scope of discussion is selective. Although Lord Nicholls' comments in *Attorney General v Blake* provide the jumping off point, this chapter is not concerned with the availability of gain-based relief for breach of contract. A great deal has already been written on that issue.[2] Consistent with the earlier quotation, the focus falls instead upon remedies that arise in response to the infringement of property rights.

---

1   *Attorney General v Blake* [2001] 1 AC 268 at 280.
2   A small sampling includes S Hedley, "Very Much the Wrong People" [2000] 4 *Web Journal of Current Legal Issues*; J Edelman, "Profits and Gains From Breach of Contract" [2001] *Lloyds Maritime and Commercial Law Quarterly* 9; S Worthington and R Goode, 'Commercial Law: Confining the Remedial Boundaries' in D Hayton (ed), *Law's Futures: British Legal Developments in the 21st Century* (Hart Publishing, Oxford, 2000) at 281; M McInnes, "Gain-Based Relief for Breach of Contract" (2001) 35 *Canadian Business Law Journal* 72.

ACCOUNT

The history of account

The history of account begins, interestingly, in law. The writ of *praecipe quod reddat* evolved during the 13th century to compel a person to render an account.[3] Initially, however, that writ was of very limited scope. It initially emerged as a check upon the fidelity of a bailiff, who was charged with the responsibility of administering a manorial estate.[4] Within a few decades, it expanded to similarly monitor the activities of a guardian in socage (who was responsible for safeguarding a ward's inheritance)[5] and a receiver (who was required to protect and return property to its rightful owner). Thereafter, the writ continued to unfold, in the usual manner, through the generous use of benign fictions. It applied, for instance, to a person who usurped the position of a bailiff or a guardian in socage, and to a person who acquired money from the claimant in exchange for a consideration that wholly failed. While not technically within any of the nominate categories of accountant, a constructive bailiff, a constructive guardian or a constructive receiver might be ordered to open his books and explain his finances.[6]

Despite those extensions, however, the common law writ of account remained profoundly flawed: a *monstrum horrendum*.[7] Some of the defects were curable. Principles were manipulated to preclude wager of law,[8] and Parliament intervened to allow the writ to be used by[9] or against[10] a personal representative. Other difficulties, largely procedural in nature, nevertheless

---

3   Praecipe writs typically had a proprietary flavour insofar as they compelled the defendant to restore a parcel of land (writ of right), a chattel (detinue) or a sum of money (debt), SJ Stoljar, "The Transformations of Account" (1964) 80 *Law Quarterly Review* 208 at 209. Although an account is not a proprietary concept, it fell easily within the language of the praecipe writ and consequently was employed in that form, CHS Fifoot, *The History and Sources of the Common Law* (Stevens & Sons, London, 1949) at 268.

4   As overseers of manorial finances, bailiffs were constantly exposed to temptation. Many succumbed. Indeed, one enterprising bailiff went so far as to draft a "how to" manual for "cooking accounts", CHS Fifoot, *The History and Sources of the Common Law*, above n 3 at 268.

5   That extension was achieved through the *Statute of Marlborough* (1267) 52 Henry III, c 17. The account was, however, limited to lands held in socage (that is, situations in which the burden upon the tenant consisted of neither military nor spiritual service, but rather, usually, payment of a fixed rent to the lord). An account was not available against a guardian in chivalry, which arose when a ward inherited land held by knight service (in which case the tenant was required to provide knights to the lord), EO Belsheim, "The Old Action of Account" (1932) 45 *Harvard Law Review* 466 at 476-477.

6   CHS Fifoot, *The History and Sources of the Common Law*, above n 3 at 271-272.

7   R Meagher, JD Heydon, M Leeming, *Meagher Gummow and Lehane's Equity: Doctrines and Remedies* (4th ed, Butterworths, Sydney, 2002) at 869.

8   *Anon* YB 14 Ed III (RS) 172; CHS Fifoot, *The History and Sources of the Common Law*, above n 3 at 273.

9   *Statute of Westminster* (1285) 13 Edward I, c 11; (1350) 25 Edward III, c 5; (1356) 31 Edward III, c 11.

10   *Administration of Justice Act* (1705) 4 & 5 Anne, c 16, s 27; *Core's Case* (1537) 1 Dyer 20a; 73 ER 42.

proved fatal. The adversarial nature of the jurisdiction generally created obstacles in cases involving multiple parties. And even in relatively simple cases, legal accounting cumbrously required three steps. A court first had to be convinced that the defendant was someone who could be held accountable. Court-appointed auditors would then examine the records and determine the extent to which a balance was owing in the claimant's favour. And finally, if the claimant did in fact enjoy a favourable balance, an action for recovery would lie against the defendant in debt. Typical of the age, the process was laden with elaborate technicalities from start to finish.

True to its nature, equity devised a system better suited to the needs of justice. The inquisitorial nature of the jurisdiction flexibly accommodated the resolution of multiple, inter-related claims. Moreover, whereas legal accounts were conducted by court-appointed auditors, equitable accounts were often performed in-house by the masters in chancery. Most significantly of all, the Chancellor was, in contrast to his colleagues in law, entitled to receive evidence from the parties and to compel discovery under oath. Those procedures substantially enhanced the claimant's ability to "scrape the defendant's conscience … closely and painfully" in an effort to discern the true state of affairs.[11] The result was perhaps predictable. From humble origins in the 14th century, the equitable account became commonplace in the 17th century, and by the middle of the 18th century effectively superseded its legal counterpart.[12] That remained true even during those periods when, owing to a general dilatoriness in chancery, the process of equitable accounting slowed to a snail's pace.[13]

The purpose of accounting

The immediate function of an account, either at law or in equity, is to expose the defendant's financial affairs insofar as they pertain to the claimant. In that sense, the process of accounting, like the process of tracing,[14] is neither a cause of action nor a remedy, but rather a preliminary exercise. The claimant typically seeks an account in order to establish an evidentiary basis for the imposition of some form of liability upon the defendant.

There is a tendency to assume that an account must be directed toward some form of gain-based liability. And indeed, the focus of this paper is on the *account of profits* that leads to an order compelling disgorgement of a wrongful

---

11   CHS Fifoot, *The History and Sources of the Common Law* (Stevens & Sons, London, 1949) at 275.

12   *Wood's Institutes* (9th ed, 1763) Book IV, chapter IV at 553. While the legal account has never been formally abolished, simple cases were eventually taken over by other processes, first debt and later indebitatus assumpsit, P Birks, 'Restitution for Wrongs' in EJH Schrage, *Unjust Enrichment: The Comparative Legal History of the Law of Restitution* (2nd ed, Duncker & Humblot, Berlin, 1999) at 177-178; S Stoljar, "The Transformations of Account" (1964) 80 *Law Quarterly Review* 203 at 223-224.

13   The last great case in legal accounting, *Godfrey v Saunders*, arose because the claimant, having waited twelve years for an equitable account to bear fruit, came before the King's Bench in the desperate hope of securing relief before his death: (1770) 3 Wils KB 73; 95 ER 940.

14   L Smith, *The Law of Tracing* (Oxford University Press, Oxford, 1997); *Boscawen v Bajwa* [1996] 1 WLR 328 at 334; *Foskett v McKeown* [2001] 1 AC 102 at 113, 128-129.

benefit. Very often, however, an account is a prelude to compensatory relief. For instance, at law, a bailiff, a guardian in socage or a receiver typically became subject to an obligation to financially repair a loss. Likewise in equity, while trustees may be required to give up wrongful gains, they are also responsible for improper shortfalls. If they failed to obtain value for the trust, the account will be surcharged; if they disposed of assets in breach, the account will be falsified. In either event, the trustees are liable to make up the difference.[15]

The traditional scope of equitable accounting

Just as legal accounting pertains to disputes arising in law, equitable accounting often pertains to issues arising in equity. Consequently, for example, a trustee may be required to account to a beneficiary with respect to trust funds, and a life tenant may be required to account to a remainderman in connection with equitable waste.[16] As a result of equity's auxiliary jurisdiction, however, an equitable account may also be invoked in resolution of *some* legal matters. Unfortunately, the precise scope of that auxiliary jurisdiction has never been settled.[17] While it previously was said that an account would be ordered only as an ancillary to injunctive relief,[18] that restriction no longer applies. Likewise, while it has been said that equity will not intervene in simple situations where the legal process would be equally effective and convenient,[19] it has been questioned whether that requirement will ever be satisfied.[20]

Against that backdrop, *Meagher, Gummow & Lehane* identifies eight situations in which an equitable account has been ordered in aid of a legal right.[21] While the object of the exercise typically is to determine the "indebt-

---

15   For an excellent examination of accounting in the trust context, see R Chambers, 'Liability' in P Birks and A Pretto (eds), *Breach of Trust* (Hart Publishing, Oxford, 2002) at 1.

16   *London Chatham & Dover Railway Co v South Eastern Railway Co* [1892] 1 Ch 120 at 138.

17   *North Eastern Railway Co v Martin* (1848) 2 Ph 758 at 762; 41 ER 1136 at 1138 (it is "impossible with precision to lay down rules or establish definitions as to cases in which it may be proper for this Court to exercise this jurisdiction").

18   *Smith v London and South Western Railway Co* (1854) Kay 408; 69 ER 173; *Price's Patent Candle Co Ltd v Bauwen's Patent Candle Co Ltd* (1858) 4 K & J 727; 70 ER 302.

19   *Taff Vale Railway Co v Nixon* (1847) 1 HLC 111; 9 ER 695.

20   R Meagher, JD Heydon, M Leeming, *Meagher Gummow and Lehane's Equity: Doctrines and Remedies* (4th ed, Butterworths, Sydney, 2002) at 870-871; SJ Stoljar, "The Transformations of Account" (1964) 80 *Law Quarterly Review* 208 at 223.

21   R Meagher, JD Heydon, M Leeming, *Meagher Gummow and Lehane's Equity: Doctrines and Remedies*, above n 20 at 871-875:
    "1. Where there are mutual accounts between the parties, in the sense that there are receipts and payments on both sides. (If there are receipts and payments on one side only, the dispute can be resolved through a simple set-off.)
    2. Where the parties share a relationship of a confidential or quasi-fiduciary nature, even though the right relied upon is legal in nature. That may be true, for instance, in an agency or employment relationship.
    3. Where the court orders a general administration of a dissolved partnership.
    4. Where the account is too complicated to be conveniently settled at law.
    5. Where the claimant asks for an injunction in response to the defendant's act of legal waste. (The availability of an equitable account for equitable waste is not similarly premised upon a request for injunctive relief.)

edness between the parties", an equitable account may also be available to determine the extent to which the defendant profited from a "treasonable" breach of contract or a violation of the claimant's intellectual property rights. Of course, as *Attorney General v Blake* has demonstrated, the categories are not closed.

MEASURES OF RELIEF

The phrase "account of profits" may be defined in a number of ways.[22] In the previous section, it was used to describe the *process* by which the defendant's finances are examined with a view to determining the extent to which he acquired a benefit by virtue of some event involving the claimant. In the present section, the phrase is used to describe the obligation that subsequently is imposed upon the defendant to pay the value of that benefit over to the claimant. Lord Nicholls employed that second definition in *Attorney General v Blake*. His primary concern was not with the underlying evidentiary process, but rather with the incidence of a particular species of gain-based liability.

Unfortunately, the concept of "gain-based" liability is also ambiguous. It is therefore necessary to briefly define the manner in which monetary remedies[23] may be calculated. Some options are largely insignificant for present purposes. Exemplary damages are set, somewhat arbitrarily, in a large amount for the purpose of punishing the defendant; nominal damages are set, somewhat arbitrarily, in a small amount for the purpose of symbolically vindicating the violation of a right. Typically, however, relief is calculated by reference to the consequences of the events underlying the claimant's cause of action. It will be

---

6. Where the defendant has violated the claimant's intellectual or industrial property rights. Although equitable accounting was previously premised upon the availability of an injunction, that restriction no longer applies. As discussed below, most claims are now governed by statute.

7. Where the claimant would have enjoyed a right to payment from the defendant if the defendant had not wrongfully prevented that right from accruing. That may be true if, for example, the defendant denied the claimant the opportunity to perform a contractual obligation and to thereby trigger a right to payment.

8. Where the defendant received a profit from a breach of contract amounting to "treasonable activities."

22 The phrase may also be used to describe the cause of action or basis upon which the defendant is subject to a gain-based liability. As previously explained, the traditional common law model of accounting involved three steps, the first of which involved a determination as to whether the defendant could be compelled to open his books. See R Grantham and CF Rickett, *Enrichment and Restitution in New Zealand* (Hart Publishing, Oxford, 2000) at 461-462.

23 An account of profits is a form of personal relief. The defendant is subject to an obligation to pay over a sum of money, but the claimant does not immediately receive a proprietary interest in any particular asset. This paper will not address the notoriously difficult question as to when gain-based relief ought to be awarded proprietarily (for example, by way of a constructive trust or lien). See R Chambers, "Constructive Trusts" (1999) 37 *Alberta Law Review* 173; R Chambers, "Resulting Trusts in Canada" (2000) 38 *Alberta Law Review* 378.

useful to touch upon four possibilities: compensation, disgorgement, restitutionary damages, and restitution. The first possibility clearly is not "gain-based," but the other three sometimes are described in that way.

Compensation

Compensation is measured by the claimant's loss. Significantly, the courts are prepared to recognise different forms of loss. The simplest cases involve readily quantifiable financial injuries. A breach of contract may have deprived the claimant of an opportunity to realise a profit of $5000; a tort may have caused the claimant to suffer an injury that required $5000 in medical treatment. But relief may be available even if the claimant cannot precisely point to an economic loss. The law may award compensation whenever the defendant infringed an interest that is considered worthy of protection. Aggravated damages have long reflected the fact that, despite the absence of any adverse financial consequences, the defendant wrongfully acted in disregard of the claimant's dignity. Likewise, within the past decade, courts have, on a number of occasions, awarded compensation with respect to losses of an intangible nature.[24] A further example, as discussed below, may occur if the defendant violates the claimant's property interests without thereby inflicting any economic loss.

Disgorgement

Disgorgement is the opposite of compensation. It reflects the defendant's gain, rather than the claimant's loss. The two measures of relief nevertheless are similar as both can be sensitively tailored to the facts. Just as the courts are prepared to respond to various forms of injury, so too they have adopted a flexible conception of profit. Indeed, they could hardly do otherwise. As the High Court of Australia has explained, it is "notoriously difficult" to determine the extent to which an enterprise profited from its wrongdoing; "mathematical exactitude is generally impossible".[25] Consequently, depending upon the circumstances, the defendant may be required to account for an entire business

---

24 *Rees v Darlington Memorial Hospital NHS Trust* [2003] 3 WLR 1091 ("conventional award" of £15,000 in recognition of loss of freedom to determine family size following a negligently performed sterilization); *Ruxley Electronics and Construction Ltd v Forsyth* [1996] AC 344 ("loss of amenity" award of £2,500 for loss of "consumer surplus" due to swimming pool being built to wrong depth); *Johnson v Unisys* [2003] 1 AC 518 (compensation for non-economic "distress, humiliation, damage to reputation in the community or to family life" arising from unfair dismissal).

25 *Dart Industries Inc v Décor Corporation Pty Ltd* (1993) 179 CLR 101 at 111. See also *Warman International Ltd v Dwyer* (1995) 182 CLR 544 at 556-558; *Colbeam Palmer Ltd v Stock Affiliates Pty Ltd* (1968) 122 CLR 25 at 37 per Windeyer J ("But what is meant here by profits, and how are they to be ascertained? In modern economic theory the profit of an enterprise is a debatable concept. Consequently, the word 'profit' has today varying senses in the vocabulary of economists. For law some definition or working rule must be accepted for the case at hand").

or merely for particular benefits; he may or may not be entitled to allowances for his expenses and efforts;[26] and so on.

Restitutionary damages

Disgorgement can be brought into sharper focus by following Dr Edelman's lead in contrasting it with "restitutionary damages".[27] Both measures of relief respond to civil wrongdoing. The primary difference between them is that while restitutionary damages reflect a benefit that the defendant wrongfully acquired *from the claimant*, disgorgement more broadly encompasses *any gain* that the defendant received as a result of committing a wrong against the claimant. Accordingly, while both measures are capable of rectifying enrichments that the defendant improperly subtracted from the claimant (as when the defendant steals cash from the claimant), only disgorgement can capture an enrichment that the defendant received from a third party as a result of breaching an obligation that was owed to the claimant (as when the defendant is paid royalties by a publisher in exchange for writing a book in breach of a contractual obligation owed to the claimant).

Restitution

This paper is concerned with gain-based responses to civil wrongdoing. References to the autonomous action in unjust enrichment are, however, unavoidable. That action consists of three parts: (1) an enrichment to the defendant, (2) an expense or deprivation to the claimant, and (3) either a positive reason for reversing the transfer or an absence of any juristic reason for the enrichment.[28] If established, a claim in unjust enrichment supports only one response: restitution. Having received a benefit that cannot in justice be retained, the defendant must give it back to the claimant.

---

26 *Boardman v Phipps* [1967] 2 AC 46; *Warman International Ltd v Dwyer* (1995) 182 CLR 544 at 561; cf *Guinness plc v Saunders* [1990] 2 AC 663.

27 J Edelman, *Gain-Based Damages: Contract, Tort, Equity and Intellectual Property* (Hart Publishing, Oxford, 2002).

28 *Banque Financière de la Cité v Parc (Battersea) Ltd* [1999] 1 AC 221; *David Securities Pty Ltd v Commonwealth Bank of Australia* (1992) 175 CLR 353; *Pettkus v Becker* (1980) 117 DLR (3d) 257. The action in unjust enrichment appears to be undergoing an important change. Restitution traditionally was premised upon proof of an "unjust factor". The claimant had to establish a positive reason for reversing a transfer of wealth, such as the fact that she had acted with an impaired intention. Recently, however, the Supreme Court of Canada held that restitution is available unless there is a "juristic reason" for the transfer. The defendant prima facie must restore every enrichment that was not received as a gift or in satisfaction of a legal obligation: *Garland v Consumers' Gas Co* (2004) 237 DLR (4th) 385; critiqued in M McInnes, "Juristic Reasons and Unjust Factors in the Supreme Court of Canada" (2004) 120 *Law Quarterly Review* 554; M McInnes, "Making Sense of Juristic Reasons: Unjust Enrichment After *Garland v Consumers' Gas Co*" (2004) 42 *Alberta Law Review* 399. Professor Birks controversially argued that the English courts had already taken that step, *Unjust Enrichment* (2nd ed, Oxford University Press, Oxford, 2005).

One explanation for that lack of remedial options lies in the fact that unjust enrichment is, in Professor Birks' phrase, a "not-wrong".[29] Most causes of action presume three elements: (1) a primary duty imposed upon the defendant in the claimant's favour, (2) a breach of that obligation, and (3) the imposition of a secondary (remedial) obligation that reflects the consequences of the breach. Unjust enrichment, in contrast, only ever involves a primary obligation. The defendant becomes obliged to effect restitution once the claim crystallises. There is never any question of either a breach or a secondary (remedial) obligation. And in the absence of any breach, there is no justification for the courts to do anything beyond reversing the impugned transfer and restoring the status quo ante. In particular, there is no warrant for shifting a loss to the defendant (as typically occurs with compensation) or conferring a windfall upon the claimant (as typically occurs with disgorgement).[30]

GAIN-BASED RELIEF FOR LEGAL WRONGDOING

Defined as an evidentiary process for determining the extent of the defendant's gain, an account of profits may be necessary for all three "gain-based" measures of relief. Indeed, as discussed below, it may even inform the calculation of compensatory relief. As used by Lord Nicholls, however, an "account of profits" is a species of disgorgement. The purpose of the remedy is to compel the defendant to give up the benefits that he acquired from someone as a result of committing a wrong against the claimant. Liability obviously is not calculated by reference to the claimant's loss (as in the case of compensation), but nor is it restricted to enrichments that economically passed to the defendant from the claimant (as in the case of restitution or restitutionary damages).

Though the position is easy enough to state in the abstract, the measure of relief represented by an account of profits is notoriously difficult to isolate in practice. The problem primarily lies in the fact that a remedy awarded for one *purpose* may have a number of different *effects*.

- Restitution and restitutionary damages provide the best examples of that proposition. Because they are defined in terms of a transfer that occurred between the parties, they inevitably involve elements of both loss-based and gain-based relief. To the extent that the claimant is able to claw back value

---

29   See for example, P Birks, "Rights, Wrongs and Remedies" (2000) 20 *Oxford Journal of Legal Studies* 1. The lack of remedial options may also be attributable to the constituent elements of proof. The court must be satisfied: (i) that the defendant received a benefit, (ii) that the claimant suffered the relevant expense, and (iii) that there is some reason to reverse that transfer of wealth. In the circumstances, restitution is the only coherent remedy. Having required proof of the claimant's loss, it would make no sense to award purely gain-based relief (that is, disgorgement). Similarly, having required proof of the defendant's gain, it would make no sense to award purely loss-based relief (that is, compensation). See M McInnes, "The Measure of Restitution" (2002) 52 *University of Toronto Law Journal* 163.

30   Birks' expanded conception of "interceptive subtraction" arguably falls foul of that proposition, P Birks, *Unjust Enrichment*, above n 28 at 66-72; cf M McInnes, "Interceptive Subtraction, Unjust Enrichment and Wrongs — A Reply to Professor Birks" (2003) 62 *Cambridge Law Journal* 697; RB Grantham and CF Rickett, "Disgorgement for Unjust Enrichment?" (2003) 62 *Cambridge Law Journal* 159 at 167.

previously held, she will, in effect, enjoy compensation. And to the extent that the defendant is ordered to give up a gain, he will, in effect, be subject to disgorgement.

• Similarly, while compensation and disgorgement may appear in pure form (that is, when a civil wrong either imposes a loss upon the claimant without generating a corresponding gain for the defendant, or creates a gain for the defendant without imposing a loss upon the claimant), they often have incidental effects.

  ◦ In discharging a compensatory order, the defendant may coincidentally effect either restitutionary damages or disgorgement (to the extent that, fortuitously, the operative loss was coterminous with a benefit that the defendant wrongfully derived from either the claimant or a third party) or restitution (to the extent that, fortuitously and without regard to the defendant's breach, the operative loss reflected an unjust transfer as between the parties).

  ◦ Likewise, in disgorging a wrongful gain, the defendant may coincidentally effect compensation or restitutionary damages (to the extent that, fortuitously, the defendant's wrongful gain was coterminous with a loss that the plaintiff suffered as a result of the underlying wrong) or restitution (to the extent that, fortuitously and without regard to the defendant's breach, the operative gain reflected an unjust transfer as between the parties).

The difficulty of identifying remedies by purpose, rather than effect, is compounded by semantic considerations. The same term may be applied to a number of discrete responses (for example, "restitution" has been used to describe not only restitution, but also, inter alia, restitutionary damages,[31] disgorgement[32] and even compensation[33]), just as a single response may bear a number of different labels (for example, the profit-stripping measure of relief has been referred to as, inter alia, "an account of profits",[34] "compound interest",[35] "disgorgement",[36] "restitution"[37] and "damages"[38]). Moreover, many of the historical precedents are inscrutable. Because cases traditionally were analysed in terms of the ancient writs (rather than the modern causes of action and measures of relief), it often is impossible to be certain whether a judge's reference to, say, the action for money had and received was intended to reveal

---

31 *Ministry of Defence v Ashman* [1993] 2 EGLR 102 at 105.

32 *United Australia Ltd v Barclays Bank Ltd* [1941] AC 1 at 18-19.

33 *Canson Enterprises Ltd v Boughton & Co* (1991), 85 DLR (4th) 129 at 137-138, 141, 145, 157-159.

34 *Attorney General v Blake* [2001] 1 AC 268 at 284.

35 *Burdick v Garrick* (1870) LR 5 Ch App 233 at 241; *Attorney General v Alford* (1855) 4 De G M & G 843 at 851; 43 ER 737 at 741; cf *Westdeutsche Landesbank Girozentrale v Islington London Borough Council* [1996] AC 669 at 693.

36 *Attorney General v Blake* [2001] 1 AC 268 at 291; *Cadbury Schweppes Inc v FBI Foods Ltd* (1999) 167 DLR (4th) 577 at 586, 589, 598.

37 *United Australia Ltd v Barclays Bank Ltd* [1941] AC 1 at 18-19.

38 *Canadian Aero Service v O'Malley* (1973) 40 DLR (3d) 371 at 392.

that the defendant was liable to disgorge a wrongful gain, or that the claimant was entitled to restitutionary damages for a wrongful transfer, or that, regardless of any wrongdoing, the defendant was required to restore an enrichment that he "unjustly" (that is, reversibly) received from the claimant.[39]

Reasonable fee

The difficulty of distinguishing between remedial *purposes* and remedial *effects* is vividly illustrated by cases in which common law courts have, in response to interference with property rights, required payment of reasonable fees. Lord Nicholls' judgment in *Attorney General v Blake* is often interpreted as treating reasonable fees and accounts of profits as the means by which law and equity respectively award gain-based relief. On closer examination, however, the proper characterisation of the legal remedy is more complex.

The common law cases[40] involve a variety of proprietary torts, including trespass arising from the wrongful occupation of land,[41] trespass arising from the wrongful use of land,[42] detention of chattels,[43] and nuisance arising from the obstruction of light.[44] The court in each instance awarded a substantial measure of relief, even in the absence of proof that the defendant's wrong inflicted an *economic* loss upon the claimant. And indeed, in many of the cases, the breach left the victim none the worse for wear from a *financial* perspective. Because the claimant in *Strand Electric and Engineering Co Ltd v Brisford Entertainments Ltd*[45] had more portable switchboards than it had customers, the defendant's retention of a single unit beyond the lease period did not deprive

---

39   J Edelman, "Money Had and Received: Modern Pleading of an Old Court" [2000] *Restitution Law Review* 547.

40   Although some of the cases discussed in this section were decided in chancery, monetary relief typically was awarded in lieu of injunctive relief for legal wrongdoing: *Carr-Saunders v Dick McNeil Associates Ltd* [1986] 1 WLR 922; *Jaggard v Sawyer* [1995] 1 WLR 269; *Wrotham Park Estate Co v Parkside Homes Ltd* [1974] 1 WLR 798; *Bracewell v Appleby* [1975] 1 Ch 408. In such circumstances, courts of equity follow the same principles as courts of law: *Johnson v Agnew* [1980] AC 367.

Equitable wrongdoing may also call for the payment of a reasonable fee. That may be true, for instance, if the defendant committed a breach of confidence: *Seager v Copydex (No 2)* [1969] 1 WLR 809.

41   *Penarth Dock Engineering Co Ltd v Pounds* [1963] 1 Lloyd's Rep; *Swordheath Properties Ltd v Tabet* [1979] 1 WLR 285; *Ministry of Defence v Ashman* [1993] 2 EGLR 102; *Ministry of Defence v Thompson* (1993) 2 EGLR 107; *Inverugie Investments v Hackett* [1995] 1 WLR 713; *Gondal v Dillon Newsagents Ltd* [2001] *Restitution Law Review* 221.

42   *Martin v Porter* (1839) 5 M & W 351; 151 ER 149; *Jegon v Vivian* (1871) LR 6 Ch App 742; *Whitwham v Westminster Brymbo Coal and Coke Co* [1896] 1 Ch D 894; *Phillips v Homfray (No 1)* (1871) LR 6 Ch App 770; *Phillips v Homfray (No 2)* (1883) 24 Ch D 439; *Bracewell v Appleby* [1975] 1 Ch 408; *Jaggard v Sawyer* [1995] 1 WLR 269; *Yakamia Dairy Pty Ltd v Wood* [1976] WAR 57.

43   *Strand Electric and Engineering Co Ltd v Brisford Entertainments Ltd* [1952] 2 QB 246; *Hillesden Securities Ltd v Ryjack Ltd* [1983] 2 All ER 184; *Gaba Formwork Contractors Pty Ltd v Turner Corporation Ltd* (1993) 32 NSWLR 175.

44   *Carr-Saunders v Dick McNeil Associates Ltd* [1986] 1 WLR 922.

45   [1952] 2 QB 246.

the claimant of an opportunity to enter into a new lease with another party. Because the hotel involved in *Inverugie Investments Ltd v Hackett*[46] habitually operated at less than full capacity, the defendant's wrongful occupation did not prevent the true owner from profitably renting out each unit within the building. Because the claimant in *Penarth Dock Engineering Co Ltd v Pounds*[47] was in the process of abandoning the property, it did not financially suffer as a result of the defendant's trespassory failure to remove a large floating dock from the premises. And so on.

Compensatory damages

The absence of an *economic loss* does not, however, necessarily preclude the availability of compensatory damages. As previously explained, courts occasionally employ an expanded conception of compensable injury. And in the present context, the payment of a reasonable fee may be characterised as reparation for a loss.[48] That is true, for instance, of the old way-leave cases, which involved the wrongful use of passageways. The defendant typically was required to pay a reasonable fee for transporting coal through tunnels beneath the claimant's land. Today, such awards are commonly treated as instances of restitutionary damages for trespass, and there is indeed some precedent for that view.[49] The original courts, however, tended to view the remedy in compensatory terms.[50]

While a compensatory analysis is appropriate, the operative injury must be carefully identified. It is a mistake to treat the reasonable fee as the price that the defendant *would have* paid if, instead of acting unilaterally, he had contracted with the claimant for a relaxation of her rights.[51] As Dr Edelman has argued,[52] the actual outcome of the parties' negotiations might have yielded something other than an objectively reasonable price. Due to an imbalance in bargaining positions, the defendant might have driven the cost down, just as the claimant might have demanded a king's ransom or refused to deal altogether.

---

46 [1995] 1 WLR 713.

47 [1963] 1 Lloyd's Rep 359.

48 *Strand Electric and Engineering Co Ltd v Brisford Entertainments Ltd* [1952] 2 QB 246 per Somervell and Romer LJJ; *Hillesden Securities Ltd v Ryjack Ltd* [1983] 2 All ER 184; *Carr-Saunders v Dick McNeil Associates Ltd* [1986] 1 WLR 922. See also *Jaggard v Sawyer* [1995] 1 WLR 269; *Wrotham Park Estate Co v Parkside Homes Ltd* [1974] 1 WLR 798; *Bracewell v Appleby* [1975] 1 Ch 408; *Tito v Waddell (No 2)* [1977] Ch 106 at 335.

49 *Phillips v Homfray (No 2)* (1883) 24 Ch D 439 at 446.

50 *Martin v Porter* (1839) 5 M & W 351 at 352; 151 ER 149; *Powell v Aiken* (1858) 4 K & J 345 at 350; 70 ER 144 at 147; *Yakamia Dairy Pty Ltd v Wood* [1976] WAR 57. The same was true in equity: *Whitwham v Westminster Brymbo Coal and Coke Co* [1896] 1 Ch D 894 at 898 (recognising that the claimant's "actual damage" was "trifling"); *Phillips v Homfray (No 1)* (1871) LR 6 Ch App 770 at 780; *Phillips v Homfray (No 2)* (1883) 24 Ch D 439 at 453, 466; *Re United Merthyr Collieries* (1872) LR 15 Eq 46 at 49.

51 RJ Sharpe and SM Waddams, "Damages for Lost Opportunity to Bargain" (1982) 2 *Oxford Journal of Legal Studies* 290.

52 J Edelman, *Gain-Based Damages: Contract, Tort, Equity and Intellectual Property* (Hart Publishing, Oxford, 2002) at 99-102, 129.

The compensatory analysis nevertheless can be saved by focusing on the reason why the claimant *could have* required the defendant to pay for the right to act in a certain way.[53] Ownership entails rights — valuable rights. To say that a person owns a piece of property is to say, inter alia, that she has the right of dominium (that is, the right to control access and use). She may choose to sell that right, or to enjoy it herself, or to do nothing at all. Regardless of the nature of her choice, however, the law necessarily respects her authority. Failure to do so would substantially, perhaps fatally, erode the underlying institution. "A property right has value to the extent only that the court will enforce it or award damages for its infringement."[54]

The violation of a property right therefore necessarily entails a loss.[55] And in the absence of any inherent economic value, the law must assign a monetary figure to the claimant's intangible injury.[56] Ubi jus ibi remedium. In doing so, it demonstrates the strength of its commitment to the protection of the underlying right. It will not allow the defendant to unilaterally expropriate a right even if, because of the surrounding circumstances, his interference with

---

53   A distinction recently has been drawn between "reparative compensation" and "substitutive compensation." The former responds to actual loss or damage. The latter, in contrast, responds to the denial or deprivation of property. It is intended to stand in the place of the property right that has been infringed. See for example, S Elliott and C Mitchell, "Remedies for Dishonest Assistance" (2004) 67 *Modern Law Review* 16.

54   *Attorney General v Blake* [2001] 1 AC 268 at 281. In *Watson Laidlaw & Co Ltd v Pott Cassels and Williamson*, Lord Shaw presented a hypothetical in which the defendant rode the claimant's horse without permission and then returned the animal unharmed. The decision is best known for the argument that Lord Shaw put into the mouth of a tortfeasor faced with a claim for compensatory damages: "Against what loss do you want to be restored? I restore the horse. There is no loss. The horse is none the worse for wear; it is the better for the exercise": (1914) 31 RPC 104 at 119. As Lord Nicholls noted in *Attorney General v Blake*, however, Lord Shaw had prefaced his remarks with the observation that "wherever an abstraction or invasion of property has occurred, then, unless such abstraction or invasion were to be sanctioned by law, the law ought to yield recompense under the category or principle ... either of price or of hire." In other words, despite the fact that the horse was unharmed, and even if the claimant would not otherwise have ridden the animal, a loss was suffered insofar as the defendant tortiously appropriated the right of dominium. That loss prima facie is recoverable by payment of a hiring fee that is quantified by reference to market value.

See also *Olwell v Nye & Nissen Co* 173 P 2d 652 at 654 (1947 Wash SC): "The very essence of the nature of property is the right to its exclusive use. Without it, no beneficial right remains. However plausible, the [defendant] cannot be heard to say that his wrongful invasion of the respondent's property right to exclusive use is not a loss compensable in law. To hold otherwise would be subversive of all property rights."

55   In *The Mediana*, Lord Halsbury LC explained that "the unlawful keeping back of what belongs to another person it of itself a ground for real damages, not nominal damages at all." Compensation therefore will lie if, for example, the defendant took away a chair for twelve months, even if the claimant would not have used the chair during that time. Damages can be calculated, in a "rough" way, by taking "a perfectly artificial hypothesis and say[ing], 'Well, if you wanted to hire a chair, what would you have to give for it for the period'": [1900] AC 113 at 118, 117.

56   The need to do so arises only if, as in the cases under consideration, the defendant's breach did not create another financial loss. The analysis is, of course, much simpler if the property itself was damaged, or if, because of the wrong, the claimant was put to some expense.

the claimant's property did not otherwise inflict a financial loss.[57] Nor will the defendant be heard to say that, since he enjoyed a superior bargaining position, he could have purchased the right for a pittance. But by the same token, the law's respect for personal property does not extend so far as to allow the owner to ex post exploit a monopoly by arguing that she would have held out for an unreasonably high price.[58] Presented with an unlawful expropriation, the law does the best that it can. Though the calculation necessarily is imperfect, the judge strikes a reasonable balance between the parties' interests by requiring payment of an objectively appropriate fee.

When read in isolation, some parts of *Attorney General v Blake* appear to reject that compensatory analysis in favour of restitutionary damages (that is, the restoration of a benefit that the defendant wrongfully acquired from the claimant). Lord Nicholls said, for instance, that relief may be measured by the defendant's gain,[59] that "there has been a move toward applying the label of restitution to awards of this character",[60] that the claimant may receive substantial relief without having suffered any financial loss,[61] and that the payment of a reasonable fee cannot be brought within the "strictly compensatory measure … unless loss is given a strained and artificial meaning".[62]

Placed into context, however, those comments reveal that Lord Nicholls actually viewed the payment of a reasonable fee as a form of compensation. The gist of his judgment is that while compensation is *normally* calculated by reference to the claimant's *financial* loss, "the common law, pragmatic as ever," recognises that there are situations in which

"… compensation for the wrong done to the plaintiff is measured by a different yardstick. A trespasser who enters another's land may cause the landowner no financial loss. In such a case damages are measured by the benefit of the trespasser, namely, by his use of the land.[63]

…

The measure of damages awarded in this type of case is often regarded as damages for loss of a bargaining opportunity or, which comes to the same, the

---

57 It sometimes is said that the defendant will be liable for a reasonable hiring fee only if the claimant was in the business of renting out the item in question: *Strand Electric and Engineering Co Ltd v Brisford Entertainments Ltd* [1952] 2 QB 246 at 249. In principle, however, the claimant suffers an intangible injury every time that the defendant violates a property right. The loss of an opportunity to bargain is simply one manifestation of the loss of dominium: *The Mediana* [1900] AC 113 at 117; *Watson Laidlaw & Co Ltd v Pott Cassels and Williamson* (1914) 31 RPC 104 at 119. Significantly, when dealing with trespass to land, the courts insist upon payment of a reasonable fee without requiring proof that the claimant was in the business of renting out the property.
58 The same pattern of analysis applies in a case of authorized expropriation of land. The court is presented with a fait accompli. It must then strike a balance between the parties' interests. Compensatory relief will not be reduced to reflect the government's overwhelming advantage in bargaining resources, nor will it be increased to reflect the fact that the owner, perhaps for sentimental reasons, would have voluntarily sold only at a unreasonably inflated price.
59 *Attorney General v Blake* [2001] 1 AC 268 at 278.
60 *Attorney General v Blake*, above n 59 at 279.
61 *Attorney General v Blake*, above n 59 at 279.
62 *Attorney General v Blake*, above n 59 at 279.
63 *Attorney General v Blake*, above n 59 at 278.

price payable for the compulsory acquisition of a right. This analysis is correct."[64]

Within that framework, the court may be interested in the defendant's gain not because it provides a direct measure of restitutionary damages, but rather because it helps to determine the fee that the defendant should have paid to the claimant for the right to act in a certain manner. The amount that a person is willing to pay to be released from an obligation may be affected by the profit that he expects to eventually realise from the anticipated project.[65]

Restitutionary Damages

Opposition to the preceding analysis stems largely from the belief that a single measure of relief (a reasonable fee) must invariably refer to a single purpose (either compensation or restitution). There is, however, no reason why different purposes cannot occasionally point to the same conclusion. As a historical matter, that proposition seems almost certainly correct. Demand for payment of a reasonable fee is an intuitively appropriate response to certain forms of wrongdoing. It simply requires a suitable vehicle for expression. As various theories of liability have waxed and waned over the years, judges have adopted different views of the defendant's obligation — sometimes in terms of compensatory damages, other times in terms of restitutionary damages.[66]

The existence of that alternative is particularly clear where the wrong consists entirely of the defendant's unilateral expropriation of the claimant's right of dominium (that is, where the breach does not give rise to either a consequential injury or a consequential enrichment). *Strand Electric and Engineering Co Ltd v Brisford Entertainments Ltd*[67] is illustrative. Electronic equipment was retained beyond the end of a rental period. Because the defendant had no real use for the equipment, it did not profit from its tort; because the claimant had a surplus of such items, it was not deprived of an opportunity to rent a unit to another customer. The defendant gained, and the claimant lost, precisely the same thing: dominium over the chattel — nothing more and nothing less. The restitutionary and compensatory analyses consequently stood on the same foundations. To say, for the purposes of the former, that the defendant enjoyed a reversible transfer is necessarily to say that it received something (that is, dominium) from the claimant. And to say that a

---

64   *Attorney General v Blake*, above n 59 at 281.

65   *Carr-Saunders v Dick McNeil Associates Ltd* [1986] 1 WLR 922 at 931; *Jaggard v Sawyer* [1995] 1 WLR 269 at 291; see also *Wrotham Park Estate Co Ltd v Parkside Homes Ltd* [1974] 1 WLR 798 at 815.

66   As previously suggested, there often is a third option. Leaving aside the impropriety of the defendant's enrichment, the claimant may be entitled to establish an action in unjust enrichment and to demand restitution (as opposed to restitutionary damages). To date, that possibility has been largely neglected by the courts: cf S Worthington, "Reconsidering Disgorgement for Wrongs" (1999) 62 *Modern Law Review* 218; J Beatson, *The Use and Abuse of Unjust Enrichment* (Clarendon Press, Oxford, 1991) at c 8; D Friedmann, 'Restitution for Wrongs: The Basis of Liability' in W Cornish et al (eds), *Restitution: Past, Present and Future* (Hart Publishing, Oxford, 1998) at c 9.

67   [1952] 2 QB 246.

reversible transfer began with the claimant is necessarily to say, for the purposes of the compensatory analysis, that it lost something.[68] Not surprisingly, then, while Somervell and Romer LJJ awarded a reasonable hiring fee as reparation for the claimant's loss, Denning LJ arrived at the same quantum by means of a restitutionary analysis.[69]

As restitutionary concepts continue to work their way into judicial consciousness, that possibility of alternative analysis is increasingly finding favour. While Lord Denning characteristically was in the vanguard,[70] other judges have begun to order the payment of reasonable fees with a view to reversing transfers, rather than repairing losses.[71] In more recent years, the English Court of Appeal has expressly endorsed both the compensatory analysis[72] and the restitutionary perspective.[73] And in a slight variation on the theme, the Privy Council has suggested that the measure of relief in such cases "need not be characterised as exclusively compensatory, or exclusively restitutionary; it combines elements of both."[74]

Disgorgement

Lord Nicholls sketched a generalised scheme in which equity requires a wrongdoer to disgorge his gains by means of an account of profits, whereas law requires a wrongdoer to repair the victim's loss through the payment of a reasonable fee. Significantly, however, both parts of that scheme are subject to exception. The equitable side of the equation is perhaps less controversial. While disgorgement may be the more familiar remedy,[75] equitable compensation has, in recent years, become firmly entrenched as well.[76] The situation is

---

68   A Tettenborn, D Wilby and D Bennett, *The Law of Damages* (Butterworths, London, 2003) at 48-49; cf J Edelman, *Gain-Based Damages: Contract, Tort, Equity and Intellectual Property* (Hart, Oxford, 2002) at 67 (arguing that there is a loss of dominium for the purpose of restitutionary damages, but not for the purpose of compensatory damages).

69   There was no evidence that the defendant positively profited from the tort, so as to raise the possibility of disgorgement. Somervell LJ nevertheless said in dicta that the "damages could not … be increased by showing that the defendant had made by his use of the chattels much more than the market rate of hire," whereas Denning LJ could "imagine cases where an owner might be entitled to the profits made by the wrongdoer by the use of a chattel": [1952] 2 QB 246 at 252, 254.

70   *Strand Electric and Engineering Co Ltd v Brisford Entertainments Ltd* [1952] 2 QB 246; *Penarth Dock Engineering Co v Pounds* [1963] 1 Lloyd's Rep 359.

71   *Gaba Formwork Contractors Pty Ltd v Turner Corporation Ltd* (1993) 32 NSWLR 175.

72   *Jaggard v Sawyer* [1995] 1 WLR 269; *Ministry of Defence v Ashman* [1993] 2 EGLR 102, per Lloyd LJ.

73   *Surrey County Council v Bredero Homes Ltd* [1993] 1 WLR 1361 at 1369 per Steyn LJ; *Ministry of Defence v Ashman* [1993] 2 EGLR 102 at 105 per Hoffmann LJ; *Ministry of Defence v Thompson* [1993] 2 EGLR 107; *Gondal v Dillon Newsagents Ltd* [2001] *Restitution Law Review* 221, noted J Edelman, "The Compensation Strait-Jacket and the Lost Opportunity to Bargain Fiction" [2001] *Restitution Law Review* 104.

74   *Inverugie Investments Ltd v Hackett* [1995] 1 WLR 713 at 718.

75   *Boardman v Phipps* [1967] 2 AC 46; *Attorney General v Guardian Newspapers (No 2) (Spycatcher)* [1990] 1 AC 109.

76   I Davidson, "The Equitable Remedy of Compensation" (1982) 13 *Melbourne University Law Review* 349; *Canson Enterprises Ltd v Boughton & Co* (1991) 85 DLR (4th) 129; *Target Holdings Ltd v Redferns* [1996] 1 AC 421.

reversed at law. Compensatory relief dominates. Indeed, some commentators have gone so far as to say that it holds a monopoly.[77] As Lord Nicholls recognised, however, the common law does occasionally "afford ... a wronged party a choice of remedies"[78] as between reparation for harm and divestment of gain. Although the preceding section illustrates that proposition, the possibility of re-casting restitutionary damages in compensatory terms takes some of the punch out of the proof. The situation is similar with respect to disgorgement damages.

Money had and received

Historically, the primary vehicle for disgorgement at law was the claim for *money had and received.* An important line of cases involves the wrongful sale of property. As Lord Romer explained in *United Australia Ltd v Barclays Bank Ltd,* the claimant has two options in such circumstances: "He may sue for the proceeds of the conversion as money had and received to his use, or he may sue for damages that he sustained by the conversion".[79] A difficulty nevertheless lies in the classification of the former remedy. The courts have not suggested that the sale proceeds represent the claimant's loss or that the relief is compensatory.[80] But nor have they consistently distinguished between restitutionary damages and disgorgement.[81] And while there is some support for the view that the defendant must *give up* (rather than *give back*) his ill-gotten gains,[82] the courts often appear to have been motivated by a desire to reverse wrongful transfers. They frequently approached the facts on the assumption that the defendant acted as the claimant's agent in selling the goods.[83] That supposed agency was, of course, a "fanciful relation," created solely for the purpose of facilitating liability.[84] It nevertheless does suggest that the remedy was regarded as a function of the claimant's ability to trace

---

77 H McGregor, 'Restitutionary Damages' in P Birks (ed), *Wrongs and Remedies in the Twenty-first Century* (Clarendon Press, Oxford, 1996) at 203 (dismissing nominal damages as "not really damages at all; they are damages in name only, and are so described," and dismissing exemplary damages as "rightly regarded as an anomaly ... and effectively outlawed"). Birks and Edelman have both argued against the "false monopoly of compensation", P Birks, 'Civil Wrongs: A New World' in *Butterworths Lectures 1990-1991* (Butterworths, London, 1992) at 55; J Edelman *Gain-Based Damages: Contract, Tort, Equity and Intellectual Property* (Hart, Oxford, 2002) at c 1.

78 *Attorney General v Blake* [2001] 1 AC 268 at 280.

79 [1941] AC 1 at 34.

80 *Hunter v Prinsep* (1808) 10 East 378; 103 ER 818; *Feltham v Terry* (1773) Lofft 207 at 208; 98 ER 613 at 613.

81 The same result could also be reached as restitution for the action in unjust enrichment. The cases are, however, generally more consistent with a tort analysis.

82 *Chesworth v Farrar* [1967] 1 QB 407; *Lightly v Clouston* (1808) 1 Taunt 112 at 114; 127 ER 774 at 775 (dicta).

83 *King v Leith* (1787) 2 Term Rep 141 at 145; 100 ER 77 at 79; *Marsh v Keating* (1834) 1 Bing (NC) 198 at 215; 131 ER 1094 at 1100; *Lamine v Dorrell* (1701) 2 Ld Raym 1216 at 1217; 92 ER 303.

84 *United Australia Ltd v Barclays Bank Ltd* [1941] AC 1 at 27.

his property into the sale proceeds[85] and to recover what the defendant had taken from him.[86]

Damages

The action for money had and received was also occasionally employed in a series of nineteenth century cases involving unauthorised coal mining operations.[87] Typically, however, the courts responded in such circumstances with *damages*. And once again, the real challenge lies not so much in determining the quantum of relief, as in identifying the remedy's classification. The difficulty largely arose from the need to make deductions. Coal in the ground is worth less than coal at the surface. The surface price represents not only the value of the coal itself, but also: (i) the out-of-pocket expenses involved in severing the material from subterranean landmass and raising it to the pit mouth, and (ii) the value of the miner's services. Unfortunately, the courts' treatment of those factors was not entirely consistent.[88] A distinction was drawn between "willful" and "innocent" tortfeasors.[89] While the willful tortfeasor was entitled to deduct the cost of raising the coal to the surface,[90] he was not given allowance for the cost of severance,[91] nor for the value of his services.[92] The innocent tortfeasor, in contrast, was entitled to deduct the expenses involved in severing and raising the coal, but again, not the value of his services.[93]

---

85   The concept of tracing featured prominently in some of the cases: *Oughton v Seppings* (1830) 1 B & Ad 241 at 244; 109 ER 776 at 777; *Powell v Rees* (1837) 7 Ad & E 426 at 428; 112 ER 530 at 531.

86   A Burrows, *The Law of Restitution* (2nd ed, Butterworths, London, 2002) at 464-465.

87   *Powell v Rees* (1837) 7 Ad & E 426; 112 ER 530 .

88   H McGregor, *Damages* (16th ed, Sweet & Maxwell, London, 1997) at 922-929.

89   The defendant could be considered "innocent" if, for instance: (i) he had a bona fide belief that he owned the land, (ii) he held a bona fide expectation that he would be granted a right to mine the coal, (iii) the land was subject to a bona fide dispute between himself and the claimant, or (iv) he inadvertently worked a piece of land that was adjacent to his own.

90   *Joicey v Dickinson* (1881) 45 LT 643.

91   The inability of the tortfeasor to deduct the cost of severance might also be explained on more technical grounds. The gist of the action was interference with personal property. Prior to the moment of severance, however, the coal was not personalty, but rather part of the realty. The relevant expenses consequently were considered immaterial to the claim in tort. The force of that objection is, however, substantially undermined by the fact that an innocent tortfeasor was not similarly precluded from deducting the cost of severance.

92   *Martin v Porter* (1839) 5 M & W 351; 151 ER 149; *Trotter v Maclean* (1879) 13 Ch D 574; *Phillips v Homfray (No 1)* (1871) LR 6 Ch App 770.

93   *Wood v Morewood* (1841) 3 QB 440. It was suggested that the value of the defendant's services were non-deductible because the claimant was entitled to extract the coal from the ground himself. And while he would have been required to incur out-of-pocket expenditures in doing so, he would not have been required to hire labour: *Re United Merthyr Collieries* (1872) LR 15 Eq 46. That argument is, however, unconvincing. In most situations, it is wholly artificial to assume that the claimant could have *personally* mined the coal. Moreover, even where the premise might have held true, the mining operation would have required time and effort, which is a type of non-monetary expenditure.

It has been suggested that the measure of relief in such cases invariably gives the claimant more than she actually lost and that it consequently must constitute disgorgement, rather than compensation.[94] The initial premise undoubtedly is correct. Compensation in tort law aims to restore the claimant's status quo ante. Before the tort was committed, the claimant had coal in the ground worth x; afterwards, she had coal in the defendant's hands worth $x + y$. To the extent that the claimant was awarded some part of y (that is, the market value of the defendant's services in a case of innocent trespass, as well as the expense involved in severance in a case of willful trespass), she was overcompensated.

The problem, however, is that just as the measure of relief exceeded compensation, so too it exceeded disgorgement. Disgorgement aims to restore the defendant's status quo ante. The goal is not to positively punish, but rather to nullify enrichments.[95] Judgment should leave the defendant with neither more nor less than he had before the wrong. But of course, to the extent that the he was required to give up some part of y (that is, the market value of his services in a case of innocent trespass, as well as the expense involved in severance in a case of willful trespass), he was liable for something that he expended, as opposed to something that he acquired. For that reason, Dr McGregor characterises that portion of the awards as "a kind of crystallised measure of exemplary damages".[96]

Accepting that relief is neither strictly loss-based nor strictly gain-based, the essential question remains: Is the award (imperfectly) aimed at compensation or at disgorgement? The decisions contain occasional statements in support of the latter. It was said, for instance, that "this Court never allows a man to make a profit by a wrong"[97] and that "the Court has adequate means, by taking an account of profits realised ... by the working of coal, to give relief in respect of wrongs attended with profit to the wrongdoer".[98] Moreover, in similar circumstances today, a judge might well be persuaded by emerging theories of gain-based liability to pursue a goal of disgorgement. On the whole, however, the cases point in the other direction.[99] The courts consis-

---

94 J Edelman, *Gain-Based Damages: Contract, Tort, Equity and Intellectual Property* (Hart Publishing, Oxford, 2002) at 138; A Burrows, *The Law of Restitution* (2nd ed, Butterworths, London, 2002) at 469.

95 *Dart Industries Inc v Décor Corporation Pty Ltd* (1993) 179 CLR 101 at 111, 114; *My Kinda Town Ltd v Soll* [1983] RPC 15 at 55; *Potton Ltd v Yorkclose Ltd* (1989) 17 FSR 11 at 14.

96 H McGregor, *Damages* (16th ed, Sweet & Maxwell, London, 1997) at 926.

97 *Jegon v Vivian* (1871) LR 6 Ch App 742 at 761.

98 *Powell v Aiken* (1858) 4 K & J 345 at 351; 70 ER 144 at 147.

99 Initially at least, the courts felt no qualms about exceeding a strictly compensatory measure: *Martin v Porter* (1839) 5 M & W 351 at 354; 151 ER 149 at 150 ("I am not sorry this rule is adopted; as it will tend to prevent trespass of this kind" per Parke B; "It may seem a hardship that the plaintiff should make this extra profit of the coal, but still the rule of law must prevail" per Lord Abinger CB); *Wild v Holt* (1842) 9 M & W 672 at 674; 152 ER 284 at 285 (the rule was "a salutary one"); cf *Livingstone v Rawyards Coal Co* (1880) LR 5 App Cas 25 at 40 ("Such was the rule of the Common Law. Whether or not that was a judicious rule at any time I do not take myself to say").

tently spoke of "damages". And while there may be no reason why that term must be confined to loss-based liability,[100] nineteenth century judges certainly did tend to equate "damages" with "compensation". Lord Denman CJ accordingly articulated the prevailing view when he awarded "compensation for the pecuniary loss suffered by the plaintiff from the trespass committed in taking his coal".[101]

Account of Profits

The preceding discussion reveals that it is difficult, though not impossible, to find purely gain-based relief entirely within the common law. Perhaps predictably, the clearest examples of disgorgement for tortious gain lie at the intersection of law and equity.[102] That is true, for instance, in some areas of intellectual property. Even where a claim is now codified or actionable at law (for example, the torts of passing off and trademark infringement), equity may intervene in an auxiliary capacity to award an account of profits. The explanation turns on the fact that the underlying rights largely began life in

---

100 J Edelman, *Gain-Based Damages: Contract, Tort, Equity and Intellectual Property* (Hart, Oxford, 2002) at c 1; cf H McGregor, *Damages*, above n 96 at 3 ("[d]amages are ... pecuniary compensation"); H McGregor, 'Restitutionary Damages' in P Birks (ed), *Wrongs and Remedies in the Twenty-first Century* (Clarendon Press, Oxford, 1996) at 202 ("there is 'restitution' and there is 'damages' ... [d]amages should be restricted to compensation for loss").

101 *Morgan v Powell* (1842) 3 QB 277 at 284; 114 ER 513 at 516. See also *Martin v Porter* (1839) 5 M & W 351; 151 ER 149; *Wild v Holt* (1842) 9 M & W 672; 152 ER 284; *Livingstone v Rawyards Coal Co* (1880) LR 5 App Cas 25 at 32 per Earl Cairns LC ("The questions is, what may fairly be said to have been the value of the coal to the person from whose property it was taken at the time it was taken"), 34 per Lord Hatherley ("the owner shall be re-possessed as far as possible of that which was his property ... there shall be compensation").

The same view also occasionally prevailed in equity. While Lord Hatherley said that equity "never allows a man to make a profit by a wrong," he also referred repeatedly to the claimant's loss and he ultimately quantified relief by reference to the price that the defendant would have been required to pay to the claimant in order to purchase the coal: *Jegon v Vivian* (1871) LR 6 Ch App 742 at 761. In the circumstances of the case, that amount was sufficient to compensate the claimant's loss, but not to eliminate the defendant's gain. Since the defendant mined the coal for commercial purposes, it would not have been willing to pay a price that encompassed the entire value — including the profit margin — that it placed upon the coal. Cf *Phillips v Homfray (No 3)* (1892) 1 Ch 465 (account of profits for value of coal taken by defendant).

102 Equity sometimes compels disgorgement of wrongful profits under the guise of awarding "compound interest." As Dr Edelman has explained:

"The only difference between this meaning of "compound interest" and an account of profits is that an award of "compound interest" will also be made where the defendant has used money obtained from a wrong in trade or commerce regardless of whether any profits are proved to have been made. Unless evidence to the contrary is shown, a court will presume that profits of compound interest have been earned because the use of money in trade of commerce will ordinarily attract compound interest."

J Edelman, *Gain-Based Damages: Contract, Tort, Equity and Intellectual Property* (Hart, Oxford, 2002) at 136-137. Although that sort of "compound interest" is usually awarded in response to a breach of fiduciary duty, it may also be triggered by fraud at law: *Southern Cross Pty Ltd v Ewing* (1988) 91 FLR 271.

chancery. It therefore is not surprising that they continue to attract equitable relief.[103]

Equity has similarly responded to other forms of legal wrongdoing.[104] *Attorney General v Blake* famously saw an account of profits imposed with respect to benefits generated through breach of contract. Within the context of property violations, the epic litigation in *Phillips v Homfray* provides another notorious, if frequently misunderstood,[105] example.[106] Coal was taken from beneath the plaintiffs' land. Inquiries were directed against the defendants with respect to: (1) the volume and market value of the coal that was removed, (2) the amount of traffic conducted through passageways beneath the claimant's land, and (3) the price to be paid for the use of those passageways. As previously noted, the second and third inquiries were likely directed to a compensatory purpose (even though modern commentators often approach them on a restitutionary basis). The first inquiry, in contrast, was unambiguously concerned with disgorgement. As the Court of Appeal clarified in the final chapter of the proceedings,[107] the tortfeasor was subject to an equitable account of profits.

---

103 It is, however, both surprising and unfortunate that the availability of such relief is inconsistent across the various species of wrongdoing. The English position is illustrative. In the absence of any statute, passing off and breach of trademark invariably trigger a right to compensation, but support an account of profits only if the defendant acted dishonestly: *Lever v Goodwin* (1887) 36 Ch D 1; *My Kinda Town Ltd v Soll* [1982] FSR 147, rev'd on other grounds [1983] RPC 15; *Edelsten v Edelsten* (1863) 1 De GJ and S 185; 46 ER 72; *Slazenger & Sons v Spalding & Bros* [1910] 1 Ch 257; *Colbeam Palmer Ltd v Stock Affiliates Pty Ltd* (1968) 122 CLR 25. In contrast, an account of profits invariably is available under the *Copyrights, Designs and Patents Act 1988*, whereas compensatory damages are confined to cases in which the defendant acted with knowledge of the claimant's rights. And finally, under the *Patents Act 1977*, neither measure of relief is available in response to an "innocent" breach. See J Edelman *Gain-Based Damages: Contract, Tort, Equity and Intellectual Property* (Hart Publishing, Oxford, 2002) at c 7; A Burrows, *The Law of Restitution* (2d ed, Butterworths, London, 2002) at 466-468.

104 According to Professor Birks, "[t]he only real brake on equity's willingness to allow an account of the profits of wrongs was the routine need to explain why equity was intervening." He concluded that "[v]ery slender excuses seemed to have sufficed", P Birks, 'Restitution for Wrongs' in EJH Schrage (ed), *Unjust Enrichment: The Comparative Legal History of Unjust Enrichment* (2d ed, Duncker & Humblot, Berlin, 1999) at 187. In *Jesus College v Bloom*, for instance, Lord Hardwicke LC said that equity could order an account of profits where it also awarded injunctive relief: (1745) 3 Atk 262; 26 ER 953.

105 The case has been said to preclude "restitution" with respect to benefits acquired through the wrongful occupation of land: see for example, *Ministry of Defence v Ashman* [1993] 2 EGLR 102 at 105-106. On the basis of a thorough reading of the various stages of litigation, however, Justice Gummow demonstrated that the case does not provide any support for that proposition, 'Unjust Enrichment, Restitution and Proprietary Remedies' in PD Finn (ed), *Essays on the Law of Restitution* (Lawbook Co, Sydney, 1990) at 60-67. See also S Hedley, "The Myth of 'Waiver of Tort'" (1984) 100 *Law Quarterly Review* 653 at 676-678; W Swadling, 'The Myth of *Phillips v Homfray*' in W Swadling and G Jones (eds), *The Search for Principle: Essays in Honour of Lord Goff of Chieveley* (Oxford University Press, Oxford, 1999) at 277.

106 See also *Edwards v Lee's Administrator* 96 SW 2d 1028 (1939 Ky CA).

107 *Phillips v Homfray (No 3)* (1892) 1 Ch 465.

THE DIFFERENCE BETWEEN LAW AND EQUITY

There is growing acceptance of gain-based relief for civil wrongdoing. Within chancery, that trend is firmly rooted in the account of profits, which is available with respect to all forms of equitable misconduct.[108] At law, however, the movement is largely academic in origin. The historical materials offer surprisingly little support — certainly far less than recent scholarship might suggest. Many of the cases that are routinely cited as illustrations of either disgorgement or restitutionary damages were actually decided on the basis of compensatory principles. And of the cases that *did* involve gain-based relief, many are explicable on the basis of either recent scholarly influences or Lord Denning's pioneering spirit.[109] Within the context of the present debate, disgorgement for legal wrongdoing enjoys solid historical support only where equity has intervened in its auxiliary jurisdiction to award an account of profits acquired either in violation of intellectual property rights that are actionable at law or, more rarely, through the tortious taking of another's minerals.

Lord Nicholls consequently was correct in suggesting that while property violations habitually generate disgorgement in equity, they usually meet with a compensatory response (sometimes in the form of a reasonable user fee) in law. It remains to be seen whether he was also correct in attributing that difference to a simple "accident of history".[110] If so, then the argument in favour of some sort of fusion should gain strength. Even allowing for the doctrine of precedent, historical accident is a poor basis for denying relief that might otherwise serve a useful purpose. Consequently, unless there is a better reason for treating equitable claimants more generously, it may be incumbent upon the courts to consider generally extending disgorgement to legal claimants as well.

Unfortunately, the cases do not clearly explain why disgorgement generally is available in equity, but not in law. The issue has seldom been addressed and the answers that have been offered are unpersuasive. In *Hogg v Kirby*, for instance, Lord Eldon LC suggested that equity relies upon the account of profits because it is "not content with an action for damages; for it is nearly impossible to know the extent of the damage; and therefore the remedy here, though not compensating the pecuniary loss except by an account of profits, is best".[111] Lord Nicholls tactfully questioned whether that "justification ... holds good factually in every case".[112] It is possible to be more emphatic.[113] Disgorgement is not more

---

108 *Boardman v Phipps* [1967] 2 AC 46 (breach of fiduciary duty); *Attorney General v Guardian Newspapers (No 2) (Spycatcher)* [1990] 1 AC 109 (breach of confidence); *Warman International Ltd v Dwyer* (1995) 182 CLR 544 (accessory liability for breach of fiduciary duty); *Paragon Finance v DB Thakerar & Co* [1999] 1 All ER 400 (fraud); J Edelman, *Gain-Based Damages: Contract, Tort, Equity and Intellectual Property* (Hart, Oxford, 2002) at 212-216.

109 Without suggesting that Lord Denning's explicit restitutionary analysis in *Strand Electric and Engineering Co Ltd v Brisford Entertainments Ltd* ([1952] 2 QB 246) and *Penarth Dock Engineering Co Ltd v Pounds* ([1963] 1 Lloyd LR 359) was incorrect or improper, it must be noted that conspicuously few judges of his era followed suit.

110 *Attorney General v Blake* [2001] 1 AC 268 at 280.

111 (1803) 8 Ves 215 at 232; 32 ER 336 at 339.

112 *Attorney General v Blake* [2001] 1 AC 268 at 280.

113 J Edelman, *Gain-Based Damages: Contract, Tort, Equity and Intellectual Property* (Hart Publishing, Oxford, 2002) at 82.

precise than compensation. To the contrary, the High Court of Australia expressed a common view when it said that the account of profits is "notoriously difficult in practice".[114] Nevertheless, just as courts of law will not be defeated by evidentiary difficulties associated with the quantification of compensatory damages,[115] courts of equity recognise that "[w]hilst ... mathematical exactitude is generally impossible, the exercise of [accounting for profits] is one that must be undertaken".[116] In any event, whatever the situation in 1803, it is now accepted that compensation is available in both jurisdictions.[117]

The nature of fiduciary obligations

The most significant explanation for equity's special affinity for disgorgement turns on the nature of fiduciary obligations. Professor Worthington provides the most powerful articulation of that idea.[118] She begins with the fact that fiduciary obligations are *proscriptive*, rather than *prescriptive*. They prohibit, rather than require. The fiduciary's duty is to *refrain* from self-serving conduct while acting on the principal's behalf, rather than to achieve any particular result. Worthington then observes that fiduciary relationships are marked by temptation and vulnerability. Because the fiduciary has been entrusted with the power to make decisions affecting the principal, there is substantial scope for abuse. The rules governing fiduciary relationships (in contrast to those governing, say, torts) must therefore do more than merely set standards and redress the consequences of breach. They must be strongly prophylactic. They must provide the greatest deterrent possible.

In the circumstances, Worthington argues that the account of profits is a uniquely appropriate remedy for breach of fiduciary duty. First, because the operative duty is simply to avoid conflicts of interest, there is no obligation to place the principal into any particular state of affairs. And because there is no relevant end-state, there generally is no place for compensatory damages, which are aimed at making the claimant whole. (In contrast, since the general duty in tort is to avoid harm, compensatory damages can be calculated to return the injured claimant to her original condition. Likewise, since the general duty in contract is to perform promises, compensatory damages can be calculated to place the disappointed claimant in position that she expected to

---

114 *Warman International Ltd v Dwyer* (1995) 182 CLR 544 at 556. Similarly, Lindley LJ once said that he did "not know any form of account which is more difficult to work out" and that "the difficulty of finding out how much profit is attributable to any one source is extremely great — so great that accounts in that form very seldom result in anything satisfactory to anybody", *Siddell v Vickers* (1892) 9 RPC 152 at 162.

115 *Chaplin v Hicks* [1911] 2 KB 786. Courts of law may, however, refuse to entertain a calculation that is so hopelessly speculative as to be impossible: *McRae v Commonwealth Disposals Commission* (1951) 84 CLR 377.

116 *Dart Industries Inc v Décor Corporation Pty Ltd* (1993) 179 CLR 101 at 111.

117 *Target Holdings Ltd v Redferns* [1996] 1 AC 42; *Aquaculture Corporation v New Zealand Green Mussel Co Ltd* [1990] 3 NZLR 299; *Canson Enterprises Ltd v Boughton & Co* (1991) 85 DLR (4th) 129.

118 S Worthington, "Reconsidering Disgorgement for Wrongs" (1999) 62 *Modern Law Review* 218; S Worthington, *Equity* (Oxford University Press, Oxford, 2003) at chapter 5. See also *Pilmer v Duke Group Ltd* (2001) 207 CLR 165 at 197-198.

enjoy.) Equity therefore focuses on the fiduciary, rather than the principal. Instead of providing compensation for the claimant's wrongful loss, it compels disgorgement of the benefits that the defendant acquired by acting in a prohibited manner.

Second, the account of profits is imposed in such a way as to both achieve justice between the parties and act *pour encourager les autres*. Given the availability of disgorgement, fiduciaries realise that they have nothing to gain by abusing their positions out of self-interest. Deterrence is achieved by stripping every wrongful enrichment, even if the breach occurred in good faith, even if the benefit was not otherwise available to the principal, and even if the principal already gained from the fiduciary's actions.[119] "This risk of wasted effort is the most effective weapon the law can muster to deter the defendant from engaging in the proscribed conduct."[120]

Deterring undesirable behaviour

That analysis undoubtedly provides a compelling explanation as to why equity responds to a breach of fiduciary duty with an account of profits. Disgorgement protects vulnerable principals by creating a powerful deterrence against self-serving behaviour. The question to be asked, however, is whether other forms of misconduct need to be similarly discouraged. Professor Worthington generally answers in the negative. She maintains that disgorgement "is available *only* when the defendant has breached an obligation of 'good faith' or 'loyalty'".[121] While that "expression is intended to have a wider compass than fiduciary duties and equitable duties of confidence",[122] the additional ground is largely theoretical. Worthington contemplates that the courts and legislatures may "import an additional 'good faith' obligation into some, if not all, dealings between individuals."[123] And that new obligation, she says, would necessarily arise in equity because it is "directed at protecting relationships; it is not, for example, a tort obligation directed at protecting affected individuals from harm (and compensating that harm)."[124]

While there is a great deal to be learned from Worthington's analysis, it is difficult to accept that purely gain-based relief is, or ought to be, so limited. To begin, even though the scope of recovery is often overstated, it is clear that both restitutionary damages and disgorgement (sometimes in the form of an account of profits) have been awarded in response to proprietary torts.[125] It is

---

119 *Boardman v Phipps* [1967] 2 AC 46 (HL); *Regal Hastings Ltd v Gulliver* [1967] 2 AC 134 (HL).
120 S Worthington, *Equity*, above n 118 at 118.
121 S Worthington, "Reconsidering Disgorgement for Wrongs", above n 118 at 218.
122 S Worthington, "Reconsidering Disgorgement for Wrongs", above n 118 at n 7.
123 S Worthington, "Reconsidering Disgorgement for Wrongs", above n 118 at 238.
124 S Worthington, "Reconsidering Disgorgement for Wrongs", above n 118 at 239.
125 Worthington insists, sometimes contrary to precedent, that the action in unjust enrichment provides the "only appropriate restitutionary vehicle for … dealing with a defendant's unauthorised *use* of the plaintiff's property", S Worthington, "Reconsidering Disgorgement for Wrongs" (1999) 62 *Modern Law Review* 218 at 219. She therefore denies that a tort may trigger restitutionary damages representing a reasonable use fee. She is silent on the question of disgorgement for tortious misappropriation or sale.

also clear that such relief has not been confined to relationships that are marked by a high degree of temptation and vulnerability. Good faith and loyalty (of the sort seen in fiduciary relationships) consequently cannot be the touchstone of gain-based relief.

The second branch of Worthington's thesis, in contrast, does appear to hold the key to the debate. The need to deter future wrongdoers undoubtedly informs the account of profits that is available in response to a breach of fiduciary duty. Indeed, given the highly sensitive nature the parties' relationship, it may be that fiduciary principles could not survive without equity's draconian response to unauthorised gains.[126] Significantly, however, while the stakes may not be quite so high, there *are* other situations in which the courts have a legitimate interest in using disgorgement as a deterrent. And not all of those situations are governed by equity.

In most instances, compensatory damages provide sufficient deterrence. Indeed, loss-based liability is usually more threatening than gain-based liability. Most wrongs cause injuries without simultaneously generating benefits. Furthermore, whereas disgorgement merely restores the defendant's status quo ante, compensation usually requires the depletion of pre-existing resources.

Nevertheless, there are situations, outside of fiduciary relationships, in which the prospect of loss-based liability fails to provide adequate deterrence. That is true when a person commits a wrong after having cynically calculated that he will be left with a net gain even if he is required to repair the victim's injury.[127]

---

126 Cf IM Jackman, "Restitution for Wrongs" (1989) 48 *Cambridge Law Journal* 302 at 304. Jackman argues that "restitution" (he did not distinguish between restitutionary damages and disgorgement) is warranted where needed to protect "facilitative institutions," which he defines as "power conferring facilities for the creation of private arrangements between individuals, such as contracts, trusts and private property." In contrast to interests like bodily integrity and reputation, which exist even outside of a legal system, facilitative institutions exist only by virtue of the law and hence are relatively more vulnerable.

Jackman's thesis works well at a descriptive level insofar as it closely corresponds to the patterns of liability that are found in the cases. It seems less compelling at an explanatory level. While the trust may rely upon the availability of disgorgement for its very existence, it is doubtful that the concept of private property is similarly dependent. The relative infrequency with which proprietary torts have generated gain-based relief (as opposed to compensatory relief which may incidentally compel disgorgement of the defendant's gain) suggests otherwise.

127 J Edelman, *Gain-Based Damages: Contract, Tort, Equity and Intellectual Property* (Hart Publishing, Oxford, 2002) at 81-86. In contrast, Edelman argues that restitutionary damages should be available anytime that the defendant wrongfully acquired a benefit from the claimant.

Restitutionary damages are relatively easy to justify precisely because they merely reverse a transfer of wealth between the parties. See also JP Dawson, *Unjust Enrichment: A Comparative Analysis* (Little Brown & Co, Boston, 1951) at 7 ("[A] claim asserting enrichment through another's loss deserves special and more favourable treatment. The sense of justice supports the conclusion drawn from simple arithmetic, that a loss translated into another's gain is much more impressive than the loss would be alone."); LL Fuller and WR Perdue "The Reliance Interest in Contract Damages" (1936), 46 *Yale Law Journal* 52 at 56 ("The 'restitution interest,' involving a combination of unjust impoverishment with unjust gain, represents the strongest case for relief. ... [T]he restitution interest presents twice as strong a claim to judicial intervention as the reliance interest, since if A not only causes B to lose one unit but

Although such behaviour may also attract exemplary damages,[128] disgorgement arguably provides the better remedy.[129] Because the gain-based remedy is rigidly tied to the value of the defendant's enrichment, it is largely immune to the criticism that civil courts ought to refrain from punitive measures.

The deterrence-based rationale for disgorgement is supported by precedent. In the context of proprietary torts, the remedy has been restricted to benefits acquired through cynical breach. Accordingly, while the victim of a trademark violation or passing off is invariably entitled to compensation, an account of profits will not be ordered unless the tortfeasor was dishonest.[130] Deterrence principles play an even stronger role if a person tortiously works another's mine. The courts have expressly manipulated the measures of relief in order to "prevent trespass of this kind".[131] Not only is the deliberate wrongdoer denied certain allowances in connection with compensatory damages,[132] he may also be subject to an account of profits by way of equity's auxiliary jurisdiction.[133]

Accepting that to be true, it must be asked why proprietary torts have so seldom generated purely gain-based relief. The answer may lie in the fact that damages awarded for a compensatory purpose frequently have the incidental effect of either reversing an unwarranted transfer or stripping an ill-gotten enrichment. So much so that, as previously explained, the academic argument in favour of gain-based relief for legal wrongdoing rests largely upon the reinterpretation of cases in which the defendant was actually ordered to repair the claimant's loss. And because the courts of law have been willing to extend the concept of compensable harm beyond the paradigm of positive economic injury, there traditionally has not been much need to invoke less orthodox measures of relief. Equity's attitude has been different simply because, given

---

appropriates that unit to himself, the resulting discrepancy between A and B is not one unit but two.").

    Disgorgement requires a higher threshold to judicial intervention because the defendant may have acquired the wealth from a third party, and because relief may therefore create a windfall for the claimant.

128 Even in England: *Rookes v Barnard* [1964] AC 1129.

129 Of course, the fact that disgorgement is rigidly tied to the value of the defendant's enrichment does limit the potential for deterrence. The wrongdoer may cynically calculate not only that his gain will exceed the claimant's loss, but also that claimant is unlikely to fully prosecute her right to disgorgement (for example, because the breach may not be detected or because the lawsuit may be settled for a reduced amount). Consequently, even allowing for the possibility of being held additionally liable for costs, the wrongdoer may rationally decide to breach his obligation. It is for that reason that exemplary damages may be calculated *in excess of* the defendant's actual gain. The courts appreciate the need to make sure that the defendant truly hurts: *Broome v Cassell and Co* [1972] AC 1027 at 1130.

130 *Lever v Goodwin* (1887) 36 Ch D 1; *My Kinda Town Ltd v Soll* [1982] FSR 147, rev'd on other grounds [1983] RPC 15; *Edelsten v Edelsten* (1863) 1 De GJ & S 185; 46 ER 72; *Slazenger & Sons v Spalding & Bros* [1910] 1 Ch 257; *Colbeam Palmer Ltd v Stock Affiliates Pty Ltd* (1968) 122 CLR 25.

131 *Martin v Porter* (1839) 5 M & W 351 at 354; 151 ER 149 at 150; *Wild v Holt* (1842) 9 M & W 672 at 674; 152 ER 284 at 285; cf *Livingstone v Rawyards Coal Co* (1880) LR 5 App Cas 25 at 40.

132 To reiterate, whereas the innocent tortfeasor is entitled to deduct both the cost of severance and the cost of raising from the value of the claimant's coal as determined at the pit mouth, the deliberate tortfeasor is only entitled to the second allowance.

133 *Phillips v Homfray (No 3)* (1892) 1 Ch 465.

historical constraints on the availability of compensatory relief, the account of profits was often thought to be the only means of correcting a breach and deterring future wrongdoing. Consequently, whereas courts of law continue to confine disgorgement to cases in which the defendant cynically committed a tort with a view to realising a net gain, chancery has never insisted upon proof of that sort of dishonesty.

Extending the account of profits for legal wrongs

There is nothing inherently equitable about the need for purely gain-based relief. The mechanisms available for the disgorgement of tortious gains are, however, inadequate. As long as a dispute remains entirely at law, the court is apt to manipulate compensatory principles and to remove the defendant's enrichment under the pretence of repairing the claimant's loss. That approach carries a number of costs. The concept of loss is stretched, some would say to a breaking point. Moreover, there is an understandable temptation to read the cases as they perhaps ought to have been decided (that is, on disgorgement basis), rather than as they were actually resolved (that is, on compensatory grounds). But, of course, since not every reader will succumb to that temptation, there is a danger of inconsistency and error. And finally, because disgorgement is often buried beneath a compensatory analysis, and achieved only indirectly, it may be overlooked or denied where it ought to succeed.

Disgorgement ought to play a more prominent and principled role within tort law. The common law could provide such relief itself, perhaps by reviving the ancient legal doctrine of account, or perhaps by openly accepting that damages may be calculated by reference to either the victim's loss or the tortfeasor's gain. The simpler route, however, would be to award an account of profits through equity's auxiliary jurisdiction. That process is already accepted and understood. There would be no need to fight for recognition of a "new" remedy. Moreover, equity would simply intervene, in the usual manner, where the common law was inadequate (the inadequacy in this instance pertaining to the need for profit-stripping deterrence).

Although the point is implicit in the preceding discussion, it bears repeating that the current proposal is *not* that the equitable account of profits should be available in response to *every* wrongful enrichment. The response to a tort prima facie should remain compensation. Disgorgement should be confined to exceptional circumstances in which reparation of the claimant's loss fails to meet the needs of the legal system. Deterrence of cynical misconduct is one such need. There may be others.[134]

---

134   Messrs Doyle and Wright argue that the account of profits should be extended to situations in which the common law remedies are "inadequate," but they do not define "inadequacy." They prefer instead for the courts to work out, over time, categories of "inadequacy", S Doyle and D Wright, "Restitutionary Damages — The Unnecessary Remedy?" (2001) 25 *Melbourne University Law Review* 1 at 12-13. See also IE Davidson and MP Cleary, 'Taking Accounts' in P Parkinson (ed), *The Principles of Equity* (2nd ed, Lawbook Co, Sydney, 2003) at 946 (arguing that the account of profits should be "available to assist in the aid of a common law right in situations … where necessary to assist the enforcement of a common law right").

17

The Importance of Specific Performance

ROBERT CHAMBERS[1]

INTRODUCTION

The modern law of contract is a well blended mixture of common law, equity, and statute. The equitable contribution to the subject comes to the surface in many places, such as the rescission or rectification of contracts, enforcement of contracts by injunctions or orders for specific performance, and relief from the effects of penalty clauses and forfeitures. Students are introduced to the rules of law and equity together as part of the law of contract, while lawyers and judges deal with those rules together in contracts cases. This is an area of law in which the fusion of law and equity works well.

Similar things can be said of the modern law of property. It too is a thorough mixture of common law, equity, and statute. It could not be learned or applied properly with the equitable contribution removed. Try to imagine the mortgage without the equity of redemption, beneficial ownership without the trust, or servitudes over land without the restrictive covenant. The equitable contributions are so fully integrated that their removal would leave behind an incomplete and often unusable shell. Equitable rules can safely be jettisoned when an entire area of law is replaced by a statutory code. For example, the equitable charge over the inventory and receivables of a business is no longer needed in jurisdictions that have adopted the American-style personal property security law, which provides for the registration of security interests in after acquired property. However, the isolated removal of an equitable principle from the law of property by a court or a legislature is dangerous, for it can have unintended and wide-ranging consequences.

This chapter is a response to just such a danger. One of the oldest rules of equity, lying at the intersection of contract and property, is under attack by the highest courts in Australia and Canada. Traditionally, when a vendor made a contract to sell an interest in land, the purchaser normally acquired that interest in equity when the contract was made, in advance of the vendor's

---

1   I thank Dr James Edelman for discussing these ideas with me and offering many helpful
     suggestions.

performance of the contractual obligation to transfer legal title. As Jessel MR said in *Lysaght v Edwards*:[2]

> "It appears to me that the effect of a contract for sale has been settled for more than two centuries... [T]he moment you have a valid contract for sale the vendor becomes in equity a trustee for the purchaser of the estate sold, and the beneficial ownership passes to the purchaser, the vendor having a right to the purchase-money, a charge or lien on the estate for the security of that purchase-money, and a right to retain possession of the estate until the purchase-money is paid, in the absence of express contract as to the time of delivering possession."

This rule depends upon the specific performance of contracts of sale. So long as the contract to sell an asset is specifically enforceable under the rules of equity, the purchaser acquires an equitable interest in that asset when the contract is made. However, if the contract is not specifically enforceable, then the purchaser does not acquire the promised interest in equity (although the purchaser might have a lien on the asset to secure the vendor's obligation to refund the purchase price). A contract is not specifically enforceable if damages provide an adequate alternative to performance or if it is not enforceable at all because it is invalid or has been frustrated or terminated.

Traditionally, most contracts to sell an interest in land were specifically enforceable and conferred an equitable interest on the purchaser. The main exceptions were cases where the contracts were defective due to mistake, undue influence, etc, or where performance was impossible, for example, because the vendor did not have and could not obtain good title. However, if a contract to sell an interest in land was valid and capable of performance, it was almost always specifically enforceable.

In contrast, most contracts to sell goods are not specifically enforceable, because damages enable the purchaser to acquire replacement goods from another vendor and therefore provide the purchaser with an adequate remedy for non-performance. However, the different treatment of land and goods is due, not to different rules, but to different outcomes when the same rules are applied to different subject matter. Normally, damages provide an adequate remedy for breach of a contract for the sale of goods but not for the sale of land. Where damages would be inadequate, specific performance becomes the normal remedy, whether the subject matter is goods or land, and the purchaser acquires an interest in the subject matter when the contract is made. As Lord Westbury LC said in *Holroyd v Marshall*:[3]

> "A contract for valuable consideration, by which it is agreed to make a present transfer of property, passes at once the beneficial interest, provided the contract is one of which a Court of Equity will decree specific performance.... [T]he vendor becomes a trustee for the vendee; subject, of course, to the

---

2   (1876) 2 Ch D 499 at 506. See SC Milsom, *Historical Foundations of the Common Law* (2nd ed, Butterworths, London, 1981) at 223-224; AB Simpson, *A History of the Common Law of Contract* (Oxford University Press, Oxford, 1987) at 346-347; AJ Oakley, *Constructive Trusts* (3rd ed, Sweet & Maxwell, London, 1997) at 275; C Harpum, *RE Megarry & H Wade: The Law of Real Property* (6th ed, Sweet & Maxwell, London, 2000) at 676-680.

3   (1862) 10 HLC 191 at 209; 11 ER 999.

contract being one to be specifically performed. And this is true, not only of contracts relating to real estate, but also of contracts relating to personal property, provided that the latter are such as a Court of Equity would direct to be specifically performed."

This rule is now under attack on two fronts, north and south. The Supreme Court of Canada has said, in *Semelhago v Paramadevan*,[4] that contracts to sell interests in land are no longer routinely specifically enforceable. Land is no different from a chattel and damages provide an adequate remedy unless the purchaser can prove otherwise. Although the court did not deal with the consequences of this change, it follows that, since contracts to sell interests in land are not normally specifically enforceable, the purchaser of an interest in land does not normally acquire the promised interest in equity. In other words, the normal contract to transfer an interest in land no longer creates property rights, but gives the purchaser only a personal right to receive, at the vendor's option, either performance of the contract or damages.

Meanwhile, the High Court of Australia has not removed the purchaser's right to specific performance of contracts to sell interests in land, but has attacked the traditional rule regarding the consequences of specific performance. In *Tanwar Enterprises Pty Ltd v Cauchi*,[5] the Court suggested that the vendor should no longer be regarded as a constructive trustee for the purchaser, but did not say clearly what property rights, if any, are created by a specifically enforceable contract to transfer an asset.

Both attacks are dangerous. They upset rules that have been well settled for centuries and it is not clear what benefits will be derived from the change. This is not to say that old rules are, or should be, immune to judicial change. However, changes must be made carefully and only after due consideration of their potential effects throughout the law. The courts that have attacked these rules of equity have not fully considered the wide range of consequences that may flow from their abolition.

The rules in question are not confined to contracts of sale, but apply generally to any specifically enforceable promise to transfer an asset. It is the reason why a contract to grant a lease, mortgage, profit, or easement, produces an equitable version of the promised right. An option to purchase is an equitable interest in land only because the exercise of that option will produce a specifically enforceable contract of sale. Changing the rules for the paradigm case, a contract for the sale of land, may shake the foundations of property law, because it must affect all contracts to transfer assets unless some justification can be found for treating contracts of sale differently.

Also, full consideration of this issue should not be confined to contracts. There is a larger principle at work, which applies both at law and in equity. Whenever someone has the power to obtain title to an asset, whether through rescission, rectification, specific performance, or even self help, that person thereby obtains a property right to that asset. Any change to the rules regarding

---

4   (1996) 136 DLR (4th) 1.
5   [2003] HCA 57 at [43]-[57]; 77 ALJR 1853 at 1860-1863. See also W Swadling, 'The Vendor-Purchaser Constructive Trust', at chapter 18 in this book.

the specific performance of contracts of sale should take into account the larger principle on which those rules are based.

Consistency in the law is essential, for the rule of law demands that like cases be treated alike. However, also at stake is another important value: legal certainty. The move away from a certain and settled rule towards the exercise of judicial discretion is almost always undesirable. Uncertainty in the law favours the rich over the poor and the strong over the weak. The costs of litigation, both financially and emotionally, can be ruinous for the ordinary citizen. It is important that, as often as possible, people are able to ascertain their legal rights and obligations, with the aid of legal advice if necessary, but without resort to litigation.

This chapter considers first the Canadian attack on the rule that, normally, contracts to sell land are specifically enforceable. It then considers the Australian attack on the rule that specifically enforceable contracts of sale produce constructive trusts. The conclusion is that these rules are too important to the law of property to be abolished.

SPECIFIC PERFORMANCE OF LAND CONTRACTS

Obiter dictum

The Supreme Court of Canada has strongly attacked the traditional rule regarding the specific performance of contracts to sell interests in land, but only in an obiter dictum, so hope remains that the rule will be fully considered by that court in some future case. In *Semelhago v Paramadevan*,[6] the vendor had breached a contract to sell a house under construction. The purchaser sued for specific performance of that contract and, at trial four years later, elected to take damages in lieu of performance.[7] The parties agreed that the purchaser had been entitled to specific performance and their appeals were argued on that basis. Their dispute was limited to the proper calculation of damages.

The trial judge doubted whether specific performance should be available, but felt constrained to apply the traditional rule and the parties did not challenge that aspect of her judgment. The Supreme Court of Canada suggested, apparently on its own initiative, that the contract was not specifically enforceable and that the outcome would have been different if the rule had been challenged. Sopinka J said, "in future cases, under similar circumstances, a trial judge will not be constrained to find that specific performance is an appropriate remedy."[8]

Although this attack on the traditional rule is not binding on lower courts, it was the judgment of six of the seven members of the court. Only La Forest J did not think the challenge to traditional rule was appropriate:[9]

---

6   (1996) 136 DLR (4th) 1.
7   Under Ontario's *Courts of Justice Act*, RSO 1990, c C.43, s 99, "A court that has jurisdiction to grant an injunction or order specific performance may award damages in addition to, or in substitution for, the injunction or specific performance."
8   *Semelhago v Paramadevan*, above n 6 at 11.
9   *Semelhago v Paramadevan*, above n 6 at 2.

"However, given the assumption under which the case was argued, I prefer not to deal with the circumstances giving rise to entitlement to specific performance or generally the interpretation that should be given to the legislation authorizing the award of damages in lieu of specific performance. In considering modification to existing law, both these interdependent factors may well require examination, and the arguments in this case were not made in those terms."

Lower courts are treating the obiter dictum in *Semelhago v Paramadevan*, not as an invitation to reconsider the traditional rule, but as the abolition of it.[10] In *John E Dodge Holdings Ltd v 805062 Ontario Ltd*, Lax J referred to it as "critical obiter".[11] In *Corse v Ravenwood Homes Ltd*, Master Funduk said, "although that is admitted obiter it is obiter of the highest order. There is obiter and there is obiter. Some has a lot more weight than others."[12] He applied the obiter dictum in *Semelhago v Paramadevan* and held that specific performance was not available, because there was nothing special about the land being sold.

Adequacy of damages

The Supreme Court of Canada did not challenge the rule that specific performance is available only when damages are inadequate. It removed the assumption that damages are normally not an adequate substitute for performance of a contract to sell an interest in land. Sopinka J said:[13]

"While at one time the common law regarded every piece of real estate to be unique, with the progress of modern real estate development this is no longer the case. Residential, business and industrial properties are all mass produced much in the same way as other consumer products. If a deal falls through for one property, another is frequently, though not always, readily available. It is no longer appropriate, therefore, to maintain a distinction in the approach to specific performance as between realty and personalty. It cannot be assumed that damages for breach of contract for the purchase and sale of real estate will be an inadequate remedy in all cases. The common law recognized that the distinction might not be valid when the land had no peculiar or special value."

Canadian judges and jurists now face the difficult task of working out the conditions under which a contract to sell an interest in land will be specifically enforceable. It will not be easy because that issue was not properly before the Supreme Court of Canada in *Semelhago v Paramadevan* and the judgment contains little guidance other than the suggestion that the contract in that case was not specifically enforceable.

What does it mean to say that damages are inadequate? No doubt it would be possible to compensate a purchaser fully for the loss of the promised land. In personal injury cases, compensation is awarded for pain, mental anguish, the

---

10 See, for example, *1174538 Ontario Ltd v Barzel Windsor (1984) Inc* [1999] OJ No 5091; *Buckwheat Enterprises Inc v Shiu* (2001) 48 RPR (3d) 72; *Ali v 656527 BC Ltd* (2004) 201 BCAC 140; *Trinden Enterprises Ltd v Ramsay* (2004) 20 RPR (4th) 138.

11 (2001) 56 OR (3d) 341 at [50]; affirmed (2003) 223 DLR (4th) 541.

12 (1998) 226 AR 214 at 218.

13 *Semelhago v Paramadevan* (1996) 136 DLR (4th) 1 at 9-10.

loss of life or limb, etc. By necessity, non-replaceable things are given monetary values. A disappointed purchaser could be awarded damages for lost expectations, disappointment, and inconvenience. If necessary, exemplary and restitutionary damages could be awarded to remove incentives for vendors to breach their contracts.[14] However, the problem in this situation is not the adequacy of compensation or deterrence, but whether damages are an adequate substitute for performance. If the purchaser can readily obtain the same asset from another vendor, then damages provide a perfect substitute for performance and there is no reason to compel the vendor to perform the contract. However, if the same asset is not readily available in the marketplace, then damages do not provide a substitute for performance and, traditionally, specific performance has been available.

Specific performance has not been limited to cases where it is impossible to obtain the same asset from another vendor, but has been awarded in cases where the asset is merely difficult to obtain or not readily available elsewhere. For example, in *Dougan v Ley*,[15] a buyer was entitled to specific performance of a contract for the sale of a taxicab, even though the buyer was able to buy another one before trial. This was because the number of cab licences was limited and, therefore, few cabs were available for sale and they were hard to obtain.

Specific performance was routinely available for contracts to sell interests in land, because damages could never provide a perfect substitute for performance. Although the purchaser might be able to find other land with similar features, it was simply not possible to obtain the same land from another vendor. Therefore, the payment of money could never be equivalent to performance since it would not put the purchaser in the same position he or she would have been in if the contract had been performed. Traditionally, damages were not adequate if they merely enabled the purchaser to obtain similar assets and therefore similar performance. This is why contracts to sell corporate shares are specifically enforceable, if the shares are not publicly traded.[16] It does not matter that the buyer could obtain shares in a similar corporation. Since the promised shares are not readily available from another seller, damages would not provide a perfect substitute for performance of the contract.

Semelhago v Paramadevan invalidated the traditional approach to the adequacy of damages. Sopinka J said, "specific performance should, therefore, not be granted as a matter of course absent evidence that the property is unique to the extent that its substitute would not be readily available."[17] Since all land is unique, Sopinka J was using the words "its substitute" to mean similar land. To obtain specific performance in Canada, a purchaser must now lead evidence that similar land is not readily available. Damages are adequate if they enable the purchaser to obtain similar performance from another vendor and it is

---

14   See M McInnes, "Gain-Based Relief for Breach of Contract: *Attorney General v Blake*" (2001) 35 *Canadian Business Law Journal* 72 at 79-80; J Edelman, *Gain-Based Damages* (Hart Publishing, Oxford, 2002) at 155, 166-169.

15   (1946) 71 CLR 142.

16   *Eansor v Eansor* [1946] 2 DLR 781.

17   *Semelhago v Paramadevan* above n 13 at 11.

assumed that the purchaser can obtain something sufficiently similar in the absence of evidence to the contrary.[18]

How does one decide whether one parcel of land is sufficiently similar to another for this purpose? Two relevant factors can be gleaned from the judgment in *Semelhago v Paramadevan*: the character of the land and the subjective value of that land to that particular purchaser.[19] Specific performance is not available unless the promised land is special to the purchaser in some particular way. There are, however, three main and significant problems with this approach. First, it contravenes the fundamental principle of equality before the law. Secondly, it introduces an unnecessary element of uncertainty. Thirdly, it has major, unintended consequences for the law of property.

Inequality

Under the rule of law, all men and women are equal before the law. Their rights should not depend on irrelevant personal characteristics, such as social class, wealth, or race. This is why justice personified wears a blindfold. By refusing specific performance unless the land has unique features of special value to the purchaser, the Supreme Court of Canada has unintentionally made the right to specific performance dependent on personal characteristics that should be irrelevant before the law.

In *Semelhago v Paramadevan*, Sopinka J quoted with apparent approval the following passage from the judgment of Gushue JA in *Chaulk v Fairview Construction Ltd*:[20]

"The question here is whether damages would have afforded Chaulk an adequate remedy, and I have no doubt that they could, and would, have. There was nothing whatever unique or irreplaceable about the houses and lots bargained for. They were merely subdivision lots with houses, all of the same general design, built on them, which the respondent was purchasing for investment or re-sale purposes only. He had sold the first two almost immediately at a profit, and intended to do the same with the remainder. It would be quite different if we were dealing with a house or houses which were of a particular architectural design, or were situated in a particularly desirable location, but this was certainly not the case."

The last sentence of the quotation is telling. Specific performance is available if the house is "of a particular architectural design" or "in a particularly desirable location", but not if it is part of a subdivision of houses "all of the same general design". Wealthier members of society buy houses with special architectural features in desirable locations. They will be entitled to specific performance, while working class families will not have that same rights to the houses they can afford. This sort of condescension is unacceptable and ignores

---

18   *11 Suntract Holdings Ltd v Chassis Service & Hydraulics Ltd* (1997) 36 OR (3d) 328 at 349; *Taberner v Ernest & Twins Developments Inc* (2001) 89 BCLR (3d) 104 at [4]; *United Gulf Developments Ltd v Iskandar* (2004) 235 DLR (4th) 609 at [17]-[18].

19   *Buckwheat Enterprises Inc v Shiu* (2001) 48 RPR (3d) 72 at [13]; *John E Dodge Holdings Ltd v 805062 Ontario Ltd* (2001) 56 OR (3d) 341 at [55], [59]; affirmed (2003) 223 DLR (4th) 541; *Ali v 656527 BC Ltd* (2004) 201 BCAC 140 at [29].

20   (1977) 14 Nfld & PEIR 13 at 21.

the importance to average homeowners of innumerable factors that make one house more desirable than another, regardless of market value. As the main character complained in the movie, *The Castle*, "but it's not a house. It's a home."[21] The family that skimps and saves to buy an average home deserves the same rights as those members of society who can afford more luxurious accommodation.

The personal characteristics of right holders may affect the economic value of their rights, but should not affect the existence of their rights. For example, suppose a claimant was injured by the defendant's negligence and therefore unable to work for three months. The value of the claim for lost income depends on what the claimant does for a living, which in turn may depend on the claimant's abilities, age, class, culture, education, race, and sex. However, the existence of the claim does not depend on those factors. Every person in the claimant's position, regardless of personal characteristics, would hold the same right to be placed in the economic position he or she would have obtained if the tort had not occurred. Similarly, the economic value of a right to specific performance of a contract of sale depends on the value of the land, which may depend on what the purchaser can afford to pay, which in turn may depend on the purchaser's age, class, education, etc. However, the existence of the right to specific performance should not be linked in any way to those personal characteristics.

The availability of specific performance should not depend on the desirability of the land sold. Nor should it depend on the particular desires of the purchaser. However, *Semelhago v Paramadevan* linked specific performance to the special value of the land to the purchaser. Sopinka J quoted with approval this statement of Sir John Leach VC in *Adderley v Dixon*:[22]

> "Courts of Equity decree the specific performance of contracts, not upon any distinction between realty and personalty, but because damages at law may not, in the particular case, afford a complete remedy. Thus a Court of Equity decrees performance of a contract for land, not because of the real nature of the land, but because damages at law, which must be calculated upon the general money value of land, may not be a complete remedy to the purchaser, to whom the land may have a peculiar and special value."

This correct statement of the law was misunderstood. Purchasers did not have to prove that the land had some "peculiar and special value" to them. It was the mere possibility that the land had that value that justified specific performance of the contract. Damages were inadequate simply because the same land was not available from another vendor. Purchasers had not been required to demonstrate that similar land would not provide an adequate substitute for performance. The right to specific performance depended not on the particular values of a particular purchaser, but on the belief that all purchasers had a right to the promised land and did not have to settle for substitutes that may or may not meet their needs or desires.

---

21   Written by S Cilauro, T Gleisner, J Kennedy, and R Sitch (1997).
22   (1824) 1 Sim & St 607; 57 ER 239 at 240.

In *Holden v Tanase*,[23] Master Breitkreuz followed the obiter dictum in *Semelhago v Paramadevan* and held that a contract to sell a house was specifically enforceable, because similar properties were not available and because the property had special value to the purchaser. The house was within walking distance of a (gridiron) football stadium, the purchaser was a "huge football fan", and it was one of very few properties in that area with an extra wide lot and finished basement. Although these factors provide perhaps the only meaningful way to distinguish this contract from the contracts in *Semelhago v Paramadevan* and *Chaulk v Fairview Construction Ltd*, above, it is wrong to make the right to specific performance dependent on the subjective desires of the parties. The rule of law requires that every person is equal before the law and that like cases are treated alike. It is unacceptable that a football fan has a right to the land, while a hockey fan must settle for damages.

Another potential problem created by the new approach is its effect on mutuality. Previously, both vendors and purchasers could sue for specific performance of a contract of sale. However, if the availability of specific performance depends on the peculiar and special values of the purchaser, how will a vendor ever succeed in obtaining an order for specific performance? For example, if the vendor in *Holden v Tanase*, above, had sued for specific performance, how could he possibly have proved that the purchaser was a "huge football fan" with a special desire for a house with a finished basement on an extra wide lot near the football stadium. The purchaser will simply deny that the land has any special subjective value, creating an insurmountable obstacle for the vendor. Although the rule that vendors can sue for specific performance has been criticised,[24] and perhaps should be changed, an unintended consequence of *Semelhago v Paramadevan* is that vendors and purchasers no longer have equal access to the remedy of specific performance.[25]

Semelhago v Paramadevan is not the first case in which the Supreme Court of Canada linked rights to personal characteristics that should have been irrelevant. In *Soulos v Korkontzilas*,[26] the plaintiff hired the defendant as his real estate agent to purchase land on his behalf. The defendant told the plaintiff that the land was unavailable and secretly purchased it for his own benefit. The Supreme Court of Canada declared that the defendant held the land on constructive trust for the plaintiff. This was an unexceptional application of the principle, derived from *Keech v Sandford*,[27] that assets acquired in breach of fiduciary duty must be given up to the victim of that breach. Disconcerting is the extra requirement introduced by the court that the plaintiff must show some special reason for seeking a proprietary remedy. In *Soulos v Korkontzilas*, special emphasis was laid on the facts that the plaintiff was Greek, the plaintiff's bank was located on the land, and "being one's banker's landlord was a source

---

23   (2002) 331 AR 11.
24   G Jones and W Goodhart, *Specific Performance* (2nd ed, Butterworths, London, 1996) at 33.
25   See *Taylor v Sturgeon* (1996) 156 NSR (2d) 147 at [19]; DH Clark, "'Will that be Performance ... Or Cash?': *Semelhago v Paramadevan* and the Notion of Equivalence" (1999) 37 *Alberta Law Review* 589 at 595-596.
26   (1997) 146 DLR (4th) 214.
27   (1726) Sel Cas T King 61; 25 ER 223.

of prestige in the Greek community of which he was a member."[28] The constructive trust was justified, in part, because of the plaintiff's "continuing desire, albeit for non-monetary reasons, to own the particular property in question."[29]

Surely, a person's rights do not depend on her or his cultural heritage. It would be absurd if the plaintiff in *Soulos v Korkontzilas* was entitled to beneficial ownership of the land because his parents were Greek, but would have lost his case if they had been Honduran, Italian, or Japanese. This is unacceptable in any nation under the rule of law and particularly surprising in a nation with a constitution that protects it citizens from "discrimination based on race, national or ethnic origin, colour, religion, sex, age or mental or physical disability."[30] However, this problem arises whenever the existence of rights are linked to the subjective values of the right holder. A person's values can be influenced by a wide range of personal attributes, such as age, culture, education, intelligence, politics, race, religion, sex, and wealth. If rights to land depend on proof that the claimant places some "peculiar and special value" on that land, those rights will vary according to personal characteristics that should be irrelevant if all claimants are truly equal before the law.

Equality before the law also dictates that it should not matter what the purchaser intends to do with the property. In *Semelhago v Paramadevan*, the trial judge thought it was relevant that the parties "were sophisticated dealers in real estate"[31] and, in *Chaulk v Fairview Construction Ltd*, emphasis was placed on the fact that the purchase was "for investment or re-sale purposes only."[32] However, motives for making a contract should not affect the rights acquired under that contract, unless they are somehow incorporated into the terms of that contract. Purchasers who want to live in the house they are buying should be treated the same as purchasers who want the house only as an investment or to demolish it for commercial development. Unless the purchaser's intentions regarding the future use of the land are incorporated in a restrictive covenant, they will not limit her or his rights to use the fee simple estate once the sale is complete. It is strange that intentions, which were not incorporated into the contract between the parties, are allowed to have any effect on the purchaser's right to enforce that contract.

The rights acquired under a contract of sale should not depend on non-contractual motives or the peculiar and special values of the parties. It is contrary to the principle of equality before the law to link those rights to factors other than the terms and subject matter of the contract. Of course, the contract might not be enforceable if it was induced by misrepresentations, duress, or undue influence or entered into by mistake. However, if the contract

---

28   *Soulos v Korkontzilas*, above n 26 at 218.
29   *Soulos v Korkontzilas*, above n 26 at 231.
30   *Constitution Act 1982*, s 15.
31   (1996) 136 DLR (4th) 1 at 5 per Corbett J.
32   (1977) 14 Nfld & PEIR 13 at 21 per Gushue JA. Also see *1174538 Ontario Ltd v Barzel Windsor (1984) Inc* [1999] OJ No 5091; *Buckwheat Enterprises Inc v Shiu* (2001) 48 RPR (3d) 72; *John E Dodge Holdings Ltd v 805062 Ontario Ltd* (2001) 56 OR (3d) 341 at [60]; affirmed (2003) 223 DLR (4th) 541 at 556.

is valid, the rights it creates should be the same regardless of the personal characteristics and desires of the right holder.

There is no need to go beyond the contract to consider whether the purchaser places any peculiar and special value on the land. The existence of a valid contract of sale establishes that the purchaser places a higher value on the land than does the vendor. The vendor has freely chosen to sell and therefore values the land less than the purchase price, while the purchaser has freely chosen to buy and therefore values the land more than the purchase price.[33] Performance of the contract gives both parties exactly what they bargained for and shifts ownership of the land to the person who values it more. This might suggest that specific performance should be available for all contracts of sale, including the sale of goods, but that remedy is unnecessary in cases where the same goods are readily available from another vendor. In those cases, damages provide a perfect substitute for performance and produce a result that is consistent with the subjective values of the parties.

Uncertainty

The second fundamental objection to the obiter dictum in *Semelhago v Paramadevan* is that it creates unnecessary uncertainty, thereby increasing the likelihood and costs of litigation.[34] There are many legal contexts in which uncertainty cannot be avoided. For example, the law relies heavily on the discretion of judges to assess the credibility of witnesses, dole out suitable punishments to criminals, and make child custody orders that further the best interests of children. Reliance on discretion increases uncertainty, but is necessary in those situations. The objection here is that the uncertainty introduced in *Semelhago v Paramadevan* was wholly unnecessary.

It is often said that specific performance is a discretionary remedy.[35] However, the exercise of that discretion had been well settled with respect to contracts to sell interests in land.[36] Specific performance was routinely available, so long as the contract was valid and capable of performance. Prior to *Semelhago v Paramadevan*, most vendors and purchasers could accurately predict the outcome of a suit for specific performance without having to resort to litigation. Specific performance now depends on proof that the land has peculiar and special value to the purchaser and that no other land with the desired qualities is readily available. Even with expert legal advice, the availability of specific performance is now highly unpredictable in Canada and likely to remain so for many years to come.

It is not clear what advantages, if any, were obtained by unsettling this previously settled area of law. There does not seem to be any significant

---

33 See OV Da Silva, "The Supreme Court of Canada's Lost Opportunity: *Semelhago v Paramadevan*" (1998) 23 *Queen's Law Journal* 475 at 490, 497.

34 N Siebrasse, "Damages in Lieu of Specific Performance: *Semelhago v Paramadevan*" (1997) 76 *Canadian Bar Review* 551 at 565-566; DH Clark, "'Will that be Performance ... Or Cash?': *Semelhago v Paramadevan* and the Notion of Equivalence" (1999) 37 *Alberta Law Review* 589 at 592.

35 G Jones and W Goodhart, *Specific Performance* (2nd ed, Butterworths, London, 1996) at 1.

36 *Goldsbrough, Mort & Co Ltd v Quinn* (1910) 10 CLR 674 at 698.

problem caused by the specific performance of contracts to sell interests in land. The problem, which was the issue in *Semelhago v Paramadevan*, concerned the proper calculation of damages in lieu of specific performance. If specific performance is available, then damages are calculated at the date of trial rather than the date of breach and the plaintiff need not take action to mitigate loss. If the court was dissatisfied with the calculation of damages in lieu of specific performance, then why not reform the law of damages?[37] The obiter dictum in *Semelhago v Paramadevan* only exacerbated the problem since there will still be many people entitled to specific performance, who can elect to take damages in lieu of performance, but there will now be many more people who have no idea whether specific performance is available, how damages should be calculated, and whether they should take steps to mitigate loss. It may well have been better simply to remove the right to specific performance altogether. At the very least, that would have produced a certain and simple rule that applied equally to all persons.

It was suggested in *Semelhago v Paramadevan* that the rules that used to apply to land were different from the rules that applied to goods and that courts should now treat land in the same manner that they have always treated goods. However, this is not what that obiter dictum accomplished. Previously, the same rule had applied to all contracts of sale, regardless of the subject matter. Damages were adequate if the same assets were readily available from another vendor, but not otherwise. Therefore, specific performance was routinely available for contracts to sell interests in land and rarely available for contracts to sell ordinary goods.

Semelhago v Paramadevan introduced a new rule for contracts to sell interests in land. Damages will now provide an adequate remedy if it is possible for purchasers to obtain sufficiently similar land. This was not the rule that applied to the sale of goods and other assets. For example, a contract to sell corporate shares is specifically enforceable if the shares are not publicly traded. Purchasers are not required to prove that those shares have "peculiar and special value" to them that could not be obtained from shares in similar corporations. Specific performance is available as a matter of course simply because those same shares are not readily available elsewhere. A question raised by *Semelhago v Paramadevan* is whether the new approach to the sale of land should also be applied to the sale of other assets.

Unintended Consequences

The third and probably most serious objection to the approach taken in *Semelhago v Paramadevan* is that it has major consequences for the law of property. No doubt this was unintended, because the court did not mention the proprietary effects of specific performance. It had been well settled that a contract to sell an interest in land confers on the purchaser an equitable beneficial interest in that land when the contract is made, but only if the purchaser is entitled to specific performance. As discussed below, there is some

---

37   See N Siebrasse, "Damages in Lieu of Specific Performance: *Semelhago v Paramadevan*" (1997) 76 *Canadian Bar Review* 551.

uncertainty about the nature of that property right pending performance of the purchaser's obligations under the contract. However, it is clear that the purchaser does acquire a proper right to the land at the outset and that specific performance is the basis of that right.

If specific performance is no longer routinely available, then most land contracts do not create property rights as they did before. This affects not only contracts to sell fee simple estates, but other contracts as well, including contracts to grant leases, options, easements, and profits. Every specifically enforceable contract to transfer an interest in land created property rights for the same reason. As discussed below, only contracts to grant mortgages are unaffected by the new rule. It is hard to imagine such a fundamental change to the law of property occurring without legislation, let alone by way of a casual obiter dictum.

Although courts are not often called on to make orders for specific performance, the conveyancing process is heavily dependent on the availability of that remedy. It is a process that begins with a contract of sale and ends with full performance of that contract by transfer of legal title and possession to the purchaser and payment of the purchase price to the vendor. Unlike contracts for the sale of specific goods, in which title usually passes to the buyer when the contract is made, a contract for the sale of land does not transfer legal title to purchaser, but is a promise to transfer legal title at a future date.

Traditionally, a contract to sell land created more than just personal rights. So long as the contract is specifically enforceable, the purchaser acquires an equitable beneficial interest in the land when the contract is made and also acquires an equitable lien when any part of the purchase price is paid in advance of conveyance. The purchaser's lien secures the right to any refund that might be due to the purchaser if the transaction cannot be completed. The vendor also acquires an equitable lien on the land to secure payment of the purchase price in full. The passing of property does not happen all at once, but occurs in stages as part of a process involving the creation of equitable property rights to shift beneficial ownership and secure financial obligations.

The proprietary effect of a specifically enforceable contract of sale means that the purchaser has an interest in the land in need of protection. The purchaser can insure that interest to obtain indemnification for losses caused by fire, etc, and can also preserve the priority of that interest by caveat or registration of the contract. However, if most land contracts are no longer specifically enforceable, then most purchasers do not acquire a beneficial interest in the land being sold, bear no risk of loss that needs to be insured, and have no property rights that can be protected by caveat or registration or enforced against third persons who might acquire competing interests in the land.[38]

Even if specific performance is not available, the purchaser might still have an equitable lien on the land to secure any right to refund of the purchase price. Traditionally, both vendor's and purchaser's liens have been linked to the remedy of specific performance and were not available for sale contracts that

---

38   *Corse v Ravenwood Homes Ltd* (1998) 226 AR 214; *1174538 Ontario Ltd v Barzel Windsor (1984) Inc* [1999] OJ No 5091.

would not normally be specifically enforced.[39] The liens seem to be justified by notions of reciprocity. If the vendor is compelled to transfer the land to the purchaser, then the purchaser should not be permitted to keep the land without paying the purchase price in full and, if the vendor has a lien for payment of the purchase price, then the purchaser should have a lien to secure any refund. Of course, the purchaser's lien becomes important only if the contract cannot be performed, but it was the possibility of specific performance that was important. Traditionally, the purchaser's lien would not arise if specific performance was normally not available because damages would provide an adequate remedy.

In *Hewett v Court*,[40] the majority of the High Court of Australia decided that the purchaser's lien did not depend on the potential availability of specific performance. The contract was not for the sale of land, but for the construction and sale of a prefabricated house to the purchasers' order. The purchasers had made substantial progress payments at stages of construction, the builder became insolvent, and the liquidator refused to complete the house or transfer it unfinished to the purchasers. The purchasers had an equitable lien on the unfinished house even though specific performance was not potentially available as a remedy. However, particular emphasis was placed on the connection between the payments and a specific asset being constructed specially for the purchasers. Deane J said:[41]

> "[F]rom the time construction commenced, the home had been specifically identified as the home being built for the appellants. The relationship between the potential debt and the partly completed home was plain. The potential debt was the potential liability to repay the deposit and the instalment of purchase price which had been paid as the price of work and materials for the construction of that particular home and, in the case of the instalment, on the basis that that particular home had reached the stage where the roof had been pitched. In those circumstances, the company would ... be acting unconscientiously and unfairly if it were to dispose of that partly completed home to another without the consent of the appellants and without, at the least, repaying to the appellants the money which it had received on the basis that that home would eventually be theirs."

Perhaps the same reasoning would entitle a Canadian purchaser to an equitable lien on land, even though there was no possibility of specific performance of the contract of sale because damages were an adequate remedy. Certainly, the purchase price is paid to acquire a specific asset. However, if damages are adequate, it is because there is similar land readily available that can provide the purchaser with a satisfactory substitute for performance of the contract. In that situation, the vendor would not "be acting unconscientiously and unfairly" if he or she refused to complete the sale or transferred the land to a third person. In contrast, specific performance was not available in *Hewett v*

39　*Re Stucley* [1906] 1 Ch 67 at 79-80, 84; *Capital Finance Co Ltd v Stokes* [1969] 1 Ch 261 at 278; C Harpum, *RE Megarry & H Wade: The Law of Real Property* (6th ed, Sweet & Maxwell, London, 2000) at 678.
40　(1983) 149 CLR 639.
41　*Hewett v Court*, above n 40 at 669.

Court because the contract was for the provision of services and not because damages would have provided a satisfactory substitute for performance.

According to *Semelhago v Paramadevan*, some contracts of sale will be specifically enforceable, provided the land has some "peculiar and special value" to the purchaser. Presumably, the traditional rules will still apply to those contracts and the purchaser will acquire both a beneficial interest in the land and an equitable lien on it, while the vendor acquires a lien. However, if the normal land contract does not give rise to these property rights, how will the parties determine whether their contract is normal or abnormal? Purchasers will not know whether they have an insurable interest in the land or a right to place a caveat on the vendor's title and vendors will not know whether they have a lien on the purchaser's land.

The new rule creates a basic problem, because the purchaser's interest depends on the availability of specific performance, which in turn depends on the "peculiar and special value" which that particular purchaser places on the land. If the purchaser has a property right to the land, presumably it should be possible for the purchaser to assign that right. However, if the contract is assigned to someone who does not place the same value on the land as the original purchaser, then damages would provide an adequate remedy for the assignee, specific performance would no longer be available, and the purchaser's beneficial interest in the land would cease to exist.[42]

If the existence of the purchaser's right to the land depends on the personal characteristics of the right holder, then it seems to lack an essential attribute of all property rights. As Mummery LJ said in *Dear v Reeves*, "a distinguishing feature of a right of property, in contrast to a purely personal right, is that it is transferable: it may be enforced by someone other than the particular person in whom the right was initially vested."[43] The problem created by *Semelhago v Paramadevan* is not merely that the purchaser's right is not freely assignable, but that it is intrinsically connected to the right holder. According to Professor Penner:[44]

"What distinguishes a property right is not just that they are only contingently ours, *but that they might just as well be someone else's*.... The contingency of our connection to particular items of property is such that, in theory, there is nothing special about *my* ownership of a particular car—the relationship the next owner will have to it is essentially identical. 'In theory' is there to point out that it is of course true that we may become emotionally or otherwise 'attached' to specific pieces of property, but while these attachments may have moral or political significance, or even legal significance in a secondary way, these attachments are utterly irrelevant if, or to the extent that, the object is treated as property. The converse proposition is that, to the extent that an individual personal relationship is the legally recognized essence of the relationship between a person and the putative object of property, that relationship fails to be a property relationship."

---

42   See *Buckwheat Enterprises Inc v Shiu* (2001) 48 RPR (3d) 72.

43   [2002] Ch 1 at 10.

44   JE Penner, *The Idea of Property in Law* (Clarendon, Oxford, 1997) at 112, emphasis in the original text.

Perhaps, after *Semelhago v Paramadevan*, contracts for the sale of land will no longer create property rights in Canada. For most contracts, it will be because specific performance is not available and, for the remainder, because the right to the land is personally connected to the right holder and therefore not property.

Other property rights are also affected by the loss of specific performance. An option to purchase land is an equitable interest in land, but only because the exercise of the option creates a specifically enforceable contract of sale.[45] The option holder has the right, upon meeting certain conditions, to purchase the fee simple estate. Essentially, the option is an offer to sell the land, which remains open for acceptance according to the terms of the option.

The reason why an option is itself an interest in land is because the option holder has the power to obtain title to the land. As Martland J said in *Canadian Long Island Petroleums Ltd v Irving Industries Ltd*, "forthwith upon the granting of the option, the optionee upon the occurrence of certain events solely within his control can compel a conveyance of the property to him."[46] This is why, apart from statute, a pre-emptive right (or right of first refusal) is not an interest in land before the conditions for its exercise are met (although it is, like most assignable personal rights, classified as "property" for the purposes of bankruptcy law).[47] The landowner cannot be compelled to sell, but if he or she offers the land for sale, then the pre-emptive right holder has the option to accept that offer. Therefore, the holder of the pre-emptive right does not have the power to obtain title until the land is offered for sale.

If the exercise of an option to purchase would not create a specifically enforceable contract, then the option is not an interest in land. Following *Semelhago v Paramadevan*, most purchasers do not have a right to specific performance, but must accept damages if the vendor chooses not to perform the contract of sale. Therefore, although holders of an option to purchase have the power to create a contract of sale, most of them will not have the power to obtain title. If an option is not a property right, it cannot be enforced against third persons, and cannot be protected by caveat or registration. Ironically, an Alberta statute declares that pre-emptive rights are equitable interests in land, but is silent about the status of options to purchase.[48]

Whatever effect *Semelhago v Paramadevan* has on contracts of sale, it must also apply with equal force to contracts to grant leases. As the High Court of Australia said in *Chan v Cresdon Pty Ltd*, "the court's willingness to treat the agreement as a lease in equity ... rests upon the specific enforceability of the agreement."[49] For the purposes of specific performance, there is no satisfactory way to distinguish the sale of a fee simple estate from the sale of a leasehold

---

45   *Commissioner of Taxes (Qld) v Camphin* (1937) 57 CLR 127 at 133-134; *Travinto Nominees Pty Ltd v Vlattas* (1973) 129 CLR 1 at 17.

46   (1975) 50 DLR (3d) 265 at 277.

47   *Mackay v Wilson* (1947) 47 SR (NSW) 315 at 325; *Pritchard v Briggs* [1980] Ch 338; *Pata Nominees Pty Ltd v Durnsford Pty Ltd* [1988] WAR 365 at 372; *Dear v Reeves* [2002] Ch 1.

48   *Law of Property Act*, RSA 2000, c L-7, s 63(1).

49   (1989) 168 CLR 242 at 252 per Mason CJ, Brennan, Deane and McHugh JJ.

estate. If a contract to buy a home is not specifically enforceable because suitably similar homes are readily available, then a contract to lease a home cannot be treated differently. Also, if a prospective tenant cannot obtain specific performance of a lease contract, then an option to renew the lease cannot be an interest in land because the option holder does not have the power to obtain a leasehold estate.

In Canada, it was common practice not to bother with the formalities needed to create a legal leasehold estate. A common law periodic tenancy can be created informally if the tenant goes into possession and pays rent,[50] but legal leases greater than three years are created only by registration or deed, depending on the jurisdiction. Since contracts to grant leases were routinely specifically enforceable, they created equitable leases that could be enforced generally against other members of society and protected by caveat or registration. However, *Semelhago v Paramadevan* has unintentionally placed in doubt the very existence of many equitable leases and options to renew leases. Landlords and tenants without a formal legal lease cannot be sure whether they are entitled to specific performance of their lease contract and, therefore, cannot be sure whether they have any lease other than the common law periodic tenancy created informally by the transfer of possession and payment of rent.

Semelhago v Paramadevan creates similar problems for several other equitable property rights. A contract to grant a profit à prendré creates an equitable profit à prendré, provided the contract is specifically enforceable.[51] A contract to grant an easement will create an equitable easement on the same basis. Previously, it was assumed that any contract to grant an interest in land would normally be specifically enforceable simply because land was unique and damages could never provide an adequate substitute for the promised interest. With that assumption removed, the existence of equitable profits and easements are placed in doubt, because it is difficult to predict whether contracts to grant those interests are specifically enforceable or not.

A property right not affected by *Semelhago v Paramadevan* is the equitable mortgage. The same basic principle applies. A contract to grant a mortgage creates an equitable mortgage because damages would not provide an adequate remedy for breach of that contract and, therefore, specific performance is routinely available. However, the inadequacy of damages is not based on the unique character of the land subject to the mortgage. The mortgagee's interest in the land is purely financial: it provides security for payment of a debt. It does not much matter what assets are mortgaged so long as the net proceeds of their sale would be sufficient to pay the mortgagor's debt to the mortgagee.

A judgment for damages would not provide an adequate remedy for breach of a promise to mortgage land because it would leave the mortgagee in the same position as if the contract had not been performed: as an unsecured creditor. Therefore, contracts to grant security rights are specifically enforced as

---

50 *Dockrill v Cavanagh* (1944) 45 SR (NSW) 78 at 80; *Chan v Cresdon Pty Ltd* (1989) 168 CLR 242 at 248.
51 *Mason v Clarke* [1955] AC 778.

a matter of course, regardless of the nature of the assets to be used as security.[52] Since the unique character of the land, goods, or other assets subject to the mortgage is not relevant, *Semelhago v Paramadevan* will have no effect on the creation of equitable mortgages.

THE EFFECT OF SPECIFIC PERFORMANCE

In Australia, specific performance is still routinely available for contracts to sell interests in land, but long-standing rules regarding the effects of those contracts are under attack. In *Tanwar Enterprises Pty Ltd v Cauchi*,[53] five members of the High Court of Australia issued a joint judgment in which they implied that the vendor did not hold the land on constructive trust for the purchaser pending performance of the contract.[54] They doubted whether the purchaser had any interest in the land, referring to the interest of the purchaser with the word "interest" in quotation marks.[55] In a separate judgment, Callinan J suggested that the purchaser might have had "an equity in the land."[56] Only Kirby J said that the purchaser had an equitable interest in the land, but he declined to identify that interest, saying that "the exact nature of the equitable interest of a purchaser in an executory contract for the sale of land is controversial".[57]

Tanwar Enterprises Pty Ltd v Cauchi is frustrating because a basic principle of equity was under attack, but with no clear indication of what was wrong with that principle or what should replace it. The central issue in the case was relief from forfeiture. A contract for the sale of land stated that time was of the essence. Financing was delayed and the purchaser (Tanwar) did not receive the necessary funds until the morning after the completion date. The vendors terminated the contract and refused to complete the transaction. Tanwar acknowledged that it was at fault, but asked the court for relief from forfeiture and specific performance of the contract. Tanwar's claims and appeals were dismissed.

The claim for relief from forfeiture was based in part on the idea that Tanwar had acquired an equitable interest in the land when the contract was made. Although the contract was specifically enforceable prior to Tanwar's default, the joint judgment appears to say (although not clearly) that Tanwar never had an interest in the land, except perhaps a lien securing the possible refund of some portion of the purchase price.[58] Perhaps that was not what the court meant. More recently, in *Zhu v Treasurer of New South Wales*, the High Court of Australia said:[59]

---

52   *Holroyd v Marshall* (1862) 10 HLC 191 at 209; 11 ER 999; *Royal Bank of Canada v Grobman* (1977) 18 OR (2d) 636; *Re Collens* (1982) 140 DLR (3d) 755.

53   [2003] HCA 57; 77 ALJR 1853.

54   *Tanwar Enterprises Pty Ltd v Cauchi*, above n 53 at [53], 1862, per Gleeson CJ, McHugh, Gummow, Hayne and Heydon JJ.

55   *Tanwar Enterprises Pty Ltd v Cauchi*, above n 53 at [43]-[57], 1860-1863.

56   *Tanwar Enterprises Pty Ltd v Cauchi*, above n 53 at [137], 1879.

57   *Tanwar Enterprises Pty Ltd v Cauchi*, above n 53 at [87], 1869.

58   *Tanwar Enterprises Pty Ltd v Cauchi*, above n 53 at [52], 1862.

59   [2004] HCA 56 at [141]; per Gleeson CJ, Gummow, Kirby, Callinan and Heydon JJ (17 November 2004). *Tanwar Enterprises Pty Ltd v Cauchi* was followed in *Jeppesons Road Pty Ltd v Di Domenico* [2005] QSC 66 at [78], where Atkinson J said that "the buyer has no

"An agreement for valuable consideration to sell property confers, if the agreement be specifically enforceable, the special equitable interest of the nature recently considered in *Tanwar Enterprises Pty Ltd v Cauchi*."

Whatever the court meant by "special equitable interest", it suggests something other than a trust. This would be a significant shift in the law of property, which deserves a deeper examination of fundamental principles and the wider context in which they are situated. As discussed below, that examination would reveal that a trust does and should arise when the contract is made, even though the purchaser has not paid the purchase price in full. Also, the property right created by a specifically enforceable contract of sale is consistent with the property rights that arise by operation of law or equity whenever the claimant has the power to acquire a specific asset.

When the purchaser has performed

Once the purchase price has been paid in full and the purchaser is entitled to possession of the land and conveyance of legal title, there is no doubt that the vendor holds the estate in trust for the purchaser. The authorities for this proposition are innumerable, but it has been acknowledged, expressly and implicitly, on many occasions by the High Court of Australia. For example, in *Stern v McArthur*, Deane J and Dawson J said:[60]

> "The relationship of trustee and beneficial owner will certainly be in existence when the purchase price specified in the contract has been paid, title has been made or accepted and the purchaser is entitled to a conveyance or transfer. At that point the purchaser is entitled in equity to the land and the vendor is a bare trustee".

At that stage of the transaction, the vendor has no real interest in the land. So long as the purchaser has the right to specific performance of the contract of sale, the rules of equity give the purchaser the power to obtain legal title and then treat the purchaser as if that power had already been exercised.[61] In other words, the purchaser is the equitable owner of the fee simple estate. Full performance by the purchaser is necessary, but not sufficient to create that relationship. If specific performance is not available, a trust will not arise. As Barwick CJ said in *Chang v Registrar of Titles*, "it is only true that the purchaser of land under a contract of sale of land becomes its equitable owner if the contract is specifically enforceable."[62] Without the power to compel conveyance, the purchaser may have a personal right to performance of the contract or payment of damages, but has no property right to the land other than a lien to secure repayment of the purchase price, if necessary.

---

interest in the land" after the seller's valid termination of the contract of sale. He did not consider the buyer's interest in the land before termination when the contract was still specifically enforceable.

60 (1988) 165 CLR 489 at 523.

61 C Harpum, *RE Megarry & H Wade: The Law of Real Property* (6th ed, Sweet & Maxwell, London, 2000) at 676; S Worthington, *Equity* (Clarendon, Oxford, 2003) at 241-243.

62 (1976) 137 CLR 177 at 181.

The relationship between the vendor and purchaser under a specifically enforceable contract of sale is best described as a constructive trust. Once the purchaser becomes entitled to receive title and possession, the vendor has only bare legal title, while the purchaser has full beneficial ownership under the rules of equity. This is, by definition, a trust.[63] The adjective "constructive" indicates only that the trust is not an express trust created directly by intention, but a trust arising by operation of the rules of equity. Although the intentions of the parties, as expressed in their contract, are relevant (and indeed central) to the creation of the trust, they are relevant as the facts on which the rules of equity operate. As Professor Birks said:[64]

> "There is a fine but important distinction between intent conceived as creative of rights, as in an express trust or a contract, and intent conceived as a fact which, along with others, calls for the creation of rights by operation of law."

These same principles apply with equal force, but some modification, to a contract of lease. Once the tenant becomes entitled to possession and conveyance of the leasehold estate, the tenant acquires that estate in equity, but only if the tenant is entitled to specific performance of the lease contract.[65] At that stage, the tenant has not yet performed all the obligations under the intended lease, since the tenant must observe the leasehold covenants and pay rent for the term of the lease. However, the tenant has done everything necessary to obtain a right to an immediate grant of a lease and is thus in a position analogous to a purchaser entitled to an immediate conveyance of a fee simple estate.

Unlike the vendor who has been paid in full, the landlord still has a beneficial interest in the land, including the right to possession at the end of the lease, the right to receive rent, and the right to performance of the tenant's leasehold covenants. However, the right to possession of the land during the term of the lease belongs in equity to the tenant. We could say that the landlord holds a portion of the fee simple estate on constructive trust for the tenant, but it is easier to call the relationship an equitable lease.

An equitable lease is different from a legal lease, just as an equitable fee simple estate is different from its legal counterpart. The two main differences between equitable and legal property rights are the manner of their creation and their priority over competing property rights. While most equitable estates are created by declarations of trust or specifically enforceable contracts, most legal estates are created by registration or deed. Also, equitable estates tend to be less durable than their legal counterparts and more likely to be subject to competing property rights acquired honestly and for value.

---

63   WG Hart, "What is a Trust?" (1899) 15 *Law Quarterly Review* 294 at 301.
64   P Birks, *An Introduction to the Law of Restitution* (Clarendon, Oxford, 1985) at 65. See W Swadling, "The Vendor-Purchaser Constructive Trust", below at chapter 18, part VI in this book.
65   *Chan v Cresdon Pty Ltd* (1989) 168 CLR 242 at 252.

When the contract is made

There is no doubt that a trust exists once the purchaser has paid the purchase price and become entitled to possession and conveyance of legal title. What interest does the purchaser have prior to that stage? The traditional view is that a trust arises as soon as the contract is made, provided specific performance would be available.[66] However, that view has been questioned on several occasions by the High Court of Australia. As Mason J said in *Chang v Registrar of Titles*:[67]

> "It has long been established that a vendor of real estate under a valid contract of sale is a trustee of the property sold for the purchaser. However, there has been controversy as to the time when the trust relationship arises and as to the character of that relationship."

Doubts about the nature of the purchaser's interest in the land reached their zenith in *Tanwar Enterprises Pty Ltd v Cauchi*, where it was suggested that the purchaser might not have any interest at all. However, despite uncertainties over the nature of the purchaser's interest, it cannot seriously be denied that the purchaser does have an interest in the land, which arises when the contract is made. Deane J was one of the strongest critics of the traditional view. In *Kern Corp Ltd v Walter Reid Trading Pty Ltd*, he said that "it is both inaccurate and misleading to speak of the unpaid vendor under an uncompleted contract as a trustee for the purchaser".[68] Although he preferred not to call it a trust, he did not doubt that, "pending payment of the purchase price, the purchaser has an equitable interest in the land".[69]

When a specifically enforceable contract of sale is made, the purchaser acquires an equitable property right to the land, which can be protected by caveat or registration and enforced against others, subject to normal priority rules.[70] The only real issue is the nature of that interest. In *Jerome v Kelly*, Lord Walker accurately described the current state of the law regarding the effect of a specifically enforceable contract of sale:[71]

> "If and so long as the contract is enforceable in that way, the seller becomes in some sense a trustee for the buyer; the buyer has an equitable interest of some sort in the subject-matter of the contract; and the contract (if protected by the machinery appropriate to registered or unregistered titles, as the case may be) is enforceable (by specific performance) against a third party who becomes owner of the property."

---

66 *Lysaght v Edwards* (1876) 2 Ch D 499 at 510; *Central Trust and Safe Deposit Co v Snider* [1916] 1 AC 266 at 272; C Harpum, *RE Megarry & H Wade: The Law of Real Property* (6th ed, Sweet & Maxwell, London, 2000) at 676.

67 (1976) 137 CLR 177 at 184. Also see S Worthington, *Proprietary Interests in Commercial Transactions* (Clarendon, Oxford, 1996) at 207-208; S Worthington, "Proprietary Remedies: The Nexus between Specific Performance and Constructive Trusts" (1996) 11 *Journal of Contract Law* 1 at 10-13.

68 (1987) 163 CLR 164 at 192.

69 *Kern Corp Ltd v Walter Reid Trading Pty Ltd*, above n 68 at 191.

70 See, for example, *Moonking Gee v Tahos* (1960) 80 WN (NSW) 1612; *Bunny Industries Ltd v FSW Enterprises Pty Ltd* [1982] Qd R 712.

71 [2004] UKHL 25 at [29].

The purchaser's interest in the land must be something between the equitable interest created by an option to purchase and the bare trust that arises when the purchaser finally becomes entitled to possession and conveyance. As discussed above, an option to purchase is an interest in land because it gives the option holder the power to obtain a specifically enforceable contract of sale and thus eventually obtain the fee simple estate.[72] The interest created by a contract of sale cannot be less than that created by the option to obtain a contract of sale. In fact, it is much more.

The most significant difference between an option to purchase and a contract of sale is that the option holder has the power to obtain title, while the purchaser has both the power and the duty to obtain title. An option holder has the opportunity to benefit from any increase in the value of the land after the option is granted, but does not bear any risk of loss, whereas a purchaser must bear the risk of loss along with the hope of gain. If the land decreases in value or its buildings are destroyed by fire, then normally the purchaser is still bound to complete the transaction, whereas the option holder is free not to exercise the option. Therefore, the purchaser has an insurable interest in the land,[73] while the option holder does not.

The hope of gain and risk of loss are attributes of beneficial ownership and indicate that the purchaser has a beneficial interest in the land. Clearly, the purchaser is not its sole beneficial owner before he or she pays the purchase price in full and becomes entitled to possession and title. The vendor also has an interest in the land at that stage, but has something less than sole beneficial ownership. The specifically enforceable contract of sale shifted some portion of that ownership to the purchaser.

In his famous essay, 'Ownership', Professor Honoré described "the standard incidents of ownership: *ie* those legal rights, duties and other incidents which apply, in the ordinary case, to the person who has the greatest interest in a thing admitted by a mature legal system."[74] According to Honoré:[75]

"Ownership comprises the right to possess, the right to use, the right to manage, the right to the income of the thing, the right to the capital, the right to security, the rights or incidents of transmissibility and absence of term, the prohibition of harmful use, liability to execution, and the incident of residuarity: this makes eleven leading incidents. Obviously, there are alternative ways of classifying the incidents; moreover, it is fashionable to speak of ownership as if it were just a bundle of rights, in which case at least two items in the list would have to be omitted."

Prior to making the contract of sale, the vendor's fee simple estate consisted of all eleven incidents. When the contract is made, the vendor continues to be

---

72   *Travinto Nominees Pty Ltd v Vlattas* (1973) 129 CLR 1; *Re Eastdoro Pty Ltd (No 2)* [1990] 1 Qd R 424; *Jacobs v Platt Nominees Pty Ltd* [1990] VR 146.

73   *Kern Corp Ltd v Walter Reid Trading Pty Ltd*, above n 68 at 172.

74   AM Honoré, 'Ownership' in AG Guest (ed), *Oxford Essays in Jurisprudence* (Clarendon, Oxford, 1961) at 107, 107; reprinted in T Honoré, *Making Law Bind* (Clarendon, Oxford, 1987) at 161.

75   AM Honoré, 'Ownership', in AG Guest (ed), *Oxford Essays in Jurisprudence*, above n 74 at 107, 113.

the legal owner of the estate, but some of those incidents become part of the purchaser's equitable interest in the land. The vendor still has the rights to possess, use, manage, and receive income from the land until the transaction is complete, but the purchaser has the right to the capital and the incidents of transmissibility, absence of term, and residuarity.

According to Honoré, "the right to the capital consists in the power to alienate the thing and the liberty to consume, waste or destroy the whole or part of it".[76] By making a specifically enforceable contract of sale, the vendor exercised that right once and for all. As Lord O'Hagan stated in *Shaw v Foster*, "by the contract of sale the vendor in the view of a Court of Equity disposes of his right over the estate, and on the execution of the contract he becomes constructively a trustee for the vendee".[77] Professor Penner provided a fuller explanation:[78]

> "In transferring property by contract, the seller relinquishes his property precisely on the condition that he will not exercise any right to dispose of it whatsoever. The seller does not make use of his property, but rather abstracts from the use of his property some measure of value, and compares it with the value of the contractual consideration offered to him... The important feature of this valuation is that it is not a prelude to using the property, which use is protected by the right of exclusive use, but is rather a prelude to never using it again. This valuation establishes the particular property right as a possible object of exchange. The owner shifts from treating the property as something to be used to enhance his interests to treating it as something to be traded."

The vendor can lease or mortgage the land pending completion (thus exercising the rights to manage the land and receive income from it), but cannot sell or give the fee simple estate to another. The purchaser has the right to the legal estate on the completion date, can protect that right by caveat or registration, and can enforce that right generally against other members of society. Also, the vendor is no longer free to consume, waste, or destroy the land or its fixtures, but has a duty to take reasonable care of the land pending completion.[79]

After the contract is made, the capital value of the land belongs to the purchaser. The vendor is still entitled to payment of the purchase price in full and has a lien on the land for that amount, but that price is no longer linked to the value of the land. It is the contract price set when the vendor agreed to exchange the land for its capital value. Normally, the debt due to the vendor is fixed and any changes to the value of the land affect only the purchaser's interest. The purchaser has the right to the capital value of the land and can exchange that value by assigning her or his rights under the contract of sale.

The incidents of transmissibility, absence of term, and residuarity all relate to the fact that ownership has the potential to continue indefinitely. Those incidents are attributes of the purchaser's interest, not the vendor's. The

---

76 AM Honoré, 'Ownership', in AG Guest (ed), *Oxford Essays in Jurisprudence*, above n 74 at 107, 118.

77 (1872) LR 5 HL 321 at 349. Also see G Elias, *Explaining Constructive Trusts* (Clarendon, Oxford, 1990) at 9-16, 50-56.

78 JE Penner, *The Idea of Property in Law* (Clarendon, Oxford, 1997) at 91.

79 *Phillips v Silvester* (1872) 8 Ch App 173; C Harpum, *RE Megarry & H Wade: The Law of Real Property* (6th ed, Sweet & Maxwell, London, 2000) at 677.

vendor's right to possession comes to an end on the completion date and the purchaser has an unlimited right to possession thereafter. Transmissibility means that "the interest can be transmitted to the holder's successors and so on ad infinitum".[80] If the purchaser dies, her or his successors acquire the purchaser's interest in the land. In contrast, the vendor' interest in the land will be treated as money if the vendor dies, according to the equitable doctrine of conversion. A right to inherit only the vendor's land would not include any land subject to a specifically enforceable contract of sale when the vendor died.[81]

The trust relationship

When a specifically enforceable contract is made, the purchaser immediately acquires an equitable interest in the land, sharing beneficial ownership with the vendor. That interest arises by operation of the rules of equity and not directly because the vendor intended to confer it on the purchaser. The traditional (although admittedly not very helpful) term for an equitable beneficial interest created by operation of law is a constructive trust.[82] The vendor has long been called a constructive trustee, but that language has fallen out of favour with the High Court of Australia. As discussed above, the Court does not doubt that a trust exists once the purchaser has paid the full purchase price and is entitled to conveyance and possession, but doubts that a trust arises before that stage is reached.

The rejection of the traditional view of the relationship between vendor and purchaser seems to be based on the fact that the vendor also has a beneficial interest in the land before the purchase price is paid on the completion date. In *Kern Corp Ltd v Walter Reid Trading Pty Ltd*, Deane J said:[83]

> "It is wrong to characterize the position of such a vendor as that of a trustee. True it is that, pending payment of the purchase price, the purchaser has an equitable interest in the land which reflects the extent to which equitable remedies are available to protect his contractual rights and the vendor is under obligations in equity which attach to the land. None the less, the vendor himself retains a continuing beneficial estate in the land which transcends any 'lien' for unpaid purchase money to which he may be entitled in equity after completion. Pending completion, he is beneficially entitled to possession and use. Pending completion, he is beneficially entitled to the rents and profits. If the purchaser enters upon the land without the vendor's permission and without authority under the contract, the vendor can maintain, for his own benefit, an action for trespass against the purchaser."

No doubt the relationship between vendor and purchaser changes when the purchase price is paid in full on the completion date. The vendor becomes a bare trustee, with no further interest in the land. However, the fact that the vendor has

---

80   AM Honoré, 'Ownership' in AG Guest (ed), *Oxford Essays in Jurisprudence* (Clarendon, Oxford, 1961) at 107, 120.

81   *Lysaght v Edwards* (1876) 2 Ch D 499 at 515; C Harpum, *RE Megarry & H Wade: The Law of Real Property*, above n 79 at 682.

82   See P Birks, *An Introduction to the Law of Restitution* (Clarendon, Oxford, 1985) at 89-90; G Elias, *Explaining Constructive Trusts*, above n 77 at 148-149.

83   (1987) 163 CLR 164 at 191-192. Also see *Stern v McArthur* (1988) 165 CLR 489 at 521-522.

a beneficial interest at an earlier stage of the transaction does not prevent their relationship from then being a trust. It is common for trustees to have interests in the trust assets. Trustees are normally entitled to use the trust assets to reimburse themselves for all expenses and liabilities properly incurred as trustees.[84] Trustees can also be beneficiaries of their own trusts, whether those trusts arise by intention or by operation of law. For example, the transfer of assets to A in trust for A and B can create a perfectly valid express trust[85] and, if A and B contribute unequally to the purchase of land jointly by A and B, they may hold it on resulting trust for themselves in proportion to the values of their contributions.[86]

A trust can exist even though the trustee has a substantial personal interest in the trust assets. Conversely, a person can be a trust beneficiary with only a very limited interest in the trust assets. For example, the beneficiary under a discretionary trust might have no right to receive a distribution from the trust and yet be a trust beneficiary with the right to enforce the trust against the trustees and anyone who wrongly interferes with the trust.[87] Trust relationships come in a wide variety of shapes and sizes and can exist even though beneficial ownership of the trust assets is shared by the trustee and beneficiary. The essential feature common to all trusts is that the trustees are required by the rules of equity to use the trust assets at least partly for the benefit of others. Although the execution of a specifically enforceable contract of sale does not create a bare trust, it does produce a trust relationship.

Another objection to the trust seems to be that it is inconsistent with the contractual relationship between the vendor and purchaser. As Jacobs J said in *Chang v Registrar of Titles*:[88]

> "Where there are rights outstanding on both sides, the description of the vendor as a trustee tends to conceal the essentially contractual relationship which, rather than the relationship of trustee and beneficiary, governs the rights and duties of the respective parties."

With respect, this suggests a false dichotomy. Contracts and trusts are not mutually exclusive. Contracts are sources of legal relationships, while a trust is a kind of legal relationship. Contracts give rise to a wide variety of different relationships, such as banker-customer, creditor-debtor, doctor-patient, and employer-employee. Each relationship is defined in part by the terms of the contract between the parties and in part by the general law applicable to that type of relationship. For example, we would not say that, because a solicitor and client have a contractual relationship, they cannot also have a fiduciary relationship.

Contracts can create trusts. For example, a loan of money to be used only for a specific purpose can create an express or resulting trust.[89] A contract between a husband and wife, in which they agree not to revoke their wills, can

---

84   *Thompson v Lamport* [1945] 2 DLR 545.
85   GT Bogert, *Trusts* (6th ed, West, St Paul, 1987) at 96-98.
86   *Calverley v Green* (1984) 155 CLR 242.
87   *Schmidt v Rosewood Trust Ltd* [2003] 3 All ER 76.
88   (1976) 137 CLR 177 at 190.
89   *Barclays Bank Ltd v Quistclose Investments Ltd* [1970] AC 567; *Twinsectra Ltd v Yardley* [2002] 2 AC 164. See W Swadling (ed), *The Quistclose Trust: Critical Essays* (Hart Publishing, Oxford, 2004).

create a constructive trust that arises when the first party dies.[90] There is nothing unusual about the constructive trust created by a contract of sale. The trust is defined both by the terms of the contract and by the general law applicable to vendors and purchasers. Describing the vendor as a trustee does not conceal, but reveals an important aspect of their relationship, which is that the purchaser has an equitable beneficial interest in the land being sold.

There may be objections that it is not appropriate to import into the vendor-purchaser relationship the normal duties of express trustees. No doubt that is true. The typical express trust involves onerous duties of obedience, care, loyalty, impartiality, etc, that do not and should not apply to vendors, who have dealt with their purchasers at arms length and are free to act selfishly, except as constrained by the contract of sale. However, there is a wide range of different trust relationships and some are far more onerous than others. It is probably true that not all trustees are fiduciaries.[91] As Mr Hackney said:[92]

> "In what sense is it right to call the unknowing infant resulting trustee, into whose name property has been secretly and voluntarily transferred, a fiduciary? Such a person can have none of the duties or powers of the express trustee and ought to have only an obligation to restore the property on demand, if still in possession of it. Even reckless disregard of property one does not know one has (the infant, grown old, but still unknowing, negligently loses the property) should not produce liability. No more should innocent transfer on."

In *Armitage v Nurse*, Millett LJ said:[93]

> "There is an irreducible core of obligations owed by the trustees to the beneficiaries and enforceable by them which is fundamental to the concept of a trust.... The duty of trustees to perform the trust honestly and in good faith for the benefit of the beneficiaries is the minimum necessary to give substance to the trusts."

To this can be added the duty to account to the beneficiaries for the trust assets received and disbursed.[94] Most trusts involve more onerous duties, but nothing more is required for a trust relationship to exist. By calling the vendor a trustee, does not add any duties to those created both by the contract of sale and by the general law that governs the relationship of vendor and purchaser. There is nothing objectionable about the notion that the vendor must perform the contract honestly and in good faith and, if he or she wrongly sells the land to someone else, must account to the purchaser for the sale proceeds.[95]

The constructive trust created by a contract of sale does not attract all the equitable duties to which most express trustees are subject, nor does it attract all the statutory provisions that govern express trusts. Trustee statutes usually

---

90   *University of Manitoba v Sanderson Estate* (1998) 155 DLR (4th) 40.
91   See LD Smith, 'Constructive Fiduciaries' in P Birks (ed), *Privacy and Loyalty* (Clarendon, Oxford, 1997) at 249; R Chambers, *Resulting Trusts* (Clarendon, Oxford, 1997) at 194-200.
92   J Hackney, *Understanding Equity and Trusts* (Fontana, London, 1987) at 167.
93   [1998] Ch 241 at 253 per Millett LJ.
94   *Jones v Shipping Federation of British Columbia* (1963) 41 WWR 636.
95   *Bunny Industries Ltd v FSW Enterprises Pty Ltd* [1982] Qd R 712.

define trusts to include "implied and constructive trusts".[96] However, courts have refused to apply those definitions to constructive trusts if it would otherwise lead to undesirable results.[97]

In *Chang v Registrar of Titles*,[98] the purchaser made a contract to buy land in Melbourne that was registered in the name of the Republic of China (in Taiwan). After the Australian government recognised the People's Republic of China (in Peking) instead of the government in Taiwan, the purchaser could not obtain performance of the contract and applied under the *Trustee Act 1958* (Vic) for an order vesting the estate in the purchaser. The application failed, primarily because there is no trust if specific performance is not available. However, Barwick CJ also said, "it seems to me that an unpaid vendor, as the vendor here may prove to be, cannot be regarded as a trustee under the *Trustee Act*".[99] That did not mean that the vendor was not a constructive trustee, but only that the provisions of the *Trustee Act* did not apply to that trust before the purchase price was paid in full and the purchaser was entitled to conveyance.

The equity of redemption

There is one form of equitable beneficial ownership other than a trust: the mortgagor's equity of redemption. Regardless of the many forms that mortgages have taken over the ages, courts of equity have had the ability to see through the form to the substance and recognise that the mortgagor is the beneficial owner of the mortgaged land, while the mortgagee has only a security interest.[100] There is some similarity between a mortgage and a contract of sale, in that both the mortgagee and the vendor have a property right to the land to secure payment of a sum of money. Normally, the vendor can retain title until the purchase price is paid in full and has a lien on the land if title is transferred before full payment. However, prior to the completion date, the vendor's interest in the land is greater than that of a mortgagee, since the vendor is also entitled to possession and the income from the land.

Some contracts of sale are instalment contracts, under which the purchaser obtains possession of the land and pays the balance of the purchase price, with interest, in instalments over a long period of time. After the purchaser takes possession, their relationship becomes completely analogous to a mortgage. The vendor's only interest in the land is as security for payment of the balance of the debt due under the contract of sale. Like a common law mortgagee, the vendor holds legal title for security purposes only and beneficial ownership belongs to the purchaser, subject to the vendor's security interest. Despite the similarity to a common law mortgage, the purchaser's interest in the land is not normally called an equity of redemption. Nevertheless, courts of equity have

---

96   See, eg, *Trustee Act 1925* (UK), s 68(17); *Chang v Registrar of Titles* (1976) 137 CLR 177 at 184.
97   *Taylor v Davies* [1920] AC 636; *Clarkson v Davies* [1923] AC 100; *Re Blake* [1932] 1 Ch 54; *JLO Ranch Ltd v Logan* (1987) 54 Alta LR (2d) 130.
98   (1976) 137 CLR 177.
99   *Chang v Registrar of Titles*, above n 98 at 182.
100 *Re Forrest Trust* [1953] VLR 246.

not lost their ability to see through the form of the transaction and identify the substance of the relationship.[101]

It might be useful to refer to the purchaser's interest under an instalment contract as an equity of redemption once the purchaser has taken possession of the land. However, that is unlikely to happen and, in any event, that label does not accurately describe the interest that exists before the purchaser takes possession. Prior to the transfer of possession, the contract of sale is significantly different from a mortgage and is best described as a trust. The trust is a general term that applies to a wide variety of relationships in which one person has an equitable beneficial interest in an asset that belongs at law to another. It indicates clearly that the purchaser has such an interest, without misleading anyone about the nature of that interest.

The wider context

A constructive trust will arise when a contract of sale is made, but only if the purchaser has a right to specific performance of the contract. Other property rights, such as the option to purchase, equitable lease, and equitable mortgage, also depend upon the availability of specific performance. The key to the existence of each of these property rights is the power to obtain a specific asset. Under normal conditions, the right holder need not accept damages, but can compel the other party to the contract to transfer the asset as promised. The right holder's claim to that asset takes precedence over the other party's right to it.

The right to specific performance creates a property right because the purchaser's claim can be enforced, not just against the vendor, but also against other persons. According to the rules of equity, it takes priority over the rights of anyone who received the promised land as a donee or with notice of the purchaser's claim. The equitable priority rules can be altered by registration, but that does not alter the basic principle that the purchaser's right to the land can and normally should be enforceable generally against other members of society, subject to the defence of bona fide purchase or some variation of that defence, such as indefeasibility of title.

The fundamental idea is that a claim to a specific asset, which prevails over the rights of the other party to the transaction, should also be enforced generally against others, so long as it does not prejudice the rights of third persons acquired for value in good faith. This basic principle is not limited to specifically enforceable contracts, but applies whenever someone has the power to obtain title to a specific asset. Generally speaking, the power to obtain title to an asset is a property right to that asset, regardless of the source of that power. This is true of incomplete gifts and of assets recoverable through rescission or rectification. While most of these property rights are equitable, the principle also operates at common law.

A gift is not complete until legal title is transferred to the donee. In most cases, that is accomplished by delivery of possession of goods, money, or

---

101 *Stern v McArthur* (1988)165 CLR 489 at 527-529; N Chin, "Relieving Against Forfeiture: Windfalls and Conscience" (1995) 25 *University of Western Australia Law Review* 110.

cheques. However, legal title to some assets, such as corporate shares or Torrens land, is transferred by registration. This creates problems from time to time, because the delivery of documents to the donee does not complete the gift. There are cases in which the donee obtained the necessary transfer documents, but the donor died before those documents were registered. Normally, the donee has no right to compel the donor to complete an intended gift, except perhaps by way of promissory estoppel.[102] However, if the donee has the power to complete the gift without the donor's help, then the rules of equity treat the gift as if it was already complete.[103] In other words, the donor holds the intended gift on constructive trust for the donee once the donee acquires the power to obtain legal title to that asset.

Rights to rescission and rectification can create property rights for similar reasons. Sometimes, the right to rescind or rectify a transaction enables the right holder to recover an asset previously transferred to the other party. That power to obtain title to the recoverable asset is a property right that is enforceable not just against the other party, but also against donees and persons with notice of the right.

There are cases in which the right to recover an asset through rescission was regarded from the outset as equitable beneficial ownership of the recoverable asset.[104] However, the modern view is that the claimant's property right begins as a power and does not become beneficial ownership until the claimant elects to rescind the transaction.[105] As Lord Millett said in "Restitution and Constructive Trusts":[106]

"The plaintiff has the right to elect whether to affirm the transaction or rescind it. If he elects to rescind it, it is usually assumed that the beneficial title revests in the plaintiff, and the authorities suggest that it does so retrospectively. But the recipient cannot anticipate his decision. Pending the plaintiff's election to rescind, the recipient is entitled, and may be bound, to treat the payment as effective.... It is not inappropriate to describe the transferee as holding the property on a constructive trust for the transferor but only after rescission, in much the same way as we describe the vendor as holding property on a constructive trust for the purchaser but only after the parties have entered into a specifically enforceable contract for sale. If so, the right to reconveyance is a form of specific performance (or 'specific unperformance') which equity makes available because a money judgment is an inadequate remedy."

---

102 *Ogilvie v Ryan* [1976] 2 NSWLR 504; *Pascoe v Turner* [1979] 1 WLR 431; *Giumelli v Giumelli* (1999) 196 CLR 101.

103 *Re Rose* [1952] Ch 499; *Re Amland Estate* (1975) 4 APR 285; *Macleod v Canada Trust Co* (1980) 108 DLR (3d) 424; *Mascall v Mascall* (1984) 50 P&CR 119; *Corin v Patton* (1990) 169 CLR 540; *Pennington v Waine* [2002] 4 All ER 215.

104 *Stump v Gaby* (1852) 2 De GM&G 623; 42 ER 1015; *Gresley v Mousley* (1859) 4 De G&J 78, 45 ER 31; *Dickinson v Burrell* (1866) LR 1 Eq 337; *Melbourne Banking Corp v Brougham* (1882) 7 App Cas 307; American Law Institute, *Restatement of the Law of Restitution* (St Paul, 1937) at 650.

105 P Birks, *Unjust Enrichment* (2nd ed, Oxford University Press, Oxford, 2005) at 183-184.

106 PJ Millett, "Restitution and Constructive Trusts" (1998) 114 *Law Quarterly Review* 399 at 416; reprinted in WR Cornish *et al* (eds), *Restitution Past, Present and Future: Essays in Honour of Gareth Jones* (Hart Publishing, Oxford, 1998) at 199, 215-216.

Before electing to rescind, the claimant's property right might be called an "option to rescind", because it is analogous to the option to purchase. In both situations, the right holder has a power in rem to obtain title to a specific asset. The exercise of an option to rescind or purchase, as the case may be, changes the right from a power to beneficial ownership. If the option to rescind is equitable, the exercise of that option produces equitable ownership, which is either a constructive or resulting trust.[107] However, if the transaction was induced by fraud or duress, the claimant may have an option to rescind at common law, in which case its exercise will cause legal ownership to be restored to claimant.[108]

The equitable option to rescind is sometimes called a "mere equity".[109] This is potentially confusing, because that term is often used to indicate that an equitable right is personal and not property.[110] In many cases, rescission will not have any proprietary effect. It will relieve the parties of their obligations under a contract, but not alter their property rights in any way. However, rescinding the transfer of an asset will cause ownership of that asset to be restored to the transferor. In those cases, the option to rescind is itself a property right to the recoverable asset, which can be enforced not just against the transferee, but also against someone who acquired the asset from the transferee as a donee or with notice of the option to rescind.

The label "mere equity" indicates that the option to rescind is more fragile than most equitable interests and more likely to be defeated by competing interests acquired for value without notice.[111] Legal options to rescind are also more fragile than other legal interests and can be defeated by the defence of bona fide purchase.[112] As Professor Birks pointed out, we would not refer to a legal option to rescind as a "mere common law".[113] Perhaps the time has come to abandon the term "mere equity" or at least restrict it to equitable personal rights.

The power to recover an asset through rectification is also a property right. Rectification is available in equity when, by mutual mistake, the documents executed by the parties do not correspond to their actual agreement. Also, registers (of land, shareholders, etc) can be rectified if incorrect or forged documents are registered. If the execution or registration of a defective document caused the unintended transfer of an asset from one party to the other, rectification of that document or register will restore that asset to the transferor. Pending rectification, the transferor has an equitable property right to the recoverable assets.[114] That right has been called a

---

107 *El Ajou v Dollar Land Holdings plc* [1993] 3 All ER 717 at 734; reversed [1994] 2 All ER 685.
108 *Carr & Universal Finance Co Ltd v Caldwell* [1965] 1 QB 525; *Barton v Armstrong* [1976] AC 104.
109 *Phillips v Phillips* (1861) 4 De GF&J 208 at 218; 45 ER 1164; *Latec Investments Ltd v Hotel Terrigal Pty Ltd* (1965) 113 CLR 265; R Chambers, *Resulting Trusts* (Clarendon, Oxford, 1997) at 171-184.
110 See, for example, *National Provincial Bank Ltd v Ainsworth* [1965] AC 1175.
111 *Latec Investments Ltd v Hotel Terrigal Pty Ltd* (1965) 113 CLR 265; R Chambers, *An Introduction to Property Law in Australia* (LBC Information Services, Sydney, 2001) at 417-423.
112 *Hunter BNZ Finance Ltd v CG Maloney Pty Ltd* (1988) 18 NSWLR 420.
113 P Birks, "Property and Unjust Enrichment: Categorical Truths" [1997] *New Zealand Law Review* 623 at 638.
114 *Blacklocks v JB Developments (Godalming) Ltd* [1982] Ch 183; *Malory Enterprises Ltd v Cheshire Homes (UK) Ltd* [2002] Ch 216.

constructive trust.[115] Perhaps the right to recover assets through rectification begins as a power and becomes beneficial ownership only when it is asserted. However, there is no election to rectify that corresponds to the election to rescind. If the source of the right to rectification is the mutual mistake of the parties, neither party has the unilateral right to affirm the transaction. If the document was forged, there is no underlying transaction to affirm.

CONCLUSION

The recent attacks on the traditional rules regarding the specific performance of land contracts have come by way of obiter dicta and passing criticisms. Though indirect, they must be taken very seriously since they come from the highest courts in Australia and Canada. The traditional rules are defended here, not because they are traditional, but because they are integral to the law of property. They are not immune to change, but changes should be made only after careful consideration of the full importance of those rules and the far reaching effects of changing them.

The attacks on the traditional rules have been indirect because the complaints are not really about the rules themselves, but about related issues. In *Semelhago v Paramadevan*,[116] the issue on appeal was the proper calculation of damages in lieu of specific performance. No doubt that is a difficult problem in need of further attention, but the solution is not to avoid the problem by removing the right to specific performance. The change proposed by the Supreme Court of Canada may well make havoc of substantial portions of the law of property. Furthermore, it is inconsistent with the rule of law, because it links specific performance to the subjective desires of individual purchasers and thereby contravenes the fundamental principle of equality before the law.

In *Tanwar Enterprises Pty Ltd v Cauchi*,[117] the issue on appeal was relief from forfeiture. Again, this is a difficult problem in need of further attention, but the solution is not to avoid the problem by denying the purchaser's interest in the land. Though seemingly not as drastic as the proposal in *Semelhago v Paramadevan*, it would also have a substantial effect on the law of property. Without an interest in the land, purchasers could not protect their rights by caveat or registration, enforce their rights against others, or insure against loss. Holders of options to purchase would suffer a similar fate.

More troubling are the inconsistencies that would be introduced if purchasers did not have interests in land. The proprietary effect of specific performance is merely one instance of a general principle of both equity and the common law. The power to obtain title to a specific asset is enforceable, not just against the other party to the transaction, but generally against other members of society, subject to defences that protect interests acquired for value in good faith. The denial of the purchaser's interest is contrary to that principle and hard to justify as an isolated exception.

Footnotes

115 *Taitapu Gold Estates Ltd v Prouse* [1916] NZLR 825; *Blacklocks v JB Developments (Godalming) Ltd* [1982] Ch 183.
116 (1996) 136 DLR (4th) 1.
117 [2003] HCA 57; 77 ALJR 1853

The effect of the change proposed in *Tanwar Enterprises Pty Ltd v Cauchi* would be reduced if the court did not deny the existence of the purchaser's equitable interest, but merely denied that it was a trust. However, that creates inconsistencies within the law of trusts. In substance, the purchaser shares beneficial ownership of the land with the vendor under the rules of equity. Equitable beneficial ownership is, by definition, either a trust or an equity of redemption. While the interest of a purchaser in possession of land under an instalment contract of sale might be regarded as an equity of redemption, that label does not accurately describe the purchaser's interest in any other situation. The relationship between legal owner and equitable beneficial owner has long been called a trust and there is no convincing reason to make an exception for the relationship between vendor and purchaser.

18

The Vendor-Purchaser Constructive Trust

William Swadling

Introduction

Perhaps the most famous, and certainly the most controversial case in the area of fusion is that of *Walsh v Lonsdale*.[1] As every law student knows, Lonsdale agreed to grant to Walsh a seven-year lease of a mill. Though no grant was ever made, Walsh entered into possession of the premises. But instead of paying rent yearly in advance, as agreed, he paid it quarterly in arrears. Lonsdale demanded a year's rent in advance and when it was not forthcoming, distrained on Walsh's chattels. Walsh sought damages for illegal distress, arguing that distress, a common law response, was not available since the grant of the seven-year lease had never been made. The only lease in existence, it was claimed, was the periodic one which arose by implication when Walsh went into possession and paid rent quarterly. In respect of that lease, said Walsh, he was not in arrears. His claim for damages nevertheless failed.

Sir George Jessel MR said that Walsh held under an agreement for a lease. He held under the same terms in equity as if a lease had been granted, it being a case in which both parties admitted that relief was capable of being given by specific performance.[2] That being so, the effect of the Judicature Acts 1873-75 meant that he could not complain of the exercise by the landlord of the same rights as he would have had had the lease been granted:[3]

> "There is an agreement for a lease under which possession has been given. Now since the *Judicature Act* the possession is held under the agreement. There are not two estates as there were formerly, one estate at common law by reason of the payment of the rent from year to year, and an estate in equity under the agreement. There is only one Court, and the equity rules prevail in it. The tenant holds under an agreement for a lease. He holds, therefore, under the

---

1 (1881) 21 Ch D 9.
2 In common law Canada it can no longer simply be assumed that a contract for the sale of an interest in land will be specifically enforced: *Semelhago v Paramadevan* [1996] 2 SCR 415. The point is discussed in detail by Professor Chambers in "The Importance of Specific Performance" in this book at 434–448.
3 Above n 1 at 14-15.

same terms in equity as if a lease had been granted ... [B]eing a lessee in equity he cannot complain of the exercise of the right of distress merely because the actual parchment has not been signed and sealed."

It should immediately be said that it is not the purpose of this chapter to ask whether the Master of the Rolls was correct in his analysis of the effect of the Judicature Acts,[4] though it is doubtful that he was.[5] The aim instead is the more modest one of asking why, in a case like *Walsh v Lonsdale*, an equitable estate comes into being at all.

The most common case in which such an estate arises is that of contracts for the sale of freehold titles to land. In *Lysaght v Edwards*,[6] the testator, who held a title to a number of parcels of land, both outright and as a trustee, had before his death entered into a contract to sell one of the titles he held outright. He died before the conveyance was executed. By his will, he left all the titles he held outright to Hubbard and Muller jointly, and those he held on trust to Hubbard alone. For the purpose of the execution of the conveyance, it was vital to know who now held the title to the land contracted to be sold. Had it passed to Hubbard and Muller jointly, or to Hubbard alone? That depended on whether the vendor was a trustee of the title at the time of his death. Sir George Jessel MR said that he was, with the consequence that the title had passed to Hubbard alone. He said:[7]

"the moment you have a valid contract for sale the vendor becomes in equity a trustee for the purchaser of the estate sold, and the beneficial ownership passes to the purchaser".

However, the rule as just stated is deficient, for it is not every contract of sale which makes the vendor a trustee of the right he has contracted to sell. Not only must there be a valid contract of sale, but the contract must be one of which a court of equity will grant specific performance. As Lord Parker of Waddington said in *Howard v Miller*:[8]

"It is sometimes said that under a contract for the sale of an interest in land the vendor becomes a trustee for the purchaser of the interest contracted to be sold ...; but however useful such a statement may be as illustrating a general principle of equity, it is only true if and so far as a Court of Equity would

---

4   Sir George Jessel was not an impartial observer in this whole process. As Solicitor-General he had piloted the *Judicature Act 1873* through the House of Commons.
5   It is interesting to note that a contrary view was expressed by the same judge two years earlier in *Salt v Cooper* (1880) 16 Ch D 544 at 549, where he said that the object of the Act "has been sometimes inaccurately called 'the fusion of Law and Equity'; but it was not any fusion, or anything of the kind; it was the vesting in one tribunal the administration of Law and Equity in every cause, action or dispute which should come before the tribunal."
6   (1876) 2 Ch D 499.
7   (1876) 2 Ch D 499 at 506. The precise issue which *Lysaght v Edwards* resolved was the date from which the trust arose. Until this case, it was uncertain whether it did so at the date of contract or only later, when the vendor's title was proved or accepted by the purchaser. The Master of the Rolls held that the contract arose at the later point, for it was only then that a "valid" contract came into being. The trust, however, then operated retrospectively to the date of contract.
8   [1915] AC 318 at 326.

under all the circumstances of the case grant specific performance of the contract."

If, for whatever reason, specific performance will not issue, no trust will arise. So, for example, if I agree to sell you a parcel of shares in a public company, you will not have the benefit of a trust, for shares in a public company are not unique, an award of expectation damages generally being an adequate response to any breach on my part of the contract of sale.[9] But if I contract to sell you shares in a private company, for which there is no market, such a contract is specifically enforceable[10] and you will have the benefit of a trust in your favour.

Finally, it should be noted that the trust in no way depends on the purchase money having been paid. However, if it has not, the vendor has an equitable lien for the purchase price over the right contracted to be sold.[11]

CONSEQUENCES

A number of consequences flow from the operation of the rule that a specifically enforceable contract of sale constitutes the vendor a trustee of the right contracted to be sold for the purchaser.[12] The four main ones are as follows:

Devolution of rights on death

Until 1925, it was the case that real and personal property went in different directions on an intestacy. Personal property[13] went to the next of kin, real property[14] to the heir. But where the deceased had contracted to sell some of his real property before his death and that contract was still executory, it passed to the next of kin, for the land was deemed to have been turned into money. Equally, where a deceased had before his death contracted to buy land, the benefit of that contract passed to the heir as realty. Realty and personalty nowadays devolve in the same way on intestacy, so the rule will only be relevant in the rare case of a deceased who deliberately leaves his real and personal property to different persons.

---

9   *Duncuft v Albrecht* (1841) 12 Sim 189; 59 ER 1104. For a general discussion of the conditions of an award of specific performance, see G Jones and W Goodhart, *Specific Performance* (2nd ed, Butterworths, London, 1996) at 31-38.

10 *Ensor v Ensor* [1946] 2 DLR 781.

11 *Rose v Watson* (1864) 10 HLC 672; 11 ER 1187; *Nives v Nives* (1880) 15 ChD 649; *re Birmingham* [1959] Ch 523; *London & Cheshire Insurance Co Ltd v Laplagrene* [1971] Ch 499.

12 Of which a full account can be found in AJ Oakley, *Constructive Trusts* (3rd ed, Sweet & Maxwell, London, 1997) at chapter 6.

13 The common law rules on what amounted to personal property need to be read in the light of the *Inheritance Act 1833* and the *Law of Property Amendment Act 1859*.

14 The common law rules on what amounted to real property were amended by the *Statute of Distribution 1670*, the *Administration of Intestates' Estates Act 1685*, and the *Statute of Frauds 1677*.

Passing of risk

The basic rule being *res perit domino*, the risk of destruction will, by operation of the vendor-purchaser trust, pass to the purchaser at the moment of contract. Thus, if I contract to buy a title to land from you and a building on that land is struck by lightning prior to completion, it is at my risk and it is therefore me who should have taken out insurance. The risk of destruction can, of course, be reallocated by the contract itself, and it is in fact common practice for contracts for the sale of land to provide that the risk shall remain with the vendor until completion.[15]

Attenuated relationship of trustee and beneficiary

We saw that the availability of specific performance turns the vendor into a trustee of the right contracted to be sold for the purchaser. It cannot, however, be said that this is a trust with the usual incidents of trusteeship, at least not until the purchase money is paid. Before that time, as Sir Thomas Plumer MR explained in *Wall v Bright*:[16]

> "The vendor is ... not a mere trustee; he is in progress towards it, and finally becomes such when the money is paid, and when he is bound to convey. In the mean time he is not bound to convey; there are many uncertain events to happen before it will be known whether he will ever have to convey, and he retains, for certain purposes, his old dominion over the estate. There are these essential differences between a mere trustee, and one who is made a trustee constructively, by having entered into a contract to sell; and it would, therefore, be going too far to say that they are alike in all respects; the principle that the agreement is to be considered as performed, which is a fiction of equity, must not be pursued to all practical consequences."

The same point was made by Lord Cairns in *Shaw v Foster*,[17] who said that "the vendor, whom I have called the trustee, was not a mere dormant trustee, he was trustee having a personal and substantial interest in the property, a right to protect that interest, and an active right to assert that interest if anything should be done in derogation of it. The relation, therefore, of trustee and cestui que trust subsisted, but subsisted subject to the paramount right of the vendor and trustee to protect his own interest as vendor of the property".[18]

Thus, the vendor is entitled to keep the rents and profits until the date fixed for completion[19] and to retain possession of the property until the contract is

---

15   Thus, condition 5.1.1 of the Standard Conditions of Sale (England and Wales) provides that: "the seller will transfer the property in the same physical state as it was at the date of the contract (except for fair wear and tear), which means that the seller retains the risk until completion."

16   (1820) 1 Jac & W 494 at 503; 37 ER 456 at 459.

17   (1872) LR 5 HL 321.

18   *Shaw v Foster*, above n 17 at 338.

19   *Cudden v Tite* (1858) 1 Giff 395; 65 ER 971.

completed by payment of the price.[20] He is also entitled to keep moneys paid out under insurance policies he has entered into on the property.[21]

Insolvency

But by far the most important consequence today is the protection the purchaser receives in the event of his vendor's insolvency, for rights held by an insolvent on trust are not available to satisfy his debts.[22] Thus, in a contest between the purchaser of land and the vendor's general creditors, the former can claim that the right contracted to be sold is not available to satisfy the debts of the latter. This can lead to anomalous results. Take once again the case of a contract for the sale of shares. Assume that P1 enters into a contract for the sale of a parcel of shares in a public company and P2 enters into a contract with the same vendor for the sale of a parcel of shares in a private company. Both pay the purchase price in full, but before title is transferred to either of them, the vendor becomes insolvent. P1 will be left to a claim against the vendor's insolvent estate and is unlikely to come away with anything. P2, by contrast, will be the beneficiary of a trust of the shares he has contracted to buy, with the result that those shares will come out of the insolvency. One purchaser will go away empty handed, while the other will obtain all that he bargained for. However, it is difficult to see in what way the merits of either purchaser are different.

APPLICATION

The vendor-purchaser contract apart, the trust also arises for the same reason in a number of other areas, specifically marriage settlements and certain types of equitable mortgage. However, one situation in which it has no application is that of fixed or floating charges over future property.

Marriage settlements

In the case of a marriage settlement concerning future property, a constructive trust will arise in favour of those within the marriage consideration when assets matching the description of those promised to be settled are received by the covenantor. An example is provided by *Pullan v Koe*.[23] By a marriage settlement made in 1859, a wife covenanted to transfer to trustees after-acquired property of the value of £100 and above. Twenty years later, she received £285. But instead of paying it over to the trustees as per the covenant, she paid it into her husband's bank account. Some of the money was used by the husband to buy two bearer bonds, which he still had at his death in 1909. It was argued that the only possible claim was on the covenant, and that that was now statute-barred.

---

20 *Gedge v Duke of Montrose* (1858) 26 Beav 45; 53 ER 813; *Phillips v Sylvester* (1872) 8 Ch App 173.
21 *Rayner v Preston* (1881) 18 Ch D 1.
22 *Insolvency Act 1986*, s 283(3).
23 [1913] 1 Ch 9.

Swinfen Eady J, however, held that the £285 received by the wife was held by her at the point of receipt on constructive trust for those within the marriage settlement, and that the bonds, since they represented the traceable value of the subject-matter of that trust, were held on the same trusts, the covenant being one of which a court would have decreed specific performance.[24]

Equitable mortgages

A second context in which this doctrine is used is in relation to mortgages. Where a contract for a mortgage is entered into but no mortgage is actually granted, the application of the rule that equity treats as done that which ought to be done gives the lender a mortgage in equity.[25] The same thinking applies to imperfect legal mortgages,[26] and mortgages created by deposit of title deeds.[27]

Charges over future property

It is sometimes said that there is a third situation in which the doctrine is applied, that of fixed or floating charges over future property.[28] That is not, however, true.

At common law, it is not possible to mortgage rights which the mortgagor does not have at the time the mortgage is created. For after-acquired rights to be caught by a mortgage, a fresh conveyance has to be executed every time a new asset is acquired. But this is not the case in equity, where it is possible to grant either a fixed or floating charge over both existing and future property. There is no need for a new instrument to be executed each time a new asset is received.[29] The charge will attach to the right without more simply on receipt. The question is whether this doctrine depends on the availability of specific performance. It is difficult to see why it should. First, the ability to charge existing rights in equity in no way depends on the availability of specific performance;[30] why then should the position be any different with respect to future rights? Secondly, it is often the case that the assets subject to these

---

24   The availability of specific performance in this case is puzzling, for it is generally thought that a promise to pay money will not be specifically enforced, damages being a perfectly adequate remedy in such a case. It may be, however, that there is an exception in the case of a promise to pay money to a third party, a rule possibly recognised by the House of Lords in *Beswick v Beswick* [1968] AC 58.

25   *Ex p Wright* (1812) 19 Ves 255; 34 ER 513.

26   *Parker v Housefield* (1834) 2 My & K 419; 39 ER 1004.

27   *Russel v Russel* (1783) 1 Bro CC 269; 28 ER 1121. Mortgages by deposit of title deeds, or more likely land certificates, have, since 1989, been ineffective unless they comply with s 2 of the *Law of Property (Miscellaneous Provisions) Act 1989*: *United Bank of Kuwait plc v Sahib* [1997] Ch 107. The 1989 Act requires contracts for the sale of land to be in writing and signed by both parties.

28   See, for example, MJ Bridge, *Personal Property Law* (3rd ed, Oxford University Press, Oxford, 2002) at 180-181.

29   *Lunn v Thornton* (1845) 1 CB 379; 135 ER 587.

30   *Metcalfe v Archbishop of York* (1836) 1 My & Cr 547; 40 ER 485.

charges are fungible, and therefore not the sort of assets of which a contract to transfer would normally be specifically enforced.

The confusion seems to have arisen from the speech of Lord Westbury LC in *Holroyd v Marshall*.[31] The case concerned a mortgage by deed of the machinery in a mill, the security being expressed to cover not only the machinery existing at the date of the agreement but that which might be later substituted for such machinery. It was agreed on all sides that the substitute machinery was not caught by the mortgage at law because there had been no subsequent conveyance of any rights to the substitute machinery when it was received. The argument instead turned on the effect of the mortgage in equity. The judgment creditor said that the substitute machinery would only be caught if there was a delivery of possession to the mortgagee or some act equivalent to it to perfect title, an argument which was accepted by Lord Campbell in the court below.[32] It failed, however, before the House of Lords. In the view of the Lord Westbury:[33]

> "It is quite true that a deed which professes to convey property which is not in existence at the time is a conveyance void at law, simply because there is nothing to convey. So in equity a contract which engages to transfer property which is not in existence, cannot operate as an immediate alienation merely because there is nothing to transfer. But if a vendor or mortgagor agree to sell or mortgage property, real or personal, of which he is not possessed at the time, and he receives the consideration for the contract, and afterwards become possessed of property answering the description in the contract, there is no doubt that a Court of Equity would compel him to perform the contract, and that the contract would in equity transfer the beneficial interest to the mortgagee or purchaser immediately on the property being acquired."

The only other substantive judgment was given by Lord Chelmsford, the third judge, Lord Wensleydale, being content merely to express his agreement with the order proposed. But while Lord Westbury's reasoning seems to depend on the availability of specific performance, Lord Chelmsford places no reliance on the doctrine whatsoever. For him, the charge came into existence the moment the future property was received, and there was no need for any further act to perfect the mortgagee's title. The difference is noted by Pennington, who, in his seminal article on the origins of the floating charge, wrote:[34]

> "Lord Westbury conceived the mortgage of after-acquired property as creating a contract for the creation of a proper mortgage which equity will specifically enforce when the property is acquired, and because of the availability of specific performance, the mortgagor becomes a trustee of the property for the mortgagee, and the mortgagee's proprietary rights thus obtained are binding on third parties. Lord Chelmsford, too, sees the original mortgage as a contract, but a contract which is self-executing as soon as the mortgagor acquires the property in question, so that whether the mortgagee could obtain

---

31   (1862) 10 HLC 191; 11 ER 999.
32   (1860) 2 De G F & J 596; 45 ER 752.
33   *Holroyd v Marshall*, above n 31 at 210-211, 1006-1007.
34   RR Pennington, "The Genesis of the Floating Charge" (1960) 23 *Modern Law Review* 630 at 635-637.

an order of specific performance or not, he obtains equitable proprietary rights automatically."

The reasoning of Lord Chelmsford was preferred by the House of Lords in *Tailby v Official Receiver*,[35] a case concerned with an assignment of present and future book debts. The Court of Appeal had held such an assignment void as to future book debts because specific performance would not be granted.[36] The House of Lords disagreed, holding that the availability of specific performance was not a precondition of the validity of the assignment. Lord Watson said:[37]

> "There is but one condition which must be fulfilled in order to make the assignee's right attach to a future chose in action, which is, that, on its coming into existence, it shall answer the description in the assignment, or, in other words, that is shall be capable of being identified as the thing, or as one of the very things assigned."

The references to specific performance in Lord Westbury's speech in *Holroyd v Marshall* were to be read as requiring merely certainty as to what assets were caught by the charge. As Lord Herschell explained, "I think the language used referred only to that class of cases to which he had alluded in an earlier part of his opinion, where it could not be predicated of any specific goods that they fell within the general descriptive words of the grant."[38] This was also the view of Lord Macnaghten:[39]

> "It is difficult to suppose that Lord Westbury intended to lay down as a rule to guide or perplex the Court, that considerations applicable to cases of specific performance, properly so-called, where the contract is executory, are to be applied to every case of equitable assignment dealing with future property. ... [Great] confusion ... would be caused by transferring considerations applicable to suits for specific performance – involving, as they do, some of the nicest distinctions and most difficult questions that come before the Court – to cases of equitable assignment or specific lien where nothing remains to be done in order to define the rights of the parties, but the Court is merely asked to protect rights completely defined as between the parties to the contract, or to give effect to such rights either by granting an injunction or by appointing a receiver, or by adjudicating on questions between rival claimants."

The upshot is, therefore, that fixed and floating charges over future property do not arise because of the application of some version of the vendor-purchaser constructive trust.

MISAPPLICATION

There are two situations in which the vendor-purchaser constructive trust has been misapplied. The first is where anticipated performance of the contract

---

35   (1888) 13 App Cas 523.
36   *Official Receiver v Tailby* (1887) LR 18 QBD 25.
37   *Tailby v Official Receiver*, above n 35 at 533.
38   *Tailby v Official Receiver*, above n 35 at 531-532.
39   *Tailby v Official Receiver*, above n 35 at 547.

has led to the contracting party receiving more than he could have ever obtained from actual performance, what we might call "over-anticipation". The second occurs where there was no primary or even secondary duty to convey a specific right.

Over-anticipation

As we have seen, the vendor-purchaser constructive trust anticipates the eventual result at law. Since the purchaser can compel performance of the contract of sale, he will eventually become the holder of the right he has contracted to buy. Equity jumps the gun, as it were, and deems that result to have occurred before it actually does. The rule does not, however, give the purchaser anything more than he would eventually obtain from performance of the contract. In fact, it gives him slightly less, for an equitable right, in that it can be destroyed by the intervention of a good faith purchaser of a legal title for value without notice,[40] is not as strong as a legal one. In one case, however, the application of this doctrine gave the purchaser a right far stronger than he could have ever obtained at law.

In *Bristol Airports plc v Powdrill*[41] an airline company was the lessee of a number of aircraft. It was indebted to Bristol Airport in respect of unpaid airport charges, and by statute the airport authority was entitled to seize and sell aircraft of which the debtor company was the operator. The airline company was insolvent, and, to enable it to continue trading, it had been placed under an administration order pursuant to section 8 of the *Insolvency Act 1986*. Section 11(3) of the same Act provides that "no ... steps may be taken to enforce any security over the company's property ... except with the consent of the administrator or the leave of the court." The question for the Court of Appeal was whether the airport authority required the leave of the court to exercise its statutory power of detention. The authority argued that it did not, on the ground, inter alia, that the aircraft, being held under leases, were not the "property" of the insolvent company, it being accepted on both sides that a lease of goods had no proprietary effect at law. The Court of Appeal held that even if a lease of goods was not a legal property right, the aircraft were still the company's property by virtue of the specific enforceability of the contract of hire. Leave was therefore required before the aircraft could be seized. Sir Nicolas Browne-Wilkinson V-C, as he then was, gave the leading judgment. He said:[42]

> "Although a chattel lease is a contract, it does not follow that no property interest is created in the chattel. The basic equitable principle is that if, under a contract, A has certain rights over property as against the legal owner, which rights are specifically enforceable in equity, A has an equitable interest in such property. I have no doubt that a court would order specific performance of a contract to lease an aircraft, since each aircraft has unique features peculiar to

---

40   *Pilcher v Rawlins* (1872) LR 7 Ch App 259.
41   [1990] Ch 744.
42   *Bristol Airports plc v Powdrill*, above n 41 at 759.

itself. Accordingly in my judgment the 'lessee' has at least an equitable right of some kind in that aircraft which falls within the statutory definition as being some 'description of interest ... arising out of, or incidental to' that aircraft."

But though the conclusion that a chattel lease is a property right in equity may well be correct in the specialised context of the *Insolvency Act 1986*, particularly in view of the extremely wide definition of "property" contained therein,[43] his lordship's invocation of the vendor-purchaser constructive trust in this context is misplaced, for two reasons. The first is that this was a case of an executed and not an executory contract. As Lord Selbourne LC explained in *Wolverhampton & Walsall Rly Co v London & North Western Rly Co*,[44] the equitable remedy of specific performance "presupposes an executory as distinct from an executed agreement, something remaining to be done, such as the execution of a deed or a conveyance, in order to put the parties in the position relative to each other in which by the preliminary agreement they were intended to be placed".[45] In this case, however, possession of the aircraft had been delivered by the lessor to the lessee and nothing remained to be done on the part of the lessor.

The second problem is that, as we have seen, a lease of land when executed by deed creates a proprietary right at law, and an application of the maxim "equity looks upon that as done which ought to be done" only anticipates the final result, albeit in equity and not at law. But at law, a lease of a chattel, even if created by deed or carved in stone, was assumed by Sir Nicolas Browne-Wilkinson V-C as creating no property right,[46] for, if it had, there would have been no need to resort to any equitable doctrine. And since, in his view, actual performance would not create property rights, anticipated performance could not do so either. For if it did, equity would not simply be jumping the gun, but destroying altogether the division between personal and proprietary rights, for now the question whether a particular right was personal or proprietary would turn not on the numeras clausus rule laid down in cases such as *Hill v Tupper*[47] and *King v David Allen (Billposting)*,[48] but on the availability of specific performance; yet given that a contractual licence to occupy land is both specifically enforceable[49] but still not a property right,[50] we know that this cannot be the case.

---

43   Section 436 provides that "'Property' includes money, goods, things in action, land and every description of property wherever situated and also obligations and every description of interest, whether present or future or vested or contingent, arising out, or incidental to, property". As Sir Nicolas Browne-Wilkinson V-C remarked, "it is hard to think of a wider definition of property": *Bristol Airports plc v Powdrill*, above n 41 at 759.
44   (1873) LR 16 Eq 433.
45   *Wolverhampton & Walsall Rly Co v London & North Western Rly Co*, above n 44 at 439. This passage was approved by Lord Macnaghten in *Tailby v Official Receiver* (1888) 13 App Cas 523 at 547.
46   For a full discussion of whether it does, see WJ Swadling, 'The Proprietary Effect of a Hire of Goods', in N Palmer and E McKendrick, *Interests in Goods* (2nd ed, Lloyds of London Press, London, 1998) at 491-526.
47   (1863) 2 H & C 121; 159 ER 51.
48   [1916] 2 AC 54.
49   *Verrall v Great Yarmouth BC* [1981] QB 202
50   *Ashburn Anstalt v Arnold* [1989] Ch 1.

No primary or secondary duty to convey specific rights

A second misapplication of the vendor-purchaser constructive trust occurred in the decision of the Privy Council in *Attorney-General for Hong Kong v Reid*,[51] which concerned a claim for restitution of gains made through wrongdoing. There is no doubt that the commission of a wrong generates a right to damages in the victim of the wrong. Those damages might be measured in a number of different ways: by reference to the plaintiff's loss (compensation); by reference to the defendant's gain (restitution); or by reference to some other measure (nominal damages, punitive damages, aggravated damages). No-one has ever suggested that a constructive trust should arise to give effect to an award of compensatory damages, exemplary damages, nominal damages or even aggravated damages. Surprisingly, however, the suggestion has been made in respect of an award of restitutionary damages. Of course, differently to the case of the other heads of damages, there may now be a res over which a constructive trust can be impressed. But the fact that there is the possible subject-matter of a constructive trust does not of itself justify its imposition.

The question of the raising of a trust in favour of the victim of a wrong has, Canada apart,[52] arisen in relation to only one particular wrong, that of breach of fiduciary duty. It seems to be taken for granted in all other cases of wrongdoing where damages can be measured on a restitutionary scale, for example, infringement of copyright[53] or breach of patent,[54] that there is only a personal right to restitution. That in itself should make us suspicious of a trust response to the wrong of breach of fiduciary duty. Yet the Privy Council gave precisely that in *Attorney-General for Hong Kong v Reid*, though through a misapplication of the vendor-purchaser constructive trust doctrine.

Reid was a high-ranking official in the office of the Hong Kong Director of Public Prosecutions who was convicted of taking $HK12.4 million in bribes to obstruct the prosecution of certain criminals. He was sentenced to eight years in prison. With some of the bribe money he had purchased rights to land in New Zealand, and the Hong Kong government sought a declaration that he held those rights for it on constructive trust. The Hong Kong government argued that as a fiduciary Reid held each bribe on constructive trust from the moment of its receipt, with the result that anything which was traceably the product of the bribe was likewise held on trust. The Privy Council agreed. In giving the opinion of the Board, Lord Templeman reasoned as follows:[55]

> "When a bribe is offered and accepted in money or in kind, the money or property constituting the bribe belongs in law to the recipient. Money paid to the false fiduciary belongs to him. ... Equity, however, which acts in personam, insists that it is unconscionable for a fiduciary to obtain and retain a benefit in breach of duty. ... The false fiduciary who received the bribe in breach of duty must pay and account for the bribe to the person to whom that duty was owed.

---

51 [1994] 1 AC 324.
52 *Lac Minerals Ltd v International Corona Resources Ltd* [1989] 2 SCR 574.
53 *Copyright, Designs and Patents Act 1988*, s 96(2).
54 *Patents Act 1977*, s 61(1).
55 *Attorney-General for Hong Kong v Reid*, above n 51 at 331.

In the present case, as soon as Mr Reid received a bribe in breach of the duties he owed to the Government of Hong Kong, he became a debtor in equity to the Crown for the amount of that bribe. ... As soon as the bribe was received it should have been paid or transferred instanter to the person who suffered from the breach of duty. Equity considers as done that which ought to have been done. As soon as the bribe was received, whether in cash or in kind, the false fiduciary held the bribe on a constructive trust for the person injured."

This is an incorrect application of the maxim that "equity considers that as done which ought to be done" for two reasons. First, what should have been done was that Mr Reid not take any bribes in the first place. But if we deem Mr Reid never to have taken bribes then there will not even be a personal claim to his enrichment. The truth is that the vendor-purchaser constructive trust arises because of the fictionalised performance of the primary obligation of the vendor to perform his promise, not his secondary obligation to pay damages for a failure to perform that promise.[56] It is not, therefore a doctrine which can apply to wrongdoing at all,[57] and *Reid* was, at least in the view of Lord Templeman, who uses the phrase "breach of duty" four times in the passage set out above, a case of restitution for wrongs.[58] But a second and more substantial objection is that the argument mistakes the nature of the fiduciary's duty to account. The duty entails the making of an account and the payment of any debt found due at the end of that accounting process. But the debt, should there be one, can be satisfied by that payment of money derived from any source belonging to the person liable to account. It is not, unlike an agreement to sell title to a particular parcel of land, an obligation to transfer rights in specie, and it is for that further reason that the vendor-purchaser constructive trust can also have no application in a case such as *Reid*.

EXPLAINING THE TRUST

As *Howard v Miller*[59] demonstrates, the vendor-purchaser trust arises from the fact that specific performance is available to compel the vendor to perform the contract. But it is not immediately obvious why the availability of specific performance should have the effect of creating a trust. The answer generally given is that it in turn triggers the application of the equitable maxim, "equity

---

56 On the difference between primary and secondary obligations, see Lord Diplock's speech in *Photo Production Ltd v Securicor Transport Ltd* [1980] AC 827 at 848-849 and the essay by P Birks, 'Obligations: One Tier or Two?' in P Stein and A Lewis (eds), *Studies in Justinian's Institutes in Memory of JAC Thomas* (Sweet & Maxwell, London, 1983) at 18-38. Other writers prefer the language of antecedent and remedial rights, though their meaning is the same: Sir Thomas Erskine Holland, *The Elements of Jurisprudence* (13th ed, Clarendon Press, Oxford, 1924) at 147-148; GW Paton and DP Derham, *A Text-book of Jurisprudence* (4th ed, Clarendon Press, Oxford, 1972) at 297-298.

57 For an excellent discussion of the concept of "wrongdoing", see P Birks, 'What is a Civil Wrong?' in D Owen (ed), *Philosophical Foundations of Tort Law* (Clarendon Press, Oxford, 1995) at 31-51.

58 Lord Millett in his chapter in this book takes the view that the case was not concerned with wrongdoing at all. See "Proprietary Restitution" in this book at 323–324.

59 [1915] AC 318.

looks upon that as done which ought to be done". But even that does not tell us why a trust should arise, for it is not the creation of a trust which the vendor ought to do but the vesting of absolute title in the purchaser,[60] and even then, not at the date of the contract but at the time fixed for completion.

We might also notice that the raising of a trust is not the inevitable consequence of the application of this rule. Take again the case of *Walsh v Lonsdale*.[61] As the contract was specifically enforceable, the court treated the lease as having been granted. But the language of trusts is completely absent from the case. Indeed, it is difficult to see how it could have been used, for the freeholder had no right which it would have been appropriate for him to hold on trust for his prospective tenant. He had a fee simple title, but if it was that which was caught by the trust, the lessee could have then exercised his rights under *Saunders v Vautier*[62] and obtained for himself the freehold, which the vendor was certainly never obliged to transfer.[63] Given this fact, it is difficult to see why the terminology of trusts in invoked where it is not the creation of a new interest which has been promised but the transfer of one that already exists. Why not simply say that there is an equitable title in the purchaser and a legal title in the vendor and leave it at that?

The real problem with explaining the vendor-purchaser constructive trust is that we are here dealing with the application of a fiction[64] and fictions do not explain themselves. Indeed, the one thing we must not do with fictions is to take them seriously. A famous example of a court doing just that is the decision of the House of Lords in *Sinclair v Brougham*,[65] where claims in unjust enrichment were said to be explained on the basis of contracts implied in law, with the result that such a claim could not succeed where an express contract to repay would have been void. The shadow that case cast over the subject made rational analysis impossible until the House of Lords dispelled the implied contract explanation nearly four decades later in *Fibrosa Spolka Akcyjna v Fairbairn Lawson Combe Barbour Ltd*.[66] A more recent example of the debunking of a

---

60 The same difficulty is also present in cases of marriage settlements, where identical reasoning applies. If in such a case A covenants with B that he will convey certain rights to B to hold on trust for C, and C is within the marriage consideration, then the moment A receives rights caught by the covenant he will hold them as constructive trustee for C: *Pullan v Koe* [1913] 1 Ch 9. Yet if A had done what he ought to have done, it is B and not A who would now be the trustee.

61 (1881) 21 Ch D 9.

62 (1841) 4 Beav 115; 49 ER 282.

63 This argument also shows the weakness of the constructive trust found by Lord Denning MR in *Binions v Evans* [1972] Ch 359. That was a case in which a purchaser of a freehold title to land took it "subject to" the rights of a contractual licensee. The Master of the Rolls held that though the licensee had no right capable of binding a third party at the outset, the later purchase "subject to" her rights made the purchaser a constructive trustee for her. But what his lordship singularly fails to do in that case is to identify the subject-matter of the constructive trust, which, since the only relevant right held by the purchaser was the fee simple, could only have been that. Despite this difficulty, the same thinking was applied by the Court of Appeal in *DHN Food Distributors v Tower Hamlets LBC* [1976] 1 WLR 852.

64 As was acknowledged by Sir Thomas Plumer MR in *Wall v Bright* (1820) 1 Jac & W 494 at 503; 37 ER 456 at 459. The passage is cited above, text to n 16.

65 [1914] AC 398.

66 [1943] AC 32.

fiction is provided by the brilliant work of Professor Smith on tracing. For years, courts thought of the rules of tracing in terms of presumptions, one such presumption, said to be the combined effect of *re Hallett*[67] and *re Oatway*,[68] being that a trustee is presumed to be acting honestly when making expenditures from a fund in which, in breach of trust, he has mixed trusts funds with his own. But such a presumption was always impossible to reconcile with the lowest intermediate balance rule in *Roscoe v Winder*,[69] for a presumption of honesty would mean that funds later coming into the account could be explained as the errant trustee making good the expenditures in breach of trust. However, it was not until Lionel Smith taught us not to think in terms of presumptions that we could finally reconcile the two.[70] Unfortunately, in the case of the vendor-purchaser constructive trust no attempt has been made to move beyond the incantation of a fiction. This section asks whether it can possibly be done. It starts by attempting to locate the event which triggers the trust to see if this throws any light on its rationale. It then looks at a justification given by Elias, the author of the only book seeking to explain the various incidences of constructive trusts. And it concludes by looking at the only explanation so far put forward by the courts, that though the passing of the legal title requires a conveyance, the equitable title passes by dint of the contract alone.

To what event does the vendor-purchaser trust respond?

There can be no doubt but that rights, including trusts, arise as a response to events which happen in the world. For example, my act of negligently running over your foot gives rise to a right in you to damages against me. Professor Birks has suggested that the events which generate rights can be conveniently classified under four broad headings: consent, wrongs, unjust enrichment, and other miscellaneous events. It should be stressed that the purpose of this classificatory scheme,[71] as with all systems of classification, is to try to understand the world, in our case the legal world, around us. It is not meant to impose a straight-jacket on legal reasoning. As Birks once wrote, "had he been averse to taxonomy or a bad taxonomist, Darwin would have observed but would not have understood. Taxonomy changes nothing, but it promotes understanding. Without it there is only a chaos of unsorted information, what Thomas Wood, writing on the condition of English law in 1722, called 'a heap of good learning.'"[72]

Consent

There are some who say that the vendor-purchaser trust is an express trust, with the inference that the trust therefore arises because of a manifestation of

---

67   *Re Halletts' Estate*, sub nom *Knatchbull v Hallett* (1879) LR 13 Ch D 696.
68   [1903] 2 Ch 356.
69   [1915] 1 Ch 62.
70   LD Smith, *The Law of Tracing* (Clarendon Press, Oxford, 1997).
71   Which Birks candidly admits might not be the best way of classifying the law: P Birks, "Equity in the Modern Law: An Exercise in Taxonomy" (1996) 26 *University of Western Australia Law Review* 1 at 7.
72   P Birks, "Equity in the Modern Law: An Exercise in Taxonomy", above n 71 at 3-4.

consent on the part of some person that a trust should come into being. Thus, in Pomeroy's *A Treatise on Equity Jurisprudence*[73] the following passage appears:[74]

> "It is commonly said that a trust is created by a contract for the sale of land; that the vendor holds the legal title as a trustee for the purchaser. Whatever of truth there is in this mode of statement, whatever of a real trust relation exists, it certainly has nothing in common with constructive trusts; it rather resembles an express trust."

But this cannot be right. At no point does the vendor intend to make himself a trustee of his title for the purchaser. His only intent is to bind himself to a subsequent transfer of that title to the purchaser, which is a very different thing. Might it then be said that a man intends the natural consequences of his acts, and, since vendor-purchaser trusts are almost automatic in these cases, that an intent to contract is an intent to create a trust? This will not work. First, it fails to explain the first incidence of such a trust. There must have been a first time that such a trust arose, and it could certainly not be said that that particular vendor knew that a trust would arise. Secondly, it assumes a knowledge of trusts law which is usually not present in vendors. Although there is no need for a settlor to have an intimate knowledge of the law of trusts in order to create a trust,[75] he does at least have to intend to bind himself to hold rights for another. We know from cases such as *Milroy v Lord*,[76] *Jones v Lock*,[77] and *Richards v Delbridge*[78] that such an intent will not be lightly found. And just as in those cases an intention to transfer absolutely or an intention to transfer to a third party on trust was said to contradict an allegation that the title holder had declared himself a trustee, so too could a contract of sale under which a promise is made to convey absolutely at a later date be said to contradict any assertion that the vendor immediately declared himself a trustee for the purchaser.

The final nail in the consent coffin is that a trust vendor-purchaser trust will arise even where it is expressly excluded by the parties. Suppose a contract for the sale of land included an express term which provided that no trust would arise between vendor and purchaser pending completion. It is difficult to see how this could stop a vendor-purchaser trust arising, for the trust depends on the availability of specific performance, not on the intention of the parties.

Wrongs

As we have already seen, there is one case in which a constructive trust has arisen as a result of wrongdoing, *Attorney-General for Hong Kong v Reid*,[79] though, as we also saw, it is incorrectly decided. But even if it were possible for

---

73 JN Pomeroy, *A Treatise on Equity Jurisprudence as Administered in the United States of America* (2nd ed, Bancroft-Whitney, San Francisco, 1892).

74 JN Pomeroy, *A Treatise on Equity Jurisprudence as Administered in the United States of America*, above n 73 at Section 1046.

75 *Re Schebsman* [1944] Ch 83; *Paul v Constance* [1977] 1 WLR 527.

76 (1862) 4 De G F & J 264; 45 ER 1185.

77 (1865) LR 1 Ch App 25.

78 (1874) LR 18 Eq 11.

79 [1994] 1 AC 324.

wrongdoing to trigger a trust, the vendor-purchaser trust cannot be said to be responding to any wrong. The only possible candidate would be breach of contract, but, since the trust arises before the time for performance is due, it can hardly be said to be responding to any breach. As was noted above, it directly enforces a primary obligation to perform, not a secondary obligation to pay damages for breach of a primary obligation. And it is only the latter which is a wrong.

Unjust enrichment

There are some isolated cases of unjust enrichments triggering trusts. A notable example is *Chase Manhattan v Israel-British Bank*,[80] where Goulding J held that a mistaken payment was held by the transferee on trust for the transferor. Leaving aside the debate over the correctness of such decisions, it is clear that the vendor-purchaser trust cannot be seen as a response to the vendor's unjust enrichment at the expense of the purchaser, for the vendor need not receive any enrichment from the purchaser. As we have seen, the trust arises even before the purchase money is paid. And even in the case where the purchase money is paid, the enrichment received from the purchaser is the sale price, but that is not what is held on trust. Moreover, a fundamental rule of the law of unjust enrichment is that there can be no unjust enrichment where benefits have been transferred pursuant to a contract unless and until that contract is first set aside.[81] In the case of the vendor-purchaser trust, this almost never happens.

Other miscellaneous events

Perhaps the reason lies beyond consent, wrongs, and unjust enrichment. But though there are certainly trust-creating events beyond these nominate heads, for example the statutory trust which arises when a title holder of land attempts to convey it to tenants in common,[82] no explanation based on other events seems ever to have been proffered. But here it must lie, for, as we have seen, it fits no nominate head. Of course, one reason why it might belong in this miscellany is that it is an anomaly. What we have seen so far certainly suggests that this might be the case.

The explanation of Elias

The only serious attempt at explaining the incidence of the vendor-purchaser trust is that of Elias. His explanation does not conform to the events-based classification used above, for its focus is not on the event triggering the legal response but on the reasons for that response. It is important to notice that these are different approaches. For example, the reason why mistaken payments have to be repaid is to effect restitution. The same purpose applies to the profits

---

80   [1981] Ch 105.
81   *Pan Ocean Shipping Co v Creditcorp (The Trident Beauty)* [1994] 1 WLR 161.
82   *Law of Property Act 1925*, s 34(2).

of wrongdoing. But the underlying cause of the former is unjust enrichment, and of the latter a breach of duty.[83]

In a difficult work,[84] more moral philosophy than legal doctrine, Elias seeks to explain the incidence of all constructive trusts, not just the vendor-purchaser constructive trust. In his view, all constructive trusts arise to give effect to one of three "aims": perfection, restitution, and reparation. Under the heading of "perfection" come such constructive trusts as that which arose in *re Rose*,[85] secret trusts, and the vendor-purchaser constructive trust itself.[86] Under the heading of "restitution" come cases of constructive trusts triggered by the defendant's unjust enrichment and those which force wrongdoers to make restitution of gains. Under the final heading of "reparation" are those "constructive trusts" which cause wrongdoers to make good losses. We are not concerned with the last two of these heads, but the obvious criticism to apply to the third, as Lord Millett has helpfully pointed out, is that such cases do not involve trusts at all but are instead personal claims to the payment of money.[87]

So far as the perfection cases are concerned, the argument is complex. The first stage comprises a justification for the binding effect of promises. Adopting the writings of Fried,[88] Elias says:[89]

> "By promising, one disposes of one's options to act contrarily to the content of the promise. … [T]he mere fact that the choicemaker has changed his mind is not a good reason for declining to uphold the choice. If we do not uphold the choice simply because he has changed his mind, we will in effect be saying that he is not a sufficiently worthy person to have the power to dispose. The power to dispose of one's options in favour of another person is an integral aspect of the fundamental capacity of the individual to make and realize such dispositive or other plans as he pleases. We could not take that capacity seriously – we would begin to say that there should be no power to dispose at all – if we took the bare plea 'I have changed my mind' seriously."

Fried was not, of course, arguing for constructive trusts but merely justifying the enforcement of promises in situations where the promisee had suffered no detriment in reliance on the promise.[90] In such a situation, the usual means of enforcement will be by way of an order that the promisor pay damages to the promisee. How then do we get from a money award to a trust? Elias explains it thus:[91]

---

83 The most useful discussion of this point is to be found in P Birks, "Unjust Enrichment and Wrongful Enrichment" (2001) 79 *Texas Law Review* 1767.

84 G Elias, *Explaining Constructive Trusts* (Clarendon Press, Oxford, 1990).

85 [1952] Ch 499.

86 G Elias, *Explaining Constructive Trusts,* above n 84 at 16.

87 *Dubai Aluminium Co Ltd v Salaam* [2003] 2 AC 366 at 404.

88 C Fried, *Contract as Promise: A Theory of Obligation* (Harvard University Press, Cambridge, 1981) at 20-21.

89 G Elias, *Explaining Constructive Trusts,* above n 84 at 9.

90 Atiyah had argued that in the absence of detriment to the promise, a promisor should not be held to his promise, even a promise supported by consideration: PS Atiyah, *Essays on Contract* (Clarendon, Oxford, 1986) at 10-56.

91 G Elias, *Explaining Constructive Trusts* (Clarendon Press, Oxford, 1990) at 34.

"[E]ach of the three [aims] is sufficiently cogent not to be confined to any particular method of giving relief. It is intuitively proper, for example, that (1) if I make a gift, the object of my bounty should become the owner of that property (perfection), or (2) if the property is lost and found, the finder does not automatically become the owner thereof as against me (restitution), or (3) one who I cause to spend time and money on my property should have a lien (reparation). Otherwise we would not be taking the three arguments seriously.

Carrying these intuitive convictions to a more general and more carefully formulated level, we may put the following proposition forward: where any of the three arguments should give the plaintiff rights against the defendant at all, there is a coherent premise for allowing the plaintiff the option of having property rights in any sufficiently factually relevant property. No ulterior aim is or need be furthered in allowing property rights to arise or persist initially in the furtherance of the three aims. We are to begin by giving each argument the full range of means of relief (including property rights) which bear it out genuinely. We are to begin, as it were, giving each argument 'full faith and credit'. The integrity of our basic commitment to an argument is what very rightly gets claims for property rights which affirm it going at all. Otherwise even basic claims like 'property passes under a gift' or 'title remains good against finders and thieves' would never get going at all. (If the integrity of our basic commitment to the perfection and restitution arguments did not suffice, we would say 'a donor is liable to pay the cash value of the property, but title to the property never passes to a donee' or 'a finder or thief gets a good title forthwith, but he may remain liable to pay the cash value of the property'.) And, because we believe that the law should be internally consistent, we should generalize such basic claims and endorse the proposition put forward at the beginning of this paragraph."

The argument in these two paragraphs is exceedingly difficult to follow. Focusing solely on the perfection aim, what Elias seems to be saying is that if we do not allow donors to make effective gifts then we fail to take the perfection argument seriously. But it is difficult to see what the argument is here, for the law does allow people to make perfectly good gifts. It seems that we do, therefore, take the perfection argument seriously. But reading between the lines, Elias's argument must be that the common law does not take perfection seriously enough, and that equity has to step in with a constructive trust in situations in which the common law falls down. If it does not, he says, the ability of donors to make gifts at law would be undermined. This is difficult to accept, for the common law rules on the making of gifts can hardly be said to be onerous. Indeed, it is telling that they are nowhere discussed in his book, with the consequence that there is no consideration whether the rules might in fact be perfectly sensible. But even if it were true to say that the common law fails to take seriously people's ability to make gifts, it does not then explain the vendor-purchaser constructive trust for the very simple reason that the vendor in such a case is not trying to transfer rights (far less to make a gift), but is instead entering into a legally binding promise to transfer rights at a future date. However, the common law rule which says that the right does not pass at the date of contract but only on conveyance can hardly be said to contradict the perfection argument at all, for at the point of contract there is no immediate attempt to transfer or promise immediately to transfer. Indeed, once the vendor-purchaser constructive trust is considered in the light of this so-called "perfection" aim, the reverse is in fact true, for it causes the right to pass at a time before that at which the vendor intends it so to do.

Equitable title passes by dint of contract

The only judicial utterances on this topic explain the vendor-purchaser trust as arising because the common law and equity have different rules for the passing of title. While title only passes at common law on the execution of the appropriate form of conveyance,[92] it is said that the position in equity is different, for in equity the contract itself is effective to pass title. Thus, in the quote from *Lysaght v Edwards*[93] given above,[94] we see Sir George Jessel MR saying that the "beneficial ownership passes to the purchaser" at the moment of contract. The same language also appears in at least two decisions of the House of Lords in the nineteenth century, *Holroyd v Marshall*[95] and *Rose v Watson*.[96]

We have already encountered *Holroyd v Marshall*, where the different approaches of Lords Westbury and Chelmsford to the requirement of specific enforceability to charges over future property were noted.[97] For the present, we should note that in the passage from Lord Westbury's speech cited above[98] the learned judge talks of the property having "passed in equity to the mortgagees, to whom Taylor [the debtor] was bound to make a legal conveyance, and for whom he, in the meantime, was a trustee of the property in question."[99] The idea of property "passing" in equity comes out even more clearly in an earlier passage from Lord Westbury's speech in the same case, where he said:[100]

> "In equity it is not necessary, for the alienation of property, that there should be any formal deed of conveyance. A contract for valuable consideration, by which it is agreed to make a present transfer of property, passes at once the beneficial interest, provided the contract is one of which a Court of Equity will decree specific performance."

The same thinking is evident in Lord Westbury's speech in *Rose v Watson*.[101] The respondent was a purchaser under a contract for the sale of land who had made a number of part-payments of the purchase price. Before the conveyance, he terminated the contract on the ground of the vendor's repudiatory breach in failing to secure that certain representations which induced him to enter into

---

92 The form of conveyance will of course change with the nature of the rights which have been contracted to be sold. While, for example, a deed will be effective to transfer title to unregistered land, it will not do the job where shares are concerned.

93 (1876) 2 Ch D 499.

94 Text to n 7.

95 (1862) 10 HLC 191; 11 ER 999.

96 (1864) 10 HLC 672; 11 ER 1187.

97 Text to nn 31-39.

98 Text to n 33.

99 *Holroyd v Marshal*, above n 95 at 211, 1007.

100 *Holroyd v Marshall*, above n 95 at 209, 1006. "Beneficial interest" would here seem to be being used as a synonym for "equitable interest". For a similar usage, see the opinion of the Privy Council delivered by Viscount Radcliffe in *Commissioner of Stamp Duties (Queensland) v Livingston* [1965] AC 694 at 712.

101 *Rose v Watson*, above n 96.

the contract were made good. After the contract had been entered into, and with notice of its existence, the appellants had taken a mortgage over the estate. The vendor now being insolvent, the respondent purchaser claimed a lien over the estate contracted to be sold. The appellant mortgagee's argument that such a lien had ceased to be available on the respondent's termination of the contract of sale was rejected by the House of Lords, for by paying over the purchase money the respondent acquired a pro rata interest in the land, and thus a lien on the land. And the reason why the purchaser had acquired an interest in the land, said Lord Westbury LC, was because:[102]

> "When the owner of an estate contracts with a purchaser for the immediate sale of it, the ownership of the estate is, in equity, transferred by that contract. Where the contract undoubtedly is an executory contract, in this sense, namely, that the ownership of the estate is transferred, subject to the payment of the purchase-money, every portion of the purchase-money paid in pursuance of that contract is a part performance and execution of the contract, and, to the extent of the purchase-money so paid, does, in equity, finally transfer to the purchaser the ownership of a corresponding portion of the estate."

The argument that the contract is effective to pass the equitable or beneficial interest while the legal title awaits the formal conveyance is, however, fundamentally misconceived, for it assumes the existence of two titles in the vendor, one legal, the other equitable. A number of cases show that this is not the case, that equitable interests are not carved out of legal estates but engrafted upon them.

Probably the best discussion of this topic is to be found in the judgment of Hope JA in the New South Wales Court of Appeal in *DKLR Holding Co (No 2) Ltd v Commissioner of Stamp Duties*.[103] Although the case later went on appeal,[104] the judgment of Hope JA was not doubted on this point. A company, 29 Macquarie (No 14) Pty Ltd, was the registered proprietor of title to certain land. It arranged with another company, DKLR Holding Co (No 2) Ltd, for the latter to hold the title on trust for the former once a change in registration was effected. The question was whether ad valorem stamp duty was payable on the document effecting the registration of DKLR as proprietor. DKLR argued that

---

102 *Rose v Watson* (1864) 10 HLC 672 at 678; 11 ER 1187 at 1190. Exactly the same thinking was expressed more recently by Lord Walker of Gestingthorpe in *Jerome v Kelly (Inspector of Taxes)* [2004] 1 WLR 1409 at 1419-1420, who said:

> "It would therefore be wrong ... to treat an uncompleted contract for the sale of land as equivalent to an immediate, irrevocable declaration of trust (or assignment of beneficial interest) in the land. Neither the seller nor the buyer has unqualified beneficial ownership. Beneficial ownership of the land is in a sense split between the seller and buyer on the provisional assumptions that specific performance is available and that the contract will in due course be completed, if necessary by the court ordering specific performance. In the meantime, the seller is entitled to enjoyment of the land or its rental income. The provisional assumptions may be falsified by events, such as rescission of the contract (either under a contractual term or on breach). If the contract proceeds to completion the equitable interest can be viewed as passing to the buyer in stages, as title is made and accepted and as the purchase price is paid in full."

103 [1980] 1 NSWLR 510.

104 *DKLR Holding Co (No 2) Pty Ltd v Commissioner of Stamp Duties (NSW)* (1982) 149 CLR 431.

only nominal duty was payable, since all that would be transferred to them would be a bare legal estate, with 29 Macquarie retaining the equitable interest. The argument was rejected. Hope JA said:[105]

> "[T]he person seised of land for an estate in fee simple has full and direct rights to possession and use of the land and its profits, as well as full rights of disposition. An equitable estate in land, even where its owner is absolutely entitled and the trustee is a bare trustee, is significantly different. ... [A]n absolute owner in fee simple does not hold two estates, a legal estate and an equitable estate. He holds only the legal estate, with all the right and incidents that attach to that estate .... [A]lthough the equitable estate is an interest in property, its essential character still bears the stamp which its origin placed upon it. Where the trustee is the owner of the legal fee simple, the right of the beneficiary, although annexed to the land, is a right to compel the legal owner to hold and use the rights which the law gives him in accordance with the obligations which equity has imposed upon him. The trustee, in such a case, has at law all the rights of the absolute owner in fee simple, but he is not free to use those rights for his own benefit in the way he could if no trust existed."

29 Macquarie could not therefore retain an equitable interest because they had no such interest before the transfer. Their equitable interest only arose on the transfer. As Hope JA explained:[106]

> "It is because equity will recognize and enforce the obligation which the plaintiff undertook to fulfil, if and when it became owner of the land, that 29 Macquarie will acquire an equitable estate in the land. The plaintiff's obligation, and not a 'retention' of a beneficial interest by 29 Macquarie, will be the source of that estate."

The reason why the confusion arises, the reason why a person absolutely entitled is thought to have both a legal and an equitable interest, is because of the use of the word "beneficial" to describe both the holding of a person vested with an unencumbered legal title and that of a person entitled under a trust. Similar language inevitably leads to an assumption that they are the same thing. But as Hope JA pointed out, that would be a mistake:[107]

> "It can, no doubt, be said that [29 Macquarie] was the beneficial owner of that land, but it held no separate equitable interest in the land; the statement merely means that it was the legal owner, and there was no equitable right in anyone to regulate or control the way in which it might exercise the rights which the legal ownership gave to it."

That a beneficial interest is not the same thing as an equitable interest under a trust comes out clearly from the judgment of Aickin J in the High Court in the same case, where the judge was careful to keep the two apart:[108]

> "A preliminary argument advanced on behalf of DKLR was that the transfer of the land to it by 29 Macquarie was effective to transfer only the 'bare legal

---

105 *DKLR Holding Co (No 2) Pty Ltd v Commissioner of Stamp Duties (NSW)*, above n 103 at 519.
106 *DKLR Holding Co (No 2) Pty Ltd v Commissioner of Stamp Duties (NSW)*, above n 103 at 523.
107 *DKLR Holding Co (No 2) Pty Ltd v Commissioner of Stamp Duties (NSW)*, above n 103 at 521
108 *DKLR Holding Co (No 2) Pty Ltd v Commissioner of Stamp Duties (NSW)* (1982) 149 CLR 431
     at 463.

estate' and to leave remaining in 29 Macquarie the entire beneficial interest. It was said that immediately prior to the transfer 29 Macquarie held both the unencumbered legal estate and the entire equitable interest in that property and that all that it had done was to transfer the legal estate. In my opinion this argument is based upon a fundamental misconception as to the nature of legal and equitable interests in land or other property. If one person has both the legal estate and the entire beneficial interest in the land he holds an entire and unqualified legal interest and not two separate interests, one legal and the other equitable."

A useful metaphor which has been used in this area is to speak of the equitable interest being "impressed" upon the legal estate. Thus, Brennan J, again in the High Court, said:[109]

"An equitable interest is not carved out of a legal estate but impressed upon it. It may be convenient to say that DKLR took only the bare legal estate, but that is merely to say elliptically that 29 Macquarie transferred to DKLR the property in respect of which DKLR had declared that it would be a trustee. The charter of 29 Macquarie's interest was DKLR's declaration, not the memorandum of transfer; and DKLR's declaration was moved by the transfer to it of the property to be held on the trust declared."

An equally good metaphor is to think of the equitable interest as being "engrafted" on the legal estate. This is the language of McLelland J in the later case of *re Transphere Pty Ltd*.[110] Having referred to the judgment of Hope JA in *DKLR*, he said:[111]

"An absolute owner holds only the legal estate, with all the rights and incidents that attach to that estate. Where a legal owner holds property on trust for another, he has at law all the rights of an absolute owner but the beneficiary has the right to compel him to hold and use those rights which the law gives him in accordance with the obligations which equity has imposed on him by virtue of the existence of the trust. Although this right of the beneficiary constitutes an equitable estate in the property, it is engrafted onto, not carved out of, the legal estate."

The same thinking can be seen in the decision of the House of Lords in *Westdeutsche Landesbank Girozentrale v Islington LBC*.[112] Money had been paid by a German bank under a contract later discovered to be void for want of capacity of the other party, an English local authority. A claim was made that the money had been received by the local authority on resulting trust for the bank. One argument for the bank was that since it only intended to part with its beneficial ownership of the moneys in performance of a valid contract, neither the legal nor the equitable title had passed to the local authority at the date of payment. And though the legal title to the money had vested in the local authority by operation of law when the moneys became mixed in the authority's bank

---

109 *DKLR Holding Co (No 2) Pty Ltd v Commissioner of Stamp Duties (NSW)*, above n 108 at 474.
110 (1986) 5 NSWLR 309. McLelland J, as MH McLelland QC, was counsel for DKLR in *DKLR Holding Co (No 2) v Commissioner of Stamp Duties (NSW)* (1982) 149 CLR 431.
111 *re Transphere Pty Ltd*, above n 110 at 311.
112 [1996] AC 669.

account, the bank, it was claimed, "retained" its equitable title. Lord Browne-Wilkinson described the argument as "fallacious":[113]

> "A person solely entitled to the full beneficial ownership of money or property, both at law and in equity, does not enjoy an equitable interest in that property. The legal title carries with it all rights. Unless and until there is a separation of the legal and equitable estates, there is no separate equitable title. Therefore to talk about the bank "retaining" its equitable interest is meaningless. The only question is whether the circumstances under which the money was paid were such as, in equity, to impose a trust on the local authority. If so, an equitable interest arose for the first time under that trust."

As this shows, it is not possible to say, as Lord Westbury does in both *Holroyd v Marshall* and *Rose v Watson* and as Sir George Jessel MR does in *Lysaght v Edwards*, that the vendor-purchaser constructive trust arises because there are different rules for the passing of the equitable and legal titles. It is not possible because there is no equitable interest separate from the legal title to pass. The equitable title in the purchaser is the creation of the court. It did not exist prior to the contract. But if this is right, we are now left with no explanation whatever for why the interest arises.

CAN THE INSOLVENCY CONSEQUENCES BE DEFENDED?

We saw above how the vendor-purchaser trust will operate in the context of the insolvency of the vendor so as to render the right contracted to be sold unavailable to the vendor's creditors. This section asks whether that result can be defended.

Surprisingly, almost no-one has ever put forward a defence of the insolvency protection given by the vendor-purchaser constructive trust. But equally, no-one seems ever to have argued against it. The only person to address the question is Elias, who devotes a chapter of his book to the issue.[114] We have already examined his arguments as to why the vendor-purchaser constructive trust arises and found them wanting. Unfortunately, he fares no better in his defence of the insolvency protection it gives.

His argument is run in terms of priority, and seeks to defend the priority of all constructive trusts, howsoever arising. The discussion is again both obscure

---

113   *Westdeutsche Landesbank Girozentrale v Islington LBC*, above n 112 [1996] AC 669 at 706. The point is also well put by Birks:
"[O]wnership is not in the normal course of things a matter of equitable meat stuffed inside a common law skin. People are not as they go about their daily lives owners at law and in equity of their cars, shares, books and so on. In the normal way of things they have no equitable interest at all. Equity has nothing to say. A legal title can become a bare right, a *nudum ius*, if equity intervenes. Until equity intervenes, we hold *pleno iure*, with the full benefits of ownership. It follows that, if B transfers to T in circumstances in which equity intervenes to say that T shall take only the *nudum ius* and that the benefits of ownership shall remain with B, the benefits of ownership remain with B because a new equitable interest has sprung up, not because B's transfer has taken his legal title across to T leaving his equitable title behind": P Birks, "Trusts Raised to Reverse Unjust Enrichment" [1996] *Restitution Law Review* 3 at 10.
114   Chapter 5 is entitled 'The Fears (2): Priority'.

and difficult to replicate. Elias starts by defending the priority constructive trusts give outside insolvency.[115] What Elias is here discussing are contests between the beneficiary of the constructive trust and purchasers from the trustee of the right which forms the subject-matter of that trust. Given that constructive trusts interests will always yield to a bona fide purchaser of a legal title for value without notice, Elias says that any fears of undue priority are exaggerated. Those who might be bound by the trust right, he says, are only volunteers,[116] and consequently deserve no protection. That argument is then extended into insolvency law, where Elias says that an insolvency priority for the constructive trust beneficiary is the natural result of taking his three aims seriously:[117]

> "If the trustee in bankruptcy could receive and keep the property, he would gain through the plaintiff's loss. Taking the restitution argument seriously implies that he should have to give up the property to the plaintiff to the extent of the plaintiff's claim. The trustee in bankruptcy is not a purchaser without notice. He is in truth a mere volunteer claiming through the insolvent. He deserves no more protection that did the mistress of the rogue in the *Banque Belge* case."

And later:[118]

> "the central point [is] that basically the ordinary claimant is a mere volunteer who should have to make restitution to the plaintiff who has a good premiss for owning rights in the property."

There are a number of problems with his arguments. First, his use of the word "priority" in this context is mistaken, for the removal of assets from the pool available to satisfy the creditors' claims is not an issue of priority. When insolvency lawyers use the word "priority", they mean to refer to situations in which the legal system departs from the normal rule of pari passu distribution amongst creditors and exceptionally gives one set of creditors a first claim on the asset pool before those of other creditors. So, for example, certain claims by employees for wages and holiday remuneration in a corporate insolvency are by statute paid before any distribution is made to the company's general creditors.[119] What Elias is discussing is not a priority among creditors, but a judgment as to what assets are available to satisfy the creditors' claims, preferred or not. But as Goode explains:[120]

> "The principle of pari passu distribution of assets does not apply to the rights of secured creditors, suppliers of goods under agreements reserving title, creditors for whom the company holds assets on trust. This, however, is not because these are exceptions to the rule but because such assets do not belong to the company and thus do not fall to be distributed among creditors on any basis."

---

115 G Elias, *Explaining Constructive Trusts* (Clarendon Press, Oxford, 1990) at 118-130.
116 The fact that good faith purchasers of *equitable* titles does not seem to get in the way of his thesis. Elias simply says that the rule is 'unfortunate' and should be changed in this regard: G Elias, *Explaining Constructive Trusts*, above n 115 at 123.
117 G Elias, *Explaining Constructive Trusts*, above n 115 at 142.
118 G Elias, *Explaining Constructive Trusts*, above n 115 at 143.
119 *Insolvency Act 1986*, ss 175 and 386, sched 6.
120 Sir Roy Goode, *Principles of Corporate Insolvency* (2nd ed, Sweet & Maxwell, London, 1997) at 152 (footnotes omitted).

The second problem is that his argument is in any case circular. It assumes that the constructive trust is justified and then says that any attempt to take away the rights it gives would conflict with the "restitution" aim articulated earlier. What it fails to notice, however, is that the rights under these trusts have been awarded by courts, and it is the court which is therefore giving "priority" to one set of creditors over another. We accept that individuals can create property rights or trusts in favour of others and thereby remove assets from the pool available to satisfy the insolvent's debts.[121] But should courts be allowed to do the same? Should they not instead stand neutral between creditors? As we have seen, the court-created vendor-purchaser constructive trust gives the purchaser of shares in a private company more favourable treatment than the purchaser of shares in a public company, the purchaser of land more favourable treatment than the traffic accident victim. It is this disparity of treatment which Elias does not address. And it is that disparity which is difficult to defend.

CONCLUSION

The vendor-purchaser constructive trust is one of the oldest, if not the oldest constructive trust known to English law. Perhaps it is its long history which has turned it into a venerable institution, one whose legitimacy has never been questioned. Indeed, one judge has gone so far as to say it could not be questioned. In *Shaw v Foster*, Lord O'Hagan said:[122]

> "Although a great deal of time was occupied in a learned disquisition on the effect of a contract of sale, as creating an equitable estate in the purchaser, I do not apprehend that there is any doubt, or that the noble and learned lord whose judgment we are considering could have meant to suggest any doubt, upon that subject. The law is clear. It is, as Lord St Leonards has said, 'one of the landmarks of the Court': *Baldwin v Belcher*;[123] and it ought not to be called into question." [123]

But it is part of the task of the academic branch of the legal profession to call into question what to judges might seem unquestionable doctrine. As Lord Goff has pointed out,[124] judges have to deal with the case before them and do not generally have the opportunity to take a wider view of the legal landscape. Even the highest appellate tribunals have to dispose of the case in hand and are at the mercy of counsels' arguments. Academics are not so constrained, and can take time to see whether any particular "landmark" is out of place.

The conclusion reached by this chapter is that the vendor-purchaser constructive trust cannot be justified. It rests on a fiction and has no rational basis. It gives protection in insolvency where no priority is deserved. Interestingly,

---

121 Subject, of course, to rules against fraudulent preferences.

122 (1872) LR 5 HL 321 at 349.

123 (1844) 1 Jo & Lat 18.

124 Sir Robert Goff, 'The Search for Principle' reprinted in W Swadling and G Jones (eds), *The Search for Principle: Essays for Lord Goff of Chieveley* (Oxford University Press, Oxford, 1999) at 313-329.

some common law jurisdictions cope without it. Thus, the *Restatement of Trusts* provides that "a contract to convey property is not a trust, whether or not the contract is specifically enforceable".[125] In similar vein is the *Indian Transfer of Property At 1882*, section 54 of which provides that a contract of sale of immovable property gives the purchaser no equitable title pending completion and that the trustee/beneficiary relationship does not come into existence. Perhaps English law should follow the lead of its former colony and also legislate this particular trust out of existence.

---

125 American Law Institute, *Restatement of the Law of Trusts* (2nd ed, American Law Institute Publishers, St Paul, Minnesota, 1959) at para 13.

19

Equity, Contract and Conscience

PETER W YOUNG

INTRODUCTION

I introduce this chapter first by outlining its purpose, then by making a personal explanation and finally by mapping out its scope.

The modern law of contract and contract-related matters have, in my view, come about by the interaction between principle of law and principles of equity over the last 650 years. It is inadequate to view the history of contract merely by tracing the history of assumpsit. When looking at the activity of the equity courts, a more complete picture emerges. I hope this chapter will go some way towards establishing that proposition.

The chapter is written from my personal perspective. I must note that I am one of the last traditional equity lawyers left on a superior court bench who has had practical experience of pre-*Judicature Act* procedures. New South Wales was one of the last places in the common law world to have a separate equity jurisdiction. Up until 1972 in New South Wales, one could still plead a defence of "no equity" to a claim on the equity side of the court. In New South Wales, the procedure at law, of a trial by a jury of four, for all civil cases meant that many commercial matters had to be disguised as equity suits. We became expert in being able to distinguish a common law claim and an equitable claim.

I came to the bar in 1963 at the age of 22. Even those who came to the bar 10 years later missed this procedural nicety and to them it must seem to matter little. I hope that this chapter, outlining the way in which the two streams of contract law have been built into the strong law that we have today will encourage continued thinking in both streams.

Like all good ex-debaters, I should define terms. I need not define the term "equity", as by it I mean to denote the Chancery Court in England and the Equity Division in New South Wales and courts elsewhere exercising the principles that govern those courts. I do need, however, to define "contract".

"Contract" as a legal category is a rather nebulous one. "Contract" means more than mere agreement. No legal system will wish to enforce all agreements. Within the wide concept of agreement comes a narrower group of agreements which the law will enforce. In the common law system, this was defined by cause of action. However, to confine contract to the causes of action in covenant or assumpsit would be wrong. Some commercial agreements outside these areas were enforced in the local and mercantile courts. Unfortunately, it is difficult to define contract, for the present exercise, otherwise than as those agreements which could be enforced at common law. But realise that this definition does not quite cover the field. It is noteworthy that modern trade practices statutes tend to use conjoint phrases such as "contract", "agreement", "arrangement" or "understanding" in their attempt to cover the field.

This analysis of equity's role in contract is first considered in four historical periods, roughly covering the period from the Black Death until the present day. As will be seen, this is not completely satisfactory, as not all significant developments were polite enough to confine themselves to any one particular period. Following this historical review specific performance and trusts will be discussed. The former is pure contract: the latter is a situation where the common law could have applied contractual principles and destroyed the trust, but declined to do so.

Some situations at the periphery of contract will be considered and I will look at the development of proprietary estoppel, negligent misstatement and the trade practices legislation, all of which have expanded the contract field.

A large proportion of this chapter discusses the early period. Some may consider this a waste. However, this period is of great importance because equity never actually loses jurisdiction. The common law or statute may take over a field from equity and equity will subside as, if there is a full remedy at law, there is no need for it. However, history shows that circumstances change and gaps appear in the common law's coverage and equity once again comes to the fore.

THE EARLY PERIOD

I will take as the early period from the Black Death of 1348 up to 1600, that is, just before *Slade's Case*[1] was decided. This was the time when the common law gave way to commercial pressure and allowed what we would call contract cases to be dealt with by jury trial instead of by way of wager of law.

At the commencement of this period, most cases we would probably call "contract" were dealt with in the local courts, the Court Baron and the merchant's courts. However, as inflation set in and the King's Courts were establishing themselves as *the* courts, these courts passed out of significance. We have some slight idea of how they administered contract law, but our material is a little flimsy. We know, for instance, from the Selden Society's *The Court Baron*,[2] that the Bishop of Ely's Manorial Court at Littleport in the Reign of Edward II was entertaining claims for specific performance of contracts to manufacture.

However, the prime concern is the King's Courts of Common Law. In those courts, and, it would seem in most of the superior courts of Europe, the only contracts that were enforced, and then only by an award of damages, were contracts that were in a strict form. In England, they had to be by deed.

---

1   (1602) 4 Co Rep 91a; 76 ER 1072.
2   Selden Society, *The Court Baron* (Quaritch, London, 1891) at 115.

During this period, the prime common law remedy is sometimes said to be covenant in the Common Pleas. Simpson says that actually the action of debt sur obligation (also in the Common Pleas) was the most common.[3] Both were actions for damages, which only lay where there had been a promise by deed. Assumpsit was developing, but, as the contract historians now frankly acknowledge, there was dithering as to how far to develop assumpsit and for a long while it lay only for misfeasances.[4]

However, even before *Slade's Case*, the Common Law was enforcing some parol contracts where there was a quid pro quo which usually occurred where detinue could be filed in the case of sale of goods. Indeed, as Ames points out, the word "contract" at the time of the Year Books denoted a case where a duty arose out of a quid pro quo.[5]

These Common Law limitations need to be mentioned to show why it was necessary for the Chancellor to fill some of the gaps.

I have taken the majority of the material for this section of this chapter from that excellent work by Professor Barbour, *History of Contract in Early English Equity*.[6] That work[7] clearly demonstrates that there was a substantial equity jurisdiction in contract cases during the late Middle Ages. Unfortunately, the surviving records are almost entirely plaintiff's claims only without indication as to how the claim was determined, so the picture is incomplete.

It would appear that, during the political instability caused by the Wars of the Roses (1455-1487), equity took a greater interest in contract because it might be impossible for a politically incorrect party to get justice at the hands of a local jury. The accession of the Tudors in 1485 and the expansion of the Common Law writ of assumpsit meant that by the time of *Slade's Case*[8] it became less and less necessary for the equity court to concern itself as much with contract and, as whenever else that happened, the court's exercise of equitable jurisdiction declined.

Indeed, Spence says that the Common Lawyers consciously made this expansion to exclude the growing jurisdiction of the Chancery Court.[9] He notes that in YB 21 Hen VII fo 41,[10] Fineux CJ said, "...if one makes a bargain with me that I shall have his land to me and my heirs for £20 and he refuses to perform it; I shall have an *Action on the Case*, and there is *no occasion for a subpoena*."

However, it must be noted that the jurisdiction to relieve against penal bonds, which is considered in the next section, began to be exercised during the

3   AB Simpson, "The Penal Bond with Conditional Defeasance" (1966) 82 *Law Quarterly Review* 392 at 415.

4   *Bukton v Tounesende ("The Humber Ferry Case")* (1348) in Baker and Milsom, *Sources of English Legal History: Private Law to 1750* (Butterworths, London, 1986) at 358.

5   FB Ames, "Parol Contracts Prior to Assumpsit" (1894) 8 *Harvard Law Review* 252.

6   WT Barbour, *History of Contract in Early English Equity* (Clarendon Press, Oxford, 1914).

7   WT Barbour, *History of Contract in Early English Equity,* above n 6 particularly at 66ff.

8   (1602) 4 Co Rep 91a; 76 ER 1072.

9   G Spence, *The Equitable Jurisdiction of the Court of Chancery* (Hein & Co, Buffalo, 1981), Vol 1 at 243.

10   YB 21 Hen VII fo 41 in G Spence, *The Equitable Jurisdiction of the Court of Chancery,* above n 9 at Vol 1 at 243.

chancellorship of Sir Thomas More. Lord Mansfield says in *Wyllie v Wilkes*[11] that More summoned the judges of England and entreated them to alter the stance of the common law, but in vain, and promised to keep issuing injunctions until they came to their senses. However, Simpson notes that the exercise of the jurisdiction was rare before the time of Elizabeth 1 (1558-1603).[12]

Barbour sets out various types of contract cases where equity intervened in the fifteenth century. No summary can do full justice to this research, but the following is an attempt.

The mere fact that the common law or the local courts did not provide any, or any adequate remedy, was not in itself sufficient reason for equity to intervene: there must be something else. That something else was found in the ecclesiastical concept of causa, which was a vague and indefinite term, in fact applied differently by particular chancellors.

Basically, equity intervened where the defendant had pledged his faith to his promise, or where the contract was connected with marriage or where there was reason in conscience to require enforcement.

The following appear to be the most common causes for equity's intervention in cases of contract:

1. The plaintiffs were allegedly too poor or powerless to sue at law.
    Many of the local courts were under the thumb of local magnates. If the local magnate or his friends were the persons sued, there would be no real hope of the plaintiff getting justice, so that the plaintiff could, in such an event, approach the Chancellor. If the plaintiff was too poor to maintain proceedings in the ordinary courts, justice would be denied if he could not come to equity.

    Spence notes that the practice in the early years of Henry VI was to hear the cases of the poor litigants first and that such litigants might be excused from paying costs if a reasonable Bill was dismissed.[13]

2. The plaintiff was the King or parties which represented him.

3. The contract was made abroad or within the royal palace.
    The Common Law Courts asserted no jurisdiction unless a fiction was employed pretending that the contract was made in England.[14] Admiralty also took some of this jurisdiction by the fiction that the contract was made on the High Seas.[15]

4. The plaintiff, though endeavouring to do so, was unable to serve the defendant with process.

---

11 (1780) 2 Doug 519 at 522-523; 99 ER 331 at 333.
12 AWB Simpson, "The Penal Bond with Conditional Defeasance" (1966) 82 *Law Quarterly Review* 392 at 416.
13 G Spence, *The Equitable Jurisdiction of the Court of Chancery*, above n 9, Vol 1 at 387.
14 AKR Kiralfy, *Potter's Historical Introduction to English Law and its Institutions* (4th ed, Sweet & Maxwell, London, 1958) at 207.
15 AKR Kiralfy, *Potter's Historical Introduction to English Law and its Institutions*, above n 14 at 195.

The jurisdiction of the royal courts at law depended upon service on the defendant and his entering an appearance to acknowledge the jurisdiction.

5. The contract was tainted with fraud.

6. The contract was by deed and the common law formalities were preventing the true arrangement between the parties being considered. An illustration of this class of case is where there had been a parol variation of an obligation by deed, or where the deed secured some lesser obligation. A further case is a contract of suretyship otherwise than by deed or where there was a suit on a promise made by executors not by deed. Other cases involve a lost deed.

7. Promises to benefit a third party, or cases where there had been an assignment of an obligation.

8. Cases involving equitable set-off.

9. Cases of partnership and agency.

10. Contracts for the sale of land.

11. Cases where the contract was oppressive.

Additionally, there were some particular contracts where equity intervened in earlier years but where later development of the common law made it inappropriate to do so thereafter. This class of case included contracts where there was no specific undertaking to pay a fixed sum, cases where the promise was not fulfilled at all as opposed to those where it was badly fulfilled, promises to erect a building, contracts for transport or to provide special personal services.

Most of the categories of contract listed above either passed into the jurisdiction still exercised today (for example, those numbered 5, 8, 9 and 10 above), or vanished when the political situation became more settled (those numbered 1-4 above). From time to time, equity became involved with other contracts which were being used to exploit the poor, such as contracts of apprenticeship and mortgages. When legislation removed the social problems, or the common law became adequate, equity withdrew. One of the prime examples of this is that, in Elizabethan times, Equity was very much concerned with contracts by apprentices.[16] However, as other common law and social machinery developed to protect apprentices, this jurisdiction became obsolete.

Despite all this, equity continued to be interested in certain types of contract. Category 7 (above) covers two types of situation. First, those which later became covered by the indebitatus count of money paid at the request of the defendant, such as where Z paid Y to ransom a prisoner at the request of X.[17] Secondly, the category covered problems where contractual rights were assigned, a concept initially rejected by the common law.

---

16 G Spence, *The Equitable Jurisdiction of the Court of Chancery* (Hein & Co, Buffalo, 1981), Vol 1 at 698. Spence notes this in his chapter on obsolete equities.

17 WT Barbour, *History of Contract in Early English Equity* (Clarendon Press, Oxford, 1914) at 107.

One of the problems to which equity gave relief was that caused by the fact that the common law could only deal with proceedings between two parties. Thus, if six different members of the public asserted similar rights against a defendant, unless there was an agreement about a "test case", each of the six actions would have to be tried. In a variety of situations, of which the most common was cases of confusion of boundaries, equity short-circuited this process by allowing one proceeding.

It was this principle that permitted intervention in cases where there had been an assignment of an obligation. It was this principle too, that allowed, in certain cases, a third party to enforce a promise made on his behalf.

The original content of categories 6 and 7 (above) was rendered obsolete when the common law changed its views. However, it may be that this part of equity is merely sleeping. A possible area of the law in which it may be reactivated is where people sue on a trust for a promise.[18] Another area occurs where there is a notional contract with an Aboriginal community under s 41 of the *Native Title Act 1993* (Cth) where individuals are suing in respect of obligations assumed under the notional contract, particularly in cases where the other party has assigned the contract.[19]

The information available is too scanty for any comprehensive conclusion to be drawn. However, it is clear that there were at least some situations where the Chancellor entertained proceedings by beneficiaries in their own name. One class of case where this was permitted was, where a beneficiary under a marriage settlement complained that the settlement was not being implemented. Barbour gives as an example *Gambon v Gambon*.[20] Another situation is where a father can sue in chancery for breach of a marriage settlement made for the benefit of his daughter.[21]

These cases came to a head in *Dutton v Poole*.[22] However, they were effectively overruled in *Tweddle v Atkinson*[23] during what I will describe as the rigid third period.

Another situation where the Chancellor allowed a third party to sue in his own name occured where there had been an informal assignment and the assignor was dead.

I should also make a few remarks about oppressive contracts (category 11 above). *Ashburner's Principles of Equity*[24] reckoned that the cases of relief against penal bonds were merely an example of this head of equity.[25]

---

18   *Trident General Insurance Co Ltd v McNiece Bros Pty Ltd* (1988) 165 CLR 107 at 120; P Young, "Third Party Contract Rights" (1992) 9 *Australian Bar Review* 39.

19   See for example, *Carriage v Duke Australia Operations Pty Ltd* [2000] NSWSC 239.

20   Extracted in WT Barbour, *History of Contract in Early English Equity*, above n 17 at 213.

21   *Drury v Aysshefeld* (1432) in WT Barbour, *History of Contract in Early English Equity*, above n 20 at 189.

22   (1678) 2 Lev 210; 83 ER 523.

23   (1861) 1 B & S 393; 121 ER 762.

24   D Browne, *Ashburner's Principles of Equity* (2nd ed, Butterworths, London, 1933) at 262.

25   See also J Story, *Commentaries on Equity Jurisprudence*, (3rd ed, Sweet & Maxwell, London, 1920) at §1316.

There is insufficient material to answer the question as to which principles were applied in equity to deal with contractual disputes in the late Middle Ages.[26] The best guess is that where a matter of conscience was involved, the Rules of Conscience applied: the "conscience" that was applied was the rule God would have applied when judging the defendant's soul and, as *Doctor and Student*[27] reveals, resort may be to the manual for those hearing confessions for more details. However, where the equity court had heard a case because of some procedural problem with obtaining relief at common law, equity followed the law.

The concept of consideration in equity first occurs where people purport to revoke uses or trusts. In *Anon* (1452)[28] the Exchequer Chamber held that if the trust was declared of the feoffor's "mere will" (an expression that is later picked up in the term "voluntary" conveyance) there is nothing in conscience to prevent a change of mind, particularly if altered circumstances give reason for change, but, if it were made for cause, it is irrevocable.

In the *Duke of Buckingham's Case*[29] it can be seen that counsel actually espoused the proposition that a trust "made on good consideration" is irrevocable.

The contrast is between "mere will" and something done after consideration for a valid reason. This latter class includes, acts done for pious reasons (which become an insignificant class), acts done for natural love and affection, acts done in connection with a marriage in the family, as well as acts done after bargains or where there is some quid pro quo.

By 1500, it was recognised that the action in deceit would lie where there had been a breach of an undertaking in a conveyance to a stranger.[30] However, this is as far as the remedies in the King's Bench had progressed.

The gaps included:

(a) no remedy for agreements made outside England;
(b) no action for breach of a contract to convey land;
(c) no way of enforcing marriage settlements;
(d) no action against a surety;
(e) little remedy available against an agent who breached his undertaking;
(f) no action for breach of contract to sell chattels;
(g) no action against a married woman; and,
(h) no action against a legal personal representative.

The position at law was partly remedied in 1504[31] when assumpsit was first recognised as a remedy where the defendant had made a promise in the form of an undertaking. The breach of the undertaking was not the prime source of the liability. The undertaking merely made an act wrongful to which the law would

---

26 WT Barbour, *History of Contract in Early English Equity* (Clarendon Press, Oxford, 1914) at 82.
27 C St Germain, *Doctor and Student* (Selden Society, London, 1974).
28 AWB Simpson, *A History of the Common Law of Contract* (Clarendon Press, Oxford, 1975) at 337-338.
29 (1504) YB 20 Hen V11 f10 pl 20.
30 See JB Ames, "The History of Assumpsit" (1888) 2 *Harvard Law Review* 1 at 13.
31 (1504) Keil 77 pl 25; 72 ER 239.

otherwise attach no consequences; it was the damage resulting from the act which was wrongful because it was contrary to the undertaking that was the gist of the action.[32]

Equity however, filled in some of the gaps. Indeed, the activities of the Chancellor probably sped the common law courts into expanding assumpsit from misfeasance to nonfeasance, a process which commenced in 1504, but was not complete until *Slade's Case* in 1602. This is apparent from the comments of Fineux CJ (KB) noted previously.[33]

Equity was even known to give a remedy in detinue where it was satisfied that at law the defendant would wage his law and avoid returning the plaintiff's goods.[34]

Finally in this section I should refer to a passage from Spence:[35]

"In one case the court relieved a merchant of Venice from the consequences of the defendant having *waged his law*, that is discharged himself by his own oath and that of his co-jurors, in an action for recovery of money, he having in his answer admitted that he had received the money, and, that he had not repaid it. This interference of the Court of Chancery no doubt had its effect in causing this ancient mode of proof, which the courts of law could not and the legislature would not repress, to go into disuse."

Spence cites the reference as Cal 120-122 temp Hen VII and notes that the Bill also sought that the defendant be punished for perjury.

1600-1800

I have chosen these limits for the second period because of *Slade's Case*,[36] which marks a milestone at the commencement of this period and the importation into English law of continental theories of contract which marked its end.

I have already remarked that after the accessions of the Tudors, equity's jurisdiction in contract became less necessary. In the present period, there was gradual development until the time of Lord Nottingham (1675-1682). Equity had no option but to enter the field of contract in a big way when the common law declined to recognise that a bond had been informally satisfied. It would seem that Italian bankers devised a method of guaranteeing contractual performance by having the contractor enter into a bond to pay a high sum if he did not perform. The bond, being a specialty, could only be discharged by exact performance of the condition or by payment of the amount. Equity interfered to recognise that some bonds could be informally satisfied and would restrain actions at law on them. Equity recognised that the real intention of the parties was to secure performance of the underlying promise. Thus, if the issue of how

---

32   WT Barbour, *History of Contract in Early English Equity* (Clarendon Press, Oxford, 1914) at 46.

33   Above nn 8-9 and accompanying text.

34   *Baby v Bramfeld* (1423) extracted in WT Barbour, *History of Contract in Early English Equity*, above n 32 at 187.

35   G Spence, *The Equitable Jurisdiction of the Court of Chancery* (Hein & Co, Buffalo, 1981), Vol 1 at 695-696.

36   (1602) 4 Co Rep 91a; 76 ER 1072.

much damage had been suffered by the non-fulfilment of the promise was quantified and paid, equity should restrain actions at law on the bond.

Something should now be said about consideration. It is a fair comment that up until about 1711, the doctrine of consideration, as we now know it, had no part to play in the contract cases decided in equity. This statement is not earth-shattering as the doctrine as we now know it was not even applied at law. Scholarly studies have shown that there was a considerable development of the doctrine at law from 1550-1950 and that there were at least three distinct phases where the term "consideration" had differing content. As Simpson points out, the term "consideration" seems to have derived from the factors that were considered by the person making the promise before he made it.[37] There is no need to discuss this matter here. Suffice it to say, that the concept applied at common law may have derived from equity and originally had significance in the old forms of action. In due course, it became the yardstick as to which promises by parol would be enforced and which would not.

Thus in *Doctor and Student*, transforming the spelling into modern usage, the Doctor says:[38]

> "first, you should understand that there is a promise called an advowe, and that is a promise made to God, whosoever makes an advowe upon a deliberate mind intending to perform it, is bound in conscience to do it though it be only made in the heart without pronouncing of words and of other promises made to man upon a certain consideration if the promise is not against the law. But if his promise be so naked that there is no manner of consideration why it should be made, then I think him not bound to perform it for it is to suppose some error in the making of the promise but if such a promise be made to a university, to a City, to the church, to the clergy or to poor men of such a place...then I think he is bound in conscience to perform it."

As has been seen, equity required a cause before it would interfere. The notion or cause and the notion of consideration originally had some common roots, but their content was not the same. Although it is impossible to be dogmatic, it would seem that the concept of cause was a merger of two earlier doctrines: (i) that a nude promise was not enforced but a vested promise was enforced; and, (ii) that an agreement supported by cause was enforced, but a causeless agreement was not.[39]

I now pass to consideration in equity, taking up the story at about 1700. Cases in the eighteenth century show that the equity court is only willing to enforce contractual obligations if there is consideration as would ground an assumpsit, or if there was what equity termed good or meritorious consideration. This latter term, according to *Blackstone's Commentaries*[40] is of blood or of natural love and affection. It should be noted that the common law had rejected

---

37   AWB Simpson, *A History of the Common Law of Contract* (Clarendon Press, Oxford, 1975) at 331.

38   C St Germain, *Doctor and Student* (Selden Society, London, 1974), Dialogue 2, Ch xxiv at 229.

39   See AWB Simpson, *A History of the Common Law of Contract*, above n 37 at 384.

40   W Blackstone, *Commentaries on the Laws of England* (Sweet & Maxwell, London, 1829), Vol 2 at 297, 444-5.

love and friendship as consideration in assumpsit in *Harford v Gardiner*[41] though there are some apparent exceptions in the sixteenth century cases.

Ballow[42] says that whilst with executed gifts, the bare pleasure of doing good stands in place of a cause, a bare promise to give or a gift imperfect and executory requires that there must be a consideration as a motive for relief, a stronger consideration than is on the other side. When expanding on this text with notes, Fonblanque[43] says, "if, therefore, the agreement be unreasonable, equity will not interpose" and cites *Stanhope v Toppe*.[44]

However, by 1780, equity had shifted ground. Whilst in 1720 the court looked to consideration to see whether it would enforce a contract, it also took cognisance of reasonableness and undervalue. The common law moved to the position that as long as consideration had some value the court did not enquire into its adequacy and equity moved along the same lines. Thus in *Griffith v Spratley*[45] in the full court of the Exchequer exercising equitable jurisdiction, Eyre LCB said with the agreement of the other three barons, "I never can agree that inadequacy of consideration is *in itself a principle* upon which a party may be relieved from a contract, which he has wittingly and willingly entered into."

It should be noted that at least in one respect the common law would enforce some contracts which equity would not. If a contract was by deed, it would be enforced by way of action for damages at common law. However, equity would not enforce a contract by deed in favour of a volunteer.

Prior to Lord Mansfield's time, there was an equitable action in account where the defendant had a fiduciary obligation to render an account to another. This was mainly because he held monies to the use of the other. That obligation to account could be terminated by the parties agreeing that the obligation to account had been completely performed and extinguished, and replaced by a common law debt. Where that occurred, an account stated arose between them. If an action for account were commenced after an account stated, the defence of plene computavit would succeed.

Lord Mansfield so adjusted (to use a neutral term) the action of indebitatus assumpsit that there would now be at law an action for money had and received to the use of the plaintiff. As Professor Langdell noted,[46] this reform completely ignored the old distinction.

Another aspect that must be considered is the approach of common law and equity to the restrictions on enforceability of contracts imposed by the *Statute of Frauds 1677*.

Common law, as it was bound to do, obeyed the statute to the letter. However, in equity, the court considered that it could be fraud for a person to escape from a contract by pleading the statute. In such cases, the court would order a person to enter into a contract which complied with the statute.[47]

---

41   (1588) 2 Leon 30; 74 ER 332.
42   H Ballow, *A Treatise of Equity* (Browne & Buckburgh, London, 1737) at 37-38.
43   J Fonblanque, *Fonblanque on Equity* (J & WT Clarke, London, 1820), Vol 1 at 350.
44   (1720) 1 Brown 157; 1 ER 483.
45   (1787) 1 Cox 383 at 388-389; 29 ER 1213 at 1215.
46   CC Langdell, "A Brief Survey of Equity Jurisdiction" (1889) 2 *Harvard Law Review* 241 at 255.
47   *Waltons Stores (Interstate) Ltd v Maher* (1988) 164 CLR 387 at 433.

Fonblanque on Equity[48] gives a good picture of equity and contract at the end of this period. In "Of the Subject Matter of Covenants",[49] the general flow of the chapter shows that equity and the common law were mostly at one with the types of contracts they would enforce and those which they would decline to enforce for illegality, impossibility etc. Only minor differences appear, such as the enforcement of contracts made for natural love and affection, and restrictions on creditors of a husband who were seeking to pursue former assets of a wife under a marriage settlement.

1800-1960

It should not be thought that by choosing this time period, I am suggesting that it was one where there was homogeneity of thought. I know that this was far from the case. Lord Mansfield dominated the final part of the previous period. However, by 1840, Mansfield was being reviled as an arch heretic, a position from which he did not recover until about 1970.

At the commencement of the nineteenth century, Equity and Chancery judges had different approaches to contract. The common law emphasised the marketing ideals of buyer beware, that with free bargaining in arm's length transactions, people must rely on themselves and not on what they were told. Equity, however, was concerned with fraud, misrepresentation, mistake and breach of fiduciary obligation, all of which put brakes on a free-market.[50]

I need to go through the nineteenth century law of contract in some detail to show how, in this century, common law principles prevailed over equitable principles.

However, I preface this with the remark that, even without the pressures shortly to be discussed, even early on in the nineteenth century, equity changed its general approach to contract and came to adopt the same approach as had been taken by courts of common law.

I start by referring to the English edition of *Cheshire & Fifoot's Law of Contracts*,[51] where the writers remind us that, prior to 1790 when Joseph Powell published his *Essay upon the Law of Contracts and Agreements*, there existed no systematic treatise expounding the English law of contract. Indeed, there was no systematic law of contract, until it was "invented" by academics in the nineteenth century. In 1806, RJ Pothier's *Treatise on the Law of Obligations or Contracts* was translated and published in England. It had originally been published in France in 1761-1764. It was very well received by English academic lawyers. Other continental writings were also influential, particularly the German jurist, Savigny.

---

48   J Fonblanque, *Fonblanque on Equity* (J & WT Clarke, London, 1820). I have the 1820 edition, but it is essentially Ballow's work of 1737 updated.

49   J Fonblanque, *Fonblanque on Equity*, above n 48 at Book 1, Chapter 4.

50   This is condensed from the admirable summary by PS Atiyah in *The Rise & Fall of Freedom of Contract* (Clarendon Press, Oxford, 1979) at 672-673.

51   M Furmston, *Cheshire & Fifoot's Law of Contracts* (9th ed, Butterworths, London, 1976) at 13.

Books on contract soon started to appear. In England we had Chitty (1826), Addison (1847), Leake (1867), Pollock (1876), and Anson (1879), some of which in their latest editions are still current.

The introduction into English law of concepts abstracted from Pothier and others and the process of rationalisation by these authors of a myriad of single instance decisions, to some extent gradually changed the common law of contract, particularly in relation to basic concepts such as consideration. In many respects, this process made the law far more rigid.

The same process occurred in the United States. Grant Gilmore says:[52]

"...the common law had done very nicely for several centuries without anyone realizing that there was such a thing as the law of contracts. ... Courts had, of course, been deciding cases about contracts ever since there had been courts. But the idea that there was such a thing as a general law – or theory – of contract seems never to have occurred to the legal mind until Langdell somehow stumbled across it."

Apart from Langdell, there was *Contracts in the Common Law* by Holmes, and later Williston and Corbin.

Gilmore, who often one must read down because he overstates the position, says that what then occurred was that the academics jammed the case law into the compartments that their theories told them existed. They promoted those cases which neatly fitted into the compartments as "Leading Cases" and forgot about the cases that did not so fit. At the same time, the merchant classes were becoming stronger as Britain led the world trade in the period of the Industrial Revolution. Sure and certain rules of which the community were aware, but not always the consumers, were to be rigidly enforced.

Then, there occurred, what Atiyah calls the fundamental subordination of equity to the common law, in England at the time of the Judicature Acts.[53] Atiyah notes that the bulk of the judges sitting in the High Court were common lawyers who not only knew no equity, but prided themselves in such ignorance. Furthermore, the office of Lord Chancellor, which for centuries had been held by an equity lawyer, was now held by common lawyers. Even the Master of the Rolls from 1883-1897, Lord Esher, was a common lawyer who sneered at equitable principles. The House of Lords, instead of being mainly composed of former Lord Chancellors, all being equity lawyers, was now mainly comprised of common lawyers. This led the way to absurd decisions such as *Derry v Peek*[54] made by a House with no equity lawyer. This decision was, to quote Atiyah, "not only the final triumph of common law over Equity; it was the final triumph of market principles in the law of contract."

Indeed, the theory that somehow or other the common law principles of contract were sacred, spread even to sane equity lawyers. Thus, in 1914, Lord Parker said in *Kreglinger v New Patagonia Meat and Cold Storage Company Ltd*[55] that it was startling that the court should be asked to assist in the repudiation of a fair and reasonable bargain. Of course the acme is the statement by Lord Cairns

---

52   G Gilmore, *Death of Contract* (Ohio State University Press, Ohio, 1974) at 5.
53   PS Atiyah, *The Rise & Fall of Freedom of Contract* (Clarendon Press, Oxford, 1979) at 672-673.
54   (1889) 14 App Cas 337.
55   [1914] AC 25 at 47.

LC in *Doherty v Allman*[56] that if a party has promised by contract not to do a certain thing then equity has virtually no discretion but to grant an injunction to confirm the contractual promise. A similar statement had been made as early as 1852 by Lord St Leonards LC in the celebrated case of *Lumley v Wagner*[57] that "this Court… will not suffer [parties] to depart from their contracts at their pleasure" leaving the injured party to his or her remedy in damages.

The retired New South Wales silk, Chester Porter, in his autobiography, *Chester Porter, Walking on Water*[58] says:[59]

> "equity started off as a means of easing the strict rules of common law liability, but modern equity judges deal with a great variety of work… I did find a tendency in equity to hold people to their contracts, even when there had been considerable unfairness. In this regard I think the old common law jury was better for the battlers trying to overcome the results of being duped or bullied by big business. I think brilliant judges often failed to see the world through the eyes of honest but foolish people."

Porter sees the enactment of consumer protection and contract review legislation as a consequence of equity's failure to intervene sufficiently in cases of oppressive contract.

The rigidity of the common law of contract made it inevitable that relief had to be given to clearly meritorious claimants in some other way. One development was what was once called "Quasi-Contract". Another necessary development was the doctrine of proprietary estoppel which can be traced back at least to *Dillwyn v Llewelyn*.[60] This development is considered later in this chapter.

Gilmore says that the concepts of quasi-contract and promissory estoppel are twins, quasi-contract enables a plaintiff to be reimbursed for some benefit that he or she had conferred on the defendant; promissory estoppel allows a plaintiff to recover loss suffered by reliance on the defendant's promise or representation.[61]

Of course, quasi-contract was a development at law and proprietary estoppel principally in equity. They both, however, demonstrated the need 150 years ago for a more just solution to problems in the area of contract.

One needs to be careful in this period to ensure that one gets the full picture of a contractual dispute. Sometimes part of the dispute was heard at law and another part in equity. The most notorious example of this is *Ford v Beech*[62] where the Exchequer Chamber on appeal from the Queens Bench considered the question as to whether any suspension of an obligation to pay a promissory note barred an action forever, but then the Chancery Court in *Beech v Ford*[63] had to consider the same contract on equitable principles.

---

56   (1878) 3 App Cas 709 at 719-720.
57   (1852) 1 De GM & G 604 at 619; 42 ER 687 at 693.
58   C Porter, *Chester Porter, Walking on Water* (Random House, Sydney, 2003).
59   C Porter, *Chester Porter, Walking on Water*, above n 58 at 55.
60   (1862) 4 De GF & J 517; 45 ER 1285.
61   G Gilmore, *Death of Contract* (Ohio State University Press, Ohio, 1974) at 88-89.
62   (1848) 11 QB 852; 116 ER 693.
63   (1848) 7 Hare 208; 68 ER 85.

Towards the end of this period, we see some new developments under Lord Denning, the most dramatic being the *High Trees* doctrine. My reading of this development is that it reintroduced equitable principles. However, Atiyah disagrees.[64] He says that promissory estoppel and *High Trees* were merely a development of the common law and there is nothing particularly equitable about them. I will return to this topic later in this chapter.

I need to say something about privity of contract. I noted at the beginning of this chapter that the more expansive ideas of equity on the subject had been kyboshed in *Tweddle v Atkinson*.[65] However, equity had other ways of providing some remediation in this area.

I can do no better than quote the words of Lockhart J in giving the judgment of the Full Federal Court in *Aussie Airlines Pty Ltd v Australian Airlines Ltd*, a judgment with which Spender and Cooper JJ agreed. Shortly before the passage below, Lockhart J had pointed out that benefits of a promise under a contract may be held on trust, just as any other property may be held on trust. He then said:[66]

> "privity of contract prevents a third party from suing at law on the contract; but it does not prevent him suing in equity to enforce the trust by compelling the promisee to sue the promisor at law or in equity."

He cited *Lloyd's v Harper*[67] and *Royal Exchange Assurance v Hope*[68] and then went on to examine a series of cases in which a trust of a chose in action was established and others where that claim failed.

1960 ONWARDS

This period saw a recovery of equitable remedies being deployed in contract cases. Of course, a number of the sacred principles of the previous period had become incorporated in decisions of the highest courts of the land and it took a little time before that level of court modified its approach or lower courts found ways of distinguishing such authorities.

Furthermore, although our research shows that there was really a law of contracts, not a law of contract, and that the law of sale of goods and negotiable instruments developed independently and were not derived from general contract law, the die had been cast and it was too late to revert to the eighteenth century position. We are fixed with the situation for good or ill, that in these cases, as with all other cases, at law and in equity, the general principles of contract worked out by the academics in the nineteenth century rule us.

As I mentioned at the commencement of this chapter, the unique situation of New South Wales being a State without a *Judicature Act* until 1972 meant that many contractual disputes had to find their way into courts of equity and

---

64   PS Atiyah, *The Rise & Fall of Freedom of Contract* (Clarendon Press, Oxford, 1979) at 676.
65   (1861) 1 B & S 393; 121 ER 762.
66   *Aussie Airlines Pty Ltd v Australian Airlines Ltd* (1996) 68 FCR 406 at 415.
67   (1880) 16 Ch D 290.
68   [1928] 1 Ch 179.

were handled by equity counsel and equity judges. This inevitably put an equity flavour into the administration of contract disputes.

Furthermore, although it is an oversimplification, English contract law tended to develop in the context of commercial contracts, contracts in which time is often of the essence by the very nature of the contract. In New South Wales, on the other hand, the main development of contract law has been in cases concerning contracts for the sale of land. These contracts concern equitable interests in property and, in New South Wales, time is not necessarily of the essence. New South Wales courts generally came to be more relaxed about time clauses than their English counterparts.

It was not surprising then, that the conflict would one day arise. It did so in an appeal from Hong Kong to the Privy Council in a conveyancing case, *Union Eagle Ltd v Golden Achievement Ltd*.[69] That sound Chancery lawyer, Godfrey J in the Hong Kong Court of Appeal, applied traditional equitable principles to excuse a ten minute delay in completing a contract after the expiry of the time for completion. He was in the minority. The Privy Council consisted predominately of commercial lawyers used to strict time limits in mercantile contracts. They relied on shipping and commercial cases as to the essential nature of time and, moreover, declined to develop the English law as to relief against forfeiture. The result has been an embarrassing decision which has been paid lip service to in Australia, but has been side-stepped ever since.

The field of duress is one where equity's influence has been noticeable. Traditionally, at common law, duress meant physical pressure which brought about a lack of consent. In equity, there were the allied principles of unconscionable conduct and undue influence. The principles were different in focus. When action was taken to enforce the relevant contract, duress looked to the reality of the consent of the defendant to enter into the bargain, while equity looked to the conscience of the plaintiff as to whether it was conscionable for him to enforce it.[70]

The most widely held view is that economic duress is a common law development.[71] However, there are respectable arguments for saying that it developed in equity.[72] Whatever its origin and whatever the theoretical focus on the plaintiff or the defendant, in practice, as economic duress has developed, the distinction between duress strictly so called and unconscionable conduct has become blurred. Thus, in *Bridgewater v Leahy*,[73] we find the judges when discussing equities giving focus to the reality of consent. In any event, the equitable doctrines have had a profound influence on the development of the concept of economic duress.

The general principle is that equity intervenes to give a remedy only where the common law remedy it provides is inadequate. Of course, there has to be some equitable ground for acting: the mere fact that there is no proper remedy

---

69   [1997] AC 514; [1997] 2 All ER 215.
70   *Blomley v Ryan* (1956) 99 CLR 362 at 401-402.
71   *Crescendo Management Pty Ltd v Westpac Banking Corporation* (1988) 19 NSWLR 40.
72   See RA Conti, "Economic Duress" (1985) 1 *Australian Bar Review* 106 and various dicta in *Barton v Armstrong* [1976] AC 104.
73   (1998) 194 CLR 457 at 478.

at common law is not enough to trigger equity's intervention. It is this factor that currently maps out the role of equity in contractual disputes.

The doctrine of good faith in contract cannot be said to be one inspired by equity. However, more and more contractual relations are being overshadowed by principles of fiduciary obligations. Thus contracts of partnership involve fiduciary duties of loyalty which may be more significant than some of the contractual terms of the partnership agreement.

Theoretically, a modern court of equity has jurisdiction over all contractual disputes. However, there is only room for applying equitable principles and remedies when the ordinary rules do not give a just result. As damages are the ordinary remedy when a contract has been broken, it is usually only when damages are not an adequate remedy that equity intervenes. This essentially means that it is only if the subject matter is particularly special or there is some factor such as trust, insolvency or preservation of property that equity will become involved. The principal situation where damages is not an adequate remedy is where the contract concerns land.

However, recently in England, we have seen other involvements of equity such as that in *Attorney-General v Blake*,[74] where the equitable restitutionary method of assessing damages was introduced into the common law.

In October, 2001, Professor Treitel gave a series of lectures at Oxford which have been published under the title, *Some Landmarks of Twentieth Century Contract Law*.[75] The word "equity" does not, so far as I can see, appear in the book at all. The three areas of contract law which attracted Treitel were Agreements to Vary Contracts, Privity, and Types of Contractual Terms. The development of each of the first two areas has been influenced by equity. The former, especially by *High Trees*, the latter both by the rule that there might be a trust of a promise and also to an extent by the equity, still not completely settled as to its scope, that those who have notice of contractual rights may be held to act unconscionably if they act contrary to them.

Of course, there have been many developments in the common law of contract where there has been no discernable influence of equity. The idea of a buyer's computer sending a signal to the seller's computer that the buyer needs two tonnes of kitty litter with the result that the seller company despatches that product and gets paid for it, has hardly caused a stir. Pleading the transaction in strict pleading terms may be difficult, but we have made life easy by abolishing common law pleadings.

The traditional view that one must have an offer and corresponding acceptance and that a counter-offer revokes an offer could not stand in its full rigour in late twentieth century commercial conditions. Both rules have had to be modified, virtually to write in the word "normally". However, apart from the fact that the New South Wales decisions to modify were made by equity judges, equity cannot claim influence here.

The equity judge over the last forty years has probably been less inhibited by the classic compartments of contract than earlier judges. The equity courts

---

74   [2001] 1 AC 268; [2000] 4 All ER 385.
75   G Treitel, *Some Landmarks of Twentieth Century Contract Law* (Oxford University Press, Oxford, 2002).

have recognised that the "ordinary" way of people becoming bound by their promises is to make a contract in the standard common law way. They have also said that they are not sympathetic to business people who fail to formalise a contract relying on some equitable principle to achieve the same aim.[76] However, there have been countless cases in equity where strict contract provisions have been modified to prevent unconscionability.

One area where this has occurred is with relief against forfeiture. In England, it was only in 1973 in *Shiloh Spinners Ltd v Harding*[77] that the equitable jurisdiction to relieve against forfeiture was reasserted.[78]

SPECIFIC PERFORMANCE

Sir Henry Maine remarked that in all legal systems, the idea that a court would order specific enforcement of a contract was late in coming and was forced on the legal system because of pressure from the increase in commercial activity.[79]

As I mentioned earlier, material has been recovered from the Bishop of Ely's Manorial Court at Littleport in the Reign of Edward II of specific performance or contracts to manufacture.

All the authorities are agreed that the origin of specific performance is obscure, but that, by 1450, such claims were commonplace.[80] Barbour suggests that many of the early cases were situations where the contract was informal or where there was a pure non-feasance by the defendant at a time when assumpsit did not extend to cover non-feasances. However, there are also some early examples where damages were not an adequate remedy. An illustration is *Langton v Byngham*,[81] where the Chancellor of the University of Cambridge sued for specific performance on an agreement to sell land to the University for the site of a new college. The position of the land made it of unique value to the University so that damages could not be an adequate remedy.

Specific performance may be granted where there is no binding contract at law. A prime example is *Crook v Corporation of Seaford*[82] where there was no contract under seal binding a local authority, but an informal agreement and acquiescence in the acts of the purchaser in clearing the land, meant that, in equity, the authority must be ordered to perform the agreement.

TRUSTS

Maitland noted that most simple trusts emanate from agreements.[83] A requests B to act as trustee for C and B accepts A's proposal. Indeed, Maitland says that

---

76 See, for example, *Milchas Investments Pty Ltd v Larkin* (1989) NSW ConvR [55-487].

77 [1973] AC 691.

78 See *Stern v McArthur* (1988) 165 CLR 489 at 500-501.

79 HS Maine, *Ancient Law* (London, John Murray, 1930) at chapter IX.

80 WT Barbour, *History of Contract in Early English Equity* (Clarendon Press, Oxford, 1914) at 122.

81 (1433) extracted in WT Barbour, *History of Contract in Early English Equity*, above n 80 at 221.

82 (1870) LR 10 Eq 678 (affirmed on appeal (1871) LR 6 Ch App 551).

83 FW Maitland, *Equity also the Forms of Action at Common Law* (Cambridge University Press, Cambridge, 1909).

it is impossible to define a contract so that the definition does not cover at least three quarters of all the trusts that are created.[84]

Why then do we not deal with trusts as contracts at law?

Maitland gives some answers to this question. The first answer he gives[85] is practical, that the common law judges knew that if they did enforce the agreements, the use or trust would be useless to the gentry in estate planning.

Maitland's main answer is that "trusts fell under the jurisdiction of the Court of Chancery and for that very reason Courts of Law did not enforce them. Just now and again they threatened to give an action for damages against the defaulting trustee — but they soon abandoned this attempt to invade a province which equity had made its own."[86]

There is also the logical and technical answer. If A promises B to hold property for C, A may not want to enforce the contract at all. Indeed, if A dies shortly after the trust is set up, A's heir may be completely opposed to the trust. C is not a party to the contract at law and thus cannot sue on the promise: B had no interest in doing so and A is unwilling to perform. The common law of contract will not solve the problem. Equity steps in to enforce a completely constituted trust or one where the promise was given for consideration.

However, the complexities of modern commercial life plus the narrowing of the gap between equity and common law after the *Judicature Act*, has meant that there are now combined cases of contract and trust coming before the courts. The clearest case is where there is a public unit trust with a manager who is also a beneficiary. The manager may well have equitable rights as a beneficiary, but may also have contractual rights as a party to a side deal encapsulated in a Deed of Management.[87]

CHALLENGES TO CONTRACT

During the last century, there has been an expansion of the type of promises that might be enforced by the courts and, in this respect, there has been a break with the traditional rules of contract as it is commonly supposed to exist. The most significant of these have been:

- proprietary estoppel;
- *High Trees* estoppel;
- conventional estoppel; and,
- negligent misstatement.

Estoppels first became significant in the law of contract after the *Statute of Frauds 1677*. As Professor Stoljar suggests, equity needed to intervene in cases where there was clear evidence that there had been a true concluded agreement, but one party fraudulently refused to perform.[88] Stoljar points out that it was the fact, though why is not clear, that early cases dealing with this problem

---

84   FW Maitland, *Equity also the Forms of Action at Common Law*, above n 83 at 54.
85   FW Maitland, *Equity also the Forms of Action at Common Law*, above n 83 at 32.
86   FW Maitland, *Equity also the Forms of Action at Common Law*, above n 83 at 54.
87   See for example, *Parkes Management Ltd v Perpetual Trustee Co Ltd* (1977) 3 ACLR 303.
88   S Stoljar, "Estoppel and Contract Theory" (1990) 3 *Journal of Contract Law* 1 at 3.

spoke in terms of estoppel.[89] This line of cases developed so that equity would enforce by injunction promises made by the parties which never actually found their way into their formal written agreement.[90]

What we now call proprietary estoppel first came to the fore in *Dillwyn v Llewelyn*.[91] Lord Westbury held that he was following along the lines of the cases where equity acted so as not to make the *Statute of Frauds* a cloak for fraud.[92] Since then, of course, the doctrine has developed so that, as *Snell* puts it:[93]

> "where by his words or conduct one party to a transaction freely makes to the other a clear and unequivocal promise or assurance which is intended to affect the legal relations between them…and, before it is withdrawn, the other party acts upon it, altering his or her position so that it would be inequitable to permit the first party to withdraw the promise, the party making the promise or assurance will not be permitted to act inconsistently with it."

As we have seen, such an equity may lead to the grant of an order that the defendant enter into a formal contract which can be the subject of an order for specific performance. Alternatively, the court may grant specific performance without taking the formal intermediate step.

The Courts have made it clear that they will not permit a person who has declined to enter into a contract, effectively to change his mind by later saying that there was a proprietary estoppel.

A good illustration is *Crabb v Arun District Council*.[94] In that case, there was no contract between the parties, but the English Court of Appeal granted an injunction to confer on the plaintiff property rights which the Council had led him to believe would be granted and on which belief he had acted to his detriment. Atiyah titled his case note on *Crabb*: "When is an Enforceable Agreement not a Contract? Answer: When it is an Equity".[95]

PJ Millett (later Lord Millett) replied that the similarity of the result of a contract case and a proprietary estoppel case may deceive.[96] He said, "both law and equity seek the same result, to do justice by refusing to allow a party to disappoint the legitimate expectations of another. But not all expectations are legitimate, and the law and equity do not necessarily draw the line in the same place. The gist of the claim in contract is consideration; for the law draws the line between bargains, which will be enforced, and voluntary transactions, which will not. The gist of the claim in equity is prejudice; equity will not permit a party who has stood by while another prejudices his position in the belief, created or encouraged by him, that he has or will obtain a legal right, afterwards to deny that right."

---

89 See for example, *Dann v Spurrier* (1802) 7 Ves 231; 32 ER 94; *Gregory v Mighell* (1811) 18 Ves 328; 34 ER 341.

90 See for example, *Jackson v Cator* (1800) 5 Ves 688; 31 ER 806; *Pigott v Stratton* (1859) 1 De G F & J 33; 45 ER 271.

91 (1862) 4 De GF & J 517; 45 ER 1285.

92 *Dillwyn v Llewelyn*, above n 91 at 521-522, 1286-1287.

93 J McGhee, *Snell's Equity* (31st ed, Sweet & Maxwell, London, 2005) at ¶10-08.

94 [1976] Ch 179.

95 (1976) 92 *Law Quarterly Review* 174.

96 PJ Millett, "*Crabb v Arun District Council* – A Riposte" (1976) 92 *Law Quarterly Review* 342 at 346.

Promissory estoppel and conventional estoppel are devices whereby a formal contract may be varied temporarily or permanently. Promissory estoppel was given life by the famous decision of Denning J in *Central London Property Trust Ltd v High Trees House Ltd*,[97] usually just referred to as *High Trees*. The principle has developed since 1947, and there is no need to spend much space on it here. Essentially, in its raw form the principle states that if a person gives another the expectation that he or she will postpone their rights and the other acts on that to their detriment, the postponement cannot be withdrawn except on reasonable notice.

Conventional estoppel, which forbids parties from departing from their joint assumptions stems from cases such as *Grundt v The Great Boulder Pty Gold Mines Ltd*.[98] Both doctrines operate to abrogate the common law rule that one looks only to the formal contract as finally drawn up to decide the rights of the parties. Stoljar notes that each doctrine leads to de facto modification of the parties' contractual rights.[99]

Negligent misstatement flows from cases such as *Mutual Life & Citizens' Assurance Co Ltd v Evatt*,[100] which hold that if a special relationship exists, negligent statements warranting reliance may be actionable. I will not dwell on this subject as it is purely a development of the common law. However, it is to be noted that care has to be taken with this concept or it will encroach into the field now occupied by contract and provide a different criterion as to what promises are to be enforced.

THREE CASE ILLUSTRATIONS

I thought it would be useful to discuss three cases on the very edge of contract which I have had to decide over the last 19 years which illustrate the problems at the interface. None of these cases is very significant in itself. Two of them are only reported in specialised series of law reports.

The first in point of time is *Beaton v McDivitt*.[101] I heard this case in September, 1985. McDivitt was an elderly "greenie" and Beaton was a young man of the same persuasion. In 1977, McDivitt invited Beaton to build a rock hut on McDivitt's land. Beaton did so. Both parties contemplated that the land would shortly be rezoned to allow a subdivision at which time McDivitt would voluntarily convey the land on which the rock hut was built to Beaton. Seven years later no such rezoning had occurred. The parties fell out in 1985 and McDivitt wished to evict Beaton.

I held that although Beaton's reliance to his detriment on McDivitt's promise was consideration, the equitable doctrine of proprietary estoppel did not apply, but that the contract had been frustrated.

The court of appeal constituted by Kirby P, Mahoney and McHugh JJA, held I was wrong in virtually every finding, yet, dismissed the appeal, McHugh JA

---

97   [1947] KB 130.
98   (1937) 59 CLR 641.
99   S Stoljar, "Estoppel and Contract Theory" (1990) 3 *Journal of Contract Law* 1.
100 [1971] AC 793; 122 CLR 628.
101 (1985) 13 NSWLR 134 (Young J); (1987) 13 NSWLR 162.

dissenting. It must have worried them a bit as the appeal was argued on 17 December, 1986, yet judgment was not brought down until 14 October, 1987.

Kirby P and Mahoney JA held that there was no contract as there was no consideration. McHugh JA held that there had been no frustration and that proprietary estoppel applied. Kirby P said that there was no proprietary estoppel. Mahoney JA agreed with me that there was frustration: Kirby P did not consider this point.

The moral of the case is that it is extremely difficult sometimes to mould the facts of real life into the categories set by the nineteenth century academics. There was an application for special leave to appeal to the High Court, but I believe that this was dismissed on the grounds that there was no point of principle involved!

The second case is *Corpers (No 664) Pty Ltd v NZI Securities Ltd*.[102] The plaintiff was the corporate vehicle for a group of barristers who wished to purchase the building they occupied for fifty-one million dollars. They proposed to the defendant or its holding company that it should lend sixty-five million dollars for the purchase price, the cost of converting to strata title plus the stamp duty and first year's interest. This proposed deal was attractive to the defendant's Sydney office as it was the mortgagee of the building and the then owner was in default. Its officer suggested that he would recommend the deal if the defendant and the plaintiff shared the profit 40/60. This was agreed to. A senior person at head office approved the deal. However, his authority was in fact capped at forty million.

On 13 December 1988, the defendant wrote to the plaintiff that the transaction had been approved and that it could proceed with the purchase of the building. A further letter of February 1989 confirmed this. Both letters were signed by persons with high sounding titles in the defendant's organisation. The plaintiff then signed a contract to buy the building for fifty-one million dollars and then sued the defendant to come good with the loan.

There was no contract between the parties. The plaintiff relied on the doctrine of proprietary estoppel. It succeeded, though only for equitable damages under *Lord Cairns Act*, because it had been induced to enter into the contract to buy the building as a result of the statements made by apparently high officials of the defendant that it was safe to do so.

The third case is *Milchas Investments Pty Ltd v Larkin*.[103] The plaintiff was one of a group of companies owned by the Fink family. The defendant was, amongst other things, a property developer. One of the Fink family, who had no authority to sign a contract for sale, negotiated with the defendant for the sale of a building in Kings Cross, Sydney. He did, however, have authority to make representations.

No formal contract was ever exchanged. However, the defendant put on a caveat alleging that he had a contract through conduct. When the plaintiff filed suit to remove the caveat, the defendant filed a cross-claim for specific performance and also relied on unconscionable conduct to compel the same result. The contract cases failed because, as there was no exchange, there was no

---

102 (1989) NSW ConvR 55-475.
103 (1989) NSW ConvR 55-487.

compliance with the *Statute of Frauds* and Mr Fink did not have the plaintiff's authority to enter into a binding contract.

As to the equitable claim, it was held that the mere fact that there is a failure to enter into a contract after a promise to do so does not constitute unconscionable conduct. Furthermore, I said that the proprietary estoppel principle is not to be implied as a back up submission in every case where the parties have failed to enter into a binding contract, a submission which in 1989 was very common.

The problem in equity has been to draw the line between contract and proprietary estoppel. At common law, there is a similar interface problem between contract and negligent misstatement. If one extends the latter too far, one ends up with the situation where promises are enforced without consideration.

SOME FUSION, SOME FISSION

Atomic reactions are not my specialty, but, from what I think I know of the subject, fusion is a reaction where light elements come together, fission is the opposite reaction, where a heavy nucleus splits apart (for example, Uranium 235 becomes Plutonium, Strontium, Caesium and Barium etc). Each reaction generates a lot of heat and energy.

In law, fusion certainly generates a lot of heat, but fission does not: probably because it is mainly unobserved.

In contract, the interplay between principles of law and equity have sometimes produced fusion and sometimes fission. Examples of fusion occur where the two streams have agreed on a common policy as to penalties etc, or where they have, by virtue of the *Judicature Act*, come to a common rule as to time. Examples of fission tend to occur when the common law is affected by statute which goes too far in correcting the supposed evil, so leaving a class of case where it would be unconscionable to enforce the common law rights. Equity then steps in. Again, social circumstances may change so that there needs to be an adjustment before the common law and to give time for Parliament catch up. Again equity will intervene.

Perhaps the best illustration of fission is in connection with confidential information. Traditionally, one was either bound by an express or implied term of a contract to keep information confidential or one was not so bound. However today, there is a two-pronged attack available to those whose confidences have been abused: (1) contract; and (2) equity.[104]

There are many other examples. The principal one is the interest of the mortgagor under a mortgage. Under the typical English mortgage, the mortgagor only has a short period in which he or she has legal (contractual) rights to recover the land. After that period, the mortgagor has only equitable rights which are truly called an "equity of redemption". In Australia, the mortgagor has principally legal rights as he or she has a legal interest in the land and the time for redemption might be 25 years away. However, in addition to

---

104 See for example, *Robb v Green* [1895] 2 QB 315.

those legal rights (sometimes misnamed "equity of redemption") the mortgagor also has a true equity of redemption in equity. Equity, of course, only intervenes if the common law rights are insufficient to do justice.

Again, where a contract for the sale of land fails, the question as to what shall happen to the deposit and any instalments paid under the contract often has to be decided. The cases show that if certain factors exist, the questions are decided under the common law of penalties, however, in other situations, the purchaser has to rely solely on principles of equity.[105]

The distinction is, of course, of significance. When one has a common law property right, that right will usually hold good against all the world. When one has an equitable right of property, that right may not only be defeated by a person with a legal right that was assumed as a bona fide purchaser without notice of the equitable right, but also in order to vindicate that equitable right, the holder will have to "do equity" to other interested parties. This latter requirement can be vital.[106]

Mistake is perhaps in a category of its own. If it has to be categorised it is a case of fission. What has usually happened is that the common law has developed its remedies and then the equitable remedy ceases to be invoked. With mistake, the common law approach has been found to be inadequate for modern conditions and equity has taken over.[107] Indeed, the editors of the Australian edition of *Cheshire & Fifoot's Law of Contract*[108] say "in the light of this development, the role for common law mistake rendering a contract void may have been reduced to virtual extinction."[109]

Up to this point, I have discussed the contribution of equity to the development of the law popularly called, "Contract." However, there has been an undercurrent of defence against the notion that there has been fusion of principle. Accordingly, I should end by a few observations of fusion and fission generally.

To a considerable extent, the first reaction to any chapter on the fusion of law and equity must be to yawn and say to oneself, "So what?" The next reaction is to ask what the author really means by "fusion".

Lehane J, when reviewing *Gareth Jones on Specific Performance* in the *Cambridge Law Journal* wrote:[110]

> "to ask that those who assert that law and equity are fused should explain what they mean, how it happened and what follows from it is not merely to indulge an idiosyncratic belief that things were better before 1873 or, still less, to suggest that law and equity then became incapable of future development."

It is indeed important that those who proclaim fusion should define their terms. If the answer to the question, "what do you mean by fusion?" is "fusion

---

105 *McDonald v Dennys Lascelles Ltd* (1933) 48 CLR 457; *Lexane Pty Ltd v Highfern Pty Ltd* [1985] 1 Qd R 446 at 455.

106 See for example, *Davis v Williams* (2003) 11 BPR 21 at 313.

107 See for example, *Taylor v Johnson* (1983) 151 CLR 422.

108 N Seddon and M Ellinghaus, *Chesire & Fifoot's Law of Contract* (8th Australian ed, LexisNexis Butterworths, Sydney, 2002).

109 N Seddon and M Ellinghaus, *Chesire & Fifoot's Law of Contract*, above n 108 at 596[12.3].

110 (1987) 46 *Cambridge Law Journal* 163 at 165.

of the courts in which equitable and legal remedies are awarded", the yawns can continue. However, if what is meant is that one can now ignore the differences between legal rights and equitable rights, one is really saying that the law has changed by stealth and this approach must be resisted.

What has really happened is that the *Judicature Act* has acted as a catalyst to the development of both the common law and equity. There has been some fusion of rules as the common law has adopted principles from equity and equity from the common law. There has been some fission in that each has developed new principles. There has also been a considerable overlay of statutory rights.

AND WHAT NOW?

The best answer I can give to this question is, "I don't know". I have looked at various twentieth century articles on "Whither Equity?" and their lack of prediction of what did in fact occur makes me shy from the task. I will only quote from one of them, Baker's "The Future of Equity",[111] because it contains vital warnings, not only predictions.

The article commences, "talk of fusion is widespread, surprising one may think in an age of ever greater specialisation." It concludes:[112]

> "before we lose the old equitable jurisdiction, so painfully built up over the centuries, in the search for a nicer justice, we would do well to remember the admonition of another greater equity judge of this century,[113]
>
> > 'We are as little justified in saying that a court has a certain jurisdiction merely because we think it ought to have it, as we should be in declaring that the substantive law is something different from what it has always been declared to be, merely because we think it ought to be so. It is even possible that we are not wiser than our ancestors.'"

Those words should be taken on board by those legal philosophers who wish to adjust the rules that have grown up over the ages to fit some pattern of justice of their own creation.

However, I venture to think that most see less significance given to the distinction between what is a rule of law and what is a rule of equity in the next decade. However such slackness of thought will lead to the same sort of problem as when it was in vogue in the late nineteenth century and phoenix-like, the principles of equity will rise again.

Jeffrey Hackney, when reviewing the 30th edition of *Snell's Equity*, strongly attacked the concept of having a book entitled "Equity" because such a work was really a pot-pourri of miscellaneous concepts of differing origins.[114] He concluded that the basic message to writers of texts on equity was, "thank you, but no more *Snells*."[115] The message was that, in his view, the production of

---

111 PV Baker, "The Future of Equity" (1977) 93 *Law Quarterly Review* 529.
112 PV Baker, "The Future of Equity", above n 111 at 539-540.
113 Lord Simonds, LC in *Chapman v Chapman* [1954] AC 429 at 444.
114 (2001) 117 *Law Quarterly Review* 150.
115 J Hackney, Review of *Snell's Equity*, above n 114 at 154.

such works would shortly cease. The late Professor Birks in his review of the 4th edition of *Meagher, Gummow & Lehane's Equity Doctrines and Remedies*[116] made it clear that he agreed with those comments.[117]

However, the market place does not seem to agree. The production of significant new works on equity tends to show this is not the way the real world is thinking.

A worrying current development in Australia is the view of some governments that it should invest statutory tribunals with powers to grant equitable relief. This policy is flawed. Apart from the undesirability of investing bodies with such powers where their members do not have tenure, these tribunals are not used to administering equitable principles. They forget to take undertakings as to damages, a vital matter for persons involved in equity proceedings. They overlook the maxim that "he or she who seeks equity must do equity" and sometimes the complainant ends up with both the money and the box. This fault is not confined to tribunals. Inferior courts of common law, invested with equity powers which they exercise infrequently, make the same mistake as has also occurred with common law judges of superior courts.

Furthermore, tribunals, even tribunals with power to make conditional orders, are usually not invested with the machinery to police undertakings and conditions. The experiments in procedural reforms of the 1850s showed that the most one can do is to give common law courts the power to grant absolute and perpetual injunctions. Advance beyond that stage and problems occur unless all the judicial officers administering equitable principles are thoroughly versed in equitable principles and procedures. In practice this is hardly ever the case.

However, if I can have my last word on fusion, I can confidently predict that in 2104 if any lawyer or, more likely, legal historian, reads and considers the material produced on this topic in the past 50 years, he or she will say, "isn't it absurd that those people wasted so much time and energy on a subject that has so little significance to the law."

---

116 R Meagher, JD Heydon, M Leeming, *Meagher Gummow and Lehane's Equity: Doctrines and Remedies* (4th ed, Butterworths, 2002, Sydney).
117 (2004) 120 *Law Quarterly Review* 344 at 344-345.

Conclusion

William Gummow

To read through all the papers which formed the basis for the chapters in this book has been an interesting, but not entirely reassuring, task. I will be forgiven if I do not now refer to all of them. To some authors this may be a matter of regret, to others a matter of relief. The identification of the larger of these classes is a matter for speculation by the reader when considering what now follows.

There are two points which I wish to make at the outset. One concerns the use of the word "fusion" in the title for the conference which formed the basis of this book. The fact of the matter is that that term will not be embraced by judges as providing a catch-all general answer to doctrinal issues. I very much doubt if the judges of the Equity Division, as they get on with their difficult tasks from case to case, ruminate upon "fusion". Those who teach law should realise this.

Indeed, and this is the other point, in Australia rather too much modern academic writing is an exercise in the promotion of the writer's view of what the law ought to be without prior analysis of how the law came to be in its present state. To proceed on the footing that the law ought to be X, and that the law is therefore X, and any decision of an ultimate appellate court to the contrary therefore must be in error, and to teach students accordingly, is unsatisfactory.

Some general observations are in order.

First, to speak with Lord Millett and with the Chief Justice of Canada[1] of the distinctive character of equitable principles and doctrines is not to refuse to look outside a closed box of historical obscurantism. To the contrary, it is this complex phenomenon, necessarily untidy given the nature of human affairs to which it continues to respond, which enriches the judge-made law and gives remarkable powers of adaptation to social and economic change. Many of the animating ideas of equity are encapsulated in its maxims. These are not all consistent. That, in turn, provides leeways for choice of the appropriate result in a given case.

Secondly, and by way of development of the first observation, equity meets a need of any sophisticated and successful legal system. The point has been well put by Professor Waddams, now of the University of Toronto. He writes with a deep knowledge of Admiralty and Ecclesiastical legal history, as well as of what

---

1   *Canson Enterprises Ltd v Boughton & Co* [1991] 3 SCR 534, at 543 per McLachlin CJ, quoted in *Youyang Pty Ltd v Minter Ellison Morris Fletcher* (2003) 212 CLR 484 at 500-501[40]; P Millett, 'Proprietary Restitution' at chapter 12 in this book.

we call "the common law". His work, *Dimensions of Private Law*, published in 2003, surveys the Anglo-American law of obligations.

Professor Waddams writes:[2]

"Attempts to reduce [the law of obligations] to a single explanatory principle, or to a precisely classified or categorized map, scheme, or diagram are likely to distort the past by omitting or marginalizing material inconsistent with proposed principles or schemes. Many legal issues cannot be allocated exclusively to one category. Often several concepts have worked concurrently and cumulatively, so that competing explanations and categories are not so much alternatives, of which only one can be correct, as different *dimensions* of a complex phenomenon, of which several may be simultaneously valid and necessary." (original emphasis)

I agree with every word of this. Perhaps unsurprisingly, I agree also with what Professor Hedley, the Chief Judge in Equity and Lord Millett have had to say on this theme.

Thirdly, the *Judicature Act 1873* (UK) was addressed not simply to the courts of common law and of equity but across the board of the legal system. What should be made of the attitude of Admiralty to questions of jurisdiction, and to the award of compound interest? What should be done, if anything, to the differences in undue influence doctrine in courts of probate and in courts of equity dealing with dispositions inter vivos? It may be observed that a completely satisfactory answer to that last question is yet to be given.[3]

Fourthly, as Sir Anthony Mason points out in chapter 1, no one now seriously contends that, contrary to its words, the *Judicature Act* established that in a conflict or variance between law and equity it is the former, rather than the latter, which prevails.

Fifthly, no one who has looked into the history of the relations between law and equity could believe that the administration of the one was wholly insulated from the other.[4]

Sixthly, no one seriously suggests that some Ice Age descended upon equity with the commencement of the 1873 legislation. *In Re Hallett's Estate; Knatchbull v Hallett*,[5] *Barnes v Addy*[6] and *Lysaght v Edwards*[7] all were decided in this very period of the introduction of the Judicature system. The development of these areas of equity, and consideration of those very decisions, is still very much with us – as several of the chapters in this book have shown.

Seventhly, an essential question always is why any particular change in judge-made doctrine should be made. Thus, whether there should be an exemplary damages remedy in trust or in other aspects of the exclusive jurisdiction is a large question. Certainly even the common law of tort has fluctuated

---

2   SM Waddams, *Dimensions of Private Law: Categories and Concepts in Anglo-American Legal Reasoning* (Cambridge University Press, Cambridge, 2003), frontispiece.
3   See P Ridge, "Equitable Undue Influence and Wills" (2004) 120 *Law Quarterly Review* 617.
4   See the collection of examples in R Meagher, JD Heydon, M Leeming, *Meagher Gummow and Lehane's Equity: Doctrines and Remedies* (4th ed, Butterworths, Sydney, 2002) at [1-205].
5   (1879) 13 Ch D 696.
6   (1874) 9 Ch App 244.
7   (1876) 2 Ch D 499.

on the subject since *Rookes v Barnard*[8] was decided by the House of Lords 50 years ago.[9] Again, whether a remedy for breach of contract in the nature of an account of profits should be allowed is another large question. Equity went beyond the remedy of damages against the Holmes bad man and awarded specific performance. But it did not always do so. To ask whether equity now should go further respecting an account of profits is to pose a question as to the basic nature of the contractual relationship. No doubt the defendant in *Attorney General v Blake*[10] was a bad man, but one might have wished for a fuller exploration of those fundamentals of contract law in the speeches in the House of Lords.

Eighthly, the universalist assumptions or pretensions of the English High Court of Chancery with respect first to Irish and then colonial litigation, and exemplified in *Penn v Lord Baltimore*,[11] are well known. Those pretensions today may be expected to cause problems with questions of jurisdiction, notably the use within the European Union of the anti-suit injunction, and also with questions of choice of law. On that latter question, Professor Yeo's paper is a valuable contribution.

The last general observation concerns statute law. The inclusion in the title to the conference of the words "The Interaction of Common Law and Equity" is misleading. It invites myopia by underestimating the significance of the role of statute. Much of what in some chapters has been called the common law is, in truth, statute law. For example, at common law there was no *Statute of Limitations*, and the question in Chancery was one of adopting the statute by way of analogy. Delay and laches and acquiescence, although not always clearly distinguished as between themselves, were all distinct principles in equity, disjoined from any question of adopting the *Statute of Limitations* by analogy.

Likewise, at common law, contributory negligence was a complete bar.[12] In *Pilmer v Duke Group Ltd (In liq)*,[13] the High Court discouraged analogical borrowing in the exclusive jurisdiction in equity from the statutes relaxing the rigour of the common law respecting contributory negligence.

Much of the concern of equity has been with the unconscientious use of legal rights, a phrase which encompasses statutory rights and immunities. Thus, to speak of "part performance" is to invoke the long history of equity's response to the *Statute of Frauds*. To speak of set-off, as Dr Derham has done in his characteristically learned and practical presentation, is to speak in part of equity's attitude to unconscientious assertion of a "legal" set-off under the *Statutes of Set-off*.[14]

Many statutory regimes would not have functioned effectively without a leavening of equity. As it happens, two of these regimes were under way at the time of the Judicature reforms. One was that of the *Companies Act 1862* (UK).

---

8   [1964] AC 1129.
9   See *Gray v Motor Accident Commission* (1998) 196 CLR 1.
10 [2001] 1 AC 268.
11 (1750) 1 Ves Sen 444; 27 ER 1132.
12 See *Astley v Austrust Ltd* (1999) 197 CLR 1 at 11.
13 (2001) 207 CLR 165.
14 SR Derham, *Set Off* (3rd ed, Clarendon Press, Oxford, forthcoming).

Much of what has become modern company law was developed from the efforts of the nineteenth century Chancery judges to adapt fiduciary and trust law notions to the working out of that statutory regime.

Another statutory regime was the Torrens system. In Australia, the operation of the Torrens system, with its notion of indefeasible title, has been facilitated by the "personal equity" and by the adaptation of equitable priorities to disputes between competing unregistered interests. What scope, if any, there is for like use of equitable principles in the operation in England of the *Land Registration Act 2002* (UK) remains to be seen.

From time to time, statutory changes appear to take the ground away from established equitable doctrines and remedies. Section 2 of the *Law of Property (Miscellaneous Provisions) Act 1989* (UK) had the effect of removing the substratum for the doctrine of part-performance in specific performance suits, and thus the substratum for the institution of the equitable mortgage by deposit of title deeds. There has followed in England a tussle as to the extent to which principles of estoppel may be invoked with respect to a contract which is void for want of compliance with the new statute.[15]

The final thing I wish to say is obvious but insufficiently remarked so far at the Conference. It is extremely heartening to see such a well-attended conference upon matters of private law. Equity is hard law, even to those who have spent much of their professional lives wrestling with it. That makes it all the more interesting to teach and to apply in practice, particularly in commercial practice.

I often hear from Law Deans across the country that private law, in particular property law, is unpopular with younger teachers. The organisers of the Conference from which this book was initiated are younger teachers, so the calamity cannot be complete. They are to be congratulated on their initiative.

---

15   R Megarry and H Wade, *The Law of Real Property* (6th ed, Sweet & Maxwell, London 1999) at [12-043], [19-039]; *United Bank of Kuwait Plc v Sahib* [1997] Ch 107.

Index

Gaian taxonomy, 2–3, 79–84, 89, 262
  modernised Gaian structure of the
    law, 90
  persons/things/actions distinction, 82
  public/private, 81–2
  satisfactoriness, 81–8

Getzler, Dr, 13

Gift
  completion, 458–9
  legal title, transfer of, 458

Goff, Lord, 70, 358

Good faith
  Equity inquiring into, 35–6
  obligation of, 35

Goode, Professor Sir Roy, 93–4, 317

Government
  regulation by, 82
  role of, 81–2

Grantham, Professor, 78, 120,
  140

Griffith, Sir Samuel, 51

Gummow, Justice, 61–2, 246

Hardship
  equitable defence, 386
  frustration and, 386
  mistake and, 386

High Court of Australia
  coherence of law, 14, 62
  unity of Australian legal system, 62

History
  argument based purely on, 20
  fusion debates, 247
  justification and, 20
  knowledge of, 12
  law, of, 12–13

Hohfeld, Professor, 121

Illegality
  defence of, 386
  unclean hands and, 386

Information
  property, as, 83

Injunctions
  Common Law Courts, grant by, 48
  property rights, protecting, 104
  public law, in, 43
  tort, claims in, 104

Innocent misrepresentation
  damages for, 58

Insolvency
  property rights, protection of, 113–16
  vendor, of, protection of purchaser,
    467, 485–7

Intellectual property
  account of profits, 423–4
  'property', 83

Intestacy
  real and personal property, 465

Jacobs, Sir Kenneth, 12

Jessel, Sir George, MR, 12, 48, 58, 243,
  283

Jewish law
  dual system, 309

Jones, Professor, 358

Jordan, Sir Frederick, 54–55, 67, 242–3

Judicial discretion
  role of, 378
  uncertainty in the law, 434, 441–2

Jury trial
  gradual abolition, 49

Kahn-Freund, Professor, 162